VIRGINIA
HANDBOOK

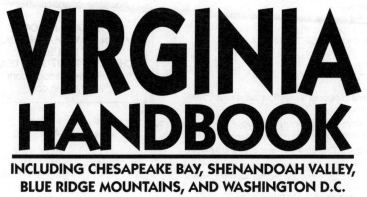

VIRGINIA HANDBOOK

INCLUDING CHESAPEAKE BAY, SHENANDOAH VALLEY, BLUE RIDGE MOUNTAINS, AND WASHINGTON D.C.
FIRST EDITION

JULIAN SMITH

MOON
TRAVEL
HANDBOOKS

VIRGINIA HANDBOOK
FIRST EDITION

Published by
Moon Publications, Inc.
P.O. Box 3040
Chico, California 95927-3040, USA

Printed by
Colorcraft Ltd.

© Text and photographs copyright Julian Smith, 1999.
All rights reserved.

© Illustrations and maps copyright Moon Publications, Inc., 1999.
All rights reserved.

Sidetrip to D.C. chapter by Kevin Jeys and Jeff Shear.

Some photos and illustrations are used by permission
and are the property of the original copyright owners.

ISBN: 1-56691-141-9
ISSN: 1099-8853

Editor: Emily Kendrick
Editorial Assistance: Gregor Johnson Krause, Matt Orendorff
Map Editor: Gina Wilson Birtcil
Copy Editor: Fred Lollar
Production & Design: Carey Wilson
Cartography: Chris Folks, Mike Morgenfeld, Allen Leech
Index: Sondra Nation

Front cover photo: Old Albemarle County Courthouse, Charlottesville © Charles Shoffner

All photos by Julian Smith unless otherwise noted.
All illustrations by Bob Race unless otherwise noted.
All illustrations in the Washington, D.C. chapter courtesy of Dover Publications, Inc.

Distributed in the United States and Canada by Publishers Group West

Printed in China

Please send all comments,
corrections, additions,
amendments, and critiques to:

**VIRGINIA HANDBOOK
MOON TRAVEL HANDBOOKS
P.O. BOX 3040
CHICO, CA 95927-3040, USA
e-mail: travel@moon.com
www.moon.com**

Printing History
1st edition—March 1999

CONTENTS

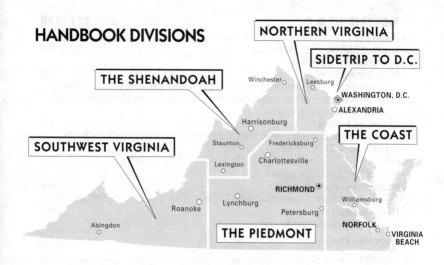

HANDBOOK DIVISIONS

NORTHERN VIRGINIA

SIDETRIP TO D.C.

THE SHENANDOAH

SOUTHWEST VIRGINIA

THE COAST

THE PIEDMONT

Winchester

Leesburg

WASHINGTON, D.C.

ALEXANDRIA

Harrisonburg

Staunton

Fredericksburg

Charlottesville

Lexington

RICHMOND

Williamsburg

Roanoke

Lynchburg

Petersburg

NORFOLK

VIRGINIA BEACH

Abingdon

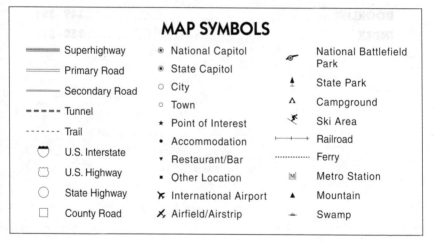

MAP SYMBOLS

Symbol	Description
═══	Superhighway
━━━	Primary Road
───	Secondary Road
-----	Tunnel
-------	Trail
⬭	U.S. Interstate
◌	U.S. Highway
○	State Highway
□	County Road
⊛	National Capitol
⊙	State Capitol
○	City
○	Town
★	Point of Interest
•	Accommodation
▾	Restaurant/Bar
▪	Other Location
✈	International Airport
✗	Airfield/Airstrip
⚞	National Battlefield Park
▲	State Park
∧	Campground
⛷	Ski Area
⊢──⊣	Railroad
··········	Ferry
Ⓜ	Metro Station
▲	Mountain
⚓	Swamp

MAPS

ABBREVIATIONS

DCR—Department of Conservation
    and Recreation
mph—miles per hour
pp—per person
VTC—Virginia Tourism Corporation

AAA—American Automobile Association
s—single occupancy
d—double occupancy
AT—Appalachian Trail

ACKNOWLEDGMENTS

A wise man once likened writing a guidebook to pushing a wheelbarrow full of toads. I'd like to thank everyone who helped heft this particular load of croakers, starting with Scott Adams, Chris Baker, Chris Bannon, Marnie Boren, Tim and Melissa Caudill, Joe Cummings, Robert & Corinne Gaines, Jennifer Ingrum, Jeff Lefkowitz and Kathryn Doyle, Steve Metzger, April Olberding, Elizabeth Roberts, and Michael Speaks.

Offering loads of assistance through various chambers of commerce, tourism councils and the like were Anne Atkinson, Lorraine Brooks, Mary Ann Corbett, Deborah DeMarco, Catherine Fox, Steve Galyean, Peggy Gaul, Julie Grimes, Karen Hedelt, John Holloman, Cheryl Kilday, Jo Ann Mitchell, Kirsten Niemann, Debby Pedgett, Peter Rippe, Lisa Sumdrla, Suzanne Taylor, and Vivian Curtis.

Most of the pictures in this book were taken with a Stylus Zoom 105 camera loaned by Olympus America, Inc.

Special thanks go to Tim Freilich (and Lysah and Scott) at Chez Altamont, Julia Scott at the Virginia Tourism Corporation, and of course my parents, for everything.

WE'D LOVE TO HEAR FROM YOU

Writing a guidebook is a never-ending process, with the printed page only a snapshot of the constant flux of prices, recipes, operating hours, openings, and closings. We welcome your comments, corrections, even the occasional polite rant—anything that will make the second edition of the *Virginia Handbook* better, or at least more fun to read. Thanks ahead of time, and send it all to:

Virginia Handbook
c/o Moon Publications
P.O. Box 3040
Chico, CA 95927-3040
e-mail: travel@moon.com

In a season on the blue roads, what had I accomplished? I hadn't sailed the Atlantic in a washtub, or crossed the Gobi by goat cart, or bicycled to Cape Horn. In my own country, I had gone, had met, had shared. I had stood as witness.

          – William Least Heat Moon, Blue Highways

INTRODUCTION

President John F. Kennedy once described Washington, D.C., as a city of northern charm and southern efficiency. Just across the Potomac spreads a state that's pretty much the opposite, and proud of it. From the banking towers of Richmond to the most remote Blue Ridge farm, Virginia embodies the best of the two worlds it bridges—southern charm, northern efficiency—and combines them into a wealth of reasons to pay a visit.

Any American who's sat through the seventh grade knows Virginia is awash in United States history, oozing from it every pore like few other states in the Union. Starting well before the first European landing in 1607, Virginia's story is really the story of the United States. The American Revolution ended a few miles away from Jamestown, and more Civil War battles raged here than anywhere else.

Virginia's gorgeous scenery is one reason the state has always been such a magnetic lure, first for settlers and now for visitors. To the west, the sublime Shenandoah Valley borders the Blue Ridge Mountains, which tumble eastward into the patrician pasturage of the Piedmont and Tidewater. Virginia's coast is a world in itself, embracing vistas of open ocean, windswept islands, and the moody waters of one of the largest bays in the world.

All around the state lies an abundance of antique stores, plantation homes, B&Bs, historic monuments, and world-class museums. Cities of all sizes host concerts, fairs, and festivals throughout the year, while the buds of spring and the fiery autumn colors set their own calendar. Lovers of the outdoors are drawn to mountain biking, river rafting, fishing, skiing, and hiking galore from one end to the other.

Best of all, though, in this state of 40-cent soda machines and billion-dollar aircraft carriers, urban sprawl and wild ponies, are the Virginians themselves. Any visitor who ventures beyond the interstates and must-see hordes will quickly discover Virginia's true treasure: her inhabitants, most of whom are, for lack of a better word, just so darned *nice*.

THE LAND

Heaven and Earth never agreed to frame a better place for man's habitation. Here are mountains, hills, plaines, valleyes, rivers, and brookes, all running into a faire Bay, compassed but for the mouth, with fruitful and delightsome land.

—Captain John Smith, 1607

Virginia stretches from the Appalachian Mountains to the Atlantic Ocean, encompassing the three distinct physical regions of the mid-Atlantic. The state's 40,767 square miles start in rugged mountains in the west, then spread across a flat, fertile middle region called the Piedmont. A defined drop-off, about even with Richmond, marks the beginning of the Coastal

Plain or Tidewater, drained by rivers flowing into Chesapeake Bay. Across the bay the southernmost splinter of the Delmarva Peninsula (named for the three states that share it) faces the open Atlantic. This Virginia peninsula is called the Eastern Shore.

More than anything, Virginia's landscape is defined by water. Natural waterways attracted the first colonizers to sheltered harbors and lured explorers upriver into the heart of the country. Four major rivers—the Potomac, York, Rappahannock, and James—reach as far as the West Virginia border for their headwaters. Incredibly fertile soil provided the early colonists with productive farmland. The serpentine rivers carried flatboats laden with cotton and tobacco downriver on their first step to the warehouses of Europe. And always the mountains stood to the west, a dramatic backdrop where life has changed little for hundreds of years.

Natural History

During the Paleozoic Era (620-230 million years ago), all of Virginia west of the Blue Ridge and

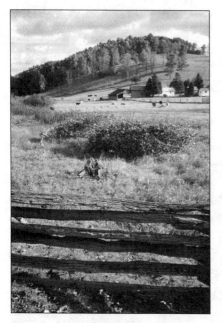

idyllic rural Virginia

part of the Piedmont lay under a great inland sea. Geologic upheavals thrust beds of sediment to mountainous heights. Today we can see evidence of those upheavals—marine fossils embedded in limestone hillsides. The Appalachian Mountains began to rise in the Mesozoic Era (230-70 million years ago), only to be gradually worn down by wind and water into their present rounded contours. Debris washed down from the eastern slopes created the deltas and flood plains of ocean-bound rivers, creating rich farmland all the way to the coast.

Reaching into two geographic provinces, Virginia hosts northern and southern species of flora and fauna at the extremes of their natural ranges. Visitors can see two seasons in a day simply by driving from the base of the Blue Ridge, where spring buds are blooming, to the top, where bare trees of winter remain. It's also possible to see northern tree species such as fir and spruce in the mountains, then head east and find alligators in cypress swamps and shells on sandy beaches, all in the same day.

THE MOUNTAINS

Virginia's hills are part of the **Appalachian chain** that forms the eastern Continental Divide, separating the watersheds of the Atlantic Ocean and the Gulf of Mexico. Once as tall and jagged as the Rockies, the much older Appalachians have mellowed with age into a soothing western skyline. Though the mountains appear gentle, looks can be deceiving—frozen drifts can still trap your 4WD vehicle at the right time of year if you're not careful. The entire chain runs from Alabama to Canada, but "Appalachia" (as much a cultural term as a geological one) only reaches as far north as south-central New York. In Virginia, narrow crests and steep slopes ease into smoother mountaintops in the south part of the range. Weathered granite outcroppings top many peaks, while slightly acidic groundwater has eroded an underlying stratum of limestone into a myriad of caves, bridges, sinkholes, and pillars.

The **Blue Ridge Mountains** form the easternmost fringe of Virginia's slice of the Appalachians, soaring from the nearly flat farmland of the Piedmont. West of the Blue Ridge the **Allegheny Mountains** undulate into West Virginia like waves of stone, separated by rivers flowing in long, narrow valleys. Almost all of Virginia's southwestern end lies at over 1,600 feet, ranging as high as 3,000 feet on the Cumberland and Kanawha Plateaus that extend into Kentucky.

Between the Blue Ridge and the Alleghenies stretches the **Shenandoah,** a valley, a river, and a way of life. Stretching from Staunton, VA, to Harper's Ferry, WV, the fruitful basin produces apples, chickens, corn, and cattle in such profusion it was nearly contested to death during the Civil War. Down the middle runs thin Massanutten Mountain, splitting the North and South

---

BEST VIRGINIA TOWN NAMES

Bumpass (pronounced BUM-puss, luckily)

Busthead	Possum Trot
Bustleboro	Scuffleburg
Modest Town	Simplicity
Mollusk	Village
Nuttsville	

Forks of the Shenandoah River for 50 miles until they join at Front Royal and flow north to the Potomac. Shallow and placid for most of its length, the Shenandoah River draws mineral nutrients from limestone springs to provide sustenance for minnows, crayfish, and their larger predators. Most of Virginia's other major rivers also have their headwaters in or beyond the Blue Ridge, including the York, James, and Rappahannock. The **New River,** to the southwest, is actually the oldest in North America, and second only to the Nile as oldest in the world. It began flowing before the Appalachians were formed, explaining why it's one of the few major rivers that flow south to north, across the grain of the mountains.

Flora and Fauna

Temperate forests include 26 tree species, from deep green eastern hemlocks to fragrant-budded tulip trees. The tulip buds give off a spicy aroma, and the trunks of the old trees once reached over 25 feet in diameter. Indians fashioned dugout canoes from these giants. Settlers boiled and ate the acorns of white oaks, before cutting down the trees for their fine wood. Flowering dogwoods erupt in the spring along with azaleas and purple flame, or rose rhododendrons (called laurels locally). The pink and white flowers of trilliums blanket the northeast foothills. Green and yellow violets, Dutchman's-breeches, lady's slippers, skunk cabbage, and 85 species of ferns all sprout in the undergrowth at various times.

Common animals in the mountains include rabbits, foxes, chipmunks, skunks, and raccoons. Many of Virginia's million or so white-tailed deer browse roadside grasses in Shenandoah National Park, while bobcats are rarely seen. Black bears are also uncommon; classified as omnivores, they subsist mostly on nuts, berries, and the tender parts of trees. Among the birdlife, the turkey vultures (buzzards) are the most impressive to watch, soaring on updrafts with a six-foot wingspan. Their red heads are a good field mark. Black vultures are smaller and less common. Another big blackbird, the raven alternates flapping with gliding, and croaking in one of a dozen particular ways. Wild turkeys, the largest birds in the hills, really look like those Thanksgiving decorations, and if you do enough hiking

you'll probably lose a few heartbeats to the sudden launch of a ruffed grouse. Red-tailed hawks can spot rodents and small reptiles from hundreds of feet in the air before diving for a meal.

THE PIEDMONT

Virginia's midsection runs from the base of the Blue Ridge (hence the term Piedmont, which translates roughly as "foot of the mountain") east across low, rolling hills rising no higher than 1,000 feet. It's separated from the coastal plain by the **fall line,** a topographic stripe where the central plain's harder metamorphic rock crumbles into the sandier soils of the coast. Many of the state's rivers, winding slowly across the flat countryside, turn into whitewater over the edge of the fall line, which roughly parallels I-95 as it runs from Alexandria to Petersburg.

Ranging from 50 miles wide in the north to almost 200 miles wide at the North Carolina border, Virginia's Piedmont has endured more human impact over the years than other parts of the state. Centuries of tree-clearing, farming, city-building, and suburb-spreading have turned much of the gently forested slopes into pastures, ponds, and pavement. The Piedmont, though transformed, still retains a patrician grace most evident in the horse country near Charlottesville and Lexington, where miles of whitewashed fences border deep green meadows.

Flora and Fauna

Oaks prevail among the trees that are left, though mostly in second- and third-stage stands of chestnut, red, and white varieties. Maples, cypress, and black gum line the wide, meandering rivers, while south of the James coniferous

bobcat

forests of pine begin to replace deciduous species. Springtime brings the vibrant pink and magenta blooms of redbud and the creamy white petals of flowering dogwoods. Morning glories and bluebells display two of the more gaudy blossoms among the flowers.

Those animals that have learned to coexist with people are abundant, including deer, raccoons, opossums, and squirrels, along with the occasional quail and wild turkey in the underbrush. Edge communities—where two ecosystems meet, such as pasture and forest or forest and lake,are good places to spot wildlife, especially birds. Indigo buntings can be spotted in hedgerows, and red-winged blackbirds prefer marshy land near water. Artificial lakes and riverbanks are prime habitat for muskrats, beavers, and kingfishers. By night your flashlight might catch the reflecting eyes of an opossum or bobcat. Reptiles include snapping and eastern box turtles and a nighttime cacophony of bullfrogs, gray treefrogs, and spring peepers. The northern water snake is most common, bearing a superficial resemblance to the poisonous (but nonswimming) copperhead.

THE COAST

The Tidewater

Once past the fall line the coastal plain begins its gentle descent to sea level. Over 3,300 tortuous miles of shoreline display a vast network of marshes, creeks, and rivers that widen into estuaries drawn and pushed by the ocean tides. Dry hardwood groves likewise transform into **flooded forests** of bald cypress and black gum. These wetter, less accessible forests have escaped the logger's ax more than their upland relatives, allowing their rich, wet soils to support largely unaltered ecosystems. Sixteen species of warbler flit through the Spanish moss in the Great Dismal Swamp, continuing south across the state line into North Carolina. Unusual species like green anole—a lizard that looks like a salamander—and Creole pearly eye butterflies inhabit the otherworldly recesses of Virginia's coastal swamps. Tannin, a natural acid, stains waters brown and keeps bacteria from growing. This led early sea captains to add these waters to their water stores on long journeys.

Impenetrable, boggy tangles of shrubs and trees called **pocosins** are rare and little-studied, once thought to be breeding grounds for all manner of poisonous snakes.

Mixing mineral salts from the ocean and fertile soil washed downriver from the Piedmont, **salt marshes** are some of the richest habitats in the state, indeed in all of North America. Organic matter decaying in these "great protein factories" helps each acre generate up to twice as much organic material as an acre of farmland, attracting migratory birds by the millions every spring and fall. Swans, geese, and ducks all float in the brackish waters at different times of year. Look for the black-tipped blue bill of the redhead, a diving duck, and listen for the supernatural hoot of barred owls at night.

Chesapeake Bay

The coastal plain flows into one of the largest estuaries in the world, fed by 100,000 streams and rivers in Maryland and Virginia. With an average depth of only 20 feet, the Chesapeake Bay meets the Atlantic at the superb natural harbor of Hampton Roads, mixing fresh and salt water into a rich blend that supports a staggering diversity of life. The bay's name comes from the Algonquian word *Chesepioc,* meaning "great shellfish bay," and bushels of oysters and crabs are still yanked up to the sunlight by the unique breed of Chesapeake watermen (or waterpeople, nowadays) as they have been for generations. Wading birds such as ibis, egrets, and great blue herons stalk the shoreline for smaller creatures. Ospreys and bald eagles—once brought to the edge of extinction by pesticides, hunting, and habitat destruction—soar overhead.

The Shore

At the ocean's edge stretch long, shallow lagoons and salt flats just a spit of sand away from open water. Change is the only constant along the beaches, especially in the case of the **barrier islands,** which line the seaward side of the Eastern Shore. These narrow strips of sand are thought to shelter a greater variety of birds than any other ecosystem in the country. Here the whistle of the endangered piping plover echoes over beaches in perpetual motion; beaches that are simultaneously eaten away and built up by the constant pounding waves. Tall marsh grass-

VIRGINIA TOURISM CORPORATION

Residents still make their living from the sea on Tangier Island.

es provide protection against erosion, at least long enough for stumpy trees to gain a foothold before being inundated by the waves to begin the cycle again. Muskrats ply tidal pools for shellfish as the rare least tern lays its eggs in shallow pits in the dunes. Thanks to the warming effect of the Gulf Stream you'll find many southerly plant and animal species at the northern extreme of their range along the Virginia coast, including live oak, sea oats, sawgrass from the Everglades, and the chicken turtle, with a neck longer than its shell.

CLIMATE

It's hard to decide whether summer's gentle prelude or its fiery swan song is more beautiful, but weather-wise, spring and fall are Virginia's most enjoyable seasons. On average the state manages to escape both the frigid northern winters and the incapacitating summer swelter of the Deep South, though high humidity levels can make temperatures in both seasons feel more extreme.

Spring's warm weather brings forth buds and blossoms throughout the mountains and Piedmont, though temperatures can still dip into the 30s at night (or even 20s in the mountains). Rivers swollen with melting snow surge across the Piedmont past electric groves of blooming bluebells, marigolds, violets, and daffodils. According to local lore, spring climbs the Blue Ridge

at 100 feet a day, pushing skyward the green line of new leaves dotted with the flowers of dogwoods, pink azaleas, and purple and white rhododendrons. Migrating birds leave their winter nesting grounds along the coast, while others arrive in breeding plumage ready to build a nest and start a family.

Summer brings high temperatures and humidity. Averages of 80° F seem more like 100° when there's enough water in the air to drink through a straw. Suddenly the coast is a lot more attractive than the muggy Piedmont, even with the sudden thunderstorms that condense in the afternoons. The mountains are also cooler than the lowlands in summer; nights can be downright nippy, making jackets and sleeping bags necessary for overnighters. Wildflowers bloom in succession the entire season, as newborn fawns and chicks take their first tentative wobbly steps.

The famous **autumn** colors peak near the middle of October with a vivid palette of yellow, gold, orange, red, and green, courtesy of maples, oaks, hickories, and assorted evergreen trees. Bird migrations peak during this season, sending hawks, shorebirds, and songbirds for the warmer climates of the southern U.S., the Caribbean, and Latin America. Harvest time brings roadside produce stands and huge barrel rolls of hay scattered throughout farmland in the Shenandoah and Piedmont. Balmy Indian summer weather gradually gives way to nighttime temperatures in the 40s by October.

In **winter,** the shore is bleak but still beautiful in its emptiness, as boardwalks stand empty and the wind whips whitecaps across the gray water. Snowfall in the Piedmont quickly turns into slush, but can still block unplowed back roads for days. Temperatures in both regions average near 30° F, rarely dipping into the teens for very long. You can experience clear, cold air and bare-branch views from the mountains, as long as the Skyline Drive and Blue Ridge Parkway aren't closed by snow. Waterfalls and seeps turn into garlands of ice, and the occasional ice storm or freezing fog can coat everything in a glittering film of frost.

CONSERVATION

The DCR's (Department of Conservation and Recreation) comprehensive **Virginia Natural Heritage Program,** Web site: www.state.va.us/~dcr/vaher.html, was started in 1989 with a goal of identifying, protecting, and managing Virginia's wide range of ecosystems. In less than a decade, scientists, resource managers, landscape architects, and computer jockeys have worked together to identify over 1,000 conservation sites to date containing rare species or communities. It was recognized by The Nature Conservancy in 1994 as one of the most outstanding natural heritage programs in the Western hemisphere.

Save the Bay

One of Virginia's main environmental challenges is keeping the Chesapeake Bay healthy. This incredibly complex ecosystem (or rather, collection of ecosystems) is doing better than it was a quarter century ago, thanks to strict fishing limits and restrictions on the flow of industrial pollutants and nutrient-laden farmland runoff. But there's still plenty of work to be done. Algae and silt cloud the water to the point of inhibiting the growth of underwater grasses that shelter crabs and fish. Annual algal "blooms" thrive on the nitrogen, phosphorus, and other chemicals introduced into the bay by polluting industries, car exhaust, and agricultural and residential runoff. The tiny plants then decompose through a process that eats up the oxygen in the water, creating "dead zones" incapable of supporting fish.

In 1996 health problems such as skin rashes, respiratory trouble, and memory loss began to appear among bay fishermen. Fish soon started showing up dead by the thousands, covered with strange red skin lesions. By August 1997, these "kills" had spread from the Pocomoke River in Delaware through Maryland to the top of Virginia's Eastern Shore, claiming as many as 10,000 fish at a time. When the culprit—a bacteria called *Pfiesteria piscicida*—was discovered, Maryland closed the Pocomoke and two other tributaries and local seafood sales plummeted. It's thought the bacteria, normally harmless, is turned toxic by excessive nutrients running into the bay from local pastures, where chicken manure is used as fertilizer (chickens outnumber people in the area by 500 to 1). The Rappahannock River was later found to have a 75% lesion rate.

One proposed solution to restore the bay to its former glory is to bring oyster populations back to their ancient levels. A century ago the bay sheltered so many oysters their huge shell banks were a navigation hazard to boats, and together they could filter the entire volume of water in the bay in 3-4 days. Only one percent of that is left now, meaning it takes a year to filter the same water. Scientists' computer models predict even 10% of the original levels would go a long way toward restoring the ecosystem, pointing to the example of zebra mussels in the Great Lakes. Even though they're considered non-native pests, the mussels have cleaned the water enough to bring back aquatic animals and plants gone for three decades. Bumper crops of stinging jellyfish might be reduced in the Chesapeake Bay as a side benefit of increasing oyster levels.

Virginia and Maryland are developing disease-resistant strains of oysters, and dumping more than three million bushels of oyster shells on old reef spots every year in the hope of re-seeding faded breeding grounds. The most vocal resistance is coming from local fishermen, who balk at the idea of setting aside a quarter of the current oyster beds as sanctuaries to prevent overfishing. They argue that natural biological rhythms and disease are the culprits, not human activity. In the end it might take a non-fishing subsidy to equal the success achieved with the rockfish population, which was brought back from the edge of disaster though a cooperative

CONSERVATION ORGANIZATIONS

Chesapeake Bay Foundation
162 Prince George St., Annapolis, MD 21401,
tel. (888) SAVE-BAY (888-728-3229),
Web site: www.cbf.org

Founded in 1966, the Chesapeake Bay Foundation is now the largest regional environmental organization in the country. Some 87,000 members form local BayWatcher groups, which clean streams and plant trees. You can help out during the annual Clean the Bay Day the first Saturday in June; call (757) 640-555, ext. 4444, for more information. It maintains a field office in Norfolk at 100 W. Plume St., tel. (757) 622-1964.

The Conservation Fund
1800 N. Kent St., Ste. 1120, Arlington, VA
22209-2156, tel. (703) 525-6300, fax 525-4610

Another group dedicated to long-term conservation solutions that balance economic and environmental concerns, the Conservation Fund has been instrumental in preserving 1.3 million acres for future generations. Its Civil War Battlefield Campaign has helped protect 5,600 acres on 25 battlefields throughout the country.

Friends of the North Fork of the Shenandoah
P.O. Box 746, 122 South Commerce St.,
Woodstock, VA 22664, tel. (540) 459-8550,
fax 459-8805, e-mail: friends@shentel.net,
Web site: www.gmu.edu/bios/shenando/north

Close to 1,000 members have worked together since 1988 to help protect the North Fork, its tributaries, and its entire watershed.

Sierra Club
P.O. Box 14648 , Richmond, VA 23221-0648,
tel. (804) 722-5550,
Web site: www.sierraclubva.org

Thirteen local groups make up the Virginia chapter of this venerable association founded by John Muir in 1892. Monthly meetings, outings, and volunteer activities help members and anyone who's interested stay aware of local conservation issues and how to influence political change for the environment.

The Nature Conservancy
1815 N Lynn St., Arlington, VA 22209, tel. (703) 841-5300, fax 841-1283, Web site: www.tnc.org

This private organization was formed in 1951 "to protect lands and waters needed to preserve plants, animals, and natural communities that represent the diversity of life on Earth." As of 1997 it owned or helped guard 10 million acres in the U.S. and 57 million acres abroad. Two hundred thousand of those acres are spread through 26 reserves in Virginia, including the priceless Virginia Coast Reserve along the Eastern Shore. The Virginia chapter is based in Charlottesville at 1233 A Cedars Ct., tel. (804) 295-6106.

**Virginia Department
of Conservation and Recreation**
1500 E. Main St., Ste. 312, Richmond, VA
23219, tel. (804) 786-1712.,
e-mail: sla@dcr.state.va.us,
Web site: www.state.va.us/~dcr/dcr_home.htm

The state's leading conservation agency manages nearly 70,000 acres of state park or natural areas, along with projects focusing on land management issues and soil and water conservation. Volunteer internships with potential for academic credit are possible, involving a commitment of at least 120 hours over four weeks. For more information contact the Natural Heritage Information Manager, tel. (804) 786-8377, fax 371-2674.

Virginia Ducks Unlimited
8632 Mount Vernon Highway, Alexandria, VA
22309, e-mail: webmaster@ducks-unlimited-va.
org, Web site: www.ducks-unlimited-va.org

The world's largest private wetlands conservation organization began raising money to protect wetlands and any creatures lucky enough to live in them in 1937. Today the organization counts over half a million members, who contribute to projects in the U.S., Canada, and Mexico. Ducks Unlimited was instrumental in the passing of the North American Waterfowl Management Plan, an international agreement with the goal of rebuilding North America's waterfowl populations to their 1970s' levels. Over 20,000 acres in Virginia to date have been set aside thanks to its efforts.

Virginia Wildlife Federation
1001 East Broad St. LL5, Richmond, VA 23219,
tel. (804) 648-3136

This local affiliate of the National Wildlife Federation focuses its efforts on endangered habitat, water quality, land management, and wetlands conservation. Local educational projects form the core of its approach, which also includes advocacy and litigation initiatives.

effort among Maryland, Virginia, and Delaware agencies. And with the bay area's population expected to grow 12% or more by 2010, the pressure is on.

The Blue Ridge Turns Purple
Visibility has never been perfect from the crest of the Blue Ridge; even early accounts of the views begin, "On a clear day . . . ." Just like in the Smoky Mountains of North Carolina, water vapor combined with airborne dust and organic compounds given off by trees forms a natural hill-shrouding haze, especially in summer. In recent years, though, industrial smog and auto exhaust have added their own purple blanket that began gradually reaching the peaks around 1976. Increasing amounts of acid rain hurt trees and fish in Shenandoah National Park, as runoff churned up by livestock and poultry produces the same results in mountain rivers and streams as it does in the Chesapeake Bay. Local conservation groups like Friends of the Shenandoah try to keep tabs on water quality and industry, but the job can be overwhelming.

One promising example of conservation in the high country is a compromise reached over the Laurel Fork Special Management Area in Highland County (see the **Shenandoah** chapter). In July 1996, Thornwood Gas of Pennsylvania received permission from the U.S. Forest Service to build a 34-mile pipeline along the boundary of the management area. Local residents, worried that the company would start to drill in the pristine woodlands, formed an opposition coalition and began to consider prohibitive lawsuits. The Nature Conservancy then stepped in and brokered an unprecedented agreement. Thornwood Gas was allowed to build the pipeline, but only by burying it alongside existing roads. Plus the company agreed not to drill, but instead to transfer 1,700 acres of surface rights to The Nature Conservancy and to draw gas in compliance with non-damaging subsurface rights owned by the U.S. Bureau of Land Management.

HISTORY

Good Old Dominion, blessed mother of us all.

~Thomas Jefferson

PRECOLONIAL ERA

No one is sure when the first humans crossed the ice bridge over the Bering Strait to enter the Americas—estimates range as high as 50,000 years ago—but anthropologists generally agree that they subsisted on seasonal hunting and gathering. Musk ox and caribou fell to stone-tipped spears and wooden clubs, supplying the primitive nomads with food, clothing, and material for tools. Roots, nuts, and berries filled in when game was scarce, and temporary encampments were moved to follow the herds or flee the harsher seasons.

Approximately 11,000 years ago, the glaciers of the most recent ice age retreated to 200 miles north of present-day Virginia. The future state's first inhabitants arrived from the west to find unfamiliar species of bison, deer, turkeys, bears, and elk moving up from the south. These family groups often camped alongside streams, leaving behind only chipped stone tools and discarded flakes to record their passing.

Within a few thousand years the ice age ended completely, taking with it the larger prehistoric mammals such as mastodons and wooly mammoths. Temperatures continued to climb, relegating cold-weather tree species such as hemlocks, birches, and firs (which once flourished at lower elevations) to the Appalachian peaks. Human populations increased slowly but surely, so that by the time of Christ, the **Woodland Period** was in full swing. Amid lowland forests of hickory, oak, and chestnut a more settled lifestyle emerged. Rudimentary agriculture produced crops of corn, squash, and beans, while fragile pottery made continuous migration less practical. The discovery of the bow and arrow made hunting and warfare more efficient. Relatively small numbers kept native Virginians' impact on their environment to a minimum, even-though they occasionally burned large swaths of forest just to flush out game and drove entire herds of bison over the edges of cliffs, killing more than they could possibly use at one time.

engraving after a
drawing by John
White

DOVER PUBLICATIONS, INC.

Welcome to the "New" World

When they arrived in 1607, the first European settlers found the Tidewater area under tho control of the **Powhatan Confederacy,** an Algonquian group whose lands stretched from North Carolina to the Potomac River. Thirty tribes containing some 10,000 people lived in palisaded villages by rivers or on hillsides under the leadership of Wahunsonacock, called Chief Powhatan by the Europeans.

The Powhatans fished and hunted, and grew corn, squash, pumpkins, and herbs in summer gardens. Dressed in animal hides and woven plant fibers, they decorated themselves with feathers, tattoos, and jewelry made of shells, clay beads, and pearls. High priests called *Periku'* offered sacrifices to *Okee* or **Mannith,** worshipped as the "Creator of All Things."

Farther west and north lived the **Monacans** and **Manahoacs,** occupying the eastern edge of the Blue Ridge and the upper banks of the James, Potomac, and Rappahannock Rivers into the Allegheny Mountains. These traditional enemies of the Powhatans shared a common Siouxan cultural heritage and language. Other native groups included the **Nansemond,** who were such good farmers they became known as the granary for the early English colony; the **Rappahannock** near present-day Richmond; and small groups of **Cherokee** up from the south.

THE COLONIAL PERIOD

Jamestown

At the turn of the 17th century, England was painfully aware that it needed to get a foothold in the New World, which Spain had been busily colonizing, converting, and pillaging for the last century. Three decades of attempts finally bore fruit in 1607, when three ships—*Sarah Constant, Goodspeed,* and *Discovery*—brought 143 settlers to the mouth of the Chesapeake Bay. In contrast to the conquistadors financed by the Spanish Crown, the English expedition was a private venture organized by the London-based Virginia Company. Captain Christopher Newport led the ships 30 miles up the James River, named after the English king, where on May 14, 1607, the colonists tied their ships to trees, disembarked, and set about building the first permanent English settlement in the Americas.

Soon James Fort stood guard over Virginia, the name given to all of North America not under the control of the Spanish or French, after the English Virgin Queen (Elizabeth I). The land was rich, game plentiful, and the natives, at least at first, were friendly, but the colony still almost failed within its first few years. Inept leaders, with the exception of adventurer John Smith, were ill-suited to the hard decisions and harder labor. Despite warnings to avoid damp, low-lying areas, they built their settlement in a salt marsh, which led to famine and disease. The winter of 1609-10 became known as the Starving Time, during which things got so bad one colonist killed and ate his wife ("for which hee was executed, as hee well deserved," wrote a fellow sufferer; "now whether shee was better roasted, boyled or carbonado'd I know not . . . "). The colony was abandoned in May 1610 by its 60 remaining colonists; however, their departing boat was met by two ships bearing Gov. Thomas Gates from England, and the survivors were convinced to stick it out.

Colonist John Rolfe, who had married John Smith's alleged 13-year-old savior Pocahontas in 1614 (not for any "carnall affection; but for the good of this plantation, for the honour of our countrie"), began a legacy a few years later by planting the first crop of West Indian tobacco (*Nicotiana tabacum*). With some selective breeding the large-leaf tobacco plant would prove a stable revenue crop in high demand back home in England. Representative government, in a limited sense, began in June 1619, when the first legislative assembly in the New World convened for six days in a "generall Assemblie" in the Jamestown church. The first boatload of 20 African slaves arrived that same year.

Things Get Worse Before They Get Better

Fewer than 1,200 out of 4,000 arrivals survived to 1624, victims to Indian attacks and a major epidemic in 1622-23 that killed 500 people. Though friendly at first with gifts of food and advice, the Powhatans turned hostile when they realized the Europeans were here to stay. Within two years all the main native towns had been seized, Chief Powhatan had fled, and any colonists venturing beyond the walls of the settlement took their lives in their hands. A tempo-

---

VIRGINIA'S TRIBES TODAY

In 1990 the state's native groups—defined by proof of existence for a minimum of 200 years—made up 0.2% of the population. The **Pamunkey** (pa-MUN-kee) live along the river of the same name in King William County, which contains the supposed burial site of Chief Powhatan. In the same country live fewer than 100 **Mattaponi** (ma-ta-poe-NIGH) on a reservation along the Mattaponi River dating to 1658. A smaller group called the Upper Mattaponi live off the reservation. Charles City County is home to 1,000 **Chickahominy** mingled with the non-native population. Half that many **Monacans** make up the westernmost surviving group, and 300 **Nansemond** live in Norfolk, Chesapeake, Virginia Beach, and Portsmouth near their ancient hunting grounds around the Great Dismal Swamp. About 750 of the **United Rappahannock** were moved from Richmond County to King and Queen County.

Events

Typical powwows echo with heavy drums, dancing, and chanting by participants in buckskin clothes and eagle and turkey feathers. Native American veterans proudly display their U.S. Army uniforms beneath the flags of their county and tribe. Chiefs lead processions, followed by braves in war paint, women, and children. Native American food and crafts are featured. The **Monacan Pow-Wow**, tel. (804) 929-0334, is held in June, along with the **Virginia Indian Heritage Festival** in Jamestown and a **Mattaponi Pow Wow.** The United Rappahannock tribe hosts the **American Indian Heritage Celebration** at the George Washington Birthplace in Westmoreland County, tel. (804) 769-1508, in early August, followed closely by the **Nansemond Indian Tribe Association Pow Wow and Festival** at Lone Star Lakes Lodge, off Rt. 10 and Pembroke Lane near Suffolk, tel. (804) 232-0248. A general **Indian Heritage Festival and Pow Wow** happens at the Virginia Museum of Natural History, 1001 Douglas Ave., Martinsville, tel. (540) 666-8600, in early September.

Our men were destroyed with [such] cruell diseases as Swellings, Flixes, Burning Fevers, and by warres, and some departed suddenly, but for the most part they died of meere famine. There were never Englishmen left in a foreigne countrey in such miserie as wee were in this new discovered Virginia.

—George Percy, early colonist

CAPTAIN JOHN SMITH

The savior of Jamestown saw more action before setting foot in the New World than most of us see in a lifetime. Born in 1580 in Lincolnshire, England, Smith spent his childhood on his family's farm before being apprenticed as a teenager to a local merchant. At age 16 he ran away to fight in France for Dutch independence from Spain, worked on a merchant ship in the Mediterranean Sea, and went to Transylvania to battle the Turks. Knocked out in battle and left for dead, Smith was captured and sold to a Turkish pasha who sent him as a present to his heartthrob in Constantinople. The lady, reportedly smitten with her English prisoner, sent him to her brother, who abused him so badly Smith killed his master and fled. With an iron collar still around his neck, he escaped through Russia, ending up back in England in time to buy stock in the newly formed Virginia Company in 1605; he was 26 years old.

On December 20, 1606, Smith and 142 other hopeful settlers sailed west. A stubborn, disputatious nature quickly got him in trouble with the trip leaders, who accused the adventurer of conspiracy and had him arrested. At their arrival in Chesapeake Bay, though, the sealed expedition orders were opened and revealed that Smith had been named a member of the governing council. When other leaders initially kept him from assuming the position he set out west to look for a passage to the Pacific. He got far enough to discover the falls on the James River near Richmond, at least, then returned to find the settlement in dire straits. Local natives had becoming increasingly hostile, and the ill-prepared colonists were reduced to a daily ration of one pint of wormy grain boiled in water. In the words of one settler, "Our drinke was water, our lodgings, castles in the air."

Smith assumed leadership and set out to whip the settlement and its inhabitants into shape. Sturdy houses and defenses were constructed and relations with the Powhatans were improved to allow colonists to trade for corn, fish, and other food. Around this time Smith began a series of expeditions up the "Patawomeck" and "Topoahannock" Rivers on which he based his famous 1606 map of Virginia. Accurate enough to serve local navigators for a century, Smith's map was used to survey the Mason-Dixon line between Pennsylvania and Maryland, which separated free states from slave states during the Civil War.

While searching for the source of the "Chickahamania" River in December 1607, Smith was captured by the Powhatans, who took him to a lodge on the banks of the York. In a later account he described Chief Powhatan as "a tall well propotioned man, with a sower looke . . . proudly lying upon a Bedstead a foote high, upon tenne or twelve Mattes, richly hung with manie Chaynes of great Pearles about his necke . . . with such a grave Maiesticall countenance, as drave me into admiration to see such state in a naked Savage."

According to his own account, Smith was then condemned to death and laid out on the clubbing block when Powhatan's 13-year-old daughter Pocahontas rushed forward and begged her father to spare his life. Whatever the case, he was eventually freed and returned to lead the colony, which had been hampered by laziness and inept leadership and was struggling through the winter of 1607. Appointed president of Jamestown in September 1608, Smith enforced a rigid discipline, strengthened fortifications, and started general military training. Idlers were spurred on with the edict, "He who does not work, will not eat." His efforts saw the group through the next hard winter until more settlers arrived with provisions in the summer of 1609. That September he was wounded severely enough in a gunpowder explosion to force him to return to England; he never went back to Virginia.

On later journeys, Smith explored and mapped the Maine and Massachusetts coastlines, dubbing the area New England with the approval of Prince Charles. On another voyage he was captured by pirates, escaped, and returned to England penniless. One final colonizing attempt in 1617 ended in failure. For the rest of his life Smith praised the wonders of the western continent in books such as *A Description of New England* (1625), *The Generall Historie of Virginia, New England, and the Summer Isles* (1624), and *The True Travels, Adventures and Observations of Captaine John Smith in Europe, Asia, Africa and America* (1630). He died in London in 1631.

rary truce followed the marriage of Powhatan's daughter Pocahontas to colonist John Rolfe in 1614, but relations quickly deteriorated. A surprise attack in March 1622 under Powhatan's successor Opechancanough killed 400 settlers. In 1624 the Virginia Company's charter was revoked, and Jamestown came under British government rule, making it the first royal colony.

Nonetheless, by 1634 the colony counted 5,000 inhabitants, concentrated along the James and York Rivers, the Eastern Shore, and the Hampton Roads area. Most settlers under Gov. Sir William Berkeley (1642-52 and 1660-77) were small-scale farmers, artisans, and tradesmen, many of whom had worked their way out of indentured servitude and found themselves owning land for the first time. Tobacco quickly became the major crop, creating a demand for slave labor. The first boatload of "20 and odd Negroes" had arrived in Hampton Roads in 1619 as indentured servants rather than slaves, but by 1660—the year before slavery was legalized—the colony counted one black for every 20 whites. Five hundred more colonists were killed in a 1644 Indian attack, one that lead to the capture and murder of the blind, elderly Chief Opechancanough. A treaty of submission signaled the beginning of the long, slow western displacement of Native tribes.

Early Unrest and Bacon's Rebellion

Supporters of Charles I, who was deposed and killed in 1644, fled to the New World and set down the roots of a gentry society with firm historical ties to England, hence Virginia's nickname of the Old Dominion. Tobacco sales were funneled through a handful of London merchants, driving prices down and making it more and more difficult for small Virginia farms to turn a profit. Charles II, placed in power in 1660 following the English Civil War, tried to grant all of Virginia's northern neck, then the entire colony, to English nobility.

Further impolitic decisions like this provoked a rebellion in 1676 led by 26-year-old Nathaniel Bacon. After the colonial government had refused to help frontier settlers fight off repeated Indian attacks, Bacon spearheaded an unauthorized campaign against the Susquehanna tribe and was labeled a rebel and traitor by aging Governor Berkeley. During the fighting that en-

sued, Bacon occupied the General Assembly, burned Jamestown, and spoke out against the increasingly corrupt and self-serving government. After Bacon's untimely death the rebellion soon collapsed, but the point had been made.

Expansion and the Golden Age

Through the late 17th and most of the 18th century the colony spread steadily west from the Tidewater. In March 1669, German scholar John Lederer became one of the first white men to reach the crest of the Blue Ridge. Scotch-Irish and Germans moved down from Pennsylvania into the Shenandoah Valley near the middle of the 18th century, sparking friction with French settlers and their native allies that resulted in the French and Indian War (1754-1763).

This same era also became known as the "Golden Age" of plantations, financed by huge tobacco profits and based largely on the snobby society of English estate owners. A core of First Families with names such as Carter, Randolph, and Byrd formed a "bourgeois aristocracy" that defended self-government jealously, as long as it served their own interests. Speculation in land and slave trading brought in even more money, while the basic concepts and advocates of American liberal thought were being born. By 1715, the colony counted one black for every three whites.

The Eve of Revolution

The more than 120,000 persons living in the British colony in 1715 made a modest subsistence in a stable, if narrowly based, plantation economy. Colonists were still prohibited many rights extended to English subjects across the Atlantic, though, and royal edicts kept overriding acts passed by the Virginia House of Burgesses. In 1763 a ridiculous, unenforceable law prohibiting westward expansion angered frontier settlers and coastal land speculators alike. Taxation without representation reached its peak when Britain passed the Stamp Act of 1765, which was designed to help extract money from the colonies for the recent war in England. Following a fiery speech by Patrick Henry (in which he implied the colonies might be better off without George III, to which the crowd responded with cries of "Treason!"), the Virginia General Assembly passed the Stamp Act Resolves which decreed that only Virginia had the right to tax Virginians. Repealed in 1766, the Stamp Act was replaced by heavy import duties the next year.

In 1773 the perpetrators of the Boston Tea Party received the support of the local government, even as the British Parliament closed the port to all commerce and sent in troops to maintain order. When Virginia's Governor Dunmore dissolved the General Assembly in response, the burgesses met at Raleigh Tavern in Williamsburg to propose a meeting in Philadelphia to discuss seriously separation from England. George Washington, Patrick Henry, and Benjamin Harrison all made it to the first Continental Congress in September 1774, where a militia was organized to defend the colonies. At the March 1775 Virginia Convention at St. John's Church in Richmond, Patrick Henry made his most famous speech. Although nobody present actually wrote it down, witnesses recalled it ending along these lines: "I know not what course other may take; but as for me, give me liberty, or give me death."

THE REVOLUTIONARY WAR

For the first three years of the American Revolution, Virginia managed to escape the fighting beyond supplying leaders, troops, supplies, and the occasional landmark document. In May 1776, the same month Gov. John Dunmore fled to England, radicals and conservatives united in the decision for independence at the Virginia Convention in Williamsburg. By the time the ink had dried on the U.S. Constitution (penned mostly by Virginian Thomas Jefferson), two other papers had been completed: George Mason's Virginia Bill of Rights, asserting that "all power is vested in, and consequently derived from, the people" (this later served as the model for the Federal Bill of Rights); and Virginia's first constitution, ending 169 years as an English

colony. Patrick Henry was chosen as governor of Virginia, and no one seemed to notice the slight irony that although Virginians had sounded the loudest demands for liberty, Virginia was still closest in sentiment to England of all the colonies. It was the Virginia gentry who were to lead the struggle for independence. "These gentlemen from Virginia appear to be the most spirited and consistent of any," wrote John Adams upon the arrival of the Virginia delegates to the first Continental Congress.

George Washington had been elected commander-in-chief of the Continental Army soon after the first shots were fired at Lexington and Concord. Many of his fellow Virginians made a name under him, including cavalry leader Col. Light Horse Harry Lee, father of Robert E., and George Rogers Clark, who managed to win the Northwest Territory from Britain in 1778-79 after a hard-fought winter campaign. Help from French forces under the Marquis de Lafayette proved crucial.

When Thomas Jefferson became governor of Virginia in 1779, he found the state treasury practically emptied by the expense of supplying the scrappy Continental Army. Life in Virginia remained more or less unaffected by the war, until English ships invaded via Hampton Roads in 1779, forcing the capital to be moved to Richmond for safety. Jefferson resigned his position in June 1780, narrowly avoiding capture by the British, thanks to Capt. Jack Jouett, who rode all night to warn him at his Monticello home. Seven other legislators were captured.

Infamous traitor Benedict Arnold—one of Washington's most trusted commanders before becoming a brigadier general in the British Army—and troops destroyed Richmond in January 1781. Before the year was out, however, Britain's Gen. Lord Charles Cornwallis found himself surrounded on the Yorktown peninsula between 10,000 Continental troops under Washington and 8,000 under Lafayette, with

Benedict Arnold

the French fleet of Admiral de Grasse preventing escape by sea. On October 19, Cornwallis marched his troops (many of whom were, according to one witness, "much in liquor") across Surrender Field between the ragged Continental Army and the spotless French forces. A band played "The World Turned Upside Down," and a new country was born.

After the Revolution

The U.S. Constitution was adopted at the Philadelphia Constitutional Convention in 1787. Virginia's approval of it spurred a debate that pitted Virginians who had helped draft it, including George Washington and James Madison, against fellow statesmen wary of an omnipotent national government, led by Patrick Henry and George Mason. The Bill of Rights proved a good compromise, and proratification forces prevailed 89-79. In 1788, Virginia became the new nation's 10th state. George Washington was elected president a year later, Thomas Jefferson became his secretary of state, and the new country was off and running.

BETWEEN THE WARS

Setting Up a New Country

Early American politics were marked by conflict over how much power the national government should have. Thomas Jefferson and James Madison championed states' rights, arguing that the federal apparatus should stick to what was specifically outlined in the Constitution and leave everything else to state and local governments. Federalists, on the other hand, followed the lead of New Yorker Alexander Hamilton in pushing for the widest possible role of the federal government. Regardless, Virginians dominated national politics for the first four decades, supplying four of the first five presidents, including an uninterrupted stretch from 1801-25. Also during that time Virginian John Marshall served as chief justice of the U.S. Supreme Court.

Antebellum Life

The first half of the 19th century is still remembered as one of the more idyllic times in Virginia's history, evoking the plantation nostalgia of hoop skirts, gentlemen on horses, and sun-drenched fields of cotton and tobacco. Of course, it *was* an ideal time—for a select few. All others worked themselves to the bone to make a living (or, in the case of slaves, simply to survive). Small-scale agriculture was still the norm—an average farm in 1850 was only 340 acres—and most farmers were too poor to own slaves, instead relying on family members for help in raising peanuts, potatoes, corn, hogs, chickens, and cattle. Rutted roads connected scattered towns where courthouses served as social hubs and mercantiles sold everything from medicines to bolts of cloth. Any necessary tools or buildings were fashioned by the farmers themselves or hired artisans.

Family connections were paramount, and served to emphasize—in a polite way—the gap between the gentry and the rabble. The gap existed even in worship, the upper class attended Presbyterian and Episcopal services while the populace primarily attended Methodist, Lutheran, and Baptist churches. Above all, the concepts of civility, humility, and honest hard work shaped Virginia society. "The Virginian," wrote historian Percival Renier, "liked to think of himself as a plain and homespun-appearing gentleman with a noble pedigree, which naturally put him above airs and snobbery and fine clothes . . . ." State politics were split between the demands for representation from burgeoning western counties, universal taxpayer suffrage, and freedom for slaves on one hand, and on the other the interests of wealthy eastern landowners and merchants who granted certain grudging concessions.

The Slavery Issue

The narrow-minded policies and political conservatism of the aspiring aristocrats of the east eventually began to mire Virginia's antebellum period in economic and political stagnation. Granted, the Founding Fathers were a hard act to follow, but the Virginia politicians faltered again and again, allowing the port of Hampton Roads to fall far behind those in New York, Baltimore, and Boston, and resisting the construction of a canal between the Potomac and the Ohio Rivers. New England became the nation's textile center instead of Richmond, public education suffered (with the exception of the University of Virginia), and a population exodus caused the state to

VIRGINIA'S EIGHT PRESIDENTS

The Old Dominion has supplied more U.S. presidents than any other state.

George Washington
1789-1797

William Henry Harrison
1841 (died during term)

Thomas Jefferson
1801-1809

John Tyler
1841-1845

James Madison
1809-1817

Zachary Taylor
1849-1850
(died during term)

James Monroe
1817-1825

Woodrow Wilson
1913-1921

lose 13 congressmen between the years 1810 and 1860.

Fostering the decline was the increasingly inefficient but entrenched plantation economy. Tobacco exhausted the soil and brought in less and less money, but even though the slave trade had been abolished in 1778, the practice of slavery continued, and came to be seen as the rotten root of a weakening tree. By the turn of the century more than one-third of Virginia lived in bondage. Thomas Jefferson—the slave-owner who had written about the equality of man—had foreseen a conflict at the turn of the century:

forced separation of a slave family

> *Indeed I tremble for my country when I reflect that God is just: that His justice cannot sleep forever: that considering numbers, nature and natural means only, a revolution of the wheel of fortune, an exchange of situation, is among possible events . . . .*

Northern states began to clamor for emancipation as slave revolts gained momentum. In 1800 a huge slave named Gabriel was to have led 1,000 others in a thwarted rebellion in Richmond. Thirty years later, black preacher Nat Turner led 60 slaves to kill 58 whites—mostly women and children—in Southampton County near the North Carolina line. Though the Rebels were caught within 48 hours, the event threw gasoline on the fire—pro-slavery forces blamed abolitionist propaganda and killed innocent blacks in retaliation.

Most arguments against slavery came from the industrialized North, where factories provided plenty of work for men of any color and smaller farms made a large labor force unnecessary. The disregard for the slaves' human rights was an issue in the new western territories, while Southern abolitionists resented the political stranglehold held by the pro-slavery planter aristoc-

racy. In the end, economics was probably the most important factor: the poor farmer in Georgia and the owner of a Massachusetts textile factory found it equally impossible to compete against slave labor.

Slave owners dreaded that these regions would unify against them. They found too much of their declining income tied up in human beings—close to half of the taxable wealth of the Tidewater was in slaves—and argued that the system was better, for everyone but the slaves, than the alternative of wage slavery for whites. It was also argued that there were too many slaves to simply set free, or so their owners said. Most southern whites found it impossible to imagine the transition to a stable, prosperous society in which two races worked side by side as equals. And who would pay to ship the freed slaves out west, or back to Africa?

An 1832 plan for gradual emancipation failed in the Virginia General Assembly, putting the issue to rest until the Mexican-American War (1846-48), which again raised a central issue, last heard in the Missouri Controversy of 1819: the status—slave or free—of new territories admitted into the Union. A slight economic recovery in the 1850s, including Virginian Cyrus McCormick's invention of the mechanical reaper in 1831, the construction of more railroads, and the flourishing of Richmond's slave-powered Tredegar Iron Works, did little to distract from the debate.

Prelude to War

In October 1859 the country was rocked by a raid on the federal arsenal at Harper's Ferry (now in West Virginia) led by abolitionist extremist John Brown. Seventeen whites and five free blacks tried to steal enough weapons to arm slaves for a rebellion, and in the process killed the mayor and other townspeople. The group was eventually captured by U.S. Marines under the command of a young lieutenant colonel named Robert E. Lee. Their death sentences gained the abolitionist cause a white martyr and forced slave owners to face the reality that opponents of slavery were willing to fight, and die, for their cause. Brown's dying words echoed over the widening chasm: "The sins of this guilty land can only be purged with blood."

The final straw came in 1860 when Abraham Lincoln was elected president on a Republican platform, pledging to keep slavery out of the territories. On December 20, South Carolina seceded from the Union, followed soon after by Mississippi, Alabama, Florida, Georgia, Louisiana, and Texas. When Fort Sumter on the South Carolina coast was attacked by Southern artillery on April 10, Lincoln called for 75,000 volunteers to put down the "insurrection." Originally against secession, Virginia nonetheless withdrew on April 19. Fireworks exploded above Richmond as "ten thousand hurrahing men and boys" carried torches through the streets to celebrate the occasion. Six days later Virginia became part of the Confederate States of America.

"They say Virginia has no grievance," reported one contemporary writer; "she comes out on a point of honor."

THE CIVIL WAR

In creating a new country, the American Revolution had left two major issues unresolved: the true dominion of the federal government over individual states, and the contradiction between the words in the Declaration of Independence that ensured the equality of man and the fact that in America more people owned other people than in any other country in the world. Before

---

Any understanding of this nation has to be based, and I mean really based, on an understanding of the Civil War. It . . . defined us as what we are and it opened us to being what we became, good and bad things . . . It was the crossroads of our being, and it was a hell of a crossroads.

—SHELBY FOOTE, THE CIVIL WAR

---

those questions would be answered, four years of fighting made muddy wastelands of the same acres fought over in the Revolutionary War less than a century before and close to 700,000 Americans died—more than in both World Wars put together.

As a border state only a rifle shot from Washington, D.C., and home to the Confederate capital, Virginia suffered more major battles and witnessed more casualties than any other state. Both the first major clash of the Civil War and the peace treaty that signaled its end happened in the Old Dominion (on property owned by the same man), while the four intervening years left her graveyards full, her society in ruins, and literally tore the state in half.

Early Fighting

The Civil War began in earnest at the **First Battle of Bull Run** on July 21, 1861. Convinced the Rebels would turn and flee at the first hint of trouble, Washingtonians rode out from the city and spread out picnics on a hillside near Manassas to watch the battle. Fewer than half of the 57,000 troops present actually fought, and confusion reigned. Blue and gray uniforms appeared on both sides, along with highland kilts and baggy trousers straight from North Africa. The early Confederate flag resembled the Stars and Stripes so closely that gunners mistakenly fired on their own troops. On their retreat to Washington, routed Federal soldiers found themselves entangled with the carriages of fleeing spectators, and all hopes of a quick victory were extinguished.

Battle of the Ironclads

Union troops retreating from Portsmouth had burned, among other things, a steam frigate called the **Merrimac.** Desperate for any kind of naval weapon to help break the tightening noose of the Union blockade, Confederate shipbuilders restored the charred hulk, covered it with steeply sloping iron plates, and rechristened her the **Virginia.** In March 1862, the reborn ship steamed into Hampton Roads like a "floating barn belching smoke," according to one witness, rammed a carriage-sized hole through one Union warship, sank another with cannon fire, and drove off three more as shells and bullets bounced off her sides. The next morning the Union unveiled its own metal ship called the **Monitor,** built with

the C.S.S. Virginia *and the* Monitor

a round turret and a flat deck even with the waterline. Four hours of fighting and maneuvering accomplished little besides demonstrating the ships' resistance to gunfire. Hampton Roads remained under Union control, Gen. George B. McClellan was able to move troops by water to occupy Norfolk, and the *Virginia* was blown up to escape capture. The *Monitor* sank in a storm off North Carolina in December.

The Rebels Forge Ahead

Virginia's Confederate Tidewater area was evacuated following the defeat of the *Virginia,* and the first struggles for Richmond began. During what became known as the **Seven Days battles** in late June 1862, General McClellan propelled his newly trained Army of the Potomac to within sight of Richmond, but was pushed back by Robert E. Lee's inspired tactics. Gen. Thomas "Stonewall" Jackson helped Lee by tying up Union reinforcements in the Shenandoah Valley. Close to 35,000 soldiers died, but the threat to Richmond was lifted, for the moment. At the **Second Battle of Manassas** in Aug.-Sept., Union Gen. John Pope made the mistake of ordering pursuit when the Confederates weren't really retreating. Lee, Jackson, and Gen. James Longstreet took the advantage, attacking with such ferocity that Pope barely managed a nighttime withdrawal back across the Bull Run River to safety.

With renewed confidence, Lee moved north, but the capture of a copy of Confederate marching orders led to a clash with McClellan at Antietam (an-TEET-um) near Sharpsburg, MD, on September 17.

This battle remains the single deadliest day in American history, leaving 12,410 Union soldiers and 10,700 Rebels sprawled in the dirt. Lincoln saw an opportunity he had been waiting for, and on January 1, 1863, issued the Emancipation Proclamation, freeing all slaves in areas not held by Union forces. This edict, which Lincoln called "the central act of my administration, and the greatest single event of the 19th century," thus turned the Civil War into a fight over slavery, pure and simple. England and France couldn't afford diplomatic recognition of the Confederacy without appearing to support the "peculiar institution" they had outlawed long ago, and the Southern cause became forever linked with human bondage.

Lee still seemed invincible, beating back Federal attacks on Virginia time and again. At **Fredericksburg** on December 13, 1862, Gen. Am-

---

SOLDIERS AND POLITICIANS

Seven U.S. presidents served in the Union army during the Civil War. All were generals except McKinley, who was a major.

Chester A. Arthur
James A. Garfield
Ulysses S. Grant
Benjamin Harrison

Rutherford B. Hayes
Andrew Johnson
William McKinley

brose Burnside, though warned by Lincoln, didn't move quickly enough in crossing the Rappahannock, which allowed Lee to entrench his forces on higher ground and win the battle. The battle of **Chancellorsville,** April 27-May 6, resulted in triumph and tragedy for the Rebels. Lee sent Jackson on a daring flanking maneuver toward a weak point in Gen. Joseph Hooker's line of 160,000. The Federals were pushed back across the Rappahannock in defeat. During the evening of May 2, however, Jackson was mistakenly fired on by his own troops, and died eight days later. "I know not how to replace him,"

mourned Lee, who had no choice but to press on without his star commander. Union forces were carrying the war's western theater, threatening the South's control of the Mississippi River and occupying Tennessee. Nevertheless, General Lee and Jefferson Davis, president of the Confederacy, plotted an attempt to take the Federal capital. In June the Army of Northern Virginia crossed the Potomac.

The Tide Turns

Three days of fighting at **Gettysburg** in early July 1863, ended Confederate hopes of taking

THE CIVIL WAR IN VIRGINIA

BALL'S BLUFF
(21 OCTOBER 1861)

BULL RUN
(21 JULY 1861 "FIRST MANASSAS") AND
(29-30 AUGUST 1862 "SECOND MANASSAS")

CHANCELLORSVILLE
(27 APRIL-6 MAY 1863)

WILDERNESS
(5-6 MAY 1864)

SPOTSYLVANIA
(8-12 MAY 1864)

FREDERICKSBURG
(13 DECEMBER 1862)

LEE SURRENDERS AT
APPOMATTOX COURTHOUSE
(9 APRIL 1865)

PETERSBURG
(16-18 JUNE 1864)

INDECISIVE BATTLE
VIRGINIA (MERRIMACK)
VS. MONITOR
(9 MARCH 1862)

SEVEN DAYS BATTLES FOR RICHMOND (1862)

A. MECHANICSVILLE, JUNE 26
B. GAINE'S MILL, JUNE 27
C. SAVAGE'S SATION, JUNE 29
D. FRAYSER'S FARM
(GLENDALE), JUNE 30
E. MALVERN HILL, JULY 1

FEDERAL VICTORY   CONFEDERATE VICTORY

0   15 mi
0   15 km

© MOON PUBLICATIONS, INC.

Washington, D.C., in spite of a final desperate charge by 11,000 Rebel soldiers under Gen. George Pickett into the face of point-blank gunfire. During the retreat Lee told Pickett, "The men and officers of your command have written the name of Virginia as high today as it has ever been written before." One in three soldiers survived Pickett's Charge. When the smoke cleared, the Battle of Gettysburg—the bloodiest of any American war—had claimed over 50,000 casualties. Vicksburg, MS, fell on July 4, 1863, and though two more years of fighting would follow, the Confederate cause was all but lost.

Virginia's westernmost districts had voted against secession in 1861, and now that Union forces controlled the entire region from the Ohio River to the mountains, they took action. In 1863 all of Virginia's counties beyond the Alleghenies and two at the northern end of the Shenandoah Valley were accepted into the Union as West Virginia.

A Slow End

By 1864 the Confederate economy was floundering. The Union naval blockade kept the shoreline sealed, causing barrels of flour to sell for $200 and spurring bread riots in Richmond. Morale plummeted and more Confederate soldiers began to desert as it became obvious that only a miracle could bring a Southern victory. Though few citizens would publicly suggest surrender, many blamed Jefferson Davis and the Confederate government for the deteriorating situation. The last realistic hope was that the Southern armies could prolong the fighting long enough for public disgust in the North to unseat Lincoln in the 1864 elections, bringing the possibility of a negotiated peace.

Instead, Ulysses S. Grant, newly appointed commander of all Union armies, moved south with Richmond and General Lee's battle-weary Army of Northern Virginia in his sights. "Wherever Lee goes," Grant ordered Gen. George Meade, "there you will go also." Lee repeatedly outguessed Grant's flanking maneuvers as the Confederate army, under-supplied and half as large, dogged the Federals in a string of fierce battles that led slowly southward. During the **Battle of the Wilderness** (May 5-6, 1864), the opposing forces clashed in dense undergrowth. Over 25,000 troops—two-thirds of them Federals—

died in the confused fighting, many in wildfires set by cannon bombardment. At least 12,000 more fell struggling for one square mile of ground called the "Bloody Angle" in the **Battle of Spotsylvania Court House** (May 8-21) nearby. Union victories came at a heavy price. In two months during the spring of 1864, the Federals lost 77,452 men in Virginia—more soldiers than there were in Lee's entire army.

Realizing he stood little change of defeating Lee in straightforward combat, Grant moved south to lay siege to Richmond and Petersburg, the Confederate capital's vital supply center. Through the summer and fall of 1864, the Confederates watched helplessly as Gen. Philip Sheridan razed the fertile Shenandoah Valley and Gen. William Sherman began his famous "march to the sea" from Atlanta to Savannah, cutting a path of destruction through the Georgia heartland.

Richmond was evacuated and burned by its inhabitants on April 3, 1865, sending the Confederate government fleeing west to Danville. After fighting a final series of skirmishes in retreat across Virginia, Lee asked Grant for a meeting six days later on April 9. Grant later wrote, "I felt . . . sad and depressed at the downfall of a foe who had fought so long and valiantly, and had suffered so much for a cause, though that cause was, I believe, one of the worst for which a people ever fought." The terms of surrender were drawn up and signed in the parlor of the Wilmer McLean House at Appomattox Court House, and on April 12 the ragged but unbowed Confederates turned over their arms and flags in a formal ceremony. The opposing armies saluted each other, and the war was over.

The Dust Settles

Virginia was readmitted to the Union in 1870, three years after Congress had placed the South under military rule. It's hard to overestimate the effect of defeat on the consciousness of the South, and Virginia and her inhabitants in particular. Society as they knew it had been utterly transformed from orderly and stratified to chaotic. Richmond and large parts of Fredericksburg and Petersburg lay in ruins, along with large sections of dozens of other cities and towns. Local currency was worthless, 350,000 slaves no longer had to take orders, and the rest of the work force—two whole generations of men—

was left demoralized, wounded, or dead. By 1877, Virginia's total war loss was estimated at $457 million, a staggering amount when divided among only 1.2 million inhabitants.

Paying the debt, including $45 million owed even before the war, became the central political issue of the late 19th century. Decades of dissension followed as "Readjusters" took the reins of government in an effort to reduce the debt and interest. Before a compromise was reached, hundreds of schoolhouses were shut down due to lack of funds. By the turn of the century, the economy had begun to gain momentum again—once free from the narrow-minded control of the planter aristocracy, Virginians were able to diversify into smaller-scale agriculture, mining, commerce, and manufacture. Railroads again stretched across the state, and suburbs sprouted as the larger cities were rebuilt.

In contrast, the decades following the Emancipation Proclamation marked one of the lowest points in the history of American blacks. Slavery was over but freedom was still drowned by the hostile voices of many white Southerners. Even though a new state constitution drawn up in 1867 ratified universal male suffrage for both races, a series of rulings preserved slavery in everything but name for years. Restrictive Black codes, poll taxes, and the 1896 Supreme Court decision in *Plessy v. Ferguson* kept minorities in a parallel existence that was definitely "separate" but far from "equal." Voting by blacks fell 90% (as did the turnout of poor whites, though not as much) when handwritten applications were required for voter registration. While there was much less racial violence in Virginia than in states farther south, the mere appearance of the Ku Klux Klan in certain regions was enough to discourage any protest.

Meanwhile the myth of the Old South began to take root in books, songs, and popular culture. The past, real or imagined, provided comfort during the hard times following the Confederate defeat. The horrors of the war—still evident in missing limbs, ruined buildings, and mass graves—began to take on the sheen of chivalry, with gallant young soldiers fighting and dying in vain defense of their homeland. Nineteenth-century novelist James Branch Campbell noted that Southerners were creating "in the same instant that they lamented the Old South's extinction, an Old South which had died proudly at Appomattox without ever having been besmirched by the wear and tear of existence."

20TH CENTURY

As the digits clicked over from double nines to double zeros, Virginia found itself an increasing contender on the national playing field. Chemical fertilizers made farmers less dependent on tobacco and diversification into industry continued. World War I stimulated the economy even more by sparking an enormous expansion of the Newport News shipyard, bringing in money and workers. Tourism began to bring in significant income, and once again a Virginian sat in the White House—Woodrow Wilson served two presidential terms 1913-21. The Great Depression slowed mining and the wheat and tobacco markets, but the state suffered less than others thanks to the frugality of a new captain at the helm.

The Byrd Years
The governorship of 1926-30 marked the beginning of half a century of political impact for Democrat Harry F. Byrd., Sr. Tracing his lineage to 17th-century merchant and land speculator William Byrd, this leading Southern progressive brought Virginia's government into the modern age with a policy of honesty and efficiency. During his tenure as governor, various laws revised the tax system, expanded highways, set aside more money for social-welfare programs including schools and mental hospitals, and promised severe penalties for lynching. A solid core of Virginia conservatism remained, though; in 1928 the state voted for a Republican presidential candidate for the first time since 1872. Roosevelt's New Deal was viewed with skepticism even as it made the government the state's leading source of revenue from 1932 on. World War II brought thousands of soldiers to military camps throughout the state and caused Hampton Roads to mushroom even more to support the shipyards and the Norfolk Naval Base.

By mid-century, Virginia had shifted from a rural state to an urban one as the population,

KEY DATES IN VIRGINIA HISTORY

1607	Jamestown settled
1610	Jamestown almost fails due to winter famine, inept leadership and poor planning
1612/13	John Rolfe plants first crop of West Indian tobacco
1619	House of Burgesses, the first representative assembly in the New World, convenes at Jamestown
	First blacks brought to Virginia
1624	Virginia becomes a royal colony when London company's charter is revoked
1676	Bacon's Rebellion against Governor Berkeley's administration fails
1693	College of William and Mary founded in Williamsburg
1699	Colonial capital moved to Middle Plantation (now Williamsburg)
1774	British Gov. John Murray dissolves House of Burgesses
	Newly formed Virginia Convention calls for first Continental Congress
1775	Patrick Henry advocates rebellion in famous speech to House of Burgesses
	Revolutionary War begins at Lexington and Concord, MA
1776	Declaration of Independence signed in Philadelphia
	Virginia Convention adopts state constitution and bill of rights
1779	Richmond becomes state capital
1781	Lord Corwallis surrenders to Gen. George Washington at Yorktown, ending American Revolution
1788	Virginia ratifies U.S. Constitution
1789	George Washington becomes first president of United States
1831	Nat Turner's slave rebellion
1859	John Brown's raid on Harpers Ferry
1861	Civil War begins
	Virginia secedes from the Union, joins Confederate States
	Richmond becomes Confederate capital
1863	West Virginia splits from Virginia, admitted to Union
1865	Lee surrenders to Ulysses S. Grant at Appomattox, ending Civil War
1870	Virginia readmitted to Union
1889	Newport News opens Simpson Dry Dock, the largest in the world
1954	U.S. Supreme Court decision to end segregation in public schools meets massive resistance in Virginia
1957	Chesapeake Bay Bridge-Tunnel completed
1969	First Republican elected governor of Virginia since 1886
1971	State constitution rewritten
1990	L. Douglas Wilder, the country's first African-American governor, is elected in Virginia

which had doubled since the turn of the century, leapt by 25% 1940-50. Thanks to the stability of the Byrd administration, employment rose and rural blacks and big labor began to emerge as potent political forces.

Race Relations

Blacks in Virginia continued to struggle against a statewide system of segregation that kept non-white schools inferior and prohibited minorities from sitting on juries and holding public office. Even without the incidents of violence that plagued the deeper South, many black citizens emigrated from Virginia to Washington, D.C., and the northeast in search of better lives. When the unanimous 1954 Supreme Court decision in **Brown v. Board of Education** declared segregation inherently unequal and therefore illegal, a massive statewide resistance blossomed. This would mark the last attempt to hold onto the old order in an embarrassing departure from the usual Virginian civility.

Spurred on by Sen. Harry Flood Byrd (son of Harry, Sr.), the General Assembly voted to withhold state funds from any school honoring racial integration. By 1958, public schools in Charlottesville, Norfolk, and Front Royal—attended by children of both races—had closed. A year later Gov. Lindsay Almond bowed to popular protest, business pressure, and the federal courts by accepting limited integration (all the while railing against the "livid stench of sadism, sex immorality, and juvenile pregnancy" that he believed resulted from the integration of public schools in Washington, D.C.). Schools in Prince Edward County remained closed until 1964, focusing national attention on the fact that black children received no public education while white children attended private institutions. The 1965 Civil Rights Voting Act and the 24th Amendment to the Constitution ended the struggle, at least in the eyes of the law, and assured minorities in Virginia and elsewhere of their right to representation.

Recent History

Virginia's economic and technological boom is best evidenced in the northern part of the state. Fairfax County, home to 41,000 residents in 1940, counted 533,000 in 1973—a 1,200% increase. The result has been, in the eyes of many, a lesson in development gone wrong—pastoral farmlands transformed into faceless suburbs. On a brighter note, the country's first test-tube baby was delivered at Norfolk General Hospital on December 28, 1981.

Meanwhile, state politics have made the transition to a true multi-party democracy controlled for the most part by Democrats. Harry F. Byrd, Sr., died in 1966, and a series of liberal Democrats then came to power. After three successive gubernatorial elections were won by Republicans, a Democrat again carried the election in 1981. In 1990, L. Douglas Wilder became the first elected black governor in the state and the country. Born in Richmond to children of former slaves, Wilder received a Bronze Star for heroism in the Korean War and a law degree from Howard University. He gained attention as the state's first black senator in 1969 for his efforts to change the state song and establish a holiday for the birthday of Martin Luther King, Jr. Wilder won the race for governor by fewer than 7,000 votes.

By the early '90s Virginia's population was well over 6 million, with two-thirds of Virginians living in cities; the state's per-capita income ranked 12th in the country. The extraordinary transformation from half a century ago—when two-thirds of only 2.7 million people lived in rural areas—owes much to the release of the past, primarily in the form of segregation. Crossing the Potomac from Washington, D.C., used to be a step back in time to a proud but impoverished land living out its dreams of yesterday and insulated from the rest of the nation. Today it's a step forward into busy financial and manufacturing centers and a modern agricultural system tied into the global market, where the past still echoes but no longer impedes.

ECONOMY AND GOVERNMENT

ECONOMY

With the nation's capital just across the Potomac, it's no surprise the federal government dominates Virginia's financial picture. Four hundred fifty square miles of military facilities, including the Pentagon in Arlington and the Marine Corps base in Quantico, provide a substantial chunk of the state's gross product. In 1990 the Department of Defense employed 108,000 people spread throughout 29 military installations. It's slightly ironic that traditionally conservative Virginia has been buoyed so much by the mid-century expansion of military and federal agencies within her borders, making the state one of the top five recipients of federal funds in the country.

Shipbuilding leads the manufacturing sector, followed by tobacco processing and light industry, producing chemicals, clothing, machinery, wood products, and food. High-tech firms are concentrated in northern Virginia, while mining consortiums supervise the extraction of coal, granite, sand, clay, and other minerals from the southwestern hillsides. Tourism brought in almost $10 billion in 1995, making it the third-largest retail industry and employer (one in 18 residents works in tourism).

Agriculture is the next big earner, centered on dairy products, livestock, fruit, and grains. Over 30% of Virginia's 93,000 acres of peanut farms crowd the mouth of the Chesapeake Bay. As the productivity demands of the 20th century have forced farms to become more and more mechanized, many smaller family operations have closed, sending ex-employees to the cities in search of work. Surviving farms have tended to shrink. In 1990 there were about 46,000 farms throughout the state averaging 193 acres each.

The coastal fishing industry is the state's smallest revenue producer, despite hundreds of millions of pounds of fish and shellfish pulled from the Chesapeake Bay each year.

GOVERNMENT

The executive branch of Virginia's state government consists of three elected positions: governor, lieutenant governor, and attorney general. Each serves a four-year term, but governors cannot be re-elected. Seven judges are appointed to the supreme court, the highest of four judiciary levels, for 12-year terms. The 10-member Virginia Court of Appeals was started in 1985.

Virginia's legislative body is the General Assembly, consisting of 40 senators serving four-year terms and 100 delegates elected every two years. It meets every January in Richmond for sessions of 30 or 60 days. The state constitution, adopted in 1971, is Virginia's seventh since 1776.

A moderately conservative electorate has voted for Republican presidents in nine out of 12 elections since 1948. Democrats, though, dominated state politics from 1883 to1970, when Linwood Holden became the first Republican governor in 87 years. However, the General Assembly has remained mostly Democratic, and the party reclaimed the gubernatorial office in 1982 and held it until George Allen's 1994 victory. Current Republican Gov. Jim Gilmore was elected in 1998.

A final interesting note: The most recent presidential candidate from Virginia, nominated in 1984, 1988, and 1992, was Independent hopeful Lyndon LaRouche, Jr.

THE PEOPLE

To be a Virginian, either by birth,
marriage, or adoption,
Or even on one's mother's side
Is an introduction to any state in the union,
A passport to any foreign country,
And a benediction from Almighty God.

Settlement

For a group with such a strong historical identity, Virginians are a surprisingly diverse lot. And it's not as if they haven't had time to blend; the first settlers stumbled ashore and kissed the earth in 1619, and people have been arriving ever since. Early colonists almost all came from rural England, mostly the Midland and southern counties near London. Arrivals from Wales and France in the 18th century had to make room for the large numbers of Irish, German, and Scotch-Irish farmers who flowed into the Shenandoah Valley from New Jersey, Pennsylvania, and Maryland. Native tribes were decimated by imported diseases they had no immunity against, until a mere fraction of tens of thousands of Native Americans remained alive.

The first blacks arrived in 1619 as indentured servants, but by the end of the century thousands of African slaves were being hauled ashore and sold as labor on huge Tidewater plantations. Virginia quickly became the most crowded state in the New World, relatively speaking, with a population that doubled every quarter century after 1680. By the eve of the Revolutionary War the colony counted 550,000 inhabitants, almost half of whom were black.

The state broke the one-million mark near the beginning of the 19th century, but lost many during the carnage of the Civil War and due to the secession of several western counties, which became West Virginia in 1863.

Current Statistics

In 1995, nearly three-quarters of Virginia's 6,618,000 inhabitants lived in the metropolitan corridor stretching south from Washington, D.C., to Richmond and east to Hampton Roads. Virginia Beach led in population, followed by Norfolk, Richmond, Newport News, and Chesapeake. Just over 75% of Virginians describe themselves as Caucasian. Almost 20% are black, concentrated in the Piedmont and coast area—central Richmond and Charles City county on the Historic Peninsula are both over three-quarters African-American.

Other minorities, mostly Hispanic, Asian, and Middle Eastern, make up the remaining five percent. In the last decade Hampton Roads had one of the country's fastest-growing Jewish communities, as well as growing numbers of immigrants from India.

The state's per capita income is slightly above the national average, with about 11% below the poverty line and about 11% earning over $75,000 in annual household income.

Attitudes

It's almost impossible to summarize a state this varied, but if any quality holds true across the board, it's affability. A wave is the surest sign, whether it's from the driver of a pickup passing on a back road or a complete stranger helping you parallel-park. Locals are more than happy to point you in the right direction or to give you their two cents on the most recent scandal across the Potomac; just be patient, as folks tend to choose their words carefully.

A mild but deeply rooted conservative streak, also called "a touch of old Southern values," runs beneath day-to-day affairs in more traditional parts of the state. This pride in the past can alternately—or simultaneously—glorify Virginia's rich heritage and sustain less welcome parts of it. Race relations, while better than in most Southern states, have been slightly inflamed in recent controversies over the designation of January 15 as Lee-Jackson-King Day (rather than just Martin Luther King, Jr. Day) and former Gov. George Allen's quickly rescinded decree that April be declared Confederate History and Heritage Month.

In the early '90s, former Gov. L. Douglas Wilder, the grandson of former slaves, led the fight to retire the state song "Carry Me Back To

Old Virginia," written by black minstrel James Bland in the 1870s. The song, which depicts a slave fondly remembering the days when he "labored so hard for old Massa/Day after day in the fields of yellow corn," infuriated black legislators and mortified many white legislators as well. It hadn't been played at official functions since the 1970s, but wasn't officialy retired by the General Assembly until 1997. A year later a replacement had yet to be found.

Virginia is a pious state, too, with a religious conservatism evidenced by broadcasts of the "700 Club" from Pat Robertson's Christian Broadcasting Network in Norfolk and by Jerry Falwell's Liberty University near Lynchburg. A tradition of religious acceptance dating back to Thomas Jefferson's 1785 Statute for Religious Freedom. Today Protestants—mostly Methodists, Southern Baptists and Presbyterians—outnumber other religious groups. You will come across pockets of Quakers and Mennonites in the Shenandoah and Hunt Country, and Richmond has one of the largest Jewish populations of any city its size in the country.

ON THE ROAD

With so many activities readily available to them, it's a surprise Virginians ever get anything done. Simply put, if you can do it on the East Coast, you can probably do it here, from shopping to surfing and most everything in between.

Hours and admission prices vary depending on the season. Children's prices generally apply to kids under 12, with tots admitted for free. Senior admission falls somewhere in between the adult and child price. Taking pictures is against the rules in many museums and historical houses; ask first.

OUTDOOR RECREATION

GENERAL RESOURCES

Information on the state's incredible range of open-air activities, as well as its 67,000 acres of state parks, can be ordered from the **Department of Conservation and Recreation** (DCR), 203 Governor St., Suite 302, Richmond, VA 23219, tel. (804) 786-1712 or (800) 933-7275, Web site: www.state.va.usdcr/dcr-home.htm. See individual chapter listings for more details. The Great Outdoor Resource Page (Web site: www.gorp/com/gorp/location/va/va.htm) lists tour operators, data, and links for Virginia. Finally, a great source for articles and activity listings in the western part of the state is *Blue Ridge Outdoors,* a free monthly tabloid-format magazine distributed throughout the state; you can also get it directly from Portico Publications, Ltd., 100 W. South St., Suite 1, Charlottesville, VA 22902, tel. (804) 295-1645, e-mail: outdoor@cstone.net.

HIKING AND CAMPING

The simplest way to enjoy Virginia often reveals her humblest, but most profound, pleasures. Whether it's an evening amble down a country lane or a pre-dawn slog up some rocky peak, walking only requires two legs, a pair of boots, and a little time and effort. For this small investment you can find yourself in a nearly forgotten corner of the state, resting by an icy waterfall or enjoying a fifty-mile view—or maybe just down the road, discussing bait fish with the folks at the local market.

Shenandoah National Park draws D.C. residents by the station wagon-full, and for good reason, as it encloses some of the choicest acres in Appalachia. Most visitors never go more than an hour from the asphalt, though, leaving the backcountry to the more determined. Through the park coils the famous Appalachian Trail, tramped by hundreds of through-hikers and thousands of day-ramblers every year. Further south lies the Mount Rogers National Recreation Area and Breaks Interstate Park, both rugged and less trafficked.

Other established trails such as the Washington and Old Dominion, Virginia Creeper, and New River started out as railroad beds before being reborn as foot-power freeways. For details on these routes (which are also open to bikes and horses), refer to the relevant chapters in this book or call the **Rails-to-Trails Conservancy** in Washington, D.C., at (202) 797-5400.

Underlying it all stretches over three million acres of the George Washington and Jefferson National Forests, covering most of the mountains and over one-eighth of the entire state. More information on the national forests can be found at local district offices (listed in the regional sections), the respective Forest Supervisors (Jefferson: 5162 Valley Pointe Parkway, Roanoke, VA 24019; George Washington: Harrison Plaza, P.O. Box 233, Harrisonburg, VA 22801), or the U.S. Forest Service main office at 14th and Independence SW, P.O. Box 96090, Washington, DC 20090-6090, tel. (202) 205-1760. For the "Hike of the Month" in Virginia Wilderness areas, steer your Web browser to home.att.net/~rscarroll/index.html.

BICYCLING

Mountain Biking

Fat-tire fanatics will quickly find that Virginia's high country offers some of the best steep dirt on the East Coast. Many excellent foot trails are also open to knobby tires—just heed the creed (see special topic, **Dirt Rules**). Difficulty ranges from countless miles of easy-grade fire roads to single-track descents to turn your hair white. These last are taken full advantage of by annual downhill events throughout the state. Interstate 81 provides handy access to trails and approach roads following the length of the Blue Ridge.

Various books can tell you where to go, and a handful of tour companies (see **Organized Tours**) can take you there. National Forest district offices are good sources of information on trail conditions and maps as are local bike shops, some of which also rent bikes. If you're looking for a more sedate ride, every former-railroad trail has a host of agencies that offer rentals and shuttle service to cyclists; obtain information from **Rails-to-Trails Conservancy** in Washington, D.C., tel. (202) 797-5400.

For more information on trails and events look up the **Virginia Cycling Association**, an organization of 20 or so local clubs, on the Internet at www.bikeracing.com/index.html. The **Eastern Virginia Mountainbike Association**, P.O. Box 7553, Hampton, VA 23666, specializes in the Tidewater area (e-mail: emva@beachway.com, Web site: www.beachway.com/evma/). The Virginia State Championship Mountain Bike Series began in 1998 with rides at six locations including Massanutten Resort and Mountain Lake near Blacksburg. Contact the Virginia Championship Commission at 2719 Summit Ridge Rd., Roanoke, VA 24012, tel. (540) 977-4335, e-mail: ksinman@roanoke.infi.net.

Road Biking

Paved roads running through the rural countryside make road riding just as rewarding as off-road adventures. A weekend in the saddle can be as diverse as a salt-breezed spin along the Eastern Shore to a turn through the rolling hills of the Piedmont, all along back roads far from the roar of the interstates. Both the Tour DuPont and the Tour de Trump follow the Skyline Drive and Blue Ridge Parkway along the crest of the mountains. Colonial Parkway connects Jamestown, Williamsburg, and Yorktown across the neck of the Historic Peninsula. Three major cycling circuits (part of Interstate Bicycle Routes 1 and 76) cross the state, including 500 miles of the Trans-America Bikecentennial Trail and sections of the Maine-to-Virginia and Virginia-to-Florida routes, both with Richmond as the hub. For maps and more information contact the **State Bicycle Coordinator** of the Virginia Department of Transportation (see special topic, **Drivers' Resources**); the coordinator can also send you brochures on state cycling laws and local bicycle clubs.

The annual **Bike Virginia** ride brings thousands of cyclists together for leisurely multi-day rides down some of the state's most scenic back roads. In 1998, they toured the Shenandoah for six days ($175 per adult) and the rim of the Chesapeake Bay for one ($40). Space on the tours is limited, and reservations include shuttle bus service, camping space, and repair support. Contact the Bicycling Education Association, P.O. Box 203, Williamsburg, VA 23187-0203, tel. (757) 229-0507.

Riders from both camps can benefit from the **Adventure Cycling Association,** a nonprofit organization that helps support the development and maintenance of over 24,000 miles of roads and off-road trails nationwide. Among other benefits, members can join organized tours and transport their bicycles free on Northwest Airlines. ACA's Cyclosource mail-order branch, tel./fax (800) 721-8719, stocks long-distance gear, books, and excellent route maps (both the TransAmericaBicycle Trail and the Atlantic Coast Route cross Virginia).

Wherever you go, don't overestimate your abilities or underestimate the terrain. Take foul-weather gear, tire patches, a pump, and enough food and water to keep you going in case the next rest stop is 10 miles farther than you thought. In the countryside, angry dogs can be a nuisance and occasionally a danger. Outrunning them is an option (most will give up the chase once you leave their territory), as is shouting and dismounting to put your bike between Cujo and yourself. Save kicking, Macing, or whacking with a pump for a last resort.

HORSEBACK RIDING

Hundreds of miles of trails are open to riders, including the Virginia Creeper and New River. The Virginia Highlands Horse Trail in the Mount Rogers National Recreation Area is probably the state's most popular, with campsites specifically designed for horse traffic. Various lodges, farms, and outfitters throughout the Shenandoah and southwest Virginia can set you up for a day ride, including guided rides from Skyland Lodge in Shenandoah National Park. The Virginia Horse Center near Lexington hosts national equine events. Contact the **Virginia Horse Council,** P.O. Box 72, Riner, VA 24149, tel. (540) 382-4113, for a statewide list of stables and public horse trails.

Riding takes on a more patrician air in the Piedmont area and the Hunt Country of northern Virginia, where horses have been a cornerstone of life for generations. **Fox hunts** evoke Old England—riders in traditional uniforms galloping after packs of baying hounds. In American hunts, the event itself is more important than the actual fox, which is rarely caught. You'll have to be invited by a member of a hunt (local club) to ride even on a mock hunt; most observers follow by car. During the Nov.-March season, you might be able to catch the blessing of the hounds, a ritual in which a priest or minister invokes divine guidance on the pack. For information on local hunts, order the annual September roster issue ($1.50) of the ***Chronicle of the Horse,*** 301 W.

DIRT RULES

The **International Mountain Biking Association (IMBA),** P.O. Box 7578, Boulder, CO 80306, tel. (303) 545-9011, advocates a set of guidelines designed to insure that mountain bikers will always be welcome in the back-country:

Ride on Open Trails Only. Stay out of wilderness areas, don't trespass on private land, and respect road and trail closures.

Leave No Trace. Stick to well-worn, hard-packed trails and forest roads whenever possible, and don't encourage erosion by mud-bogging right after a rainstorm.

Control Your Bicycle. Don't give fellow bikers a bad rap by hitting someone else.

Always Yield Trail. Cyclists should give way to both hikers and horses on the trail. Let them know you're coming, then slow down or even stop to let them pass.

Never Spook Animals. Give horses a wide berth (consider dismounting), and leave the cows alone.

Plan Ahead. Don't strand yourself by over-estimating your abilities, and always wear a helmet.

Washington St., Middleburg, VA 20117, tel. (540) 687-6341, Web site: www.chronofhorse.com, and then contact the local clubs themselves.

Long before Virginia-born Secretariat won the Triple Crown in 1973, **horse races** have raised the blood pressure of both species involved. Dozens of steeplechases and assorted flat-track events take advantage of the state's prime horse stock, which goes back to thoroughbred stallions like Bulle Rock, imported from England in 1730. Races are held from spring to fall at places such as Foxfield near Charlottesville, where dressy tailgate parties distract college students and race fans alike. The Plains, near Middleburg, hosts the Virginia Gold Cup in May and the International Gold Cup in October. Contact the **Virginia Steeplechase Association,** P.O. Box 1158, Middleburg, VA 22117, tel. (540) 687-3455, for a schedule, or try www.middleburgonline.com/steeplechase on the Internet.

Polo matches usually include the traditional divot-stomping at halftime. Recent referendums have begun to reverse religious-inspired prohibitions on pari-mutuel **betting,** making new tracks like the Colonial Downs in Richmond the place to lay your money down.

CLIMBING

At least 30 recognized climbing areas scattered along the Blue Ridge provide a respectable alternative to West Virginia's Seneca Rocks, with a fraction of the crowds. Most cliffs are 40-60 feet high and can be toproped. Access is easy and legal to routes in national forests and state and national parks, and you might even find some winter ice at places such as Crabtree Falls

and White Oak Canyon. Great Falls on the Potomac is one of the most popular sites in the D.C. area, with over 100 routes of all levels.

Don't trespass on private land, and clean up any mess you make to help insure future climbers will be welcome. Jeff Watson's *Virginia Climber's Guide* (see the Booklist) is the best, and only, source.

RAFTING, KAYAKING, AND CANOEING

Few things embody the Virginia landscape as much as flowing water, etching the Piedmont before widening into the watery highways of the Tidewater and the Chesapeake Bay. Some 380 miles of Virginia's waterways have been declared State Scenic Rivers for their beauty, historic significance, or recreational value. All told, nearly 200 rivers, creeks, and channels are open to boaters of every kind, many with excellent public access. Calmer waters fill tidal estuaries and more than 30 lakes ranging 500-50,000 acres. Dozens of outfitters and tour companies can put you on the water (see **Organized Tours,** below).

The foothills of the Blue Ridge are only the beginning of the journey for Virginia's biggest rivers, whose upper reaches often churn with whitewater, like the Russell Fork as it roars through the canyons of Breaks Interstate Park. Rafters and kayakers in search of a challenge should also look east to the fall line, where wide, slow rivers suddenly gush over a natural ledge that runs the length of the state. Even though the park itself is closed to boaters, the Potomac River seethes near Great Falls Park into one of the finest white-water stretches in the east. The

Steeplechasing has a rich tradition in Virginia.

James River can reach class V, depending on the season, within sight of Richmond.

In between the chutes and holes lie placid stretches ideal for canoes and inner tubes—the Clinch, Maury, Mattaponi, upper James, and the South Fork of the Shenandoah are just a few of the most popular watercourses. A canoe is also the best way to explore the spooky depths of the Great Dismal Swamp or the boggy reaches of the Nottaway and Blackwater rivers near Suffolk. Always bring food, drinking water, sunscreen, and a change of clothes in a waterproof container (trash bags work). River shoes and insect repellent can also come in handy.

The **Virginia Professional Paddlesports Association,** Shenandoah Heights Rd., Front Royal, VA 22630, is a good place to direct water sports questions. **Blue Ridge River Runners,** P.O. Box 10243, Lynchburg, VA 24501, tel. (804) 392-5054, advocate river safety and the protection of Virginia's waterways, and can help arrange paddling instruction (e-mail: wa4pgm@ moonstar.com, luna.moonstar.com/~wa4pgm/ brrr.htm). On the Internet two good sites for checking river levels are www.awa.org/awa/river-project/virginia/index.html (the American Whitewater Association) and www.moonstar.com/ ~wa4pgm/yakva.htm. Rafting companies are listed under **Organized Tours,** below.

BOATING

On the Chesapeake Bay and the Atlantic, it may take more effort and money to hit the water, but it's almost guaranteed to be well worth it. **Excursion** or **cruise** boats, from restored wooden schooners to modest motorboats, take passengers on sightseeing junkets. The trips, which can last anywhere from an hour to all day, usually feature narration on points of interest and drinks, snacks, or even a full sit-down meal (on the luxury dinner yachts up the Potomac). You'll find more locals than tourists aboard **water taxis** and **ferries,** which simply shuttle between one shore and another.

Charter boats, under both sail and mechanized power, can be rented for a day or longer to go after trophy fish or to explore the farthest reaches of the seaward islands. Expect to have your references and credentials thoroughly checked if you plan to rent one "barebones," meaning without a captain. A hired skipper will tack on at least $100 to the price, which tends to be around $250 for two days (often a minimum rental). Charters often leave from **marinas,** shoreside establishments that are combination truck stop, mini-mart, and RV campground. Mooring slips, electrical hookups, holding-tank pumps, fresh water fill-up, bait, tackle, and crusty advice are standard, with the occasional laundry, grocery, and shower facilities thrown in for good measure.

Various local schools offer **classes** in the operation and navigation of sailing and power boats. Your next step will probably be a **rental,** either of a full-sized craft or a smaller daysailer, windsurfer, or rowboat. Most major lakes and countless locations along the bay and coast have public launching ramps for boat trailers. Contact the DCR for a map of public access to the Chesapeake Bay and its tributaries, and look at the *Virginia State Road Atlas* (see Booklist) for other river and lake access points.

SURFING

Virginia Beach is without a doubt the most popular surfing area on the coast. Be careful of local regulations: surfing is prohibited in some spots and within 300 feet of piers; wear a leash to avoid a $50 fine. Summer surfing hours typically run from sunrise to 10 a.m. and 5 p.m. to sunset. A good break curls near the jetty off 1st Street near the Lighthouse Restaurant. Conditions are just as promising along the Eastern Shore, but difficult access keeps many surfers away. You'll need a flat-bottomed boat to explore the outer islands of the Virginia Coast Reserve.

Swells are usually small (1-5 feet), but can grow to 9-10 feet during the winter and spring nor'easters or late summer hurricanes. Early fall is most dependable. You'll probably need at least a partial wetsuit in the spring and fall, and an early start is essential to enjoy the summer warmth without the crowds. Bottoms are sandy. Virginia Beach is full of surf shops, some of which rent boards.

For more details order *The Surf Report,* Vol. 8, #12, from Surfer Publications, P.O. Box 1028, Dana Point, CA 92629, tel. (714) 496-5922, fax 496-7849. The Virginia District of the **Eastern**

Surfing Association, Web site: www.surfesa.org, can be contacted at P.O. Box 4619, Virginia Beach, VA 23454, e-mail: saltaire@pinn.net. For online surf conditions try www.mcnetwork.com/surf/.

FISHING

The over 75,000 registered anglers (annually) have statewide conservation efforts to thank for the quality of fishing in Virginia. Both fly and bait casters can go after native Eastern brook trout in the hillside streams of Shenandoah National Park, part of 2,800 miles of trout waters within the Blue Ridge. Bass are ubiquitous throughout the state—the upper James River can't be beat for smallmouth, with more trophy fish per mile than any other Virginia river. Sunfish and catfish are also plentiful, joined by crappie and white perch downstream near Richmond.

Head to the South Fork of the Shenandoah River for redbreast sunfish, then try the New River for yellow perch, muskellunge, and walleye, and the Chickahominy near Walker's Dam in late spring for bluegill, chain pickerel, and herring. Almost all of the state's lakes and reservoirs also offer excellent fishing: Smith Mountain Lake near Roanoke is Virginia's top spot for striped bass, and largemouth bass fishing in the John H. Kerr Reservoir along the North Carolina border can't be beat. Charter boats ply the Chesapeake Bay for trout, bluefish, flounder, drum, and sharks, while deep-sea boats leave Virginia Beach in search of marlin, sailfish, and sea bass. Peak saltwater season is May-Sept.

The **Virginia Department of Game and Inland Fisheries,** P.O. Box 1104, 4010 West Broad St., Richmond, VA 23230-1104, tel. (804) 367-1000, can provide details on fishing spots and regulations, along with an annual guide to freshwater angling throughout the state. Freshwater licenses are available to nonresidents for $30 from sporting goods stores, bait shops, and marinas (saltwater permits are $7.50). They're required except for the first Saturday and Sunday in June, when non-trout fishing is free statewide. Fly-casters should check out www.sklarew/com/vaflyfish on the Internet.

HUNTING

Hunting ranks near the top of the list of Virginia's most popular activities—though more among locals. So many permits are sold every year that, when combined with the sale of fishing licenses, it's almost enough to completely support the Virginia Department of Game and Inland Fisheries. Over 350,000 licenses are sold annually for every type of hunting imaginable, starting with guns, arrows, trapping, and falconry. In the western part of the state, most hunting occurs in the national forests, while back east hunters use private land or hunting clubs. With close to a million deer roaming the state, it's no surprise that white-tails are one of the most popular targets during the Nov.-Jan. season (dates vary for black-powder and bow hunters). Other fall seasons encompass duck, small-game (rabbit and squirrel), quail, and bear. Waterfowl season includes Canada geese along the Eastern Shore, and turkey season spans five weeks in the spring.

Licenses and regulations vary locally, and a hunter education certificate is necessary for first-timers and younger hunters. Order the annual *Virginia Hunter Guide* from the **Virginia Department of Game and Inland Fisheries,** P.O. Box 1104, 4010 West Broad St., Richmond, VA 23230-1104, tel. (804) 367-1000. Local hunt clubs will know about public and private shooting ranges for clay, trap, and skeet.

BIRDWATCHING

The uninitiated may dismiss it as a mysterious, pointless waste of time and energy, but once you've caught the birding bug, you'll always wince at how much you were *missing* before peering through binoculars and poring over checklists taught you to see all of nature in a vivid new way. The spring and fall migration periods are the best times for birding in almost any part of the state, from hawk-spotting along the Blue Ridge to waterbirds following the Atlantic Flyway up and down the coast. A number of guidebooks (see Booklist) are indispensable for birders, and most Virginia parks and reserves can supply, or a least point you toward, a list of local species.

CAVES AND CAVERNS

Though not technically *out*-doors, Virginia's underground acres can provide a glimpse of a fascinating side of the state—the underside. Over millions of years, the steady drip of mineral-laden water has worn away rooms and passages and filled them with a moonscape of fantastic formations with names such as soda straw, cave drapery, and flowstone. Stalactites hang tight to the ceiling, often bearing a drop of water at the tip ready to slide off and leave another hairsbreadth of ore behind. Stalagmites grow up underneath, occasionally meeting their sus-pended twin and joining into a column. Everything happens excruciatingly slow—it can take over 100 years for a feature to grow one inch.

No matter how sturdy they seem, don't touch any formations; the oils from your fingertips can stop the accumulation of minerals (notice how slick and dead-looking the places you're allowed to touch are). Keep an eye out for bats hanging asleep along the walls and ceiling; if they're woken up in the middle of their winter hibernation, they'll use up too much stored energy and won't be able to survive until spring. (And just for the record, bats are not dangerous; just imagine them as mice with wings). Caves are cool year-round (55-65° F) so bring your jacket, and con-

---

DIRTY, DARK, AND FUN

If you're interested in something more adventurous than a stroll down a well-lit, well-trodden underground path, then spelunking in private caves may be just your speed. Numerous regional grottoes (clubs) can get you started and recommend private guides. Expect cool temperatures, hibernating bats, confusing passages, and one of the only opportunities on earth to experience total darkness. Tight squeezes might mean you have to push your backpack though first, or assume the "Groucho walk"—bent over at the waist with your head up to watch for stalactites. Guides show the way, and provide assurance and helmets with carbide lamps. Emergency kits, instruction in their use, and three sources of light per person should be standard. Wear sturdy boots, reasonably warm clothes you won't mind getting muddy, and bring food and water in a small backpack. *Never* go underground without an experienced guide.

Local Clubs

Blue Ridge Grotto
2528 Montgomery Ave. SW
Roanoke, VA 24015-4225
tel. (540) 989-7693 or 989-0483

Battlefield Area Troglodyte Society (BATS)
P.O. Box 3472, Fredericksburg, VA 22402-3472
tel. (540) 891-5581 or (703) 775-0685

Charlottesville Grotto
P.O. Box 625, Ivy, VA 22945-0625
tel. (804) 977-7046 or 823-7757

Fairfax Underground Network (FUN)
7713 Shreve Rd., Falls Church, VA 22043-3315
tel. (703) 573-1068 or 451-7663

Front Royal Grotto
4001 Tanager Ct, Front Royal, VA 22630
tel. (540) 635-3394 or 635-1503

Madison University Student Grotto
VREC Building, James Madison University,
Harrisonburg, VA 22807
tel. (540) 833-2576 or 574-2337

Mid-Virginia Underground
RR 2, P.O. Box 49-B, Stanardsville, VA 22973
tel. (804) 932-3200 or 985-3976

New River Valley Grotto
P.O. Box 3056, Radford, VA 24143
tel. (540) 731-4812 or 633-2017
Web site: www.runet.edu/~jfox/nrvg

Richmond Area Speleological Society
5300 W. Marshall St. Suite 10
Richmond, Virginia 23230
tel. (804) 673-CAVE (804-673-2283),
748-7764 or 272-4310

Tidewater Grotto
P.O. Box 62642, Virginia Beach, VA 23462
tel. (757) 485-0350 or 420-6126

VPI Cave Club
P.O. Box 558, Blacksburg, VA 24063-0558
Web site: www.vt.edu:10021/org/cave

sider the range of your flash before snapping pictures wildly.

Virginia's most impressive and accessible caves—almost all in the Shenandoah—have been tamed and opened to the public. These commercial caverns feature paved paths, handrails, colored lights, and towering monuments with ridiculous names like "Dairy Queen Cone." Wide reflective lakes (always called "Fairy-"something) are often only inches deep and peppered with dozens of tiny growths. Guided tours are mandatory.

SKIING

In 1959, The Homestead, in the Shenandoah area, added the first ski slopes in the South to its long list of activities. Since then three other resorts have opened on Virginia's western mountains. Conditions can be great for this far south: I've carved six inches of fresh powder at Massanutten on a few occasions. During the ski season of mid-Dec.-mid March, temperatures seldom drop below the teens even at night. All four resorts welcome snowboarders (The Homestead boasts a 250-foot halfpipe), and most offer snowmaking and slopeside lodging. For information and a discount coupon applicable on certain weekends, call (800)-743-7669, (800 THE-SNOW).

GOLF

With its mild climate and endless undulating acres of grass, Virginia has sprouted over 150 public, resort, and semi-private golf courses. A few rival any in the country, including Wintergreen Resort and The Homestead. One course in Williamsburg clings so tightly to its Highland roots that sheep roam the grounds and a Scottish bagpiper plays at dusk each day. The **Virginia State Golf Association,** 830 Southlake Blvd., Suite A, Richmond, VA 23236, tel. (804) 378-2300, e-mail: info@vsga.org, Web site: www.vsga.org. mail/html, publishes the *Virginia Fairways Annual Golf Guide,* or call the Virginia Tourism Corporation's golf number, (800) 932-2259, for statewide information. On the Internet try www.virginiagolf.com. You can order the free *Golfer's Guide* tabloid from The Golfer's Guide, Inc., 9616 Sir Barry Ct., Richmond, VA 23229, tel. (804) 750-1704.

MORE OUTDOOR RECREATION

Many water sports, including sailing, scuba diving, and jet-skiing, are offered by various businesses along the coast, especially in Virginia Beach.

Hot-air balloons and **skydiving** planes lift enthusiasts above the fields of the Piedmont and northern Virginia (bringing them back to earth at slightly different speeds). The seasonal **college sports,** such as football, basketball, soccer, and baseball demonstrate the local spirit like nothing else. See the pertinent chapters for details on all of these pastimes and more.

CIVIL WAR-RELATED ACTIVITIES

With the most Civil War battlefields and sites of any state—one-third of the country's total—Virginia has the market cornered on Civil War sightseeing. From the first major battle at Bull Run to Robert E. Lee's surrender at Appomattox Court House, the Old Dominion boasts over two dozen spots where you can appreciate the war's effects on the lives of soldiers and everyday citizens. Most of the National Battlefield Parks, administered by the National Park Service, are concentrated in the northern and eastern parts of the state. All charge entrance fees, but several special passes are available. A Golden Eagle Passport—good at any national park for a year—costs $50. U.S. Citizens over 62 can buy a Golden Age Passport ($10) for lifetime access to any National Park, while disabled visitors can receive a free Golden Access Passport with similar privileges. Fees in all national parks are suspended on August 25 for Founders Day, celebrating the establishment of the National Park Service.

Presentations, exhibits, brochures, and park rangers are there to teach you about the history of each site before you take the tour, which can be self-guided or led by rangers. Picnic areas and gift shops are part of the package, but you'll have to look elsewhere for food and lodging.

REENACTMENTS

Even if history isn't your thing, you may well become more interested after watching one of these. Held on various anniversaries at sites throughout the state, reenactments are history brought to vivid life, worlds away from dull textbook prose. The attention to detail is amazing—for serious reenactors *everything* has to be authentic, down to the scratchy wool of their pants and the frames on their eyeglasses. Many carry original weapons and accessories (antique sabers and firearms can run in the thousands of dollars). Although rifle fire is prohibited in national battlefield parks except under carefully controlled circumstances, in other areas you'll see antique arms put to every intended use save actually perforating another soldier.

In the field, the smoke of campfires and artillery firings mingles with the rattle of drums and the clop of horses's hooves. Back in camp you can watch a surgeon demonstrate his amputation technique, or a local matron hand out hoecakes to hungry soldiers. Tens of thousands of spectators gather for the larger events, each paying a small fee (typically $5-10) to watch. Individual battlefields and sites can tell you about

Civil War reenactment at Meadow Farm Museum/Crump Memorial park, Richmond

VIRGINIA TOURISM CORPORATION

Civil War reenactment
at Chimborazo Park,
Richmond

VIRGINIA TOURISM CORPORATION

reenacting schedules or put you in touch with local reenactment organizations. Also try magazines such as *Civil War Times Illustrated,* Cowles Magazines, 2245 Kohn Rd., P.O. Box 8200, Harrisburg, PA 17105-8200; the *Camp Chase Gazette,* 3984 Cincinatti-Zanesville Rd. NE, Lancaster, OH 43130; and *The Union Times,* UADF, 7214 Laurel Hill Rd., Orlando, FL 32818. A good Web site for general information on the Civil War in Virginia is www.civilwar-va.com.

CIVIL WAR TRAILS

Inaugurated in 1997, these planned itineraries focus on five different phases of the conflict in Virginia. Three special driving itineraries ("1862 Peninsula Campaign: Civil War in the Tidewater," "Lee vs. Grant: The 1864 Campaign," and "Lee's Retreat") and two regions (the Shenandoah Valley and northern Virginia) have been marked and mapped with interpretive signs describing each site's significance. Special arrow signs point you down remote back roads far from the modern world, past private homes still bearing bullet scars, churches that once housed the wounded, and streams where soldiers rested over a century ago. Maps and information can be ordered free from **Virginia Civil War Trails,** tel. (888) 248-4592.

ORGANIZED TOURS

In addition to local tour companies, several national operators can lead you through Virginia's tourist attractions, back roads, or outdoor recreation. Reservation and cancellation policies vary; you usually have to reserve your spot with a deposit, which can be refunded as long as you don't cancel too close to the date of departure. All prices quoted are pp based on double occupany.

BUS TOURS

Most of these are primarily booked through travel agents. **Globus** offers "The Civil War," covering Washington, D.C., the Shenandoah Valley, northern Virginia, Richmond, Maryland, and Pennsylvania (8 days, $1,009-1,049); and "The Historic East," through Washington, D.C., Charlottesville, Williamsburg, Maryland and Pennsylvania (8 days, $959-999). Their **Cosmos** budget branch covers much of the same area in "America's Glorious Heritage" (9 days, $689-729). **Colette Tours's** "Heritage of America" ranges from New York to Williamsburg (9 days, $1,099-1,149). **Maupintour,** 1515 St. Andrews Dr., Lawrence, KS 66047, tel. (785) 843-1211, covers the Washington, D.C. area, Williamsburg, Shenandoah National Park, and the Piedmont along with Philadelphia (8 days, $1,475)

Gadabout Tours, 700 E. Tahquitz Canyon Way, Palm Springs, CA 92262, tel. (800) 952-5068 or (760) 325-5556, offers a fall tour of the Shenandoah and Colonial Williamsburg, including Washington, D.C., and Gettysburg (9 days, $1,626-1,666) along with a jaunt through the Washington, D.C. area in the spring and fall (10 days, $1,895-1,975). **Mayflower Tours,** 1225 Warren Ave., P.O. Box 490, Downers Grove, IL 60515, tel. (800) 323-7604, has "Washington, D.C., Williamsburg, and Pennsylvania Dutch" (8 days, $1,159-1,188). Local operator **VanGuide, Inc.,** 12 Wachovian Way, Raphine, VA 24472, tel. (800) 685-7265 (ext. 7315) or (540) 377-2110, runs guided van and bus tours for about $10 per hour. Their trips, which clients may customize, roll through the Charlottesville area and the Shenandoah Valley.

Gray Line, tel. (202) 289-1995, fax 484-0573, sends daily bus tours to Colonial Williamsburg ($64 adults, $54 children), Monticello and Charlottesville ($64 pp), and Mt. Vernon and Old Town Alexandria ($24 adults, $12 children); all leave from Union Station at 50 Massachusetts Ave. NE in Washington, D.C.

CYCLING TOURS

Backroads, 801 Cedar St., Berkeley, CA 94710-1800, tel. (800) GO-ACTIVE (800-462-2284) or (510) 527-1555, fax 527-1444, e-mail: goactive@backroads.com, Web site: www.backroads.com, covers the Shenandoah Valley and Blue Ridge Parkway over six days. Riders stay in country inns at night ($1,395). With **Vermont Bicycle Tours,** P.O. Box 711, Bristol, VT 05443-0711, tel. (800) 245-3868 or (802) 453-4811, fax 453-4806, e-mail: info@vbt.com, Web site: www.vbt.com, you can choose from "Horse and Wine Country" (4 days, $995), the Shenandoah Valley (2-5 days, $349-995), and a weekend in Colonial Williamsburg ($795). More ambitious riders can contact the **Adventure Cycling Association,** 150 E. Pine St., P.O. Box 8308, Missoula, MT 59807-8308, tel. (800) 755-2453, fax (406) 721-8754, e-mail: acabike@aol.com, Web site: www.adv-cycling.org, for details on the annual TransAmerica ride from Williamsburg to Portland, OR—it totals 4,450 miles and is spread out over 93 days with full support ($2,975).

OUTDOOR TOURS

Sierra Club Outings, 85 2nd St., 2nd Floor, San Francisco, CA 94105, tel. (415) 977-5522, fax 977-5795, e-mail: national.outings@sierraclub.org, Web site: www.sierraclub.org/outings, organizes "Cycling Through Civil War History," a one-week trip through battlefields and other sites in Virginia, Maryland, and Pennsylvania ($575). They'll also arrange for you to work alongside U.S. Forest Service personnel in the Mt. Rogers Wilderness Area during a one-week service trip ($275). **New**

England Hiking Holidays, P.O. Box 1648, North Conway, NH 03860, tel. (800) 869-0949 or (603) 356-9696, e-mail: nehh@aol.com, Web site: www.nehikingholidays.com, rambles through the Blue Ridge, exploring Civil War history and country inns along the way (5 days, $995-1045). The Potomac Appalachian Trail Club and Appalachian Trail Conference both organize day and overnight hikes as well; see the special topic **The Appalachian Trail** for details.

Birders could do much worse than **Field Guides Incorporated,** P.O. Box 160723, Austin, TX 78716-0723, tel. (800) 728-4953 or (512) 327-4953, fax 327-9231, e-mail: fgileader@aol.com, Web site: www.fieldguides.com. Their "Virginia's Warblers" tour covers the Piedmont, Shenandoah Valley, and West Virginia (5 days, $755). **Smithsonian Study Tours and Seminars,** 1100 Jefferson Dr. SW, Ste. 3077, MRC 702, Washington, D.C., 20560, tel. (202) 357-4700, fax 633-9250, Web site: www.si.edu/tsa/sst, offers a wide range of seminars and study tours in Virginia covering topics as diverse as classic railroads, architecture, and winter birding. They range from $47 for a one-day Civil War tour to $1,655 for a tour of art collections in Richmond and Williamsburg.

HOLIDAYS AND FESTIVALS

Every town has its own list of annual celebrations, from Monterey's Highland Maple Festival to Norfolk's Harborfest. At any given event, chances are you'll find live music, dancing, parades, displays of regional crafts, and tables groaning under platters of local food. Historical figures from a particular city are often remembered—or even brought to life by reenactors—on their birthdays, and local events are commemorated in services or parades. Some events charge admission, anywhere from $5 to $20 per adult, and the more popular ones start selling tickets months ahead of time.

Most national holidays, including Easter, the Fourth of July, and Labor Day, get their own celebrations, while Christmas and the week after bring religious services, buildings lit with strings of bulbs, and candlelight tours of historical sites. **First Night** heralds in the New Year in many cities, often an alcohol-free, family-oriented, cultural-performance event. During **Historic Garden Week** at the end of April, the grounds and gardens of some 200 locations statewide (most otherwise closed to the public) are open to visitors. Contact the Garden Club of Virginia, 12 E Franklin St., Richmond, VA 23219, tel. (804) 644-7776, Web site: www.vagardenweek.org, for details.

A good source on festivals in Virginia, besides the VTC and local chambers of commerce, is the Old Dominion edition of *Southern Festivals,* a bi-monthly newspaper published by Kim Lowry & Associates, 8709 Wellsley Way, Raleigh, NC 27613-1363, tel. (888) 257-0956, fax (919) 870-9729, e-mail: jlowry@ipass,net, Web site: www.southfest.com.

Many businesses and all government offices are closed on national holidays. These include: New Year's Day (January 1), Martin Luther King, Jr.'s Birthday (Monday closest to January 15), President's Day (Monday closest to February 22), Memorial Day (May 30), Independence Day (July 4), Labor Day (first Monday in September), Columbus Day (October 12), Veteran's Day (November 11), Thanksgiving Day (fourth Thursday in November), and Christmas Day (December 25).

SHOPPING

Crafts
Virginia handicrafts come in an amazingly broad range of styles and quality. Virginia pottery is near the top of the quality list, produced in such historic ceramics centers as Strasburg. Along the coast you can watch decoy carvers at work, or take a class yourself. Keep an eye out for bronze wildlife sculptures and signs advertising "woodcarvings for sale" outside private homes. Craftspeople in Jamestown and Colonial Williamsburg keep historical skills alive as they produce silver pitchers, hand-blown glass, shoes, and musical instruments, many of which are for sale.

Heading west you'll come across hooked rugs, table linens, and quilts from the looms of local weavers, along with hand-forged iron and brass from places such as Virginia Metalcrafters in Staunton. Woodcrafters turn out tools, toys, musical instruments, and cane-seat chairs and other furniture. Throughout the state artisans benefit from **art centers** like the Torpedo Factory, housed in an old munitions plant in Alexandria. Some, including Norfolk's d'Art Center and The Arts Depot in Abingdon, offer classes as well as display and sales areas.

Antiques

Serious buyers and casual browsers agree that shopping for antiques can eat up a week as easily as an afternoon. Barns and attics throughout the state have been raided to stock tiny shops and huge antique malls, with old stuff by the truckload for sale restored or "as-is." Prices are lower in Virginia than in Washington, D.C., drawing many shoppers down from the Capitol in search of that elusive but always possible Great Find. The list is practically endless, but includes old toys, quilts, magazines, food cans, advertising posters, clothing, and lawn ornaments. **Furniture** ranges from country standbys like cupboards, dressers, wardrobes, rope beds, and blanket boxes to distinctive Hepplewhite, Sheraton, and empire desks, chairs, and chests. **Civil War relics** such as swords, guns, uniforms, and utensils can get pricey, but smaller items—for instance prints, maps, and minnie balls (bullets)—are often more affordable. Packaging and/or delivery can often be arranged on the spot.

Before you plunk down $400 on that creaking, weather-beaten farm table, it helps to know a little about antique pricing. Shop around to get an idea of price ranges, and look for various reference books that advise how to get the most for your money. Two tabloid magazines list dealers and antique events: the weekly *Antiques & Auction News,* Rt. 230 West, P.O. Box 500, Mount Joy, PA 17552, tel. (717) 653-4300, and the monthly *Southern Antiques,* P.O. Drawer 1107, Decatur, GA 30031-1107, tel. (404) 289-0054, fax 286-9727. The bi-monthly *Antique Traveller,* tel. (703) 437-4971, e-mail: pscpub@aol.com, covers northern and southeastern Virginia along with parts of West Virginia, Maryland, and Washington, D.C.

Local Specialties

For a souvenir you can eat, consider taking home a particularly Virginian **food;** hams, pound cakes, wine, preserves, and peanuts are the most typical. Local cookbooks, especially those found along the coast, will bring back dinnertable memories for years. **Minerals** are popular, especially at "rock shops" at the entrance to most commercial caverns. Some sell geodes (hollow stone balls filled with crystals) that you can crack open yourself.

Taxes

The state levies a 4.5% sales tax, which is occasionally augmented by a local tax of 0.5%.

ACCOMMODATIONS

Price Ranges

This book uses the following rate categories, based on double occupancy during high season: **budget** (under $35), **inexpensive** ($35-60), **moderate** ($60-85), **expensive** ($85-110), **premium** ($110-150), and **luxury** (over $150). A 5% **lodging tax** is added to the state sales tax for a total increase of 9.5%.

Hotels and Motels

Virginia law dictates that maximum prices must be posted in rooms. Beyond that, though, accommodation rates can vary drastically depending on the timing, your persistence, and the manager's desire to fill an otherwise empty room. **High season** (May-Sept. and the October fall foliage displays) can jack up prices as much as 50%, as can holidays and local events such as college athletic games and graduations. Always ask about discounts—business/corporate, government, senior (AARP), auto club (AAA), and military rates are almost always lower. Weekend rates, except in resort areas like Virginia Beach, can save you a bundle if you stay Friday and/or Saturday night. Longer stays of a week or more are also discounted. Hotel chains' main reservation numbers (see special topic, **Virginia Hotel Chains**) can tell you the location of their nearest representative, list facilities, and even keep a room waiting.

VIRGINIA HOTEL CHAINS

HOTEL	TELEPHONE	ON THE INTERNET
Best Western	(800) 528-1234	www.bestwestern.com
Budgetel Inn	(800) 428-3438	www.budgetel.com
Comfort Inn	(800) 228-5150	www.comfortinn.com
Days Inn	(800) 325-2525	www.daysinn.com
EconoLodge	(800) 553-2666	www.econolodge.com
Hampton Inn	(800) HAMPTON (800-426-7866)	www.hamptoninn.com
Hilton Hotels	(800) 445-8667	www.hilton.com
Holiday Inn	(800) 465-4329	www.holiday-inn.com
Howard Johnson Lodge	(800) 654-2000	www.hojo.com
Hyatt Hotels	(800) 233-1234	www.hyatt.com
Marriott Hotels and Resorts	(800) 321-2211	www.marriott.com
Motel 6	(800) 466-8356	www.motel6.com
Omni	(800) 843-6664	www.omnihotels.com
Quality Inn	(800) 288-5151	www.qualityinn.com
Radisson	(800) 333-3333	www.radisson.com
Ramada Inn	(800) 272-6232	www.ramada-hotels.com
Sheraton Hotels	(800) 325-3535	www.sheraton.com
Super 8 Motels	(800) 800-8000	www.super8motels.com
Travelodge	(800) 255-3050	www.travelodge.com

More Personal

Bed and breakfasts, though more expensive, can often be a reason for visiting in themselves. Staying at one is like being a guest in someone's house, which is often exactly what you are, except that someone caters to your every whim and the building is often an outstanding antique. Nobody opens a B&B to retire early (though many owners already are), so you know your hosts are in it for the joy of meeting people and sharing their love of the area. Owners have often grown up nearby or even in the same house, making them an ideal source of local guidance and trivia. Multicourse, silver-service breakfasts are the norm instead of the exception—no muffin-and-instant-coffee "Continental" farce here. Smoking is usually permitted only outside, if at all (one brochure reads, "The house is 200 years old and the fire department five miles away."). Private bathrooms are standard, or there'll be a separate bath just down the hall—these, for some reason, often have large, claw-foot tubs. Guests can often use a kitchen or kitchenette to prepare food.

Country inns straddle the line between hotels and B&Bs, with the formalized quality of service of the former and much of the charm of the latter. Led by the world-class Inn at Little Washington, Virginia's inns offer privacy and luxury in a romantic, indulgent setting.

Advance reservations are desirable for both inns and B&Bs, especially during weekends, high season, and special events. Popular ones fill up months or even years in advance. A deposit in the form of one night's fee is often required, and a minimum length of stay may be imposed during the high season. Cancellation requires prior notice—at least 24 hours, or as much as one week—to avoid paying a service charge. Deals on multi-night stays are possible. Rates given are per room, double occupancy.

The **Bed and Breakfast Association of Virginia,** P.O. Box 791, Orange, VA 22960, tel. (540) 672-0870, can provide a list of its members statewide (e-mail: bbav@symweb.com, Web site: www.symweb.com/bbav or www.bbonline.com/va). Other helpful sources are the **Bed and Breakfast Line** of the Virginia Tourism Corporation, tel. (800) 262-1293, and **Bed & Breakfast Inns Online,** www.bbonline.com/va. Regional B&B associations are listed in the various chapter introductions.

Camping

Whether you want to get completely away from it all or just relocate and bring most of it with you, camping is the most flexible and affordable way to travel for an extended period. Campgrounds vary widely, but most are open from March or April through November or December. Reservations and/or deposits may be necessary at private campgrounds in resort areas or during peak seasons.

Public campgrounds include those at state parks, state fishing lakes, and wildlife management areas. Free primitive camping is permitted in the backcountry of the Jefferson and George Washington National Forests except where specifically prohibited. Backcountry and campsite camping are possible in the Shenandoah National Park; see the Shenandoah chapter for details. You can rent cabins at various state parks, including Douthat and First Landing/Seashore, for $50-80 per night or $230-430 per week depending on the season. Call the Department of Conservation and Recreation for details and reservations.

Private campgrounds usually include grills, drinking water, flush toilets, hot showers, coin laundry, and a camp store. More elaborate sites, typified by **KOA Kampgrounds,** tel. (800) KOA-9114 (800-562-9114), Web site: www.koakampgrounds.com, come complete with pools, game rooms, hot tubs, saunas, and volleyball courts. Occasionally they'll have small **cabins** with a/c and heat for about the price of a budget motel room. Features such as bicycle rental, miniature golf, and summer children's programs cost extra.

Hookups for water, electric, and sewer are charged as a whole or occasionally available separately. RV drivers can contact the **Recreation Vehicle Industry Association,** Dept. 3A, P.O. Box 2999, Reston, VA 22090, for an information packet listing RV publications and local clubs. **Camper Clubs of America,** tel. (800) 369-CAMP (800-369-2267), offers a $5-per-night guarantee to 225 private campgrounds nationwide, as well as no-cost reservations, for a fee of $200 per year.

Youth Hostels

Virginia has official Hostelling International (HI) outposts in Bluemont, Urbanna, Virginia Beach, and on the Blue Ridge Parkway at the North Carolina state line. Even without the member's discount, these modest lodgings are much cheaper than a hotel room at around $15 pp per night (less for members). Membership is $25 per year, and can be acquired at any hostel or from **Hostelling International-American Youth Hostels,** 733 15th St. NW, Ste. 840, Washington, DC 20005, tel. (202) 783-6161, fax 783-6171, Web site: www.hostels.com., or HI's **Potomac Area Council,** 1108 K St. NW, Lower Level, Washington, DC 20005, tel. (202) 783-4943. Hostels are usually closed during the day, and lock their doors at 10 p.m.

Homestays

U.S. Servas, Inc., 11 John St., Ste. 407, New York, NY 10038, tel. (212) 267-0252, fax 267-0292, e-mail: usservas@igc.apc.org, oversees a worldwide network designed to promote peace and foster inter-cultural understanding through person-to-person contact. After an initial interview, travelers 18 and over pay $55 per year to rent a list of hosts who offer room and board for two nights. Becoming a Servas traveler is an excellent way to meet interesting local people, and can easily repay your initial investment. At last count their East Coast list had some three dozen hosts in Virginia out of 1,886 in the United States.

Rentals and Exchanges

A number of companies can arrange rentals of private homes: try **Property Rentals International,** 1008 Mansfield Crossing Rd., Richmond, VA 23236, tel. (804) 378-6054 or (800) 220-3332, fax (804) 379-2073, e-mail: villas@erols.com, Web site: www.imall.com/stores/pri; **Rent-a-Home International,** 7200 34th Ave. NW, Seattle, WA 98117, tel. (206) 789-9377 or (800) 488-7368, fax (206) 789-9379, e-mail: rentahomeinternational@msn.com, Web site: www.rentavilla.com; and **Hideaways International,** 767 Islington St., Portsmouth, NH 03801, tel. (603) 430-4433 or (800) 843-4433, fax (603) 430-4444, e-mail: info@hideaways.com, Web site: www.hideaways.com. If you're interested in a longer-term home exchange, try **HomeLink International/ Vacation Exchange Club,** P.O. Box 650, Key West, FL 33041, tel. (305) 294-1448 or (800) 638-3841, fax (305) 294-1148; or **Loan-a-Home,** 2 Park Ln., Apt. 6E, Mount Vernon, NY 10552, tel. (914) 664-7640.

FOOD

Classic Country Cuisine (a.k.a. Home Cookin')

As soon as the Jamestown settlers were able to make it through a few winters in a row, they set about starting a tradition of rich dining that lives on in Virginia homes and restaurants today. All the fruits of the fertile land went into the pot and onto the table, including fish from the rivers, bays, and ocean, corn from the Indians, produce brought from the Old World, and farm animals of every description. Every well-stocked dining room had a "groaning board" bent under the weight of overflowing platters.

Today restaurants like Williamsburg's Shield Tavern, Charlottesville's Mitchie Tavern, and Leesburg's Green Tree serve the legacy in its truest form. Wherever you go in Virginia, though, you're liable to enjoy it in some form or another. Odds are better farther into the countryside, or at a restaurant that advertises home cookin' as a specialty.

One quick disclaimer—this is not health food. Deep-fried, salted for weeks, and loaded with butter, home cooking Virginia-style can pack on the pounds quicker than a chocolate tour of Switzerland. But heck, people have been eating it for generations, and they keep living to a ripe old age, so it's not as if your arteries will clog overnight.

And anyway, it is *good.* The classic meal, served at a restaurant such as The Homeplace near Roanoke, goes something like this: sides of coleslaw, beans (butter or baked), black-eyed peas, mashed potatoes (plenty of gravy), cornbread, grits, and fresh, flaky, steaming biscuits sidle up to a centerpiece of crispy fried chicken, juicy roast beef, or salty country ham. Occasionally soup—vegetable, chili, or hearty Brunswick Stew (with the original rabbits and squirrels replaced with chicken, ham, or beef)—is served on the side. Peanut soup is a local staple, just the right balance of sweet and spicy. Salad can mean anything from tossed greens and dressing to canned fruit served on cottage cheese. Iced tea is the drink of choice, followed closely by local apple cider. Dessert is often homemade peach cobbler or pecan pie.

Main courses almost always include some kind of meat. "Country-fried" or "chicken-fried" steak is covered in batter before cooking, and barbecue usually means pork, with a more delicate flavor than the vinegar-fueled kick of barbecue served farther south. Pot roast, rib-eye steak, chicken and dumplings, and baked pork chops are all popular, but **ham** is by far the most distinctive Virginia centerpiece. The tradition began in colonial days, when pork proved easier to preserve by smoking, drying, sugar-curing, or pickling than other meats. Over the years, ham (technically the thigh of a hog) has evolved into a few variations. Virginia ham, also known as Williamsburg or country ham, is dry-cured with salt and then smoked. Smithfield ham, named after the small town on the James River west of Norfolk, is slowly smoked over a hickory fire and then aged, skin and all, for up to a year. This, along with a coating of pepper applied during curing, gives it a stronger, smokier taste than other, less mature hams. Local stores often have Smithfield hams hanging in burlap sacks, which customers remove before soaking overnight and cooking. The secret is to slice it paper thin, ideal for the traditional ham-and-biscuit.

Breakfast is often as serious an undertaking. Biscuits and gravy, chicken-fried steak, and ham slices may all make an appearance next to your eggs and coffee.

CRAB LINGO

backfin	large fin containing choice meat
buster	within hours of shedding
dead men	gray lungs (and how you'll feel if you eat them)
doubler	male and female crab caught in mating embrace
jimmy	legal-sized male
peeler	ready to molt
pot	crab trap
sook	mature female

working the shedding floats for soft crab, Tangier Island

VIRGINIA TOURISM CORPORATION

Seafood

The daily catch, served up in weather-beaten cafes on the Eastern shore and Virginia Beach's great oceanfront restaurants, is the state's other gourmet specialty. Ask your server whether the selection is native or not—fresher is better. Dozens of Virginia's 200 species of **fish,** including rockfish (striped bass), bluefish, shad, trout, pike, and crappie, are served broiled, fried, smoked, and baked.

The most famous Chesapeake shellfish is *Callinectes sapidus,* the famous **Chesapeake blue crab** whose scientific name translates as "savory, beautiful swimmer." An average of 50 million pounds of these are plucked from the bay every year, making up half the nation's entire catch. Cracking open and eating crabs is an acquired art form, but well worth the effort; males are easier to pick apart, while the millions of eggs inside females can make the experience even messier. Crab cakes, made with cornmeal or cracker crumbs and eggs, are a more manageable alternative.

Soft-shells are brought up within an hour after molting, as they sit dazed on the bottom waiting for their new shells to harden. Those caught just before shedding are stored in floating boxes and watched around the clock until they get around to it. They're fried in batter and eaten whole, often on a bun—a true saltwater delicacy. Crab imperial (mixed with bread, egg, mayonnaise, and Worcestershire), deviled crabs with horseradish and chili powder, and cream-based soups like bisque and sherry-laced "she-crab" are all recipes worth trying. If you're interested in catching your own, try renting a small crab pot from a sporting goods store, or netting crabs in the shallows with fish or chicken leftovers as bait.

It was a brave soul who ate the first raw **oyster,** but somehow the slimy mouthful caught on. Chincoteague oysters on the halfshell are the best. Oyster season runs Sept.-April, with a peak around the holidays. **Clams** are served raw or steamed, and are usually cherrystones (a.k.a. little-necks, hard-shells) or manoes (steamers, longnecks, or soft-shells). True Virginia-coast chowder isn't the creamy New England style or red Manhattan style; here it's made with a clear base filled with potatoes, celery, onions, and herbs. Everything comes with a handful of small balls of fried cornmeal dough called **hush puppies.**

VIRGINIA WINE

Of all the eastern states, Virginia enjoys the best climate—and mindset—for growing and enjoying quality vintages. Vineyards between 37-39° north latitude, the same as California's north coast, avoid both the harsh northern cold and the prolonged humid southern summers. Production is limited, with most bottles sold at wineries, festivals, wine shops, and supermarkets alongside beer (hard liquor by the bottle is found only in state-run Alcohol Beverage Control stores). Quality of Virginia wine has taken a quantum leap in the '90s, according to one winemaker—who knows, maybe the state's second-place complex (to the West Coast wine country) will some day carry it to first.

History
Early Jamestown settlers grew grapes with the help of French *vignerons* sent by the Virginia Company, but even with the Assembly's "Acte 12" compelling each farmer to plant 12 grapevines or be punished, imported vines died and hardy local varieties turned sour. A multitude of factors, including cold weather, insects, disease, and the American Revolution undermined the 1769 Act for the Encouragement of the Making of Wine. Thomas Jefferson, the "Father of American Wine," even went so far as to import an Italian expert to help him plan Monticello's vineyards, but it wasn't until 1835 that Richmond viticulturist Dr. D.N. Norton bred the first "nonfoxy" American wine grape, encouraging local vintners to give it another go. By 1979 Virginia counted six wineries.

Ronald Reagan presented former Soviet president Mikhail Gorbachev with a bottle of Virginia Seyval at the 1988 Moscow summit, four years before *Wine Spectator* magazine dubbed Virginia "the most accomplished of America's emerging wine regions." The awards had started rolling in, including the 1993 and 1995 *Wine Spectator* Critic's Choice awards bestowed on Williamsburg Winery, placing it among the world's 200 best. By 1997, Virginia was sixth in the country in fine wine production, with 47 wineries covering 1,500 acres.

Varieties
Whites like chardonnay and Riesling grow best in the Old Dominion. They tend to be light- to medium-bodied, closer to wines from Burgundy or the Pacific Northwest than California, thanks to Virginia's comparably cooler climate. More complex whites bear the mark of oak-barrel aging. Chardonnay is the most widely planted variety, resulting in a balanced, crisp bottle that's easy to match with food. Riesling comes next, producing a semi-dry to dry wine. Reds like cabernet sauvignon are more temperamental—"God couldn't grow a good merlot in Virginia," says one vintner.

Visiting Wineries
Wineries can be found from the coast to the mountains, with the highest concentration in the Piedmont. Visiting one combines a drive through beautiful countryside with the satisfaction of buying a quality vintage directly from the person who made it (plus, prices are always best at the winery). Tastings are given free or for a small charge, allowing you to pick your favorite from a wide selection. Tours of the facilities can be guided or self-guided, leading you past crusher-stemmers, presses, fermentation tanks, oak aging barrels, and bottling setups. Many wineries allow you to enjoy your purchase immediately with a picnic on the grounds, and a few offer gourmet restaurants on the premises. October has been dubbed Virginia Wine Month, with 33 different events held at wineries. During the rest of the year wineries host everything from jazz concerts to food festivals.

Local wineries are listed in special topics in each chapter. Visiting hours vary, so it's always a good idea to call before showing up.

Resources
For a free list of wineries and events contact the **Virginia Wine Marketing Program,** Virginia Department of Agriculture & Consumer Services, Division of Marketing, P.O. Box 1163, Richmond, VA 23209, tel. (800) 828-4637 or (804) 786-0481. On the Internet stop by www.vawine.com.

TRANSPORTATION

*I've never been lost, but I was bewildered
once for about three days.*

—Daniel Boone

BY CAR

Like most of the U.S., Virginia is best explored in your own vehicle. Luckily a convenient network of interstate highways provides easy access to every corner. I-81, running the length of the western border, and I-95, connecting Washington, D.C., with Richmond and North Carolina, are the main north-south arteries. Interstate 66 links the nation's capital with I-81, and I-64 runs from the Norfolk area through Richmond to Staunton, continuing west from Lexington into West Virginia.

The speed limit on rural interstates is 65 mph; otherwise it's 55 mph or as marked. Radar detectors are illegal in Virginia. State-maintained routes may have a name (i.e., Old Mill Road) as well as a number (Rt. 645), so keep this in mind as you look for that out-of-the-way B&B. Give the tourism office (VTC) a call for a free map of the state's thousands of miles of official and proposed **scenic byways.**

If you plan on doing a lot of driving, then joining the **American Automobile Association (AAA)** can come in handy. Emergency roadside assistance, free maps, tourbooks, and campbooks are all included in the year-long membership. Contact your local AAA office for details.

Driving Hazards

In winter, state maintained roads are generally plowed quickly, thought a fast, heavy snowfall

---

RESOURCES FOR DRIVERS

VIRGINIA DEPARTMENT OF HIGHWAYS AND TRANSPORTATION

Administrative Services Division, 1221 E. Broad St., Richmond, VA 23219, tel. (800) 835-1203, Web site: www.vdot.state.us

24-HOUR HIGHWAY HELPLINES

Provides information on work zones, highway incidents, and bad weather.

Statewide	tel. (800) 367-ROAD (800-367-7623), TTY (800) 828-1120
Hampton Roads Area	tel. (800) 792-2800 or (757) 928-1111 ext. 7623
Chesapeake Bay Bridge-Tunnel	tel. (757) 331-2960
Jamestown Ferry	tel. (757) 331-2960
New River Valley Area	tel. (540) 382-0200, ext 7623
Roanoke Valley Area	tel. (540) 981-0100, ext. 7623

STATE POLICE OFFICES

Division 1	Rt. 1, four miles north of Richmond, tel. (804) 553-3444 or (800) 552-9965
Division 2	Rt. 29, three miles northeast of Culpeper, tel. (540) 829-7401 or (800) 572-2260
Division 3	Rt. 613, two miles west of Appomattox, tel. (804) 352-7128 or (800) 552-0962
Division 4	I-81, two miles east of Wytheville, tel. (540) 228-3131 or (800) 542-8716
Division 5	Rt. 13 in Chesapeake, tel. (757) 424-6820 or (800) 582-8350
Division 6	Rt. 11, one mile west of Salem, tel. (540) 380-1500 or (800) 542-5959
Division 7	Rt. 620 in Fairfax, tel. (703) 323-4500 or (800) 572-4510

MAJOR CAR RENTAL COMPANIES

COMPANY	TELEPHONE	ON THE INTERNET
Alamo	(800) 327-9633	www.goalamo.com
Avis	(800) 831-2847	www.avis.com
Budget	(800) 527-0700	www.budgetrentacar.com
Dollar	(800) 800-4000	www.dollarcar.com
Enterprise	(800) 325-8007	www.pickenterprise.com
Hertz	(800) 654-3131	www.hertz.com
National	(800) 328-4567	www.nationalcar.com
Thrifty	(800) 367-2277	www.thrifty.com

can take a day or two to clear. Nearly invisible **black ice** is the biggest winter driving hazard, especially at night and in the early morning before the sun melts it. **Fog** on the mountains is another concern; it's most often encountered along the Skyline Drive and Blue Ridge Parkway. Visibility can plunge to 50 feet or less, so go slow and turn on your headlights. (Some passes, like I-64 near Waynesboro, have lights in the roadway to make driving in fog safer).

Car Rental

You have to be 25 years old to rent from most agencies, though some will accept drivers over 21. To save money, shop around for the best rates and consider local companies. Fly-drive packages and long-term rentals, especially if booked ahead of time though a travel agent, can be much less expensive. Ask if the quoted price includes local taxes and unlimited mileage, and get clear on dropoff/refueling charges, cancellation penalties, one-way fees, insurance coverage, and deposits.

BY BUS

Greyhound, tel. (800) 231-2222, Web site: www.greyhound.com, connects most Virginia cities and tourist destinations. Tickets are cheaper if you buy them 7-21 days in advance. Their Ameripass offers discounted unlimited travel for 7, 15, 30, or 60 days. Ask about other discounts for students, seniors, and military personnel. Children 2-11 travel for half-price, and companions assisting a disabled traveler are free with 48 hours' notice. Call the toll-free number for route and fare

information; local terminal numbers will handle all other inquiries.

BY TRAIN

Traveling on **Amtrak,** 60 Massachusetts Ave. NE, Washington, DC 20002, tel. (800) USA-RAIL (872-7245), TTD (800) 523-6590, Web site: www.amtrak.com, is closer in price to flying to the state but more comfortable and convenient. Amtrak's *Metroliner* connects New York City to Washington, D.C.'s **Union Station,** 50 Massachusetts Ave. NE, tel. (202) 484-7540. From there, Metrorail lines run to destinations in northern Virginia.

In the rest of the state service varies between one or more roundtrips daily to 3-6 per week, with Amtrak Thruway buses connecting some cities. Drive aboard the Auto Train in Lorton, which can take you all the way to Sanford, Florida. A Student Advantage Card ($20) provides 15% discounts for one year; call (800) 962-6872 for information. Special seating, boarding assistance, and discounts for disabled travelers are available with 24 hours' notice, and service dogs ride free. Once again, use the toll-free number for route and fare questions; otherwise, local terminal numbers for baggage and other questions are given under individual city listings.

BY AIR

Most major airlines fly into one of two major airports in northern Virginia: **Washington Dulles International Airport** near Herndon, or **National Airport** on the Potomac between Arlington and Alexandria. National handles domestic flights from east of the Mississippi. There are also major airports near Richmond, Norfolk, Newport News/Williamsburg, Charlottesville, and Roanoke.

The cheapest flights are almost always roundtrip and date-restricted (usually requiring a Saturday-night stay). You'll have to book in advance and purchase within a day or two to secure the fare. Try different airports and smaller or regional carriers, and look in the Sunday travel sections of larger U.S. newspapers for the most up-to-the-minute deals.

MAJOR AIRLINE CONTACT NUMBERS

The following major airlines, with telephone numbers and Web sites listed, schedule flights to Virginia.

Airline	Phone	Website
American Airlines	(800) 433-7300	www.americanair.com
Continental Airlines	(800) 525-0280	www.flycontinental.com
Delta Airlines	(800) 221-1212	www.delta-air.com
Midway Connection	(800) 446-4392	www.midwayair.com
Northwest Airlines	(800) 225-2525	www.nwa.com
Trans World Express	(800) 221-2000	www.twa.com
United Airlines, United Express	(800) 241-6522	www.ual.com
USAir, USAir Express	(800) 428-4322	www.usairways.com

INFORMATION AND SERVICES

WHEN TO GO

If you're lucky enough to choose any time of year to visit, then seasonal weather will be one of your prime concerns (see **Climate** in the Introduction chapter). Even when considering other factors, though, spring and fall are probably the best overall times to visit to Virginia. In April, May, and September you'll find lulls in the tourist season *and* great weather.

In the spring, equestrian events like races and hunts thunder through northern Virginia, and crowds aren't yet a problem. Be warned that many tourist attractions don't open until April or May. Summer is high tourist season, even though high temperatures and humidity send most visitors to the beaches, historic sites, and theme parks along the coast. Fall's famous colors bring a second high season, though smaller than in the summer. In winter, the least crowded season, you can have entire days to yourself— if you can handle the cold. Many sights close, especially in the mountains. Local festivals happen throughout the year.

HEALTH AND SAFETY

For emergencies anywhere in the state, dial 911 from any phone (no charge), or phone the Virginia State Police (see special topic Resources for Drivers). Hospitals in larger cities are excellent, though emergency-room treatment is always more expensive than visits scheduled with an appointment. A number of agencies offer specialized travelers' insurance in various combinations of health, accident, trip-cancellation and trip-interruption, and lost-luggage protection (see special topic Insurance Companies).

Outdoors

Whenever you go into the wild, always tell someone where you're going and when you expect to be back, and then contact them when you return. It's a good idea to carry a first-aid kit, available pre-packaged at most camp stores, and bring extra clothing layers (including a waterproof layer) and a safety kit that includes a Swiss army knife, waterproof matches, compass, topographical map, flashlight, emergency blanket (pocket-sized, mylar), signal whistle, and emergency food.

Even the clearest, highest mountain streams stand a good chance of containing **giardia,** a bacteria transmitted in human and animal waste that causes severe diarrhea. Filter or treat all water with iodine pills or drops. **Mosquitoes** are an annoyance everywhere in the summer and fall, along with **bees, wasps, yellowjackets, and hornets.** Female **black widow spiders,** identifiable by a tiny red hourglass on the abdomen, live in dark, woody places like rotting logs and under benches and tables. Their bite causes severe abdominal pain. If you are bitten, consult a physician. **Lyme disease** is transmitted through deer tick bites. It's not as common here as in New England, but still appears every so often. Use insect repellent and check yourself after passing through tick territory—high grass or underbrush. If you notice a large red circular rash around a bite, seek medical treatment—it's life-threatening if untreated.

Virginia is home to three species of poisonous snakes. **Rattlesnakes** live in the mountains, **cottonmouth moccasins** inhabit swamps, and **copperheads** are everywhere. Don't stick your feet or hands anywhere you can't see ahead of time, and if you encounter one, back off slowly. They're more afraid of you than you are of them, and strike out of fear at sudden movements. Swimming in the ocean could expose you to a brush with the dreaded **jellyfish.** The best thing to minimize the sting (besides staying out of the water) is, believe it or not, meat tenderizer.

Plants to avoid include **poison ivy, poison oak,** and **poison sumac.** To help watch out for offending flora, remember the saying, "leaves of three, let it be." The irritating oil transmitted by contact with these plants can be washed off with soap and water, and over-the-counter cortisone creams can relieve the itching. Several local types of **mushrooms** and **berries** are also dangerous if ingested—don't eat any if you don't know what you're doing.

Weather-Related Problems

Being wet and tired in the cold mountains can lead to **hypothermia,** a dangerous plunge in the body's core temperature. Symptoms include shivering, slurred speech, and loss of coordination and mental clarity. Warm the affected person up by skin-to-skin contact, warm them with liquids (no alcohol), and evacuate as a last resort. **Lightning** is a danger on exposed ridges—stay away from lone trees and conductive materials such as power lines and metal fences. The summer sun along the coast can cause a nasty **sunburn,** so cover up with clothes and lotion, at least for the first week or so.

Crime

Although things have improved in the last few decades, the downtown areas of larger cities like Richmond, Norfolk, and Alexandria still pose a threat of **robbery,** especially at night. Check with hotel staff regarding safe and dangerous areas. To discourage **break-ins** and **car theft,** don't leave valuables in plain view in your vehicle, and always lock the doors. Consider an antitheft device like The Club in questionable neighborhoods.

MAPS

The **AAA map** of Virginia is the handiest for general navigation. For every last back road and some city maps, pick up a copy of the large-format *Virginia State Road Atlas* published by ADC (1996, $12.95). Hikers can order U.S. Geo-

---

TRAVEL INSURANCE COMPANIES

Access America; P.O. Box 90315, Richmond, VA 23286; tel. (800) 284-8300 or (804) 673-1491

Carefree Travel Insurance; P.O. Box 9366, 100 Garden City Plaza, Garden City, NY 11530; tel. (516) 294-0220 or (800)-323-3149

Tele-Trip; Mutual of Omaha Plaza, P.O. Box 31716, Omaha, NE 68131; tel. (800) 228-9792

Travel Assistance International; 1133 15th St. NW, Ste. 400, Washington, DC, 20077; tel. (202) 828-5894 or (800) 821-2828; fax (202) 828-5896

Travel Guard International; 1145 Clark St., Stevens Point, WI 54401; tel. (715) 345-0505 or (800) 782-5151; fax (800) 826-1300

Wallach and Co., Inc.; 107 W. Federal St., P.O. Box 480, Middleburg, VA 20118-0480; tel. (540) 687-3166 or (800) 237-6615; fax (540) 687-3172

WEATHER RESOURCES

Weather Channel Connection	tel. (900) 932-8437 (95 cents per minute)
Richmond Weather Report	tel. (804) 268-1212
Roanoke Weather Report	tel. (540) 982-2303
Newport News Weather Report	tel. (757) 877-1221
Statewide Weather and Traffic Conditions	Web site: www.state.va.us/home/conditon.html

logical Survey (USGS) **topographical maps** from the Distribution Branch, P.O. Box 25286, Federal Center, Denver, CO 80225. These are also available from **Omni Resources,** 1004 South Mebane St., P.O. Box 2096, Burlington, NC 27216-2096, tel. (800) 742-2677, fax (336) 227-3748, e-mail: custserv@omnimap.com, Web site: www.omnimap.com, which also carries city and recreational maps and the *Virginia Atlas & Gazetteer.*

If you're into maps as art (like me), order a catalog from **Raven Maps & Images,** P.O. Box 850, Medford, OR 97501-0253, tel. (800) 237-0798, fax (541) 773-6834. At 35" by 65", their *Virginia, Maryland, Delaware, and the District of Columbia* map is too large to carry in the car with you, but with tinted elevation and shaded relief it's nice enough to frame and hang on the wall ($25 plain, $45 laminated).

INFORMATION

The **Virginia Tourism Corporation** (VTC), 901 E. Byrd St., Richmond, VA 23219, tel. (800) VISIT-VA (800-847-4882) or (804) 786-2051, fax 786-1919, Web site: www.virginia.org, can send you information on almost anything having to do with tourism in the state. The state also maintains an **information center** in Washington, D.C. at 1629 K St., tel. (202) 659-5523 or (800) 934-9184, open Mon.-Fri. 9 a.m.-5 p.m. On the Internet, the Commonwealth maintains a general state Web site at www.state.va.us/.

MONEY

ATMs are widely available in mid-sized and larger cities, but uncommon in smaller towns. For the locations of ATMs accepting cards bearing the Cirrus logo, call (800) 424-7787; for Plus call (800) 843-7587. Credit card use follows a similar pattern: accepted in cities, but in small towns you'll come across restaurants and museums that won't take them. In an emergency, you may be able to convince a local merchant or gas station attendant to give you cash change on a credit card purchase. **American Express,** tel. (800) 221-7282, has offices in Richmond, 1412A Starling Drive, tel. (804) 740-2030, and Roanoke, 22 E Campbell Ave., tel. (540) 982-2200.

STUDENT TRAVEL

The **Council on International Education Exchange** (CIEE), 205 E. 42nd St., 16th Fl., New York, NY 10017, tel. (800) 226-8624 or (212) 661-1414, fax 822-2699, Web site: www.ciee.org, issues the International Student Identity Card (ISIC) and under-26 Youth Cards that can secure you the occasional admission deal, as well as cheap flights with its worldwide **Council Travel** network. **STA Travel,** tel. (800) 777-0122, Web site: www.sta-travel.com, is another student-oriented, international travel agency with branch offices across the country. Canadian students should contact **Travel CUTS,** 187 College St., Toronto, Ontario M5T 1P7, tel. (416) 979-2406 or (800) 667-2887, for rail passes and discounted flights.

GAY TRAVELERS

Even though it's not part of the Deep South, Virginia still leans toward the conservative, so discretion is advised. Most larger cities, though, support some sort of gay scene, which you can find out about through a number of channels. The **Dulles Triangles,** P.O. Box 3411, Reston, Virginia 20195-1411, tel. (703) 787-0744, Web site: www.geocities.com/WestHollywood/8885, is a gay social club in the northern Virginia area. Look to the Internet for gay guides to the Norfolk area (members.aol.com/DavMarLtd/GGN/index.htm and www.gay-tidewater.com).

The **International Gay Travel Association,** P.O. Box 4974, Key West, FL 33041, tel. (800) 448-8550, fax (305) 296-6633, combines travel agents and tour operators. *Out & About,* 8 W. 19th St., Ste. 401, New York, NY 10011, tel. (212) 645-6922 or (800) 929-2268, fax 929-2215, is a monthly newsletter ($50 for 10 issues) covering resorts, hotels, cruise lines, and airlines. The *Fodor's Gay Guide to the USA,* by Andrew Collins (Fodor's Travel Publications, 2nd edition, 1998) is another good source.

TRAVELERS WITH DISABILITIES

Wheelchair access varies, so it's always best to call ahead and check. Upscale hotels are usually accessible, while B&Bs—often in old houses—probably aren't. Some theaters and restaurants have ramps and elevators, and some caverns and Civil War sites feature paved trails. All National Park Service visitor centers are wheelchair accessible. Most restrooms and buildings in Shenandoah National Park are accessible, along with some picnic grounds and campgrounds.

Resources
The VTC provides a special number, (800) 742-3935, for fielding questions regarding special needs travel. Reach its TDD Relay Center at (800) 828-1120. The **Opening Door, Inc.,** 8049 Ormesby Lane, Woodford, VA 22580, tel. (804) 633-6752, is a local nonprofit organization that publishes the *Virginia Travel Guide for the Disabled,* listing access information on Virginia hotels, restaurants, shops, and attractions (also available from VTC). For more information on disabled travel contact **Mobility International USA,** P.O. Box 10767, Eugene, OR 97440, tel. (541) 343-1284, fax 343-6812, TTY (541) 343-1284; the **Society for the Advancement of Travel for the Handicapped,** 347 5th Ave., Ste. 610, New York, NY 10016, tel. (212) 447-7284, fax 725-8253; and the **Travel Information Service,** tel. (215) 456-9600.

TRAVELING WITH CHILDREN

Dozens of spots in Virginia are as fun for children as their parents—if not more. Theme parks like Paramount's Kings Dominion, Busch Gardens, and Water Country USA are obvious first choices. You may be surprised how quickly children warm up to history when it's brought to life at places like Colonial Williamsburg, the Museum of American Frontier Culture, and Virginia's Explore Park. (Nothing sparks a kid's interest like a

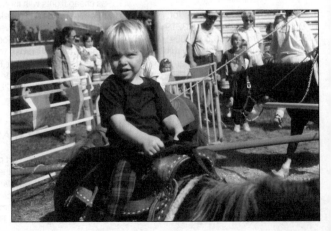

There's plenty of attractions for kids in Virginia. Here, a young one braves the pony ride at the Virginia Garlic Festival in Amherst.

mountain man in full buckskin explaining how to hunt bear, or a blacksmith pounding red-hot iron over a forge.) Even Civil War sites, which could easily bore young minds to tears, offer the occasional battle re-enactment or fascinating museum. Other hands-on exhibitions are designed with kids in mind, like the Shenandoah Valley Discovery Museum in Winchester or Roanoke's outstanding Science Museum of Western Virginia. Theaters often host children's plays, and storytellers, musicians, face-painters, and puppeteers frequent festivals.

Local baby-sitting agencies can be found in the yellow pages or through hotel desks. The Family Travel Times, 40 5th Ave., New York, NY 10011, tel. (212) 477-5524, publishes the quarterly *Travel With Your Children,* for $40 per year.

SENIOR TRAVELERS

Many hotels and attractions offer discounts for seniors—ask when making reservations or at the gate. The **American Association of Retired Persons,** 601 E St. NW, Washington, DC, 20049, tel. (202) 434-2277, is the country's largest seniors' organization, with member discounts on hotels, car rentals, air travel, and tours worldwide. **Elderhostel,** 75 Federal St., Boston, MA 02110-941, tel. (617) 426-7788, organizes study vacations on college campuses for about $300 per week. It's open to people 55 and over (one half of a couple is sufficient). Sears' travel club **Mature Outlook,** P.O. Box 10448, Des Moines, IA 50306, tel. (800) 336-6330, features a magazine and discounts of up to 50%.

TIME ZONES

Virginia is in the eastern time zone, five hours behind Greenwich mean time. **Daylight saving time** sets clocks one hour ahead on the first Sunday in April ("spring forward") and back one hour on the last Sunday in October ("fall back").

BUSINESS HOURS

Stores are generally open Mon.-Fri. 10 a.m.-6 p.m., and occasionally on Saturday. Shopping centers can be open daily, late on weeknights and Sunday noon-5 or 6 p.m. Public and private office hours run Mon.-Fri. 9 a.m.-5 p.m., and banks are open Mon.-Fri. 9 a.m.-5 p.m., with occasional extended hours on evenings and Saturday mornings. Post office doors open at 8:30 a.m. on all days but Sunday, and stay open until 5 p.m. on weekdays and 12:30 p.m. on Saturday. Museum and gallery hours vary, but many are closed on Monday. Just about everything closes on Thanksgiving, Christmas, and New Year's Day (even sites listed as open daily), and other national holidays may mean closings as well.

TIPPING

As any former restaurant server will tell you (and there are plenty of us out there), a 15% tip on bills is standard, since waiters make considerably less than minimum wage before tips. Leave 20% or more to reward outstanding service. Taxi drivers typically receive 15% and airport porters and bellhops about $1 per bag.

THE PIEDMONT: MR. JEFFERSON'S COUNTRY

Two and a half centuries later, the man who left his indelible stamp on the central part of Virginia is still spoken about with a curious mixture of awe and familiarity, like a distinguished uncle who's just in the next room. These rolling hills, achingly beautiful in the late-afternoon sunlight, echo almost every aspect of a true renaissance life.

Thomas Jefferson was born on his father's farm at Shadwell in 1743, and plows still turn the rich soil of large parts of Albemarle and Orange counties every spring. Along with the land for Monticello, Jefferson inherited a taste for things patrician, a value system carried on with gusto by the Piedmont's current upper crust. Grand 19th-century homes anchor wealthy neighborhoods in Richmond, while in rural areas shaded country lanes lead to historic estates, each with its own name and legion of caretakers. Packs of foxhounds in the care of riders on purebred horses are blessed outside Grace Episcopal Church on Rt. 231 in an annual ritual Jefferson would have undoubtedly appreciated.

Though the author of the Declaration of Independence failed in his first few attempts at coaxing a decent grape from the fertile Virginia soil, central Virginia now cradles the highest number of wineries in the state. Jefferson's fascination with classical architecture lives on in the neoclassical lines of the state capitol in Richmond, the porticoes of Monticello, and the unmistakable rotunda of the University of Virginia in Charlottesville.

Above all, the third American president carried himself with an air of humility—he described how he found the greatest happiness when up to his elbows in his gardens or tinkering on one of the items on an endless list of projects and mechanical schemes. And despite all the New Money that has poured into the Piedmont lately—along with celebrities like Rita Mae Brown, Sam Shepherd, and billionaire John Kluge—central Virginia is still simple at heart. Whether it's the hand-poled Hatton Ferry across the James River at Scottsville, a well-worn tractor resting in a field of alfalfa, or the way everyone knows your name down at the general store after a couple of visits, this part of the state carries on Jefferson's greatest, quiet legacy: that of things of quality, appreciated slowly.

Highlights

Almost all Virginia interstates lead to Richmond, which has been bursting with history ever since

Patrick Henry gave his "liberty or death" speech in St. John's Church in 1775. As headquarters of the Confederacy, Richmond guarded the home of Jefferson Davis; the home is now part of the state's foremost Civil War museum. Today Richmond remains Virginia's political and commercial capital, humming with life in restored historic neighborhoods full of museums, restaurants, shops, and nightclubs.

Other Piedmont cities well worth a visit include the traditional tobacco center of Lynchburg, frighteningly cozy Charlottesville, and Fredericksburg, contested in some of the Civil War's hottest fighting. Civil War buffs have made a living out of exploring the Piedmont's wealth of battlefields and sites, from the trenches around Richmond to Appomattox Court House, where Robert E. Lee surrendered in April 1865.

Many founding fathers picked the Piedmont to build their homes, which survive today as

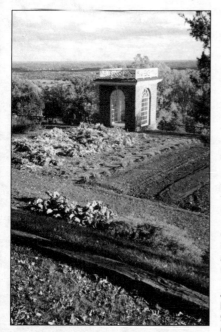

the gardens beneath Monticello

museums, including Thomas Jefferson's Monticello and Poplar Forest, James Madison's Montpelier, and James Monroe's Ash Lawn-Highland. Outdoor enthusiasts can cycle down the Piedmont's asphalt ribbons for weeks, or shoot the James rapids through the heart of Richmond. Rivers such as the Rapidan, Rappahannock, and James snake from one end of the region to the other, providing ample opportunities for boating, swimming, and fishing. To the southwest, Smith Mountain Lake offers all of the above and more.

Access
All roads lead to Richmond—or interstates, in this case. I-64 connect Virginia's capital with the Blue Ridge, Charlottesville, and the coast, while I-95 skewers Richmond on its way from Washington, DC to North Carolina. I-85 is an alternate route south, while I-295 encircles Richmond and reaches down to Petersburg. Beyond the Interstates, federal highways such as US 15, US 60, and US 522 offer more direct (and scenic) drives in between major Piedmont cities. US 29 is the quickest route between Charlottesville and Washington, DC via I-66—just watch those speed traps around Culpeper. Smaller state roads like Rt. 20, Rt. 231, and Rt. 40 are the slowest and prettiest yet, taking their sweet time as they meander across the farmlands and up into the Blue Ridge foothills.

Resources
The **Jefferson's Virginia** promotion, tel. (888) 293-1776, Web site: www.jeff-virginia.org, provides access to nine Jeffersonian historic sites throughout the state, from Natural Bridge to the College of William and Mary. The block tickets ($57 adults, $25 children 6-12) are much cheaper than separate admissions. **Reservations Plus** can arrange hotel rooms and golf packages near Richmond, tel. (800) 444-2777, and Fredericksburg, tel. (800) 373-1776.

Former lawyer and dairy farmer Frank Walker, Jr. started **Tourguide, Ltd.,** 10199 Little Skyline Dr., Orange, VA 22960, tel./fax (540) 672-9414, in 1994. His step-on guide services for Civil War battlefields and local history are $150-200 per day.

RICHMOND AND VICINITY

Since its miraculous rebirth from the ashes of the Civil War, the capital of Virginia has learned to look forward as well as back. Without ignoring its role as one of America's consummate Southern cities—and all the respect for tradition that entails—Richmond has become a busy, affluent, eclectic metropolis that's more than sufficient to anchor its mother state in the past and propel it toward the future.

Visitors, swayed by descriptions a decade or two out of date, might expect a crumbling, dreary place full of unrepentant ghosts and the stale smell of tobacco. Granted, some parts of downtown still aren't all that pleasant. Others, though, have undergone an amazing transformation. Some of the liveliest nightlife in the state has bloomed by the James River, while to the west streets are packed at noon with browsers and the business lunchtime crowd. Other historic neighborhoods go about their business and tend their historic buildings as proud and conservative as ever.

Greater Richmond, which includes the city and Chesterfield, Hanover, and Henrico counties, is home to 850,000 people, of whom 30% are African-American. The number climbs to 80% when focused on the 203,000 inhabitants of the city itself. A high percentage of younger residents are here attending schools such as the University of Richmond, Virginia Commonwealth University and its Medical College of Virginia branch, Virginia Union University, and the Union Theological Seminary.

Richmond has always been one of Virginia's most vital commercial hubs, and even as trade along the James has faded it has found new ventures to take over. More than a dozen Fortune 500 companies have their corporate headquarters here, including Reynolds Metal, which introduced Richmond and the world to aluminum foil in 1947. Richmond's title of "Tobacco Capital of the World" lives on in cigarette billboards, cigar shops, and the sprawling, state-of-the-art headquarters of Philip Morris—the city's largest private employer—south of the James. Nonethe-

THE PIEDMONT

less, *Health* magazine recently rated the Richmond metro area as the healthiest city in the country.

Revitalization is a never-ending process, and Richmond's latest direction is the $1-billion Downtown Master Plan, designed to guide development until 2010. In the blueprints are a biotechnology research park, the restoration of the Jefferson Hotel and Main Street Station, and complete facelifts to the Richmond Convention Centre and the Sixth Street Marketplace. The transformation of 32 acres of Tobacco Row along the river from 5th to 17th Sts., complete with walkways, plazas, and apartment buildings, is con-

sidered one of the most ambitious redevelopment projects in the country.

HISTORY

Christopher Newport and Captain John Smith scouted the stretch of the James by Richmond in 1607, within weeks of the English settlers' landing. The name came from William Byrd II, who decided the falls at this spot on the James reminded him of Richmond-on-Thames in England. Several forts gave protection to the bustling port, which was plotted out in 1737.

© MOON PUBLICATIONS, INC.

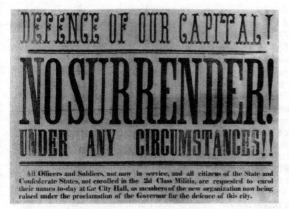

DEFENCE OF OUR CAPITAL!

NO SURRENDER!

UNDER ANY CIRCUMSTANCES!!

All Officers and Soldiers, not now in service, and all citizens of the State and Confederate States, not enrolled in the 2d Class Militia, are requested to enrol their names to-day at the City Hall, as members of the new organization now being raised under the proclamation of the Governor for the defence of this city.

In April 1780 the colonial capital was moved from Williamsburg to Richmond to protect it from the invading British, but to no avail. Famous traitor Benedict Arnold put the town of 700 to the torch in January 1781. Richmond recovered, thanks in large part to a canal system completed in 1840 that connected to the western Piedmont. The canal bypassed the falls and helped the city become a regional hub for transport, milling, banking, and trade. By the turn of the 19th century, Richmond's population had passed 5,000, and local culture blossomed. Planters brought their families into town in the winter to enjoy the stars of Europe and America performing on city stages. Edgar Allen Poe wrote brilliant, scathing book reviews for *The Southern Literary Messenger* from August 1835 through January 1837, and at one party Charles Dickens acquired his nickname of the "artful dodger" as his host boasted how the famous author had dodged Philadelphia and Baltimore in favor of Richmond.

The most industrialized city in the south at the start of the Civil War became the Confederate capital on May 29, 1861. Jefferson Davis presided over this city flush with Southern pride and host to lavish balls where hoop-skirted belles flirted with officers in crisp uniforms. After three years of fighting, however, hope had given way to reality. Richmond's population tripled as wounded and captured soldiers flooded the city. Belle Isle in the James became one of the war's largest prison camps, local factories cranked out thousands of weapons for Confederate troops, and basic necessities such as food and clothing grew scarce as the sound of gunfire approached with enemy armies.

The Union army marched within hearing distance of the city's church bells in 1862 and again in 1864, but it wasn't until April 1865 that Robert E. Lee's Army of Northern Virginia found itself cornered. Davis and the Confederate government fled to Danville as the defensive lines at Petersburg collapsed on April 3. Retreating troops marched out by the light of fires raging in the riverside commercial district, set ablaze to keep its supplies out of Yankee hands.

Once again Richmond rebuilt itself. Still an important shipping center, the city enjoyed an economic boom near the turn of the 20th century. During this time, tobacco factories, flour mills, and iron foundries were constructed. Three major railways fed 1,245 manufacturing plants. Prohibition and the Great Depression came and went, shaking but sparing the city that by the late 1930s was the fastest growing industrial center in the country. The historian Mary Newton Standard wrote how "business buzzes, traffic roars, skyscrapers soar to heaven, and numberless smokestacks proclaim that everything in the world, from matches to locomotives, is made in Richmond."

Dozens of antebellum homes in the downtown area fell to the wrecking ball of progress while wealthy citizens built Tudor estates to the west. A growing black population made the integration of city schools an inevitability and has shifted the political power structure away from its traditional Southern paradigm.

The Army of the Confederate Government having abandoned the City of Richmond, I respectfully request that you will take possession of it with organized force, to preserve order and protect women and children and property.

—Mayor Joseph C. Mayo's message to Ulysses S. Grant at the fall of Richmond, April 2, 1865

ORIENTATION

Downtown Richmond, the heart of the Greater Richmond Metropolitan Area, spreads along the northern side of a bend in the James River. Navigation is simple: the only kink in the simple grid street layout is in Carytown and The Fan, where everything has a 30-degree slant. Aside from this, and the fact that most main avenues are one-way, Richmond is an easy city to navigate. Parking is another matter—tickets appear quicker than flies at a barbecue, and the main nightlife districts in Shockoe are notorious for their lack of spaces (even though they're free on weekends). Broad St. (US 60) is the main east-west thoroughfare, running the entire length of the city. As you'll soon find out, Richmonders love to carve their city up into neighborhoods, though they're not always so eager to delineate them clearly.

Safety: In 1996 the violent crime rate for the metro area was 597 crimes per 100,000 people,

about the same as in Raleigh-Durham, NC, and Boston, MA. The city proper, though, has experienced a 40% jump in crime since 1987, so it's better to drive than walk through the downtown area at night, especially from one neighborhood to the next (say, Jackson Ward to Shockoe Slip). Wandering within popular, well-lit districts like Carytown and The Fan is considered safe. Some hotels offer shuttle service, and trolleys run until 11 p.m. Beyond that, drive or call a cab.

NEIGHBORHOODS

Central Richmond

Richmond's historic heart beats in the neighborhood of **Court End,** between Leigh St. and the state capitol (see below). Centuries-old mansions and churches sit next to the dome of the Richmond Coliseum, modern office buildings, and the halls of the Medical College of Virginia (MCV), a branch of Virginia Commonwealth University.

White House and Museum of the Confederacy: The largest collection of Confederate relics in the world starts with pieces of the C.S.S. *Virginia* out front and continues inside. For its location in the heart of the rebel capital, the presentation is surprisingly objective, with only a slight Southern slant peeking through from time to time. The moving collection ranges from the prosaic—over 500 flags, dozens of swords, pistols, and rifles, and soldiers' letters home—to the particular, in its prized assortment of personal effects from Confederate luminaries.

J.E.B. Stuart's plumed hat, Stonewall Jackson's revolver, and a re-creation of Robert E. Lee's field tent with his table inside are highlights, along with the sword and coat Lee wore to Appomattox and the pen with which he signed the surrender documents. Upstairs you'll find changing exhibits addressing the experiences of blacks, women, and other civilians during the war, while downstairs hangs "The Last Meeting of Lee and Jackson," a monumental 1869 oil painting depicting the commanders' final parley at Chancellorsville.

Next door stands the building leased by the Confederate government as a home for Jefferson Davis, his family, and a dozen or so slaves Aug. 1861-April 1865. Built in 1818, it became the Federal headquarters during Reconstruction.

RICHMOND AREA CLIMATE

SNOWFALL   MAXIMUM TEMP.
RAINFALL   MINIMUM TEMP.

Lavish period decorations include many original Davis pieces, such as his favorite horsehair rocking chair (sat in by Lincoln less than 48 hours after the evacuation of Richmond) and a marble bust of the president of the Confederacy buried by a neighbor to keep it safe from Union troops. Notice the "gasaliers," hanging glass globes lit by coal gas, and the toy cannon in the nursery (the Davis kids were apparently hellions).

Both buildings are on the Medical College of Virginia campus at 1201 E. Clay St., tel. (804) 649-1861. Open Mon.-Sat. 10 a.m.-5 p.m., Sunday noon-5 p.m.; $8 adults, $5 children 5-18 (separate admissions are available).

Capitol Square: A statue of George Washington on horseback surveys this grassy oasis dominated by the classical lines of the **Virginia State Capitol,** tel. (804) 786-4344. The original central section, begun in 1785, was designed by—who else— Thomas Jefferson, based on the Maison Carrée, a first-century Roman temple in Nîmes, France. Even though it wasn't yet completed, the Virginia Assembly held its first meeting here in 1788. The Jean Antoine Houdon statue of George Washington that stands under the cupola was unveiled the same year. It's considered one of the most valuable marble sculptures in the country, since it was the only one Washington posed for in person. House and Senate chambers were added to the structure in 1904-06. Open Mon.-Sat. 9 a.m.-5 p.m., Sunday 1-5 p.m., with free tours every half tour.

To one side is the **Governor's Mansion,** tel. (804) 371-8687, the oldest continually inhabited governor's residence in America. Call for a current schedule of free 15-minute tours. **Old City Hall** fills Leigh St. with a block of Victorian Gothic pomp in gray stone. Built in 1886-95, the structure was restored in the mid-1980s. The first floor is open to visitors—don't miss the ornate splendor of the painted pillars and two-story atrium. Across Leigh St. stands **New City Hall** with

Visitors can tour the Governor's Mansion in Richmond.

a 19th-floor observation deck (open daily until dusk), and a **visitor information center** fills the bottom of the Old Bell Tower (1824) at the southwest corner of the square.

Valentine Museum: A collection of photos, old clothing, and antique tobacco tools captures the "Life and History of Richmond" from the 17th to 20th centuries. The museum abuts the Wickham House, built in 1812 by John Wickham, Richmond's wealthiest citizen and the lawyer who defended Aaron Burr against charges of treason in 1807. It's hard to decide which is more beautiful—the rare set of neoclassical decorative wall paintings, or the Oval Parlor, designated one of the "100 most beautiful rooms in America." Behind the museum is a small garden, cafe, and the studio of Richmond sculptor Edward Valentine, moved here in 1937 from its original spot at Leigh and 8th Streets. The museum, 1015 E. Clay St., tel. (804) 649-0711, fax 643-3510, Web site: www.valentinemuseum.com, is open Mon.-Sat. 10 a.m.-5 p.m., Sunday noon-5 p.m.; $5 for adults, $3 children 7-12.

John Marshall House: The home of the third U.S. Supreme Court chief justice (1801-35) reflects the astonishing career of one of the most brilliant men to ever hold the post. Revolutionary War veteran, lawyer, ambassador to France, secretary of state—Marshall did it all. He even had the temerity to oppose his cousin, Thomas Jefferson, in the political arena. The house was built in 1788-90 in the federal style, and contains many original architectural features and relics from Marshall's life and times. The house, 818 E. Marshall at 9th St., tel. (804) 648-7998, is open Tues.-Sat. 10 a.m.-5 p.m. (Oct.-Dec. until 4:30 p.m.); $3 for adults, $1.25 children 7-12.

Richmond Children's Museum: The M-word can strike fear into the heart of the bravest 10-year-old, but this playhouse will leave youngsters age 2-12 begging for more. After dressing up for the kid-sized doctor's office, TV studio, and grocery store, children can learn about com-

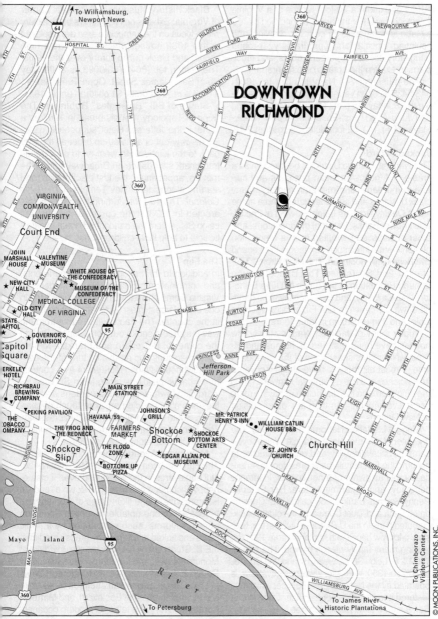

DOWNTOWN RICHMOND

puters or explore a 40-foot replica of a Virginia limestone cave. For the artistically inclined there's a stage and materials for painting, drawing, and sculpting. Special family programs year-round bring storytellers, puppeteers, chefs, and musicians to explain their crafts or just entertain.

The museum, 740 Navy Hill Dr., tel. (804) 643-5436, is open year-round Saturday 10 a.m.-5 p.m., Sunday 1-5 p.m., Monday 9 a.m.-5 p.m., and June-Aug. Tues.-Fri. 9 a.m.-5 p.m. (Sept.-May until 1 p.m.); $2 for adults, $3 children 2-12.

Jackson Ward

This National Historic District is best known as a cradle of African-American business and culture in the early- and mid-20th century. Many black business and social leaders found a home along Quality Row, as Leigh St. west of 2nd St. was known. Banks, fraternal organizations, and other businesses benefited from a foundation of prominent figures such as Maggie Walker and Bill "Bojangles" Robinson. The Hippodrome Theater on 2nd St. (called The Deuce) swung through Prohibition to the tunes of Duke Ellington, Cab Calloway, and Billie Holiday, who handed down the crown to Ella Fitzgerald, Nat King Cole, and James Brown in later years.

Today many of Jackson Ward's stately row houses have been restored as homes and offices, while others show signs of the ravages of time. Almost all, though, have shallow covered front porches and fine ornamental ironwork, giving the neighborhood the distinction of having more decorative wrought iron than any other outside of New Orleans.

Maggie L. Walker National Historic Site: The daughter of a former slave, Maggie Walker overcame physical disability and racial prejudice to become the first female bank president in America, as well as owner of a newspaper, insurance company, and department store. Her St. Luke Penny Savings Bank is now called The Consolidated Bank and Trust Company, the oldest black-operated bank in the U.S. Walker lived at this two-story brick row house with her family from 1904-34, leaving many family pieces behind. The house, 110 1/2 E. Leigh St., between 1st and 2nd Sts., tel. (804) 780-1380, Web site: www.nps.gov/malw, is operated by the National Park Service, which has restored it to its 1930s appearance. Open Wed.-Sat. 9 a.m.-5 p.m.; admission free.

Black History Museum and Cultural Center of Virginia: Exhibits on Richmond's black history with a focus on the immediate area are displayed in this 1832 house, which served as a high school and black public library over the years. The center, tel. (804) 780-9093, is at 00 Clay St. at Saint James Street. Open Tues.-Sat. 11 a.m.-4 p.m.; $2 adults, $1 children under 18.

Statue of Bill "Bojangles" Robinson: The "King of Tapology" got his break in 1907 as a waiter in the Jefferson Hotel, supposedly dancing his way out of a mixed-up order all the way back to the kitchen. He went on to perform his trademark stair dance on Broadway and in the movies, appearing in the first black "talkie" and starring alongside Shirley Temple in *The Little Colonel.* The 10-foot aluminum sculpture was erected in 1973 at the corner of Adams and Leigh Sts., where the dancer had donated a traffic light to help local children cross in safety.

The Fan

In addition to thrift shops, worn-in apartments, and combination deli-laundromats, students of Virginia Commonwealth University enjoy living in one of the largest intact Victorian neighborhoods in the country. The Fan takes it name from the way the streets spoke out from Monroe Park at the corner of Belvedere and Franklin. Million-dollar mansions and renovated turn-of-the-century townhouses along Monument Ave. contrast funky pastel buildings along Main St. west toward Carytown, with rooftop gardens and cobblestone alleys adding an extra touch of character. South of the I-95 downtown expressway, The Fan turns purely residential, with brightly painted houses along tree-lined streets.

Monument Avenue: The northern border of The Fan has been called one of the most beautiful boulevards in the world, and even if statue-happy Richmond has worn you down already, it is impressive. Huge likenesses of Confederate heroes—with one notable exception—pose on raised platforms, each surrounded by a traffic circle and linked to the next by grassy medians. **J.E.B. Stuart** sports his trademark plumed hat at Monument Ave. and Lombardy St., followed by **Robert E. Lee** at Allen Ave. and **Jefferson Davis** at Davis Street. **Stonewall Jackson** faces boldly north (on purpose) at Boulevard, and **Matthew Fontaine Maury,** the father of modern oceanography, stands at Belmont Avenue. (Ironically, Maury's work helped the Union blockade seal up the Southern coast during the Civil War.)

Monument Avenue's latest addition almost didn't make it. Born in Richmond in 1943, **Arthur Ashe, Jr.** began playing tennis at age seven and went on to win the U.S. Open and Wimbledon, becoming the first black man to receive a number-1 international ranking. After retiring, Ashe used his fame to promote black athletics and education, even writing a book about the history of black athletes. Controversy surrounded the decision to erect Ashe's likeness in such traditional company, but it was unveiled in 1996 nonetheless. Fittingly, the statue renders him offering a tennis racket and book to children reaching up at his feet.

South of the Fan

Byrd Park: Three lakes, picnic shelters, sports fields, trails, and tennis courts fill one of Richmond's most popular parks, along Boulevard south of I-195. During the summer you can rent paddle boats on Boat Lake and feed the ducks on the other two. **The Carillon,** a 240-foot tower with 56 bells, recently underwent $1.4 million worth of renovations and is a centerpiece of the city's Fourth of July fireworks. Outdoor concerts, children's performances, and the Festival of the Arts in July and August are held in the **Dogwood Dell** outdoor amphitheater.

Maymont: The former dairy farm of Maj. James Dooley, Confederate veteran and millionaire, and his wife Sallie May has become the city's most family-friendly sanctuary. A Romanesque Revival mansion, completed in 1893, is full of European and Asian curios acquired over years of traveling, including oriental rugs, stained glass, frescoes, and porcelain. Maymont's grounds, though, are its real treasure: 100 acres of rolling open parkland, a riot of buds, birds, and blossoms in the spring and inviting at any time of year. Three decades of work went into the herb, formal Italian, and Japanese gardens that slope down toward the James River. Children love the aviary, farm barn, and Mary Parsons Nature Center, with outdoor habitats for animals like bears, bobcats, bison, and foxes.

Maymont is run by the nonprofit Maymont Foundation, tel. (804) 358-7166. Everything is free except **tram rides** ($2 adults, $1 children) and **carriage rides** ($3 adults, $2 children) offered April-November. Annual events start with a Flower and Garden Show in February and continue to a Family Easter and Christmas open house. Call about periodic Barn Days, garden tours, and history and nature programs. The nature center and mansion are both open Tues.-Sun. noon-5 p.m. (June-Aug., Tues.-Sat. 10 a.m.-5 p.m., Sunday noon-5 p.m.). You can enter from Hampton and Pennsylvania Sts. on the east side or Spotswood St. on the northwest corner.

Hollywood Cemetery: It's hard to imagine a more tranquil resting place than this bluff over the James River. Acres of headstones, winged monuments, and mausoleums alternate between eerie and almost inviting, depending on the whims of weather and the time of day. Jefferson Davis, James Monroe, and John Tyler are the three most famous residents, along with J.E.B. Stuart and 21 other Confederate generals, six Virginia governors, and the first battle casualty of the Civil War. A 90-foot pyramid of rough stone marks the graves of 18,000 Confederate soldiers. The cemetery, tel. (804) 648-8501, is open daily 8 a.m.-5 p.m., but you can walk around until 7 p.m. Enter off of Albemarle St.

James River Park: A substantial chunk of riverbank and several islands have been set aside as a nature and recreational reserve in the middle of Richmond. Four hundred fifty acres of urban wilderness stretch from the Robert E. Lee (US 1/301) bridge upriver to the **Pony Pasture** and **Huguenot Woods** section beyond the Powhite Parkway (Rt. 76) bridge. An elevated footbridge leads to **Belle Isle,** with a great view of the Richmond skyline, 19th-century industrial ruins, and the remains of a notorious Civil War POW camp that held as many as 8,000 prisoners at one time. Migrating thrushes and warblers flock to Pony Pasture in the spring, accompanied by the blooms of Virginia bellflowers, morning glories, and Dutchman's breeches.

A **visitors center,** tel. (804) 780-5311, sits along Riverside Dr. on the south bank, a mile east of Huguenot Bridge. Pick up information on fishing and multi-use trails like the Geology Interpretive Trail near Belle Isle, crossing a favorite 19th-century dueling ground. Naturally, it's the floating that draws the most visitors: the calm stretch of river from Huguenot Woods to the visitors center is fine for tubing, but beyond that you'll need a raft or kayak and experienced guide (see **Recreation** below).

Carytown
Cary St., west of Boulevard, strings together an eclectic mix of antique stores, unusual restaurants, and students on skateboards clattering down brick sidewalks.

Virginia Museum of Fine Arts: Richmond's most outstanding collection is on par with any along the eastern seaboard. Everything from Egyptian sculptures to Andy Warhol's "Triple Elvis" makes an appearance in the multifarious museum, which boasts original works by Monet, Renoir, Picasso, and Degas along with strong showings from the ancient Mediterranean, medieval Europe, and American art nouveau and art deco.

The museum, 2800 Grove Ave. at Boulevard, tel. (804) 367-0844, Web site: www.vmfa.state.va.us, is open Tues.-Sun. 11 a.m.-5 p.m. (Thursday until 8 p.m.) for a $4 suggested donation. Free guided tours of highlights are offered. Locals rate the museum shop as outstanding, and the **Arts Cafe** is convenient for a bite on the outside patio among the sculpture garden.

Riverfront
The former riverside site of Richmond's Tredegar Iron Works, origin of most Confederate cannon balls and artillery pieces during the Civil War, is now home to a **WW II and Korean War Memorial. Brown's Island,** at the bottom of 7th St., is one end of Richmond's **Canal Walk** along the old James River-Kanawha Canal. Historic markers tell the history of the riverfront from here to the other end at 12th and Main Streets. Plans are underway to develop the canal from 5th to 17th Sts. with hotels, shops, pedestrian walkways, and jet-propelled tour boats zooming across the water.

Shockoe Slip
The Confederate capital's warehouse and commercial district, reduced to charred rubble in 1865, has been resurrected within the last few decades into a lively local hot-spot. Fashionable shops and art galleries are open by day, and at night old-fashioned street lamps light the cobblestone avenues in front of renovated warehouses now holding restaurants and nightclubs. A portion of Thomas Jefferson's Virginia Statute for Religious Freedom has been emblazoned on the wall of a parking lot at the corner of Cary and 14th Streets.

Shockoe Bottom
Farther east under the I-95 overpass, Shockoe Bottom was once Richmond's oldest commercial district, replete with produce markets and warehouses. Tall sailing ships hailed from Africa with bodies for the district's slave auction houses, while canal barges and rail lines brought in raw materials for towering brick tobacco factories. Until recently, Shockoe Bottom was plagued by periodic flooding—a 1972 surge courtesy of Hurricane Agnes caused $350 million in damage—but a multi-million dollar flood wall now protects dozens of restaurants, pubs, and shops.

Tobacco Row, between 20th and Pear Sts., is the target of Richmond's latest urban redevelopment project, aimed at transforming crumbling warehouses into apartment buildings. There are also plans to restore the unmistakable **Main Street Station,** whose ornate clock tower once welcomed countless rail travelers to the city, to its former glory. The **17th Street Farmer's Market** has been active since 1779, making it perhaps the oldest in the country.

Shockoe Bottom Arts Center: In 1994 artist Deanna Brizendine and her son Rusty Davis acquired the bottom floor of an abandoned American Tobacco Company factory. With Old Town Alexandria's Torpedo Factory in mind, they opened dozens of studio spaces to artists of all stripes. The Arts Center is slowly expanding to all four floors, and holds monthly juried exhibitions and an evening reception the second Friday of each month. The first Saturday of each month is said to be the best time to catch artists in their studios. The center, 2001 E. Grace St. at 21st, tel. (804) 643-7959, is open Tues.-Sat. 10 a.m.-5 p.m., Sunday 1-5 p.m.

Edgar Allan Poe Museum: The genius of ghoul was raised and married in Richmond, spending more time here than in any other city. Poe gained his first national attention here on the staff of the local *Southern Literary Messenger.* The Old Stone House—actually the oldest residence in Richmond, built in the 1730s—houses his personal effects and daguerreotypes of his famous haunted visage. Sip a lemonade in the Enchanted Garden before embarking on a

FIGHTING FOR RICHMOND

The Confederate capital saw two major Civil War campaigns reach her doorstep. The first, in 1862, crushed the possibility of a short war, and the second two years later set the stage for the war's end.

The Seven Days' Battles

Gen. George B. McClellan's Peninsular Campaign advanced to within sight of Richmond in June 1862. Robert E. Lee, recently named commander of the Confederate army, recalled Stonewall Jackson and his troops from the Shenandoah Valley and struck first on June 26 with 90,000 men. McClellan's army was flushed out of Mechanicsburg, but struck back at Beaver Dam Creek with a vengeance that left earthworks "waist deep in blood," in the words of one officer.

The next day 55,000 Rebels attacked at Gaines' Mill, securing a last-ditch victory after being driven back repeatedly from the blue line along Boatswain's Creek. The heaviest fighting of the Seven Days' Battles resulted in 15,000 casualties, twice as many Confederate as Federal. McClellan began a fighting retreat, clashing with Lee at Savage's Station on June 29 and White Oak Swamp and Glendale (Frayser's Farm) on June 30. On July 1 the Union army managed to reach the gunboats waiting on the James River at Harrison's Landing. Under orders to protect the withdrawal, Maj. Gen. Fitz-John Porter lined his troops up in battle formation along Malvern Hill and mowed down enemy ranks as they crossed open ground. Gunboat artillery helped slaughter 6,000 advancing troops, causing Confederate Gen. E.M. Law to remark later, "It was not war—it was murder."

The Seven Days' Battles convinced McClellan to abandon his advance on Richmond for the time being, refusing Lincoln's offer of another 50,000 men by saying it would not be enough. A week of fierce combat had cost 35,000 lives and untold suffering. One Georgian soldier wrote home, "I have seen, heard, and felt many things in the last week that I never want to see, hear, nor feel again."

The Beginning of the End

By 1864 Richmond was heavily protected behind two rings of defensive earthworks and a series of forts erected on the outskirts of the city. Ulysses S. Grant had taken command of Union forces and put Richmond in the crosshairs once again. After much strategic maneuvering by both sides, Confederate troops dug in at Cold Harbor just in time for Grant's assault on June 3.

A massive frontal attack in sweltering heat threw 60,000 men against the impregnable Confederate lines in what quickly became the bloodiest charge of the war. Over 7,000 Federal soldiers were cut down with appalling speed by Rebel rifles and artillery. Some witnesses said the outcome was decided in fifteen minutes; others said eight. Knowing they were doomed, Union soldiers pinned their names to their uniforms to notify their next of kin of their death—the early origin of dog tags. A diary found on one soldier's body ended with: "June 3. Cold Harbor. I was killed."

Ten more days of fighting in 100° F weather proved the futility of infantry assaults against strongly held trenches, changing the course of the Civil War and all wars thereafter. Grant eventually withdrew and crossed the James toward Petersburg, where a 10-month siege would lead to the fall of Richmond and the end of the Civil War.

General Robert E. Lee

General George B. McClellan

guided tour of the house, where you'll see his walking stick, childhood bed, and a model of Richmond in Poe's day.

The museum, 1914 E. Main St., tel. (804) 648-5523 or (888) 21E-APOE (888-213-2763)' Web site: www.poemuseum.org, is open Tues.-Sat. 10 a.m.-5 p.m., Sunday and Monday noon-5 p.m.; $6 adult, $5 children.

Church Hill

A mosaic of 19th-century architectural styles adorns the city's oldest residential neighborhood, named for St. John's Church. Lovingly restored homes in Victorian, Greek revival, and federal style gaze out over the city and river.

St. John's Church: Built in 1740-41, Richmond's oldest house of worship is also one of the oldest wooden buildings in Virginia. It's best known as the site of Patrick Henry's "Give me liberty or give me death" speech to George Washington, Thomas Jefferson, and the rest of the Second Virginia Convention on March 23, 1775. The parish dates to 1611, and services are still held here. Edgar Allen Poe's mother, is buried in the surrounding cemetery, which was the only public burial ground in Richmond until 1826.

Half-hour tours of the church, 2401 E. Broad St., tel. (804) 648-5015, are given Mon.-Sat. 10 a.m.-3:30, Sunday 1-3:30 p.m.; $3 for adults, $1 children 7-18. Henry's speech is reenacted in full the Sunday closest to March 23, with a smaller-scale reading every Sunday at 2 p.m. from the end of May to the beginning of September.

Richmond National Battlefield Park Visitors Center: Stop by here, the site of one of the Confederate's largest wartime hospitals, before beginning the tour of Richmond's battlefields. At its peak, Chimborazo Hospital was the largest of its kind in the world, eventually treating 76,000 patients in 150 buildings and 100 tents.

Chimborazo Visitor Center, tel. (804) 226-1981, Web site: www.nps.gov/rich, is open daily 9 a.m.-5 p.m.; admission is free. Park rangers can answer any questions left after your tour of the museum and a short film, and they rent out tapes for a self-guided **auto tour,** which runs to the east and south of the city. A 130-mile loop takes you past 10 sites from the 1862 campaign (Chickahominy Bluff, Beaver Dam Creek, Gaines Mill/Watt House, Glendale/Frayser's Farm, Malvern Hill, and Drewry's Bluff) and the fighting

in 1864 (Garthright House, Parker's Battery, Cold Harbor, and Fort Harrison). There's an unstaffed visitors center at Cold Harbor on Rt. 156, open daily 9 a.m.-5 p.m., and another one at Fort Harrison, open June-Aug. 9 a.m.-5 p.m.

OTHER SIGHTS

Virginia Holocaust Museum

Opened in 1997 by a group of volunteers, some of whom survived concentration camps themselves, this small museum offers a poignant look into the horrors of Europe during WW II. Self-guiding tours with CD players and headphones lead you through a re-created box car and family room frozen in mid-capture. Archives and a library are available to researchers.

The museum, 213 Roseneath Rd., tel. (804) 257-5400, is behind Temple Beth-El at Roseneath and Grove Streets. It's open Mon.-Fri. 9 a.m.-5 p.m., Saturday 2-5 p.m., Sunday 1-5 p.m. for free, but donations are appreciated. E-mail: info@va-holocaust.com, Web site: www.va-holocaust.com.

Science Museum of Virginia

It's hard to miss the monumental Union Station (topped by a green copper dome), which houses an excellent body of hands-on displays on neat-o subjects like aviation, computers, crystals, astronomy, and static electricity. A 100-foot Foucault pendulum in the rotunda lobby is so big it's swing is nudged the rotation of the earth, and even the infrared toilet flushers have explanatory cards. IMAX films and planetarium shows are shown in the 270-degree Ethyl Universe Theater.

The museum, 2500 W. Broad St., tel. (800) 659-1727 or (804) 367-6552, Web site: www.smv.mus.va.us, is open Mon.-Sat. 9:30 a.m.-5 p.m., Sun 11:30 a.m.-5 p.m., for $8 adults, $7 children 4-12 including a theater show. Admission to the museum only ($5 adults, $4 children) and theater only ($4 all) is also available.

Virginia Aviation Museum

Fans of the early days of air travel will love this hangar full of restored vintage planes at the Richmond International Airport. The impressive collection includes the 1927 Fairchild FC-2W2 used by Admiral William Byrd (a Virginian) to make the first flight over Antarctica, and a luxury monoplane that carried Clark Gable, Carole Lombard, and William Randolph Hearst. Open daily 9:30 a.m.-5 p.m.; $5 adults, $3 children 4-12.

Lewis Ginter
Botanical Gardens at Bloemendaal

Patrick Henry once owned these grounds north of Richmond where Lewis Ginter, founder of the American Tobacco Company, opened the Lakeside Wheel Club in the 1880s for Richmond's cycling gentry. Ginter's niece began converting the property into gardens, which she named Bloemendaal after Ginter's home in the Netherlands and left to the city at her death. The largest perennial gardens on the East Coast include plants native to Africa, Asia, and the Americas, including the Standard Reference Collection of the American Ivy Society. Streams gurgle past wildflower meadows, a formal Victorian garden, and a typical English "cottage" garden.

The gardens, 1800 Lakeside Ave., tel. (804) 262-9887, are at the intersection of Hillard Rd. (Rt. 356) and Lakeside Ave. (Rt. 161), 1.5 miles north of I-95 exit 80. They're open daily 9:30 a.m.-4:30 p.m. for $4 adults, $2 children 2-12. The Bloemendaal House has a horticultural gift shop, and the Lora and Claiborne Robins Tea House serves light meals.

ACCOMMODATIONS

A construction boom in the 1980s resulted in a new hotel opening up just about every other month in Richmond, leaving the city with 11,000 rooms in 150 hotels and motels. The most distinctive—and expensive—lodgings congregate downtown, led by the truly unique Jefferson Hotel. More generic options scatter into the Greater Richmond area, with a concentration near the Richmond International Airport.

Bensonhouse of Richmond, e-mail: b.our. guest@bensonhouse.com, Web site: www.bensonhouse.com, operating out of the Emmanuel Hunzler House, (see below) can arrange stays in private homes throughout Richmond.

Downtown

Lowest rates near the James go to the passable **Massad House Hotel,** 11 N. 4th St., tel. (804) 648-2893, fax 780-0647. Inexpensive. The 363 rooms at the **Omni Hotel,** 100 S. 12th St., tel. (804) 344-7000, fax 648-6704, start in the moderate range. The 16-story hotel overlooks the canal and river, and has a restaurant and deli. A row of 1840 Greek Revival townhouses has been converted into the lovely **Linden Row Inn,** 100 E. Franklin St., tel. (804) 783-7000 or (800) 348-7424, fax (804) 648-7504. Period Victorian furnishings decorate 71 rooms and parlor suites, and guests have access to the first-class sport facilities of a YMCA a few blocks away. Expensive, suites premium.

Because it's in The Fan historic district, the **Emmanuel Hunzler House,** 2036 Monument Ave., tel. (804) 355-4885 or 353-6900, can't hang a sign out front, but the fully restored 1914 Italian Renaissance townhouse is well worth searching out. Dark mahogany paneling starts in the entry and leads into the living room, with a large marble fireplace. An elevator and shallow stairs—legacies of a former disabled owner—lead upstairs to four guest rooms, one of which has a jacuzzi and its own fireplace. Rates include a full breakfast and a big gray cat (to pet, not to keep). Expensive-premium.

Mr Patrick Henry's Inn, 2300-02 E. Broad St., tel. (800) 932-2654 or (804) 644-1322, is only a block from St. John's Church on Church Hill. All rooms have fireplaces, and a few have balconies overlooking the formal garden and patio. A celebrated Colonial restaurant is open for lunch and dinner Mon.-Sat. Expensive to premium. Right next door is the **William Catlin House Bed & Breakfast Inn,** 2304 E. Broad St., tel. (804) 780-3746, built for its namesake in 1945 by one of the country's finest masons. Robert and Josephine Marin have since outfitted it with oriental rugs, crystal chandeliers, and canopied four-poster beds with goosedown pillows. A full breakfast is included with rooms (expensive) and suites (premium-luxury).

The best high-rise hotels in central Richmond are the **Crowne Plaza Richmond,** 555 E. Canal St., tel. (804) 788-0900, fax 788-7087, and the **Richmond Marriott,** 500 E. Broad St. at 5th, tel. (804) 643-3400, fax 788-1230 (both premium). On the other end of the scale, in size if not in luxury, is the **Berkeley Hotel,** 1200 E. Cary St., tel. (804) 780-1300, fax 343-1885. This small, European-style place in the heart of Shockoe Slip earned four AAA stars thanks to its excellent service and terraces over the street. Its Berkeley Restaurant, open daily, is whispered to be as good, and perhaps a better value, than The Jefferson's hallowed Lemaire. Premium.

Jefferson Hotel

Maj. Lewis Ginter, of botanical-garden fame, spared no expense when he created the country's finest hotel in Richmond's most fashionable neighborhood near the turn of the century. Millions from Ginter's cigarette fortune went into its design and construction, and in 1895 the Jefferson opened in time for the wedding-of-the-year—the union of Charles Dana Gibson and Irene Langhorne, the original "Gibson Girl." An eye-popping smorgasbord of styles from rococo to Edwardian has wowed a who's-who of famous guests over the years, including Charlie Chaplin, Sarah Bernhardt, and nine presidents. After a steady decline through the 20th century, this National Historic Landmark received a multi-million-dollar facelift in the late '80s and early '90s that brought back much of its original splendor.

A tourist destination almost as much as it is a hotel, the Jefferson starts with the opulent Rotunda Lobby, with a 70-foot ceiling and huge faux-marble pillars dripping with carved nuts and fruits. A central staircase (often credited, incorrectly, with inspiring the set designers of *Gone With the Wind)* flows upward to the Palm Court, where sunlight pours through a Tiffany stained-glass dome onto a life-sized statue of Thomas Jefferson by Edward Valentine. The court once featured a grass lawn around a pool filled with live alligators; today classical music wafts over guests enjoying a traditional afternoon tea.

Along with a salon, gift shop, and health club, the Jefferson, at Franklin and Adams Sts., tel. (800) 424-8014 or (804) 788-8000, fax 225-0334, offers the formal **Lemaire Restaurant,** whose seven dining rooms have earned it awards for best brunch and best overall restaurant in Richmond. Open for all meals Mon.-Fri., Saturday for breakfast and dinner, and Sunday brunch. **T.J.'s Grill and Bar** serves more causal and less expensive fare like black-eyed pea hummus and grilled focaccia pizzas. Luxury.

Outside of Downtown

In the inexpensive category you can choose from the **Best Western Airport Inn,** 5700 Williamsburg Rd., tel. (804) 222-2780, fax 226-4056, and the **Econo Lodge Airport,** 5408 Williamsburg Rd., tel./fax (804) 222-1020, both by—you guessed it—the airport. There's a **Days Inn,** 1600 Robin Hood Rd., tel. (804) 353-1287, fax 355-2659, a short distance northwest of downtown, and a **Travel Inn,** 6511 Midlothian Tpk., tel. (804) 745-7500, on the south side of the river on US 60.

The **Airport Inn Motel,** 5121 S. Laburnum, tel. (804) 222-4200, fax 222-2828, and the **Comfort Inn Richmond Airport,** 5240 Airport Square Ln., tel. (804) 226-1800, fax 226-0958, both offer comfortable moderate-level lodgings near the . . . well, you know. Follow Broad St. west about eight miles to reach the **Fairfield Inn by Marriott,** 7300 W. Broad St., tel. (804) 672-8621, fax 755-7155. Moderate.

The **Holiday Inn Central,** 3207 North Blvd., tel. (804) 359-9441, fax 359-3207, is next to the city visitors center near I-95 exit 78. Expensive. For premium hotel lodgings try the **Sheraton Inn Richmond Airport,** 4700 S. Laburnum Ave., tel. (804) 226-4300, fax 226-6516, or the **Hyatt Richmond,** 6624 W. Broad St., tel. (804) 285-1234, fax 288-3961, at I-95 exit 143.

Camping

The closest campgrounds to Richmond are still some distance out of the city center. In Ashland, off I-95 exit 89, located 10 miles north of downtown, you'll find the **Americamps Richmond-North/Best Holiday Trav-L-Park,** 11322 Air Park Rd., tel. (804) 798-5298, has hook-up sites for $18-23. **Pocahontas State Park,** tel. (804) 796-4255, about eight miles south of Richmond, has sites for $11, and the Paramount's Kings Dominion theme park welcomes campers for $18-25.

FOOD

For a conservative city, Richmond has an astonishing variety of restaurants. From cheap retro diners to upmarket haute cuisine, every style and ethnicity you can imagine is represented among hundreds of eateries. You might even detect a postmodern jab at the city's slowly eroding traditionalism in places like The Frog and The Redneck.

Central Richmond

East meets South at **P.G.T. Beauregard's Thai Room,** 103 E Cary St. at 1st St., tel. (804) 644-2328, Richmond's first and still by far best Thai restaurant. Waitresses in traditional costume take your orders for satay (skewered) beef, spring rolls, and specials like salmon steamed in a bamboo basket. Cool down after a spicy plate of green curry beef with a dish of homemade ice cream. The open brick cafe in back is perfect for warm summer evenings. Open for lunch Mon.-Fri., dinner Mon.-Saturday.

Bright pastels and reggae set the stage for **Winnie's Caribbean Cuisine,** 200 E Main St. at 2nd St., tel. (804) 649-4974, where you can wash down a jerk pork and roti (thin homemade stuffed bread) with a Red Stripe, ginger beer, or Ting (grapefruit) soda. Curries and vegetarian dishes are moderately priced for lunch and dinner Mon.-Sat. **Cafine's,** 401 E. Grace St., tel. (804) 775-2233, is a stylish coffeehouse/cafe by day and dance house by night (see "Entertainment," below). Overstuffed sandwiches, pizzas, and various soup-salad combinations are around $6 for lunch Tues.-Fri. and slightly more for dinner Friday and Saturday.

Hand-crafted desserts are the forte of **Homemades by Suzanne,** 10 S. 6th St., tel. (804) 755-2116, where the cheesecakes, carrot cakes, and pies of every description are to die for. They also make up salads and boxed lunches popular with the business crowd, delivered or to go. Open Mon.-Fri. 9 a.m.-3 p.m. The '50s-style **Third Street Diner,** 218 E. Main St., tel. (804) 788-6072, is a good place for a late-night bite, open 24 hours, seven days a week. Dozens of small eateries in the north section of the **Sixth Street Marketplace** on Broad St. cater to tourists and downtown lunch-breakers.

The Fan

One side of "Cajun Corner" at W. Main and Addison Sts. is claimed by the lavender **Gumbo Ya Ya,** 2232 W. Main St., tel. (804) 358-9292, a Creole cafe with a sizable bar. Start out with a plate of jalapeño poppers before moving on to a shrimp Creole étouffée or catfish po'boy. Open daily for dinner. Opposite sits **Southern Culture,** 2229 W. Main St., tel. (804) 355-6939, with an interesting, well-seasoned amalgam of Louisiana, Caribbean, southwestern, and Mexi-

can flavors. If the entrées like pasta jambalaya and seafood okra gumbo ($7-17) look too big, then one of the huge salads—or even desserts—might well be enough.

At **World Cup,** 204 N. Robinson St., tel. (804) 359-5282, you can enjoy coffees and teas from around the world on map-topped tables. They also offer sodas and light fare like bagels and sandwiches, along with live music on Monday evenings in the summer. Open daily from 7 or 8 a.m.-11 p.m. The **Strawberry Street Cafe,** 421 N. Strawberry St., tel. (804) 353-6860, is always packed for lunch with fans of its healthy, filling food and bathtub salad bar. Homemade soups, amazing gourmet sandwiches (try the hot, open-faced crab), and entrées like spinach lasagna and Mediterranean wraps are served daily for lunch and dinner.

They say Americans are bad at geography, but the **Texas-Wisconsin Border Cafe,** 1501 W. Main St., tel. (804) 355-2907, is stretching it a bit far. Anyway, this intriguing, low-key place offers bratwurst and kielbasas from the Great Lakes region alongside enchiladas and "widow-maker" chili from down near Mexico. Elk heads and bull horns face each other over the junk-laden bar. Open daily for all meals. **Mamma'Zu,** 501 S. Pine St., tel. (804) 788-4205, inhabits an unpretentious old diner, but it's a hidden gem with some of the best Italian food in Richmond. Made-to-order pizzas and calamari Napoletana run $7-9 for lunch (Mon.-Fri.), and dinner entrées from the chalkboard list are $10-15 (Mon.-Sat.).

North of the Fan

Named for a 19th-century Virginia governor who always gave a little more, **Extra Billy's,** 5205 W Broad St., tel. (804) 282-3949, offers button-popping servings of baby-back ribs, pork barbecue, and beef brisket. Grab an onion-string appetizer and bucket of beer, and dig in. Open Mon.-Sat. for lunch, dinner daily.

Carytown

Look for the big sun over the outdoor patio to find **Nacho Mama's,** 3449 W. Cary St., tel. (804) 358-6262, serving Richmond's best burrito along with combo dinners and a mouthwatering Mexican crab cake platter. Lunch specials run $6, along with a few vegetarian options and the requisite range of margaritas. The cozy bistro **Ris-**

torante Amici, 3343 W. Cary St., tel. (804) 353-4700, serves fresh Northern Italian cuisine and great *tiramisu*. Entrées are around $10 for lunch (Mon.-Sat.) and closer to $20 for dinner (daily), with pastas in the $13 range.

For a quick Carytown bite stop by the vegetarian deli inside **Ellwood Thompson's Natural Market**, 4 N. Thompson St., tel. (804) 359-7525, or **Mary Angela's Pizza, Pasta & Subs**, 3345 W. Cary St., tel. (804) 353-2333, which whips up NY-style pizza and subs for $4-5 (open for lunch Mon.-Sat., dinner daily). **Farouk's House of India**, 3033 W. Cary St., tel. (804) 355-0378, has a $6 lunch buffet and a wide vegetarian selection. Subcontinental specialties like tandoori chicken and naan bread are available for lunch Tues.-Sun. and dinner Mon.-Sun.

The **Cary Street Cafe**, 2631, W. Cary St., tel. (804) 353-7445, sits a few steps outside the bustle of Carytown. Another range of veggie options include the ELT (eggplant instead of bacon), spinach lasagna, and sautéed summer squash cakes. A weekday happy hour takes advantage of the room-length bar inside. Open Mon.-Fri. 3 p.m.-2 a.m., Saturday and Sunday 11 a.m.-2 p.m.

Shockoe Slip

If there's one restaurant you shouldn't miss in Richmond, even if only to peek inside, it's **The Tobacco Company**, 1201 E. Cary St., tel. (804) 782-9555. Dim light, wicker chairs, iron scrollwork, and plenty of plants evoke Richmond's turn-of-the-century heyday when this began as a tobacco warehouse, down to a wooden cigarshop Indian and roaming cigarette girl. An antique elevator rises slowly through the three-story glass-roofed atrium toward a brass chandelier from the lobby of a Federal Reserve Bank in Chicago.

The Victorian lounge on the first floor is great for a mint julep in the afternoon, and is only one of The Tobacco Company's options for live music in the evenings. And amid all this spectacle is some of the city's better food. A "Contemporary American" menu is heavy on the seafood, beef, and veal, with an excellent four-seafood pasta ($16-22). The second-floor dessert buffet has to be one of the best refined-sugar-for-your-dollar deals in the state. Open daily for lunch and dinner.

Local celebrity chef Jimmy Sneed joined forces with partner/mentor Jean Louis Palladin to open another Shockoe institution, **The Frog and the Redneck**, 1423 E. Cary St., tel. (804) 648-3764, Web site: www.frogandredneck.com. Sneed now runs it with another partner, but it's still one of downtown's most popular eateries. Whimsical cartoons on the wall trace the evolution of fine dining, which Sneed offers his own capricious take on: Redneck Risotto made from grits and "homemade pasta with stuff," to name two. Pastas are around $10, entrées $20-30, and there's a five-course tasting menu for $45 pp. A huge wine list is divided into "Frog" (French) and "Redneck" (Virginia) selections. The restaurant is open for dinner Mon.-Sat., but you can sample Sneed's handiwork for lunch at the **Frog Bar & Cafe** next door, open Mon.-Fri. for lunch. Individual pizzas ("the best you'll ever eat") and sandwiches like leg of lamb and seared skirt steak are $6-9. The covered patio has some of the tastiest happy-hour bites around.

Two of the best Asian restaurants in the city face each other across Cary St. in the center of Shockoe Slip. Stone lions flank the entrance of **Peking Pavilion**, 1302 E. Cary St., tel. (804) 649-8888, an elegant Chinese dining room with lunch specials for $6-7 and dinner plates for around $10. Dinner specials like Szechwan Three Delicacies and Peking Imperial ($11-23) are worth the splurge. Open daily for lunch and dinner. **Hana Zushi**, 1309 E. Cary St., tel. (804) 225-8801, is Richmond's only true sushi bar, serving the Japanese delicacy à la carte at the bar ($3-4 each) or on combination plates for $9-12. They also have a full selection of teriyaki, tempura, and sake and Sapporo beer to top it off. Open Mon.-Fri. for lunch and Mon.-Sat. for dinner.

The **Richbrau Brewing Company**, 1214 E. Cary St., tel. (804) 644-3018, owns the distinction of being the first brewpub to open in Richmond. It's classier than you might think, with everything from beer-battered fish & chips to maple pecan chicken ($10-18) to go along with the homemade beers. Try a Big Nasty Porter (it's not so bad) or the Old Nick Pale Ale. They also make root beer and cream soda. Open daily for dinner 4-11 p.m.; the bar and upstairs are open later.

PIEDMONT AREA WINERIES

Afton Mountain Vineyards
tel. (540) 456-8667
Near Afton; 234 Vineyard Lane

Autumn Hill Vineyards/Blue Ridge Winery
tel. (804) 985-6100
Near Stanardsville; 301 River Dr.

Barboursville Vineyards and Historic Ruins
tel. (540) 832-3824; e-mail: bvvy@comet.net
Near Barboursville; south on Rt. 687 and Rt. 777

Burnley Vineyards
tel. (540) 832-2828
Near Barboursville; west on Rt. 641 off Rt. 20

Chermont Winery, Inc.
tel. (804) 286-2211
Near Esmont; James River Rd. (north shore of
James River)

Dominion Wine Cellars
tol. (540) 825-8772
Near Culpeper; Rt. 3 exit off US 29

Greyhaven Winery
tel. (804) 556-3917
Near Orchid; I-64 east exit 159 to Rt. 522 north

Horton Cellars
tel. (540) 832-7440
Near Gordonsville; Rt. 33 west for 4 miles

Jefferson Vineyards, LP
tel. (804) 977-3042
Near Charlottesville; three miles past Monticello
on right, 1399 Thomas Jefferson Parkway (Rt.
53)
Site of Thomas Jefferson's first *vinifera* vines.

Lake Anna Winery
tel. (540) 895-5085
Near Glenora; I-95 Thornburg exit to Rt. 208 west

Misty Mountain Vineyards Inc.
tel. (540) 923-4738
Near Madison; Rt. 231 north from US 29 to Rt.
651 west

Montdomaine Cellars
tel. (804) 961-8947
Near Carters Bridge; Rt. 627 west from US 29
south of Charlottesville

Mountain Cove Vineyards
tel. (804) 263-5392
Near Lovingston; Rt. 718 to Rt. 651
Fiesta de Primavera in May.

Oakencroft Vineyard & Winery
tel. (804) 296-4188;
Web site: www.oakencroft.com
Near Charlottesville; 3.5 miles west of US 29 on
Barracks Road

Prince Michel & Rapidan River Vineyards
tel. (800) 869-8242
Near Leon; US 29 south of Culpeper
Wine museum, four-star restaurant, tel. (800)
869-WINE (800-869-9463)

Rebec Vineyards
tel. (804) 946-5168
Near Amherst; Rt. 29 five miles north of town
Garlic festival in October.

Rose Bower Vineyard & Winery
tel. (804) 223-8209
Near Farmville; south on US 15 to Rt. 665 to Rt.
604 to Rt. 686

Rose River Vineyards & Trout Farm
tel. (540) 923-4050
Near Syria; west on Rt. 670, left on Rt. 648

Stonewall Vineyards & Winery
tel. (804) 993-2185
Near Concord; north five miles on Rt. 608, left on
Rt. 721
Annual Halloween Jazz on the Lawn

Tomahawk Mill
tel. (804) 432-1063
Near Chatham; Rt. 57 west, 4.5 miles, right on
Rt. 799, 3.4 miles, left on Rt. 649, three miles

Totier Creek Vineyard & Winery
tel. (804) 979-7105
Near Charlottesville; Rt. 20 past Thomas
Jefferson Visitors Center, 10.5 miles, right on Rt.
720, one mile

White Hall Wineyards
tel. (804) 823-8615
Near White Hall; Rt. 810 north, left on Rt. 674
(Breakheart) to Sugar Ridge Road

Wintergreen Winery, Ltd.
tel. (804) 361-2519, fax 361-1510
Near Nellysford; Rt. 151 south to Rt. 684 west

For information on wineries in the Charlottesville
area, contact the Jeffersonian Wine Grape
Growers Society, Rt. 5, Box 429, Charlottesville,
VA 22901, tel. (804) 296-4188.

Shockoe Bottom

For a healthy dose of soul food (meaning cooked with plenty of love), stop by **Johnson's Grill,** 1802 E. Franklin St., tel. (804) 648-9788. If the meatloaf, pork chops, and spare ribs ($4-6.50) don't bring tears to your eyes, the homemade peach and apple cobbler will. Open Mon.-Fri. for breakfast and lunch from 6 a.m.

Lazy ceiling fans, palms trees, and a haze of cigar smoke would make Fidel feel right at home in **Havana '59,** 16 N. 17th St., tel. (804) 649-2822. Step up to the wide bar under strings of tiny lights and order a *mojito,* the Cuban mint julep, or take a table and enjoy a bowl of Cuban black bean soup or a plate of *ropa vieja,* a quintessential Caribbean mix of barbecued shredded beef with peppers, tomatoes, onions, and garlic. Despite an unfortunate location right under the I-95 overpass, **Bottoms Up Pizza,** 1700 Dock St., tel. (804) 644-4400, thrives thanks to outstanding pizza with thick sourdough crusts served inside or on two open decks. Try one of their specialty pies like the Remocaldo Renegade, with crabmeat, spinach and artichoke hearts, to learn why this place keeps getting voted the best pizzeria in the city. Upstairs, with its pink-lit bar, is a popular place to meet for a late-night bite before hitting the Shockoe scene. Open for lunch and dinner daily.

All the things that make a classic diner—table jukeboxes, breakfast all day, and the "Rochester Garbage Plate"—come together in the **River City Diner,** 1712 E. Main St., tel. (804) 644-9418. This endearing '50s throwback is open for breakfast and lunch Sun.-Mon., all meals Tues.-Thurs., and 24 hours on Friday and Saturday. **Millie's Diner,** 2603 E. Main St. at 26th St., tel. (804) 643-5512, puts a gourmet spin on countertop meals with entrées like Thai spicy shrimp and grilled quail on polenta. It's still definitely a diner—there's a jukebox on the counter and the grill sizzles right next to the door—but the food guarantees you'll have to wait for a table if you don't show up early. Open Tues.-Sun. for lunch and dinner.

NIGHTLIFE

With so many college-age residents, Richmond certainly has no deficit of bars, pubs, and music halls, but the city's traditional attitude ensures plenty of more refined alternatives (some of which may require dressing up). Most of the action centers on Shockoe neighborhood restaurants, thanks to Virginia licensing laws, which require establishments that serve alcohol to serve food as well.

Look for up-to-the-minute information on evening entertainment in the *Richmond Times-Dispatch,* various entertainment papers like the *Richmond Music Journal, Focus, Punchline,* and *Style,* or the handbills plastering any utility pole. Tickets for larger events can be ordered through **Ticketmaster,** tel. (800) 736-2000.

Shockoe Bottom

Main St. between 17th and 18th throbs with music on weekend evenings, as places like **Shotz,** 4 N. 18th St., tel. (804) 649-7468, and **Sunset Grille,** 1814 E. Main St., tel. (804) 643-4701, each tries to out-volume its neighbors in luring college-age fun-seekers. **The Flood Zone,** 11 S. 18th St., tel. (804) 643-1117, is the city's biggest and most popular music venue. Set in (what else) an old tobacco warehouse, the Flood Zone boasts three bars and a balcony. Upwards of 1,000 people can cram in for concerts and dance nights. The first of every month brings the Capital City Barn Dance, a family-oriented evening of country music and entertainment.

The **Moondance Saloon,** 9 N. 17th St., tel. (804) 788-6666, hosts blues, rockabilly, and rock acts, while **Poe's Pantry and Pub,** 2706 E. Main St., tel. (804) 648-2120, tends toward the bluegrass, acoustic, and jazz. Poe's also has open-mike nights and blues jams. Guitars and cue sticks are the instruments of choice at the **Rack-n-Roll Cafe,** 1713 E. Main St., tel. (804) 644-1204.

Shockoe Slip

This area tends to attract a more mature crown than the Bottom, frequenting places such as the **The Tobacco Company** lounge, which brings quality blues, rock, acoustic, and jazz acts Tues.-Sat. evenings. The **Tobacco Club** downstairs draws the professional crowd for pop and top-40 music, with a moderate dress code befitting the classy setting. Just as stylish is the rooftop of **Havana '59,** where patrons sip rum-and-Cokes while a DJ spins below. A Victorian billiards lounge/sport bar above the **Richbrau Brewing**

Co. dining room is popular with 20- and 30-somethings, offering foosball, darts, and live music. For a dose of the urban blues head to **Medly's Restaurant,** 1701 E. Main St., tel. (804) 648-2313, and for a laugh try the **Fox River Cafe and Comedy Club,** 109 S. 12th St., tel. (804) 643-5653.

The Fan

Coffeeshops and alternative tunes, mostly along Main St. from VCU to Boulevard, cater to a hip college crowd. **Trademarks,** 1707 E. Franklin, tel. (804) 649-1079, and **Twisters,** 929 W. Grace St., tel. (804) 353-4263, both feature up-and-coming local bands. The latter also has DJs and disco nights. On weekends, jazz floats from the intimate confines of **Bogart's Backroom,** 203 N. Lombardy St., tel. (804) 353-9280, one of the oldest clubs in the area. **Mudbones,** 2 N. Meadow St., tel. (804) 359-9572, is an Italian restaurant that also hosts live jazz on weekends, and the **Cary Street Cafe** welcomes an eclectic mix of acoustic and bluegrass in between open-mike nights.

Elsewhere

In midtown there's the **Boom Nightclub** at Cafine's at Grace and 4th Sts., open Fri.-Sun. 9 p.m.-3 a.m. **Alley Katz,** 10 Walnut Alley Ave., tel. (804) 643-2816, is a distinctive venue for local and national bands that tend toward the mainstream more than the dissonant. It's off Labernum Ave. near the state fairgrounds. Finally, **Potter's Pub,** 7007 Three Chopt Rd., tel. (804) 282-9999, is the place for folk music. This one is in the Village Shopping Center—take Kensington Ave. west until it turns into Patterson, and keep going until it intersects with Three Chopt Rd. at the city limits.

THE ARTS

Music

The **Virginia Opera,** tel. (804) 643-6004, has gained national attention since its inception at the Official State Opera in 1975. Eleven productions a season are held at the Carpenter Center (see below). Even older, the **Richmond Symphony,** tel. (804) 788-4717, began in 1957, and went on to receive the American Society of Composers, Author and Publishers' Award for the

fifth time in 1996. Two hundred annual performances range from classical Masterworks to All-Star Pops with guest artists like Itzhak Perlman and Bruce Hornsby. Most of the shows happen at the Carpenter Center and the Landmark Theater (see below).

Dance

A beloved holiday performance of *The Nutcracker* is only one great production of the **Richmond Ballet,** tel. (804) 359-0906, the state's only professional troupe and one of the finest on the East Coast. The **Concert Ballet of Richmond,** tel. (804) 798-0945, performs more modern works at the Women's Club Auditorium at 211 E. Franklin St. and various outdoor festivals.

Theaters and Performance Spaces

Everyone who visits Richmond should see a movie at the **Byrd Theater,** 2908 W. Cary St., tel. (804) 353-9911, in a setting as palatial as anything on Broadway. Tickets are only $1 pp ($2 in the balcony on Saturday), and if you're lucky you'll come on a night when the organ player rises out of the stage before the show. Another Roaring-20s movie house has been transformed into the **Carpenter Center for the Performing Arts,** 600 E. Grace St. at 6th St. Marketplace, tel. (804) 643-9432 or 225-9000. A ceiling painted to look like the open sky caps a lavish array of Moorish adornments, plush rugs, and a sweeping grand staircase. With 2,000 seats, the Carpenter Center is large enough to host the Richmond Ballet and opera performances as well as concerts and traveling Broadway productions.

Richmond's Landmark Theater, 6 N. Laurel at Main, tel. (804) 780-4213, began in 1918 as a Shriner meeting hall with 4,600 seats, six lobbies, 42 hotel rooms, and a bowling alley. It was known as The Mosque until 1995, when a $6-million renovation brought back 3,500 seats, both reproductions and originals. It has hosted the same range of performances as the Carpenter Center, including Garrison Keillor's "American Radio Hour." **The Empire Theater,** 114 W. Broad St., tel. (804) 344-8040, is Richmond's oldest theater (1910) and home to Theater IV, offering family, Off-Broadway, and adventurous performances for older audiences.

Outdoor concerts, children's performances, and the Festival of the Arts in July and August come to the **Dogwood Dell** in Bryd Park. The **State Fairgrounds at Strawberry Hill** accommodates Virginia's largest monthly flea market, tel. (804) 431-9500, along with many annual festivals (see **Events,** below). Major rock acts such as Sting and Tina Turner swing by the **Classic Amphitheater,** tel. (804) 228-3213.

Groups and Organizations

TheatreVirginia, based in the Virginia Museum of Fine Arts, puts on a nationally acclaimed variety of drama, comedies, and musicals during its Sept.-April season. The **Arts Council of Richmond,** 1401 W Main St., tel. (804) 355-7200, is a nonprofit organization aimed at the promotion of arts in the metro area, while **Downtown Presents,** 550 E Marshall St., Ste. 202, tel. (804) 643-2826, sponsors events and festivals in central Richmond.

SHOPPING

Funky gift, thrift, and clothing shops share space in Carytown with pricey boutiques and stores selling housewares and furniture. Drop in on places like **Galaxie 409,** 409 Strawberry St., tel. (804) 278-9411, and **Loco Color by Hannex** 3220 W. Cary St., tel. (804) 353-5382, for a taste of the unusual. **La Lune Design,** 3407 W. Cary St., tel. (804) 358-6505, sells clothing, jewelry, and art, as does **Bygones Vintage Clothing,** 2916 W. Cary St., tel. (804) 353-1919, next to the Byrd Theater.

Carytown is also the first stop for antiques, where **The Antique Gallery,** 3140 W. Cary St., tel. (804) 358-0500, has over 50 dealers in a mini-mall setting. The **West End Antiques Mall,** 6504 Horsepen Rd., tel. (804) 295-1916, also has a good selection, as does the smaller **Martha's Mixture Antique Sales & Restoration,** 3445 W. Cary St., tel. (804) 358-5827. Try the **Antique Boutique and Delectable Collectibles,** 1310 E. Cary St., tel. (804) 775-2525, in Shockoe, and **Adams' Antiques,** 1423 W. Main St., tel. (804) 355-0254, in The Fan.

Millie Jones sewed her first flag ("It's a Boy") a quarter of a century ago, and since then her colorful banners have become a Richmond tradition

that's spreading to the rest of the state. Other flag shops have followed, but Millie's **Festival Flags,** 322 West Broad St., tel. (804) 643-5247, is the real thing. The **Richmond Arsenal,** 7605 Midlothian Tpk., tel. (804) 272-4570, doesn't sell firearms, but it is full to the rafters with Civil War relics. For new, used, and rare books on all things American, Southern, and Virginian, stop by **Owens & Ramsey Booksellers,** 2728 Tinsley Dr., tel. (804) 272-8888. They also have a selection of maps and fine art prints.

North of The Fan, **Ghana House by Rawquartz,** 517 N Harrison St., tel. (804) 355-2962, stocks a kaleidoscopic array of wooden masks, sculptures, crafts, and clothing from West Africa. **Tinkers,** 2409 Westwood Ave., tel. (804) 359-3301, is Richmond's choice for folk art. You can watch artists at work in their studios at **Arts on the Square,** tel. (804) 648-5015, in the Sixth Street Marketplace, before picking something you like from their galleries. The section of the marketplace south of Broad St. has a host of smaller gift shops. **My Romance,** 1206 E Cary St., tel. (804) 643-4438, is typical of Shockoe's upscale offerings. Chandelier and classical music provide a luxurious setting for the lingerie, soaps, candles, and fragrances.

RECREATION

Tours

The paddle wheeler **Annabel Lee,** tel. (804) 644-5700, leaves from 3011 Dock St. in Shockoe Bottom for leisurely dining cruises on the James River. Lunch ($23.50) and dinner ($32-37) are offered March-Dec. Wed.-Sun., and on Tuesday an all-day Plantation Lunch trip ($52 including continental breakfast) leaves at 10 a.m. for the Westover, Evelynton, and Berkeley plantations downriver.

The **Historic Richmond Foundation,** 707-A E. Franklin St., tel. (804) 780-0107, organizes a two-hour walking tour of the downtown area on Sunday afternoons April-Oct. for $5 pp. It also runs three guided bus tours focusing on Richmond's past and present highlights and its role as capital of the Confederacy. These run $13-16 adults, $10-13 children 6-18, and pickup can be arranged from downtown hotels and the Capitol Square visitors center.

Spectator Sports

The **Richmond Braves**, tel. (804) 359-4444, continue a strong local baseball tradition that has left Richmond without a baseball team only one year since 1884. The Atlanta Braves' top AAA farm team plays at the 12,000-seat Diamond ballpark, one of the finest minor-league stadiums in the country. The **Richmond Kickers**, tel. (804) 644-5425, compete in the United States Interregional Soccer League (USISL), and won the U.S. Open Cup in 1995. Their April-Sept. season takes place at the University of Richmond Stadium at Douglas Ave. and McCloy Street.

Puck-heads will want to catch the **Richmond Renegades**, tel. (804) 643-7825, who won the East Coast Hockey League's Riley Cup championship in 1994-95, only four years after forming. The Renegades play at the **Richmond Coliseum**, 601 E. Leigh St., tel. (804) 780-4956, which at 14,000 seats is the largest indoor entertainment facility in Virginia. The Coliseum hosts a wide range of professional and college sports and other events. It's been losing good concerts to the Classic Amphitheater lately, but still offers everything from pro wrestling and monster-truck extravaganzas to ice shows and the circus.

All of the **universities and colleges** in town have their own sports teams, from the U of R's Spiders on down, that compete on campus and in city venues such as the Coliseum. Call the athletic departments of the University of Richmond, tel. (804) 289-8388; Virginia Commonwealth University, tel. (804) 828-7267; and Virginia Union University, tel. (804) 257-5890, for schedules and locations.

Horse-racing fans breathed a sigh of relief in 1997 with the opening of **Colonial Downs**, tel. (804) 966-7223 or (888) 482-8722, the first pari-mutuel betting racecourse in the state since the 1800s. With a five-level grandstand, restaurants, lounges, and monitors, the track is one of the largest and most luxurious of its kind in the country. The fall thoroughbred season culminates with the Breeder's Cup. Colonial Downs is near exit 214 off I-64 heading east to Williamsburg and Newport News, and there's a 200-screen Off-Track Wagering Facility at 4700 Broad St., tel. (804) 423-2211.

On weekends in March and September crowds of close to 100,000 descend on the **Richmond International Raceway**, tel. (804) 345-7223, in the state fairgrounds at Strawberry Hill, to watch America's fastest-growing (and most-photographed, according to Kodak) spectator sport, that thunderous mix of gas fumes and adrenaline known as NASCAR. The track, Virginia's largest sports facility, hosts various Winston Cup events, from the Pontiac Excitement 400 in March to the Miller Genuine Draft 400 in September, among other races. Tickets can get scarce, so call ahead.

Rafting and Kayaking

As one of the few cities in the world with serious whitewater churning through its center, Richmond knows its rapids, which can hit class IV and V near Hollywood Cemetery and Belle Isle. Milder sections of the James welcome paddlers and tubers during the March-Nov. season. A licensed outfitter is definitely the way to go if you're up for tackling the urban froth: the **Richmond Raft Company,** 4400 E. Main St. at Water St., tel. (804) 222-7238 or (800) 540-7238, leads trips for $35-50 pp, both class-III and -IV quickies to serious spills over the fall line.

Adventure Challenge, 8225 Oxer Rd., tel. (804) 276-7600, e-mail: info@adventurechallenge.com, Web site: www.adventurechallenge.com, runs whitewater kayaks down the James ($25-70 pp), Appomattox, and Anna Rivers. They also organize skiing shuttles in the winter. Jay Lewis' **Old Dominion Adventures,** 501 S 14th St. on Mayo Island, tel. (804) 343-1711, e-mail: kayakoda@erols.com, offers canoe and kayak trips, instruction, and rentals for the day or weekend. Their sea kayak excursions head to Assateague and Chincoteague on the Eastern Shore.

Other Outdoor Recreation

Two Wheel Travel, 2934 W. Cary St., tel. (804) 359-2453, rents hybrid bicycles for $20 the first day and $10 each additional day. Call the **Richmond Area Bicycling Association's Ride Line,** tel. (804) 266-2453, for information on group rides for families, mountain bikes, and racers, along with local cycling maps and tips. The **Richmond Department of Recreation and Parks,** tel. (804) 780-5733, in City Hall at 900 E. Broad St., is the best source of information on Richmond's 60 parks. They organize various outdoor adventure classes, trips, and seminars throughout the year.

EVENTS

Many of Richmond's annual events happen at the Strawberry Hill Fairgrounds, tel. (804) 228-3200, north of downtown at the intersection of Labernum Ave. (Rt. 197) and Meadowbrook Rd. (Rt. 627). To get there from downtown, take 5th St. north from Leigh St. a mile and a half to Brookland Park Blvd., take a left, bear right onto Meadowbrook Rd. after two blocks, and keep going another mile.

Vote for your favorite tongue-scorcher at the **Chili Cook-Off** at Strawberry Hill in March. April's **Easter on Parade** fills Monument Avenue with an old-fashioned parade, carnival rides, and jazz, blues, and Dixieland music. That same month brings Richmond's rite of spring: the **Strawberry Hill Races,** a steeplechase event and so much more. City-wide carriage parades and balls get everyone in the mood for the extravagant tailgate parties the day of the races, some of which are so elaborate there's a competition for the best theme and costumes. All proceeds go to charity.

May's perfect softball weather ushers in the **Round Robin Softball Tournament,** said to be the largest in the world. Over 400 teams from 20 states compete on Memorial Day weekend in parks around the city. That same month the **Tour DuPont,** one of America's premier cycling events, rolls through downtown Richmond on a different course every year. Tens of thousands line the streets to watch riders sprint to the finish line at 10th and Cary Streets.

Up to 50 free concerts comprise **The BIG Gig,** a.k.a. Richmond's International Festival of Music, in July. Jazz, rock, country, and classical performances are held in the Nina Abady Festival Park, the Carpenter Center, and elsewhere.

Everything that makes fairs great—rides, live-stock exhibits, fattening food, the circus—happens for 10 days in late September at the **State Fair of Virginia** at Strawberry Hill. Loosen your belt a few more notches for the **International Food Festival** at the Richmond Centre the same month.

In October the **Second Street Festival** celebrates Jackson Ward's African-American Heritage with theater, soul food, vendors, and rag-time and gospel music. Also in October, the **Richmond Children's Festival** in Byrd Park is modeled on a different culture every year, with music, entertainers, crafts, and food.

The December holidays bring **open houses** at historic homes like Maymont and the Lewis Ginter Botanical Gardens, along with **Holiday House Tours** in various neighborhoods. Call (804) 643-3643 to tour Church Hill, and (804) 344-7998 for downtown and The Fan. A local favorite is the **Grand Illumination** of the tree and holiday displays at the James Center, tel. (804) 344-3232, accompanied by choral concerts and wagon rides. Richmonders are also fond of the **Tackiest Christmas Decorations Tour,** which links places so gaudy they stop traffic. Look in the *Richmond Times-Dispatch* in early December or late November for a map.

TRANSPORTATION

Getting Around

In 1888, Richmond became the first city in America to boast an electric trolley system, and its rubber-wheeled cars have been revived by the **Greater Richmond Transit Company,** tel. (804) 358-4782, along two downtown routes. The red route connects Shockoe Bottom to City Square, Jackson Ward, and points west to Monroe St., and the blue route travels from Shockoe Bottom around the State Capitol to the Richmond Centre and as far south as the river. Trolleys run every 15 minutes Mon.-Sat. 11 a.m.-11 p.m. (every 25 after 8:30 p.m.) and cost only 25 cents pp. Stop by the GRTC's information booth in the Sixth Street Marketplace for maps.

Local **taxi** companies, including Yellow Cab, tel. (804) 222-7300, Veterans Cab Association, tel. (804) 329-3333, and Metro Taxicab Service, tel. (804) 353-5000, can take you to the airport from downtown for $15-20.

Getting There and Away

Plans are afoot to restore Main St. Station in Shockoe Slip to serve as a train depot once again, but until then there's **Amtrak,** 7519 Staples Mill Rd., tel. (804) 553-2903, north of I-64 exit 185 in western Richmond. Taxi fare to downtown runs around $13. The **Greyhound-Trailways** terminal, 2910 N. Blvd., tel. (804) 254-5910, is near I-95 exit 78.

Once known as Byrd Field, the **Richmond International Airport,** tel. (804) 226-3052, sits off I-64 exit 197 east of downtown. There's no bus service into the city, but **Groome Transportation,** tel. (800) 552-7911 or (804) 222-7222, offers 24-hour service ($19 per couple). Most downtown luxury hotels also run shuttles. Car rental agencies include Thrifty, tel. (804) 222-3200; Budget, tel. (804) 222-5310; National, tel. (804) 222-7477; Avis, tel. (804) 222-2562; and Hertz, tel. (804) 222-7228.

INFORMATION

The headquarters of the **Metro Richmond Convention & Visitors Bureau,** 550 E. Marshall St., tel. (800) 365-7272 or (804) 782-2777, fax 780-2577, are on the second floor of the Sixth Street Marketplace. They operate three **visitors centers:** one at the airport, tel. (804) 236-3260; one at 1710 Robin Hood Rd., tel. (800) 370-9004 or (804) 358-5511; and one in the Bell Tower in Capitol Square, tel. (804) 648-3146. Each sells blocks of tickets ($15 pp) for admission to over three dozen of the city's finest historic houses, museums, and churches; tickets are good for a month. E-mail: mrcvb@richmondva.org, Web site: www.richmondva.org.

For Richmond information online, try the websites of *Richmond* magazine (www.richmag.com), *Style Weekly* (www.styleweekly.com), and the *Richmond Times-Dispatch* (www.gatewayva.com).

NEAR RICHMOND

Paramount Kings Dominion

Ten roller coasters—the most on the East Coast—are the main draw to the Piedmont's favorite amusement park. Start with a few of the classic wooden rattlers, like the 1975-vintage Rebel Yell and The Grizzly, consistently voted one of the best in America by enthusiast groups, before risking gastrointestinal distress on something more modern. Volcano: The Blast Coaster shoots passengers from the top of a "live" volcano at 70 mph, and The Outer Limits: Flight of Fear uses an electromagnetic launching system to shoot cars horizontally onto a darkened indoor track.

Other rides include the Xtreme Skyflyer in Wayne's World, sort of a swinging bungee jump, and guaranteed soakers such as Whitewater Canyon, the Log Flume, and Hurricane Reef, a six-acre water park with 15 water slides. For children, there's KidZville and Nickelodeon Splat City, and a one-third model of the Eiffel Tower with a view of the whole park.

Kings Dominion, tel. (804) 876-5000, Web site: www.pkd4fun.com, is on Rt. 30 off I-95 exit 98. Tickets are $32 for adults and children over seven, and $23 for children 3-6. It's open late April-early Sept., on weekends only outside of June-Aug. Call for exact hours. Hurricane Reef is open weekends in May, then daily until early Sept., noon-8 p.m.

PETERSBURG AND VICINITY

Best known as the site of the last major battle of the Civil War, Petersburg (pop. 36,000) sits sleepily alongside the Appomattox river within day-trip distance of Richmond. The friendly residents of historic Olde Towne still recall with a shiver the tornado that passed through in August 1993, causing more damage in a few minutes than the Union army did during a 10-month siege. Many businesses are still closed and lots left vacant, but most of the city's major sights escaped unharmed. Petersburg is only a short drive from the number of historic plantations along the upper James.

History
Established in 1784, Petersburg weathered a destructive visit by Benedict Arnold and 2,500 British soldiers on their way to Yorktown during the Revolutionary War. For the next hundred years the town served as a popular stopover for travelers drawn to its theater, race track, and taverns.

By June 1864, Ulysses S. Grant realized the key to taking Richmond was this vital road and rail junction just a day's ride to the south. He managed to sneak 75,000 troops almost within striking distance before Robert E. Lee caught on and scrambled to reinforce Gen. P.G.T. Beauregard's force of 15,000 before the Federals arrived.

Poor coordination kept Union forces from taking advantage of an early victory on June 15 over the northern Confederate bulwarks, and five days later the two armies settled down to 10 months of trench warfare and waiting. Opposing lines were so close that soldiers on both sides could tell time by the tolling of the courthouse clock. Supplies quickly ran low inside the city, but the unflappable Confederates held thrifty Starvation Balls rather than submit.

In time Grant was able to lengthen Union lines until they stretched from here to Richmond. Scattered skirmishes peaked on March 25, 1865, when Lee tried to break out with a failed attack at Fort Stedman to the east. The Confederate commander realized his hopeless position, and on the night of April 2, Lee evacuated Petersburg and Richmond and led his army on its final march west.

AFRICAN-AMERICAN HISTORY IN PETERSBURG

Petersburg's rich vein of African-American history starts with the First Baptist Church at 236 Harrison St., which opened in 1774 as the earliest organized black church in America (guided tours by appointment). By the mid-19th century, the city had the largest free black population in Virginia, though two-thirds remained slaves. Former slaves who had been given their freedom (manumitted) or bought it themselves organized small, self-contained communities in places like Pocahontas Island on the Appomattox River near Petersburg. Joseph Jenkins Roberts, the first president of Liberia 1848-1855 (and again 1871-76), left his hometown in 1829, and 1888 saw the election of Virginia's first black congressman, Petersburg resident John Mercer Langston. The visitors center has more information on local black history.

SIGHTS

Olde Towne
Petersburg's historic hub centers on the Appomattox River where the **Appomattox Iron Works** (under repair in 1997) hunkers on aptly named Old Street. Call the visitors center for details on the following sights.

The beautiful Exchange Building, built in the 1840s as a commodities market, is the home of Petersburg's **Siege Museum,** 15 W. Bank St. Farmers once gathered to trade and auction produce under the Greek revival dome in the two-story central hall, but now the focus is on civilian life during the terrible 10 months before the city fell. Hoop skirts, tourniquets, and cannon balls show what civilians faced from day to day as Grant waited on the doorstep. Unusual pieces, like an experimental revolving-barrel cannon and the shell-dented brass steeple of the Tabb Street Presbyterian Church, round out

GEORGE'S LIE

George Washington visited Petersburg near the turn of the 19th century and recorded being forced to tell a lie in order to leave in peace:

Having suffered very much by the dust yesterday, and finding that . . . a number of other Gentlemen were intending to attend me part of the way today, I caused their enquiries [sic] respecting the time of my setting out, to be answered that, I should endeavor to do it before eight o'clock; but did it a little after five.

the collection. Open daily 10 a.m.-5 p.m.; $3 adults, $2 children. Tours for the Trapezium House and Farmers Bank start here.

Eccentric Irish bachelor Charles O'Hara built the **Trapezium House of 1817,** Market and High Sts., without a single right angle or pair of parallel walls, supposedly because his West Indian servant warned him evil spirits lurked in proper geometry. Open April-Oct., daily 10 a.m.-5 p.m. Built the same year, the **Farmer's Bank,** 19 Bollingbrook St., survives as one of the country's oldest bank buildings. A cashier lived on the upper floor with his family, lowering the heavy safe into a floor vault beneath his office at night. Open April-Oct., Mon.-Fri. 10 a.m.-5 p.m. Tours of each ($3 adults, $2 children) leave from the Siege Museum.

The prominent Bolling family built **Centre Hill Mansion,** 1 Centre Hill Circle between Adams and Tabb Sts., in 1823. Originally in the Federal style, Centre Hill was remolded as a Greek Revival building in the 1840s. Victorian antiques, ornate woodwork, and plaster designs adorn the main floors, while downstairs is the mouth of a tunnel that once went all the way to the river. Open daily 10 a.m.-5 p.m.; $3 adults, $2 children.

Outside of Olde Towne

Proving it's not just for backyard barbecues and company picnics, the **Softball Hall of Fame,** 3935 S. Crater Rd., tel. (804) 733-1005, honors the men and women who have left their mark

in the ranks of the professional U.S. Slo-Pitch Softball Association (USSSA). World Champion jerseys, trophies, and videos fill the museum, which is open Mon.-Fri. 9 a.m.-4 p.m., Saturday 10 a.m.-4 p.m., Sunday noon-4 p.m.; $2 adults, $1 children.

The story of the U.S. Army Quartermaster Corps, the oldest corps in the army, is told in the **Quartermaster Museum,** tel. (804) 734-4203, at Fort Lee three miles east of downtown along Washington St. (Rt. 36). Everything from Ulysses S. Grant's saddle to General Patton's Jeep (with custom Mercedes seats) is displayed Tues.-Fri. 10 a.m.-5 p.m., Saturday and Sunday 11 a.m.-5 p.m.; free.

Petersburg National Battlefield Park

Comprising six major units, this park protects Petersburg's Civil War legacy. Start at the main unit, 2.5 miles east of downtown on Washington St. (Rt. 36), where a **visitors center,** tel. (804) 732-3531, Web site· www.nps.gov/pete, has an hourly map presentation that relates an overview of the battles. Take the trail past the grassy knolls of Confederate defensive earthworks to the massive Dictator mortar that once hurled 250-pound shells into the heart of Petersburg (at night citizens could watch the lit fuses arc overhead before impact). From here a four-mile auto tour, also popular with cyclists and walkers, leads past other spots along the battle line including the gaping hole left by the surreal Battle of the Crater (see special topic, **The Crater Fiasco**).

Other units include the **Poplar Grove National Cemetery** southwest of downtown, filled with 6,000 Union casualties; **Five Forks,** farther west along Rt. 460, where Gen. Sheridan took 2,000 Confederate prisoners on April 1, 1865; and Grant's siege headquarters at **City Point,** where the Appomattox empties into the James. Most of the siege's 30,000 Confederate casualties are buried in **Blandford Cemetery,** off of Crater Rd. (US 301/480) south of Washington St. A set of Tiffany stained glass windows was donated to the 18th-century **Blandford Church,** at Rochelle Ln., by Southern states in memory of their Civil War dead.

The park is open daily 8 a.m.-5 p.m. (until 7 p.m. June-Sept.), $4 per car, $2 per bicycle or pair of shoes. During the summer costumed interpreters add a living touch to the experience.

Living history programs at Petersburg National Battlefield Park re-create life during the Civil War.

Pamplin Park

This private Civil War site south of Petersburg features an interpretive center with a fiber-optic battle map, interactive video programs, and war relics. Trails lead along some of the best-preserved Civil War fortifications in existence. Get an idea of life during the winter of the Petersburg siege (1864-65) in a reconstructed soldier's hut, and across the road stop by Tudor Hall, the 1812 plantation home of the Boisseau family. It was used as headquarters by a Confederate general. Guided tours and reenactments happen periodically; call for a schedule. Pamplin Park, tel. (804) 861-2408, fax 861-2820, is on Duncan Rd. (Rt. 670), a little over a mile south of I-85 exit 63 via US 1. It's open daily 9 a.m.-5 p.m. (later in summer); $3 adults, $1.50 children 6-11.

ACCOMMODATIONS

Moderate

A treasury of French antiques fill **La Villa Romaine,** 29 S. Market St. at Market St., tel. (804) 861-2285 or (800) 243-0860 ext. 1234, fax (804) 861-6780, Web site: lavilla.tierranet.com, from a carved armoire to matching twin Louis XVI beds. A full European breakfast is included, and guests after a little something special can opt for a chauffeured Rolls Royce tour of the area. **La Casita Real,** 241 S. Sycamore St. at Wythe, tel. (804) 863-4208 or (800) 586-9070, overlooks Poplar Lawn Park. Five rooms and suites fill the house, built in 1889. E-mail: b&b@midatlantic.net, Web site: www.midatlantic.net/b&b.htm.

A turret tops the Queen Anne Victorian mansion now know as **The Owl and the Pussycat,** 405 High St., tel. (804) 733-0505, fax 862-0694. Choose from the Owl, Pussycat, and Boat room—guess which one the owners' two cats prefer. E-mail: owlcat@ctg.net, Web site: www.ctg.net/owlcat/. Three miles west of downtown on Washington St. is the **Mayfield Inn,** 3348 W. Washington St., tel. (804) 861-6775 or (800) 538-2381, where Robert E. Lee stayed with his staff before abandoning Petersburg. Four acres of grounds around the 1750s mansion include a pool and enchanting gardens. A full country breakfast comes with a night in one of the four rooms.

Facing each other just east of I-95 exit 52 are the **Best Western of Petersburg,** 405 E. Washington St., tel. (804) 733-1776, fax 861-6339, and a **Ramada Inn,** 501 E. Washington St., tel. (804) 733-0730, fax 861-3807.

Expensive

Built in 1763, the **Folly Castle Bed & Breakfast,** 323 W. Washington St., tel. (804) 861-3558 or (800) 863-0089, takes its name from the fact that such a large Georgian home for its childless owner seemed, well, a bit ill-advised. In 1885 its owners moved it 100 feet so they could enjoy a fashionable West Washington Street address. Suites include access to a peaceful garden with waterfall and lily pond.

Camping

The **South Forty KOA,** 2809 Courtland Rd., tel. (804) 732-8345, is south of Petersburg, half a mile beyond I-95 exit 41 on Rt. 35. Sites with hookups are $20-25.

FOOD

Next to the visitors center on Old St., the **Farmer's Market,** tel. (804) 732-3378, occupies an octagonal brick building built in 1888 on the site of Petersburg's first tobacco warehouse. Local farmers still sell seasonal produce from stalls outside, a stipulation of the building's 1806 deed of sale for $1. Economical lunch salads and sandwiches are in the $5 range, and dinner entrées from BBQ to surf and turf run $10-15. Line dancing, comedy shows, karaoke, and live bands fill the center stage throughout the week. Open Tues.-Sun.

Leonardo's Deli & Cafe, 7 Bollingbrook St., tel. (804) 863-4830, serves light fare, coffees, and Italian sodas Monday 8 a.m.-5 p.m., Tues.-Wed. 8 a.m.-9 p.m., Thurs.-Fri. 8 a.m.-10 p.m., and Saturday 5 p.m.-midnight. It's located next to the Farmer's Bank. A block beyond down Sycamore is the **Dixie Restaurant,** 250 N. Sycamore, tel. (804) 732-5761, a local institution with rock-bottom prices and famous hot dogs (ask about the Dixie Dog song). Open Mon.-Sat. for all meals. Head west down Bank St. past the Siege Museum to **Portabella,** 105 W. Bank St., tel. (804) 732-6233. Petersburg's most stylish bistro offers gourmet sandwiches for $7-8 (try the smoked roasted pork or the ham-pineapple-brie on a croissant) for lunch Wed.-Fri. Dinner entrées like sautéed sea scallops are $12-23, served Tues.-Sun. along with a wide selection of wines.

ENTERTAINMENT AND RECREATION

Shopping
The sign says Complete Home Furnishings at the **Trading Post,** 314 N. Sycamore, tel. (804) 733-4772, but you'll find much more in this salvage shop supreme. Everything from railroad collectibles to coffee and spices trades hands at the **South Side Station Marketplace,** tel. (804) 733-5050, a flea market housed in two buildings along the river. It's open Tues.-Sunday. Antique addicts can get their fix within a few blocks of the visitors center at **Cockade Antiques,** 1 W.

THE CRATER FIASCO

The idea was simple and daring: covertly dig a 500-foot tunnel under the Confederate trenches at Petersburg, fill it with explosives, and with one lit match avoid a torturous siege and perhaps even end the Civil War early. Union officials dismissed the idea as "claptrap and nonsense," but Lt. Col. Henry Pleasants managed to convince Maj. Gen. Ambrose E. Burnside that his corps of Pennsylvania coal miners could pull it off.

Burnside in turn persuaded a reluctant Ulysses S. Grant to give the go-ahead, and on June 25, 1864, digging began. How Union sappers managed to dig a tenth of a mile directly under hundreds of listless Confederate troops without being heard is anyone's guess, especially with two Confederate counter-tunnels in the vicinity, but on July 23 the cramped passage was completed. It took four days to pack the end with 8,000 pounds of gunpowder and seal the shaft for 38 feet, and at 3:30 a.m. on July 30 the fuse was lit.

Nothing happened. A nervous volunteer was sent below with another match, and at 4:45 a.m. the earth beneath the sleeping Confederates erupted. Nine entire companies were suddenly airborne above a hole 170 feet wide and 30 feet deep. Nearly 300 men were killed outright or mortally wounded.

Brig. Gen. James Ledlie's division spearheaded the assault into the smoking hole, but were so shocked by the carnage they found that they milled about in confusion. The enraged Rebels regrouped and struck back, firing on the clump of blue uniforms without mercy. A black Union division (originally picked to lead the attack, but switched at the last minute to avoid charges of racism) was ordered in to help, but found itself trapped as well. Many were shot by Confederates after surrendering. By 1 p.m. the Union troops had been pushed back to their original line after suffering 3,798 casualties, more than twice as many as their opponents.

Grant later called the event "the saddest affair I have witnessed in the war."

FOOD AND FUN IN EMPORIA

Emporia, a small city in south-central Virginia, hosts two annual events celebrating regional food. The second weekend in June the **Virginia Pork Festival,** tel. (800) 482-7675 or (804) 634-6611, fax 348-0119, features 20 tons of food, from ribs and barbecue to pigs' feet and chitterlings. All you can eat, along with five stages of country, bluegrass, and rock, is yours for $20 pp. E-mail: vapork@admit1fest.com, Web site: www.admit1fest.com/vapork.

The **Virginia Peanut Festival,** tel. (804) 348-3378, e-mail: vapeanutfest@admit1fest.com, Web site: www.admit1fest.com/vapeanutfest, arrives in late September with music, carnival rides, peanut parade, classic car show, and the Miss Emporia-Greensville Peanut Festival Pageant. Part of the peanut celebration is the Great Peanut Bicycle Tour, which winds through the peanut country of southern Virginia and northeast North Carolina. The four-day tour is $45 pp, not including food samples along the way, and it draws around 1,500 cyclists. For more information contact the Emporia Bicycle Club, tel. (800) 449-2453, e-mail: gpt@3rddoor.com, Web site: www.3rddoor.com/~gpt/.

Old St., tel. (804) 861-2417, and **Woody's Antiques,** 3 W. Old St., tel. (804) 861-9642.

Outdoors
A four-mile **river trail** along the near shore of the Appomattox was planned to open in 1999. Starting at Pocahontas Island, the trail will be open to foot and cycle traffic, with canoe inlets and walkways to various river islands.

EVENTS

A Civil War-themed **Starvation Ball** on New Year's Day brings period costumes, music, and Jeff Davis punch to Centre Hill Mansion. In mid-April the Petersburg Art League sponsors a citywide **Artfest** at Poplar Lawn Park at Sycamore and Fillmore. You can take **Hallows Eve tours** of Blandford Cemetery in late October. Call the visitor's center for more information.

TRANSPORTATION

Amtrak, tel. (804) 526-4077, has a station at 3516 South St. in Ettrick, across the river on US 36 past Virginia State University. **Greyhound/Trailways,** tel. (804) 732-2905, is at 108 E. Washington St. at Adams. Local bus service is provided by Petersburg Area Transit, tel. (804) 733-2413.

INFORMATION

The 1815 home of mayor George Jones, has become the Petersburg **visitors center,** 425 Cockade Alley at Old St., tel. (800) 368-3595 or (804) 733-2400. Just south of the US 1/301 bridge, the McIlwaine House is open daily 9 a.m.-5 p.m. From April-Oct. you can buy block tickets to certain Petersburg sights. The Campaign Pass ($15 adults, $7 children) includes the Siege Museum, Trapezium House, Centre Hill, Farmer's Bank, Blandford Church, and the National Battlefield Park. The Cockade City Pass ($11 adults, $8 children) covers everything but the park.

FREDERICKSBURG AND VICINITY

The largest city between Washington, D.C., and Richmond, Fredericksburg eases up against a bend in the Rappahannock River just below its tumble over the fall line. The home of Mary Washington College and dozens of antique and relic shops, Fredericksburg (pop. 22,000) counts estates, battlefields, and a historic riverfront area among its attractions. Herb and flower gardens busting with tulip magnolias, crepe myrtles, and Bradford pear blossoms separate trim, neatly spaced houses in the downtown National Historic District. It's a popular escape from the Capitol and a good base for exploring the Northern and Middle Necks (see the **Coast** chapter).

History

Fredericksburg was established in 1727, named for the Prince of Wales and father of King George III. Wagons loaded with tobacco, flax, wheat, hemp, and flour rolled into the port city from surrounding farms for shipment downriver and on to Europe. George Washington spent part of his childhood at Ferry Farm across the Rappahannock. He attended school briefly in town and returned decades later to buy his mother Mary a house on Charles St. Trade was brisk at the Rappahannock falls, and Fredericksburg thrived for a time. Three-masted schooners docked in her port, and wealthy plantation owners enjoyed horse races and lavish balls.

Revolutionary fervor reached a peak in Fredericksburg in the 1770s as the courthouse green rang with the shouts of officers drilling their troops. In 1777 Thomas Jefferson, George Mason, and other founding fathers met in the Rising Sun Tavern to draw up the Virginia Statute of Religious Free-

dom, which would eventually become the First Amendment to the U.S. Constitution.

Its strategic position on the river, midway between the two capitals, put Fredericksburg and its 4,000 inhabitants in the middle of some of the Civil War's hottest fighting. From 1861-65 it changed hands seven times, but it was in 1862-63 that the city saw its worst moments. A Union bombardment two days before the Battle of Fredericksburg reduced most of the city to rubble.

THE VIRGINIA STATUTE OF RELIGIOUS FREEDOM

Passed by the Virginia Senate on January 16, 1786, Thomas Jefferson's landmark Virginia Statute of Religious Freedom separated church and state so effectively it became the basis for the First Amendment to the U.S. Constitution. Along with the University of Virginia and the Declaration of Independence, it was one of three things he ordered to be included in his epitaph: " . . . and not a word more . . . because by these, as testimonials that I have lived, I wish most to be remembered." (About one-third of the statute appears here.)

I. WHEREAS Almighty God has created the mind free, so that all attempts to influence it by temporal punishments or burdens, or by civil incapacitations, tend only to beget habits of hypocrisy and meanness . . .

II. BE IT . . . ENACTED BY THE GENERAL ASSEMBLY that no man shall be compelled to frequent or support any religious worship, place, or ministry whatsoever, nor shall be enforced, restrained, molested, or burdened in his body or goods, nor shall otherwise suffer on account of his religious opinions or belief; but that all men shall be free to profess, and by argument to maintain, their opinion in matters of religion, and that the same shall in no wise diminish, enlarge, or affect their civil capacities.

III. . . . AS WE ARE FREE to declare, and do declare, that the rights hereby asserted are of the natural rights of mankind, and that if any act shall hereafter be passed to repeal the present, or to narrow its operation, such act will be an infringement of natural right.

Thirty thousand occupying soldiers found little left to loot before their officers imposed order. Lincoln visited on May 20 to meet with his generals, and Clara Barton tended wounded Federal soldiers inside the Presbyterian church. In 1863 and 1864, Lee repeatedly trounced Grant in the fields to the west, resulting in 17,000 bodies to fill the Fredericksburg National Cemetery, part of the Fredericksburg and Spotsylvania National Military Park.

SIGHTS

Most of Fredericksburg's historic sites are preserved in a 40-acre National Historic District along the river. George Washington's younger brother Charles built the **Rising Sun Tavern,** 1306 Caroline St., tel. (540) 371-1494, around 1760. It served as a stagecoach stop and post office during its heyday, when a beer cost three times as much as a bed (which you might have had to share with four other people) and the bathwater was changed after every third person. Self-described "wenches" in colonial costume guide you through the separate rooms for women (resting and primping) and men (drinking and gambling), explaining along the way why tankards have glass bottoms, and the genesis of expressions such as "mind your Ps and Qs" and "cold shoulder." Open daily 9 a.m.-5 p.m. (Dec.-Feb. 10 a.m.-4 p.m.) for $4 adults, $1.50 children.

Some of the remedies at the **Hugh Mercer Apothecary Shop,** Caroline and Amelia Sts., tel. (540) 373-3362, are guaranteed to make you glad you weren't born 200 years ago. Mercer practiced here for 15 years, treating George Washington, among many other patients. He was killed in the Revolutionary War. Nowadays tour guides demonstrate tooth extractors, amputation tools, and the 18th-century inoculation technique for smallpox. Don't miss the tools for inducing bleeding, including a jarful of live leeches and a hand-held razor device (back then it was thought that human bodies

held 12 quarts of blood, a mistake that may have helped kill Washington.) Others medicines aren't so bad: cobwebs for open wounds, coltsfoot for asthma, and saffron to "quicken the brain." A pair of handblown glass bottles, exquisitely painted from the inside, stands on the shelves. Open daily 9 a.m.-5 p.m. (Dec.-Feb. 10 a.m.-4 p.m.); $4 adults, $1.50 children.

Mary Ball Washington spent the last 17 years of her life in the **Mary Washington House,** 1200 Charles St., tel. (540) 373-1569, bought for her by her son George. The simple home still contains some original pieces like china bearing the Washington family wheat pattern. Behind the building is a separate kitchen and a small garden that's been restored to Mary's standards. Open daily 9 a.m.-5 p.m., (Dec.-Feb. 10 a.m.-4 p.m.); $4 adults, $1.50 children. Furnishings, arts, weapons, and personal objects make up the collection of the **James Monroe Museum and Memorial Library,** 908 Charles St., tel. (540) 654-1043, e-mail: jmmuseum@mwc.edu, Web site: www.flstarweb/com/museum/tour. The fifth President was the only one besides Washington to fight in the Revolutionary War, and the only one to have a foreign capital named after him (Monrovia, Liberia). Mary Washington College administers the museum, which holds many pieces from the Monroe White House. Open daily 9 a.m.-5 p.m. (Dec.-Feb. 10 a.m.-4 p.m.); $4 adults, $1.50 children.

The **Fredericksburg Area Museum and Cultural Center,** 907 Princess Anne St., tel. (540) 371-5668, holds three floors of excellent exhibits

Fredericksburg Area Museum and Cultural Center

from the prehistoric to the present. The first floor is geared toward kids, with changing exhibits like the Age of Reptiles. They'll also like the Indian wigwam. On the second floor, Revolutionary-era pieces include a beautiful inlaid Hepplewhite sideboard and early 18th-century survey documents. Firearms and a shell-splintered door represent the Civil War, followed by Ku Klux Klan relics and whites-only signs that touch on 20th-century racial issues. A re-created council chamber and Civil War photos fill the third floor. Open Mon.-Sat. 10 a.m.-5 p.m., Sunday 1-5 p.m. (Dec.-Feb. Mon.-Sat. 10 a.m.-4 p.m., Sunday 1-4 p.m.); $4 adults, $1 children.

Incredible plasterwork by the same itinerant artist who decorated Mount Vernon is a highlight of the **Kenmore Plantation and Gardens,** 1201 Washington Ave., tel. (540) 373-3381, e-mail: mailroom@kenmore.org, Web site: www.kenmore.org. One of the rooms in the elegant 18th-century mansion, built for George Washington's brother-in-law and his wife, is considered one of the 100 most beautiful in the country. A wide lawn balances the elaborate boxwood gardens behind. Stop by the kitchen for a nip of tea and a cookie. Open March-Dec. Mon.-Sat. 10 a.m.-5 p.m., Sunday noon-5 p.m.; $6 adults, $3 children.

In 1752, Washington entered the **Masonic Lodge No. 4,** 803 Princess Anne St. at Hanover St., tel, (540) 373 5003, as an apprentice. Now a museum, the lodge includes the Bible on which Washington swore his Masonic oath. Open Mon.-Sat. 9 a.m.-4 p.m., Sunday 1-4 p.m.; $2 adults, $1 children. A few other buildings in downtown Fredericksburg are worth a visit, starting with the Greek Revival **Presbyterian Church,** at George and Princess Anne Streets. Built in 1833, it still has a cannon ball from the Union barrage imbedded in one wall. **St.**

George's Episcopal Church, on Princess Anne St. between George and William St., has a number of Tiffany windows. Union troops set up temporary barracks in the basement of the Victorian Gothic **courthouse** across George St., and watched the nearby battles from its cupola.

Colonial ladies once mounted horses from the small **slave auction block** at the corner of Charles and William Sts., and the **horse-chesnut tree** on Faquier St. between Charles and Edward is the only one left of 13 planted by George Washington to symbolize the original states.

DOWNTOWN FREDERICKSBURG

© MOON PUBLICATIONS, INC.

For information on the National Cemetery and visitors center at Marye's Heights, see **Fredericksburg and Spotsylvania National Military Park,** below.

ACCOMMODATIONS

Inexpensive

There's a **Best Western Johnny Appleseed,** 543 Warrenton Rd., tel. (540) 373-0000, fax 373-5676, near the intersection of US 17 and I-95; and the **Best Western Thunderbird Inn,** 3000 Plank Rd., tel. (540) 786-7404, fax 785-7415, sits next to the Spotsylvania Mall. Or, try the **Days Inn Fredericksburg South,** 5316 Jefferson Davis Hwy., tel./fax (540) 898-6800.

Moderate

The **Fredericksburg Colonial Inn,** 1707 Princess Anne St., tel. (540) 371-5666, fax 371-5697, looks like a everyday quality motel from the outside, but inside it has 22 rooms and 8 suites decorated with Civil War antiques, and a museum of Civil War relics and arms just off the lobby. At the south end of Old Town is the **Selby House,** 226 Princess Anne St., tel. (540) 373-7037, the only true B&B in town. Owner Jerry Selby is a Civil War buff with a dozen authentic rifles in his collection. He gives battlefield tours for $30 each or $100 per day.

Expensive

In this category are the **Sheraton Fredericksburg Inn,** 2801 Plank Rd., tel. (540) 786-8321, fax 786-0397, and the **Holiday Inn Fredericksburg South,** 5324 Jefferson Davis Hwy., tel. (540) 898-1102, fax 898-2017.

Premium

The **Kenmore Inn,** 1200 Princess Anne St., tel. (540) 371-7622 or (800) 327-7622, fax (540) 371-5480, has an award-winning restaurant with outdoor dining and an English Pub with jazz and blues on weekends. Guests can relax on the veranda facing Princess Anne St. or in front of the fireplace in the sitting room. Two-day packages, in the $300 range, include a romantic dinner for two, a light meal in the pub, and continental breakfasts. Facing the visitors center is the **Richard Johnston Inn,** 711 Caroline St., tel. (540) 899-7606, occupying a pair of joined townhouses built in the late 1700s by the mayor of Fredericksburg. Six sumptuous bedrooms and two suites are dressed out with antiques such as a huge mahogany queen bed from the 1830s, and a pair of Great Pyrenees will make quick friends of dog lovers (and maybe a few converts).

FOOD

Breakfast and Lighter Fare

Start things off with a $4 breakfast at the **Caroline Street Cafe,** 1002 Caroline St., tel. (540) 374-1136, which also sells burgers and sandwiches from 7:30 or 8 a.m. (10:30 on Sunday). **Goolrick's Pharmacy,** 901 Caroline St., tel. (540) 373-3411, is a step back in time with its 1940s soda fountain and lunch counter. They serve an inexpensive breakfast, homemade soups, and sandwiches along with the obligatory egg creams and floats. Pick up a box lunch for the battlefields at the **Olde Towne Wine and Cheese Deli,** 707 Caroline St., tel. (540) 373-7877, with Boar's Head sandwiches, fresh soups, and a Friday evening New Orleans dinner. Open Mon.-Sat. 11 a.m.-5 p.m.

Hyperion Espresso, 301 William St., tel. (540) 373-4882, serves the black diesel in an eye-catching setting, and **The Java Connection,** 615 Caroline St., tel. (540) 371-4435, also has bagels, chai, sweets, and a gift shop. **Barefoot Green,** 1017 Sophia St., tel. (540) 373-2012, is a restaurant, market, and carryout with seafood platters for $6-8. Open Thurs.-Sun. 11 a.m.-5 or 6 p.m.

More Substantial

Le Lafayette, 623 Caroline St., tel. (540) 373-6895, offers French cooking with a modern twist in a 1771 Georgian home known as The Chimneys. Gallic favorites like duck-liver paté and veal scallopine are served Tues.-Sun. for lunch and dinner. An alternate take on French is **Le Petit Auberge,** 311 William St., tel. (540) 371-2727, home to yet another D.C. chef who fled to the quieter reaches downstate. Local paintings hang on bare brick walls in the dining room adjoining a small pub. Excellent entrées like wild bay rockfish and baked brie are $5-15 for lunch and $10-20 for dinner, and there's an early-bird meal for $14, 5:30-7 p.m.

Smythe's Cottage and Tavern, 303 Faquier St., tel. (540) 373-1645, squeezes into a tiny, blue 19th century cottage. Notice the upside-down picture of Ulysses S. Grant in the tap room, and enjoy local staples like ham and biscuits, peanut soup, and Brunswick stew. Dining is available inside or on outside tables. Open for lunch and dinner Wed.-Mon.

Generous portions of authentic northern Italian dishes are standard at the **Ristorante Renato,** 422 Williams St., tel. (540) 371-8228. Lunch and dinner specials includes side dishes, dessert, and even a glass of wine (for dinner). Open for lunch Mon.-Fri., dinner daily. It may seem like an oxymoron, but **Sammy T's,** 801 Caroline St. at Hanover St., tel. (540) 371-2008, serves healthy pub fare like bean and grain burgers and an apple-cheddar melt. Sandwiches are around $6 and entrées $5-9. Open daily for all meals.

ENTERTAINMENT AND RECREATION

Shopping

You could outfit a mansion (or a brigade) with all the antiques and Civil War artifacts for sale along Caroline Street. Try the **Picket Post,** 602 Caroline St., tel. (540) 371-7703; **Historically Yours,** 820 Caroline St., tel. (540) 899-6229; and the **Antique Corner of Fredericksburg,** 900 Caroline St., tel. (540) 373-0826, for starters. Every weekend starting at 7 a.m. you can peruse seasonal produce, crafts, and antiques at the **Manor Mart Flea Market,** along US 1 just south of town.

Outdoors

The folks at **Outdoor Adventures,** 4721 Plank Rd., tel. (540) 786-3334, run canoe and kayak trips on Potomac Creek and the Rapidan and Rappahannock Rivers. Prices start at $35 for an afternoon and $200 for an overnight. They also rent camping gear and have classes in kayaking, rock climbing, and backpacking. **Friends of the Rappahannock Ecotourism,** 3219 Fall Hill Ave., tel. (540) 373-3448, e-mail: cleanriver@ pobox.com, Web site: www.cybercity.com/for, is a volunteer group aimed at preserving the river's beauty and health. Offered are interpretive canoe tours, guided hikes, and overnight trips for $5-40. For more paddle sports, check with **Rappa-**

hannock Outdoors, 3219 Fall Hill Ave., tel. (540) 371-5085, or **Clore Brothers Outfitters,** 5927 River Rd., tel. (540) 786-7749.

Tours

The Living History Company, tel. (540) 899-1776, leads a wide range of guided tours, from daylight history walks to lantern-lit "Phantoms of Fredericksburg" battlefield rambles. Town tours are $10 adults and $6 children, and battlefield rambles cost $40-80 for 2-4 hours. Buy tickets at the visitors center for **Trolley Tours of Fredericksburg,** tel. (540) 898-0737, which cover the major sights in town in 45 minutes. These run April-Nov. and cost $10 adults, $5 children.

Nightlife

Mary Washington students name **The Underground,** under the George St. Grill at 106 George St., tel. (540) 371-9500, as *the* place in town for acoustic and rock acts. Blues and folk are scheduled Wed.-Sat. at the **Irish Brigade Pub,** 1005 Princess Anne St., tel. (540) 371-9413.

EVENTS

The **Peach Blossom Festival** the first weekend in April sees celebrity chefs, crafts shows, and music concerts downtown and by the river. In June, the **Great Rappahannock Whitewater Canoe Race** paddles past. Some people take it seriously, and some slap together the most ridiculous craft that will float. The story of October's **Dog Mart** begins in pre-Revolutionary days when Indians were said to have traded furs for the settler's exotic animals. Revived in 1927, it's evolved into a small festival with music, food, and a dog parade. Also in October, on the first Saturday, there's a **Cheesecake Festival.** Think fattening dessert, not Jane Fonda in *Barbarella*—this is an occasion to sample numerous varieties of cheesecake in the sweet, "savory," and "special" categories. Check with Karla's Great Cheesecakes, 41 Cool Springs Rd., tel. (540) 371-3754, for information.

TRANSPORTATION

There's an **Amtrak** station at Princess Anne St. and Lafayette Blvd., with commuter service via

Alexandria to D.C.'s Union Station, and a **Greyhound/Trailways** depot at 1400 Jefferson Davis Hwy., tel. (540) 373-2103.

INFORMATION

Stop by the **Fredericksburg Visitor Center,** 706 Caroline St., tel. (800) 678-4748 or (540) 373-1776, for walking tour maps and a short movie on the area. They also have free parking passes and block tickets to area sights: the Hospitality Pass covers seven major sights in town for $19.75 adults, $7 children, and the self-explanatory Pick Four is $13.75 adults, $5.50 children. Open daily 9 a.m.-5 p.m.

ACROSS THE RIVER

Belmont

The home of American painter Gari Melchers (1860-1932) has been turned into a museum and park overlooking the river and city. The house dates to the turn of the 18th century, and was left untouched during the Federal occupation because its owner was a Union sympathizer. Many of Melchers's original furnishings, including a linen press and a series of plates designed to teach children the story of the Prodigal Son, reflect his fascination with Holland and the simple lives of the Dutch peasants that he painted repeatedly. A granite studio holds these works and famous portraits of Teddy Roosevelt and Mark Twain.

The house and studio, tel. (540) 654-1015, are open for tours Mon.-Sat. 10 a.m.-5 p.m., Sunday 1-5 p.m. (Dec.-Feb. Mon.-Sat. 10 a.m.-4 p.m.) for $4 adults, $1 children. By dictate of his widow's will, the gates to the peaceful parklike grounds—perfect for a picnic—are never locked.

Ferry Farm

In 1738 the Washington family moved to a small farm on the east bank of the Rappahannock, near a dock from which ferries ran to the newly founded city of Fredericksburg. Here, the future president, still only a child, would begin his education and grow up alongside three brothers and a sister. Ferry Farm is also the source of two of the more enduring Washington myths—the cherry tree and the silver dollar thrown across the river. At his death in 1743, Augustine Washington left Ferry Farm to George, who turned to surveying for income. Nine years later he inherited Mount Vernon from his half-brother Lawrence, leaving his mother in possession of Ferry Farm until he sold it in 1774 and moved her into town.

Excavations are still in progress, so there's not much to see beyond an archaeology lab, surveying office, and icehouse pit. Self-guided tour brochures point out what used to be where. The farm is under the auspices of Kenmore Plantation, tel. (540) 373-3381, and open daily dawn-dusk.

FREDERICKSBURG AND SPOTSYLVANIA NATIONAL MILITARY PARK

From 1862-64 some of the most brutal engagements ever fought on North American soil shook the landscape around Fredericksburg. It's estimated that 100,000 soldiers were killed on four major battlefields within 15 miles of the city.

Park headquarters are across the Rappahannock from Fredericksburg in **Chatham Manor,** 120 Chatham Ln., tel. (540) 371-0802, Web site: www.nps.gov/frsp. This Georgian mansion was built in 1771 with a commanding view from the riverside heights. A series of Union officers established command posts here, and Walt Whitman, Clara Barton, and Abraham Lincoln all passed through during the fighting (making it the only building both Lincoln and George Washington visited).

Battle of Fredericksburg

During the cold winter of 1862, Union Gen. Ambrose Burnside, who had replaced McClellan after his defeat at Antietam, MD, pursued Robert E. Lee south toward Richmond. Despite Lincoln's urgings for speed, Burnside had hesitated long enough to allow the Army of Northern Virginia to dig in on the high ground west of Fredericksburg by early December. Pontoon bridges across the icy Rappahannock were finally erected, in the face of Confederate sniper fire, and on December 13, 120,000 Federal troops poured across the river to attack Lee's force of 70,000.

Stonewall Jackson initially drove Gen. George Meade's forces back from Prospect Hill. Burnside then sent 30,000 troops to take Marye's Heights from 5,000 Confederate soldiers who were crouched behind a stone wall along the Sunken Road, and the real slaughter began. Wave after wave of Federal soldiers were mowed down by rifle fire from ahead and artillery shells from above. None came closer than 100 feet to the wall, but Burnside's orders held and the futile attacks continued until 8,000 men lay broken and dying.

A 19-year-old South Carolina infantryman named Richard Kirkland was so tormented by the cries of the wounded that he left the safety of the stone wall to offer men water from his canteen. Union gunners ceased fire at this act of mercy, and the Angel of Marye's Heights entered Civil War legend. Kirkland's deed is commemorated on the Sunken Road in a monument done by the same sculptor who created the Marine Corps Iwo Jima Memorial in Arlington.

Never had anyone present seen such a massacre. Viewing the battle, Lee said to Gen. James Longstreet: "It is well that war is so terrible, or we should grow too fond of it." "It can hardly be in human nature," wrote a Northern war correspondent, "for men to show more valor, or generals to manifest less judgment." Pacing in his tent the next day, Burnside was overheard muttering "Those men. Those men."

The **Fredericksburg National Cemetery** now occupies Marye's Heights in the center of the city. Over 15,000 soldiers are buried here, of whom only 15% have ever been identified. As you stand on the crest of the hill, imagine thousands of Federal troops swarming from the fields to the east "like some huge blue serpent," in the words of one Confederate witness, "about to encompass and crush us in its folds." At the foot of the slope a **visitors center**, tel. (540) 373-6122, sells tickets good for a week at the surrounding sites ($3 pp). You can also rent a tape to guide you along the 75-mile auto tour. It's open daily 9 a.m.-5 p.m.

Battle of Chancellorsville

Union spirits ran low after the debacle at Marye's Heights. In late April 1863 Gen. Joseph "Fighting Joe" Hooker replaced Burnside and set about reorganizing the Union forces and restoring morale. So as not to repeat Burnside's mistake, Hooker divided his 134,000 troops into two

It rained. The procession of weary soldiers became a bedraggled train, despondent and muttering, marching with churning effort in a trough of liquid brown mud under a low, wretched sky. Yet the youth smiled, for he saw that the world was a world for him, though many discovered it to be made of oaths and walking sticks. He had rid himself of the red sickness of battle. The sultry nightmare was in the past. He had been an animal blistered and sweating in the heat and pain of war. He turned now with a lover's thirst to images of tranquil skies, fresh meadows, cool brooks—an existence of soft and eternal peace.

Over the river a golden ray of sun came through the hosts of leaden rain clouds.

—Stephen Crane,
The Red Badge of Courage,
on the aftermath of Chancellorsville

groups and moved them across the Rapidan and Rappahannock Rivers to attack Lee from the west in a pincher movement.

True to form, Lee took the initiative and rushed west to attack first at Chancellorsville, after making the risky decision to leave 10,000 men under Maj. Gen. Jubal Early to defend the Fredericksburg position. Though outnumbered more than two to one, Lee threw his forces against the Union defensive lines. Jackson was sent with 25,000 troops on a 12-mile march to attack the Federal army from the west, which the savvy commander managed to pull off undetected—had he failed and Hooker attacked Lee's remaining 15,000, the Confederates would have been crushed.

As it happened, Jackson's brigade charged from the woods behind a terrified horde of deer and rabbits, destroying the Union right flank.

Fierce gunfire left nearby trees useless as lumber afterwards. The victory was short-lived, though, as Jackson was mistakenly shot by his Confederate guards while out scouting the battlefield at dusk on May 2. He died eight days later.

Meanwhile, Gen. John Sedgewick had finally wrested Marye's Heights away from Jubal Early. J.E.B. Stuart took over Jackson's position and drove Hooker back to the Rappahannock. The Union general withdrew his forces across the river and was relieved of command by Lincoln shortly thereafter. The Confederate army had won a huge victory, but lost one of their finest commanders.

The **Chancellorsville Visitor Center** on Rt. 3, tel. (540) 786-2880, is open daily 9 a.m.-5 p.m. A four-mile loop trail covers major sites and can be shortened to a 20-minute walk. A **battle reenactment** is held nearby in early May; call the Virginia Battlefield Trust, tel. (540) 374-0900, for more information.

Battle of the Wilderness

In March 1864 Ulysses S. Grant became commander-in-chief of all Union forces. He also gained a determination to track down and annihilate Lee at all costs. By May 5 Grant had marched almost within sight of the Confederate position around Fredericksburg. Once again Lee struck first in the tortured undergrowth west of Chancellorsville known as The Wilderness.

Federal coordination and their advantage of numbers dissolved in the confusion. Heavy gunfire ignited the dense brush, burning wounded soldiers to death in a hellish confusion of smoke and bullets. One Union survivor remembered it as "a blind and bloody hunt to the death, in bewildering thickets, rather than a battle." After two days of fighting both armies had lost close to 15% of their ranks: the Federals 17,500 and the Confederates 8,000.

The **Wilderness Exhibit Shelter** is on Rt. 20, 1.3 miles west of Rt. 3.

Battle of Spotsylvania Court House

Refusing to accept defeat at The Wilderness, Grant resolved to lead his army south, a decision greeted with cheers by his soldiers. Lee, however, won the race to Spotsylvania Court House, which controlled the shortest route to Richmond. Federal troops found themselves facing an entrenched Confederate army of 50,000, dug in behind hastily constructed earthworks.

"I propose to fight it out on this line if it takes all summer," Grant wrote Lincoln, but the battle was decided in just two weeks of the war's most savage combat. On May 20 the Battle of Bloody Angle raged around a bulge in the Rebel line called the Mule Shoe. Twenty hours of desperate hand-to-hand fighting in the pouring rain saw men trampled into knee-deep mud and others shot and bayoneted through gaps in the wooden breastworks. Point-blank cannon fire cut two-foot oaks in half, prompting one solider to remark later, "We had not only shot down an army, but also a forest." Days later the square-mile patch of ground that had cost 13,000 lives was abandoned by both sides.

Both armies, each a third smaller, eventually moved southeast together for 11 more months of fighting. While the Union could replace its fallen soldiers, the Confederacy could not, and Lee's goal changed to delay instead of victory.

The **Spotsylvania Exhibit Shelter** is on Rt. 613. Loop hiking trails up to seven miles long pass the Bloody Angle and Lee's final line.

Stonewall Jackson Shrine

After his accidental wounding, Jackson was moved to a plantation office in Guinea Station, where he died on May 10. Historians on duty lead tours through the building, tel. (804) 633-6076, which is open Fri.-Tues. 9 a.m.-6 p.m. (daily in the summer).

Accommodations

The morning of December 13, 1863, Robert E. Lee took breakfast in the dining room of a mansion across the street from his Fredericksburg headquarters. The fifth generation of the Howison family still owns the building, which they've turned into the **Braehead B&B**, 123 Lee Dr., tel. (540) 899-3648, fax 373-6989. Antiques, collected over a century and a half, include an 1868 piano and a silver service shipped to New York aboard the *Great Eastern* liner in 1851. Expensive.

Campers can choose from **Aquia Pines Camp Resort**, tel. (540) 659-3447, on US 1 just north of I-95 exit 143 ($20-27), or the **Rappahannock River Campground,** tel. (540) 399-1839, on the south side of the river on Rt. 683 from Rt. 619 ($5-15).

CHARLOTTESVILLE

Home to an eclectic mix of old values and liberal intellectualism, "C-Ville" combines fraternity parties and yoga groups, colonial architecture and Wal-Marts, all in a setting that's close to perfect—the Blue Ridge Mountains half an hour west, the ocean two hours east, and in every direction the acres roll and rivers wind. It's no wonder, then, that a 1995 article in *Outside* magazine listed Charlottesville (pop. 40,000) as one of the 10 most inviting small, outdoorsy cities in the country.

It's a wealthy town (just head out into the countryside in any direction to find estates galore) but surprisingly down-to-earth, with a strong community feeling. Coffee shops and bookstores abound near the University of Virginia, and the downtown mall teems with locals and tourists alike on summer evenings. In contrast, traffic chokes the glass-and-plastic corridor of US 29 north toward D.C., lined with shopping malls, office buildings, and supermarkets. A diverse local music scene boasts some impressive talent, and new plays and gallery shows open like dogwoods in the springtime.

HISTORY

Named in 1762 for Queen Charlotte, wife of George III, Charlottesville depended on Rivanna River trade until well into the 1800s. English soldiers and officers and Hessian mercenaries were incarcerated in barracks from 1799-80 (the origin of the name of Barracks Rd.), and a year later Col. Banastre Tarleton raided the town intent on capturing Thomas Jefferson and other revolutionary leaders. British troops destroyed stores of tobacco and seized the county courthouse, but a heroic 40-mile ride by Capt. Jack Jouett through pitch-dark forests—on a par with Paul Revere's historic gallop—enabled Jefferson to escape.

Along with Jefferson, Charlottesville has hosted over the years James Monroe, James Madison, and the exploring duo of William Clark (born in Buena Vista) and Meriwether Lewis (born near Ivy). Though it was positioned along one of the main roads from the coast to the mountains,

it remained a small town until the early 19th century. In 1822 Jefferson wrote:

In our village . . . there is a good degree of religion, with a small spice of fanaticism . . . Episcopalian and Presbyterian, Methodist and Baptist meet together . . . listen with attention and devotion to each others' preachers, and all mix in society in perfect harmony.

When Jefferson opened the University of Virginia in 1825, the town consisted of 600 people, a courthouse, a church-in-progress, and a handful of taverns. River traffic faded after the Virginia Central Railroad reached Charlottesville in 1848, and many University buildings became hospitals during the Civil War. Sheridan's troops did little damage when they occupied the town in 1865. When chartered as a city in 1888, Charlottesville's population was 4,200.

ORIENTATION

Charlottesville really has two downtown areas: the elbow of University Ave./Main St. known as "the Corner," and the historic district around the downtown mall. West Main St. connects the two. The first few miles of US 29 north toward Culpeper is crammed with shopping centers, fast-food restaurants, and service stations. Often the easiest way to get from one end of town to the other is to hop on the US 250 bypass, which loops around the northern side, or on I-64 as it cruises by to the south.

SIGHTS

University of Virginia
In his epitaph, Thomas Jefferson wished to be remembered—right next to penning the Declaration of Independence—as the father of the University of Virginia. At the time, his idea of an "academical village" was pushing the envelope; in the guise of the first secular college in the

CHARLOTTESVILLE AREA CLIMATE

SNOWFALL — MAXIMUM TEMP.
RAINFALL — MINIMUM TEMP.

sand for a beach blowout in February). Centuries-old secret societies hold mystical ceremonies, paint their symbols on buildings, and disburse the occasional unsolicited donation to needy causes. In school lingo, a "freshman" is called a "first-year" and so on up the ladder—and don't let anyone hear you call the *grounds* a "campus."

But gradual change seeps in among the most entrenched traditions. Once an old-boy's club of the highest order, U.Va. went coed in the early '70s. A sizable "alternative" subculture supports bands with strange names and more than a few left-leaning publications. Large percentages of the student body claim African-American or Asian ancestry.

The Lawn has been declared a World Heritage Site as well as an "outstanding achievement of American architecture" by the American Institute of Architects. At the head of the grassy, sloping expanse stands the striking white dome of the Rotunda, modeled after the Pantheon in Rome. Jefferson envisioned the grounds as a living architectural museum where students couldn't help but be inspired to learn, so each of the 10 **pavilions** reflects a different classical style. Notice how they're set farther apart heading downslope, to account for perspective when seen from the Rotunda. The pavilions are still divided between professors' residences and classrooms, though now only a select few seniors—sorry, *fourth-years*—get to live in the Lawn's tiny brick rooms, which is still considered an honor even if the bathrooms are outside and around the corner. Many rooms have their own story—one occupied by Edgar Allan Poe has been sealed off with glass. Behind each is a unique garden lined by distinctive serpentine brick walls (for stability as well as beauty).

The Rotunda is open daily 9 a.m.-4:45 p.m. Free, lively tours are offered five times a day every month but December by the University Guides, whose ranks are filled in an annual competition. For more information on the University and events call (804) 924-0311, or stop by the **University Information Center,** tel. (804) 924-7166, on Ivy Rd. near the US 250 bypass intersection.

The outstanding **Bayly Art Museum,** tel. (804) 924-3592, is a block down Rugby Rd. from the Rotunda. Opened in 1935, it boasts a permanent collection of art from the 15th to 19th centuries with an emphasis on American works, especially those from Jefferson's era (1775-1825). A dozen

country, Jefferson planned to bring the values and intellectual excitement of the Enlightenment to America. Ground was broken in 1819 within sight of Monticello, where in his later years Jefferson could gaze down on his pet project. The school opened in 1825 with 68 students and 10 teachers, consisting of the present-day central Lawn and surrounding buildings.

Today, UVA ("U-V-A," or simply "The University") is one of the highest-rated state universities in the country, excelling in English—former poet laureate Rita Dove teaches writing—and its numerous graduate schools: business, law, and medicine. Most of the approximately 20,000 Cavaliers (the nickname comes from the school's nationally ranked football team) hail from northern Virginia suburbs, and competition for admission among out-of-staters is fierce. Tradition lives on in the fraternities and sororities clustered along Rugby Road, where parties reach epic proportions (one house fills its entire ground floor with

CHARLOTTESVILLE

DETAIL

MARTHA'S CAFE
TWO MOONS KITCHEN
LIQUID SMOOTHIE AND JUICE BAR
CAFE EUROPA
RED ROOF INN
BODO'S BAGELS
THE VIRGINIAN
WHITE SPOT
UNIVERSITY HOSPITAL
ORBIT BILLIARDS & CAFE
1817 HISTORIC BED AND BREAKFAST

To Barboursville
To Clifton, The County Inn, Keswick Hall
To Richmond
To Ash Lawn-High and
MONTICELLO HOME
To Carter's Mtn.
MICHIE TAVERN
Riverview Park
CHARLOTTESVILLE-ALBEMARLE INFORMATION CENTER
To The Inn at Monticello and Charlottesville KOA
To Airport
ENGLISH INN OF CHARLOTTESVILLE
HOLIDAY INN UNIVERSITY AREA
BODO'S BAGELS
BLUE RIDGE BREWING COMPANY
SOUTHERN CULTURE
DOWNTOWN MALL
AMTRAK
GREYHOUND/TRAILWAYS
BLUE BIRD CAFE
HAMPTON INN AND SUITES
UNIVERSITY HOSPITAL
BUDGET INN
UNIVERSITY HALL
KLOCKNER STADIUM
BEST WESTERN CAVALIER INN
UNIVERSITY OF VIRGINIA
ROTUNDA
THE LAWN
CABELL HALL
ANNA'S PIZZA #5
SCOTT STADIUM
UNIVERSITY POLICE AND VISITOR INFORMATION CENTER
OBSERVATORY HILL
To Foxfield
To Waynesboro
To Bellair Market, Boar's Head Inn, Waynesboro
SEE DETAIL

0 0.5 mi
0 0.5 km

© MOON PUBLICATIONS, INC.

or so temporary exhibits, from Rodin to Australian aboriginal bark paintings, get floor space every year. Open Tues.-Sun. 1-5 p.m., free.

Downtown Mall
Charlottesville's pedestrian mall on W. Main St. between 2nd St. E and 6th St. E has become an example for similar structures around the country. Trees, fountains, benches, and whimsical statues mingle with outdoor cafes, unique shops, and vendors selling everything from Mennonite bread to Rastafarian incense. The controversial addition, in the mid 1990s, of a six-screen movie theater and ice rink to the west end has turned out to be a crowd-drawing blessing in disguise, even though it opened a cross-street to traffic.

At the eastern end is the **Virginia Discovery Museum,** tel. (804) 977-1025, with hands-on science and history exhibits, including an authentic colonial log house and a working beehive. It's open Tues.-Sat. 10 a.m.-5 p.m., Sunday 1-5 p.m.; $4 adults, $3 children under 13.

Other Downtown Sights
A few blocks off the mall sits the **Albemarle County Courthouse,** 501 E. Jefferson St. at 5th St. E, the historical hub of downtown activity since its completion in 1860. Jefferson's will and some of his correspondence are stored inside. The **McGuffey Art Center,** 201 2nd St. E. between Jefferson and Market, tel. (804) 295-7973, occupies an old school named for Dr. William McGuffey, author of the *McGuffey Eclectic Reader* series for children at the turn of the 20th century. Close to 50 artists have workshops and studios here, sharing gallery space with rotating exhibits and dance performances. Open Tues.-Sat. 10 a.m.-5 p.m., Sunday 1-5 p.m.; free.

Monuments
Robert E. Lee astride Traveler graces a small park at the corner of Jefferson and 1st St. E., and a dynamic **Stonewall Jackson** urges Little Sorrel forward from Jefferson and 4th St. East. The **Lewis and Clark** statue at Main St. and Ridge St. is the subject of occasional protests for its depiction of their female Indian guide, Sacajawea, in a kneeling, subservient position. **William Clark,** explorer of the Northwest territory, stands at W. Main St. and Jefferson Park Ave.

UVA's Rotunda was modeled after the Pantheon in Rome.

ACCOMMODATIONS

Services
Guesthouses Bed and Breakfast, Inc., tel. (804) 979-7264, fax 293-7791, e-mail: 105275.1620@compuserve.com, Web site: www.va-guesthouses.com, arranges stays in B&Bs and private cottages throughout Albemarle County. It's open Mon.-Fri. noon-5 p.m.

Inexpensive
The **Red Roof Inn,** 1309 Main St., tel. (804) 295-4333, is right on the Corner. At the intersection of Emmet St. (US 29) and Ivy Rd./University Ave. are a **Budget Inn,** 140 Emmet St., tel. (804) 293-5141, fax 293-5143, and the **Best Western Cavalier Inn,** 105 Emmet St., tel. (804) 296-8111, fax 296-3523.

Moderate
The antique-themed **English Inn of Charlottesville,** 2000 Morton Dr., tel. (804) 971-9900, fax (804) 977-8008, sits in the elbow of US 29 and the Rt. 250 bypass, opposite the **Holiday Inn University Area,** 1600 Emmet St., tel. (804) 293-9111, fax (804) 977-2780.

Expensive
The new **Hampton Inn and Suites,** tel. (804) 923-8600, is at 900 W. Main St. Just as central is the **1817 Historic Bed & Breakfast,** 1211 W. Main St., tel. (804) 979-7353 or (800) 730-7443,

fax (804) 979-7209, Web site: www.symweb. com/1817. It's actually two townhouses built by Thomas Jefferson's master craftsman James Dinsmore, who left his mark on Monticello, Montpelier, and Poplar Forest. If anything in the convertible clutter strikes your fancy, you might be able to take it home: Candice Deloach runs the place as an antiques store too, with the help of Mississippi and Virginia, a pair of black labs. Rates include a "continental plus" breakfast, and The Tea Room Cafe serves lunch daily, featuring entrées such as tarragon chicken salad and avocado melts.

The **Omni Charlottesville**, 235 W. Main St., tel. (804) 971-5500, fax 979-4456, anchors the east end of the Downtown Mall. It has two pools, a fitness center, and the Virginia Wine Country Restaurant featuring local vintages. Since it was built in 1856, **200 South Street**, tel. (800) 964-7008 or (804) 979-0200, fax 979-4403, e-mail: clancyb@cfw.com, it has passed through various phases as a boarding house, brothel, and girls' finishing school. A columned neoclassical veranda wraps all the way around the cream-colored building, perfect for an evening cup of tea. English and Belgian antiques and a private collection of local historical photos decorate the interior. Rooms include whirlpool baths, canopy beds, and a continental breakfast.

Premium

Take Monticello Ave. (Rt. 20) south past I-64 and the visitors center to reach **The Inn at Monticello**, 1188 Scottsville Rd. (Rt. 20) tel. (804) 979-3593, fax 296-1344, Web site: www.innatmonticello.com. Built around 1850 at the foot of Monticello Mountain, this country inn roared in the 1920s with a horse racing track and swimming pool in the front yard. Twin fireplaces face each other across the main entrance room where famous gourmet breakfasts are served. Upstairs are five bedrooms, some of which have fireplaces, private porches, and period antiques. To fill the afternoons there's a croquet, a hammock, and checkers on the front porch.

Luxury

Opened on the Downtown Mall in 1997, the **Downtown Inn**, 213 E. Water St., tel. (804) 977-3746, fax 977-6991, occupies the second floor of a 1901 building, above a restaurant and catering business. Convertible guest rooms with pressed-tin ceilings share a six-person hot tub under a skylight and a common sitting room overlooking the mall. The **Boar's Head Inn & Sports Club,** tel. (800) 476-1988 or (804) 296-2181, fax 972-6024, e-mail: bhi@cfw.com, Web site: www.boarsheadinn. com, is on Rt. 250 two miles west of town. The 53-acre country estate has 175 rooms and suites furnished with Colonial art and reproductions. Dining choices include the four-star Old Mill Room and the somewhat more casual Racquets Restaurant. A daily wine tasting is held off the main lobby. Guests have access to their famous Sport Club with its Birdwood championship golf course, a top-rated tennis facility, pool, and gym. If this isn't enough, try an afternoon at the Just Rewards spa or a flight in a hot air balloon (see **Recreation,** below).

It's a little farther to **Keswick Hall,** 701 Country Club Dr., Keswick, tel. (804) 979-3440 or (800) 274-5391, fax 977-4171, but guests who can afford it won't be disappointed. Sir Bernard Ashley (husband of designer Laura) turned this 1912 Italianate villa into an exclusive country club/resort intended to feel like someone's home rather than a hotel. Hence there's no concierge desk, but there is a lounge with a fireplace opening onto a patio overlooking the hills rolling into the distance. Laura Ashley fabrics decorate each room in a different theme, all reflecting the couple's hobbies, such as sailing and lepidoptery. Guests are spoiled with head chef Rick Small's French and Italian cuisine, including a Sunday brunch of smoked fish, eggs benedict, imported cheese, and champagne ($25 pp). Accommodations include temporary membership to the Keswick Club, boasting one of Arnold Palmer's favorite golf courses on the East Coast, tennis courts, spa, and pools. To get there take Rt. 250 east to Shadwell, take Rt. 22 east for 1.5 mile and follow the signs. E-mail: keswick@keswick.com, Web site: www.keswick.com.

In the same direction off Rt. 729 is **Clifton: The Country Inn,** 1296 Clifton Inn Dr., tel. (804) 971-1800 or (888) 971-1800, fax (804) 971-7098, e-mail: reserve@cstone.net, Web site: www.cliftoninn.com, named by *Country Inns* magazine as one of the 12 top inns in America. The manor house was built around 1800 as an office for Thomas Mann Randolph, Thomas Jefferson's son-in-law, who liked it so much he moved in. Each of the 14 rooms is unique, and private guest cottages like the Livery, Carriage House, and Randolph's Law Office are all within a stone's throw of the Rivanna River. A lap pool flows into a waterfall near the hot tub and clay tennis court. Rates include a continental breakfast and afternoon tea. Chef/innkeeper Craig Hartman's nightly five-course gourmet dinners are $50-60 pp.

Camping

The **Charlottesville KOA**, 3825 Red Hill Rd., tel. (804) 296-9881, is on Rt. 708 south of the city. You can get there via I-64 east exit 118A and US 29 south, or I-64 west exit 121 and Rt. 20 south. It's open March-Nov., with full hook-up sites for $20-25 and cabins for $30.

FOOD

On The Corner

Two UVA alumni opened the **Liquid Smoothie and Juice Bar**, 104 14th St. W, tel. (804) 295-3775, a vegetarian cafe with a brain-freezing array of fruit smoothies. Sandwiches like roasted red pepper hummus on wheat fall in the $4 range, accompanied by homemade soups (try the ginger and apple with squash), wheatgrass shots, and soya milk chai. If you need a boost ask for an extra shot of ginseng, kava-kava, or St. John's Wort in your Energizer or Mood Enhancer. Open Mon.-Fri. 8 a.m.-10 p.m., Saturday 10 a.m.-10 p.m., Sunday 11 a.m.-8 p.m. Just around the corner, **Cafe Europa**, 1331 W. Main St., tel. (804) 295-4040, offers a Greek version of light, healthy fare, with soups, salads, sandwiches, and baklava served daily for all meals.

Continuing on the nutritious theme, **Two Moons Kitchen**, 109 14th St. W, tel. (804) 923-3494, serves up fat burritos like the Birdie Num-Num or the Burning Pig, (or invent your own from a selection including organic bison and summer squash salsa). Vegan tamales, flan, and gingered lemonade are other options. Open daily for lunch and dinner. They've also expanded to the Downtown Mall with **Two Moons To Go**, 110 2nd St. E., tel. (804) 293-5709, open for lunch only.

Martha's Cafe, 11 Elliewood Ave., tel. (804) 971-7530, has healthy, vegetable-heavy entrées inside and on the patio of a charming old house. At the end of the same street the **Buddhist Biker Bar & Grill**, tel. (804) 971-9181, has a modern menu with a wry twist. Lamb lentil chili, duck tacos, and the "Big ol' hunk of beef" (ribeye) are $9-14, served on the brick patio and two outdoor decks in nice weather. Open daily for dinner.

The Virginian, 1521 W. Main St., tel. (804) 984-4667, is Charlottesville's oldest restaurant. It's been a keystone of the Corner proper since 1921, and still offers the same dependable eats and beer as always. Entrées start at $9 for pasta and include an $11 catfish platter and $13 filet mignon. Sandwiches, soups, and quiches run $5-6. Open daily for lunch and dinner. By now we've left the realm of the heart-friendly, but that's the attraction of the **White Spot**, 1407 University Ave., tel. (804) 295-9899. This quintessential greasy spoon is famous for its Gusburger, topped by a fried egg and usually devoured at 2 a.m. during the stumble home. Open daily for all meals.

West Main Street

The **Blue Ridge Brewing Co.**, 709 W. Main St., tel. (804) 977-0017, was opened by William Faulkner's grandsons in 1988 as the first brewpub in the state. Appetizers such as smoked trout wontons and romano artichoke dip are standouts, along with the beers—try an Afton Ale or Humpback Stout to go with your salmon pasta. There's also a long daily specials list ($9-14). Open for lunch and dinner. A few doors down is **Southern Culture**, 633 W. Main St., tel. (804) 979-1990, true to its roots with baked Virginia ham, Georgia peach cobbler, and sweet potato pie. Cajun and Caribbean influences put jambalaya and jerk pork on the menu—served leisurely but worth the wait. A popular bar almost fills the first floor. Open daily for dinner.

Another few steps brings you to the **Blue Bird Cafe**, 625 W. Main St., tel. (804) 295-1166, a good place for a sunny California-style lunch on the front patio. Jumbo salads, veggie burgers, and tuna steaks barely leave room for homemade desserts like chocolate bourbon pecan pie. Open Mon.-Fri. for lunch, dinner daily, and Sunday brunch.

Downtown Mall

Asian-leaning contemporary is the idea at **Eastern Standard**, tel. (804) 295-8668, where pomegranate lamb chops and other entrées are $15-22 for dinner Wed.-Sat. It's on the second floor above **Escafe,** more economical but just as stylish. Appetizers like spicy sesame noodles are $2-8, followed by pasta and chicken entrées for $7-14. The bar is one of *the* places to been seen downtown. Open for dinner Tues.-Sun. A lot of research went into creating the ultimate coffeehouse, resulting in the **Mudhouse,** tel. (804) 984-6833, with comfy sofas, Internet computer, and live music some weekend nights.

The **Monsoon Cafe,** tel. (804) 971-1515, draws influences from all over Asia for its Thai noodles, Burmese ginger curry, miso soup, and Vietnamese coffee. Think twice before specifying your spiciness, from 1 ("mild") to 5 ("lick the sun"). Local artist Stephen Keane did the wild paintings on the walls and tables. It's in the back of a small shopping arcade just to the right of the Mudhouse, and open Mon.-Fri. for lunch, daily for dinner. **Sylvia's,** tel. (804) 977-0162, has the best pizza on the mall; order it by the slice or a whole pie. Just next door is the **Hardware Store,** tel. (804) 977-1518, a real (former) hardware store—shelves perch over the old-time soda fountain and condiments are served in a tool box. An encyclopedia of inexpensive sandwiches ($4-6) fills the menu, along with meter beers, sundaes galore, crepes, and knishes. **Bashir's Gourmet Take Out,** tel. (804) 923-0927, was twice voted Best Ham in New York City for its apricot-glazed ham sandwich, served on a roll with a slice of brie. Other dishes show Armenian and Hungarian influences. Open Mon.-Sat. 7 a.m.-7 p.m. or later.

The Pepsi sign out front doesn't seem to promise much, but the **C&O Restaurant,** 515 E. Water St., tel. (804) 971-7044, across from the old train station, is often called the best in town. Brick walls and worn wood floors give it the feel of an old country home inside, the perfect setting for innovative French cooking. Try an appetizer like wild mushrooms in puff pastry ($3-8) before digging into a Cuban steak or rockfish baked in parchment ($12-18). Open Mon.-Fri. for lunch, daily for dinner. Across the Mall the **Court Square Tavern,** 5th St. at Jefferson St., tel. (804) 296-6111, offers tavern favorites like shepherd's pie and a brewer's bible of beers in an atmosphere fitting its historic location.

Elsewhere

The **Bellair Market,** 2401 Ivy Rd., tel. (804) 971-6608, is another case where looks are deceiving. From the deli inside this Exxon gas station comes specialty sandwiches as good as any in town. Mouthfuls like the Keswick, Montpelier, and Ednam are $4-6, with some vegetarian options. Who knows what happened to the first four, but **Anna's Pizza #5,** 115 Maury Ave., tel. (804) 977-6228, serves some of the best in town. **Foods of All Nations,** 2121 Ivy Rd., tel. (804) 296-6131, is an international gourmet grocery *par excellence,* with everything from sandwiches to sushi available to go.

And last is a Charlottesville tradition: **Bodo's Bagel Bakery,** serving thousands of authentic New-York style "water" (i.e., boiled) bagels every day. A long line at mealtimes is a given at each of its three locations—1418 N. Emmet St. (Rt. 20), tel. (804) 977-9598; 505 Preston Av., tel. (804) 293-5224; and 1609 University Ave., tel. (804) 293-6021—but whether you're on a budget or not, you just can't beat the bagel sandwiches for $1.50-3, famous Caesar salads, and homemade soups. Open early for breakfast and lunch daily, until 8 p.m. Mon.-Sat., 3 p.m. on Sunday.

ENTERTAINMENT

The local *C-Ville Weekly* is a good source for entertainment news and schedules. The Piedmont Council of the Arts operates an **Artsline,** tel. (804) 980-3366, with details on local happenings.

Performing Arts

Charlottesville's premiere performance space is **Live Arts,** 609 E. Market St., tel. (804) 980-2779, with a year-round schedule of theater, poetry, dance, performance art, and music. The **Community Children's Theater,** tel. (804) 961-7862, organizes kid's shows at the Charlottesville Performing Arts Center, 1400 Melbourne Rd., tel. (804) 979-9532, and at the Performing Arts Center of the Charlottesville High School on Grove Rd. Call the **Charlottesville and University Symphony Orchestra,** tel. (804) 925-6505, for their most recent performance schedule.

At the University, the **McIntire Department of Music,** tel. (804) 924-3984, is the place to ask about shows by the Jazz Ensemble, Collegium

Musicum, or various singing groups such as the University Singers and Hullabahoos. Call the **Drama Department,** tel. (804) 924-3376, for information on seasonal plays.

Theaters

Independent cinema is the hallmark of the **Vinegar Hill Theater,** 220 W. Market St., tel. (804) 977-4911, which recently opened a restaurant. U.Va.'s **Cinematheque,** tel. (804) 924-7900, also shows artsy films and college classics in the basement of Newcomb Hall. Opened in 1912, the **Jefferson Theater,** on the Downtown Mall, tel. (804) 980-1331, has hosted the Three Stooges and Harry Houdini over the years. Now it's one of those second-run movie houses that mysteriously—but thankfully—stays in business despite only charging $1.50 per seat.

Nightlife

For its size, Charlottesville has an astonishing amount of local musical talent. It's best known as the home of The Dave Matthews Band (and as the "next Seattle" in an often-scoffed *Newsweek* quote). Dave himself used to tend bar at Miller's, and local jazz guru John D'Earth has toured with Bonnie Raitt and Bruce Hornsby. Other star-quality resident performers include guitarist Tim Reynolds and drummer Robert Jospe. Even local rockers seem to stay a notch above the usual white noise.

If you only have one night to go out, catch D'Earth's jazz group on a Thursday night at **Miller's,** tel. (804) 971-8511, on the Downtown Mall—you don't hear bop this hopping for so little money very often. Red neon lights the smoky bar, which used to be a hardware store. Also on the Mall, the **Jewish Mother,** tel. (804) 984-0204, has a restaurant downstairs and a bar area above where local and national bands play.

Students and townspeople alike pack the grassy amphitheater at the western end of the mall for the beer truck and live music sponsored by Charlottesville's **Fridays After Five** concert series, tel. (804) 296-8548. Bring a blanket and a snack and get down to everything from funk and rock to blues and country. Concerts are held April-Sept.

On the Corner is **Orbit Billiards & Cafe,** 102 14th St. NW, tel. (804) 984-5707, which hosts the occasional folk or blues jam. **Trax,** 120 11th St. SW, tel. (804) 295-8729, has been Char-

lottesville's top live-music club for years, hosting everyone from Wynton Marsalis to Pavement. Tickets are available at the door, Plan 9 records, Mincer's on the Corner, or from tel. (800) 594-8499 for big-name shows. **Max** next door has country music and line dancing.

Sushi bar by day, musical hot-spot by night, **Tokyo Rose,** tel. (804) 295-7673, books cacophonous local groups and established indie-rockers. If you're going to catch the Next Big Thing, chances are it'll be here. The **Outback Lodge,** 917 Preston Ave., tel. (804) 979-7211, brings regional and national blues and rock to Preston Plaza at Rose Hill Dr., and hidden among the fraternity mansions of Rugby Road is the **Prism Coffeehouse,** 214 Rugby Rd., tel. (804) 977-7476, Web site: www.theprism.org, a local gem that hosts national bluegrass, folk, and acoustic acts.

RECREATION

Spectator Sports

Cavalier **football** games at U.Va.'s Scott Stadium are as much a display of tradition as school spirit. Semi-formal attire is the norm, especially among the fraternities and sororities. Wait for the song after each home-team touchdown, sung (or at least hummed) to the tune of "Auld Lang Syne." A strong **soccer** program has turned out powerhouse teams and sent members to the Olympics. Games are held in Klockner Stadium next to University Hall, where you'll catch **basketball** games. Call (800) 542-8821 or (804) 924-8821 or browse www.virginiasports.com for schedules.

Two major steeplechase events are held every year at **Foxfield,** tel. (804) 293-8160, about five miles out Barracks Rd. into the countryside after it turns into Garth Rd. One occurs the last Saturday in April, the other the final Sunday in September, and both are full-day occasions complete with tailgate picnics, socializing, and hip-flask nipping (among Cavaliers, at least).

Outdoors

At the **Ivy Creek Natural Area,** 2.3 miles west on Hydraulic Rd. from US 29 north, thirteen trails explore 215 acres of maples, walnut, poplars, and hemlocks. Call the Ivy Creek Foundation, tel. (804) 973-7772, for information. **Riverview Park** borders a bend of the Rivanna River east of downtown.

For the best view of Charlottesville—as good as Monticello's, if not better—take a right turn on the way up to the historic home (see below for directions). A steep, winding dirt road tops the next mountaintop over, where you'll find an apple orchard and 360-degree view from the observation deck.

Hot-air balloon flights can be booked through the **Bear Balloon Corporation,** tel. (804) 971-1757; **Bonaire Charters,** tel. (804) 293-3561; and the **Blue Ridge Flight Center,** tel. (804) 978-2114, near the airport. Prices are typically $135-185 pp.

The **Charlottesville Department of Parks and Recreation,** tel. (804) 970-3589, has more details on local outdoor pursuits.

Other Activities

You can carve the rink at the **Charlottesville Ice Park,** tel. (804) 979-1423, even in the middle of the Piedmont's summer swelter. Anchoring one end of the Downtown Mall, it has a skating school, hockey leagues, and public skating time along with a pro shop, rentals, and lessons. A **walking tour** with the Charlottesville Historical Society, tel. (804) 296-1492, is a pleasant way to see the historic downtown area. One-hour walks leave from the McIntire Building, at 200 2nd St. NE, from April-Oct. at 10 a.m. on Saturdays; suggested donation is $3 pp.

SHOPPING

The Downtown Mall has Charlottesville's best browsing-per-block quotient. Here you'll find **Copernicus,** at 1st St., tel. (804) 296-6800, with a wide range of brain-rousing children's toys, and **Vivian's Art to Wear,** tel. (804) 977-8908, which sells clothes, sculpture, and other crafts from regional artists. The front section of the **Hardware Store** restaurant, tel. (804) 977-1518, is a minimall complete with confectioner, bookstore, and small shops selling Mexican art and jewelry.

Stop by the **Signet Gallery,** at 5th St., tel. (804) 296-6463, for ceramics, wood, leather, and glass goods, and if you have room in your luggage for an oriental rug try **T.S. Eways,** tel. (804) 979-3038, or the **Sun Bow Trading Co.,**

108 4th St. NE, tel. (804) 293-8821. For a great selection of Virginia wine and good advice on choosing, visit the **Market Street Wineshop** and Gourmet Grocery, 311 E. Market St., tel. (804) 979-9463.

EVENTS

In February and March the **UVA Jazz Festival** brings performers like Elmore Jones and Tony Williams. Every year it has a different theme, like bassists or drummers. Mid-April's **Dogwood Festival,** is Charlottesville's largest. For two weeks the delicate blooms are the occasion for fireworks, a carnival, barbecue, and city-wide parade.

The **Monticello Wine and Food Festival** in early October starts with a seven-course Bacchanalian Feast at the Boar's Head Inn. That same month the **Virginia Festival of American Film,** tel. (800) 882-3378 or (804) 924-3378, Web site: www.virginia.edu/~vafilm, celebrates the silver screen with, premieres, critical analyses, and visits from nationally known actors.

TRANSPORTATION

Getting Around

Charlottesville is best appreciated by foot, especially since convenient parking is at a premium. Things are a bit spread out, though, so it's a good thing the **Charlottesville Transit Service,** 425 Fourth St. NW, tel. (804) 296-7433, sends buses around the city and county. Hop aboard the **University Transit Service,** tel. (804) 924-7711, to get around the University area. For taxi service try **Yellow Cab,** tel. (804) 295-4131.

Getting There and Away

There's a **Greyhound/Trailways** bus terminal at 310 W. Main St., tel. (804) 295-5131. Trains leave the **Amtrak** station, 810 W. Main St., tel. (804) 296-4559, three times a week for Washington, D.C., and daily for New York and Chicago. The **Charlottesville-Albemarle Airport,** tel. (804) 973-8341, e-mail: boe@cfw.com, Web site: www.cho-airport.state.va.us, is eight miles north of town on the west side of US 29. It's served by USAir Express, Comair, Continental Express, United Express, and Colgan Air. It also has three car rental agencies: Avis, tel. (804) 973-6000; Budget, tel. (804) 974-6122; and National, tel. (804) 974-4664.

INFORMATION

The **Charlottesville-Albemarle Information Center,** tel. (804) 293-6789, fax (804) 295-2176, e-mail: caccbb@comet.net, is just south of the intersection of Monticello Ave. (Rt. 20 south) and I-64. Among the best-equipped in the state, it has a gift and book shop and a small museum on Thomas Jefferson. If you have time before you head uphill to Monticello, catch the free 30-minute film on Jefferson's life and home shown at 11 a.m. and 2 p.m. On sale is a President's Pass block ticket that covers Monticello, Mitchie Tavern, and Ash-Lawn Highland for $20 adults, $11 children 6-11 (also available at each location). The #8 "Piedmont College" bus from 5th St. and Market St. will drop you off here. Open daily 9 a.m.-5 p.m.

A great Internet site for Charlottesville info is www.cjp.com/guide.

CHARLOTTESVILLE VICINITY

NORTH OF CHARLOTTESVILLE

Barboursville Vineyards

Virginia governor James Barbour lived here from 1810-1815, in a mansion designed by Thomas Jefferson (which accounts for the octagonal central room). It burned on Christmas Day 1884, leaving a roofless brick hulk with columns pointing skyward. The ruins are a great place for a picnic accompanied by a bottle of wine from the winery. If you can, come by in late July or early August when the Four County Players, tel. (540) 832-5355, perform their annual **Shakespeare in the Ruins** under the stars.

The winery, tel. (540) 832-3824, e-mail: bvvy@barboursville.com, Web site: www.barbousvillewine.com, is near the intersection of Rt. 20 and Rt. 23. Open Mon.-Sat. 10 a.m.-5 p.m., Sun 11 a.m.-5 p.m.

Montpelier

James Madison, most well known as the chief proponent of the Federal Bill of Rights, was actually the third generation of his family to make his home here on 2,700 acres of Piedmont farmland. His father built the original red-brick Georgian house, which Madison himself enlarged upon twice under the advisement of Thomas Jefferson. In 1817 he retired to Montpelier with his wife Dolly after serving four congressional terms and the fourth presidency. Madison died in 1836 and was buried on the property; his wife died in 1849.

In 1900 the property was purchased by William and Anna Rogers DuPont, who enlarged the house further, creating a total of 55 rooms plus added outbuildings. Their daughter Marion, one of Virginia's foremost horsewomen, took over the property in 1928 and began the well-known Montpelier Hunt Races.

Today the house is undergoing continual restoration aimed at making it a memorial to Madison's life and work. As of yet it bears little resemblance to its 19th-century splendor, when French carpets, porcelain, and paintings by Gilbert Stuart filled its halls. The view of the Blue Ridge Mountains is still impressive, though, as are two and a half replanted acres of formal gardens.

Montpelier, tel. (540) 672-2728, is just south of the town of Orange on Rt. 20, and is open mid March-Dec. daily 10 a.m.-4 p.m. (weekends Jan.-Feb.); $6 adults, $1 children 6-11. Admission includes a short movie on Madison's life and a pre-recorded audio tour of the house and grounds. The **birthdays** of James and Dolly Madison are celebrated on March 16 and May 20, respectively, with graveside ceremonies and receptions at the home. The **Montpelier Wine Festival** in early May welcomes seven surrounding wineries, and the **Montpelier Hunt Races** the first weekend in November features the Virginia Hunt Cup and a $115,000 purse.

Skydive Orange

This small but experienced outfit, tel./fax (540) 942-3871, operates out of the Orange County Airport. First-timers can make their first static-line jump for $170, a tandem for $180, or even go for the Accelerated Free-Fall course for $295 (it's the course that's sped up, of course). After your first time, subsequent dives are $10-16. E-mail: skydive@cfw.com, Web site: www.skydiveorange.com.

Graves Mountain Lodge

The Graves family has offered food and lodging in Syria for almost a century and a half, starting with stagecoaches crossing the Blue Ridge and now five generations later with this rustic retreat within sight of Hawksbill and Old Rag Mountains. Two motels, 11 secluded cottages, and six rooms in an old farmhouse range from moderate to expensive. Rates include three meals a day of honest farm fare served family-style at long wooden tables. Locally caught catfish and baked ham, sugar-cured on the premises, are backed up by fruits and vegetables grown on the 5,000-acre farm.

Here at the foot of the Blue Ridge, the opportunities for hiking and fishing are almost endless. The lodge's Overnight Wilderness Outfitters, tel. (540) 923-5071, organizes horseback rides by the hour or day, and there's even a swimming pool. Yearly events pack the place to the gills, starting with the **Spring Fling Festival** during the last weekend in April. May brings the **Graves' Mountain Festival of Music**—bluegrass, that is—the weekend after Memorial Day. The second and third weekends in October are claimed by the **Apple Harvest Festival**, with hayrides, apple-picking, cider-making, and lots of country music.

Graves Mountain Lodge, tel./fax (540) 923-4231, is near Syria, reached from Rt. 231 via Rt. 670. It's open late March-Nov.

THE INN AT LITTLE WASHINGTON

Virginia's flagship country inn sits at the main (and only) crossroads of a small village at the eastern foothills of the Blue Ridge. Washington itself, once prefixed by "Little" to distinguish it from the capital, was surveyed by its 17-year-old namesake in 1749, and is the only place that was named for him before he became the first president. Almost abandoned by the 20th century, Washington now brims with B&Bs, antique stores, and life. Much of this is thanks to the inn, which was bought in 1977 by Patrick O'Connell and Reinhardt Lynch.

After 100 years as a general store, gas station, and dance hall, the building needed some serious renovations. But the work was worth it: the inn was the first place ever to get five stars from both the Mobil Travel Guide and AAA for its accommodations and food. One reviewer gave it five stars out of a possible four.

Flags and flowers drape the white clapboard facade of the modest two-story building. Inside, rich fabrics and wall-coverings set off the owners' collection of art and antiques. Eight rooms and two suites were decorated by a London stage designer whose drawings hang on the walls. Personal touches like framed tarot cards, crystal balls, and bouquets of flowers create a small world of exotic luxury. Rooms don't have TVs or radios, but they do have king-sized canopied beds and chilled champagne waiting at check-in. Suites have Jacuzzis and loft bedrooms; two more rooms fill detached guest houses.

It's hard to believe, then, that what the Inn is *really* known for is its cuisine. Chef Patrick O'Connell derives inspiration from the 18th-century portrait of French gastronome Anthelme Brillat-Savarin ("Tell me what you eat and I'll tell you what you are") in turning out meals that one critic described as "so good it makes you cry." None less than Craig Claiborne of the *New York Times* called his dinner "the most fantastic meal of my life." Something perfect from the 14,000-bottle wine cellar is only one highlight of the five-course masterpieces, whose entrées add a French zest to regional Virginia favorites like Chesapeake Bay crabmeat and wild duck. Breakfast can be served in your room or in the Terrace Room overlooking the garden, and picnic lunches are available.

The Inn is in the center of town at Middle and Main Sts., tel. (540) 675-3800, fax 675-3100. Rooms are $260-410, suites $545 and guests houses $310-420. Add another $100 on Fridays during the entire month of October, and on certain other dates. Saturdays are $175 extra. Prix-fixe dinners are $78-98 and served Wed.-Monday. Rooms and tables fill up months ahead (on some Saturday nights they've received 3,000 requests for only 65 seats), so book your stay as far in advance as possible. The inn is popular for getaways, both romantic and illicit. Ten engagements happened on one Valentine's Day, and the maître d' has said his job can sometimes be like directing a French movie.

WEST OF CHARLOTTESVILLE

Crozet

The only reason most people have heard about this tiny burg is because it's the home of **Crozet Pizza**, Rt. 240 at Rt. 810, tel. (804) 823-2132. Owner/chef Bob Crum tops the best pizza in the state, if not the East Coast, with the usual (pepperoni) and unusual (asparagus, eggplant, jalapeños). Photos of fans from around the world wearing Crozet Pizza shirts decorate the walls. Open Tues.-Sat. 3-10 p.m.; reservations are definitely recommended for dinner.

Montfair Stables, tel. (804) 823-6961, e-mail: mfstables@hotmail.com, has guided trail rides along the eastern edge of the Blue Ridge for $25 per hour, as well as private and group lessons.

SOUTH OF CHARLOTTESVILLE

Michie Tavern

On Rt. 53 to Monticello, you'll pass this restored tavern, which was originally in Earlysville, 17 miles northwest of Charlottesville. Built by William Michie (MICK-ee) in 1784, it served stagecoach travelers for decades before falling into disrepair. In 1927, a wealthy businessman paid to have it moved here and restored.

Behind the tavern proper are reproductions of "dependencies," including a smokehouse, ice house, and root cellar. The Meadow Run grist mill is said to have seen no rest since 1797. After perusing the general store and crafts shops, try an Old Dominion vintage at the Virginia Wine Museum, tel. (804) 977-1234. Admission is $6 adults, $2 children 6-11.

If you didn't pack a lunch for your visit to Monticello, a stop at the "Ordinary" will leave you bursting at the seams. This log cabin sports original wood-beam walls and ceilings, creating the perfect atmosphere for a colonial-style southern buffet served on pewter plates. You can dine 11:15 a.m.-3:30 p.m. (Nov.-March 11:30 a.m.-3 p.m.) for $10 adults, $5 children 6-11, which gives you $2 off museum admission.

An alternative for lunch is the **Simeon Farm Market,** tel. (804) 977-8200, a small gourmet grocery and sandwich shop a short distance past Monticello at the intersection of US 53 with Milton Rd. (Rt. 732).

Monticello

Even if you're not a history fanatic, you know this landmark—it's on the back of a U.S. nickel, a portrait of its creator on the flipside. If you're into history, or architecture, or at the very least can appreciate a stunning spread, don't miss Monticello, one of the country's outstanding architectural achievements.

Monticello (mon-ti-CHELL-o) was Thomas Jefferson's pet project, which he designed, expanded, and refined over four decades. The first version of the house itself was radically redesigned after a five-year trip to France, where the future president acquired a loathing for the British-style Georgian brickwork so common to contemporary colonial architecture. (Williamsburg's design, he wrote, was "the most wretched I ever saw.")

What took its place was a blend of the Italian style of architect Andrea Palladio and the French design of the court of Louis XVI. Eight rooms became 21, and Monticello Mark II was finished in 1809. Jefferson died here on July 4,

THOMAS JEFFERSON

I have sworn upon the altar of God eternal hostility against every form of tyranny over the mind of man.

President, author of the Declaration of Independence, and potent political philosopher, Thomas Jefferson began his life on April 13, 1743, in what is now Albemarle County. When his father, surveyor and cartographer Peter Jefferson, died in 1757, Jefferson followed his father's wishes and pursued a classical education, at the College of William & Mary. In school he made friends among the faculty and local government who introduced him to pleasures of urbane society, as well as the law, the natural sciences, and the pursuit of knowledge for its own sake.

After a five-year study of law and admittance to the bar, Jefferson entered politics in 1769 as a member of the Virginia House of Burgesses. Relations with Britain were already sliding downhill, and Jefferson soon found himself leading Patrick Henry and others who favored strong resistance to the mother country. In 1776, as a member of the Second Continental Congress, Jefferson found an outlet for his growing intellectual radicalism and profound, passionate skill at writing by drafting the Declaration of Independence.

As his country struggled to fight itself free, Jefferson tried to put the ideas of the declaration into action as governor of Virginia 1779-81. This proved easier said than done; his Statute of Religious Freedom encountered vigorous opposition that delayed its enactment until 1786, and his lackluster performance during the British invasion of 1780-81 inspired the editor of a local paper to label him "a coward, a calumniator, a plagiarist, [and] a tame, spiritless animal." On September 6, 1782, the worst blow fell. Martha Wayles Skelton Jefferson, with whom Jefferson had enjoyed "ten years of unche-

quered happiness," died soon after the birth of their sixth child. "A single event," he wrote, "wiped away all my plans and left me a blank which I had not the spirits to fill up." He never remarried.

Jefferson was able to escape somewhat on a five-year diplomatic trip to France from 1784-89 in the company of Benjamin Franklin and John Adams, who had helped him draft the declaration. Here he wrote his only full-length book, *Notes on the State of Virginia* (1787). This volume, which answers a series of questions posed by a French diplomat on North America and its rapidly changing society, is considered by many to be one of the most insightful works of the 18th century.

After stints as secretary of state and vice president, Jefferson became the third U.S. president in 1801, narrowly defeating Aaron Burr in a close race that characterized the early polarization of American politics. In contrast to Burr's Federalists, Jefferson's Republicans supported policies claimed both by today's Democrats, in their championship of human rights and opposition to plutocracy and oligarchy, and modern Republicans, in the idea that the best federal government is small, non-interfering, and decentralized.

During his first term (1801-05) Jefferson nearly doubled the size of the United States through the Louisiana Purchase. He originally intended to buy only a small part of the Mississippi River valley, but when a cash-poor Napoleon offered to sell everything from the Great Lakes to the Rockies and beyond for only $15 million, Jefferson jumped at the chance (even though, as he freely admitted, he had no constitutional authority to do so). Under his orders the Lewis and Clark expedition left to explore the territory.

His second term didn't go as well, thanks in part to growing controversy over the role of the federal government. Jefferson's efforts to avoid involvement in the Napoleonic Wars led to more charges of timidity and vacillation. In 1809, deeply in debt, he handed over the reins of office to James Madison.

Jefferson's later life at Monticello gave him ample time to pursue the endless interests pushed aside by a career in politics. Over his lifetime Jefferson wrote volumes of letters that give a remarkably detailed picture of the man himself. He considered himself part of an educated gentry that owed its existence to the same public that held it responsible to govern justly. At six feet two inches high, Jefferson was tall, angular, and carried himself with a relaxed dignity.

Jefferson observed the construction of the University of Virginia by telescope until its opening in 1819, when he was finally able to indulge what he called his "canine appetite" for learning. He was one of the most educated men of his time—able to understand Latin, Greek, French, Spanish, Italian, and Anglo-Saxon—to the point where, at age 71, he read Plato's *Republic* in the original Greek and pronounced it overrated.

His interest in architecture left its neoclassical stamp on dozens of buildings in Virginia and Washington, D.C., and as an amateur naturalist Jefferson collected and tried to classify fossils from all over the country. Mathematics and meteorology both fascinated him, and he always had some experiment in planting going in the fields of Monticello in the hopes of improving the prosperity of American farmers.

Yet, even as almost every event of his daily life went down on paper, certain aspects of the private man have remained a mystery. In 19,000 surviving letters, for example, not one exists between him and his wife. Then there's the question of how the country's foremost champion of natural rights and the equality of man could own hundreds of slaves. His *Notes on the State of Virginia* address the issue most directly, calling it a "great political and moral evil." But from there Jefferson falls back on limp arguments reflecting the prevailing prejudices of his era. Arguing that blacks were inferior to whites in physical beauty, foresight, and imagination, Jefferson couldn't bring himself to imagine both races living peacefully side by side. Slavery, in his view, was a necessary evil, crucial to the economy of the state and preferable to the "dynamite of class struggle" between rich and poor white planters.

Jefferson died on July 4, 1826, the 50th anniversary of the signing of the Declaration of Independence and only hours before his friend John Adams. He lies at Monticello under the inscription:

Here was buried Thomas Jefferson, author of the Declaration of American Independence, of the Virginia Statute of Religious Freedom, and father of the University of Virginia.

the famous Monticello

1826, on the 50th anniversary of the signing of the Declaration of Independence. He's buried in a family plot on the grounds.

The manor house tops a columned, classical portico with a large dome, the first of its kind in the state. Notice how the outside windows are continuous between floors, making the facade look smaller while giving it a more unified appearance. Touches of Jeffersonian whimsy fill the interior, where the first floor is open to the public. A private museum in the entrance hall holds mastodon bones, a model of the Great Pyramid of Egypt, and relics from Lewis and Clark's expedition to the Pacific Ocean. In the corner a seven-day clock has weights that slowly fall from the ceiling to the basement through special holes in the floor.

Almost every room is a different size and shape. In the study an ingenious handwriting copier allowed Jefferson to pen two letters at once, and don't miss the view from the parlor. The president's private suite features a bed alcove open to both the dressing room and the study, allowing him to rise in either room depending on his mood and the time of day.

The estate's true kingly feel, though, comes from the grounds. Over 1,000 acres of lush gardens have been restored to their original glory, doing proud Jefferson's sentiment that "no occupation is as delightful to me as the culture of the earth, and no culture comparable to that of the garden." Service quarters in Mulberry Row were placed so as not to obscure the stunning view (Monticello means "little mountain" in Italian). Even though he called it an "abominable crime," Jefferson did own about 200 slaves, whose homes and lives are currently being excavated and examined.

The estate commands a hilltop three miles southeast of Charlottesville on Rt. 53 (Thomas Jefferson Pkwy.). From I-64, take exit 121 (westbound) or 121 A (eastbound) to Route 20 South (if traveling westbound, turn south, or left, on Route 20); make a left on Route 53, just after the first stoplight. The entrance to Monticello is located on the left, approximately one and a half miles from Route 20. You'll have to park at the bottom and take a shuttle bus up to the house. Weekends can be crowded, but there are always picnic spots among the trees. Admission ($9 adults, $5 children 6-11) includes a 25-minute guided tour. Open daily 8 a.m.-5 p.m. (Nov.-Feb. 9 a.m.-4:30 p.m.), tel. (804) 984-9800 or 984-9822, Web site: www.monticello.org.

Ash Lawn-Highland

It seems Jefferson's sense of style was contagious. In 1793 James Monroe, whom some historians call Jefferson's protégé, bought 1,000 acres just south of Monticello. When George Washington sent Monroe to France for three years, Jefferson hired gardeners to give his friend's orchards a jump start. From 1799-1823 Monroe lived at Highland with his family. He felt comfort in the view of Monticello to the north, and borrowed from his mentor's style in designing his own house (which remained a much more modest affair).

Sadly, one year after his second term as president ended in 1825, Monroe was forced to sell Highland, where he had hoped to retire, due to a $75,000 debt. Subsequent owners added the name Ash Lawn in 1838 and in 1884 built a Victorian-style house next to the original building.

The College of William & Mary, Monroe's alma mater, maintains Ash Lawn-Highland as a working farm; it's 2.5 miles southeast of Monticello on Rt. 795 (James Monroe Pkwy.). A collection of period furnishings fills the main house, including some from the Monroe White House and others that were presented as gifts from South American republics in thanks for the Monroe Doctrine of non-interference in political matters. The small screens protected ladies' caked-on makeup, lard- and wax-based as was the style, from melting in the heat from the fireplace.

Keep any eye out for the chair that's been seen to rock on its own on repeated occasions. Legend has it it was Monroe's favorite, so some think the spirit is his. Another story holds that a nanny died in the chair when a stray spark from the fireplace caught her long hair on fire.

A gift shop and picnic tables await after a 40-minute house tour, which is included in the admission ($7 adults, $4 children 6-11). Open daily 9 a.m.-6 p.m. (Nov.-Feb. 10 a.m.-5 p.m.), tel. (804) 293-9539. In April period music drifts through the gardens, lit with 1,000 candles, during the **Champagne and Candlelight Tour** that coincides with Garden Week. The annual **Summer Festival** from June-Aug. features musical performances and a bonfire finale, and **Planta-**

tion Days in July includes crafts, historical reenactments, and dressage (horse dancing).

Walton's Mountain Museum

Earl Hamner, Jr., based his famous TV series on vivid memories of growing up in the rural village of Schuyler during the Depression. The show won six Emmys and two Golden Globes its first year, and went on to run for 211 episodes over eight more years. Fans will recognize locations like the Waltons' kitchen and living room and John-Boy's bedroom, all re-created in Hamner's own elementary school. Ike Godsey's country store now houses a gift shop. The museum, tel. (804) 831-2000, Web site: www.the-waltons.com, is open March-Nov. daily 10 a.m.-4 p.m.; $5 adults, $4 children 6-12. To get there take US 29 south to Rt. 6 east, go five miles, take a right and follow Rt. 800 to its end, and then a right onto Rt. 617.

Scottsville

The first seat of Albemarle County occupies a horseshoe bend in the James River, a choice location which made it the chief port above Richmond for freights and passengers during a golden era in the mid 1800s. The barges are long gone, but you can still drift downstream on a canoe or innertube from **James River Reeling and Rafting**, tel. (804) 286-4386. Rentals with shuttle service are $12-23 pp, and they also offer overnight camping and fishing trips for $35-40 pp.

Amherst

Five miles north of Amherst town are the **Rebec Vineyards,** tel. (804) 946-5168, home of the Virginia Garlic Festival the second weekend in October. Virginia's most fragrant fair has 100 vendors selling garlic in just about every form imaginable, along with pony rides for children and music on four stages. Some 12,000 people turn out to see the Garlic King and Queen elected and the garlic-eating contests. (Think you can eat 3 oz. of raw garlic in 30 seconds? Only three out of 40 contestants accomplished the feat one year.) Admission is $8 per adult ($15 with a commemorative wine-tasting glass) and $3 per child.

Wintergreen Resort

Seventeen ski slopes ranging from novice to expert earned Wintergreen *Skiing Magazine*'s title of "best ski resort in the South." Five expert trails cut through the 1,000-foot vertical drop of the Highlands, and there's a snowboard park and a learn-to-ski area. Sip a cappuccino in front of the fireplaces in the cozy stone lodge, recently improved along with other facilities to the tune of $10.5 million. Lift tickets are $30-40, or $20 at night.

Two outstanding golf courses (one designed by Rees Jones) draw guests during the summer, along with 25 tennis courts, six pools, and 20-acre Lake Monocan. You can rent bikes, horses, and ponies, or simply hike from the nature center along 30 miles of trail operated by the Wintergreen Nature Foundation. The Wintergarden Spa has hot tubs, a jacuzzi, saunas, and workout rooms. Rental choices include hundreds of mountaintop villas and dozens of slopeside homes, most of which have kitchens and fireplaces. Five full-service restaurants are nearby.

Wintergreen, tel. (800) 325-2200, fax (804) 325-8003, Web site: www.wintergreenresort.com, is on Rt. 644, off Rt. 151 south of Nellysford. You can also get there from the Blue Ridge Parkway via the Reeds Gap exit at milepost 13.

LYNCHBURG AND VICINITY

Virginia's classic tobacco town goes under a few different monikers. As the "City of Seven Hills," Lynchburg (pop. 66,000) bulges with lofty historic districts and stately inns. As the center of Virginia's conservative religious heartland, it's no surprise that it's also known as the "City of Churches"—there are more than 130 houses of worship as well as Jerry Falwell's Liberty University, Dial-the-Bible listings in the White Pages, and radio preachers who end every sentence in "-uh." And even Lynchburg's tourist slogan— "The Real Virginia"—rings true thanks to Lynchburg's combination of the new, a number of medium-sized colleges, and the old, Thomas Jefferson's Poplar Forest and Appomattox Court House nearby.

pounds of tobacco were passing through the city's warehouses every year. Lynchburg served as a major Confederate storage depot during the Civil War, and as one of four quartermaster (horse) depots in the Confederacy. On June 18, 1864, Gen. Jubal Early narrowly managed to save the city from destruction by running empty trains back and forth with much noise and commotion, convincing Union generals that imaginary rebel reinforcements had arrived.

The tobacco trade carried Lynchburg into the early 20th century, but as demand slackened the city turned to its wealth of antiquity to lure visitors. Many antebellum houses marred by mid-century neglect have been restored as homes and offices.

HISTORY

After earning his freedom from a wealthy Quaker planter, indentured Irish servant Charles Lynch went on to marry the boss's daughter and build the town's first warehouses and commercial buildings on land he had acquired along the upper James River. In 1757 his son John set up a ferry terminal at the bottom of today's 9th St., and Lynchburg was off and running as a regional commercial center.

Trade poured in along the river itself, the James River and Kanawha Canal from Richmond, and railroads from Petersburg and Alexandria. A dark, course-leafed local variety of tobacco soon became the area's main cash crop. Farmers humming popular songs like "Goin' Down to Lynchburg Town To Carry My Tobacco Down" brought huge hogsheads in from surrounding fields to dozens of warehouses along the riverbanks. Small boats called bateaux, usually manned by a trio of skilled, brawny slaves, waited on the water to take the containers to Richmond.

By the mid-19th century Lynchburg was second only to New Bedford, MA, in per capita income nationwide (whale oil still brought in more money than tobacco). Soon over 30 million

SIGHTS

Five of Lynchburg's seven hills are now historic districts near the river. Two Baptist church spires bookend **Court House Hill,** where the 139 steps of **Monument Terrace** lead past a row of war memorials to the steps of the **Old City Court House Museum,** 901 Court St., tel. (804) 847-1459. The dome-capped Greek Revival temple was used from 1855-1955, and displays a working clock made in Boston in 1925 with weights that drop through hollow columns in front. It was opened in 1976 as a local history museum entered through the restored Hustings Courthouse. Exhibits range from native Monacan tribes to life in Lynchburg during the tobacco boom. Open daily 10 a.m.-4 p.m.; $1 pp over 12.

Many of the grand houses on **Diamond Hill** were built during Lynchburg's golden age near the turn of the century. Once one of the city's most exclusive neighborhoods, Diamond Hill embraces a wealth of architectural styles including Queen Anne and Greek, Gothic, and Georgian revival. **Federal Hill** to the west was Lynchburg's first residential suburb, filled with federal-style homes along steep, dead-end streets. Once known as Quality Row as it passed through the **Garland Hill** district, Madison Avenue is still partially paved in century-old brick.

On the far side of Blackwater Creek rises **Daniel's Hill,** dominated by the octagonal bay facade of **Point of Honor,** 112 Cabell St., tel. (804) 847-1459. Built in 1815 by Dr. George Cabell, Sr. (doctor to Patrick Henry, among other revolutionary figures), the Federal mansion is named for duels once fought over matters of principle on this bluff over the James. Open daily 10 a.m.-4 p.m., with admission ($3 pp over 12) including a guided tour.

A few blocks farther up the James you'll find the **Maier Museum of Art,** 1 Quinlan St., tel. (804) 947-8136, Web site: www.rmwc.edu/maier, on the campus of the Randolph-Macon Women's College. An impressive collection of 19th- and 20th-century paintings includes works by Edward Hopper, Winslow Homer, and Georgia O'-Keefe. Open Wed.-Sun. 1-4 p.m. (Sept.-May Tues.-Sun. 1-5 p.m.); free.

The **Old City Cemetery,** open daily dawn to dusk, came into use in 1806. A loop trail starting at Taylor and 4th Sts. passes ancient family plots, Revolutionary War graves, and the final resting place of Blind Billy, a local street musician and former slave whose freedom was paid for by Lynchburg residents. Beyond the Confederate section, containing 2,200 soldiers from 14 states, you'll find butterfly and medicinal herb gardens, a lotus-studded goldfish pond, and a row of 60 varieties of antique roses from the 16th to 19th centuries.

Along the path is the **Pest House Medical Museum,** once the medical office of local physician John J. Terrell. During the Civil War, Dr. Terrell turned it into a "House of Pestilence" for his experiments isolating victims of smallpox and measles. The 1840s building contains medical tools from the era—an amputation kit, "asthma chair," and "poison chest" (presumably for medicines). You can take an exterior self-guiding tour, but the inside is only open by prior appointment. Call the Lynchburg visitors center for information.

At the **Anne Spencer House and Garden,** 1313 Pierce St., tel. (804) 846-0517, the Lynch-

THE BEALE TREASURE

Virginia's best-known lost fortune is said to consist of close to 3,000 pounds of gold, 5,000 pounds of silver, and thousands of dollars in jewels. Some say it's a hoax, but hundreds of as yet unsuccessful treasure-hunters would like to believe otherwise.

In 1817, a party of 30 Virginians led by Thomas Jefferson Beale left to try their luck mining in Colorado. They struck a rich vein of gold and silver in the south-central part of the state, which they worked for a year and a half before the accumulating wealth started to make some uncomfortable. Beale and eight others were sent back to Virginia to bury two truckloads of nuggets while the others stayed and mined.

The party arrived at Goose Creek in Bedford County in November 1818, following a faint trail through a gap in the Blue Ridge foothills near the Peaks of Otter. Snow covered their tracks as they dug a square pit six feet deep, lined it with flat stones, and placed inside iron cooking pots filled with treasure. The last concealing spadeful fell in December, and within two months they had rejoined their comrades.

After two more years of mining, Beale led another trip back to the same spot and a second load joined the first. This time he decided to leave a message for this partners in Colorado in case something happened to his group on the return. Three numerical ciphers detailing the location of the hoard, the contents of the vault, and the name of the party were put in a strongbox and given to Lynchburg innkeeper Robert Morris, with instructions to open it if no one returned in 10 years.

Beale and his crew left once more for Colorado, and Morris never saw any of the them again. Two months later he received a letter saying the keys to the code were in the mail, and then silence. As years passed Morris gradually forgot about the strongbox, until he happened upon it in the 1840s while searching for a harness in a shed. After trying to decipher the codes for years, Morris showed them to a friend, who managed to break the one describing the vault using a key based on the Declaration of Independence. The other two were made public, but remain a mystery despite the efforts of decoding experts and computer code-breakers.

burg poetess who wrote of love and the reverence of beauty in mankind and nature is memorialized in her home and the gardens that inspired many of her stanzas. Spencer (1882-1975) is considered part of the Harlem Renaissance, and is the only Virginian included in the *Norton Anthology of Modern American and British Poetry*. While living here she entertained such visitors as George Washington Carver, Martin Luther King, Jr., Thurgood Marshall, and W.E.B. DuBois, when she wasn't composing in the small garden cottage she called Edenkraal. Open Mon.-Sat. 10 a.m.-4 p.m.; free but small donations suggested.

The city's first house of worship still stands as the **South River Meeting House,** 5810 Fort Ave., tel. (804) 239-2548, also called the Quaker Meeting House. Open daily 9 a.m.-3 p.m. for free; tours can be arranged with a few days' prior notice.

Parks and Natural Areas

Daniel's Hill continues upriver into **Riverside**

© MOON PUBLICATIONS, INC.

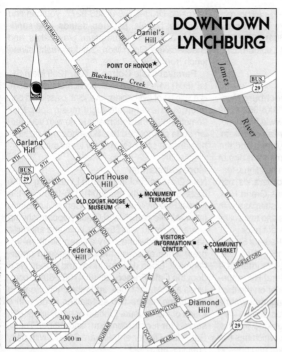

DOWNTOWN LYNCHBURG

© MOON PUBLICATIONS, INC.

Park—look for a sign along Rivermont at the Virginia School of the Arts building. Trails along the hillside lead to the keel of the packet boat *The John Marshall,* typical of the 19th-century craft that were pulled by mules as far as Richmond. This particular one carried Stonewall Jackson's body to Lexington for burial.

Three hundred acres along **Blackwater Creek** as it snakes through downtown Lynchburg from Cabell St. to Old Forest Rd. have been set aside as a Natural Area, interlaced by bicycle and foot trails and enclosing the 155-acre Ruskin Freer Nature Preserve. To find the northern end of the 6-mile Blackwater Creek Trail, take Rivermont Rd. to Bedford Rd. and then Hollins Mill Rd., following this 0.7 mile to a parking lot at Hollins Mill Dam. Another entrance off Rivermont follows signs along Elmwood Ave., Woodland Ave., and E. Randolph Place.

For more information on parks in the area contact the Lynchburg Park and Recreation Department at 301 Grove St., tel. (804) 847-1640.

ACCOMMODATIONS

Inexpensive
Lynchburg's most economical hotels are the **Econo Lodge,** 2400 Stadium Dr., tel. (804) 847-1045, and the **Timberlake Motel,** 11222 Timberlake Rd., tel. (804) 525-2160.

Expensive
In the Garland Hill district stands the **Madison House Bed and Breakfast,** 413 Madison St., tel. (800) 828-6422 or (804) 528-1503, an Italianate Victorian mansion built for a tobacco baron in the 1880s. Beautiful wrought-iron porch decorations and leaded glass in the front door window are only the beginning. Inside you'll find a library filled with volumes dating to the 18th century, elegant crystal chandeliers, and original china bathroom fixtures from the early 1900s. Meals—served on Limoges and Wedgwood china—are for guests only, but anyone is welcome to stop by for afternoon tea and scones. E-mail: madison@lynchburg.net, Web site: www.bbhost.com/1880s-madison.

Children are welcome at **Once Upon a Time,** 1102 Harrison St., tel. (804) 845-3561, since the owners have four daughters themselves. A different fairy tale theme decorates each bedroom, from the Frog Prince Room to the Three Bears Suites, and guests can write their own tales in the blank journals while relaxing in a claw-foot tub. The French Second Empire mansion was built in 1874 atop Federal Hill by the brother-in-law of the city's first millionaire, so he could overlook his factories. E-mail: hughest@inmind.com, Web site: www.inmind.com/b_and_b.

The four rooms at the Georgian Revival **Doyle House,** 2601 Rivermont Ave., tel. (804) 528-1806, e-mail: doylehouse@aol.com, feature extraordinary woodwork and floor-to-ceiling mirrors. Also in this price range are a **Hampton Inn**, 5604 Seminole Ave., tel. (804) 237-2704, and a **Comfort Inn**, 3125 Albert Lankford Dr.., tel. (804) 847-9041.

Premium

It's back to Garland Hill for the **Lynchburg Mansion Inn**, 405 Madison St., tel. (800) 352-1199 or (804) 528-5400, Web site: www.bbonline.com/va/lynchburg/, built in 1914 for James Gilliam, president of six banks, five coal firms, and the Lynchburg Shoe Company. The manor is one of Virginia's finest Spanish Georgian buildings, featuring 22 columns under a 105-foot veranda, rich cherry woodwork in the cavernous Grand Hall, and a three-story oak and cherry staircase with over 200 balustrades. Four rooms and two suites include use of the five-person spa out back.

The **Federal Crest Inn**, 1101 Federal St., tel. (800) 818-6155 or (804) 845-6155, Web site: www.inmind.com/federalcrest/, commands a stately view from the top of Federal Hill, especially from the Eagle's Nest Theater on the third floor, built as a stage for the original owner's children (and now home to a large-screen TV). Seven fireplaces, each with a unique mantel, are spread throughout the house, which has five guest rooms with down comforters and gas-log fireplaces.

The **Lynchburg Hilton**, 2900 Candler's Mountain Rd., tel. (804) 237-6333, has a restaurant, fitness center, and outdoor pool only two miles from the Lynchburg Regional Airport.

FOOD

Snacks and Starters

The **Lynchburg Community Market**, tel. (804) 847-1499, is the place for picnic fixings, baked goods, and exotic takeout. It's been open since 1783 (current hours daily 7 a.m.-2 p.m.). Just inside the entrance, **Moore's at the Market** serves a no-frills breakfast from $2-3. **The Farm Basket**, 2008 Langhorne Rd., tel. (804) 528-1107, offers box lunches and healthy fare along the lines of cucumber sandwiches on fresh-baked bread. The small eatery is open for lunch Mon.-Sat. At **Donald's Bagels and Bites**, 2225

Lakeside Dr., tel. (804) 385-9277, you can find breakfast bagels, pastries, salads, and sandwiches along with scrumptious pies, cakes, and cheesecakes. Open Mon.-Sat. for breakfast and lunch from 6:30 or 7 a.m.

Percival's Isle Coffee & Tea, 1208 Main St., tel. (804) 847-3059, e-mail: pervical@inmind.com, is a little bit of everything: java joint, classic old bar, Internet cafe, and late-night music spot. Pick something off the light menu to go with your Italian soda or imported tea, like a gourmet pizza or homemade soup. Open daily for all meals.

More Substantial

New Orleans cooking lives in Lynchburg at the **Jazz Street Grill**, tel. (804) 835-0100, in the Forest Plaza West Shopping Center. Louisiana favorites like catfish and Cajun popcorn shrimp share the menu with $5-6 po' boys and andouille sausage sandwiches. Try a Deep South microbrew while enjoying the live weekend entertainment. Open daily for lunch and dinner. Next door the **Cafe France**, tel. (804) 385-8989, combines a restaurant, deli, and wine shop. Seafood and prime rib are two specialties to go with a touch of the unusual (buffalo or emu, anyone?), served for lunch Mon.-Sat. and dinner Tues.-Saturday. Dinner entrées are $11-17 with daily specials up to $21.

Crown Sterling, 6120 Fort Ave. at US 501, tel. (804) 239-7744, bills itself as "Central Virginia's Oldest Fine Dining Restaurant," serving aged beef charcoal-grilled to perfection for dinner Mon.-Saturday. Steaks, chicken, and seafood entrées run $12-24, including teriyakis, grilled swordfish, and filets galore. A Host's Choice Dinner, complete with 8-oz. steak, glass of wine, and parfait, is $17.50. A contemporary contrast comes in the form of **Meriwether's Market Restaurant**, tel. (804) 384-3311, in the Boonsboro Shopping Center. This cheery, moderately upscale bistro offers various soup/salad/sandwiches combinations for $6-7 (try the orzo salad and oyster spinach bisque) and healthy, Mediterranean-style entrées for $14-21 during dinner. Lynchburg's best wine list and dozens of beers compliment a hand-crafted bar near a small market selling various cooking concoctions. Open for lunch and dinner Mon.-Sat., with live jazz on Wednesday.

ENTERTAINMENT

Nightlife

Cattle Annie's, 4009 Murray Pl., tel. (804) 846-2668, features both kinds of music—country *and* western—and a 4,500-square foot dance floor. Wednesday is family night, and Friday is ladies' night. Patrons of **Mudpuppy's Pub and Sports Emporium,** tel. (804) 385-4304, in the Forest Plaza West Shopping Center, can choose from 10 TVs usually showing sports, a beer at the bar, and live blues on Friday and Saturday nights until 2 a.m. **Percival's Isle** hosts live blues and funky tunes some nights, and the **Jazz Street Grill,** tel. (804) 835-0100, in the Forest Plaza West Shopping Center, sounds like Dixieland on weekends.

Fine Arts

One of the oldest continuous community theater groups in America, the **Lynchburg Fine Arts Center,** 1815 Thompson Dr., tel. (804) 846-3804, presents pop chorus concerts, resident ballet company shows, and assorted children's performances year round. Two free galleries show changing exhibits. The **Lynchburg Symphony Orchestra,** 621 Court St., tel. (804) 845-6604, puts on seven concerts per year at the Lynchburg City Stadium or the E.C. Glass Auditorium. Call **Lynchburg College,** 1501 Lakeside Dr., tel. (804) 522-8300, for details on events at the Dillard Fine Arts Building, and the Daura and Dillard Galleries.

SHOPPING

Two dozen antique shops sell bits and pieces of Lynchburg's rich history, from Victorian hatpins to antique linens. Many are along Main Street, like **Haleys,** 1024 Main St., tel. (804) 528-1329; **Scarlet's Main Street Antique Mall,** 1026 Main St., tel. (804) 528-0488; and **Sweeney's Curious Goods,** 1220 Main St., tel. (804) 846-7839. In the Boonsboro Shopping Center **Pheasant's Eye,** tel. (804) 384-3568, displays and retails works by local and regional artists including photographs, pottery, hand-blown glass, clothing, and lamps.

The Farm Basket shopping complex, 2008 Langhorne Rd., tel. (800) 432-1107 or (804) 628-1107, is a fun bunch of shops offering art, flowers, jewelry, and crafts. Wander inside to unearth the gems offered at **Farm Basket Papers,** featuring unique stationery, and **Virginia Handicrafts Inc.,** with kaleidoscopes, games, and paintings. Then take a break on the deck overlooking Blackwater Creek with a box lunch from the complex's food shop (and don't miss the homemade foods like apple butter and hot pepper jelly).

EVENTS

From Easter to Christmas the Community Market rings with music and smells like supper at annual events such as May's **Country Music Festival,** the **Main Street Music and Harvest Festival** in October, and the **Thomas Jefferson Tomatoe Faire** every August, commemorating the founding father's first taste of the feared fruit (which was once thought to be poisonous).

In June the **James River Bateaux Festival** brings a week of one of the East Coast's most unusual waterborne celebrations, centered on re-productions of 18th-century shallow-draft merchant boats. Each 60-foot craft could carry up to 20 tons of goods to Richmond and back much faster than horses and wagons. A few were discovered near Richmond in the early 1980s, allowing carpenters to rebuild the time-tested design. The festival follows the river, stopping at towns along the way for various activities.

September's **Kaleidoscope** starts with the Italian Festival of the Seven Hills and keeps going the entire month. Kaleidoscope is Lynchburg's main fall celebration and involves everything from a barbecue jamboree and bike race to a teddy bear parade and bocce-ball tournament, plus the usual concerts, crafts, and cooking.

TRANSPORTATION

Getting Around

The **Greater Lynchburg Transit Company,** tel. (804) 847-7771, serves the city and surrounding area from its main terminal at the Plaza Shopping Center.

Getting There and Away

The **Lynchburg Regional Airport,** tel. (804) 582-1150, is eight miles south of downtown on US 29. It's served by USAir Express, United Express, and Atlantic Southeast Airlines/Delta. Airport Limo, tel. (804) 239-1777, will take you into town, or you can rent a car from Avis, Budget, or Hertz. The Crescent line between New York and New Orleans stops at the local **Amtrak** station, Kemper St. at Park Ave., daily. **Greyhound/Trailways,** tel. (804) 846-6614, is at Wildflower Dr. at Odd Fellows Drive.

INFORMATION

For walking tour brochures and advice on any other aspects of the region, stop by the **Lynchburg Visitors Information Center,** 216 12th St., tel. (800) 532-7821 or tel./fax (804) 847-1811, e-mail: RealVA@aol.com.

THOMAS JEFFERSON'S POPLAR FOREST

In 1773 Thomas Jefferson inherited a 4,812-acre working tobacco farm from his father-in-law, providing the future president with a welcome source of cash income. In 1806 he laid the foundation there for a house he would come to cherish even more than Monticello: a year-round retreat from that "curiosity of the neighborhood" which had already become a magnet for visitors. Eventually Jefferson was making the three-day ride from his official residence three or four times a year, and staying here anywhere from two weeks to two months at a time.

Poplar Forest was sold at Jefferson's death and became a private home. In 1984 it was bought by a nonprofit organization that began restoration in the early 1990s. As of 1997, renovations were in full swing, with the outside almost done and the inside still gutted. Visitors are welcome to drop by and examine the extensive archaeological displays and ongoing restoration.

A winding gravel drive leads to the north portico of the house, which forms a perfect octagon reflected in the shape of two brick privies on the opposite side. Similarities to Monticello ap-

pear in the skylight over the 20-foot central room, alcove beds, and the three-piece windows that fill the parlor with light from floor to ceiling. The lawn was once dug out below the columns of the south portico, enabling servants to walk directly outside from the house's lower level. Twin earth mounds at either side were once planted with aspens and weeping willows, two of fourteen species that graced the property.

Poplar Forest, tel. (804) 525-1806, is open April-Nov. Wed.-Sun. 10 a.m.-4 p.m.; $6 adults and $1 children 6-16 (grounds only $2 pp).

BEDFORD

The self-proclaimed "World's Best Little Town" is home to the inimitable **Holy Land USA,** tel. (540) 586-2823, a curious mix of faith and farming on the property of retired supermarket owner Bob Johnson. Sheep graze and geese waddle among life-sized dioramas depicting the life of Jesus and scenes from the Bible using unmistakable imagery: the wise man's house stands firm on a rock, while the foolish man's house built on sand is a pile of scrap. A three-mile trail into placid fields passes old farm machinery and enough Bible quotations for a month of Sundays.

Holy Land USA is three miles west on Dickerson Mill Rd. (Rt. 746) from Rt. 122 just south of town, open dawn-dusk; free.

APPOMATTOX COURT HOUSE NATIONAL HISTORIC PARK

Following the falls of Petersburg and Richmond in early April 1865, Robert E. Lee led his exhausted Army of Northern Virginia on a fighting retreat west. The goal was to link up with Gen. Joseph Johnston and his Army of Tennessee in Danville, but Ulysses S. Grant's forces harried the Rebels at every step. On April 6 the Battle of Saylor's Creek cost 7,000 Confederate casualties and a third of the remaining ranks captured, including Lee's son Custis and seven other generals. Two days later Lee answered Grant's request for a discussion of surrender, though saying he would rather "die a thousand deaths."

On Sunday morning, April 9, the two generals met in the parlor of Wilmer McLean's humble

LUCKLESS WILMER McLEAN

In the summer of 1861 a Union shell tearing through his kitchen convinced an aging farmer named Wilmer McLean it was time to move, as two huge armies clashed on his farm near Manassas. Declaring he hoped "never to see another soldier," McLean took his family south and west to where he thought the war could never reach—the dusty burg of Appomattox Court House, where on 9 April, 1865, Gen. Robert E. Lee surrendered to Gen. Ulysses S. Grant in McLean's living room, ending the Civil War. As Wilmer later said, "The war began in my front yard and ended in my front parlor."

where it began

DOVER PUBLICATIONS, INC. / 2

where it ended

home in Appomattox Court House. The terms of surrender were quickly written up—the Confederates would be allowed to return home unmolested, all could keep their horses and officers their sidearms—and Lee signed the paper, ending four years of bloodshed and chaos. At a ceremony on April 12, the ragtag Rebel army laid down its flags and weapons and each man was handed a hastily printed parole. Grant prohibited

any celebration among his troops out of respect. "The war is over," he said, "the rebels are our countrymen again." Instead he ordered his men to present arms to their former enemies, who returned the salute in kind.

The McLean House was dismantled in 1893 amid plans to ship it to the capital and rebuild it as part of a war museum, but this never happened and the pieces lay rotting for decades.

Luckily the decaying village was designated a National Historical Park in 1954 and eventually restored to its 1865 appearance.

Visiting Appomattox Court House

Appomattox Court House National Historical Park is on Rt. 24, three miles north of US 460 and the town of Appomattox. Start at the **visitors center,** tel. (804) 352-8987, Web site: www. nps.gov/apco, which is open daily 8:30 a.m.-5 p.m.; $2 pp. Get your bearings with two 15-minute slide presentations and a map display of Lee's retreat, and take a look at the museum, which holds relics such as little Lula McLean's doll, the "silent witness" to the signing.

In the village, a reconstructed version of the McLean House is decorated as accurately as possible from paintings and first-hand accounts. None of the furnishings are original, thanks in part to many of those at the signing who quickly snapped up mementos of the event (i.e., anything that wasn't nailed down). Nearby Clover Hill Tavern, on the other hand, dates to 1819. The park includes a section of the Richmond-Lynchburg Stage Road where the Confederates stacked their arms during the surrender ceremony.

Park interpreters can answer questions and point you down the trails to both Lee's and Grant's final headquarters. Reenactments are held yearly the weekend closest to April 9 on Rt. 667, three miles north of US 460 toward Lynchburg. Call (804) 352-0493 for information.

Near Appomattox Court House

Stop by **The Caboose,** tel. (804) 352-2638, at the intersection of Rt. 24 and US 460 in the town of Appomattox, for inexpensive subs and ice cream. Camping is available at the same crossroads at the **Parkview Mobile Home & RV Park,** tel. (804) 352-2366 ($15) and at **Yogi Bear's Jellystone Camp Resort,** tel. (757) 993-3332, six miles west on US 460 next to Paradise Lake; $15-20. You can also find sites in **Holiday Lake State Park,** tel. (804) 248-6308, within the Appomattox Buckingham State Forest east on Rt. 24; $15.

For more information on the area, including details on the **Railroad Festival** in mid-October, contact the **Appomattox Visitor Information Center,** 5 Main St., tel. (804) 352-2621, fax 352-2621.

BUCKINGHAM

Born in India in 1914, Integral Yoga guru Sri Swami Satchidananda established the **Satchidananda Ashram-Yogaville,** tel. (800) 858-9642 or (804) 969-3121, fax 969-1303, to further his goals of peace, universal understanding, and enlightenment. The 750-acre rural retreat centers around the Light of Truth Universal Shrine (LOTUS), shaped like a 100-foot blooming lotus. Inside is a neon-lit meditation chamber and twelve altars symbolizing the 10 major religions, "Other Known," and "Those Still Unknown." Open Mon.-Fri. 10 a.m.-noon, 2-5 p.m., Friday 7-9 p.m., Saturday 10 a.m.-7 p.m., Sunday 10 a.m.-5 p.m., (longer hours in the summer); free.

The ashram hosts workshops and retreats year-round, and guests are welcome to stop by for an afternoon, day, or longer. Lodging options include camping (inexpensive), dorms (moderate), and the Lotus Inn (expensive), all of which include buffet vegetarian meals, two yoga classes, and three meditation sessions per day. E-mail: ashram@luna.moonstar.com, Web site: www.moonstar.com/~yoga.

STATE'S OLDEST COVERED BRIDGE

Virginia's oldest covered bridge, in Long Island, spans Seneca Creek near the Roanoke River. Built in 1878, it was used until it had to be replaced in 1952. It's 1.5 miles down Rt. 705 from Rt. 761, 3.3 miles south of US 501 at Gladys.

SMITH MOUNTAIN LAKE

Central Virginia's favorite aquatic escape was formed in 1966 by the damming of the Roanoke River in Smith Mountain Gap. The resulting forty-mile lake has over 500 miles of gorgeous shoreline (featured in the movie *What About Bob?* with Richard Dreyfus and Bill Murray). Oak and pine forests shelter wild turkeys, deer, and woodchucks, and year-round bird species like pine warblers, tanagers, ospreys, and the rare bald eagle are joined by migratory ducks, geese, loons, and occasionally great tundra swans.

Information and Activities

At Bridgewater Plaza, on the south side of Hales Ford Bridge (Rt. 122 south from Bedford), you'll find a **visitors center** operated by the Smith Mountain Lake Chamber of Commerce, tel. (800) 676-8203 or (540) 721-1203, fax 721-7796, Web site: www.smlchamber.com, along with one of two dozen marinas scattered along the shoreline. At just about any of these you can rent Jet-Skis, canoes, sailboats, paddleboats, and fishing boats by the hour or day as well as buy bait and equipment; try **Webster's Marine Center**, tel. (800) 325-9110 or (540) 297-5228; **Captain's Quarters,** tel. (540) 721-7777; and the **Saunders Marina** at the end of Rt. 626 on the north side, tel. (540) 297-6109 or 297-4412.

Fishing in Smith Mountain Lake is outstanding, especially for black bass, muskie, and walleye. Striped bass are in season year-round—the state record (45 lbs., 10 oz.) was taken here in 1995. Guides like **Reel Time Charters**, tel. (888) 202-3474 or (540) 970-3524, and **My Time Guide Service,** tel. (800) 817-5007 or (540) 721-5007, provide equipment and advice. Trips of two to four people can be either four or eight hours long.

Contact **Bridgewater Parasail**, tel. (540) 721-1639, for a short flight behind a drag-boat over the water. **Virginia Air Services,** tel. (540) 297-4500, runs sightseeing flights in a high-wing Wilga out of the small local airport. Of course there's plenty of **shopping** possibilities in the gourmet markets and antique stores along Rt. 122 on both sides of the bridge. Three lakefront **golf courses**—Mariner's Landing, tel. (540) 297-7888; Sycamore Ridge, tel. (540) 297-6490; and The Westlake, tel. (800) 296-7277 or (540) 721-4214—are open to the public. You can tour the **Smith Mountain Dam,** tel. (540) 985-2587, in the Recreation Area of the same name, at the east end of the lake daily 10 a.m.-6 p.m.

Smith Mountain Lake State Park

Sixteen miles of shoreline and the only public swimming beach in the lake fall within this small park, tel. (540) 297-6066, on the north shore of the lake off Rt. 626. Facilities include paddleboats for rent, hiking trails, and 50 primitive campsites for tents and vehicles ($7) open March-December.

Accommodations

Don and Mary Davis's **Stone Manor Bed & Breakfast,** 1135 Stone Manor Place, tel. (540) 297-1414, is at the west end of the lake. The beautiful stone house has three rooms, private docks, a pool, and a lighted boardwalk along 690 feet of waterfront. Moderate. To get there take Rt. 757 from Rt. 24, pass Goodview, take a right onto Rt. 653, another right at the Sycamore Ridge Gold Club sign, and continue one mile.

Campers can hole up at the state park (see above), or the **Crazy Horse Campground & Marina,** tel. (540) 721-2792, on Rt. 122 a mile north of Hale's Ford Bridge ($15-18). The **Camper's Paradise Marina,** , tel. (540) 297-6109, is along Rt. 616 on the south side, with full-hookup sites for $27.50 and moderate motel rooms.

Events

Only members of the Virginia BASS Federation can enter the **Mr. Bass Tournament** in mid-April, but anyone can watch and admire the monster catches. In June, the **Trebark ASA Pro-Am Archery Tournament** pits 250 pros and 1,000 amateurs against one another for $93,000 in prizes. Saunders Marina hosts an **Antique and Classic Boat Show and Rally** in August, with mahogany and cedar cruisers, runabouts, and sailboats on display for free. Fifteen wineries come for the **Smith Mountain Lake Wine Festival** at Barnard's Landing in late September.

BOOKER T. WASHINGTON NATIONAL MONUMENT

Turn-of-the-century America's most influential and powerful black activist was born a slave on a small Virginia tobacco farm in 1856. Freed by the Emancipation Proclamation, the Washington family moved to West Virginia, where a young Booker struggled to take advantage of a startling new opportunity: education. First he rose every day before dawn to work in a salt mine so his afternoons would be free for school. Then, at age 16, Booker walked most of the 500 miles back to Virginia to attend the Hampton Institute, one of the country's leading schools for blacks, where he would eventually become a teacher.

In 1881 Washington opened his own school, the Tuskegee Institute in Alabama. A low point in race relations, personified by the rising Ku Klux Klan, intensified the fine balance between educating fellow blacks in agriculture and industrial skills and antagonizing whites. His non-confrontational stance, calling for interracial cooperation without rocking the boat too much by abruptly abolishing social segregation, drew criticism from within his own race.

Nonetheless, Washington endured critical attacks and racial slurs to become the leading black figure of his day. His famous Atlanta Compromise Address of 1895 crystallized his conservative viewpoint, which gradually became more liberal in his later years. In 1901 he published an autobiography, *Up From Slavery,* and he died at Tuskegee in 1915.

The farm where Washington was born into servitude is on Rt. 122 west of Smith Mountain Lake. The visitors center, managed by the National Park Service, tel. (540) 721-2094, Web site: www.nps.gov/bowa, has a short video and museum displays on Washington's life. From there, a short walking trail leads past reconstructed buildings and stone outlines of the original structures, including the owners' home and the building where Washington was born. Costumed interpreters lead guided tours during the summer, and the 1.5-mile Jack-o-Lantern Trail heads off into the woods. Open daily 9 a.m.-4:30 p.m.; free.

Booker T. Washington

THE COAST

A simple concept—Virginia meets the ocean—is much more complex in reality. Comprising both the state's largest city and towns so small that everyone in the phone book could ride the same school bus (a short one), the coastline embraces some of Virginia's greatest diversity in both its landscape and its people. Aside from the sea, its major defining feature is the Chesapeake Bay, whose mouth opens onto the one of the finest—and largest, and busiest—natural ports in the world. Around this harbor spreads Hampton Roads, officially the Norfolk-Virginia Beach-Newport News Metropolitan Statistical Area, home to 1.4 million people, a quarter of Virginia's population and more than the total population of 13 other entire states.

Second only to northern Virginia in growth, the Hampton Roads area boasts the world's largest coal-shipping port, privately owned shipyard, and naval facility. A third of its workers are employed by the Department of Defense or private defense contractors. Yet around this megalopolis—close enough, in parts, to see its glow at night—stretch some of the state's most pristine acres, covering miles of undisturbed shoreline, barrier islands, marshes, and estuaries.

Highlights

Most of the two and a half million people who visit Virginia's coast every year have their sights set on the Historic Peninsula, where the United States began—twice. Only a short drive apart are Jamestown, the first European settlement in the New World in 1607, and Yorktown, site of the final battle of the American Revolution. In between is Colonial Williamsburg, one of America's most popular family destinations, where life in the 18th century is re-created down to belt buckles and bootstraps. Venerable historic plantations, including Shirley, America's oldest, and Berkeley, site of the first Thanksgiving, preside over the James River.

Along with nightlife, restaurants, and hotels, Hampton Roads offers some of Virginia's most outstanding museums, including the Mariner's Museum in Newport News and the Virginia Marine Sciences Museum in Virginia Beach. The city of Hampton is rich in African-American history, and Portsmouth—birthplace of almost 200 WW II warships—sits just across the Elizabeth River from Norfolk, home to the U.S. Navy Atlantic fleets. To the east, Virginia Beach boasts 38 miles of beaches and a scrubbed-up version of a classic boardwalk.

Hikers, boaters, and bikers need only insect repellent, sunscreen, and a water bottle to explore the depths of the Great Dismal Swamp and amazingly unsullied coastal preserves including First Landing/Seashore State Park, almost with-

THE COAST

© MOON PUBLICATIONS, INC.

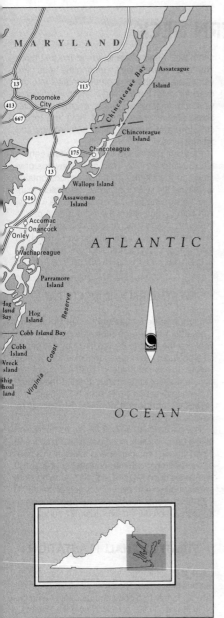

MARYLAND

Assateague
Island

Pocomoke
City

Chincoteague
Island

Chincoteague

Wallops Island

Assawoman
Island

Accomac
Onancock

Onley

Wachapreague

ATLANTIC

Parramore
Island

Hog
Island
Bay

Hog
Island

Cobb Island Bay

Cobb
Island

Wreck
Island

Ship
Shoal
Island

OCEAN

in walking distance of downtown Virginia Beach, and False Cape State Park. Reaching toward the interior of the bay, "the Necks" (local parlance for the area's skinny peninsulas delineated by rivers) offer a quiet rural escape dotted with historic mansions and Indian reservations. In a category of its very own is the Eastern Shore, home to archaic harbor towns, gourmet crab shacks, and Chincoteague's wild ponies.

Access

The only Virginia interstate that heads seaward is I-64 from Richmond, threading the Historic Peninsula as it runs east to Williamsburg and the Hampton Roads area. US 17 leaves Fredericksburg for the Middle Neck, where it joins with US 360 before crossing the York River at Yorktown. Farther south, US 460 connects Petersburg with Suffolk near Hampton Roads, and US 58 rolls east from Emporia more or less along the North Carolina state line toward Portsmouth. Two of the most scenic ways to reach the coast are Rt. 5, which passes half a dozen James River Plantations southeast of Richmond, and US 13 down the length of the Eastern Shore from Maryland.

NORTHERN NECK

Reaching bayward between broad, patient rivers, the Necks evoke the Piedmont—but with a shoreside twist. A hazy light filters across the flat farmland, where the odor of freshly mown fields mixes with the slightly salty breeze off the Chesapeake Bay, and talk at the local store is as likely to be about fixing outboards as about maintaining Chevies. Replete with local color—John Boy's Market, Ernie's Gas Station, an annual "Ugly Pick-Up" contest in the twon of Village—it's even more rural than much of central Virginia. Most visitors come for quiet walks, fishing, boating, and shopping from spring to fall (in the off season, many towns completely shut down their tourist facilities).

For more information on Northern Neck, contact the **Northern Neck Travel Council,** in Reedville, tel. (800) 393-6180, fax (804) 453-7096.

GEORGE WASHINGTON BIRTH-PLACE NATIONAL MONUMENT

The father of his country squalled into the light on February 22, 1732, on Pope's Creek Plantation, on the southern bank of the Potomac. It doesn't seem like a bad place to spend the first three and a half years of life, in among the trees here where the meandering creek empties into the river. Although the building in which Washington was born is gone, an outline in crushed oyster shells shows where it stood, next to a reconstructed farm complete with outbuildings and animal pens.

Pleasant paths lead from the visitors center, tel. (804) 224-1732, Web site: www.nps.gov/gewa, to the Memorial House, which contains an original tea table. Costumed interpreters manage the working farm, which provides a window into 18th-century life in the Tidewater. A nature trail continues to a picnic area, and at the end of the road is a family burial ground and a beach on the Potomac. The monument is on Rt. 204 off Rt. 3, open daily 9 a.m.-5 p.m.; $2 pp.

WESTMORELAND STATE PARK

Ancient marine fossils trapped in Horsehead Cliffs attest to the age (upwards of 127 million years) of the sediments that make up this peninsula between the Rappahannock and Potomac Rivers. It was set aside in 1936 as one of Virginia's first six state parks. Behind the beach and steep riverside bluffs stretch 1,295 acres of meadows and forest populated by beavers, hawks, and turkeys.

The park, on Rt. 347 off Rt. 3, has horse and hiking trails, a swimming pool, picnic areas, and a playground. You can spend the night in a one- or two-bedroom cabin (moderate) or one of 100 campsites open March-Dec.; $11. A camp store sells supplies, and the visitors center, tel. (804) 493-8821, rents rowboats and paddleboats in season. Open daily dawn-dusk; $1 per car.

STRATFORD HALL PLANTATION

George Washington isn't Northern Neck's only famous native son. The other was born on an estate his family had occupied for almost a century. In the late 1730s on a bluff near the Potomac,

---

WESTMORELAND BERRY FARM

You can pick your own raspberries, blackberries, blueberries, and strawberries at this 80-acre farm along the Rappahannock. Or you can stop by just to sample over a dozen seasonal fruits, including apricots, peaches, cherries, apples, plums, and pumpkins. A snack bar serves fruit sundaes, frozen yogurt, and other toothsome mouthfuls, and families from Fredericksburg and beyond come to enjoy wagon rides, farm animals, and crafts at the Tri-Berry Festival in June.

The Farm, tel. (800) 997-2377 or (804) 224-8967, is southwest of Oak Grove on Rt. 638, reached from Rt. 3 via Rt. 634. It's open during growing season (May-Oct.) Mon.-Sat. 8 a.m.-6 p.m. and Sunday 10 a.m.-6 p.m.

Thomas Lee built a huge mansion—shaped like an H in honor of his wife, Hanna. His nephew, Henry, moved in in 1782 and married Annie Hill Carter of Shirley Plantation. Henry went on to make a name for himself in the Revolutionary War as Light-Horse Harry Lee. But on January 19, 1807, just four years before Henry lost his fortune in land speculation and moved the family to Alexandria, Annie gave birth to a son who was destined for even greater fame: Robert E. Lee.

The Great House, one of the most majestic edifices in the state, looks like a brick castle set back a short distance from the river. Sixteen fireplaces and numerous 17th- and 18th-century furnishings fill the cavernous interior. These include many Lee heirlooms, such as a 1660 clock and the crib where Robert slept as a baby. Notice the 17-foot "inverted tray" ceiling in the Great Hall, and ask about the fireplace angels to which Robert bid good-bye as the family was packing to move. Downstairs are servants' quarters, the original kitchen, bedrooms, and a schoolroom where the teacher slept.

Stratford Hall, tel. (804) 493-8038 or 493-8371, Web site: www.stratfordhall.org, is on Rt. 214 off Rt. 3. A reception center houses a museum where you can learn about estimating the age of clay pipes by the diameter of their stems, and a gift shop selling fresh-ground corn and oats from the estate's fully functional mill. There's also a snack bar and a log-cabin dining room serving a hearty plantation lunch daily ($9 adults, $5 children). Three miles of nature trails explore the working plantation's 1,700 rural acres. Annual events include a free open house on Robert's birthday (January 19), another on African-American Heritage Day (usually the last weekend in February), and chamber-music concerts in the summer and fall with plantation dinners by candlelight. Open daily 9 a.m.-4:30 p.m.; $7 adults, $3 children.

REEDVILLE

Founded ("by Northerners," glowers one pamphlet) in 1867, this small city was reportedly the richest per capita in the country around WW I, thanks to the abundant menhaden fishing in Chesapeake Bay. Today, boats sit in the driveways of tidy houses along Main St. (Rt. 360),

which dead-ends at the water along Millionaire's Row, named for a succession of drop-dead-gorgeous Victorian mansions.

Sights

A **Fisherman's Museum,** tel. (804) 453-6529, e-mail: bunker@crosslink.net, Web site: www.northernneck.com/museum, has been set up in an 1875 waterman's house along Main St. just before Millionaire's Row. Displays of ship models, photos, and tools lead the visitor to a crabbing skiff and traditional workboat moored to the rear dock. Open Wed.-Mon. 10:30 a.m.-4 p.m. (weekends only Nov.-May); $2 adults.

Accommodations

A good reason in itself to come all the way out here is **The Morris House Bed and Breakfast Inn,** tel. (804) 453-7016, fax 453-9032, e-mail: morrishs@crosslink.net, Web site: www.eaglesnest.net/morrishouse, occupying a lavish turn-of-the-century mansion near the end of Millionaire's Row. Ornate but tasteful furnishings range from hand-crocheted bedspreads to a Victorian rocking horse. Two rooms are moderate to expensive with full breakfast, and two suites, including the Turret Suite on the entire top floor, are premium. A cottage out back with a kitchenette is premium.

Almost across the street sits **The Bailey-Cockrell House,** tel. (804) 453-5900, fax 453-2690, where Charlotte and Alf Braxton serve breakfast under a crystal chandelier just down the hall from a sitting room overlooking the water. Guests can choose from one room (expensive) and two suites (premium).

Take a left onto Fleeton Rd. before the final stretch of Main St. to reach Fleet's Point, home of the **Cedar Grove Bed & Breakfast Inn,** tel. (800) 497-8215 or (804) 453-3915. This spacious, elegant colonial revival home on the water dates to 1913 and features a sunroom and period antiques in a formal parlor. Breakfasts reflect hostess Susan Tipton's experience at the New York Culinary Institute, and tennis, croquet, bicycles, and a hammock are available to guests. Premium.

The **Chesapeake Bay/Smith Island KOA,** 2.5 miles northeast of the intersection of Rt. 652 and US 360, tel. (804) 453-3430, has campsites for $20-25. Boats to Smith Island, Maryland, leave from here from May through October.

cruising the waters of Northern Neck

VIRGINIA TOURISM CORPORATION

Food

The only real restaurant in town is **Elijah's,** tel. (804) 453-3621, near the Bailey-Cockrell House. Seafood, of course, is the specialty, along with homemade bread, desserts, and soups served outside on the wide porch. Elijah's is open seasonally for lunch on weekends and dinner Wed.-Sun. The deli counter at **Cockrell's Creek Seafood,** tel. (804) 453-6326, south on Seaboard Rd. off Fleeton Rd., sells scallops, shrimp, crabs, and other marine delicacies to take out or eat there. Open in season Mon.-Thurs. 10-4, Fri.-Sat. 10 a.m.-5 p.m.

Recreation

Pittman's Charters, tel. (804) 453-3643, sends fishing groups after stripers, croaker, trout, and bluefish aboard the 42-foot *Mystic Lady* May-Dec. Charters, including gear, run $55 pp with a minimum of seven people and can accommodate up to 23 people. **Captain Billy's Charters,** tel. (800) 850-1557 or (804) 580-7292, runs similar trips from the Ingram Bay Marina, near Wicomico Church, for $360 per day (maximum six people).

Nearby Ophelia, on Rt. 644 off US 360, is the home base for **River Rats,** tel. (804) 453-3064, fax 453-3433, e-mail: federhar@crosslink.net, Web site: www.virginia.org/riverrats. They offer sea kayak trips to Westmoreland State Park and Pope's Creek by day ($25 pp) and night ($50), rentals ($35 per day), and lessons.

Day trips to Tangier Island and lunch cruises up the Rappahannock to the Ingleside Plantation Winery are only two of the trips offered by **Tangier and Chesapeake Cruises,** tel. (804) 453-2628 or (800) 598-2628, Web site: www.eaglesnest.net/tangier. They also offer narrated lunch and dinner tours aboard a paddlewheeler to Fredericksburg, with onboard dancing, on Friday and Saturday. Boats leave May-Oct. from the Buzzards Point Marina, reached by taking a right before Reedville onto Fairport Rd. (Rt. 626), followed by a left onto Buzzard Point Road.

Events

Contact the Watermen's Museum, tel. (757) 887-2641, for details on annual events. The **Waterman's Festival and Blessing of the Fleet,** the first full weekend in May, packs tiny Reedville with crowds hankering for tons of seafood, boat rides and tours, and demonstrations of crab picking and crab-pot building. The second weekend in June brings the **Bluefish Derby,** at Buzzard's Point Marina. Anyone whose catch beats the standing state record of 25 lbs. 4 oz. can claim a $50,000 cash prize plus a new pickup, boat, and trailer.

The **Traditional Small Boat Show,** around the Fourth of July, showcases hand-crafted boats under 20 feet, and the traditional **Oyster Roast and Bluegrass on the Lawn** takes place the second Saturday in November.

IRVINGTON AND VICINITY

Christ Church

The centerpiece of this small fishing town is a monolithic house of worship completed in 1735 by Robert "King" Carter. This is one of the few unaltered colonial churches in the country. It features a high arching ceiling, shoulder-high walls between family-sized pew "boxes," and a three-level pulpit, although it has no bell tower. Services are still held here from June to Labor Day, and a museum/visitors center, tel. (804) 438-6855, is open April-Nov. Mon.-Sat. 10 a.m.-4 p.m., Sunday 2-5 p.m. The church is on Christ Church Rd. (Rt. 646) off Rt. 200 just north of Irvington.

Accommodations and Food

Along Carter's Creek you'll find both sections of the first-class **Tides Resorts,** tel. (800) TIDES-INN (800-843-7466) or (804) 438-5000, fax 438-5222, Web site: www.tidesinn.com. The Tides Inn, on King Carter Dr. (Rt. 634), is an all-inclusive getaway rated among the top 20 in the country by Condé Nast *Traveler.* Open April-Dec., it features the top-rated Golden Eagle golf course, a sandy beach, saltwater pool, and yacht cruises aboard the *Miss Anne.* Luxury. Turn off Christ Church Rd. onto Garkins Rd. (Rt. 709) at the church to find the less formal **Tides Lodges,** with 60 rooms, tennis courts, marinas, and pools. Premium-luxury.

In 1890, a schoolhouse opened in an old Methodist church near the center of Irvington. Today the building houses **The Hope and Glory Inn,** 634 King Carter Dr., tel. (800) 497-8228 or (804) 438-6053, Web site: www.hopeandglory.com, decked out with folk art and a large central lobby where classrooms once echoed with children's voices. If the four upstairs bedrooms are full, there are also four guest cottages out back near an enclosed outdoor bath with claw-foot tub, shower, and sink. The English cottage garden features a moon patch that blooms in the evening. Premium to luxury.

The **White Stone Wine and Cheese Co.,** tel. (804) 435-2000, on Rt. 3 in the town of White Stone, offers the largest local wine selection and sandwiches in a small cafe.

MIDDLE NECK

URBANNA

One of 20 port towns established by a 1680 Act of Assembly, Urbanna has weathered pirate attacks and three wars during its centuries as a tobacco export center and fishing village. Watermen still unload their day's catch on wharves shared by recreational boaters and anglers—only a short walk from Victorian homes on the National Register of Historic Places.

Sights

Opened in 1876, the **R.S. Bristow Store,** Virginia St. at Cross St., tel. (804) 758-2210, once sold patent medicines, live chickens, and wood by the cord. A century and a quarter later, it's still going strong, selling clothes, gifts, and household goods. There's a shoe section where the post office used to be, and an old-fashioned rolling ladder to reach the higher shelves. The nearby **court house building** dates to 1748, making it the oldest structure in Urbanna. It's served various functions over the years, shifting from church to Confederate Civil War barracks to its present role as women's club headquarters.

Accommodations

In addition to 13 modest rooms, the **Urbanna Inn,** 250 Virginia St., tel. (888) 758-4852 or (804) 758-4852, fax 758-0516, has one of the nicest restaurants on the Middle Neck. Entrées include seafood, poultry, meat, and pasta selections, and sorbet comes between courses. There's a fun raw bar toward the rear. Open for lunch and dinner Mon.-Fri., all meals Saturday and Sunday. Inexpensive to moderate. The **Atherson Hall B&B,** 250 Prince George St., tel. (804) 758-2809, was originally the home of a 19th-century schooner captain. Moderate. **Bradwick's White Swan B&B,** 350 Virginia St., tel. (804) 758-3367, has three rooms (inexpensive to moderate).

The cozy **Sangraal By-The-Sea,** tel. (804)

776-6500, doubles as an AYH hostel ($15 members, $20 nonmembers) and country inn ($35 pp, $70 with all meals). The owners give sailing lessons for $30 per hour and offer bareboat charters for $120 per day. It's a little tricky to find, especially at night; take Rt. 628 off Rt. 33/3 about three miles east of the turnoff for the Rt. 3 bridge across the Rappahannock. Turn north at the Wake Post Office onto Carlton Rd. (Rt. 626), and it's about half-mile farther, on the left.

Waterfront campsites at the **Bethpage Camp Resort,** tel. (804) 758-4349, about 15 miles west near the intersection of Rt. 17 and Rt. 684, are $20-22 with full hookups. This huge place has two pools, a tennis court, grocery store, and marina. Open April-November.

handmade flint points. Open Tues.-Sun. 10 a.m.-4 p.m.; $2.50 adults, $1.25 children. Take Rt. 633 or Rt. 626 south from Rt. 30, then follow the signs.

A necklace that once belonged to Pocahontas is displayed in a museum on the **Mattaponi Reservation,** tel. (804) 769-2194, off Rt. 30 opposite the Pamunkey reservation via Rt. 626 or Rt. 640. Other artifacts date back as far as 5000 B.C. Open Saturday and Sunday 2-5 p.m.; $1 pp. The Minnie Ha-Ha Educational Trading Post offers a range of activities that introduce visitors to native medicines, cooking, and pottery-making (by appointment only, $2.50 pp). Call the museum for information on traditional dances open to the public.

INDIAN RESERVATIONS

A museum on the **Pamunkey Indian Reservation,** tel. (804) 843-4792, traces the history of the largest Powhatan chiefdom. Exhaustive displays include beautiful ceremonial garments and an extensive collection of mean-looking weapons, including the world's largest collection of modern

WEST POINT

Take the plunge at the **West Point Skydiving Center,** tel. (804) 785-9707 or (757) 934-3964, offering tandem jumps after a one-hour class for $185 pp. A 4-6 hour accelerated free-fall course will have you yanking your own ripcord the same day for $285.

COLONIAL WILLIAMSBURG AND THE HISTORIC PENINSULA

America's largest and most popular living history museum presents the colonial capital as it existed on November 11, 1775, the tense eve of the Revolutionary War. One of the most ambitious historical projects ever, this isn't just a re-created farm or household—this is an entire town brought back to life and inhabited by people portraying a cadre of craftspeople, slaves, merchants, and aristocrats.

It may not be everyone's cup of tea (or ale), but Colonial Williamsburg is a remarkable feat, the product of decades of research, experiment, and refinement. The realism—aside from the hordes of tourists—is amazing. Horse-drawn carriages clop past a merchant arguing with his neighbor over the best course of political action, while nonplussed ducks wander down a dusty lane where a smith stands sweating over his

forge. And best of all, you can even take part in it yourself, whether joining a tipsy colonial gentleman singing bawdy tavern songs, learning the finer points of baking apple fritters from the man's decorous wife, immersing yourself in the latest findings at an archeological dig, or sitting on the courthouse jury to decide whether the pig thief deserves a flogging or just a day in the stocks.

Children especially love the "living" aspect of Williamsburg, rolling hoops across the Palace Green in three-cornered hats or taking lessons from the Dancing Master in the Governor's Palace. Colonial Williamsburg has done an enviable job of marketing itself as the ultimate family destination—covering both the educational and entertainment angles—and a million visitors a year seem to agree.

*truly colonial
transportation*

HISTORY

Rural acreage known as Middle Plantation got a rude awakening when its was picked as the site for the new colonial capital in 1699. The planter aristocracy of the day had decided it needed a more sophisticated spot for the business of governing and socializing than damp Jamestown, and this site, near the newly established "Free schoole & college" of William and Mary, seemed suitable.

Plans were immediately set in motion to transform a scattering of plantation buildings into a capital fit for the New World's oldest and richest colony. First to be laid out was the Duke of Gloucester St., 100 feet wide and almost a mile long, from William and Mary's Wren Building at one end to the capitol at the other. A grassy mall led to the Governor's Palace.

The town quickly became the cultural and political center of Virginia, and the focus of colonial America's most fashionable social scene. As a ceremonial city with little manufacturing base, Williamsburg swelled during "Public Times" in April and October. Rural gentry rode in from their plantations to attend sessions of the House of Burgesses and Governor's Council, delighting in a social whirl that, they said, rivaled London's. Countless balls, fairs, and races competed for attention with performances by English actors and musicians in one of the earliest theaters in America.

Williamsburg welcomed some impressive names during its heyday, including George Washington, George Mason, and Patrick Henry. Thomas Jefferson first arrived in the early 1760s as a student at William and Mary and returned later as a member of the House of Burgesses. In 1719, 13 pirates from the ship of the notorious Edward Teach (Blackbeard) were tried and condemned to death in the General Court chamber in the Capitol building. A decade later, Williamsburg boasted the first successful printing press in the colony, followed soon after by its first newspaper and paper mill.

Patrick Henry defied the British Stamp Act in his "Caesar-Brutus" speech to the House of Burgesses on May 30, 1765, throwing sparks ever closer to the fuse of revolution. When Governor Spotswood dissolved the House of Burgesses as it was about to vote to boycott British goods in 1769, its members simply reassembled at the Raleigh tavern and voted there. On May 6, 1776, the first Virginia Convention met in Williamsburg to declare Virginia an independent commonwealth, and four years later the capital was moved to Richmond to escape the invading British.

British, Continental, and French forces all billeted on the city's grassy lawns during the Revolutionary War, providing temporary relief from an economic slump that continued into the 19th century by buying goods from local merchants. Restoration began in the 1920s at the instigation of Rev. Dr. W.A.R. Goodwin, rector of the historic

---

COAST AREA WINERIES

Ingleside Plantation Vineyards
tel. (804) 224-8687; e-mail: Inglewine@aol.com
Near Oak Grove (Northern Neck); Rt. 638 south of Oak Grove
Hosts Northern Neck Seafood Extravaganza in late September.

Williamsburg Winery, Ltd.
tel. (757) 229-0999; e-mail: wine@wmbg.com; Web site: www.wmbg.com/winery
Near Williamsburg; I-64 exit 242A to Rt. 199 west, left onto Brookwood Dr., left onto Lake Powell Rd.
   for 0.75 miles
Gabriel Archer Tavern next door.

Windy River Winery
tel. (804) 361-2519
Near Beaverdam; I-95 N exit 98, Rt. 684 west 10 miles, Rt. 738 north 1.5 miles

---

Bruton Parish Church. Bankrolled by no less than John D. Rockefeller, Jr. (who signed documents anonymously as "Mr. David"), the plan met some local resistance until residents realized it was probably the best thing to happen to the city in a century and a half.

Exhaustive research in libraries and museums in Europe and America uncovered documents, drawings, and maps detailing Williamsburg's faded glory. Over 450 buildings were torn down, 91 were built, and 67 colonial structures restored (with their inhabitants allowed to stay on for life).

Eighty-eight original buildings have been meticulously restored on 173 of the town's 220 original acres. Over 500 other structures have been rebuilt as closely as possible to their original specifications, surrounded by 90 acres of lawns and gardens and a 3,000-acre buffer zone against further development. Restoration is constantly being refined as new archeological information comes to light, from hearth-stone material to hand-painted wallpaper designs.

VISITING COLONIAL WILLIAMSBURG

If you don't plan ahead, visiting Colonial Williamsburg can be an exercise, at best, in patience. Reservations for hotels and special events are essential during peak months (April, May, July, August, October, late November, and December), and early morning is always the best time to visit the more popular stops, such as the Governor's Palace and Capitol building. You can do the highlights in one day, even a single tiring morning, but a much better plan is to leave yourself a few days—even a week—to enjoy wandering the back lanes, chatting with the interpreters, and lingering over a pint at one of the taverns.

Williamsburg is open 365 days a year, with its main attractions open April-Oct. 9:30 a.m.-5 p.m. and Nov.-March 10 a.m.-4 p.m. Restaurants and taverns bustle until after dark, and the streets are always free to wander, but you'll need to buy passes to enter the historic buildings.

First stop is the **Colonial Williamsburg Visitors Center,** run by the Colonial Williamsburg Foundation, tel. (757) 220-7645 or (800) 447-8679, fax (757) 565-8938, e-mail: cwres@cwf.org, Web site: www.colonialwilliamsburg.org/travel. The center, off US 60 Bypass and the Colonial Parkway just east of Rt. 132, is an event in itself, with Burger King and Texaco branches, color-coded parking lots, and a gigantic bookstore. Ticket lines can take a while, so you might want to designate a volunteer to wait while everyone else in your party catches the 35-minute orientation film, *Williamsburg—The Story of a Patriot.*

Admission passes come in a few different versions, but you can always upgrade to the next level. The **Basic Admission,** good for one day, costs $26 adults, $15 children, and includes an orientation walk and entrance to the Folk Art Center, the Gallery, and all major buildings except the Governor's Palace and wheelwright. The **Colonist's Pass** ($30 adults, $17 children) is good for two days and includes all historic area exhibits. The **Patriot's Pass** ($34 adults,

$19 children) is good for a whole year and includes Carter's Grove, Bassett Hall, and a discount on evening events outside of the holidays. These last two are the best deals and the most convenient, since you'll probably want to see attractions not covered by the basic ticket.

You can buy individual tickets to the two museums ($10 adults, $6.50 children), the Governor's Palace, and Carter's Grove (both $17 adults, $10 children). Tickets are also available at a booth in Merchant's Square.

The Colonial Williamsburg Foundation has concocted a number of packages involving accommodations, meals, golf, and seasonal events. The **Revolutionary Fun** package includes two nights' lodging and admission to Colonial Williamsburg, Jamestown Settlement, the Yorktown Victory Center, Busch Gardens, and Water Country USA, for anywhere from $213 to $428 for a family of four. Tickets can be bought here, at Monticello, or at Virginia's Washington, D.C., information center. **Felicity in Williamsburg** is a package shaped around the life of Felicity Merriman, a character in the popular children's series, and offers girls the opportunity to perfect their curtsies and needlepoint. Prices start at $230 for a family for four for two nights.

With any ticket, you'll receive a copy of the tabloid *Visitor's Companion,* which contains a map and details on the week's events.

If you like, you can exchange your modern bucks for Colonial dollars good at Williamsburg hotels, restaurants, and stores (you can change them back when you leave).

From the visitors center, you catch a shuttle bus to the historic area.

HISTORICAL SIGHTS

Governor's Palace

This mammoth building was constructed 1708-20 to symbolize the power of the Crown in the colonies. Thomas Jefferson and Patrick Henry stepped through the door as the capital's first two governors, shortly before it burned to its foundation in 1781. It's been restored to the era of Governor Botetourt (1768-70), one of the last royal governors who was actually respected by his colonial subjects (maybe the lavish dinner parties had something to do with it).

An astounding rosette of muskets on the ceiling of the entrance hall, along with dozens of crisscrossed swords on the walls, show the true basis of British power in the colonies. Don't miss the birdcages in the butler's pantry and the 10 acres of restored gardens with topiary works, holly maze, and fish pond. The Governor's Palace is the single most popular building in Colonial Williamsburg, receiving 650,000 visitors annually, so try to get there early in the day.

The Capitol

Shaped like a bulbous H, this brick building is a reconstruction of the original structure finished in 1705 and burned in 1747. Large round windows admit light to twin chambers for the House of Burgesses and Governor's Council, as well as the General Courtroom, with its dark wood paneling, snakelike glass chandelier, and semicircular bench with chairs for the governor and council. George Washington, Thomas Jefferson, and Patrick Henry all polished their oratory in the House of Burgesses, the lower elected body that sent proposed laws to the Council for consideration. Interpreters explain how jury duty today is a garden party compared to what it was in the 18th century, when juries were denied heat, food, and water in order to encourage a speedy verdict. A military encampment in the Capitol Square explains why the House of Burgesses is currently dissolved (or was, in November 1775).

Courthouse

Many a criminal quaked at the sight of the cupola and weathervane atop Williamsburg's Courthouse, where severe punishment followed quick judgment. Criminal cases from wife-beating to murder were tried in this original building, along with more mundane matters such as debtor disputes and the issuing of licenses. Guilty parties were then fined, thrown in jail, or simply flogged at the whipping post outside. Visitors can take part in the dispensation of colonial justice on either side of the docket—as a member of the jury or a defendant. Punishments are optional.

Magazine and Guardhouse

Weapons and 60,000 lbs. of gunpowder were once stored in this octagonal structure, built in 1715 on Duke of Gloucester St. opposite the

To Williamsburg
Pottery Factory

612

Walker Mill
Reservoir

60

RICHMOND RD.

ANVIL

LONGHILL RD.

612

OLD MILL HOUSE OF
PANCAKES AND WAFFLES

LONGHILL CONNECTOR RD.

322

LONGHILL RD.

ABERDEEN
BARN

MAMA STEVE'S HOUSE OF PANCAKES

GOVERNOR
SPOTTSWOOD MOTEL

THE JEFFERSON
RESTAURANT

COLONIAL
MOTEL

LOBSTER HOUSE

162

60

HOLIDAY
INN

615

IRONBOUND RD.

THE LIBRARY
TAVERN

HSING LING

THOMPSON
GUEST HOUSE

LEWIS GUEST HOUSE

CHEZ TRINH

CARTER'S GUEST
HOUSE

162

WILLIAMSBURG
WOODLANDS

MONTICELLO AVE.

PRIMROSE
COTTAGE
B&B

LAFAYETTE

GOVERNOR'S
INN

COLONIAL
WILLIAMSBURG
VISITOR CENTER

132

COLONIAL
CAPITOL B&B

COLLEGE   OF

31   5

ST.

WILLIAM AND
MARY HALL

PAUL'S DELI

GOVERNOR'S PALACE

COLLEGE DELLY

BURTON PARISH
CHURCH

MERCHANT

Historic

WILLIAM   AND   MARY

WREN
BUILDING

SQUARE

Williamsburg

PUBLIC HOSPITAL OF 1773
DEWITT WALLACE DECORATIVE
ARTS GALLERY

WILLIAMSBURG
INN

FRANCIS
ST.

Lake
Matoaka

31

5

BOUNDARY ST.

WILLIAMSBURG
LODGE

Mill Creek
Pond

NEWPORT
HOUSE B&B

132

ADDY ALDRITCH
ROCKEFELLER
FOLK ART
CENTER

JOHN TYLER MEMORIAL HWY.

LIBERTY
ROSE B&B

COLONIAL
GARDENS B&B

COLONIAL NATIONAL HISTORICAL PKWY.

5

OLD CHICKAHOMINY
HOUSE

HENRY ST.

0   0.5 mi

0   0.5 km

199

31

To Jamestown

To Richmond

EXIT 238

143

64

132

MERRIMAC TRAIL

Queens
Lake

WILLIAMSBURG

To Yorktown

WHITE LION MOTEL

CAPITOL
LANDING RD.

5

31

163

HOLIDAY INN

KING WILLIAM
INN

PARKWAY
DR.

COLONIAL NATIONAL HISTORICAL PKWY.

NICHOLSON
ST.

162

SECOND ST.

143

Jones Pond

CAPITOL

YORK ST.

BASSETT
HALL

60

DUKE OF
GLOUCESTER ST.

PENNIMAN RD.

MERRIMAC TRAIL

QUARTERPATH
INN

PENNIMAN RD.

641

Duncan
Pond

199

BEN & JERRY'S

OAK DR.

EXIT 242

64

GOVERNMENT
ST.

Tutters Neck
Pond

199

60

143

VILLAGE SHOPS
AT KINGSMILL

To Kingsmill Resort, Anheuser-
Busch Brewery, Busch Gardens,
Water Country USA, Carter's
Grove Plantation

© MOON PUBLICATIONS, INC.

Courthouse. It later served as a meetinghouse, dance school, livery stable, and market before being fully restored and filled with flintlock muskets, cannons, bayonets, and powder barrels once again.

Raleigh Tavern

The unofficial capitol of Colonial Williamsburg was known for the quality of its entertainment as well as its discussion and gossip. Named for Sir Walter Raleigh, who founded the famous lost colony of Roanoke Island, NC, two decades before Jamestown's founding, the tavern witnessed the birth of the Phi Beta Kappa society and innumerable late-night soirees in its first few decades. Patriots including Thomas Jefferson and Light-Horse Harry Lee all endured hangovers after late nights in the Apollo ballroom (after evenings spent plotting the future of their infant country, no doubt). A table in the billiard room dates to 1738, and there's a bake shop in back that sells gingerbread and cider.

Brush-Everard House

Public Armorer John Brush built this house in 1717, making it one of Williamsburg's oldest buildings. Two-time mayor Thomas Everard moved in in the late 18th century, and it was continually occupied until 1946. It's furnished as a typical colonial craftsman might have been able to afford, with outstanding carved woodwork and a library containing books recommended by Jefferson as "the core of any educated gentleman's collection."

Bruton Parish Church

One of the country's oldest Episcopal churches stands at the foot of Palace Green, built in 1715 in the shape of a cross by Governor Spotswood, who included an enclosed covered pew for his own use. The walls and windows are original, and since services are still held here it's only open 9 a.m.-5 p.m. Mon.-Sat., noon-5 p.m. Sunday. Legend has it that a vault buried in the churchyard by Nathaniel Bacon holds gold chalices, original editions of the U.S. Constitution, the King James Bible, and the Book of Saint Peter, and proof that his father, Sir Francis Bacon, authored the plays attributed to Shakespeare. In spite of that last one, more than one researcher has dug among the graves with no luck.

Peyton Randolph House

One of Colonial Williamsburg's most elegant homes reflects the tastes of its owner, speaker of the House of Burgesses, president of the First Continental Congress, and the only native Virginian to be knighted. French military leaders Lafayette and Rochambeau lived here during the Yorktown campaign, enjoying its seven paneled rooms at the corner of Nicholson and England Streets. At Randolph's death, his cousin Thomas Jefferson purchased his books and used them to start the Library of Congress.

George Wythe House

A more conservative residence belonged to the first Virginian to sign the Declaration of Independence. (He didn't sign the Constitution, however, because it didn't contain antislavery provisions or a Bill of Rights.) As the first professor of law in America, Wythe taught Jefferson, Monroe, and future Chief Justice John Marshall at William and Mary. George Washington stayed in this house before the battle of Yorktown, and Rochambeau passed through after Cornwallis' surrender. A tree box topiary and hornbeam arbor fill the rear gardens, near an outbuilding where you can watch demonstrations of colonial cooking techniques.

Public Gaol

Offenders and the merely offensive, from pirates and runaway slaves to Tory sympathizers and the insane, all enjoyed the hospitality of Williamsburg's public jail. Built in 1704, it was used until 1910 and has been restored to its 1720s appearance. Miserable barred cells still hold the little extras—manacles, leg irons, and the like—that made every stay special.

Public Hospital of 1773

Speaking of madmen, Williamsburg's Public Hospital for Persons of Insane and Disordered Minds opened as the first facility in the country to care for the mentally ill. In the 18th century, insanity was considered a conscious choice, so along with the progressive therapies like sports and music, patients were also kept in cages, dunked in water, and held in manacles to "convince" them to mend their mindset. Conditions grew more humane in the 19th century under the administration of John Galt II, who introduced crafts shops and social gatherings for inmates. Successful treatments, though, remained elusive. Open Wed.-Mon., 11 a.m.-6 p.m.

Trade Sites

Master craftspeople, many of whom have served multi-year apprenticeships, practice Colonial-era crafts at dozens of shops and exhibits throughout the historic area. At the **gunsmith** house, an armorer explains the intricacies of a flintlock musket. You can watch handbills and newspapers being printed on an 18th-century press in the **Printing Office.** One of the best areas to watch demonstrations is near **Robertson's Windmill,** between the Governor's Palace and Randolph House, where coopers build casks and carpenters plane boards for the latest restoration. A **shoemaker, silversmith, saddlemaker,** and **wigmaker** operate along Duke of Gloucester St., and elsewhere you can catch a **milliner, wheelwright,** and **blacksmith** at work. Stop by the **Pasteur and Galt Apothecary Shop** for a disquieting display of medical knowledge (or ignorance) at the time.

College of William and Mary

America's second-oldest college was chartered on February 8, 1693, by King William III and Queen Mary II, consisting of three buildings in the angle formed by Richmond and Jamestown Roads. The **Wren Building** was named for Sir Christopher Wren, though he probably didn't design it, and is the oldest college building in the country (1695). Two wings containing a chapel and Great Hall embrace a courtyard whose fourth side was never enclosed as planned. To either side stand the **President's House,** still in use, and the **Brafferton,** originally built as an Indian School.

The college severed ties with Great Britain in 1776 and soon became the first school in the United States to have branches of law and modern languages, and operate under an honor system. Thomas Jefferson, James Monroe, and John Tyler are among its more prestigious alumni. It became state-supported in 1906 and went coeducational in 1918. Today it counts close to 8,000 students, most of whom take advantage of one of the top undergrad programs in the country, taught by over 667 faculty.

The Wren Building, restored to its 1776 appearance, is the only structure in the "ancient campus" open to the public. Call (757) 221-1540 for information.

Bassett Hall

The 19th-century home of John D. and Abby Aldrich Rockefeller has been restored to its 1930s splendor of Chippendale furniture, original paneling, and needlepoint rugs made by Abby herself. It sits amid 585 acres of woodlands across Francis St. from the Capitol, and is open by appointment to Patriot's Pass holders Thurs.-Tues. 10 a.m.-6 p.m. for audio tours.

A gunsmith displays his craft.

OTHER SIGHTS

DeWitt Wallace Decorative Arts Gallery

A gift of $14 million (the largest in Williamsburg's history) from DeWitt Wallace, the owner of *The Reader's Digest,* funded construction of this modern exhibition hall. Entered through the Public Hospital, the DeWitt Gallery houses an astonishing collection of 10,000 objects from England and America. Furniture, paintings, ceramics, textiles, silver, and glass on display dates to the 17th and 18th centuries. Highlights in the Masterworks Gallery upstairs include a Charles Wilson Peale portrait of George Washington and a case clock made for King William III in 1699. The **Gallery Cafe** serves light sandwiches, salads, soups, and wine for lunch Wed.-Mon. The gallery is open Wed.-Mon. 11 a.m.-6 p.m.

Abby Aldrich Rockefeller Folk Art Center

This world-class collection of folk art, ranging in age from the 1730s to the present, was the passion of John D. Rockefeller's wife, one of the first collectors to search out untutored rural artists in the 1920s and '30s. Everything from toys and weathervanes to painted furniture and tinware show that true inspiration can have the most humble beginnings. Notice the ship carvings and embroidered mourning pictures. Open Fri.-Wed., 10 a.m.-5 p.m.

America's Railroads on Parade

What began as a lobby display in the Citicorp building in New York City has evolved into one of the country's largest model-train layouts. Four thousand square feet of O-, HO-, and S-scale layouts re-create the 1940 New York World's Fair, the Colorado Rockies, and the skylines of Detroit, New York, and Boston (combined in a single city). The detail is amazing—notice the lobsters escaping from the pots on one tiny wharf, and the animated wood-choppers and ice skaters near the winter model of Pottersville, New York, the setting of the Jimmy Stewart classic *It's a Wonderful Life.*

America's Railroads, tel. (757) 220-8725, is in The Village Shops at Kingsmill on US 60 a few miles east of Colonial Williamsburg. It's open daily 10 a.m.-6 p.m.; $5 adults, $2.50 children 3-18.

ACCOMMODATIONS

With close to 10,000 hotel rooms, Williamsburg has no shortage of places to stay. Still, this is such a popular destination that reservations are always helpful—and essential during peak months of April, May, July, August, October, late November, and December. The **Williamsburg Hotel/Motel Association,** tel. (800) 899-9462, operates a reservation service that can help set up lodgings and meals in the area. You can also try **The Travel Tree,** tel. (757) 253-1571.

Colonial Williamsburg Foundation Hotels

For information and reservations for these accommodations in the historic area, call (800) 447-8679.

What could be more authentic after a long day in the 18th century than curling up in an actual colonial home? The foundation operates 24 **guest homes and inns,** each with its own unique history and a capacity of up to seven people. The Market Square Tavern is where Thomas Jefferson lodged as a student at William and Mary; the Quarter was a favorite of Cary Grant in the 1940s. Some of the buildings, including the Bracken Tenement and Ewing House, are original, while others are reconstructed. Many have canopied beds, fireplaces, and views of Duke of Gloucester Street. Expensive and up.

The **Williamsburg Inn,** 137 Francis St., tel. (757) 229-1000, fax 220-7096, is probably the finest hotel in the city if not the entire Historic Peninsula. No two of the 95 rooms in this five-star hotel are alike, but all are lavishly decorated with antiques. The Inn's formal Regency Dining Room is justly famous for its elegant setting and extensive wine list; the Regency Lounge provides a more casual option. English tea—including a children's version, Felicity's Tea—is served on Saturday and Sunday, and a convincing facsimile of Martha Washington attends occasionally. Guests have access to full sports facilities and three golf courses, including the nationally known Golden Horseshoe. Luxury.

Across England St. from the Abby Aldrich Rockefeller Folk Art Center stands the **Williamsburg Lodge,** 310 S. England St., tel. (757) 229-1000, fax 220-7799, a resort hotel popular with conference groups. Over 300 rooms alternate between Colonial and modern decor, and the sunken garden is perfect for an after-dinner ramble. Dining choices include the Bay Room Restaurant and the relaxed Lodge Cafe. Luxury. **Williamsburg Woodlands,** 102 Visitors Center Dr., tel. (757) 229-1000, fax 221-8942, offers 315 contemporary rooms next door to the Colonial Williamsburg visitors center in comfortably wooded surroundings. Moderate-premium. The **Governor's Inn,** 506 N. Henry St., tel. (757) 229-1000, fax 220-7019, began its career as a Sheraton a short walk from the visitors center and the historic area. Moderate-expensive.

Bed and Breakfasts

Century-old beech, oak, and poplar trees welcome you to the **Liberty Rose B&B,** 1022 Jamestown Rd., tel. (800) 545-1825 or (757) 253-1260, Web site: www.libertyrose.com, called the most romantic bed and breakfast in Williamsburg. Set on a hilltop, the two-story home features rooms with names like "Magnolia Peach" and "Savannah Lace," decorated with designer wallcoverings and vintage fabrics. Soak in an antique clawfoot tub or savor a gourmet breakfast on the sunny porch. Luxury.

Colonial Gardens, 1109 Jamestown Rd., tel. (757) 220-8087 or (800) 886-9715, fax (757) 253-1495, is just next door, with rocking chairs on the front porch and plush robes in the bedrooms. Breakfast is served on fine china in the formal dining room, and over the holidays a Christmas tree brightens each room. E-mail: colgdns@ widomaker.com, Web site: www.ontheline.com/ cgbb. Moderate to premium. German-born Inge Curtis opened **Primrose Cottage,** 706 Richmond Rd., tel. (800) 522-1901 or (757) 229-6421, fax 259-0717, Web site: www.primrose-cottage.com, as an outlet for her interests in cooking, gardening, and carpentry, and it shows in the beds of pansies and primroses in the front yard and her famous "Dutch Babies" for breakfast. Expensive to premium.

The **Colonial Capital Bed & Breakfast,** 501 Richmond Rd., tel. (800) 776-0570 or (757) 229-0233, fax 253-7667, occupies a 1926 colonial revival home across the street from William and Mary. Oriental rugs and family heirlooms fill the three-story house, whose large plantation parlor warmed by a roaring fire in the winter. E-mail: ccbb@widomaker.com, Web site: www.ccbb.com.

Expensive-premium. For historical accuracy it's hard to beat the **Newport House,** 710 S. Henry St., tel. (757) 229-1775, fax 229-6408, Web site: www.bbonline.com/va/newport/index.html, a reconstruction of a 1756 home designed by colonial architect Peter Harrison. Wood siding is carved to look like cut stone (Harrison's solution for a client who couldn't afford a stone house), and the two rooms are furnished with museum-quality English and American antiques, accurate down to the bedspread patterns. Hosts John and Cathy Miller teach English country dancing in the ballroom on Tuesday evenings and often include a historic recipe or two for breakfast. Premium.

Noteworthy B&Bs in the Williamsburg area include Laura Reeves' **Williamsburg Manor Bed & Breakfast,** 600 Richmond Rd., tel. (757) 220-8011 or (800) 422-8011, fax (757) 220-0245, Web site: www.bbonline.com/va/williamsburg/index.html, with optional but delectable dinners; and the **Williamsburg Sampler Bed and Breakfast,** 922 Jamestown Rd., tel. (800) 722-1169 or (757) 253-0398, fax 253-2669, e-mail: wbg.sampler@aol.com, proclaimed "Inn of the Year" by Gov. George Allen in 1995. Both are expensive-premium.

Guest Houses

A number of private homes in Williamsburg have been opened to guests. Simple accommodations fall within the budget range, and it's usually only a short walk or drive to the historic area. Try **Carter's Guest House,** 903 Lafayette St., tel. (757) 229-1117; the **Lewis Guest House,** 809 Lafayette St., tel. (757) 229-6116; or the **Thompson Guest House,** 1007 Lafayette St., tel. (757) 229-3455.

Hotels and Motels

Least expensive in town are the **Governor Spottswood Motel,** 1508 Richmond Rd., tel. (757) 229-6444, fax 253-2410; the **Colonial Motel,** 1452 Richmond Rd., tel. (757) 229-3621; and the **White Lion Motel,** 912 Capitol Landing Rd., tel. (757) 229-3931, fax 229-3156. All fall in the inexpensive range.

A few more dollars will bring you into the moderate category, where top honors go to the **Williamsburg Travel Inn,** 1800 Richmond Rd., tel. (757) 229-2781, fax 229-2544; the **Quarterpath Inn,** 620 York St., tel. (757) 220-0960, fax

220-1531; and the **King William Inn,** 824 Capitol Landing Rd., tel. (757) 229-4933, fax 229-9686.

Holiday Inn has the market cornered in the expensive range, with no fewer than four branches in town. There's one at 814 Capitol Landing Rd., tel. (757) 229-0200, fax 220-1642, and another at 725 Bypass Rd., tel. (757) 220-1776, fax 220-3124. Both have dining rooms, gyms, and cocktail lounges and offer the most convenient location.

Resorts

Five miles east of Colonial Williamsburg on US 60 is **Kingsmill Resort,** tel. (757) 253-1703 or (800) 832-5665, the state's largest golf and spa resort. Three golf courses on the banks of the James River include the difficult River Course, site of the Michelob Championship at Kingsmill and the Anheuser-Busch Golf Classic. Fifteen tennis courts, racquetball, nature trails, and a full fitness center/spa round out the amenities. Guestrooms and suites, with one to three bedrooms and kitchens, are luxury-category accommodations. Call for info on various packages including admission to Colonial Williamsburg and nearby attractions.

Camping

The **Anvil Campground,** 5243 Mooretown Rd., tel. (800) 633-4442 or (757) 565-2300, is the closest to central Williamsburg, but the nearby train tracks may take some getting used to. Full-hookup sites are $25 and tent sites are $18, and

the campground offers a free cookout on Friday and a 20% discount during the winter. Off I-64 exit 234 to Rt. 199 south are the **Fair Oaks Family Campground,** 901 Lightfoot Rd., tel. (757) 565-2101, next to the Williamsburg Pottery Factory ($13-16.50, year-round); and the **Kin Kaid Campground,** E. Rachant Dr., tel. (757) 565-2010, open March-Nov. ($10-12).

Take Rt. 646 north one mile from that same exit to reach the **Colonial Central KOA,** 4000 Newman Rd., tel. (757) 565-2734, open March-Sept. ($24-33).

FOOD

Colonial Williamsburg Foundation Taverns

Four reconstructed taverns carry on the tradition, begun back in the 18th century, of "savory victuals expeditiously served after the best manner." Low beamed ceilings, roaring fireplaces, and pewter plates evoke the days when wealthy planters gathered to dine on classic dishes such as peanut soup, Sally Lund bread, and Brunswick stew. All the taverns have garden seating in cooperative weather, and entrées range $6-8 for lunch and $13-22 for dinner. Call (800) 828-3767 or (757) 229-2141 for reservations, which are recommended.

Christina Campbell's Tavern, on Waller St. behind the Capitol, specializes in seafood. Mrs. Campbell's gumbo and Carolina fish muddle were favorites of George Washington, who prob-

Fish was a valuable source of protein in the Native American diet.

DOVER PUBLICATIONS, INC.

ably would have also enjoyed the strolling balladeers. Open daily for dinner. Grilled poultry, seafood, and colonial game pie are served in candlelit elegance at the **King's Arms Tavern** on Duke of Gloucester St. Top it off with a slice of pecan pie and goblet of colonial punch. Open daily for lunch and dinner.

The **Shields Tavern** next door is the oldest and largest in Williamsburg, re-creating a rustic eatery of the late 1740s. Eleven dining rooms fill with the smell of pork chops baking and beef roasting on a specially designed spit. Other tempting choices, including the catch of the day and filet mignon, go well with a mug of sparkling cider. Open daily for all meals. Adjacent to the Courthouse is **Josiah Chowning's Tavern,** opened in 1766. Mr. Chowning's black walnut ice cream is a standout after a heaping plateful of baked stuffed pork chops. After 9 p.m., you can knock back a tankard of ale in a setting rich with 18th-century music and games in Gambol's pub. Open daily for lunch and dinner.

Merchant's Square and Vicinity

Award-winning chef Marcel Desaulniers, author of the popular dessert manuals *Death by Chocolate* and *Dessert to Die For,* is reason enough to visit the **Trellis Cafe,** tel. (757) 229-8610, a California-style restaurant hung with whimsical paintings. Lunch offerings such as herbed couscous sandwiches and grilled eggplant and scallion salad run $7-9. Don't miss the shiitake-asparagus soup if you can help it. Dinner entrées include vegetarian and vegan selections alongside thin-cut calf's liver and sautéed rabbit. Full dinners run $22. Desserts, it goes without saying, are deadly. Open daily for lunch and dinner.

A Good Place To Eat, tel. (757) 229-4370, is just that, if you're looking for burgers, hot dogs, ice cream, and other such cafeteria fare. Breakfasts are $2-3. Open daily for all meals. Look one block behind it to the south for **Berrett's Restaurant and Raw Bar,** 199 S. Boundary St., tel. (757) 253-1847. This casual seafood place runs with a nautical theme as it offers every kind of fresh local seafood imaginable. Try the Crabmeat Imperial, served on puff pastry with Virginia ham.

Starters

Two places with good breakfast selections are the **Old Mill House of Pancakes and Waffles,** 2005 Richmond Rd., tel. (757) 229-3613, with over a dozen varieties, and **Mama Steve's House of Pancakes,** 1509 Richmond Rd., tel. (757) 229-7613, run by the same folks who own The Jefferson (see below). Both are open daily for breakfast and lunch. The Hunt Breakfast buffet at the Cascades Restaurant, by the Colonial Williamsburg Visitors Center, also earns wide praise.

Student Favorites

Inexpensive pizzas, subs, sandwiches, and steamed seafood are the standard favorites at **The Library Tavern,** 1300 Richmond Rd., tel. (757) 229-1012, "where silence isn't golden" and which also has a full bar and pool tables in the back. The **College Delly & Pizza Restaurant,** 336 Richmond Rd., tel. (757) 229-6627, is similar, with spaghetti and hot sandwiches, and **Paul's Deli Restaurant and Pizza,** 761 Scotland St., tel. (757) 229-8976, has Greek and Italian plates. All three are open daily for lunch and dinner until 2 a.m.

Plenty of fast-food joints line Richmond Rd. heading north, with many seafood and breakfast buffets options. And no matter how big the meal, there's always room for a scoop of **Ben & Jerry's,** on Rt. 60, open daily 11 a.m.-10 or 11 p.m.

More Substantial

In 1950, Harriet Petrell opened **The Jefferson Restaurant,** 1453 Richmond Rd., tel. (757) 229-2296, making it one of the first eateries on the Richmond strip. She can still be found knitting behind the counter while the kitchen turns out tried-and-true Virginia specialties from grain-fed catfish to Southern-fried chicken. Entrée are $13-22 including soup and salad. This unpretentious but dependable place is open daily from 4 p.m. Half restaurant, half antique shop, the **Old Chickahominy House,** 1211 Jamestown Rd. (Rt. 31), tel. (757) 229-4689, resembles an old farmhouse and serves food to match. Plantation meals in the 18th-century dining room include chicken and dumplings and homemade pie; hearty country breakfasts of ham, bacon, sausage, eggs, and biscuits are $7.75. Open daily for breakfast and lunch.

Live Maine lobsters are cooked to order at **The Lobster House,** 1431 Richmond Rd., tel.

(757) 229-7771, which also offers fresh fish, steaks, and chicken dishes. Open daily for dinner. The **Aberdeen Barn,** 1601 Richmond Rd., tel. (757) 229-6661, claims the best beef in town, and a bite of the aged prime rib might convince you. Reservations are suggested for the rustic, candlelit restaurant, open daily for dinner. **Le Yaca,** tel. (757) 220-3616, in the Village Shops at Kingsmill, serves the best French food for miles around in a rustic setting around a large open hearth. For lunch, the salad table is filled with a dozen kinds of French salads, and no dinner is complete without the outstanding onion soup and something off the lengthy wine list. Open Mon.-Sat. for lunch and dinner.

For a taste of Asia, try the char-grilled Vietnamese entrées at **Chez Trinh,** tel. (757) 253-1888, 157 Monticello Ave., in the Williamsburg Shopping Center, or the Mandarin, Cantonese, and Szechuan specialties at **Hsing Ling,** tel. (757) 220-2344, 204 Monticello Ave., in the Monticello Shopping Center.

RECREATION

Historical Diversions
Colonial Williamsburg offers a full roster of activities by day and night, from guided tours of the historic area to an evening of Vivaldi at the Palace of the Governors. Some, such as a candlelit walk around the city's haunted spots, are scheduled. Others just happen—as when wandering reenactors allow you to debate the rights of man with Thomas Jefferson or gossip with Martha Washington about her husband's snoring.

You can ride a carriage down Duke of Gloucester Street, attend a witch trial, and march to the beat of the Colonial Williamsburg Fife and Drum Corps—all in the same day, if you want. The African-American Interpretation and Presentations staff reflects the fact that half of Williamsburg's population in the 18th century were slaves. Check your *Visitor's Companion* for a daily schedule of events. Most are free, but evening presentations require a $10 ticket.

Music
J.M. Randall's Restaurant and Lounge, 4854 Longhill Rd. in the Olde Towne Square, tel. (757) 259-0406, features acoustic rock and blues. Live

bands also play at the **Library Tavern,** 1300 Richmond Rd., tel. (757) 229-1012, which is popular with William and Mary students. A DJ spins tunes from the 1950s and '60s at **Rockin' Robin,** 1402 Richmond Rd., tel. (757) 253-8818, which also has karaoke and free dance lessons on country night.

The **Old Dominion Opry,** 3012 Richmond Rd., tel. (757) 564-0200, is a family-oriented country-music theater with shows Mon.-Sat. **The Music Theatre of Williamsburg,** 7575 Richmond Rd., tel. (757) 546-0200 or (888) 687-4220, is similar but with a wider range of music. Opened in 1998, it hosts variety shows covering the spectrum from big band and jazz to show tunes and gospel, with a dash of comedy.

At William and Mary, concerts come to **Phi Beta Kappa Hall,** tel. (757) 221-2655, and the larger **William and Mary Hall,** tel. (757) 221-3346, which can hold up to 10,000 people.

Other Nightlife
The Corner Pocket, tel. (757) 220-0808, in the Williamsburg Crossing Shopping Center at Rt. 5 and Rt. 199, is an upscale, 18-and-over pool hall with a moderate dress code and high-quality tables. The Holiday Inn 1776 has a **comedy club** with shows Wed.-Sunday.

Outdoors
You can rent bicycles from **Bikes Unlimited,** 759 Scotland St. at Richmond St., tel. (757) 229-4620, or **Bikesmith,** 515 York St., tel. (757) 229-9858, and explore Colonial Williamsburg and the Colonial National Historical Parkway.

Shopping
Williamsburg is one of Virginia's shopping meccas, so the trick becomes figuring out what you want to buy, not where to buy it. Outlets galore fill malls and shopping centers in every direction from the historic center, but the most distinctive souvenirs come from specialty shops in and around Colonial Williamsburg.

Most of the items you can see being made by Williamsburg craftspeople are also for sale, either at the shops themselves or in two **Craft Houses** run by the Colonial Williamsburg Foundation. One is in the colonial shopping district of Merchant's Square, which fills the last block of Duke of Gloucester St. before William and Mary;

the other is near the Folk Art Center. At both you can buy authorized reproductions of furniture, wallpaper, china, glassware, and many other items made in Williamsburg workshops.

Alternately, head to the shops themselves to meet the artisans and discuss their work. Choose from handmade jewelry at **The Geddy Silversmith** and the **Sign of the Golden Ball,** cakes from the **Raleigh Tavern Bakery,** and antique prints at the **Colonial Post Office** (which can cancel your postcards with an original 18th-century postmark). General stores including **Greenhow** and **Tarpley's** carry tricornered hats, candles, soaps, and baskets, while **Prentice Store** sells fine linens.

Merchant's Square is home to upscale shops such as the **J. Fenton Gallery,** with unique handicrafts by Virginia artists; **Quilts Unlimited, Shirley Pewter Shop,** and **The Toymaker of Williamsburg.**

Five miles north on Richmond Rd. lurks the **Williamsburg Pottery Factory,** tel. (757) 564-3326, more of a settlement than a store, with 32 buildings spread over 200 acres. Begun as a roadside stand in 1938, Williamsburg Pottery stocks tens of thousands of discounted items—not just pottery but also prints, glassware, ceramics, and much more—and draws five million visitors a year. Amtrak trains even stop here briefly.

EVENTS

The **Summer Breeze Concert Series,** tel. (757) 565-6924, brings Virginia jazz artists to Merchants Square on Tuesday evenings during the summer. The Fourth of July starts with a fife and drum salute to the original 13 colonies, followed by a reading of the Declaration of Independence from the Courthouse steps. An evening party in the garden of the Governor's Palace and fireworks finish things off.

The Christmas holiday season is one of Williamsburg's busiest times, beginning with the **Grand Illumination,** on December 6, when the entire historic area flickers with candlelight. Homes are decorated with 18th-century ornaments made from natural materials such as pine cones and evergreen boughs, and the streets echo with concerts and carols. Special holiday

programs, feasts, fireworks, and military salutes continue through the New Year.

TRANSPORTATION

Getting Around
Bus service along US 60, passing Williamsburg Pottery and Busch Gardens, is managed by James City County Transit (JCCT), tel. (757) 220-1621. Service runs Mon.-Sat. from early morning to mid-afternoon. Colonial Williamsburg's shuttle buses are the easiest way to get around the historic area, with stops at the visitors center, Merchants Square, the Magazine, Governor's Palace, and Capitol building.

Getting There and Away
The **Williamsburg Transportation Center,** N. Boundary St. at Lafayette, houses the terminals of Greyhound/Trailways, tel. (757) 229-1460, and Amtrak, tel. (757) 229-0750. Fourteen miles east of Williamsburg, at I-64 exit 255 in Newport News, is the **Newport News-Williamsburg International Airport,** tel. (757) 877-0221, Web site: www.phr-airport.org. Shuttle services include Associated Cab, tel. (757) 887-3412, and Williamsburg Limousine, Inc., tel. (757) 877-0279. Both the transportation center and the airport have a handful of car rental agencies.

INFORMATION

In addition to the Colonial Williamsburg Visitors Center, you can contact the **Williamsburg Area Convention & Visitor Bureau,** 201 Penniman Rd., tel. (800) 368-6511 or (757) 253-0192, Web site: www.visitwilliamsburg.com, for general information, or stop by **Williamsburg Online** at www.williamsburg.com.

NEAR WILLIAMSBURG

York River State Park
A rugged landscape of gorge, forest, marsh, and bluff fills 2,500 acres where Taskinas Creek meets the York River. The site of public tobacco warehouses in the 17th and 18th centuries, when it was known as Taskinas Plantation, this park

has a much longer history than that: Fossilized whale vertebrae, sharks' teeth, and coral up to five million years old have all been found nearby.

Twenty miles of trails connect the river, creek, and freshwater ponds plied by anglers during fishing season. Mountain-bike rentals are available for a six-mile single-track and three easier trails. Guided canoe trips up the brackish tidal waters of Taskinas Creek leave from the **Taskinas Point Visitors Center,** tel. (757) 566-3036, and interpretive programs explore the park's fossils and natural offerings. The visitors center is off I-64 exit 231 to Rt. 507 north; continue to Rt. 606; within a mile, take a right, continue a mile and a half, and take a left onto Rt. 696.

Busch Gardens Williamsburg

Historic recreation takes on a slightly different meaning in Virginia's largest amusement park, repeatedly voted America's Most Beautiful for its Old World theme. Roller coasters are the stars, beginning with the Alpengeist, billed as the "world's fastest, tallest, and most inverted." Passengers hang from the track as if on a ski lift—although the similarity ends when the ride hits 67 mph and 3.7 Gs during the "cobra roll." *People* magazine voted it the number-one coaster in America in 1997.

Other wild rides along the Tyrolean motif include the water-skimming Big Bad Wolf, the Drachen Fire with its zero-G camelback hump, and the Roman-themed water flume Escape from Pompeii. You won't believe how big and beautiful the Anheuser-Busch Clydesdales near the petting zoo are, and if you get hungry (tip: *after* the Alpengeist) you'll find wurst, beer, and an oompah band in the 2,000-seat Festhaus. A monorail runs to the Anheuser-Busch brewery (see below).

Busch Gardens, tel. (757) 253-3350 or (800) 253-3350, Web site: www.buschgardens.com, is off US 60 three miles southeast of Williamsburg. It's open 10 a.m. to 7 or 10 p.m., daily May-Aug. and assorted weekends and other days in March, April, September, and October. Tickets are $33 adults, $26 children 3-6, plus another $6 for parking. You can buy a three-day pass for Busch Gardens and Water Country USA for $52 pp, and the Williamsburg Hotel/Motel Association offers a "Thrills and Spills" package deal with two nights' lodging for a family of four plus admission to both parks for $364.

Water Country USA

Anheuser-Busch also administers this, the mid-Atlantic's largest waterpark, which offers more than 30 ways to escape the summer swelter. Splash through the darkened tunnels of the Aquazoid, ride the whitewater over Big Daddy Falls, or hit escape velocity on the super-speed, 320-foot Nitro Racer waterslide. The H2O UFO and Cow-A-Bunga areas are geared toward kids, and whole families can enjoy the wave pools and dive shows.

Water Country USA, tel. (757) 229-9300 or (800) 343-7946, Web site: www.watercountryusa.com, is on Water Country Parkway (Rt. 199) near Busch Gardens. It's open daily May-Sept. 10 a.m.-6 to 10 p.m. (weekends only at either end of the season); $25.50 adults, $18 children 3-6, plus $6 parking.

Anheuser-Busch Brewery

Fans of suds can visit the source at one of the world's largest breweries, tel. (757) 253-3039, only a few miles east of Williamsburg along US 60. A free self-guiding tour teaches you about the history of beer from George Washington's own recipe to the modern mega-brewing process. At the end, there's a hospitality center with free samples (two per person), a snack bar, and a gift shop. Open daily 11 a.m.-5 p.m.

Carter's Grove Plantation

Carter Burwell, grandson of Robert "King" Carter, built this grand mansion from 1750 to 1754 along the shore of the James. The 200-foot-long manor house is described as the epitome of the Georgian style, even though later owners added Victorian and colonial revival touches. A wide arch in the paneled entrance hall leads to a sweeping flight of stairs, with sword gashes on the railing said to be the work of British brigadier Banastre Tarleton as he spurred his horse up the stairs. Both George Washington and Thomas Jefferson were reportedly turned down for marriage in the "Refusal Room" upstairs.

Around the 750-acre estate are reconstructed slave quarters, whose pine-log cabins each held as many as 24 people, and the ongoing excavation of **Wolstenholme Towne**—all that's left of a colonial settlement wiped out by Indians on March 22, 1622. Only 60 of the original 220 colonists known as the "Society of Martin's Hundred" escaped. Recent finds are displayed in the **Winthrop Rockefeller Archeology Museum.**

Carter's Grove, tel. (757) 220-7645 or (800) 447-8679, is open Tues.-Sun. 9 a.m.-4 p.m. Admission is included in a Williamsburg Patriot's Pass; separate admission is $17 adults, $10 children 6-12.

JAMESTOWN

The first permanent European colony in America began as James Fort, hastily erected in 1607 by a handful of nervous English settlers who had traded three cramped sailboats for an endless, untamed wilderness. A combination of sickness, inexperience, hostile natives, and bad management almost spelled the colony's doom in the first few years, but the leadership of Capt. John Smith and a series of fragile truces with the local tribes allowed 5,000 inhabitants to survive to 1634.

Settled in 1607, Jamestown, site of the first permanent European colony in America, fell to ruins after the colonial capital was moved to Williamsburg in 1699. A Confederate fort took the place of the original wooden stockade in 1861, a year before Jamestown Island was occupied by Union troops. In 1933, the island became part of the Colonial National Historical Park. It enjoyed that distinction until the late 1980s, when an archaeological reassessment led to the discovery of the original settlement (part of which had been hidden by the shifting currents of the James River). Further excavations uncovered the triangular footprint of the Jamestown fort in 1996.

Two separate locations provide contrasting interpretations of the site. First comes Jamestown Settlement, a re-creation of life on the pitiless frontier. Across the bridge is the real thing, on Jamestown Island, a much more low-key but equally affecting spot maintained by the National Park Service.

Jamestown Settlement

Hardy colonists and their native counterparts come to life in this living-history museum of life in 17th-century Virginia—albeit a slightly sanitized and user-friendly version—down to the smell of cooking fires and the roar of gunpowder muskets. Start at the museum, packed with artifacts and information on the English pioneers and their alternating allies and enemies, the Powhatan Indians. Catch the short movie on the settlement before you step outside for the real attractions.

First comes the **Powhatan Indian village,** a cluster of domed houses made of woven reeds over sapling frames. Here, interpreters costumed in animal skins show you how to make bone fishhooks, scrape hides, and build a canoe. Kids will enjoy grinding corn (at least for a while) and will probably ask about the ceremonial circle of wooden poles carved with faces.

A short walk down the path brings you to the river pier, where three full-size **ship reproductions** of the vessels that brought the European settlers are tied up. Cormorants fish in the water next to the *Discovery,* the *Godspeed,* and the *Susan Comfort.* Climb aboard and imagine crossing 6,000 miles of open ocean in quarters this cramped—the smallest craft is only 50 feet long, with roughly as much space as a small school bus. The *Susan Comfort,* the largest, is 116 feet long with a brightly painted hull. Reenactors will point out the brick hearth (surprising on a wooden ship) and demonstrate various shipboard activities including furling sails and dropping anchor. These are fully functioning ships, and they occasionally sail away to participate in nautical events.

The colonists must have breathed a sigh of relief to step out of the fo'c'sle and into the safety and relative spaciousness of **James Fort.** Tall wooden palisades connect three raised circular platforms at each corner. Farm fields stretch beyond the walls, while inside stand wattle-and-daub homes, a church, a guardhouse, and storehouses. Try your hand at ninepins (an early version of bowling) and cover your ears for the periodic firing of militia rifles.

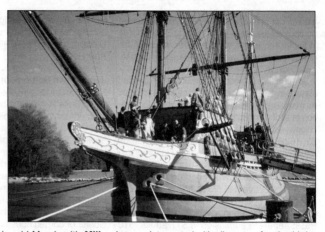

The Susan Comfort is a full-size reproduction of a European vessel brought to these shores by settlers.

Yearly events start in mid-March with **Military Through the Ages,** with demonstrations and reenactments of weapons, tactics, and camp life. The Virginia Council on Indians co-sponsors the music and dance of the **Virginia Indian Heritage Festival** in mid-June, which also brings crafts, storytelling, and food. Two holiday events happen simultaneously at the Yorktown Victory Center (see below): **Foods & Feasts of Colonial Virginia,** a three-day Thanksgiving event focusing on colonial and native food; and **A Colonial Christmas,** showcasing 17th- and 18th-century holiday decorations and traditional activities.

Jamestown Settlement, tel. (757) 229-1607, Web site: www.nps.gov/colo, is open daily 9 a.m.-5 p.m., and has a gift shop and small cafe. Tickets are $9.75 adults, $4.75 children 6-12, with a combination ticket including the Yorktown Victory Center available for $13.50 adults, $6.50 children. For more information, contact the **Jamestown-Yorktown Foundation,** P.O. Box 1607, Williamsburg, VA 23187, tel. (888) 593-4682 or (757) 253-4838, fax 253-5299.

Jamestown Yacht Basin

At the end of Rt. 31, the **Jamestown Ferry,** tel. (800) VA-FERRY (800-823-3779), heads to Scotland on the south side of the river every half hour. Narrated nature cruises on the *Jamestown Island Explorer,* tel. (703) 259-0400, also head from here into the marshes and streams of the lower James. Accounts of local history and folklore are interrupted with glimpses of native birds, fish, and animals during the 90-minute tours ($12.50 adults, $8 children). **Jamestown Beach Campsites,** tel. (703) 229-7609, has sites for $15-22 with full hookups along with a beach, pool, playground, and boat ramp.

Jamestown Island

The earlier end of Colonial National Historical Park begins with the **Jamestown Glasshouse of 1608,** next to the ruins of the original brick and river-stone furnaces. The first factory industry in the colonies folded after one shipment to England, but artisans in the reconstructed workshop still sell lovely hand-blown glassware made from the same mixture of ash and sand. Open daily 8:30 a.m.-5 p.m.

Keep driving across a narrow spit of land into the island to reach the National Park Service **visitors center,** tel. (703) 229-1733, with a museum housing one of the largest collections of 17th-century artifacts in the country. Everyday utensils including hairpins, buckles, and candlesticks invoke the very real people who suffered, survived, and died on this swampy island an ocean away from anything safe and familiar.

Pick up a map of the **James Cittie townsite,** then explore on your own or join one of the four or so ranger-led walks per day. Part of the original townsite has been inundated as the James shoreline shifted, but brick outlines mark where certain buildings once stood. The oldest standing structure is the 1639 tower of the Memorial

Church, near statues of Pocahontas and Captain John Smith. A memorial cross marks 300 shallow graves dug during the Starving Time of 1609-10. The Association for the Preservation of Virginia Antiquities (APVA), which co-manages the site, operates an archeology lab in the Dale House that displays recent finds in the ongoing excavations (open daily 10 a.m.-4 p.m.).

Along the five-mile loop drive (which can be shortened to three), you'll stand a good chance of spotting descendants of the same deer, muskrat, and waterbirds hunted by the Jamestown settlers. To augment historical markers along the way, you can rent an audio tour tape at the visitors center ($2). Living history programs and children's activities are held at the visitors center from spring to fall. Annual events include **Jamestown Weekend,** celebrating the founding of the colony, in early May; the **First Assembly Day Commemoration,** in late July; and an evening walking tour and symbolic torching of the town on the anniversary of **Bacon's Rebellion** on September 19, 1676. Open daily 9 a.m.-5 p.m.; $5 adults over 16 ($7 with the Yorktown Battlefield).

For more information on Jamestown island, contact the **National Park Service,** P.O. Box 210, Yorktown, VA 23690, , tel. (757) 898-3400, Web site: www.nps.gov/colo. **Williamsburg Limousine,** tel. (757) 877-0279, offers transportation from Williamsburg to Jamestown or Yorktown for $20 pp each per day, or $40 for both, including admission.

YORKTOWN

One of Virginia's major ports in the 18th century, Yorktown rivaled Williamsburg with its thriving waterfront at the base of a bluff beneath Main Street's regal homes. Almost 2,000 people lived here when Lord Cornwallis arrived in 1781, pursued by the American army and the French navy just offshore. Days of bombardment convinced the British general to request a meeting on October 17 and to surrender officially two days later.

Yorktown Visitors Center
The earth ramparts erected by George Washington's troops now defend this museum, filled with various relics saved from the final confrontation of the Revolutionary War. George Washington's field tents are displayed next to surrendered flags and a rifle stock broken by a British soldier in disgust. Walk through a partial reconstruction of a British warship (watch your head), and get your bearings through a narrated map presentation.

Walking tours, led by interpreters in costume and character, leave from here for the British Inner Defensive Line and the town of Yorktown. You can rent an auto tour tape ($2) for two battlefield loops, passing Surrender Field, George Washington's headquarters, and earthworks reconstructed through archaeological excavations and detailed studies of 18th-century military maps.

The visitors center, tel. (757) 898-3400, is open daily 8:30 a.m.-5 p.m. for $4 pp over 16 ($7 with Jamestown Island). It's administered by the National Park Service, P.O. Box 210, Yorktown, VA 23690, tel. (757) 898-3400, Web site: www.nps.gov/colo.

Historic Yorktown
Still a sparse but working village, Yorktown counts dozens of homes over two centuries old, many of which occupy their own "lots" (blocks) on the fringes. A path from the visitors center takes you past the 84-foot **Victory Monument,** topped by a winged statue of Liberty, to **Cornwallis' Cave** on the riverbank, a dank hole where the British general is said to have made his headquarters during the shelling. The **Nelson House** was once home to Thomas Nelson, Jr., a signer of the Declaration of Independence. It still bears scars from cannonballs directed by Nelson himself, who suspected Cornwallis was inside. The terms of surrender were drafted in the **Moore House.**

History of a different sort is remembered in the **Watermen's Museum,** 309 Water St., tel. (757) 887-2641. Boat models, marine life, and a boat-building area out back honor the "iron men and wooden boats" who have fished the local waters since the first Indians ventured out in dugout canoes. A gift shop sells work by local artists. It's on the far side of the US 17 bridge by the water. Open Tues.-Sat. 10 a.m.-1 p.m., Sunday 1-4 p.m.; $3 pp.

Accommodations: The **Duke of York Motel,** 508 Water St., tel. (757) 898-3232, fax 898-5922, sits right on the riverside. Moderate. The

Yorktown Motor Lodge, 8829 George Washington Hwy., tel. (757) 898-5451, fax 898-1766, has 42 comfortable rooms and an outdoor pool, three miles south of the bridge along US 17. Inexpensive.

Food: You can grab a bite along the water at the **Yorktown Pub,** tel. (757) 898-8793, with live music on Friday and Saturday nights. Open daily for lunch and dinner, cash and travelers checks only. **Waterstreet Landing,** tel. (757) 886-5890, serves gourmet pizzas, soups, and sandwiches at the foot of Church St. **Nick's Seafood Pavilion,** tel. (757) 887-5269, is a classier affair at the foot of the US 17 bridge. Friendly service complements a Mediterranean mélange of mirrors, statues, greenery, and even a fountain pool. Seafood dishes are $10-15, with combination plates around $14. Open daily for lunch and dinner.

Shopping: Colonial goods, including ceramics, brass, and wrought iron, can be found at the **Poor Potter Shop,** tel. (757)-898-3400, and **Period Designs,** tel. (757) 886-9482, and local artists sell their work at **Gallery on the Green,** tel. (757) 989-0191, and **On The Hill Cultural Arts Center,** tel. (757) 898-3076.

Annual Events: In late May a **Civil War Weekend** features encampments and a Confederate field hospital, followed by a **Revolutionary War encampment** in late July or early August. Yorktown's biggest celebration is the **Victory Weekend** around October 19, with costumed skirmishes, parades, patriotic music and military drills occurring here and at the Yorktown Victory Center.

Activities: From May-Oct. **Erin Kay Charters,** tel. (757) 879-8276 or (804) 642-5096, runs fishing trips and pleasure cruises on the York River and Chesapeake Bay from the Watermen's Museum. Excursions aboard the *Miss Yorktown* are $10-30 pp, including bait and tackle on fishing trips.

Yorktown Victory Center

This well-done museum and living-history center sits across US 17 from Yorktown itself. Brush up on your background knowledge along the outdoor timeline that leads inside the main building, where exhibits on people affected by the war—from slaves to common women to soldiers—are told through narrated recordings, relics, and documents. A military section displays pistols owned by the Marquis de Lafayette near the waterlogged remains of British ships raised from the York River.

Outside, at the Continental Army encampment, you can learn about medicine, food, and music in colonial armies, and become one of the 17 people needed to fire a cannon (unloaded, of course). A short distance away is a reconstructed farmsite typical of a lower- to middle-class family of the late 18th century. A tobacco barn, forge, and modest home stand next to vegetable and herb gardens and animal pens, managed by costumed interpreters who demonstrate colonial cooking, farming, and games.

The Yorktown Victory Center, tel. (757) 887-1776, is open daily 9 a.m.-5 p.m. for $7.25 adults, $3.50 children 6-12. It hosts local fife and drum corps and choral groups during the **American Heritage Music Festival,** in late April, and welcomes kids with games, entertainment, and crafts during the **Children's Colonial Fair,** near the Fourth of July. There's also a snack bar and large gift shop.

The Victory Center operates under the auspices of the **Jamestown-Yorktown Foundation,** P.O. Box 1607, Williamsburg, VA 23187-1607, tel. (888) 593-4682 or (757) 253-4838, fax 253-5299.

JAMES RIVER PLANTATIONS

The fertile banks of the lower James have been prime real estate ever since the days of the Powhatan capital at Sandy Point. During the 18th and 19th centuries, lavish mansions served as business and social centers for huge tobacco plantations. Carriages no longer clatter down long, tree-shaded gravel lanes where servants wait to escort visitors into the parlor for tea and talk of planting, but the area is still mostly forest and farmland with no major town center.

Rt. 5, also called the John Tyler Highway, leads straight from Richmond to six major plantations along the river's north bank. Annual events like garden tours, special teas, birthday celebrations, and progressive luncheons happen almost every month of the year. Block tickets granting admission to Shirley, Berkeley, Evelynton, and Sherwood Forest cost $28 for adults and are sold at each. For more information on the plantations, call (800) 704-5423, or on the Internet stop by www.jamesriverplantations.org.

Shirley Plantation

Virginia's oldest plantation sits on land settled in 1613 by Sir Thomas West. The Queen Anne mansion was begun in 1723 by Edward Hill III for his daughter Elizabeth and her new husband, John Carter, eldest son of agricultural tycoon Robert "King" Carter. Finished in 1738, the house survived both the Revolutionary and Civil Wars and is the birthplace of Anne Hill Carter Lee, mother of Robert E., who married Light-Horse Harry in the parlor. Today it's home to the 11th and 12th generations of the Hill-Carter family, plenty of heirlooms, and centuries of stories.

Highlights of the mansion include hand-carved woodwork and a unique square flying stairway that ascends for three stories without any visible means of support. A laundry house where Robert E. Lee was tutored for a time stands among the original brick outbuildings in the unique Queen Anne forecourt, next to an inviting bench under a huge willow oak overlooking the river. Corn, soybeans, and wheat have taken the place of tobacco on the remaining 800 acres of farmland.

Shirley Plantation, tel. (804) 829-5121 or (800) 232-1613, e-mail: information@shirleyplantation.com, is open daily 9 a.m.-5 p.m. (weekends only from mid-January to mid-February); $8.50 adults, $4.50 children 6-12. Half-hour tours are given until 4:30 p.m.

Berkeley Plantation

On December 4, 1619, 38 English settlers had kissed the earth and thanked the heavens upon landing partway up the James River after three months at sea. A monument marks the spot of the original Thanksgiving (followed only two years later by the first batch of bourbon whiskey distilled in the New World).

The Harrison family bought this property in 1691. Benjamin Harrison IV built the manor house in 1726, leaving his and his wife's initials in a datestone over a side door. His son Benjamin V signed the Declaration of Independence and served three terms as governor of Virginia. *His* son William Henry became the ninth president of the United States after making his name on the western frontier. George Washington stopped by from time to time, the first in a string of 10 presidents to enjoy the Harrisons' hospitality. And although he didn't live at Berkeley, William Henry's grandson Benjamin Harrison did the family proud by becoming the 23rd president of the United States.

During Union occupation in 1862, Gen. Dan Butterfield composed the haunting melody of "Taps" shortly before Lincoln visited to review McClellan's army. In this century, the property has been lovingly restored through the efforts of Malcolm Jamieson—whose father, ironically, was a Federal drummer boy. Worth a stop in themselves are Berkeley's terraced boxwood gardens, spread between the house and wide lawns leading down to the river where geese and sheep wander.

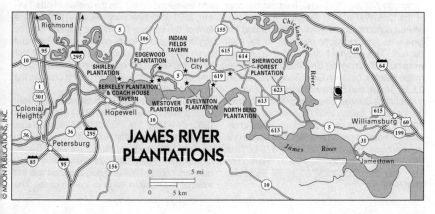

JAMES RIVER PLANTATIONS

Berkeley, tel. (804) 829-6018, is open daily 9 a.m.-5 p.m. for $8.50 adults and $4 children 6-12. The **First Thanksgiving Festival**, on the first Sunday in November, commemorates the original ceremony of gratitude with Colonial and native re-enactors. At Berkeley's **Coach House Tavern**, tel. (804) 829-6003, costumed waiters serve colonial favorites in a restored outbuilding (open daily for lunch and dinner).

Westover Plantation

William Byrd III, founder of Richmond and Petersburg, built this Georgian manor house in the 1730s. It's famous for its elegant proportions, view of the James, and ancient tulip poplars around the lawn. Westover is also known as one home of the ghost of Byrd's daughter Evelyn, who pined to death at age 18 after her Catholic parents forbade her to marry a Protestant. She told friends she would be back from the beyond, and her glowing ghost has since been reported here and at Evelynton (witnesses describe it as non-threatening).

Westover, tel. (804) 829-2882, shares an access road off Rt. 5 with Berkeley Plantation. The house is only open during Historic Garden Week in April, but the grounds and garden are open to visitors daily 9 a.m.-5 p.m. for $2 pp.

Evelynton Plantation

Originally part of the Westover property, Evelynton (EVE-lin-ton) was named after Byrd's daughter, who is said to haunt both mansions. Since 1847, it has been home to the Ruffin family, whose patriarch, Edmund, fired the first shot of the Civil War at Fort Sumter, SC, and pioneered agricultural techniques that rescued Virginia's declining tobacco economy in the 19th century. The original house and outbuildings were burned during the Civil War Battle of Evelynton Heights, between Gen. George McClellan, J.E.B. Stuart, and Stonewall Jackson.

Architect Duncan Lee designed the current manor house, built in 1937. The Ruffins still farm 2,500 surrounding acres but allow guests to peruse the house's period antiques and formal gardens outside. Evelynton, tel. (800) 473-5075 or (804) 829-5075, is open daily 9 a.m.-5 p.m. (Fri.-Mon. only Jan.-Feb.) for $7.50 adults, $3.50 children 6-12.

Sherwood Forest

The only home owned by two U.S. presidents was begun in 1730 under the name Smith's Hundred. William Henry Harrison inherited it in the 1790s but never lived here, in part because he died a month after his inaugural speech. Harrison's vice president, John Tyler, took over both the presidency and the ownership of this white clapboard house, where he retired in 1845. Tyler's grandson still lives upstairs.

Additions to the original building have made Sherwood Forest the longest wooden-frame house in the country—over 300 feet. A 68-foot ballroom was designed to accommodate guests dancing the Virginia reel. Scars in the woodwork bear witness to Civil War action, and many of the furnishings and decorations belonged to President Tyler. Original outbuildings, terraced gardens, and over 80 varieties of trees brighten the grounds. Sherwood Forest is also home to a ghost—the Gray Lady, whose rocking has been heard in the Gray Room for over two centuries.

Sherwood Forest, tel. (804) 829-5377, fax 829-2947, is open daily 9 a.m.-5 p.m. for $8.50 pp.

Accommodations and Food

Edgewood Plantation, 4800 John Tyler Hwy., tel. (804) 829-2962 or (800) 296-3343, hosts guests in a Gothic Revival home built in 1849 that has since served as post office, church, and Confederate signal post. Fireplaces and a two-story freestanding spiral staircase wait inside, while a 1725 gristmill, formal gardens, and pool surround the house. Premium to luxury. Between Evelynton and Sherwood Forest sits the **Indian Fields Tavern,** 9220 John Tyler Hwy., tel. (804) 829-5004, a turn-of-the-century farmhouse praised by *Bon Appetit* magazine for its country specialties and fresh Chesapeake seafood. It's open daily for lunch and dinner, but make reservations ahead of time or be ready to wait in a rocking chair on the veranda until a table opens up.

Across Rt. 5 is the **North Bend Plantation,** 12200 Weyanoke Rd., tel. (804) 829-5176 or (800) 841-1479, fax (804) 829-6828, Web site: www.inngetaways.com/va/north.html, built in 1819 for William Henry Harrison's sister Sarah. Union Gen. Philip Sheridan made his headquarters here in 1864 and dug trenches that still exist at the eastern edge of the property. The owners, the fifth generation of the Copland family to own North Bend, are happy to point out Sheridan's plantation desk, the 1914 billiard table, and a library full of rare and old books. Rates (expensive-premium) include a full country breakfast and swimming pool.

NORTHERN HAMPTON ROADS

NEWPORT NEWS

Virginia's fourth-largest city (pop. 182,000), Newport News was named for Capt. Christopher Newport, pilot of the **Discovery** in 1607, whose "news" was word sent back to England that the settlers had arrived safely. With no real downtown area, Newport News stretches along I-64 and US 60 toward the largest privately owned shipyard in the country, the massive Newport News Shipbuilding and Dry Dock Company facility.

Recently overtaken by Food Lion as the state's largest private employer, the shipyard still employs about one-tenth of the city's population. Despite recent military cutbacks, it still churns out nuclear attack submarines and aircraft carriers for the U.S. Navy, still according to its founder's 19th-century credo: "We shall build good ships here at a profit—if we can—at a loss—if we must—but always good ships."

Dust-blackened trains rattle south, bound for the largest coal-shipping port in the country, passing one of the country's largest municipal parks and the outstanding Mariner's Museum (well worth a day's detour in itself).

Mariner's Museum

A 3,200-pound, 18-foot golden eagle figurehead ushers you into one of the best nautical collections in the world. Thirteen galleries display the distress lantern that signaled the end of the Union's steel-hulled *Monitor,* gleaming Chris Crafts from the 1930s, and intricate scrimshaw carved by bored but talented whalers. Especially remarkable are the 16 miniature model ships made over two decades by August Crabtree. Magnifying glasses built into the display cases let you appreciate the stunning detail, down to inch-tall figureheads carved with modified dental tools. It's a wonder Crabtree didn't go blind during the 20 years it took to finish the collection, which comprises everything from Indian dugouts to Columbus's ships.

On interactive video displays in the Chesapeake Bay gallery, you can learn how to navigate. Other displays include a series of knot-tying lessons; well-worn boat-building tools; paintings, prints, and photos recording famous sea disasters; and changing exhibits covering topics such as pirates, the slave trade, and (of course) the

YOU CAN'T DRIVE THE HAMPTON ROADS

Spend a little time near the mouth of the Chesapeake Bay and you'll probably start to get confused by a fair amount of local terminology. Most important, and least distinct, is the term "Hampton Roads" itself.

In maritime parlance, "roads" means a safe anchorage, usually in a sheltered natural harbor, which the lower Chesapeake Bay has in abundance. "Hampton" comes from English nobleman Henry Wriothesley (RIZ-lee), the third Earl of Southampton, who financed early colonizing expeditions. What was originally the "Earl of Southampton's Roadstead," then, has been shortened over the years to "Hampton Roads."

You'll also hear Hampton Roads used to refer not only to where the James, Nansemond, and Elizabeth Rivers flow into the Chesapeake Bay, but to the entire metropolitan area surrounding it, from Newport News to Virginia Beach. Hampton Roads itself is usually divided further into the "South Side" (of the James)—including Norfolk, Virginia Beach, Chesapeake, Portsmouth, and Suffolk—and "the Peninsula" (as in Historic) to the north, the setting of Newport News and Hampton itself.

And even though "Tidewater" technically refers to the entire region affected by the ebb and flow of the ocean (basically all of Virginia east of the fall line), it's often used the same way "South Side" is—to refer to everything south of the James River. The Norfolk-Virginia Beach bus system, for example, is run by Tidewater Regional Transit.

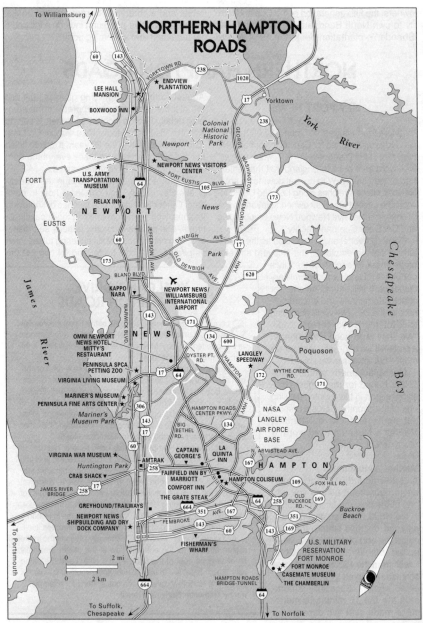

NORTHERN HAMPTON ROADS

To Williamsburg

60 143

YORKTOWN RD. 238
1020
17 Yorktown

LEE HALL MANSION ★ ENDVIEW PLANTATION
BOXWOOD INN ●

Colonial National Historic Park
Newport
238 York River

FORT
U.S. ARMY TRANSPORTATION MUSEUM ★
NEWPORT NEWS VISITORS CENTER ★
FORT EUSTIS BLVD.
105
News
173
64
RELAX INN ●
NEWPORT
EUSTIS
60
DENBIGH AVE.
17
173
Park
OLD DENBIGH AVE.
620
BLAND BLVD.
James River
KAPPO NARA ●
NEWPORT NEWS/WILLIAMSBURG INTERNATIONAL AIRPORT
WARWICK BLVD.
JEFFERSON AVE.
143
N E W S
171
134
OMNI NEWPORT NEWS HOTEL, MITTY'S RESTAURANT ●
600
LANGLEY SPEEDWAY ★
PENINSULA SPCA PETTING ZOO ★
OYSTER PT. RD.
17
64
Hampton
172
WYTHE CREEK RD.
171
VIRGINIA LIVING MUSEUM ★
Poquoson
MARINER'S MUSEUM ★
PENINSULA FINE ARTS CENTER ★
306
143
HAMPTON ROADS CENTER PKWY.
NASA LANGLEY AIR FORCE BASE
Chesapeake Bay
Mariner's Museum Park
17
BIG BETHEL RD.
134
60
VIRGINIA WAR MUSEUM ★
CAPTAIN GEORGE'S
LA QUINTA INN
N. ARMISTEAD AVE.
167
H A M P T O N
Huntington Park
AMTRAK
258
FAIRFIELD INN BY MARRIOTT
COMFORT INN
HAMPTON COLISEUM ★
109
FOX HILL RD.
CRAB SHACK ▼
JAMES RIVER BRIDGE
258
GREYHOUND/TRAILWAYS
THE GRATE STEAK
64 258
169
OLD BUCKROE RD.
Buckroe Beach
NEWPORT NEWS SHIPBUILDING AND DRY DOCK COMPANY ★
664 351 167
PEMBROKE
143 60
351
169
To Portsmouth
FISHERMAN'S WHARF
143
U.S. MILITARY RESERVATION FORT MONROE ★
FORT MONROE
CASEMATE MUSEUM
THE CHAMBERLIN

0   2 mi
0   2 km

HAMPTON ROADS BRIDGE-TUNNEL
64

To Suffolk, Chesapeake
664
To Norfolk

English settler John White's depiction of Native Americans crafting a dugout canoe

DOVER PUBLICATIONS, INC.

Titanic. The museum, tel. (757) 596-2222 or (800) 581-7245, Web site: www.mariner.org, is open Mon.-Sat. 9 a.m.-5 p.m., Sunday noon-5 p.m.; $5 adults, $3 children.

The same turn off US 60 leads to the **Peninsula Fine Arts Center,** tel. (757) 596-8175, e-mail: pfac@whro.org, Web site: www.whro.org/cl/pfac, with changing exhibitions of local and national artists (open Mon.-Sat. 10 a.m.-5 p.m., Sun 1-5 p.m.; free), and the 500-acre **Mariner's Museum Park.** A five-mile trail circles Lake Maury, where you can rent canoes ($3/hour), johnboats ($6-10/day), and fishing tackle ($5/day) from the boathouse, tel. (757) 591-7799.

Newport News Park

Covering more than 8,000 acres, this largest city park east of the Mississippi is a patchwork of meadows, swamps, lakes, and hardwood forest threaded by mountain-bike, horse, and nature trails. There's an 18-hole Frisbee golf course, a five-star archery range, and the kaleidoscopic azaleas of the Peace Garden, and visitors can rent bikes ($3 per hour) to explore 10 miles of Civil War fortifications or take out a canoe or paddleboat ($3-4 per hour) to fish on Lee Hall Reservoir. The Newport News Golf Club at Deer Run, tel. (757) 886-7923 or 886-7925, has two full courses, and an interpretive center offers naturalist walks and nature programs. You can even spend the night at one of 180 campsites, tel. (757) 888-3333, with full hookups for $15-20.

Historic Plantations

Wealthy planter Richard Decauter Lee built **Lee Hall Mansion,** 163 Yorktown Rd., tel. (757) 888-3371, in 1848-59. The Italianate Renaissance house served as headquarters for Union Maj. Gen. John Macgruder and Gen. Joseph E. Johnson during the early stages of the 1862 Peninsular Campaign. In 1998, it was being restored to its Civil War-era appearance. Plans include relocating the Civil War collection of the Virginia War Museum (see below) to the basement, and landscaping the grounds with 19th-century bulbs and plantings. Call the Newport News Visitors Center (see **Information,** below) for hours and prices.

Another mansion-in-the-works as of 1998 was **Endview Plantation,** 362 Yorktown Rd., tel. (757) 887-1862, erected around 1760 by William Harwood, Jr. One of the few surviving wooden buildings from the 18th century, Endview was visited by George Washington and 3,000 Virginia militia and served as a training ground for troops during the War of 1812. George B. McClellan paid a visit during the Civil War, as did a Confederate captain who made it his home. A permanent living-history encampment is planned to commemorate the local Battle of Seven Pines. Call the Visitors Center for details.

Virginia Living Museum

It doesn't have statues that walk or paintings that talk, but this semi-zoo does boast a bevy of wild animals in outdoor pens modeled after their natural habitats. Start in the main building, where different sections of the James River—complete with plants, catfish, and bass—have been reproduced in a series of aquariums. At the touch tank, find out why horseshoe crab blood sells for $30,000 an ounce, and try not to wake the screech owl in the World of Darkness.

Then step outside onto the nature trail to reach open-air enclosures where raccoons scurry, bobcats pace, and otters zoom away from an underwater window in streams of bubbles. Past the raucous wetlands aviary, home to great blue herons and snake-necked cattle egrets, are more pens containing white-tailed deer, wild turkeys, and bald eagles.

The main building has a planetarium and a gift shop full of neat stuff along the lines of ant farms and glowing floating plastic jellyfish. Various educational programs and outings include Chesapeake Bay eco-safaris and winter whale-watching trips. The museum, 524 J. Clyde Morris Blvd., tel. (757) 595-1900, Web site: www.valivingmuseum.org, is open Mon.-Sat. 9 a.m.-5 p.m., Sunday noon-5 p.m. (indoors only Thursday 7-9 p.m.); $6 adults, $4 children 3-12; $7 adults, $5 children with a planetarium show.

Huntington Park

At the east end of the James River bridge (Rt. 258) you'll find the **Virginia War Museum,** 9285 Warwick Blvd., tel. (757) 247-8523, with hundreds of artifacts from centuries of combat. From flintlock pistols to M-16s, sabers to WW II Japanese officers' samurai swords, anything and everything having to do with conflict in all its forms is displayed next to actual pieces of the Dachau concentration camp and the Berlin Wall. Open Mon.-Sat. 9 a.m.-5 p.m., Sun 1-5 p.m.; $2 adults, $1 children 6-15.

Younger kids will love the big wooden **Fun Fort** overlooking the water by a children's fishing pier and picnic area. The **James River Fishing Pier,** farther on, sells bait and supplies.

Other Sights

Even more animals live across J. Clyde Morris Blvd. at the **Peninsula SPCA Petting Zoo,** tel.

(757) 595-1399. A surprising collection of exotic animals, including lions, tigers, jaguars, snow leopards, mountain lions, and mandrills (a type of ape) shares a rear lot with a petting barnyard, home to goats, ducks, sheep, peacocks, and one nervous llama. You can't take any of these home with you, but you might be inspired to adopt a dog or cat inside.

The history of the transport wing of the U.S. Army (motto: "Nothing happens until something moves") is the subject of the **U.S. Army Transportation Museum,** tel. (757) 878-1115, on the grounds of Fort Eustis off 164 exit 250A. If it ever carried men or equipment, it's here, from a Conestoga wagon to Desert Storm HUMVs. Experimental designs are the most interesting—check out the one-man "aerocycle" helicopter and the 20-foot silver disk of the Avro Car Mark II, a real-life flying saucer now claimed by nesting birds in the yard outside. Open Tues.-Sun., 9 a.m.-4:30 p.m.; free.

Accommodations and Food

The **Omni Newport News Hotel,** 1000 Omni Blvd. tel. (757) 873-6664, fax 873-1732, has an indoor heated pool, a nightclub, and Mitty's Ristorante and Piano Lounge, the best Italian eatery this side of Hampton Roads. Moderate. Rooms at the **Relax Inn,** 12340 Warwick Blvd., tel. (757) 249-5395, fax 599-6035, are inexpensive, and the **Mulberry Inn,** 16890 Warwick Blvd., tel. (757) 887-3000, fax 887-3000, has a total of 232 rooms and efficiencies. Moderate.

The **Boxwood Inn,** 10 Elmhurst St., tel. (757) 888-8854, began as the turn-of-the-century home of Simon Curtis, railroad baron and unofficial "boss-man" of Warwick County. Set along the train tracks that made Curtis his fortune, the building was gradually expanded and altered into a general store, boardinghouse, post office, and county hall of records. It fell into disrepair, but through the tireless efforts of Bob and Barbara Lucas it's gradually being reborn as a B&B, restaurant, tea room, and antique shop. Barbara studied at French culinary school, so the food is excellent, and the couple plans seasonal "dinnertainments" with various themes—a medieval banquet, Civil War costume ball, Dickens Christmas dinner, and so on. Moderate to premium.

On the James River Fishing Pier sits the **Crab Shack,** 7601 River Rd., tel. (757) 245-CRAB

(757-245-2722), with a window-lined dining room and outdoor deck overlooking Hampton Roads. Fresh softshell crabs and the catch of the day come in sandwiches ($4.50-8) and on platters ($14-20). Open daily for lunch and dinner. If you think it can't get any fresher, try the sushi and sashimi at **Kappo Nara,** 550 Oyster Point Rd., tel. (757) 249-5396, open for lunch Mon.-Fri. and dinner daily.

Transportation
Local bus service is provided by **PENTRAN,** tel. (757) 722-2837, which connects to Williamsburg's JCCT and Norfolk's TRT lines. The **Greyhound/Trailways** terminal is at 9702 Jefferson Ave. (Rt. 143) at W. Pembroke Ave., tel. (757) 599-3900. **Amtrak,** 9304 Warwick Blvd. in Huntington Park, tel. (757) 245-3589, is the closest station to Hampton Roads, with shuttle bus service to Norfolk and Virginia Beach. To reach the terminal of the **Newport News Williamsburg International Airport,** tel. (757) 877-0221, Web site: www.phr-airport.org, turn onto Bland Blvd. off Jefferson Ave. (Rt. 143) near I-64 exit 255.

Information
The **Newport News Visitors Center,** 13560 Jefferson Ave., tel. (757) 886-7777, is at the entrance to Newport News Park at I-64 exit 250B. It's open daily 9 a.m.-5 p.m.

HAMPTON

The oldest English community in America leapt into the modern age with the seven Mercury astronauts, who trained at the NASA Langley Air Force Base. Hampton (pop. 141,000) overflows with history—especially about African-Americans—and boasts an attractive, modern waterfront jammed with masts and fishing boats.

History
A settlement of Kecoughtan (KICK-o-tan) Indians was overrun in 1610 by a band of settlers sent by Capt. John Smith to build a fort at the mouth of the James River. Fort Henry and Fort Charles both came in handy when relations with the native tribe went downhill. Formally established and named in 1680, Hampton was plagued by pi-

rates during its early years. In 1718, Lt. Robert Maynard is said to have captured and killed Edward Teach, alias Blackbeard, and displayed his head at the entrance to the bay as a warning to other pirates.

Hampton was spared during the Revolutionary War but attacked and occupied by the British in 1813. The *Monitor* and the *Virginia* battled within sight of Fort Story in March 1862, eight months after Hampton's inhabitants had burned most of the city to the ground to prevent its falling into Federal hands.

A rich vein of black history in the area began in August 1619 with the arrival of British America's first shipment of "20 and odd" Africans to Old Point Comfort, and continued with the establishment of the Hampton Normal and Agricultural Institute in 1868.

Hamptons Carousel
This ornate merry-go-round, tel. (757) 727-6381, graced an amusement park on Buckroo Beach from 1921 to 1985. It's been fully restored and enclosed from the elements, with all the original paintings, mirrors, and organ music intact. Open April-Dec., from noon to 6 or 8 p.m.; 50 cents pp.

Virginia Air and Space Center
Imagine an airplane hangar opening like a beetle's wings and you'll have a good picture of Hampton Roads's temple of aeronautics, full to its curving roof with jets, spacecraft, and the gizmos that keep them in the air. The Apollo 12 command module and a 3-billion-year-old moon rock commemorate the moon race, and dozens of hands-on displays explain the principles of flight and space travel. You can hop on the Internet, have your height scanned electronically, and try to keep lunch down in the tri-axis astronaut trainer.

The **Hampton Roads History Center,** upstairs, traces the area's past and includes what archaeologists believe is a pirate's skeleton. There's also a five-story IMAX theater. The center, at 600 Settlers Landing Rd., tel. (757) 727-0900 or (800) 296-0800, Web site: www.vasc.org, is open daily 10 a.m.-5 p.m.; $6 adults, $4 children ($9 adults, $7 children with an IMAX movie). In the summer, tour buses leave for the NASA Langley Base, now devoted mostly to basic aerospace research.

St. John's Church

Elizabeth City Parish, the oldest continuous Anglican parish in the country, was established the same year Europeans arrived at Hampton. This small cruciform church at 100 W. Queens Way, tel. (757) 722-2567, open Mon.-Fri. 9 a.m.-3 p.m., Saturday 9 a.m.-noon, is the fourth on this site, erected in 1728. Eight-foot-thick walls are graced by stained glass windows dating to 1883, one of which portrays the baptism of Pocahontas. Take a minute to wander the surrounding graveyard, with its ornate monuments and Confederate tombstones.

Little England Chapel

The only remaining African-American missionary chapel in the state, 4100 Kecoughtan Rd., tel. (757) 723-6803, contains exhibits on the religious lives of blacks in Virginia after the Civil War. Open Tuesday, Wednesday, Friday, and Saturday 10 a.m.-2 p.m.

Hampton University

The story of America's foremost black university goes back to the Civil War, when escaped slaves sought refuge at Union-held Fort Monroe. Federal officers declared the runaways "contraband of war" to assure their safety, and in 1868 Gen. Samuel Chapman Armstrong answered their pleas for education by opening the Hampton Normal and Agricultural Institute in the center of the city. Initially consisting of only three teachers and 15 students, Hampton University has grown into a model for African-American schools in the United States, counting Booker T. Washington among its many distinguished alumni. Still standing near the entrance is Emancipation Oak, under whose branches slaves once labored over the alphabet and the Emancipation Proclamation was first read to Hampton's populace.

Nine thousand pieces of African-American, Native American, Asian, and Pacific art occupy the galleries of the **Hampton University Museum,** tel. (757) 727-5308, including works by John T. Biggers, Elizabeth Catlett, and Henry O. Tanner's *The Banjo Lesson.* The pen Lincoln used to sign the Emancipation Proclamation is also on display, and the museum store sells hand-crafted ethnic art. Open Mon.-Fri. 8 a.m.-5 p.m., Saturday, Sunday noon-4 p.m.; free.

Fort Monroe

Fort Monroe, the largest stone fortification ever built in the U.S. was preceded by Fort George, which was washed away in a hurricane in 1749. This version was constructed 1819-34 at Old Point Comfort to protect the strategic entrance to the Chesapeake Bay. Edgar Allan Poe was stationed here 1828-29, and Robert E. Lee was here 1831-34 as a second lieutenant and engineer. Manned by 6,000 soldiers, Monroe was the only Union-controlled fort in the upper South during the Civil War. In May 1862, Abraham Lincoln visited "Fort Freedom," two months after Federal troops watched the *Monitor* and the *Virginia* shell it out from the ramparts.

Today the fort, still surrounded by a moat with a bridge wide enough for only a single car, is headquarters for the U.S. Army Training and Doctrine Command. Visitors can walk around the walls for the view of Norfolk across the water and visit the **Casemate Museum,** tel. (757) 727-3391, in whose cool, dank chambers Jefferson Davis was imprisoned for six months after the end of the war. Displays on the history of the fort and coastal artillery include relics of Davis' stay, including his intricate meerschaum pipe. Open daily 10:30 a.m.-4:30 p.m.; free.

Accommodations

Near the Hampton Coliseum you'll find a **Fairfield Inn by Marriott,** 1905 Coliseum Dr., tel. (757) 827-7400, fax 827-7400, inexpensive, and a **Comfort Inn,** 1916 Coliseum Dr., tel. (757) 838-3300, fax 838-6387, moderate. Only a few blocks away is **La Quinta Inn,** 2138 W. Mercury Blvd., tel. (757) 827-8680, fax 827-5906, moderate.

The **Radisson Hotel Hampton,** 700 Settlers Landing Rd., tel. (757) 727-9700, fax 722-4557, surveys the waterfront from wide bay windows. It has a gym and pool, and a few rooms with whirlpools for an slight surcharge. Victor's Restaurant serves all meals. Premium. On the grounds of Fort Henry stands **The Chamberlin,** tel. (800) 582-8975 or (757) 723-6511, fax 722-3636, Web site: www.chamberlin-hotel.com, built in 1928 to replace two previous buildings which both burned. The first, called the Hygeia, was a prime seaside escape in the 19th century, with a veranda where Edgar Allan Poe read poetry a month before his death. A full-scale renovation was underway in 1998 to bring it up to par with its choice location and amenities, including tennis, golf, a private beach, and a pool on the edge of the bay. Rooms are moderate to expensive, depending on whether they have water views, and suites are luxury.

You can camp at **Gosnold's Hope Park,** tel. (757) 850-5116, for $5 per night with (no hookups, but a dump station and flush toilets). It's north of downtown Hampton off Little Back River Rd., open year-round.

Food

The **Second Street Restaurant and Tavern,** 132 E. Queen St., tel. (757) 722-6811, is one of those friendly, big-screen-TV kinds of places serving buffalo wings, burgers, and assorted soup/salad combinations for $4-7. Seafood and Italian entrées ($8-14) can be broiled for the health-conscious. **Goodfellas Restaurant and Bar,** 13 E. Queen St., tel. (757) 723-4979, offers a similar menu with the addition of pizza. Both have outdoor patios and are open daily for lunch and dinner.

Look for the Dionysian painting on the wall of **The Pottery Wine and Cheese Shop,** 22 Wine St., tel. (757) 722-8466, to find this gourmet deli and espresso bar. Homemade bread and signature sandwiches are among the edible offerings. Open Mon.-Sat. 9 a.m.-6:30 p.m. For seafood head to **Captain George's,** 2710 W. Mercury Blvd., tel. (757) 826-1435, with a huge buffet, or the **Fisherman's Wharf,** 14 Ivy Home Rd., tel. (757) 723-3113, which has a great view of the Norfolk Naval Base. Both are open daily for dinner, as is **The Grate Steak,** 1934 Coliseum Dr., tel. (757) 827-1886, where you can cook your own on their open grill.

Recreation and Entertainment

Buckroe Beach, tel. (757) 727-6347, is a wide, clean stretch of sand on the Chesapeake Bay. Concerts and outdoor movies are held at a pavilion during the summer. NASCAR races roar through **Langley Speedway,** 3165 N. Armistead Ave., tel. (757) 865-1100, during the Winston Series, March-October.

Head down to the public piers near the visitors center to find the *Miss Hampton II,* a double-decker motor boat that explores the Chesapeake Bay on sightseeing cruises April-Oct.; $15 adults, $8 children. On sunny days, it passes the Norfolk

Naval Base and stops at Fort Wool, a pre-Civil War citadel built on a 15-acre man-made island. Call the visitors center for tickets and reservations. The *Venture Inn II,* tel. (757) 850-8960 or (800) 853-5002, leaves from the same place for deep-sea fishing excursions Oct.-Dec. ($45 adults, $35 children) and whalewatching trips Dec.-March ($25 adults, $20 children). You can charter the *Venture Inn II* for fishing trips, or try **Chesapeake Charter Service,** 519 Bridge St., tel. (757) 723-0998, with boats leaving twice a day June-Oct. for $16.50 pp, not including rod rental and bait.

For an evening out, it's hard to beat the **Hampton Coliseum,** tel. (757) 838-4203, which has welcomed everyone from the Rolling Stones to Metallica. Ask the ticket-seller if she knows about the Elvis Door, cut into the side of the arena in the 1970s so the King could escape straight to his limo after the show. **Fathoms Nightclub,** below the Second Street Restaurant, hosts comedy Thurs.-Sat., and blues bands play at Goodfellas.

Events

In mid-April, the **Hampton Roads Regional Chili Cook-off,** tel. (757) 727-6429, pits one fiery brew against the next for a chance to compete nationally. There's a "Crockpot" division for "recreational" (i.e. merciful) cooks, and another chili competition in early November. The **Buckroe Beach Jazz Festival,** tel. (757) 727-6300, brings swing to the sand on evenings June-Aug.

Hampton's big yearly event is the **Hampton Jazz Festival,** tel. (757) 838-4203, boasting three decades of some of the world's best musicians. It's shifting toward more soul, blues, and pop, with performers like Aretha Franklin, Ray Charles, and B.B. King. Hotel rooms fill up months ahead of time for the two-day festival in late June, so plan accordingly. The same weekend brings the **Afrikan-American Festival,** tel. (757) 838-4721, to Mill Point Park, downtown. This one is free and family-oriented, offering crafts, music, ethnic foods, and an international marketplace.

Late July's **Seafood Fling,** tel. (757) 727-2312, fills Fort Monroe with children's games, a volleyball tournament, and a 5-km race. The **Hampton Cup Regatta Powerboat Race** in mid-August is the oldest of its kind in the country. Souped-up hydroplanes hit 140 mph on their way from the Mercury Blvd. Bridge to Fort Monroe. In mid-September the Chesapeake Bay itself is cause for celebration during **Hampton Bay Days,** tel. (757) 727-6122, a week of carnivals, seafood, sports, and fireworks.

Transportation and Information

The antique-styled **Hampton Trolley** runs from the downtown waterfront to the colisuem every 40 minutes daily until late afternoon for 25 cents pp, May-Nov. A second "shopping shuttle" route runs year-round. Hampton's **visitors center,** tel. (757) 727-1102 or (800) 800-2202, Web site: www.hampton.va.us/tourism, occupies an octagonal building on the waterfront reminiscent of a screw-pile lighthouse. It's open daily 9 a.m.- 5 p.m. and distributes walking tour maps.

NORFOLK AND VICINITY

Norfolk (pop. 232,000), Virginia's second-largest city and the unofficial hub of Hampton Roads, is more than home to the world's largest naval base. The city also gives the region a "real" downtown and city-style skyline and is home to a galaxy of great restaurants, outstanding museums, and enough nightlife and shopping to keep even visiting sailors happy (now that most of the off-color waterfront joints have closed). Norfolk is a surprisingly pleasant city, with a spanking new Waterfront marketplace, plenty of green parks, and blue water in every direction. (By the way, it's pronounced NOR-fik—or NAW-fik, if you want to sound like a true old-time local.)

HISTORY

The original townsite of about 500 acres was bought near the turn of the 18th century for 10,000 pounds of tobacco. It quickly became one of colonial Virginia's largest trade centers, sending out tobacco, flour, meat, and lumber to be exchanged for sugar and molasses in the West Indies. With a spring at Main and Church the only source of drinking water, visiting sailors naturally steered for the taverns (and have been doing so, more or less, ever since).

With a little over 1,000 residents by the latter 18th century, Norfolk almost ceased to exist on New Year's Day 1776, when an 11-hour British bombardment leveled two-thirds of the city. Within two months, colonists had destroyed the rest to prevent it from sheltering Lord Dunmore's soldiers. Only a few brick structures were left standing in "chimney town," including the cannon-scarred walls of St. Paul's Church.

Such a great location couldn't go to waste, though, and Norfolk soon rebuilt itself into the largest town in Virginia. Many of its 7,000 inhabitants worked on the docks and in the warehouses that exchanged produce from the Piedmont for goods from abroad. Some historians blame the economic jealousy of upriver cities for Norfolk's failure to become a great ocean port akin to Boston or New York.

The tens of thousands of Confederate troops stationed nearby couldn't keep Norfolk, along with Portsmouth and Suffolk, from falling into

NORFOLK AREA CLIMATE

the hands of the Federals in March 1862. The first steps to becoming the world's largest coal port came with the first load of coal, which arrived in 1882 on the freight cars of the Norfolk & Western Railroad. In 1907, the Jamestown Exhibition again drew national attention to Norfolk and planted the seeds of what would become the naval base in a few abandoned buildings that were used for offices and barracks. Three years later, Eugene Ely made the first airplane flight to take off from a ship (an honor turned down by the Wright brothers).

A friendly force of soldiers, sailors, and officers invaded Norfolk during WW I, prompting construction of a working base in 1917. Huge ships steamed in and out of Hampton Roads, dropping off men for training and R&R and picking up munitions turned out by the thousands. By the end of the war, Norfolk counted 34,000 enlisted residents and was well on its way to becoming synonymous with the U.S. Navy.

Even with recent base closings, Norfolk is still the world's largest naval center. A recent downtown renaissance cleaned up seedy sections of

NORFOLK AND VICINITY

DOWNTOWN NORFOLK

HARRISON OPERA HOUSE

PAGE HOUSE INN

CHRYSLER MUSEUM

GREYHOUND/ TRAILWAYS TERMINAL

TODD JURICH'S BISTRO!

SCOPE CENTER

CHRYSLER HALL

FREEMASON ABBEY RESTAURANT AND TEVERN

D'ART CENTER

LA GALLERIA

THE DUMBWAITER

MACARTHUR CENTER

(OPENING 1999)

ST. PAUL'S CHURCH

NAUTICUS

Douglas MacArthur Memorial

PRINCE BOOKS AND COFFEEHOUSE

Town Point Park

WATERSIDE FESTIVAL MARKETPLACE

MARINA

NORFOLK WATERSIDE MARRIOTT

Elizabeth River

Harbor Park

BASEBALL STADIUM

0   200 yds
0   200 m

© MOON PUBLICATIONS INC

the waterfront and saw the creation of the Waterside Festival Market, a 12,000-seat baseball stadium for the AAA Norfolk Tides, and the futuristic NAUTICUS center. A 260-foot whale mural gracing a parking garage on Waterside Drive illustrates the revival.

SIGHTS

NAUTICUS

The $52-million National Maritime Center was opened in 1994 to much fanfare (and some con-

troversy over the price tag). Designed to resemble an aircraft carrier down to a Blue Angel fighter landing on top, this high-tech gallery offers children and adults a plethora of interactive computer displays on all things nautical, from ship design to cleaning up after an oil spill.

Experience warfare at sea in the AEGIS theater, which simulates the bridge of a destroyer, and try to rescue the Loch Ness Monster's eggs in the world's first virtual-reality game for groups (which is harder than it looks). Beautiful tropical fish and moray eels flit through aquariums near a touch tank and working aquatic laboratories maintained by Old Dominion University and the Norfolk State University.

NAUTICUS, 1 Waterside Dr., tel. (757) 664-6613 or (800) 664-1080, Web site: www.nauticus.org, is open Tues.-Sat. 10 a.m.-5 p.m., Sun noon-5 p.m. (daily Memorial Day-Labor Day); $7.50 adults, $5 children 6-17. The first floor, open to anyone who crosses the "gangplank" entrance ramp, has storage lockers, a gift shop, and a cafeteria. On the second floor, the **Hampton Roads Naval Museum,** tel. (757) 444-8971, covers two centuries of local naval history through archaeology, models, and photographs. Open Monday 9 a.m.-4 p.m., Tues.-Sun. 10 a.m.-5 p.m.

Hermitage Foundation Museum
The 12-acre summer retreat of William and Florence Sloane, built 1908-32 on the shore of the Lafayette River, now houses the largest private collection of Asian art in the country. The Mock Tudor House itself is a wonder, filled with hidden doors and stairways and incredible woodcarvings by Charles Woodsend. Then there's the collection: 1,400-year-old Chinese marble Buddhas, unique Persian prayer rugs, and a collection of minutely detailed Chinese and Japanese snuffboxes. Other ancient cultures are represented by glass vials to catch the tears of Roman mourners, intricately carved Spanish *varqueños* (traveling desks), Bronze Age burial containers for food over 6,000 years old, and other items.

The museum, 7637 North Shore Rd., tel. (757) 423-2052, is open Mon.-Sat. 10 a.m.-5 p.m. , Sunday 1-5 p.m.; $4 adults, $1 children 6-18. The lush wooded grounds are free.

Douglas MacArthur Memorial
Norfolk's 19th-century City Hall, a neoclassic monolith designed by the same architect as the U.S. Capitol, was chosen as the final resting place for Douglas MacArthur (1880-1964), one of this century's most intriguing military figures, who is buried in the building's rotunda. Displays include many personal curios, including his ever-present corncob pipe and a 1950 Chrysler Imperial limousine. A theater shows a short film on his life, and thousands of books and mementos fill the library and archives. It's open Mon.-Sat. 10 a.m.-5 p.m., Sunday 11 a.m.-5 p.m.; free.

St. Paul's Church
The only building to survive the devastation of Norfolk in 1776 stands in an island of trees and ancient gravestones amid the clangor of downtown. The first church on this site was built in 1639; this one dates to 1739 and still has a British cannonball embedded in its south wall. At St. Paul's Blvd. and City Hall Ave., the church, tel. (757) 627-4353, still supports an active Episcopal parish. It's open to visitors Tues.-Fri. 10 a.m.-4 p.m., and tours by appointment.

Huntington Tugboat Museum
The 1933 *Tug Huntington,* built in Norfolk, pushed and pulled hundreds of submarines, aircraft carriers, and passenger vessels during its half-century career. It's been restored from crew's quarters to mighty engine room and now displays photos and videos on the history of tugboats through the years. The tug, tel. (757) 627-4884, is docked at the Waterside Marina, between Town Point Park and the Waterside. Open Memorial Day-Labor Day daily 10 a.m.-5 p.m., otherwise Tues.-Sun., noon-5 p.m.; $2 adults, $1 children.

Norfolk Naval Base
The home of NATO's Atlantic operations and the U.S. Atlantic Fleet—all 150 ships and 100,000 workers—the Norfolk Naval Base stretches for 15 miles along the Elizabeth River and Willoughby Bay. Visitors can ogle monstrous aircraft carriers, amphibious assault vessels, submarines, cruisers, and destroyers on narrated tours leaving daily from the Naval Base Tour Office, 9079 Hampton Blvd., tel. (757) 444-7955, Web site: www.pinn.net/~navytour, ($5 adults, $2.50 children). You can also catch a bus from a kiosk at the Waterside, tel. (757) 640-6300. On weekends, certain ships are open to the public 1-4:30 p.m.—check at the base tour office.

Norfolk Botanical Gardens
This is the perfect antidote to Hampton Roads' urban sprawl, 155 acres of trees, shrubs and flowering plants sandwiched between the Norfolk International Airport and Lake Whitehurst. It's easy to spend a whole day wandering among beds brimming with so many varieties of plants that something's almost always in bloom. Every known variety of azalea—250 in all—bloom

submarine at the
Nortfolk Navy Base

VIRGINIA TOURISM CORPORATION

March-May, followed by the 4,000 plants in the Bicentennial Rose Garden. Add 600 camellias and one of the largest collections of rhododendrons east of the Mississippi and you have a flower-lover's nirvana. More than 30 special gardens include a tropical plant pavilion, colonial herb garden, and a unique garden in a bog, where unfortunate Confederate POWs were held during the Civil War.

The gardens, 6700 Azalea Garden Rd., tel. (757) 441-5830, Web site: www.communitylink.org/nbg, are open daily 9 a.m.-5 p.m. for $3.50 adults and $1.50 children 6-18. Twelve miles of trails wind through the greenery, including the Fragrance Garden Trail for visitors with impaired vision. You can walk or drive the paths (no bikes), or take a tram tour for $2.50 pp. A boat tour on the lake costs the same. In the main building, you'll find a horticultural gift shop and the Garden House Cafe, with a patio over the Japanese garden. It's no surprise that the gardens are popular with wedding parties and, especially the third week in April, with picnickers, who flock for the **International Azalea Festival,** tel. (757) 622-2312. The four-day event celebrates Norfolk's role in NATO, honoring a different country every year and ending with the coronation of an Azalea Queen in a special garden pavilion.

Virginia Zoological Park

A century old, this is the state's biggest zoo, with 350 animals in its collection. Most popular are three white rhinos, the African elephants,

and the Siberian tigers. Peacocks and guinea hens wander near the monkey house. In 1998, ground was broken for a special 10-acre African Okavango Delta exhibit, which will expand the zoo by one-third with lions, zebras, giraffes, and warthogs displayed in natural surroundings near a replica of an African village. Special children's events include summer safaris, crafts, and games, and changing exhibits pass through regularly. The zoo, 3500 Granby St., tel. (757) 624-9937, is open daily 10 a.m.-5 p.m.; $3.50 adults, $1.75 children 2-11. It's free 4-5 p.m. on Sunday and Monday.

Chrysler Museum of Art

Named one of the 20 best art museums in the country by *The Wall Street Journal,* the Chrysler boasts a collection ranging from pre-Columbian to modern and touching on Greco-Roman, Asian, Islamic, Egyptian, and Indian along the way. Works by Mary Cassatt, Paul Gauguin, and Edward Hopper hang just a room or two down from photos by William Wegman and an outstanding collection of decorative glass, including dozens of gorgeous Tiffany lamps, windows, and the famous flower-form vase. On the second floor resides the 6.5-pound sterling silver mace presented to the city in 1754 by Governor Robert Dinwiddie in recognition of wealthy local merchants' support of the Tory party.

The museum, 245 W. Olney Rd., tel. (757) 664-6200 or 664-6201, is open Tues.-Sat. 10 a.m.-5 p.m., Sunday 1-5 p.m.; $4 adults, $2 children. It's free on Wednesday, and you can buy combination tickets including admission to the three historic houses administered by the museum—the Moses Myers and Willoughby-Baylor Houses (see below) and the Adam Thoroughgood House in Virginia Beach. **Palettes Restaurant** serves lunch, coffee, and dessert. For a recording of weekly events, call (757) 662-2787. E-mail: chrysler@norfolk.infi.net, Web site: www.whro.org/cl/cmhh.

Historic Houses

The **Moses Myers House,** 323 E. Freemason St., tel. (757) 664-6283, was built 1789-91 by one of Norfolk's first Jewish residents, a consul and merchant originally from New York. His family lived here until 1931, when the house was opened as a museum concentrating on the lifestyle and traditions of Virginia's early Jewish immigrants. Most of the furniture, including a beautiful tall case clock, is original, Open Tues.-Sat. 10 a.m.-5 p.m., Sunday 1-5 p.m. (Jan.-March Tues.-Sat. noon-5 p.m.). A blend of Georgian and federal styles characterizes the **Willoughby-Baylor House,** 601 E. Freemason St. at Cumberland, tel. (757) 664-6283, restored to reflect the middle-class 18th century life of Captain William Willoughby's family. Cooking and medicinal herbs have been replanted in the kitchen garden. Open Tues.-Sun. (Jan.-March Tues.-Sat.) at 2 p.m. for tours with advance reservations.

Admission to either house is $3 adults, $1.50 children, with a combination ticket including the Adam Thoroughgood House in Virginia Beach available for $6.

ACCOMMODATIONS

With so many hotels right next door in Virginia Beach, Norfolk has slid a little in the lodging department. Thanks to unusual local regulations, there's only one B&B in the whole city.

Moderate

The first hotel you'll pass coming from Hampton is the **Econo Lodge,** 9601 4th View St., tel. (757) 480-9611, fax 480-1307, on the ocean side of Oceanview Ave. Keep going down the beach for the **Tides Inn,** 7950 Shore Dr., tel. (757) 587-8781, fax 480-6071, which has a few efficiencies.

The **Best Western Center Inn,** 235 N. Military Hwy., tel. (757) 461-6600, fax 466-9093, has a pool, sauna, and gym near I-264, and the **Old Dominion Inn,** 4111 Hampton Blvd., tel. (757) 440-5100, fax 423-5238, is near its namesake university. The **Comfort Inn Airport,** 6360 Newtown Rd., tel. (757) 461-1081, fax 461-4390, actually isn't very close to the airport, but it does offer a pool and free breakfast.

Expensive and Up

Closest to the airport is the **Norfolk Airport Hilton,** 1500 N. Military Hwy., tel. (757) 466-8000, fax 466-8802, with two lighted tennis courts and a spa. Expensive. Some of the rooms at the 23-story **Norfolk Waterside Marriott,** 232 E. Main St., tel. (757) 627-4200, fax 628-6452, have views of the Elizabeth River just outside. Two restaurants serve all meals.

Stephanie and Ezio DiBelardino bought a condemned 1899 Georgian revival mansion near the Chrysler Museum in 1990 and transformed it into the **Page House Inn,** 323 Fairfax Ave., tel. (800) 599-7659 or (757) 625-5033, fax 623-9451. Business is booming at Norfolk's only B&B, furnished with four-poster beds, clawfoot tubs, and 19th-century artwork. Four rooms (expensive) and three suites, including the Bath Suite with its gas-log fireplace and sunken hot tub (premium to luxury) are available in the house. They also offer a singular Boat and Breakfast option aboard their 43-foot motorsailer, with private crewed excursions optional (luxury, two-night minimum). E-mail: innkeeper@pagehouseinn.com, Web site: www.pagehouseinn.com.

FOOD

What it lacks in hotels, Norfolk more than makes up for in food. From $1 cones on the world's first ice-cream-cone machine to dinner in a restored abbey, the city has it covered—and with the headquarters of People for the Ethical Treatment of Animals (PETA) in town, you can be sure of plenty of vegetarian options. All are open daily for lunch and dinner unless otherwise noted.

Downtown

Head to the international food court at the **Waterside complex** for Cajun, pizza, tacos, sushi, burgers, and Ben & Jerry's. One standout, the **Mongolian Express,** lets you choose as much meat, veggies, noodles, and sauces as you can fit in a bowl before a cook stir-fries it in front of you for $5. Upstairs, **Reggie's British Pub,** tel. (757) 627-3575, offers fish and chips and shepherd's pie in a dark-green, oiled-wood ambiance. Entrées are around $7 for lunch and $9-15 for dinner, and, of course, there's plenty of beer, ale, and hard ciders. Live entertainment on weekends builds up to one of the biggest St. Patrick's Day parties in town.

Also in the Waterfront is **Il Porto,** tel. (757) 627-4400, serving Italian food in a rustic Mediterranean atmosphere of wall paintings and columns. Enjoy foccacia bread pizza, pastas, and $6 lunch specials such as scallops primavera on the outdoor deck over the harbor. Stop by on a Friday or Saturday evening for the acclaimed piano bar. **Schooner's Harbor Grill,** tel. (757) 627-8800, offers the standard seafood, ribs, and steaks along with a full bar. Live jazz graces the Sunday brunch. The coffeeshop at **Prince Books and Coffeehouse,** 109 E. Main St., tel. (757) 622-9223, has pastries, panini sandwiches, salads, and desserts on Mon.-Fri. 8 a.m.-8 p.m., Saturday 10 a.m.-8 p.m., Sunday 11 a.m.-5 p.m.

Produce from small, ecologically sound farms goes into the food at **Todd Jurich's Bistro!,** 210 W. York St., tel. (757) 622-3210. Jurich, one of the best chefs in the area, mixes the innovative with the down-home in dishes like a vegetarian Reuben and country-style meatloaf. Open Mon.-Fri. for lunch, daily for dinner. A high arched ceiling and stained glass windows show that the **Freemason Abbey Restaurant & Tavern,** 209 W. Freemason St., tel. (757) 622-3966, occupies a real late 19th-century abbey. Daily specials such as lobster, prime rib, and tempura fried shrimp are around $10 for lunch and $13-19 for dinner. Lighter choices like seafood quiche and house sandwiches are also available.

"Neo-classic Southern" is how the food at **The-Dumbwaiter,** 117 W. Tazewell St., tel. (757) 623-3663, is described. This funky place has two levels of seating and a retro-hip feel, with creative "large courses" (entrées) like char-grilled tuna mignon wrapped in smoked bacon for $10-19. "Small courses," including vegetarian choices and a smoked quail and a wild mushroom melange, are $4-6. Weekends bring live jazz.

Open daily from 4 p.m. **La Galleria,** 120 College Pl., tel. (757) 623-3939, is a more dapper place with contemporary Mediterranean food, specializing in pasta and wood-burning oven pizzas. Open Mon.-Fri. for lunch, Mon.-Sat. for dinner.

Ghent and Vicinity

This neighborhood, once one of Norfolk's classiest zip codes, has been rescued from a mid-century decline and turned into a hotspot of boutiques, fine restaurants, and historic homes within walking distance of Old Dominion University. The decor alone at **Elliot's,** 1421 Colley Ave., tel. (757) 625-0259, an art-deco jumble of neon, signs, and plaster animals, is worth a visit. Elliot Juren opened this restaurant/bar in 1978, making it the oldest in Ghent. It serves a mix of Mexican, Italian, and American, with plenty of seafood and vegetarian dishes including grilled portabella mushrooms and bean burritos. Open daily for lunch and dinner.

The **Wild Monkey Gourmet Diner,** 1603 Colley Ave., tel. (757) 627-6462, offers a chic spin on the traditional diner. A large wine selection is displayed, bottles and all, on the chalkboard menus advertising heaping portions of jambalaya, pork chops with port wine, and their "famous" $10 meatloaf. The contemporary **Cafe 21,** 742-G W. 21st St., tel. (757) 625-4218, cooks up Chicago-style stuffed pizzas and more unusual dishes—such as chicken and apple curry over couscous. Enjoy a tasty crab cake sandwich for lunch at the orange-and-glass bar.

More than fresh, crusty breads are on the menu at the **Baker's Crust,** 21st and Llewellyn, tel. (757) 625-3600, a popular local cafe with a crêpe bar and bakery attached. Big salads, herb rotisserie chicken, and Cajun pasta have gone over so well that there's already one in Virginia Beach and another opening in Richmond. Other good spots for a quick bite in Ghent are **Bagelworks,** tel. (757) 622-2955, in the same shopping center as Cafe 21, and the **First Colony Coffee & Tea Company,** 204 W. 22nd St., tel. (757) 622-2224.

You can munch a bit of history at **Doumar's Cones and Barbecue,** Monticello Ave. and 20th St., tel. (757) 627-4163. "Uncle" Abe Doumar invented the ice cream cone at the 1904 World's Fair, and his original hand-rolling machine is still in use at this true-as-they-come drive-in with curb service and famous limeades. Even the prices haven't changed in decades: cones are only $1, and burgers, hot dogs, and barbecue sandwiches are $2.

Elsewhere

Tabouli Mediterranean & Vegetarian Cuisine, 4140 Granby St., tel. (757) 627-1143, makes up for an unfortunate location with a delicious assortment of kabobs, falafels, and gyros. Joe Hoggard's **Ship's Cabin,** 4110 E. Ocean View Ave., tel. (757) 362-4659, serves elegant seafood overlooking the Chesapeake Bay, and on tables in the sand during the summer. Open daily for dinner. In the Ward's Corner shopping center near the Navy Base is **Uncle Louie's,** 132 E. Little Creek Rd., tel. (757) 480-1225, a local institution with two faces. On one side a cozy restaurant hides behind a gourmet deli, serving everything from deli sandwiches to whole lobsters topped off by great desserts shipped in from out of town. The other side is a bar and grill with diner-style meals by a pink neon-lit bar and pool tables. Open daily for all meals, with karaoke on Wednesday and live entertainment on Saturday nights.

ENTERTAINMENT AND RECREATION

To find out what's going on around Norfolk, pick up a copy of the *Port Folio* entertainment weekly or the Friday *Preview* section of the *Virginian Pilot.*

Nightlife

Call (757) 625-5483 for info on bands appearing locally. The **Tap House Grill,** 931 W. 21st St., tel. (757) 627-9172, has a long list of microbrews to go with live music most evenings. Side by side near Old Dominion University are the **4400 Campus Club,** 4402 Hampton Blvd., tel. (757) 451-4400, a college dance club that once made a *Playboy* magazine best-part-spot list, and **Friar Tucks,** 4408 Hampton Blvd., tel. (757) 440-9464, with live classic rock and bluegrass. The **Riverview Theater,** 3912 Granby St., tel. (757) 625-7469, has been converted from movie house to live-music stage, hosting hard-edged and lighter alternative sounds.

For an evening of jazz try **Alexander's** at the Omni Hotel at 777 Waterside Dr., tel. (757) 625-

6664, or the **Pizazz Restaurant and Lounge,** 244 Granby St. at Tazewell, tel. (757) 627-2569, which has a dress code and small cover. The **Fifth National Banque,** 1849 E Little Creek Rd., tel. (757) 483-3600, has been voted "Club of the Year" by the Virginia Country Music Association several times thanks to its huge dance floor and quality booking. **The White House Cafe,** 249 W. York St., tel. (757) 533-9290, hosts comedy acts, and **Q-Master Billiards** has two branches; one in the Waterside complex and one at 6214 Sewells Point Rd., tel. (757) 853-8900. They offer free pool with lunch and occasional discounts for couples.

Performing Arts

Norfolk's eye-catching **SCOPE Center,** tel. (757) 441-2161 or (800) 448-9009, can seat 12,000 for concerts, ice shows, and circuses. The less impersonal **Chrysler Hall,** tel. (757) 664-6464, hosts the **Virginia Symphony,** tel. (757) 632-2310, as well as Broadway shows and an annual pops series. The **Virginia Opera,** tel. (757) 623-1223, performs at the 1,600-seat Harrison Opera House, 160 Virginia Beach Blvd., tel. (757) 627-9545, and the **Virginia Stage Company,** tel. (757) 627-1234, puts on five productions a year from April-Oct. at the intimate Wells Theater on Monticello Avenue. Call the **Virginia Ballet Theater,** 134 W. Olney Rd., tel. (757) 622-4822, for its current schedule.

Spectator Sports

The AAA **Norfolk Tides,** tel. (757) 622-2222, aren't the only ones enjoying the new Harbor Park stadium. A four-star restaurant helped earn it a reputation as one of the best minor-league ballparks in the country—perfect for this farm team for the New York Mets (the Tides have already produced stars like Dwight Gooden and Daryl Strawberry). Partners with the Washington Capitols, the **Hampton Roads Admirals** hockey team, tel. (757) 640-1212, competes in the East Coast Hockey League in the SCOPE Center Oct.-March.

On the Water

Vacation homes and inexpensive apartment-hotels line seven miles of **Ocean View Beach** on the Chesapeake Bay, with public bathrooms, picnic facilities, and a 1,600-foot pier where you can rent fishing and crabbing gear. Lifeguards keep an eye out during the summer, even though there's no undertow. Ocean View Beach Park hosts free movies, concerts, and food festivals May-Aug.; call Norfolk Festevents, tel. (757) 441-2345, for a schedule. **Ocean View Watersports,** 1000 E. Ocean View Ave., tel. (757) 583-8888, e-mail: ovws@aol.com, Web site: web-age.com/ovws, rents jet skis and waverunners for $50 per hour, along with kayaks, windsurfers, paddle boats, and small sailboats.

Certified instructor Randy Gore runs **Tidewater Adventure Kayak Ecotours,** 110 W. Randall Ave., tel. (757) 480-1999, which offers beginning and intermediate kayak classes, rolling clinics, and private instruction. They also lead tours to the Back Bay, Eastern Shore, and Great Dismal Swamp. The **Chesapeake Sailing Association,** 1525 Bayville St., tel. (757) 588-2022 or (800) 296-SAIL (800-296-7245), has sailboats for rent and ASA certification classes to teach you how to use them. They're in the Willoughby Harbor Marina off I-64 exit 272.

Cruises and Tours

Sightseeing and dinner-dance cruises aboard the *Spirit of Norfolk,* 333 Waterside Dr., tel. (757) 627-7771, Web site: www.spiritcruises.com, leave from the Waterfront year-round. Prices range from $16 for a weekend moonlight party cruise to $24 lunches and $36 dinners. The *Carrie B,* tel. (757) 393-4735, leaves from the Waterside and Portsmouth's Portside for daily tours of the shipyard and naval base ($10-12 adults, $5-6 children under 12) and sunset cruises. At 135 feet tall, the red-sailed *American Rover,* tel. (757) 627-7245, is the largest topsail passenger schooner flying the stars and stripes. Daily tours of Hampton Roads nautical landmarks past and present run April-Oct.; $14-17 adults, $7-9 children.

TRT, the local bus system, runs one-hour **trolley tours** of downtown Norfolk's major attractions and historic neighborhoods. Trolleys run May-Sept. three or four times a day for $3.50 adults, $1.75 children under 12, and you can get off and catch a later one all day.

Shopping

Designed by the same team responsible for Baltimore's Harborplace and Richmond's Sixth

Norfolk's American Rover *cruises Hampton Roads' nautical landmarks.*

VIRGINIA TOURISM CORPORATION

Street Marketplace, Norfolk's new **Waterside Festival Marketplace,** tel. (757) 627-3300, has dozens of shops selling African art, Southwestern jewelry, clothes, herbs, and Virginiana. Art exhibits and music performances pass through various public spaces, and there are plenty of places to stop for a bite. The complex, open Mon.-Sat. 10 a.m.-9 or 10 p.m., Sunday noon-6 or 8 p.m., also has a TRT bus kiosk and visitors center.

Also downtown is the **d'Art Center,** 125 College Place, tel. (757) 625-4211, home to 30 studios where resident artists labor over everything from ceramics and calligraphy to sculpture and masks. You can stop by to chat or browse Tues.-Sat. 10 a.m.-6 p.m., Sunday 1-5 p.m., and every weekend a different artist gives a discussion and demonstration of his or her work. Call the center for information on art classes and changing exhibits.

Norfolk's trendiest shopping neighborhood is historic Ghent, centered on Colley Ave. and 21st St. Here you'll find places like **Artifax,** 1511 Colley Ave., tel. (757) 623-8840, selling contemporary American crafts, alongside antique stores such as **Nero's Antiques and Appraisals,** 1101 Colonial Ave., tel. (757) 627-1111, and **Hollingsworth Antiques,** 819 Granby St., tel. (757) 625-6525, in an old livery stable. The **Ghent Market & Antique Center,** 1400 Granby St., tel. (757) 625-2897, takes a whole block to accommodate an auction gallery, farmers' market, restaurant, and old-time arcade.

EVENTS

With as many annual celebrations as any city in the state, Norfolk takes its festivals seriously. It even has an office devoted just to scheduling and information, called **Festevents,** 120 W. Main St., tel. (757) 441-2345, fax 441-5198, Web site: www.festeventsva.org. Call the events hotline at (757) 640-5555, ext. 3378, for recorded information. Unless indicated otherwise, all events are held among the trees in the pleasant Town Point Park on the Waterfront. Along with those listed below, the park hosts free **Friday Concerts at The Point** May-Aug. Sailing fans will want to keep an eye out for regular **tall-ship visitations,** when ships from as far away as South America dock at the park. When you climb aboard you'll find the crews are happy to show you around.

The third weekend in April, the **International Azalea Festival and Parade,** tel. (757) 022-2312, ends with an air show featuring the Blue Angels, barnstormers, and free-fall teams celebrating Norfolk's importance to NATO. The festival culminates in the coronation of an Azalea Queen. That same month, the **Virginia Waterfront International Arts Festival,** tel. (757) 664-6492, attracts world-class performers such as Itzhak Perlman and the Moscow Chamber Orchestra for a series of concerts in Norfolk, Hampton, Portsmouth, and Virginia Beach.

Cinco de Mayo, on the weekend closest to May 5, brings mariachi bands, spicy food, and Tejano music, followed by the **Town Point Jazz and Blues Festival** midmonth. One of the largest free concerts of its kind in the East, this has featured bands like Spiro Gyra and the Fabulous Thunderbirds in the past. June's **Harborfest** attracts a quarter of a million people for water and air shows, live entertainment, fireworks, and seafood the first weekend of the month. A highlight is the Parade of Sails, a procession of fully rigged sailboats through the harbor.

Zydeco and crawdads arrive in late June during the **Bayou Boogaloo and Cajun Food Festival,** followed by the **Summer Breeze Jazz Concert** the weekend nearest the Fourth of July. Also in July, watch hundreds of sails billow past the Waterside during the **Cock Island Race,** tel. (757) 393-9933, the East Coast's largest sailboat race. **Reggae on the River** in mid-September brings national acts such as Eek-a-Mouse and the largest drum jam in Hampton Roads. Giant puppets, costumed characters, and theater shows mark the **Virginia Children's Festival** around the same time. Hone your SPAM-carving skills for the city-wide contest during the **River Rib Fest,** simultaneous with a **Clogging Classic** both also in September.

Twenty-five Virginia wineries are featured during the **Town Point Virginia Wine Festival** in mid-October, which sets the stage for **Fleet Week,** celebrating the birthday of the navy, and the Halloween **Masquerade in Ghent. First Night Norfolk,** on New Year's Eve, is a family-style event ending in fireworks over the Elizabeth River.

TRANSPORTATION

Getting Around

Norfolk, Virginia Beach, Portsmouth, and Chesapeake are connected by the **Tidewater Regional Transit System (TRT),** 1500 Monticello Ave., tel. (757) 640-6300. The Norfolk terminal is open Mon.-Fri. 7:30 a.m.-5 p.m., and there's also a kiosk in the Waterside, open daily. The *Elizabeth River Ferry,* tel. (757) 640-6300, is an old paddle wheeler kept around for its charm now that a bridge connects Norfolk to Portsmouth. It churns across the river year-round for under $1 pp, leaving every hour on the quarter-hour Mon.-Fri. 7 a.m.-midnight, and Saturday and Sunday 10 a.m.-midnight from Memorial Day-Labor Day (reduced hours the rest of the year).

Getting There and Away

You can catch a Thruway bus to the Amtrak station at Newport News at Norfolk's **Greyhound/Trail-**

ways terminal, 701 Monticello Ave., tel. (757) 625-5641. Reach the **Norfolk International Airport,** tel. (757) 857-3351, Web site: www.infi.net.orf, from I-64 exit 279 to Norview Avenue. **Norfolk Airport Shuttle,** tel. (757) 857-1231, will take you there, and to Virginia Beach for $25.

INFORMATION

The **Norfolk Convention & Visitors Bureau,** 236 E. Plume St., tel. (757) 441-1852 or (800) 368-3097, operates a visitors center on 4th View St. off I-64 exit 273 (open daily 9 a.m.-5 p.m.), and another in the Waterside complex, tel. (757) 622-3602. At the latter, open daily 10 a.m.-3 p.m. (5 p.m. in summer), Sunday noon-6 p.m., you can watch *Norfolk Reflections,* a movie on the city's history, and buy tickets to NAUTICUS and the *Spirit of Norfolk* boat tour.

PORTSMOUTH

Just over 100,000 people live in this centuries-old seaport across the Elizabeth River from Norfolk. The nation's oldest naval shipyard bristles with cranes and girders south of the narrow, tree-lined brick sidewalks of the Olde Towne district, with more historic buildings than any other city between Alexandria,VA, and Charleston, SC.

History
Portsmouth was established in 1752 on the land of a colonist executed for participating in Bacon's Rebellion. The Gosport Navy Yard arrived 15 years later, quickly becoming the busiest in the Colonies during the Revolutionary War. British soldiers ransacked Portsmouth in 1779 and burned ships in the harbor, but by 1798 Portsmouth was again so busy that, according to a witness, "one might walk . . . to Norfolk on the decks of vessels at anchor." In 1799, the shipyard turned out the *Chesapeake,* the first ship built for the new United States government. The British paid another visit during the War of 1812, when 2,600 men landed here only to be beaten back by American troops at Forts Norfolk and Nelson (today home to the U.S. Naval Hospital).

Federal forces evacuated the city and burned the naval yard soon after Virginia's entry into the Civil War, allowing Confederate shipbuilders to raise the sunken frigate *Merrimac* and turn her into the CSS *Virginia* in time to battle the Union ironclad *Monitor.* In May 1862, it was the Confederates' turn to torch the city as Union troops moved back in. The country's first battleship, the USS *Texas,* rolled off the docks in 1892, followed by the first American aircraft carrier, the USS *Langley,* in 1922. Portsmouth's docks, well on their way to becoming the largest in the country, were renamed the Norfolk Naval Shipyard in 1945.

Sights
Portsmouth's **Olde Towne** includes the **Portside** complex, a smaller version of Norfolk's Waterside with various small eateries open April-Oct. Ship models, artifacts, and uniforms fill the **Naval Shipyard Museum,** tel. (757) 393-8591, at the end of High Street. The collection, dating to the 1700s, includes an 1880 Gatling gun and antique diving helmets. Open Tues.-Sat. 10 a.m.-5 p.m., Sunday 1-5 p.m. for $1 pp.

A $5 Key Pass includes admission to the following three attractions. At the water end of London Blvd., the retired Coast Guard vessel *Portsmouth* houses the **Lightship Museum,** tel. (757) 393-8741. Commissioned in 1915, the ship guided vessels into Hampton Roads's tricky harbor for decades before being restored as a floating museum. Tour the captain's quarters, boiler room, and crew's mess Tues.-Sat. 10 a.m.-5 p.m., Sunday 1-5 p.m. for $1 pp. A kid-sized city, planetarium, and rock-climbing wall are only a few of the 65 hands-on diversions at the **Portsmouth Children's Museum,** 221 High St., tel. (757) 393-8393. Open Tues.-Sat. 10 a.m.-5 p.m., Sun 1-5 p.m.; $4 pp.

Portmouth's **Arts Center,** 420 High St. tel. (757) 393-8543, fills a restored 1846 courthouse with works by international and regional artists. Open Tues.-Sat. 10 a.m.-5 p.m., Sunday 1-5 p.m. A century of local sports heros, including Arthur Ashe, Bobby Ross, and Sam Snead, are honored in photos and personal equipment at the **Virginia Sports Hall of Fame & Museum,** 420 High St., tel. (757) 393-8031.

Entertainment and Recreation
One of the best sound systems in Hampton Roads makes a movie at the **Commodore The-**

ater, 421 High St., tel. (757) 393-6962, an experience not to be missed. Built in 1945, the art-deco theater underwent a two-year, $800,000 restoration that brought back 40-foot canvas murals and Italian lead crystal chandeliers. You can enjoy appetizers and light meals during the show ($5 adults, $3.50 children 6-13) in the 200-person dining area downstairs, but up in the 318-person balcony you'll have to be content with the usual movie snacks.

Narrated **trolley tours** of Olde Towne are offered by TRT, the regional bus company, from April-Aug. **Olde Towne Lantern Tours** are led by guides in period costumes on Tuesday evenings June-Aug. Check at the visitors center (see below) for tickets and information. Paddleboat tours of the inner harbor, shipyard, and Norfolk Naval Base leave from Portside on the *Carrie B,* tel. (757) 393-4735.

Information and Transportation
The **Elizabeth River Ferry,** tel. (757) 640-6300, leaves daily from the Portsmouth **visitors center,** tel. (757) 393-5111, at Portside. The visitors center is operated by the **Portsmouth Convention & Visitors Bureau,** 505 Crawford St., Ste. 2, tel. (757) 393-5327 or (800) 767-8782. Open daily 9 a.m.-5 p.m.

GREAT DISMAL SWAMP NATIONAL WILDLIFE REFUGE

Steeped in mystery, legend, and dread, this sodden corner of the state is actually more beautiful than it is dreary and still bursts with life despite multiple attempts to tame its wildness. Deep peat bogs echo with the strange cries of concealed animals down long, straight canals that contrast the seething disorder of the bog itself.

History
Estimates put the age of the swamp at close to 10,000 years, when the rivers flowing through it began to slow and accumulate peat. An Indian legend of a great fireball falling from the sky has led some to believe that 3,100-acre Lake Drummond—one of only two natural lakes in the state—was formed by a meteorite. Early colonists saw the swamp as an ugly hindrance

rather than a wildlife haven, and tried their best to "improve" it. In 1728, after nearly losing his life surveying the state line, Col. William Byrd gave the area its name and called it a "vast body of dirt and nastiness" that "not even a Turkey Buzzard will venture to fly over."

George Washington organized a logging company in 1763, building roads and digging drainage ditches through what he considered a "glorious paradise." One 22-mile canal bearing his name is the oldest artificial waterway in the country. Eventually most of the timber was cut, leaving the swamp a shadow of its former self. In 1973, The Nature Conservancy transferred 49,100 acres to the Department of the Interior to make into a National Wildlife Refuge. Today, the Great Dismal Swamp covers 131,770 acres in Virginia and North Carolina, of which 82,150 are in Virginia.

Habitats and Residents
Ironically, human interference has left a greater variety of habitats than if the swamp had been left alone. Mixed forest, brier thickets, pine barrens, and shrub bogs now surround the original cypress swamps, whose peaty depths can reach 18 feet. Vines including the tree-strangling supplejack, hydrangea, and Virginia creeper festoon the branches of maples, black gums, and, of course, bald cypress, with its knobby mud-level "knees" and swollen lower trunk. Poison ivy vines as thick as your arm and a sharp-spined shrub called the devil's walking stick will make you want to hew to the trails. Venture out at night and you'll probably see the ghostly glow of foxfire (a type of fungus) in the distance.

In among the greenery live otters, raccoons, foxes, mink, and white-tailed deer, along with the rare bobcat and black bear. Snakes including copperheads, rattlers, and cottonmouth moccasins all are found here, albeit infrequently, as well as 22 species of amphibians and dozens of kinds of birds. The tannic acid is too much for most fish to live in Lake Drummond, whose position in an unusual "perched bog" makes it the highest point in the swamp.

Visiting the Swamp
One hundred forty miles of hiking and biking trails follow old drainage ditches from one end of the swamp to the other. Fishing and boating are

also popular. Bring water, good shoes, *and insect repellent*—the mosquitoes are merciless. Spring is the best time to catch migrating birds and the tiny blooms of dwarf trillium. The Washington Ditch entrance, off Rt. 32 south of Suffolk via US 13, is open daily 8 a.m.-5 p.m., and there's a U.S. Army Corps of Engineers campground, tel. (757) 421-7401, off US 17, 3.6 miles north of the state line. For more information contact the refuge office in Suffolk at (757) 986-3705.

VIRGINIA BEACH AND VICINITY

Miles of beaches, inexpensive hotels, surf, sand, and sun: Virginia's premiere seaside resort has it all. It also has tacky gift shops, hotels so tall they block your tan, and over 425,000 people. Whatever your vacation preference, be it putt-putt golf or a world-class museum, you can probably find it in Virginia Beach—though you might have to share it with a few new friends.

Tourism, obviously, is the number-one industry, ever since the first beachfront hotel went up, in 1883. Virginia Beach didn't really become a national resort, though, until recently. The city's population doubled between 1980 and 1990, and by the year 2000, Virginia's most populous city is expected to hit 500,000.

The municipality invested nearly $100 million in the 1990s to make its resort area more family oriented. New benches and lighting, wider sidewalks, buried power lines, and a boardwalk bicycle trail have all transformed Pacific and Atlantic Avenues. A stepped-up police presence and anti-cruising laws help maintain the crime rate lower than in any other city this size in the country. A historic neighborhood revitalization is planned to start in 1999, and a Beatles museum is also coming.

Repeat visitors will find Virginia Beach wears two faces: one during the summertime tourist season, and a very different one the rest of the year. Off-season, the city returns to its residents and quiets considerably, becoming just perfect, in some people's opinions, for enjoying nearby state parks, the outstanding Marine Sciences Museum, and Edgar Cayce's Association for Research and Enlightenment—or simply staring out to sea from your own private stretch of sand.

SIGHTS IN TOWN

Virginia Marine Sciences Museum
You'll find yourself eye-to-eye with a harbor seal before you're even inside this place, the most popular museum in the state and one of the best in the country. From the seal tank at the entrance to a drift through a kelp forest in the 3-D IMAX theater, the Marine Sciences Museum draws 650,000 visitors per year (from the sound of it sometimes, mostly schoolchildren) with a collection that's the next best thing to—and in some cases *better* than—strapping on a scuba tank and going diving yourself.

A recent $35-million expansion tripled the size of the museum, giving it 800,000 gallons of fresh and salt water in aquariums galore. Starting with the new 300,000-gallon Atlantic Ocean Pavilion, these tanks are the highlight of any visit. See if you can count five varieties of sharks in the Norfolk Canyon Aquarium, and don't miss the sea-turtle hatchling laboratory next to the aquarium holding their cat-eyed parents. (On the Internet at www.whro.org:80/vmsm, you can peer through an underwater camera here.) A touch-tank full of stingrays are so eager to be petted they pop halfway out of the water. Just down the hall are exhibits on deep-sea diving, beach ecology, and a decoy shack with a resident carver. Try your hand at oyster tonging before taking a walk down the path to the Owls Creek Salt Marsh Pavilion, where you can watch river otters and ospreys nesting on specially built platforms.

The museum, 717 General Booth Blvd., tel. (757) 425-FISH (757-425-3474), is open daily 9 a.m.-5 p.m. with extended summer hours. Admission is $8 adults, $6 children 4-11, or $12 adults, $10 children including an IMAX movie. The museum also organizes various **day-trips** (see **Recreation,** below). E-mail: va-marine-science-museum@va-beach.com, Web site: www.va-beach.com/va-marine-science-museum.

Association for Research and Enlightenment
The work of Edgar Cayce, the famous 20th-century American psychic, is the basis for this institution and museum. After entering a self-induced

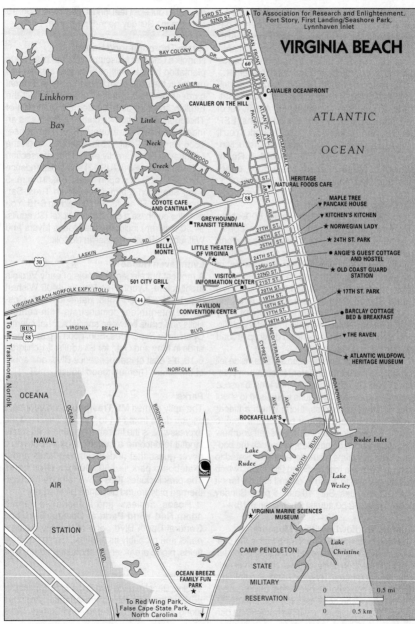

To Association for Research and Enlightenment,
Fort Story, First Landing/Seashore Park,
Lynnhaven Inlet

VIRGINIA BEACH

Crystal Lake

Linkhorn Bay

Little Neck Creek

ATLANTIC OCEAN

CAVALIER OCEANFRONT
CAVALIER ON THE HILL

HERITAGE NATURAL FOODS CAFE

MAPLE TREE PANCAKE HOUSE
KITCHEN'S KITCHEN
NORWEGIAN LADY
24TH ST. PARK
ANGIE'S GUEST COTTAGE AND HOSTEL
OLD COAST GUARD STATION
17TH ST. PARK
BARCLAY COTTAGE BED & BREAKFAST
THE RAVEN
ATLANTIC WILDFOWL HERITAGE MUSEUM

COYOTE CAFE AND CANTINA
GREYHOUND/ TRANSIT TERMINAL
BELLA MONTE
LITTLE THEATER OF VIRGINIA
501 CITY GRILL
VISITOR INFORMATION CENTER
PAVILION CONVENTION CENTER

VIRGINIA BEACH BLVD.

NORFOLK AVE.

OCEANA NAVAL AIR STATION

To Mt. Trashmore, Norfolk

ROCKAFELLAR'S

Lake Rudee

Rudee Inlet

Lake Wesley

VIRGINIA MARINE SCIENCES MUSEUM

CAMP PENDLETON STATE MILITARY RESERVATION

Lake Christine

OCEAN BREEZE FAMILY FUN PARK

To Red Wing Park, False Cape State Park, North Carolina

0   0.5 mi
0   0.5 km

trance, Cayce would deliver predictions on the future and surprisingly accurate diagnoses of patients from just their names and addresses. ARE has some 14,000 transcripts of the sessions, called "readings," including the one that convinced Cayce to move to Virginia Beach and open the center.

The Association, 67th St. and Atlantic Ave., tel. (757) 428-3588, is open to the public Mon.-Sat. 9 a.m.-8 p.m., Sun 11 a.m.-8 p.m. A daily list of free activities includes group meditations, ESP classes, and lectures on Cayce's work. You'll have to pay extra for yoga, meditation instruction, and evening lectures. The **Harold J. Reilly School of Massotherapy**, next door, offers massage, hydrotherapy, and reiki treatment.

Old Coast Guard Station

From 1875 to 1915, more than 600 ships foundered and sank off the Virginia coast, prompting the creation of 11 lifesaving stations from the North Carolina border to the Eastern Shore. This 1903 building is the only one left of five along the southern Virginia shore. Formerly called the Life-Saving Museum, the Old Coast Guard Station, 24th St. and Atlantic Ave., tel. (757) 422-1587, still traces the history of early rescue efforts—which is really the history of Virginia Beach itself, since the town grew up around the five nearby stations.

Videos, models, and full-sized artifacts inside tell the story of the hardy Surfmen, forerunners of today's Coast Guard, who risked their lives to rescue shipwreck survivors. Lyle guns were used to shoot lines to ships in distress, along which a lifecar could ferry as many as four people at a time to safety. Knowledgeable volunteers tell you how the attic is said to be haunted, ever since the bodies of wreck victims were stored there. Slated to open in 1998 is a roof-mounted "shipcam," which guests can use to zoom in on and identify far-off ships. Open Tues.-Sun. 10 a.m.-5 p.m., Sunday noon-5 p.m.; $2.50 adults, $1 children 6-18.

Atlantic Wildfowl Heritage Museum

The long history of bird hunting is told in the centuries-old DeWitt Cottage, 1113 Atlantic Ave., tel. (757) 437-8432, in prints, decoys, and marvelously detailed sculptures. Try your hand at painting a decoy on a computer screen before buying one in the gift shop, and don't miss the homemade "O-gauge" Big Gun upstairs, whose homemade barrel started out eight feet long. Open Tues.-Sun. 10 a.m.-5 p.m., Sunday noon-5 p.m.; free.

Adam Thoroughgood House

Norfolk's Chrysler Museum oversees this 1680s plantation house, built of brick and oyster-shell mortar in the style of an English cottage. Formal gardens and four rooms of antiques reflect the English ancestry of its builder, the grandson of Thoroughgood, who had come to Virginia as an indentured servant around 1620. The house, 1636 Parish Rd., tel. (757) 460-0007, is on the Lynnhaven River directly east of the intersection of Northampton Blvd. (US 13) and Independence Blvd. (Rt. 225). It's open Tues.-Sat. 10 a.m.-5 p.m., Sun noon-5 p.m. (Jan.-March Tues.-Sat. noon-5 p.m.); $3 adults, $1.50 children 6-18. You can also purchase a combination ticket ($6 adults, $4.50 children) including the Moses Myers and Willoughby-Baylor Houses in Norfolk.

Lynnhaven House

A modest but elegant example of early Virginia architecture, Lynnhaven House, 4405 Wishart Rd., tel. (757) 460-1688, dates to 1725. Costumed interpreters demonstrate 18th-century skills and crafts between special annual events. Open June-Sept. Tues.-Sun. noon-4 p.m., weekends in May and Oct., for $3 adults, $1 children 6-18. It's east of Independence Blvd. and south of the Adam Thoroughgood House.

Parks

The aptly named **Mt. Trashmore,** on your right as you drive from I-64 to Virginia Beach on the expressway, is the first aboveground solid-waste landfill to become a municipal park. But you'd never guess that underneath two lakes and a skateboard park lie 650,000 tons of garbage. The park includes Kids Cove, a huge nautical-themed playground designed by children.

Roses, azaleas, and a Japanese garden adorn **Red Wing Park,** at Oceana Blvd. and General Booth Blvd., one of the city's oldest parks and probably its prettiest. It also has ballfields, picnic areas, and a short loop nature trail.

Beaches

Virginia Beach's pride and joy, a wide expanse of pure white sand facing the Atlantic, stretches along "the Strip" from 1st to 42nd Streets. From

BONNY BARBARA ALLEN

O ne of Virginia's most famous folk ballads conforms to the classic, albeit loose, definition: a romantic song with no known author and no definitive text (this is only one of dozens of versions), told by an objective, uninvolved narrator.

'Twas early in the month of May,
The rosebuds they were swelling,
Sweet Jimmy on his death-bed lay
For the love of Barbara Allen.

He called his servant to his side:
"Go to the town she's dwelling,
Say, 'My master's sick and sent for you
For you, Miss Barbara Allen."

So slowly, slowly did she ride,
And slowly she went to him
And all she said when she arrived
Was, "Young man, you are dying."

"Oh yes, Oh yes, I'm very sick
The pain of death's upon me,
I know I'll never see another day
Unless I get you, Barbara Allen."

He turned his pale face to the wall,
She turned her back upon him.
"Farewell, farewell, to all my friends,
Be kind to Barbara Allen."

As she was riding through the town
She heard the bells a-tolling,

And every sound seemed to say,
"Hard-hearted Barbara Allen."

She looked to the east and looked to the west
She saw the corpse a-coming,
"Driver, drive here to my side
That I may gaze upon him."

The more she looked the more she sighed
And finally burst out crying;
"Mother, father, take me home,
For, mother, I am dying."

Sweet Jimmy died on Saturday night
Barbara Allen died on Sunday,
The mother died the love of them both
And was buried on Easter Monday.

They both were carried to the graveyard
And they were buried together,
And on one grave sprung a red red rose,
And on the other a briar.

They grew and grew to the church steeple top,
They could not grow any higher,
They linked and twined in a true lover's knot
For all true lovers to admire.

Memorial Day through Labor Day, lifeguards are stationed every block or so, keeping an eye out for wayward vacationers and anybody drinking, fishing, or tossing a ball or frisbee—all of which are prohibited in the summer. Surfing is also forbidden on the main beach, but wave-riders still congregate near Rudee inlet and the 14th St. pier.

The **Norwegian Lady,** at 25th St., faces the sea, where the bark *Dictator* sank in 1891. A twin of the nine-foot bronze figurehead stands in Moss, Norway.

The sand becomes less crowded (and unpatrolled) as you head north into Fort Story or south to Croatan. Chick's Beach, just west of Lynnhaven Inlet, is the most popular of the calmer beaches along the Chesapeake Bay.

NEARBY SIGHTS

Fort Story

In the middle of this U.S. Army base, tel. (757) 898-3400, stands the **Cape Henry Memorial,** replacing one erected by Jamestown colonists under Capt. Christopher Newport on April 29, 1607, in gratitude for a safe arrival on solid ground. Part of Colonial National Historical Park, the memorial also describes the naval battle that raged offshore on September 5, 1781, between 24 French ships commanded by Adm. Comte de Grasse and 19 British vessels under Rear Adm. Charles Graves. After surprising the French at anchor, the British hesitated long

French and British fleets clash off Cape Henry in 1781.

enough for the colonists' allies to line up in battle formation and win after a brief fight. Cornwallis was thus denied reinforcements, and the American Revolution brought one step closer to success.

The official symbol of Virginia Beach, the **Old Cape Henry Lighthouse,** tel. (757) 422-9421, was built in 1791, the first building authorized by the first Congress. Stones from the same quarry that supplied the U.S. Capitol, the White House, and Mt. Vernon went into the 90-foot octagonal tower set on the tallest sand hill in the area. In use until 1881, the lighthouse is now open to the public March-Oct., daily 10 a.m.-5 p.m.; $2 adults, $1 children 6-15. The ascent—up a steep spiral staircase, two ladders, and through a small hole in the floor of the upper room—is not for the weak of heart or wide of midsection, but the view is outstanding.

First Landing/
Seashore State Park and Natural Area

The inner half of Cape Henry manages to hide 2,770 acres of dunes, marshes, and cypress forest within sight of the high-rises along Virginia Beach's seaside strip. It's the most popular state park in Virginia, drawing more than a million visitors annually, yet remains an amazingly unspoiled nugget of nature for lying so close to the state's largest city.

Habitats ranging from tidal cordgrass salt marshes to live-oak and loblolly pine scrub atop

50-foot dunes shelter prothonotary warblers, also called swamp canaries, and wading birds such as green herons. Spring peepers, bullfrogs, and kingfishers ply the tannin-browned waters of gothic flooded forests in the center, one of the northernmost stands of Spanish moss and bald cypress in North America.

Stop at the **visitors center,** tel. (757) 481-4836 or 481-2131, on Rt. 343 from Seashore Dr. (US 60), for a map of 19 miles of hiking trails, including the six-mile Cape Henry trail (which runs the length of the park and is popular with mountain bikers) and the Bald Cypress Nature Trail into the heart of the swamp. This park can get crowded, especially with trail joggers, so come early and on weekdays to avoid the herds—and bring insect repellent. Primitive **campsites** near this entrance are $22 (March-Dec.) and require advance reservations in the summer and on weekends year-round. Camping cabins are also available. Admission is $2 per car ($3 on weekends).

ACCOMMODATIONS

At last count, close to 150 places offered rooms of some sort in Virginia Beach, mostly along Atlantic and Pacifc Avenues. Keep in mind that rates can swing widely from one season to the next. High season is loosely defined as May to mid-September, with a week in March for spring break. From November to February or March is the lowest season, leaving March-May and Sept.-Nov. in between. The same room can cost three times as much in June as it does in January. (In the listings below, off-season rates are included in parentheses.)

Bargaining may work at hotels and motels in the off-season, and ask about discounts for extended stays. Many accommodations, like B&Bs and condominiums, are open only during the summer.

The city offers a few helpful **central reservation telephone numbers** for securing rooms: (800) VA-BEACH (800-822-3224), City of Virginia Beach; (800) ROOMS-VB (800-766-6782), Virginia Beach Central Reservations; and (800) 213-7645, Virginia Beach B&B Reservations. You might also try **Reservations Plus,** tel. (800) 766-6782.

Moderate and Below

Angie's Guest Cottage and Hostel, 302 24th St., tel. (757) 428-4690, is a comfy house in the center of the strip with 36 beds for $14 ($10) for AYH and HI members and $17.50 ($13.50) for nonmembers. There's a porch, library, and full kitchen, and six B&B rooms that range from inexpensive to moderate. On Atlantic Ave. you'll find moderate-range rooms at the **Golden Sands Motel,** Atlantic Ave. at 14th St., tel. (757) 428-1770 (inexpensive), and the **Royal Clipper Motor Lodge,** Atlantic Ave. at 36th St., tel. (757) 428-8992, fax 491-9302 (budget).

An 1895 summer cottage, one of Virginia Beach's oldest houses, has become the **Barclay Cottage Bed & Breakfast,** 400 16th St., tel. (757) 422-1956, Web site:www.inngetaways. com/va/barclay.html. It once served as a boarding school where Ms. Lillian Barclay taught until age 80. Double-covered balconies run all the way around the building, decorated with antiques such as an 1810 sleigh bed and items donated by former students. It's open April-October. Moderate-expensive. The **Sundial Motel,** Pacific Ave. at 21st St., tel. (757) 428-2922 or 491-8218, has 31 efficiencies with refrigerator and stove. Moderate-premium.

Expensive and Up

Expensive-category hotels along Atlantic Ave. include the **Idlewhyle Motel,** 2705 Atlantic Ave.

at 27th St., tel. (757) 428-9341, fax 425-5355 (budget-inexpensive); the **Econo Lodge Oceanfront,** 2109 Atlantic Ave. at 21st St., tel. (757) 428-2403, fax 422-2530 (inexpensive); and a **Comfort Inn,** 2800 Pacific Ave. at 28th St., tel. (757) 428-2203, fax 422-6043 (inexpensive-moderate). The **Alamar Resort Inn,** 311 16th St., tel. (757) 428-7582 or (800) 346-5681, has 11 one-bedroom apartments with kitchens around a courtyard and heated pool. Each sleeps up to eight people, and there's also a rooftop sundeck. Expensive-luxury (budget-expensive).

At the opposite end of town is the **Church Point Manor House,** 4001 Church Point Rd., tel. (757) 460-2657, fax 460-2845, Web site: www.symweb.com/churchpoint. The restored 1860s farmhouse has been so nicely decorated as to make Martha Stewart proud, with wall paintings and antiques in the original and newer sections. Inviting music and drawing rooms fill the first floor, while a restaurant and pub are open downstairs on weekends. Guests can play tennis, rent bicycles, or hop in a canoe to explore the Lynnhaven River just out the back door. A total of eleven rooms, including three in the detached carriage house, are premium to luxury.

Opened in 1927, the original **Cavalier Hotel,** 42nd St. (Cavalier St.) at Oceanfront, tel. (800) 446-8199 or (757) 425-8555, fax 428-7957, Web site: www.cavalierhotel.com, was *the* place to stay in Virginia Beach between the wars. Chauffeured limos and Pullman coaches brought seven presidents and celebrities including Jean Harlow, Fatty Arbuckle, and Johnny Weismuller to enjoy the indoor seawater pool (considered good for your health) and the Cavalier Beach Club, hopping to the sounds of the orchestras of Glenn Miller and Benny Goodman, among others. The hotel on the hill became a radar training school in the 1940s and today is open seasonally. The newer **Cavalier Oceanfront,** open year-round, sits across Pacific Ave.on the beach.

Guests can dine at tables favored by presidents in the Hunt Room Grille, or in the Orion Grill, 11 stories above the beach. Two Olympic-size pools are now filled with fresh water, near hard and clay tennis courts, shuffleboard, and a golf course. The Cavalier Oceanfront has a health club and Camp Cavalier for kids. Rates, including a buffet breakfast, are premium to luxury at both (moderate-expensive).

For more oceanfront high-rise rooms try the **Holiday Inn Oceanside,** 2101 N. Atlantic Ave., tel. (757) 491-1500, fax 491-1945, premium (moderate), and the **Days Inn Oceanfront,** Atlantic Ave. at 32nd St., tel. (757) 428-7233, fax 491-1936, luxury (moderate).

Condominiums and Vacation Houses

Usually rented by the week, fully furnished houses and condominiums offer a comfortable alternative for extended stays. Prices range $700-1,200 per week in season for a two-bedroom apartment with full bath, kitchen, and dining room near the beach to $400-600 off-season. Both **The Colony,** 1301 Atlantic Ave., tel. (757) 425-8689, ext. 311, and **Beach Breeze Condos,** 1133 Tanager Trail, tel. (757) 422-0579, have two-bedroom units within a few blocks of the sand. **Oceanfront Rentals,** 311 24th St. tel. (757) 428-7473, has cottages and two-, three-, and four-bedroom houses; and **The Seasons,** 109-111 52nd St., tel. (757) 428-4441, has four four-bedroom units. For vacation-house rentals contact **Siebert Realty,** 601 Sandbridge Rd., tel. (800) 231-3037 or (757) 426-6200, e-mail: bchrltr@aol.com, Web site: ww.siebert-realty.com.

Camping

The **Best Holiday Trav-L-Park,** 1075 General Booth Blvd., tel. (757) 425-0249, is virtually a small city, with 1,000 sites, four pools, sports courts, restaurant, and a miniature golf course. Campsites with hookups are $28 ($15-18), and 14 cabins are $55 ($25). Down the road the **Virginia Beach KOA,** 1240 General Booth Blvd., tel. (757) 428-1444, has 400 sites for $27-36 ($15-20).

The **Outdoor Resorts Virginia Beach RV Resort,** 3665 S. Sandpiper Rd., tel. (757) 721-2020, spreads across the beach south of Rudee Inlet. Two pools, lighted tennis courts, a boat ramp, and playground are sandwiched between the Atlantic and Back Bay. Waterfront sites are $36-42. Also in this neighborhood is the secluded **North Shore Bay Campground,** 3257 Colechester Rd., tel. (757) 426-7911, with 140 sites for $16 (April-Oct.) and three four-person cabins for $40 with a/c. To get to both take General Booth Blvd. south to Princess Anne Rd. east, and continue east of Sandbridge Road. Colechester Rd. will be on your right, and Sandpiper Rd. is the final intersection before the water.

FOOD

Snacks and Starters

Both the **Maple Tree Pancake House,** 2608 Atlantic Ave., tel. (757) 425-6796, and **Kitchen's Kitchen,** Atlantic Ave. at 26th, tel. (757) 491-0813, serve good breakfasts from early morning on. The **Heritage Natural Foods Cafe,** 314 Laskin Rd., tel. (757) 428-0500, is a big natural-food market and New Age bookstore with a small cafe offering smoothies, baked goods, soups, and vegetarian sandwiches. Open daily 10 a.m. or noon-7 p.m.

Bagelworks, 1268 Great Neck Village Rd., tel. (757) 496-2596, has inexpensive bagel sandwiches. For a cuppa joe, try the **Webcity Cybercafe,** 116 S. Independence, tel. (757) 490-8690, Web site: www.webcitycafe.com, or the **PJ Baggan Java Cafe,** 960 Laskin Rd., tel. (757) 491-8900, which has wine, espresso, and light bites.

Seafood

Near the southern end of the Chesapeake Bay Bridge-Tunnel is **Alexander's On The Bay,** 4536 Ocean View Ave., tel. (757) 464-4999, with fine dining in a weathered-wood setting. Escargot and baked brie appetizers ($5-8) lead to lobster, duck, and steak entrées for $14-20. Pasta and sandwiches on the open-air beach deck are $7-14, led by the brimming "Bubba Gump boat" of seafood.

A tourist landmark that locals love too is **Henry's,** 3319 Shore Dr., tel. (757) 481-7300. The largest cylindrical saltwater aquarium in the east towers inside the entrance to this two-story glass and concrete building, with two decks overlooking the Chesapeake Bay. Choose from the raw bar, broiled "heart-smart" items, or regular entrées like chinook salmon and Alaskan crab legs in the $17 range (plates $25) for dinner. Open daily for lunch and dinner, with a $10 Sunday brunch buffet served 10 a.m.-2 p.m.

If the Mediterranean-style fresh fish of the day is any indication, the **Lynnhaven Fish House,** 2350 Starfish Rd., tel. (757) 481-0003, serves seafood as good as any in Virginia Beach. Dinner entrées run from $15 for Chesapeake Bay crabs to $22 for King Neptune's Banquet, and lunch plates such as seafood omelettes, casseroles, and quiches are $7-9. Open daily for lunch and dinner.

Other Choices

Leaning columns and bloom-spilling baskets give **Bella Monte,** 1201 Laskin Rd., Ste. 100, tel. (757) 425-6290, the feel of an explosion in a Tuscan flower shop. Inside the cheery Mediterranean chaos you'll find a gourmet international market, deli, and cafe that has won numerous local awards. Choose from 10-inch hand-tossed pizzas, rotisserie chicken, and watercress salads for $6-7, or chicken, pork, and pasta main dishes for $11-16. It's in the Birdneck Point Commons, open Mon.-Sat. for lunch and dinner.

The classy **Coastal Grill,** 1427 N. Great Neck Rd. in the Mill Dam Crossing Shopping Center, tel. (757) 496-3348, specializes in ocean-influenced American fare, from oysters mignonette appetizer ($7) to pan-seared fish, pork, veal, and beef entrées ($15-18). It has some sidewalk dining in front. Open daily for dinner. The **Coyote Cafe & Cantina,** 972-A Laskin Rd. in Linkhorne Shops, tel. (757) 425-8705, is a little like Santa Fe: based in the Southwest, but evolved into something beyond. A sense of chic fun pervades the restaurant, with its stuffed coyote and cartoon stills from a previous business incarnation, and its menu, from the "kick-ass" chorizo chili to Madre's Meat Loaf. Quesadillas compete with crab cakes on the lunch menu; dinner visits the realm of roast duck and sashimi. Open Mon.-Sat. for lunch and dinner daily.

An urban artsy theme sustains the **501 City Grill,** 501 N. Birdneck in Birdneck Shoppes, tel. (757) 425-7195. Bikes and art hang on the tiled wall under ceiling fans that keep the open kitchen cool. Try the southwest tuna tacos or trademark Michelob Shrimp appetizers for around $6, followed by a "truck-stop" filet mignon, pizza from the wood oven, or grilled delmonico, with a cappuccino or something from the long wine list to top it off. Open daily for dinner from 4 p.m. **The Raven,** 1200 Atlantic Ave. at 12th St., tel. (757) 425-1200, pulls off the usual beach-strip steaks, seafood, and poultry with a little more friendly flair than most. Open daily for lunch and dinner.

In a big old three-story house near Rudee Inlet, **Rockafeller's,** 308 Mediterranean Ave., tel. (757) 442-5654, is one of Virginia Beach's most popular standbys. Sit inside among the plants or out on two levels of covered balcony seating, it doesn't matter—the caesar salads, crab cakes, steaks, and pasta can't be beat. Entrées range $9-17, but every day 3:30-6 p.m. they run early-bird specials and let kids eat for only $1. Open daily for lunch and dinner, with a moderately priced Sunday brunch from 10 a.m.-2 p.m.

WATER SPORTS

Fishing

An armful of places offer half-day, full-day, and overnight **charters** in pursuit of the marlin, dolphin, tuna, sailfish, and wahoo that teem offshore at the right time of year. At Rudee Inlet, the **Virginia Beach Fishing Center,** 200 Winston-Salem Ave., tel. (757) 491-8000 or (800) 752-0509, runs mackerel trips Feb.-March for $30 per day and wreck fishing for sea bass, tautog, and blues for $40 per day in the spring, fall, and winter. Nearby you can try **Rudee Inlet Fishing Charters,** 200 Winston-Salem Ave., tel. (757) 422-5700, and **Action Charters,** 200 Winston-Salem Ave., tel. (757) 491-0794. At Lynnhaven Inlet are the **Lynnhaven Seafood Market & Marina,** 3311 Shore Dr., tel. (757) 481-4545, and **Bubba's Marina,** 3323 Shore Dr., tel. (757) 481-3513.

If all you want is to get the hook in the water, you can rent rods, reels, and crab cages from April-Oct. at the **Lynnhaven Inlet Fishing Pier,** 2350 Starfish Rd. off Shore Dr., tel. (757) 481-7071, and the **Virginia Beach Fishing Pier,** 15th St. at Oceanfront, tel. (757) 428-2333, near a small amusement park.

Scuba Diving

Explore centuries of shipwrecks for $40-50 per dive at places such as the **Lynnhaven Dive Center,** 1413 Great Neck Rd., tel. (757) 481-7949, which offers a $100 certification course in its heated indoor pool. Visibility is usually 40-50 feet, and many wrecks have some coral growth. Other places to try for trips, charters, and PADI and NAUI instruction courses include the **Mid-Atlantic Dive Center,** 5350 Kemps River Dr., tel. (757) 420-6179, and **Undersea Adventures,** at Rudee Inlet, Pier 3, tel. (757) 481-3688.

A marlin breaks the surface off the Virginia coast.

VIRGINIA TOURISM CORPORATION

Surfing

The **Graveyard Surf & Skate Shop,** 3912 Bonney Rd., tel. (757) 498-8770, is where old boards go to die, with many new and used models for sale or on consignment. Another popular source is the **17th Street Surf Shop,** 307 Virginia Beach Blvd., tel. (757) 422-6105. For a surf report, call **Wave Riding Vehicles,** 1900 Cypress Ave. at 19th St., tel. (757) 428-1877, or **Hotline Surfboards,** 608 Norfolk Ave., tel. (757) 428-6703.

Rentals

Enticer Water Sports, 308 Mediterranean Ave. at Rudee Inlet, tel. (757) 422-2277, rents jet skis daily for $67 per hour, as does **Rudee Inlet Jet Ski Rentals,** with outlets at the Virginia Beach Fishing Center, tel. (757) 428-4614, and 31st St. at Oceanfront, tel. (757) 491-1117. The latter also rents kayaks and waverunners. **SeaVenture Rentals,** 600 Laskin Rd. at Browning's Landing, tel. (757) 422-0079, has pontoon boats and waterskiing equipment.

Excursions

The **Virginia Marine Sciences Museum** offers two-hour trips year-round that explore different facets of Virginia Beach's rich waters. Whale-watching excursions (Jan.-March) go after humpbacks and fin whales with cameras instead of harpoons, and dolphin-watching trips June-Sept.

often spot pods of bottlenose dolphins. Kids love the ocean collection trips June-Aug., on which real marine treasures including seahorses, jellyfish, sand dollars, and crabs are caught and explained, then released back into the water. Each excursion is $12-14 adults, $10-12 children under 12. Call (757) 437-BOAT for information and reservations.

OTHER ACTIVITIES

The new paved bike trail along the beach will make you glad you brought your wheels or soon have you looking for some to rent. **Cherie's Bicycle and Blade Rentals,** 2417 Atlantic Ave., tel. (757) 437-8888, rents bikes, in-line skates, and safety gear and offers skating classes. They have stands on the boardwalk at 8th, 22nd, 24th, and 37th Streets. Beach-supply places such as **Atlantic Mart,** 28th and Atlantic Ave., also rent bikes and rollerblades along with boogie boards, beach chairs, strollers, and umbrellas. Remember, there's a $25 fine for riding without a helmet. Try your hand (and heart) at **parasailing** in the two-person Skyrider operated by the **Virginia Beach Fishing Center,** 200 Winston Salem Ave. W, tel. (757) 422-UFLY (757-422-8359).

The **Ocean Breeze Family Fun Park,** 849 General Booth Blvd., tel. (757) 422-4444 or (800)

678-9453, has a wave pool, water flume, and slides in the Wild Water Rapids water park. Tickets are $16.50 adults, $11.50 children. You'll have to buy individual passes for miniature golf ($5), batting cages ($2.50), and rides such as the Grand Prix cars in Motorworld. Open May.-September. Another popular (and free) diversion in Virginia Beach is to watch **Navy jets** take off from the Oceana Naval Air Station along Oceana Blvd. and London Bridge Road. Call (757) 433-3131 for a schedule.

ENTERTAINMENT

Nightlife
Beach towns always have some of the best after-hours activities going, and Virginia Beach is no exception. Summer crowds tend toward the young, tanned, and beautiful, but whatever your stripe, you'll probably be able to find *some* place that's your speed. Sunburned bodies pack venues such as **Club Rogue's,** 616 Virginia Beach Blvd., tel. (757) 422-3344, and **The Abyss,** 1065 19th St., tel. (757) 422-0748, to sweat a little more after dark. (The Abyss's dark alter ego, the Nocturnal Café, also hosts bands.) If you'd like a bite with your music, try a restaurant/nightclub such as the sushi bar **Hot Tuna,** 2817 Shore Dr., tel. (757) 481-2888.

The **Jewish Mother,** 3108 Pacific Ave., tel. (757) 422-5430, is one of Virginia Beach's hottest music spots, featuring jazz, folk, and blues most nights. You can catch acoustic performances at **Abbey Road,** 203 22nd St., tel. (757) 425-6330, and **Smackwater Jack's,** 3333 Virginia Beach Blvd., tel. (757) 340-6638, while **Desperado's,** 315 17th St., tel. (757) 425-5566, offers country music, Tex-Mex food, and one of Virginia's few mechanical bulls. Some places, like the **House of Jazz,** 314 Constitution Dr., tel. (757) 456-0884, and **Scully's Classic Rock & Roll,** 3472 Holland Rd., tel. (757) 468-7625, are self-explanatory.

For a game of pool, stop by **Q-Master II,** 5612 Princess Anne Rd., tel. (757) 499-8900, or **Bay Billiards,** 2941 Shore Dr., tel. (757) 481-9393. For a chuckle try **The Comedy Club,** tel. (757) 499-2500, at the Thoroughgood Inn in the Pembroke Meadows Shopping Center, Pembroke Ave. and Independence Boulevard.

Completed in 1996 at a cost of $1.75 million, the **GTE Virginia Beach Amphitheater,** 3550 Cellar Door Way, tel. (757) 368-3000, presents 40 or so concerts per season. Performers include the likes of Jimmy Buffett, Phish, Sting, and No Doubt. There's space for 12,500 people on the lawn in addition to 7,500 covered seats. It's on Princess Anne Rd. near Princess Anne Park.

Performing Arts
Not all of Virginia Beach's entertainment involves alcohol, flashing lights, and sweating bodies (well, maybe some sweat). Both the **Virginia Beach Symphony Orchestra,** 372 S. Independence Blvd., tel. (757) 671-8611, and the **Virginia Beach Ballet,** 4718 Larkspur Square Shopping Center, tel. (757) 495-0989, perform at the Pavilion Theater in the Pavilion Convention Center, 1000 19th St., tel. (757) 437-4774. The symphony also plays at a stage on the boardwalk at 24th St. The **Little Theater of Virginia,** 550 Barberton Dr. at 24th St., tel. (757) 428-9233, showcases local thespian talent.

Spectator Sports
You can catch the **Hampton Roads Mariners,** 1016 Independence Blvd., tel. (757) 464-1021, as they compete in the U.S. Interregional Soccer League April-Aug. at the First Colonial High School, on Mill Dam Rd. off First Colonial Rd. (Rt. 408) near its intersection with Great Neck Rd. (Rt. 279).

SHOPPING

If your tastes don't run to seashell fishermen and sunset ashtrays, there are a few places in town that sell souvenirs of a more memorable kind. **Colonial Cottage Antiques,** 3900 Bonney Rd., tel. (757) 498-0600, brings together several dealers in one of the largest antique centers in the Tidewater. **Echoes of Time Antiques,** 320-B Laskin Rd., tel. (757) 428-2332, offers vintage clothing and books along with well-used furniture, and the **Olde Virginia Mercantile,** 3101 Virginia Beach Blvd., tel. (757) 486-3432, stocks folk art and hooked rugs as well as antiques and reproductions.

Handcrafted quilts, candles, butter churns, and sleds can be found at the **Amish Shoppe,**

2956 Virginia Beach Blvd., tel. (757) 486-5925, which also has Pennsylvania-style foods. **Caravans International Marketplace,** 302 Laskin Rd., tel. (757) 425-7766, offers an eclectic collections of sarongs, batiks, carvings, and toys from Indonesia and Africa, while **Casa Luna Imports,** 323 Laskin Rd., tel. (757) 425-4109, tends toward the Latin American in its pottery, jewelry, and wall hangings.

EVENTS

Most Virginia Beach festivals involve music or sports in close proximity to the ocean. For more information, call (800) 446-8038 or (757) 491-SUNN (757-491-7866).

May brings three options: **Beach Music Weekend** mid-month, with performances on beachfront stages at 17th, 24th, and 30th Sts.; the **Big Band Weekend** later in the month; or the **Viva Elvis Festival** near the end. In early June the **North American Sand Soccer Championships** are sponsored by the Hampton Roads Soccer Council, tel. (757) 456-0578. It's followed by the **Boardwalk Art Show and Festival,** tel. (757) 425-0000, held since 1955, between 14th and 28th Sts. along the beach.

Since 1962 the **East Coast Surfing Championship** has determined the best North Atlantic rider in professional and amateur categories. This August event also includes live music, a 5-K race, and a catamaran competition offshore. The **American Music Festival** in early September welcomes over 100 national acts from pop to country in the East Coast's largest music event. Performances are held in oceanfront parks at 5th, 17th, and 24th Sts. (free at all but 5th St.). **Blues at the Beach** follows mid-month in the 17th St. park.

September also brings Virginia Beach's biggest blowout, the **Neptune Festival,** tel. (757) 498-0215. Parades, surfing, sailing, and a Sand Castle Classic alternate with the Sandman Triathlon, a U.S. Navy Air Show, and the formal King Neptune's Ball to choose the year's king. Things slow down the rest of the year, with only the **Boardwalk Exotic Auto Expo** in mid-October to break the silence. From late November to early January, though, two miles of boardwalk are illuminated with glowing sea creatures and sinking ships during **Holiday Lights at the Beach.**

TRANSPORTATION

Getting Around

During the spring and summer, **TRT trolleys,** tel. (757) 428-3388, carry passengers up and down the beach area and west along Rt. 44. One connects Rudee Inlet to 42nd St. via Atlantic Ave. (daily noon-midnight), while the Museum Express runs from 19th St. down Pacific Ave. as far as the Virginia Marine Sciences Museum and the Ocean Breeze Amusement Park (daily 8 a.m.-midnight). A third heads west along the Expressway (Rt. 44) to the Lynnhaven Mall. Fares are 50 cents pp, or you can buy a three-day pass for $3.50.

Getting There and Away

Greyhound/Trailways has a terminal at 1017 Laskin Rd., tel. (757) 422-2998. The nearest **Amtrak** station is in Newport News, but you can buy tickets at **Great Atlantic Travel,** 1065 Laskin Rd., Ste. 101, tel. (757) 422-0444. A Thruway bus connects the terminal to the Amtrak shelter and 24th St. and Pacific Avenue.

If you're driving yourself and planning to continue on into North Carolina, try this neat route: take Pacific Ave. south to Princess Anne Rd. (Rt. 615), which ends at Knott's Island at the southern end of Back Bar. From here you can take a free 40-minute car ferry to Currituck, NC, which leaves six times a day. Call (800) BY-FERRY (800-293-3779) for up-to-the-minute ferry information.

INFORMATION

The main **Virginia Beach Information Center,** 2100 Parks Ave., tel. (757) 437-4888 or (800) 822-3224, is near 21st St., open daily Memorial Day-Labor Day 9 a.m.-8 p.m. (otherwise 9 a.m.-5 p.m.). There are information kiosks along Atlantic Ave. at 17th, 24th, and 27th Sts. Visitor-oriented Internet sites include www.virginia-beach.va.us, www.va-beach.com, and www.vgnet.com/.

BACK BAY NATIONAL WILDLIFE REFUGE

A thin strip of shoreline and a set of islands in Back Bay make up this sanctuary, which preserves 7,700 acres of Virginia's southern Atlantic coast as it was before the high-rises and jet-skis arrived. Once the haunt of wealthy duck hunters from New England, Back Bay National Wildlife Refuge was established in 1938 as an important stop along the Atlantic Flyway for migrating waterbirds, especially greater snow geese.

A wide range of habitats starts among the sea oats on the mile-wide Atlantic strip, a constantly shifting stretch of sand that is predicted to eventually break free from the northern headland near Sandbridge. Maritime forests of scrub oak and loblolly pine cover the higher elevations, interspersed with wax myrtle shrubs and bayberry and blueberry bushes. Three-quarters of the refuge is marsh, covering the bay side of the strip and Long and Ragged Islands at the north end of Back Bay.

The refuge's three hundred species of birds includes 30 kinds of waterfowl, among them the endangered bald eagle and peregrine falcon. Spring is the peak migration time of songbirds and shorebirds, while hawks arrive in the fall. Tens of thousands of greater snow geese swing through from Nov.-March on their way south from Greenland and Canada's Northwest Territories. The snow goose migration peaks in December, accompanied by Canada geese and tundra swans. The mammal list includes gray foxes, river otters, mink, muskrats, and nutria (a large rodent) which compete with feral horses and pigs introduced by settlers. Back Bay is also one of the northernmost nesting spots for endangered loggerhead sea turtles, who drag themselves ashore in the summer to lay clutches of leathery eggs under the watchful eyes of refuge staff.

Visiting Back Bay

Take Sandbridge Rd. south to reach the entrance gate, open daily dawn-dusk ($4 per car). A **visitors center** (open Mon.-Fri. 8 a.m.-4 p.m., Saturday, Sunday 9 a.m.-4 p.m.) has displays and films on the ecology of the refuge. Boardwalk trails cross the beach, while others along interior dikes are open to mountain bikes. Surf and freshwater fishing is permitted from land or small boats, which many visitors use to explore the bay and islands.

Camping is permitted only in False Cape State Park to the south, reached by a five-mile hike after parking outside the refuge gate. Two-hour guided **tram rides** through Back Bay and False Cape in open-sided electric trams run twice a day from April-Oct.; $6 adults, $4 children under 18. Call (757) 498-BIRD (757-498-2473) for details. For more information on Back Bay, contact the refuge office at 4005 Sandpiper Rd. in Virginia Beach, tel. (757) 721-2412.

FALSE CAPE STATE PARK

This state park encloses six miles of pristine beaches, shore forest, and marsh at the primitive southern end of Virginia's barrier spit, named False Cape because sea captains commonly confused it with Cape Henry, at the entrance to the Chesapeake Bay. Halfway down the spit lie the brick foundations and old cemetery of the town of Wash Woods, moved because of shifting dunes that threatened to inundate it.

Only environmental education classes are permitted to drive in, so False Cape State Park is accessible to the general public only by a six-mile hike or bike ride though Back Bay National Wildlife Refuge, or by boat through Back Bay. During the winter, the entrance may be closed; check with the **park office,** 4001 Sandpiper Rd. in Virginia Beach, tel. (757) 426-7128, for details, and information on various guided hikes and programs. **Camping** permits can be obtained through the First Landing/Seashore State Park.

THE EASTERN SHORE

"Junk and Good Stuff" reads a sign outside a store on US 13, inadvertently but rather neatly (if simplistically) summing up the whole of the Eastern Shore in more ways than one. The long, flat neck of the Delmarva Peninsula, dividing the Chesapeake Bay from the Atlantic from Maryland to Cape Charles, is something of an anomaly, a throwback, an often-forgotten corner of crusty watermen, rusty pickups, and salt breezes. It's also one of the most subtly enticing parts of Virginia.

They say that when you cross the Chesapeake Bay Bridge-Tunnel from Virginia Beach you step back in time, and it's not all hyperbole. A rural 1950s feeling pervades all 70 miles of the Eastern Shore, so after a while it's the modern cars on US 13 that start to look out of place, not the vine-covered buildings slowly being re-claimed by the earth on either side. Fewer than 50,000 residents—more than in Charlottesville, fewer than in Lynchburg—are divided into "born-heres" (occasionally "stuck-heres") and recently arrived "come-heres," many of whom have opened B&Bs in small historic towns.

Agriculture is the biggest money-maker on this peninsula, and most of the low-lying fields are covered with acres of potatoes, soy beans, and other crops. Seafood comes next, from net-fuls of finfish to oyster beds and crab pots seeded the length of the bay. Pockets of poverty evidence the recent slipping of both industries.

Visiting the Eastern Shore

A slower pace of life means that it might take a little longer to get your crabcakes on the table and your water refilled here, but use the time to savor

THE CHESAPEAKE BAY BRIDGE-TUNNEL

Stretching across the mouth of the Chesapeake Bay like a gap-toothed smile, this engineering wonder lets thousands of drivers a day save a hundred-mile detour between Hampton Roads and the Eastern Shore. Officially named the Lucious J. Kellam, Jr. Bridge-Tunnel, after the Eastern Shore businessman who conceived it, the longest bridge-tunnel system in the world comprises 17.65 miles of US 13 from Virginia Beach to Cape Charles.

Construction began in 1958 to replace ferry service that had operated since the 1930s. Over the following six years, some 825,000 tons of concrete and 55,000 tons of steel were cast into pilings and sections of roadway on shore, hauled out on barges, and fit together like the world's biggest Lego project. The most impressive feat was the raising of four man-made islands in water averaging 40 feet deep. Each one, large enough to hold Yankee Stadium, serves as one end to two mile-long tunnels sunk beneath the main shipping channels.

Two hundred million dollars later, the bridge opened, allowing the first ceremonial vehicle to cross 12 miles of trestled roadway, dip under the bay twice, and pass over two high-clearance bridges near Fisherman Island off Cape Charles. (The idea of one long bridge was scrapped by Navy strategists, who said it would be too easy for enemies to destroy and block the navigable lanes with debris during wartime.)

Improvements begun in 1995 are intended to relieve traffic congestion caused by as many as 15,000 vehicles a day in summer months. Another $200 million will add new one-way bridge sections parallel to the original ones, reducing the number of head-on collisions. Traffic lanes will share the same tunnels.

Sea Gull Island, the southernmost of the man-made islands, is home to a restaurant, gift shop, and 625-foot fishing pier, tel. (757) 464-4641, with bait and tackle for sale and rent. And even though you might not believe that all this thundering traffic is conducive to wildlife viewing, the artificial islands are among the best places in Virginia to watch migratory seabirds in the winter. Scoters, ruddy turnstones, scaup, eiders, and other duck species including buffleheads, gadwalls, and common goldeneyes all make appearances in the winter, especially after a hard freeze.

The bridge-tunnel, by the way, is an exercise in private enterprise, as permitted by Virginia law. A $10 toll is charged each way. Call (757) 331-2960 for more information.

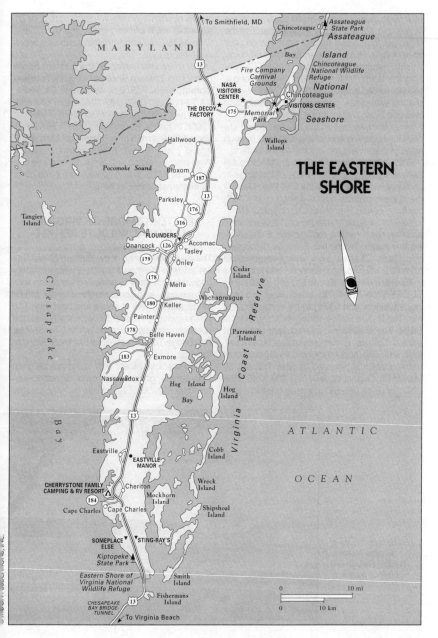

To Smithfield, MD

Chincoteague

Assateague
State Park

Assateague

MARYLAND

13

Island

Bay

Chincoteague
National Wildlife
Refuge

Fire Company
Carnival
Grounds

National

NASA
VISITORS
CENTER

175

THE DECOY
FACTORY

Chincoteague

VISITORS CENTER

Memorial
Park

Seashore

Hallwood

Wallops
Island

Pocomoke Sound

Bloxom

**THE EASTERN
SHORE**

187

Tangier
Island

13

Parksley

176

316

Chesapeake

FLOUNDERS

126

Onancock

Accomac

Tasley

179

Onley

178

Melfa

Cedar
Island

Virginia Coast Reserve

180

Keller

Wachapreague

Painter

178

Parramore
Island

Belle Haven

183

Exmore

Nassawadox

Hog Island
Bay

Hog
Island

Bay

13

ATLANTIC

Eastville

Cobb
Island

OCEAN

EASTVILLE
MANOR

CHERRYSTONE FAMILY
CAMPING & RV RESORT

Cheriton

Wreck
Island

184

Mockhorn
Island

Shipshoal
Island

Cape Charles

Cape Charles

SOMEPLACE
ELSE

STING-RAY'S

Kiptopeke
State Park

Smith
Island

Eastern Shore of
Virginia National
Wildlife Refuge

Fishermans
Island

0   10 mi

0   10 km

CHESAPEAKE
BAY BRIDGE
TUNNEL

13

To Virginia Beach

your surroundings. There aren't as many things to see and do, per se, as in other parts of the state, but then again that all depends on your point of view. Roadside stands selling produce, shrimp, peanuts, and flowers line US 13, running the length of the Eastern Shore along a historic railroad route. Countless "creeks"—wide, shallow estuaries—perforate the "bayside" and "seaside," just waiting to be explored by boat. A few public beaches on the bay and ocean are open for swimming and fishing, and trails through miles of marshland are goldmines for birders.

Back in town, fans of historic architecture will have a field day with hundreds of buildings in continual use since before the Civil War. Many fit the classic country-house design of the 19th century, consisting of four connected structures—"big house," "little house," "colonnade," and "kitchen"—with a roofline like a descending bar graph. Towns like Eastville, Accomac, and Cape Charles brim with centuries-old churches, courthouses, schools, and homes.

Eastern Shore Escapes, tel. (888) VA-SHORE (888-827-4673), offers weekend birding, kayaking, and biking tours in cooperation with The Nature Conservancy, stopping at local B&Bs. The excursions, offered April-Oct., start around $200 pp. E-mail: esescapes@esva.net, Web site: aaa.accomack.com/escapes. Local transportation is provided by **Star Transit,** 59 Market St., Onancock, tel. (757) 789-5246, 789-5247, or (800) 386-5816, whose buses run the length of US 13 in Virginia daily. Fares are $1 pp within each of two zones, one from Cape Charles to Onley and another from Onancock to Chincoteague.

For more information on the Eastern Shore contact the **Eastern Shore of Virginia Tourism Commission,** P.O. Box 460, Dept. 98, Melfa, VA 23410, tel. (757) 787-2460, fax 787-8687, which runs a visitors center just south of Melfa at 19056 Industrial Parkway, tel. (757) 787-2460, open daily 9 a.m.-5 p.m. (Nov.-April Mon.-Fri. 9 a.m.-5 p.m.). E-mail: esvatourism@esva.net, Web site: www/esva.net/~esvatourism. You can find local B&Bs online at www.bbonline.com/va/easternshore/index.html.

EASTERN SHORE OF VIRGINIA NATIONAL WILDLIFE REFUGE

The southernmost tip of the Eastern Shore was set aside in 1984 as a sanctuary for migratory birds. Most of the 775 protected acres are saltwater marsh, with some maritime forest, grasslands, and thickets of myrtle and bayberry. The refuge includes most of Fishermans Island, the northernmost island crossed by the Chesapeake Bay Bridge-Tunnel, as well as Skidmore Island to the east.

Bird species resident year-round include great blue herons, great horned owls, woodpeckers, and black ducks. Shorebirds including cattle

The Eastern Shore of Virginia National Wildlife Refuge is a birder's paradise.

egrets, glossy ibis, and willets pass through in the spring, but the major migration takes place from late August to early November, when large groups of songbirds and raptors wait at the south side of the bay until weather conditions permit a crossing. Ospreys nest on special platforms in the spring and fall, and in the winter you have a good chance of spotting American kestrels, northern harriers, and snow geese.

The refuge **visitors center** is on the left just past the northern end of the bridge-tunnel. It has a viewing room over a marsh complete with binoculars and spotting scopes. A half-mile interpretive loop trail passes a 60-foot observation tower and old concrete gun emplacements that protected Norfolk's Naval Base during WW II. You can canoe or hike on your own from dawn to dusk. Ask about guided tours of Fishermans Island (Saturday mornings Oct.-March), and contact the U.S. Fish and Wildlife Service at 5003 Hallett Circle in Cape Charles, tel. (757) 331-2760, for more information.

KIPTOPEKE STATE PARK

One of the few public beaches on the Eastern Shore started out as the northern terminus of the ferry to Virginia Beach, which moved to Cape Charles in 1949. Kiptopeke, which means "Big Water" in the Accawmack Indian language, now protects half a mile of sand (lifeguarded Memorial Day-Labor Day), as well as trails, a fishing pier, boat launching ramp, and full-service campground ($18, $26 with hookups). Entrance is $2 per car ($3 on weekends and free on Wednesday), and naturalist programs are offered during the summer.

The Virginia Society of Ornithology maintains a bird-banding station and raised observation platform to take advantage of the park's location on the Atlantic Flyway. Some 80,000 raptors pass through in early September and October, including sharp-shinned and Cooper's hawks, ospreys, bald eagles, and peregrine falcons. The tours, presentations, and workshops of the **Eastern Shore Birding Festival,** in October, coincide with the peak fall migration. Call the park office at 3540 Kiptopeke Dr. in Cape Charles, tel. (757) 331-2267, for information on guided canoe tours through the park's marshes during the hawk migration.

CAPE CHARLES

This quiet town sprang up in 1884 as the southern terminus for the New York, Philadelphia, and Norfolk Railroad. Ferries carried automobiles and freight trains across the Chesapeake Bay to Norfolk and Hampton until the 1950s, when the freight business faded and the newly opened Chesapeake Bay Bridge-Tunnel killed the auto ferry. Today Cape Charles offers only hints that it was once the busiest town on the Eastern Shore, but its appeal hasn't faded completely.

Most of Cape Charles is a historic district. With over 500 buildings erected between 1885 and 1940, this is one of the largest collections on the East Coast. Colonial revival, neoclassic, and Victorian homes decorated with gingerbread woodwork line residential streets named after famous Virginians, fruits, and trees. Keep an eye out for several Sears Roebuck mail-order-house designs from the 1920s.

Sights
The **Cape Charles Museum and Welcome Center,** tel. (757) 331-1008, sits across Rt. 184 from the vividly named Meatland supermarket on the way into town. The building the museum occupies used to be a generator house for Delmarva Power and still has one gigantic generator (which still turns over) embedded in the floor. Old photos, decoys, and boat models trace the history of Cape Charles. Open late April to early November, Thurs.-Sun. 10 a.m.-5 p.m.; free.

While you're admiring the architecture, take a look at two houses—at 212 and 214 Randolph Ave.—that have settled into the swampy ground so much over the years that their eaves now touch.

Accommodations
Ebullient innkeeper Chris Bannon runs the **Sea Gate Bed & Breakfast,** 9 Tazewell Ave., tel. (757) 331-2206, in a lovingly restored 1861 house. A curving porch wraps around the entire front of the building, which was once split into a duplex. Moderate. E-mail: seagate@polit.infi.net, Web site: www.bbhost.com/seagate. Corinthian columns flank the foyer of the **Cape Charles House,** 645 Tazewell Ave., tel. (757) 331-4920, fax 331-4959, set in a 1912 colonial revival frame house with high ceilings and maple plank floors. Expensive.

E-mail: stay@capecharleshouse.com, Web site: www.capecharleshouse.com.

Rooms in the **Wilson-Lee House,** 403 Tazewell Ave., tel. (757) 331-1954, embody styles ranging from Victorian to art deco, but each one has terrycloth robes and queen-sized beds. All are expensive except the James W. Lee room (premium), decorated with original blueprints of the house. E-mail: WLHBnB@aol.com, Web site: www.wilsonleehouse.com. The west-facing **Bay Avenue Sunset,** 108 Bay Ave., tel. (757) 331-2424 or (888) 422-9283, makes good on the promise in its name with spectacular twilight shows over the Chesapeake Bay. Expensive (moderate Jan.-Feb.) E-mail: sunsetbnb@aol.com, Web site: www.baysunsetbb.com.

Camping
The **Sunset Beach Inn,** tel. (757) 331-4786 or (800) 899-4786, has 54 pull-through campsites with full hookups for $30, plus a pool, restaurant, and boat ramp, a few miles south of Cape Charles on US 13. A mile and a half west of US 13 on Rt. 680 you'll find the **Cherrystone Family Camping & RV Resort,** tel. (757) 331-3063, with three pools, a beach, sports courts and a playground spread over 300 acres. They rent sea kayaks, paddleboats, and bikes, and have 700 campsites for $15-21. Hookups are another $6. In season, there is a minimum length of stay.

Food
In Cape Charles proper is **Rebecca's,** 7 Strawberry St., tel. (757) 331-3879, a homey local place with great clam chowder. Open Wed.-Mon. for lunch and dinner. For the real treat, though, head back out to US 13 and a little over four miles south, where Ray Haynie's **Sting-Ray's,** tel. (757) 331-2505, serves gourmet seafood platters in the back of a big red Exxon station. It may not look like much, but wait until you try the softshells and crab imperial, maybe alongside a bottle from one of the best wine selections on the Eastern Shore. They also serve inexpensive sandwiches, breakfasts, and the usual ribs and chili. Open daily from 6 a.m. If that's not your style, you can always find **Someplace Else,** tel. (757) 331-8430, which in this case is a roadhouse right across the street with great burgers and a bar.

Shopping
Charmer's Antiques, 211 Mason Ave., tel. (757) 331-1488, inhabits a turn-of-the-century mercantile building. Half of it has been turned into a country-store museum; ask about admission. Paintings, woodcarvings, stained glass, and prints by local artists are sold at the **!2 Peach Street Gallery,** 12 Peach St., tel. (757) 331-1715, and the **Cape Charles Trading Company,** 113 Mason Ave., tel. (757) 331-1442, has a little bit of everything—clothes, books, candles, and even a few antiques.

Events and Information
In May, June, and September Cape Charles holds an **Applaud the Sun Harbor Party,** to celebrate its location on the largest harbor between Norfolk and Maryland. The **Eastern Shore Music Festival and Chili Cookoff,** tel. (757) 332-5175, Web site: esvamusicfest.esva.net, brings country, rock, blues, and R&B in early August, followed by a hometown parade during **Cape Charles Day** in September.

For details on these and anything else about the town, contact the **Cape Charles-Northampton County Chamber of Commerce,** P.O. Box 87, Cape Charles, VA, 23310, tel. (757) 331-2304.

EASTVILLE

In 1766, 10 years before the Declaration of Independence, the county court of this tiny village—then called Peachburg—declared the Stamp Act of Parliament unconstitutional. By the early 19th century, it boasted 217 inhabitants who were, in the words of one visitor, "not to be surpassed for their morality and hospitality to strangers."

The **Old Courthouse** on Courthouse Square guards the oldest continuous court records in America, having escaped rats, rot, and fire since they were begun in 1632. The building dates to the turn of the century. Next door, the **Clerk's Office** has a small museum inside, including leg irons and a device for measuring slaves' heights. Barred windows mark the **Debtor's Prison,** built around 1814, with an old whipping post in front that may make you grateful for the comparatively civilized techniques of modern collection agencies.

Courthouse green is on Courthouse Rd. (US 13 Business). Step into the modern Circuit Court building, tel. (757) 678-0465, for keys to the three buildings above during business hours.

Accommodations and Food
There aren't any signs on US 13 pointing out the **Eastvile Manor,** 6058 Willow Oak Rd. (Rt. 631), tel. (757) 768-7378, but that's how owners Bill and Melody Scalley like it. Word of mouth seems to be doing them pretty well—people are willing to drive up from Norfolk, even with the toll, for a meal in the 1866 Victorian home. A former chef for the Four Seasons and the Mayflower in Washington, D.C., Bill stirs up treats such as pan-fried lump crab cakes and beef tenderloin, accompanied by chilled cantaloupe soup, mushrooms in puff pastry, and fresh herbs and edible flowers from the garden. Dinner is served Wed.-Sat., and a suite upstairs with a double whirlpool (luxury) can be split into two rooms (premium).

WACHAPREAGUE

Two hundred folks live in the "Flounder Capital of the World," whose name means "Little City by the Sea" in an Indian tongue. Wachapreague (WAH-cha-preeg) is a good base for charter fishing or exploring the islands and marshes of the Eastern Shore's Atlantic edge.

Three brothers named Powell established a wharf and shipping firm here in 1872. Weekly freight and passenger steamers left for points north around the turn of the century, when wealthy visiting sportsmen enjoyed a dance hall, pool room, movie houses, and an elegant hotel (which burned in 1978).

Accommodations and Food
On the waterfront, the **Wachapreague Motel,** 17 Atlantic Ave., tel. (757) 787-2105, e-mail: island@wachapreague.com, has 30 rooms, efficiencies, and two-bedroom apartments in the moderate and expensive categories. They also book trips with several local charter boats and run the **Island House Restaurant,** tel. (757) 787-4242, overlooking the marsh across the street (check out the third-floor lookout tower).

Fifth-generation Wachapreague natives Pat,

OFFSHORE EDEN

The Nature Conservancy oversees the outermost fringe of Virginia's Eastern Shore, the largest stretch of unspoiled coastal wilderness in the country. With 50,000 acres spread over 14 barrier islands, the Virginia Coast Reserve has been designated one of 10 Last Great Places in America by its custodians and an International Biosphere Reserve by the United Nations.

Beaches, lagoons, pine forests, marshes, and scrub woodlands shelter as many as 80,000 pairs of nesting birds at a time, including every species found along Virginia's coast. Visiting is limited to day use, but the boating, swimming, beachcombing, and picnicking are unsurpassed. Getting there is the only catch, since it requires a boat or canoe. Parramore, Shipshoal, and Revel Islands are closed to the public, and much of Cedar Island remains in private hands. Check with The Nature Conservancy, P.O. Box 158, Brownsville Farm, Nassawadox, VA 23413, tel. (757) 442-3049, for regulations and information on the dozen or so naturalist-led trips they run every year, mostly in the spring and fall.

Tom, and Mike Hart, run **Burton House,** 9 Brooklyn Ave., tel. (757) 787-4560, and **Hart's Harbor House,** 11 Brooklyn Ave., tel. (757) 787-4848. The two century-old homes have a total of 10 guest rooms (moderate-expensive) and four cabins (inexpensive). Rates include full breakfasts and afternoon tea, and guests of both houses can borrow bikes to explore the town. They're on the Internet at www.bbonline.com/va/bbav/wachapreague.html.

You can also grab a bite at the **Wachapreague Seaside Marina** to the right of the Island House, and at **Carpenter's Grocery,** Main St. at Brooklyn, tel. (757) 787-9527.

Recreation
Both the **Wachapreague Seaside Marina,** tel. (757) 787-4110, and **Wachapreague Boat Rentals,** tel. (757) 787-4913, are on the docks, each with its own Bait & Tackle operation and 16-foot fiberglass boats for rent for around $60 per day. Fishing charters run $300-700, depending on time of year and what you're after.

Events

The Wachapreague Hotel sponsors the **Spring Flounder Tournament** in April, and the **Eastern Shore Release Tournament** is sponsored by the Eastern Shore Marlin Club, tel. (757) 787-1125 or 442-3704. August is the time for the **ARC Annual Fish Fry & Melfa Rotary Auction,** tel. (757) 787-7824.

ONANCOCK

One of the Eastern Shore's prettiest towns sits on Onancock Creek near one of two deepwater harbors on the peninsula. Chock full of 19th-century houses with gingerbread trim and wrap-around porches, Onancock (o-NAN-cock) has enough cultural offerings and quiet allure to entice you for a stay of a weekend or more.

The name, meaning "foggy place" in an Indian language, comes from a native tribe whose king Ekeeks introduced Englishman John Pory to oysters and "batata" (potatoes) in 1621. (After burning his mouth on a steaming tuber, Pory groaned "I would not give a farthing for a truckload.") The settlement, founded in 1680 as Port Scarburgh, weathered frequent raids by British privateers during the Revolutionary War. Growth arrived with steamships plying the Chesapeake Bay, leaving Onancock one of the largest communities on the Eastern Shore.

For Internet info on Onancock, try www.onancock.com or hometownamerica.com/va/ACC/Onancock.html.

Sights

On Market St. (Rt. 179) before the center of town stands **Kerr Place,** tel. (757) 787-8012, one of the Eastern Shore's finest antique manor homes. Built in 1799 by a Scottish merchant, the elegant federal mansion once presided over an estate of 1,500 acres. It's been restored by the Eastern Shore of Virginia Historical Society, who have set up offices and a museum of Eastern Shore history inside. Intricate woodwork and plaster carvings decorate the walls and ceiling around period artwork and furniture. Notice the false window in the brick facade, included for symmetry. Open March-Dec. Tues.-Sat. 10 a.m.-4 p.m.; $3 pp.

The venerable **Hopkins Brothers Store** and its attached Eastern Shore Steamboat Company Restaurant are scheduled to have undergone a complete makeover. One of the oldest general stores on the East Coast, it was built on the wharf in 1842. Call (757) 787-3100 for details.

Accommodations

Marge and Mike Carpenter's **76 Market Street Bed & Breakfast,** 76 Market St., tel. (757) 787-7600 or (888) 751-7600, is only a short walk from downtown and the wharf area. Three rooms in the 19th-century Victorian home all have a/c, and guests can enjoy a TV room and great full breakfasts. Moderate. E-mail: stay@76MarketSt.com, Web site: www.76MarketSt.com. Built in 1890, **The Spinning Wheel,** 31 North St., tel. (757) 787-7311, fax 787-8555, bills itself as a folk Victorian B&B. Rates are moderate, and the owners offer a midweek package including two nights' lodging and ferry tickets to Tangier Island for $160. E-mail: evergreen@esva.net, Web site: www.esva.net/~evergreen/spinningwheel.

The **Colonial Manor Inn,** 84 Market St., tel. (757) 787-3521, fax 787-2448, Web site: www.onancock.com/inn/html, got its start as a boarding house in the 1930s, making it the oldest operating inn on the Eastern Shore. Two acres of grounds and full breakfasts served at the huge dining table are included in the price. Iinexpensive-expensive. Back out Rt. 179 toward US 13 sits **Montrose House,** 20494 Market St., tel. (757) 787-7088 or (800) 241-6667, fax (757) 278-8997, Web site: www.visitnepa.org/members/montrose.html, a beautiful country home in the classic four-part design of the early 19th century. A rear screened porch overlooks herb and perennial gardens graced by statues and trellises. Twelve rooms include eight with private baths. Inexpensive. Owner Richard Caden also runs Confetti's Cafe, tel. (757) 787-8887, in Roses Shopping Center toward US 13.

Food

Chef/owner Armando Suarez from Argentina has decorated **Armando's,** 10 North St., tel. (757) 787-8044, with treasures accumulated over a lifetime of music-loving, including antiques, congas, and jazz posters. The menu, with Pablo Neruda quotes and a dish named after his daughter, lists pastas and other dishes combining Spanish, Argentine, and Italian influences (the sauces alone are worth a visit). Outside seating is available on an ivy-draped brick patio. Open for dinner Tues.-Sun. The **Market Street Inn**, 47 Market St., tel. (757) 787-7626, serves standards including tuna steak and seafood quiche for all meals Mon.-Saturday.

Recreation and Entertainment

Coffee bar and sandwich shop by day, **Perk**, 57 Market St., tel. (757) 787-2750, turns into **Club Tsunami** at sundown, with live music, comedy, and the occasional no-alcohol family night. Local actors stage works such as *Biloxi Blues* and *Dracula* at the **North Street Playhouse**, 4 North St., tel. (757) 787-2358 or 787-4107, which can fit 50 spectators in air-conditioned comfort.

Tony Pruitt operates **Chesapeake Bay Charter Fishing**, tel. (757) 787-8929, aboard the 47-foot *Shana Marie*. Early-morning and night charter trips are available.

Shopping

Bizzotto's Gallery Cafe-Market, 41 Market St., tel. (757) 787-3103, sells artsy ceramics right next to **Crockett's Gallery**, tel. (757) 787-2288, with nautical-themed works by a Tangier-born artist. Look to **Walter and Walton's Emporium**, 23 Market St., tel. (757) 787-1995, for antiques, furniture, decoys, and Asian art, and head east on Market St. to Hill St. to find the **Blue Crab Bay Co.**, tel. (757) 787-3602 or (800) 221-2722, fax (757) 787-3430. Delicacies such as Virginia hams, she-crab soup, and cocktail mixes have turned this place into a thriving mail-order business as well, offering beach party packs and gift baskets.

Near Onancock

Off US 13 near Onley, **Turner Sculpture**, tel. (757) 787-2818, fax 787-7064, is the largest personal foundry and gallery in the country. Renowned sculptors William and David Turner count the National Audubon Society, the American Museum of Natural History, and the White House among dozens of public commissions for their realistic wildlife bronzes. Here in the gallery, over 300 different animals are frozen in vivid poses that work especially well in the aquatic creatures—otters, dolphins, humpback whales, and the like. Prices range from $50 for palm-size works to the thousands for larger pieces. Open daily 9 a.m.-5 p.m. E-mail: turner@esva.net, Web site: www.esva.net/~turner.

ONANCOCK TO CHINCOTEAGUE

Tasley

A snug old tenant house has been reopened as **Flounders**, 24391 Lankford Hwy. (Rt. 13), tel. (757) 787-2233, offering fresh local seafood and vegetables in front of a fireplace that comes in handy in the winter. Croaker, flounder, and rockfish platters are $11-17 for dinner and $5-9 for lunch, served Tues.-Sat.

Accomack

A wealth of colonial architecture fills the tree-shaded streets in this historic burg, founded as Drummondtown in the 18th century. On Courthouse Green stands the turn-of-the-century **Courthouse** next to the Victorian brick **Clerk's Office**, where the Accomack County Orders of 1714-1717 bear the vitriolic inscription "God Damn the King" over the more traditional "God Save the King."

Elaborate paintings inside the Greek revival **St. James Episcopal Church**, built in 1838, simulate columns, doors, and arches. Call (757) 787-2462 to arrange a visit to the 1784 **Debtor's Prison**, rendered obsolete in 1849 by a state law that abolished imprisonment for debt.

Parksley

The **Eastern Shore Railway Museum**, 18468 Dunne Ave., tel. (757) 665-RAIL (757-665-7245), starts with a gift shop and collection of antique cars in the 1906 New York, Philadelphia, and Norfolk Railroad passenger station. An original freight station across the yard holds uniforms, maps, and lanterns from back when railroads were the lifeline of the Eastern Shore, while the yard itself is full of dining cars and cabooses from the Richmond, Fredericksburg & Potomac, Norfolk & Western, and Wabash lines, including a 1927 Pullman Diplomat coach and a baggage car with an HO-scale model train layout inside. Open daily (Thurs.-Tues. Nov.-March) 10 a.m.-4 p.m., Sunday 1-4 p.m.; $2 adults.

CHINCOTEAGUE

From killdeer nesting in the parking lot at the visitors center to gales that redefine the sandy shoreline, life on Chincoteague Island is shaped by the natural world. Known for its annual pony swim and auction, the largest community on the Eastern Shore combines a seasonal beach resort with a timeless offshore sanctuary for plenty of coastal life besides the famous fillies.

History

The story goes that on October 25, 1662, this island, sandwiched between the mainland and Assateague, was granted to Capt. William Whitington by Wachawampe, emperor of the Gingo Teagues. Over time the tribe's name would evolve into Chincoteague (SHINK-a-tig), meaning "Beautiful Land Across the Water." A tiny settlement was destroyed by a tidal wave that swept over both islands in 1821, but the area was gradually resettled over the next decades.

In 1861, a 132-2 vote to remain part of the Union set Chincoteague against the rest of its parent state. Several attempts by mainlanders to storm the island were repulsed. The railroad arrived in 1876, ending an era of lawlessness, illiteracy, and bare feet with the introduction of schools, churches, a newspaper, and new homes.

Incorporated as a town in 1908, Chincoteague was connected to the mainland by an automobile causeway in 1922. It was Marguerite Henry's 1947 book, *Misty of Chincoteague,* though, that propelled the town into the collective imagination of children worldwide as only a book about horses can. Many local residents appeared in the movie made from the children's story in the 1960s, and the town has been synonymous with ponies on the beach ever since.

Orientation

The town of Chincoteague occupies most of the island of the same name, connected to the mainland and US 13 by Rt. 175. A long, straight causeway crosses marshland and a drawbridge to Main St., running the length of the island's western shore. Head north (left) on Main St. for a few blocks and turn east (right) onto Maddox Blvd., where signs lead to the visitors center and the Chincoteague National Wildlife Refuge (see below).

Sights

Decoys of every shape and species fill the cedar-smelling **Refuge Waterfowl Museum,** 7059 Maddox Blvd., tel. (757) 336-5800, alongside traps, boats, and hunting weapons. Learn how to reload a shotgun shell like a turn-of-the-century market hunter, and stop by on a weekend when there's a resident carver at work. Don't miss the antique hunting carriage in a side room. Open Thurs.-Mon. 10 a.m.-5 p.m.; $2.50 adults, $1 children. A few blocks further the **Oyster and Maritime Museum,** 7125 Maddox Blvd., tel. (757) 336-6117, holds the huge frenel lens from the Assateague Island Lighthouse and exhibits on the history of the local oyster industry. Open Thursday, Saturday, and Monday noon-4 p.m.; $3 adults, $1 children. The new **Island Aquarium,** tel. (757) 336-6508, in Landmark Plaza on N. Main St., features touch tanks and other exhibits on life in the marshes and waters of the Chesapeake Bay. Open Mon.-Sat. 10 a.m.-9 p.m., Sunday 1-5 p.m.; $3 adults, $2 children.

Hotels and B&Bs

As befits a seasonal resort town, many hotels in Chincoteague close or drop their prices by as much as a third in the off-season.

The T-shaped **1848 Island Manor House,** 4160 Main St., tel. (757) 336-5436 or (800) 852-1505, fax (757) 336-1333, was built by a local Union surgeon and a postmaster who married a pair of sisters. Apparently the wives didn't get along under the same roof, prompting their husbands to split the house in two and move half next door. It's since been re-joined and decorated in federal style. Moderate rates, including full breakfasts and afternoon tea, rise to expensive on weekends. E-mail: imh@shore.intercom.net, Web site: www.chincoteague.com/b-b/imh.html.

Miss Molly's Inn, 4141 Main St., tel. (757) 336-6686 or (800) 221-5620, fax (757) 336-0600, occupies a Victorian home built in 1886 by J. T. Rowley for his daughter Molly, who lived there until age 84. Marguerite Henry stayed here while writing *Misty of Chincoteague.* Prices (moderate to premium) include full breakfasts in the gazebo and scones at teatime. E-mail: msmolly@shore.intercom.net, Web site: www.quickpage.com/M/missmollys. A wraparound veranda and scallop shingles adorn **The Watson House,** 4240 Main St., tel. (800) 336-6787 or (757) 336-1564, fax 336-5776, Web site: www.chincoteague.com/b-b/watson.html, built in the late 1800s by David Robert Watson. In addition to the main house, guests can stay in a three-bedroom cottage and two-bedroom townhouse, and have access to complimentary bicycles and beach chairs. Moderate to premium. Also in the moderate category are the **Beach Road Motel,** 6151 Maddox Blvd., tel. (757) 336-6582, and the **Lighthouse Inn,** 4218 Main St., tel. (757) 336-5091.

A stone's throw from Chincoteague Sound, the **Year of the Horse Inn,** 3583 Main St., tel. (757) 336-3221 or (800) 680-0090, was the first B&B in town in 1978. It has a private pier and three rooms with refrigerators and balconies. Expensive. Both the **Refuge Motor Inn,** 7058 Maddox Blvd., tel. (757) 336-5511, fax 336-6134, and the **Driftwood Motor Lodge,** 7105 Maddox Blvd., tel. (757) 336-6557, fax 336-6558, are also expensive.

Four large guest rooms and a third-floor sitting room fill **The Inn at Poplar Corner,** 4248 Main St., tel. (800) 336-6787 or (757) 336-1564, fax 336-5776, Web site: www.bbonline.com/va/poplarcorner/index.html, under the same owners as the Watson House. Premium. Barbara and David Wiedenheft, the owners of Miss Molly's Inn, also operate the **Channel Bass Inn,** 6228 Church St., tel. (757) 336-6686 or (800) 221-5620, fax (757) 336-0600, dating to 1892. Some of the six rooms and one suite have a view of the Chesapeake Bay, and the public is welcome to stop by for Barbara's famous scones at afternoon tea in the Tea Room—just call (757) 336-6148 for reservations. E-mail: smolly@shore.intercom.net, Web site: www.chincoteague.com/bb/channel.html.

Furnished Cottages
Another option for extended stays on Chincoteague range in price $400-600 per week to $300 per weekend in season. Most have cable TV, a/c, full kitchens, picnic tables, and grills. Try **Duck Haven Cottages,** 6582 Church St., tel. (757) 336-6290, **Holiday Cottages,** 6113 Taylor St., tel. (757) 336-6256, and **Island Pride Cottages,** 4375 Chicken City Rd., tel. (757) 336-6345.

Camping
The **Maddox Family Campground,** 6742 Maddox Blvd., tel. (757) 336-3111, has 550 sites open March-Nov. for $22-27 depending on whether you want hookups or not. They also offer a pool, showers, and crabbing equipment.

Sites at the **Pine Grove Campground & Waterfowl Park,** 5283 Deep Hole Rd., tel. (757) 336-5200, are $18 from April-Dec. **Tom's Cove Campground,** 8128 Beebe Rd., tel. (757) 336-6498, fax (757) 336-6153, has waterfront sites within sight of the pony swim for $21-29, open March-November.

Food
Dining in Chincoteague is a lesson in convergent evolution: most of the 23 restaurants are named after someone and offer family-style food, usually seafood, for all meals daily. Many are only open Memorial Day-Labor Day. Steak, seafood, and chicken entrées run $10-15. Popular spots include **Bill's Seafood,** 4040 Main St., tel. (757) 336-5831, **Etta's Channel Side Restaurant,** 7452 East Side Dr., tel. (757) 336-5644, and the **Island Family Restaurant,** 3441 Ridge Rd., tel. (757) 336-1198.

The **Landmark Crab House,** Landmark Plaza, 6162 Main St., tel. (757) 336-5552, serves Chincoteague's famous oysters for dinner daily, and encloses the Waterfront Lounge, with a Brunswick bar from Chicago dating to 1897. **Don's Seafood Restaurant,** 4113 Main St. at Smith, tel. (757) 336-5715, also has a lounge with a raw bar and dancing past midnight. Wood-roasted chicken and barbecue are a welcome change from seafood at **Paul's Restaurant,** 6447 Maddox Blvd., tel. (757) 336-1400, and you can grab seafood packed to take home at Captain Fish's Steaming Wharf in the **Russel Fish Co.,** 3855 Main St., tel. (757) 336-6986.

For a light bite or sweet snack, stop by **Sugarbakers,** 4095 Main St., tel. (757) 336-3712, a combination bakery and cafe, or the **Island Creamery,** 6251 Maddox Blvd., tel. (757) 336-6236, with fudge and ice cream. **Pony Tails,** 7001 Maddox Blvd., tel. (757) 336-6688, sells saltwater taffy and candy.

Fishing and Hunting
Dozens of places in Chincoteague rent boats and fishing tackle for visitors interested in exploring the fringes of Chincoteague Bay. Expect to pay $40-50 per day for a mid-sized fishing boat for three to four people, and around $100 for a 12-person pontoon boat for four hours. Try **Barnacle Bill's Bait & Tackle,** 3691 S. Main St., tel. (757) 336-5188, and **Captain**

Bob's Fishing Camp, 2477 S. Main St., tel. (757) 336-6654. Both **East Side Rental,** 7462 East Side Dr., tel. (757) 336-3409 or (800) 889-1525, and **Snug Harbor Marina and Cottages,** 7536 E. Shore Dr., tel. (757) 336-6176, rent jet skis as well.

Charters let you venture offshore for the big ones: tuna, marlin, swordfish, and shark. Call ahead for reservations at places like **Charters By Kay,** 6435 Dogwood Ln., tel. (757) 336-6517, or call the captains themselves. Both the **Bucktail,** tel. (757) 336-5188, and the **Mar-shell,** tel. (757) 336-1939, have been recommended. Half-day trips are around $400.

The **Chincoteague Hunting and Fishing Center,** 6531 Maddox Blvd., tel. (757) 336-3474, is the place to go for advice, gear, and guiding services aimed at the island's incredible diversity of seasonal waterfowl. Pintails, canvasbacks, snow geese, and eiders are all plentiful in the winter, or you can hunt deer, turkey, or quail just about year-round. Hunting trips are $125 pp per day.

Tours and Excursions

Captain Barry's Back Bay Cruises, 4256 Anderson Ave., tel. (757) 336-6508, leave from Landmark Plaza on N. Main St. for early-morning birdwatching, afternoon "Adventure Quests," champagne sunset cruises, and moonlight excursions for $10-30 pp. For a quarter of a century the 40-foot **Osprey,** a former fishing boat, has been taking visitors on narrated sightseeing cruises to the Atlantic mouth of the Chincoteague channel and back. The trips run June 20-Labor Day, and tickets ($10 adults, $5 children) can be bought at the Refuge Motor Inn (see above).

Jay Cherrix, son of a Chincoteague waterman, runs sea-kayak trips through **Tidewater Expeditions,** 7729 East Side Dr., tel. (757) 336-3159 or 336-6811. Guided paddles are $42 for two people and leave from sunrise to sunset. They also rent kayaks for $10 per hour or $40 per day pp.

Bicycle Rental

Both **The Bike Depot,** at the Refuge Motor Inn (see above), and the **Piney Island Country Store,** 7085 Maddox Blvd., tel. (757) 336-5188, rent regular and tandem bikes along with four-person pedal-carts.

Shopping

Another unmistakable sign of beach resorts is dozens of stores selling everything from crafts, dolls, and candles to framed seascapes and Christmas goodies, and Chincoteague is no exception. Places including **Church Street Peddlers,** 6292 Church St., tel. (757) 336-6507, and **Island Galley and Gifts,** 6219 Maddox Blvd., tel. (757) 336-3076, have a little bit of everything. Ronald Justis's **Decoys Decoys Decoys,** 4039 Main St., tel. (757) 336-1402 or (800) 877-6911, has one of the largest selections on the East Coast, while copper and folk art are the main offerings at **White's Copperworks,** 6373 Maddox. Blvd., tel. (757) 336-1588.

The **Ark II Gallery,** 3777 Willow St., tel. (757) 336-6219, sells wildlife prints, sculpture, and paintings, and **Skipjack,** 4103 Main St., tel. (757) 336-1768, specializes in nautical crafts and gifts. The stone- and earthware Carol Myers' **Main St. Pottery,** 3891 Main St., tel. (757) 336-1546, ranges from whimsical to practical. Local artist Nancy West has woven clothing, oil paintings, and unique jewelry at **Island Arts,** 6196 Maddox Blvd., tel. (757) 336-5856, while Wales native Hal Lott sells silkscreens through **Lott's Arts & Things,** 4281 Main St., tel. (757) 336-5773.

Events

Many of Chincoteague's annual events require advance tickets; call the Chincoteague Chamber of Commerce for information.

In April, 150 local and national artists congregate for the **Easter Decoy and Art Festival.** It includes plenty of home-cooked food, but not nearly as much as the **Seafood Festival,** at Tom's Cove Campground (see above) the first Wednesday in May. All you can eat of bushels of raw oysters, shoals of fish, and tens of thousands of clams are yours for the price of a ticket—but the event is popular, so you have to buy that ticket in advance from the Eastern Shore Chamber of Commerce in Melfa. If you can, stick around for the **Blessing of the Fleet** at the town dock later in the month

June brings the **Homestyle Music, Shrimp and Beef Fest** at the Volunteer Fire Company Fairgrounds and the **Power Boat Regatta** in Memorial Park. The **Pony Swim and Auction,** though, is Chincoteague's biggest happening, and one of the largest on the Virginia coast. Held since 1925, this event is preceded by the two-week Fireman's Carnival. On the last Wednesday of June, members of the Chincoteague Volunteer Fire Company dress up as cowboys and round up the herd of wild ponies that live in the Chincoteague National Wildlife Refuge. After swimming across the channel, the horses step ashore at Memorial Park at the southern end of the island. Here they're penned until Thursday, when 50,000 or more people gather for the famous auction for about $200 each. This event fills the town to capacity, so book accommodations well in advance.

The Maddox Family Campgrounds host the **Chincoteague Oyster Festival** the Saturday of Columbus Day weekend in October.

Information

The Chincoteague Chamber of Commerce operates a **visitors center,** 6733 Maddox Blvd., tel. (757) 336 6161, Web site: www.chincoteaguechamber.com, in a traffic circle about a mile west of the bridge to Assateague Island. Here you can buy a documentary video ($20) or audio tour tape ($5.50) on the town. Open Mon.-Sat. 9 a.m.-4:30 p.m., plus Sunday 12:30-4:30 p.m. Memorial Day-Labor Day.

Near Chincoteague

NACA (National Advisory Committee on Aeronautics) opened an aeronautical research center at Wallops Island in 1945. NACA became a full federal agency, NASA, in 1958, and over the years, the facility has tested and launched thousands of orbital and sub-orbital rockets and balloons. A recent agreement will allow launches of commercial satellites from the facility. The agency runs a **Visitors Center,** tel. (757) 824-1344, tracing the history of flight, rockets, and space travel through video displays, photos, and real relics of the space program. Space-suit demonstrations and model rocket launchings take place during the summer. Open Thurs.-Mon. 10 a.m.-4 p.m. March-June and Sept.-December. During July and August, it's open daily 10 a.m.-4 p.m. From December through February, the visitor center is closed; free.

On US 13 just north of the turnoff onto Rt. 175 for Chincoteague is **The Decoy Factory,** tel. (757) 824-5621, the largest of its kind in the world. You can watch workers put decoys together or buy just about anything you need to make your own, from $10 miniature kits to monthly species specials.

CHINCOTEAGUE NATIONAL WILDLIFE REFUGE

Assateague Island, a thin ribbon of sand 37 miles long, extends from Ocean City, MD, to just past Chincoteague Island. The entire spit has been designated a National Seashore, and Virginia's southern one-third of the island was set aside in 1943 as the Chincoteague National Wildlife Refuge to protect dwindling habitat for migrating snow geese.

There's much more to the fishhook tip of sand than the graceful white birds with black wingtips, though. Virginia's portion of the wild pony herd draws plenty of visitors, while enough birds pass through during migrating season to guarantee additions to most birders' life lists. And even though they're not open to camping, 10 miles of wild oceanside beaches offer wave-soothed solitude for hikers who venture off the more popular pathways.

Habitats

Tidal salt marshes and mudflats line the ragged landward side of the island, facing Chincoteague Island and Chincoteague Bay. Pine and hardwood forests fill the interior, dotted with pools and the large bight of Toms Cove at the southernmost end. The smooth Atlantic edge is almost pure sand, slowly being pushed southward by the endless caress of the ocean.

Species

Over 300 species of **birds** depend on the rich harvest of mollusks, insects, and crustaceans, provided by Assateague Island's freshwater impoundments, marshes, mudflats, and tidal pools. Herons, egrets, gulls, terns, and sandpipers arrive in the summer, followed in the fall by migrating shorebirds and peregrine falcons, which are easier to spot on Assateague than almost anywhere else on the East Coast. Migrating waterfowl, including mallards, pintails, black ducks, Canada geese, and greater snow geese, take advantage of the island's mild winter climate during their thousand-mile journeys. Keep an ear out for the distinctive call of the willet, and be aware of area closures (usually most of Toms Cove Hook) to protect the nesting sites of the endangered piping plover.

Most famous of Assateague's 44 mammal species are undoubtedly the **wild ponies,** separated into two herds by a fence at the Maryland state line. The Virginia herd is technically owned by the Chincoteague Volunteer Fire Company and allowed to graze on federal land by special permit. It's fun to hear that they swam ashore from a shipwrecked Spanish galleon, but it's more probable (and prosaic) that they're the descendants of herds hidden on the island in the 17th century by mainland colonists trying to avoid livestock taxes. (This means they're actually stunted horses, not true ponies.)

With their shaggy manes and stubby legs, they look cute enough to pet, which many people do. Bad idea. These are *wild* horses, and visitors get bitten and kicked every year (and promptly blame the refuge staff) for their own foolishness. The horses' short stature, and their bloated bellies (which can't handle human handouts), most likely results from generations of salty marsh grass and brackish water.

Your best chance of spotting them is from the Woodland Trail in Black Duck Marsh, but you might bump into a few just about anywhere. They tend to stick to the beach in the summer, where the constant breeze keeps the legendary Assateague mosquitoes at bay—at least somewhat.

A small herd of Japanese **sika deer** was released by a Boy Scout troop in 1923 at the northern end of the island, and the deer now outnumber the native **white-tailed deer.** If you come across a large, relatively unfazed rodent with a big bushy tail, it's probably an endangered **Delmarva fox squirrel.**

Visiting the Refuge

The refuge entrance, at the end of Maddox Blvd., is open daily 6 a.m.-8 p.m. for $5 per car. A $15 Federal Duck Stamp is good for all federal national wildlife refuges for a year. The U.S. Fish and Wildlife Service operates the **Refuge Visitor Center,** tel. (757) 336-6122, open daily 9 a.m.-4 p.m., with wildlife information, trail brochures, and schedules of interpretive activities.

Parts of the beach are open to surfing, fishing, swimming, clamming, and crabbing. Fifteen miles of trails include the 1.6-mile Woodland Trail, to an overlook over pony-favored Black Duck Marsh; the 3.2-mile Wildlife Loop, open to vehicles 3 p.m.-dusk; and the Toms Cove Nature Trail, out along the southern tail. Miles of untracked beach stretch north from the National Park Service's **Toms Cove Visitor Center,** tel. (757) 336-6577, open daily 9 a.m.-5 p.m., at the entrance to Toms Cove Hook. Cyclists are welcome on paved trails. Boaters should check ahead of time for permitted landing sites.

Camping isn't allowed in the refuge, but it is across the state line in the **Assateague State Park,** 7206 National Seashore Lane, Berlin, Maryland 21811-9742, tel. (410) 641-3030 or 641-1441. **Assateague Island Tours** runs a narrated motor tour of the refuge from April-Sept. Check at the refuge visitors center or Bayside Arts and Crafts in Chincoteague, tel. (757) 336-6798, for reservations and a schedule. Visit the Assateague Island National Seashore on the Internet at www.nps.gov/asis.

Both the Park Service and the U.S. Fish and Wildlife Service offer naturalist programs in the refuge daily during the summer and on spring and fall weekends. Annual events start with the **International Migratory Bird Celebration** in May, with guided walks, speakers, and workshops, and continue through **National Wildlife Refuge Week** in October. **Assateague Island Waterfowl Week,** in late November during the southward migration of Canada and snow geese, is the only time visitors can drive to the northern end of the refuge.

TANGIER ISLAND

Only 10 miles of Chesapeake chop from the mainland, Tangier seems decades away from even the atavistic air of the Eastern Shore. The insularity of this tight little fishing community is something you don't come across every day. The pace of life is a little different and the accent hard to place, making a visit as much a cultural experiences as a sightseeing jaunt. Even in a state with as many curious nooks as Virginia has, Tangier still stands out.

VIRGINIA TOURISM CORPORATION

ing him to write what would become the "Star-Spangled Banner."

A cholera outbreak in 1866 forced an almost total evacuation, and "The August Storm" of 1933 inundated everything on the low-lying island but the top floors of houses. Three years later, the Army Air Corps had to drop supplies onto the school playground when "The Big Freeze" clogged the entire northern bay with a foot of ice. Electricity arrived in 1946, and satellite dishes have begun sprouting in the last decade.

Tangier Today

A little over five square miles in area, the island consists of three inhabited "ridges" only a few feet above the Chesapeake waterline. Most is marsh and wetlands, hunting grounds for Virginia rails, muskrats, herons, and egrets. About 680 people live on Tangier—fewer than half as many as did at the turn of the century—and most are related. A third are Crocketts, with the names of other settlers including Pruitt, Dise, Parks,

Boats are the principal form of transportation on the island.

History

Indians fished and hunted on the island for centuries, but the first settlement wasn't until 1686, 20 years after native tribes, according to legend, sold the island for two overcoats. Cornishman John Crockett, along with his eight sons and their families, was the first to arrive. By the 19th century, the island was home to 100 residents, half of them Crocketts, who made a living fishing and grazing livestock.

The outside world intruded during the Revolutionary War, when British troops used the island as a base for raiding American ships. During the War of 1812, 12,000 more redcoats stood under the pines in preparation for an attack on Fort McHenry. Local reverend Joshua Thomas harangued the invaders, claiming (or perhaps merely predicting—correctly) that the word from above was that they could not take Baltimore. In 1814, Francis Scott Key boarded a British boat on Tangier to negotiate the release of an American prisoner. During his voyage, Key witnessed the Battle of Baltimore, inspir-

---

THE TOWN THAT TURNED PAUL NEWMAN DOWN

The Great Movie Controversy of 1998 showed clearly that the increasing influx of tourists hasn't changed the stubbornly independent local attitude of Tangier all that much.

Actor Paul Newman had selected Tangier as the perfect place to film *Message in a Bottle,* a movie starring himself and Kevin Costner. Everything looked great until a core of religious fundamentalists on the town council forced a last-minute change of plans. In spite of a petition bearing 200 names, the possibility of $23,000 worth of repairs to the town dock, and work for hundreds of hard-up island residents, a 6-0 vote said the PG-13 script, with its profanity, sex, and alcohol, was inconsistent with community values and therefore unwelcome.

Many indignant islanders pointed out that swearing, procreating, and even illicit drinking were far from rare on Tangier—and that legions of locals had taken the boat to Salisbury, MD, to see the disaster epic *Titanic.* But the arguments fell on deaf ears, and Newman, who had scoped out the island incognito, had to look elsewhere for a film site.

and Wheatley covering most of the remainder. Crabbing and clamming sustain the classic fishing community, whose men leave before dawn to check the farms alongshore where the famous local softshells are raised.

Tangier has always been a tightly knit community, demonstrated near the turn of the century when a gossipy book by Thomas Crockett rattled so many local skeletons that his descendants later gathered up and destroyed as many copies as they could find. During a WW I visit, President Woodrow Wilson found Tangier's doors locked when islanders suspected his aides of being a German raiding party off a submarine. When, in the 1930s, Accomack County officials sent over a metal jail, island residents threw it into the water, saying they had no need for one.

A peculiar accent, the product of generations of isolation, evokes England's West Country, turning "time" and "mind" into "toime" and "moind." Front yards (the highest ground on the island) are often crowded with graves and headstones, and highly religious roots continue to sprout—a 1995 revival left a third of the population born-again Christians. All children attend one school, rebuilt in the mid-1990s, and health care comes in the form of mainland physicians who come twice a week (dentists and optometrists visit monthly).

Everyone knows each other, of course, and welcome visitors with a wave from golf carts, bright cruiser bicycles, and a handful of cars and trucks. Stacked crab pots fill back yards lined with chain-link fences, and motorboats zoom around the wharf area, a maze of pilings and crab shanties.

Accommodations and Food

Since it generally sees only one boat a day most of the year, reservations are essential on Tangier. Shirley and Wallace Pruitt run **Shirley's Bay View Inn** on Ridge Rd., tel. (757) 891-2396. Wallace, who was born in the 1806 house, runs fishing parties and boat excursions. Rooms in the house and in four cottages behind are open year-round, with a/c, cable TV, and breakfast included. Moderate. The **Sunset Inn,** tel. (757) 891-2535, is also on Ridge Rd., with moderate-range cottages.

Hilda Crockett's Chesapeake House, tel. (757) 891-2331, is in town a few blocks south of

JULIAN SMITH

Shirley's Bay View Inn

the church. This local institution, open since 1940, offers inexpensive rooms mid-April through late October including dinner and breakfast. The restaurant is also open to the public, serving all-you-can-eat meals for $12.25, daily 11:30 a.m.-6 p.m.

Near the docks are the **Fisherman's Corner Restaurant,** tel. (757) 891-2571, and the **Islander Restaurant,** tel. (757) 891-2249, both serving fresh seafood during tourist season (roughly April-Oct.). In between is a grocery store with a deli counter, and Main Ridge Rd. has a few sandwich and ice cream shops. Alcohol is technically forbidden on Tangier.

Shopping and Recreation

A handful of **gift shops** are the only places in town that take credit cards. Sandy's Gifts, on King Street, has a small museum, and some enterprising islander has set up an honor-fee recipe rack on a fence near the Islander Restaurant. Head to the south end of the island for a nice beach. A number of places, including Wanda's Gift Shop, rent bicycles, which can be left sitting around anywhere (where's a thief going to go?). **RB's Rentals,** tel. (757) 891-2240, rents golf carts, canoes, kayaks, motor boats, and bicycles from the town dock.

Information

For more details on Tangier, contact the **town offices** at 4301 Joshua Thomas Lane, P.O. Box 244, Tangier, A 23440, tel. (757) 891-2438.

Transportation

A **mailboat,** tel. (757) 891-2240, leaves Crisfield, MD, Mon.-Sat. at 12:30 p.m. year-round, returning at 8 a.m. the next day ($10 one-way). Also in Crisfield, **Tangier Island Cruises,** 1001 W. Main St., tel. (410) 968-2338, sends the 300-passenger *Steven Thomas* to the island from May-Oct. at 12:30 p.m., returning the same day at 4 p.m. ($18 pp roundtrip).

Tangier & Rappahannock Cruises, tel. (804) 453-2628, sends tour boats from the Buzzards Point Marina near Reedville, VA, daily May-Oct. at 10 a.m., returning at 3:30 p.m. ($18.50 pp roundtrip), with a narrated tour on the island. **Tangier-Onancock Cruises,** 16458 W. Ridge Rd., Tangier, tel. (757) 891-2240, leave from Onancock Mon.-Sat. June-Sept. at 10 a.m., returning at 1:30 p.m. ($18 pp roundtrip). The 90-minute cruise aboard the 65-foot *Captain Eulice* is narrated, with an option for a guided tour around the island.

Finally, **Chesapeake Aviation,** tel. (757) 787-2901, operates a year-round charter flight service leaving from Melfa on the Eastern Shore for $130 roundtrip, covering up to three passengers.

SOUTHWEST VIRGINIA

Virginia's rugged western tail—by far the least-tamed, and most-forgotten, part of the state—dangles in the hilly country bordered by North Carolina, Tennessee, Kentucky, and West Virginia. The area has no sweeping Civil War battlefields or well-dressed Founding Fathers to anchor it in memory. History here has a rougher edge to it, beginning with the frontier families who pushed their way into the rippling hills, set up shop, and began a legacy that still exists. Pockets of Brethren and Friends (Quakers) keep alive the faith handed down from 18th-century German farmers. The hillsides were gouged into to make way for coal mining and railroads, creating new towns and giving rise to others—while covering everything with a layer of fine grit. Today, endless back roads wind past hillsides laid bare by strip mines, and cities struggle to find a way to fill the economic vacuum left by the departure of the industries.

Highlights

Most visits to southwest Virginia start and end at the "Star City" of Roanoke, a former railroad town reborn as a lively, forward-thinking metropolis. Interstate 81 shoots straight southwest past Blacksburg (wired in more ways than one on the brainpower of Virginia Tech university) and Abingdon, which is blessed with the outstanding tourist trinity of the Barter Theater, Martha Washington Inn, and the Virginia Highlands Festival.

Beyond that, you have back roads, tobacco barns, and mountain music. The hills here are alive with the sounds of fiddles, banjos, and stomping feet at famous hoe-downs such as the Galax Fiddler's Convention, the Carter Family Memorial Music Center, and the Floyd Flatfoot Jamboree.

Southwest Virginia's true heart, though, is outdoors—the natural wonders of this slice of the Appalachian Plateau rival any in the east. Countless rivers and streams carve the hills with deep, parallel valleys, capped by the quarter-mile deep gorge of Breaks Interstate Park. The Cumberland Gap National Historical Park preserves the gateway to the American west in much the same condition it was in when Daniel Boone blazed the trail.

Thousands of acres of beech, maple, hickory, and ash stand within the Jefferson National Forest, including the 117,000 acres of the Mount Rogers National Recreation Area, which contains the highest peak in the state. Outdoor pursuits are almost endless, from hiking the Appalachian Trail and mountain biking or horseback riding along the Virginia Creeper and New River Trails to rafting the Russell Fork River. Even the view from the driver's seat of a car can be worth the trip—especially along I-77 north to West Virginia or the southern section of the Blue Ridge Parkway.

Access

Interstate 81 runs most of the length of south-western Virginia, paralleled by the slower, more scenic US 11. Interstate 77 slices across briefly from North Carolina to West Virginia. West and north of Abingdon, most rural roads are two-lane, meandering, and gorgeous. The only major airport is in Roanoke, the nearest Amtrak service 45 miles north, in Clifton Forge.

Resources

In Abingdon, the **Heart of Appalachia Visitor Information Center**, tel. (888) 827-6867 or (540) 623-2209, fax 623-2320, stocks details on the entire Appalachian Mountain region, as does the **Highlands Gateway Visitor Center** in Max Meadows, tel. (800) 446-9670 or (540) 637-6766, fax 637-6328. And if you plan to be among the thousands who flock here during autumn, the Roanoke Convention and Visitors Bureau is kind enough to maintain a special fall colors Web site at www.roanoke.com/parkway. *New River Outdoors Magazine,* 2600-H Foxhunt Lane, Blacksburg, VA 24060, tel. (540) 552-0049, e-mail: ksingle@roanoke.infi.net, was started in 1997. A nine-issue annual subscription runs $13.50.

ROANOKE AND VICINITY

Settled in a bowl in the mountains and split by the Roanoke River, Roanoke, the largest city in southwest Virginia (pop. 231,000), offers metropolitan convenience with a surprising amount of flair. The "Capital of the Blue Ridge" serves as transportation and medical center for the entire region and was the first community in North America to offer citywide recycling. Various polls have put it in the top 10 or 20 cities nationwide for quality of life, lack of stress, and tourism potential. Much of this potential is due to Roanoke's vibrant downtown area, anchored by Market Square and the justifiably famous Center in the Square arts complex.

History

The city's unenviable original name, Big Lick, refers to the area's salt deposits, sought out by animals, which were in turn hunted by Native Americans. The first European settlers arrived near the end of the 1700s, stopping along the Great Road down the Shenandoah Valley. By the early 1800s, the town's central streets had been laid out and, with the completion of a road over the Blue Ridge from Lynchburg, Big Lick was on its way to becoming a crossroads for western Virginia.

Explosive growth arrived with the steam and clatter of the railroads shortly after the Civil War. In 1881, the Shenandoah Valley and Norfolk & Western Railroads chose the town of 700 as a junction point, changing its name in the process to the more presentable Roanoke, from the native word *rawrenock,* meaning "shell money."

By 1892, some 25,000 people called the valley home. The Virginia Railway arrived in 1906, bringing coal traffic and passengers including Mark Twain, who rode on the first coach into the city. The largest rayon plant in the world opened here in the early 1900s, but even so,

Tobacco drying in a barn is a common sight in rural southwestern Virginia.

SOUTHWEST
VIRGINIA

KENTUCKY

Breaks
Interstate
Park

Grundy

John W. Flannagan
Reservoir

Wise

Big Stone Gap

Lebanon

Cumberland Gap National
Historical Park

Jonesville

Natural Tunnel
State Park

Abingdon

Gate
City

River

Powell

River

Clinch

TENNESSEE

Damascus

Bristol

Cherokee
Lake

Boone Lake

Holston
Lake

toward the middle of the century, Roanoke's economy began to slip.

During the award-winning downtown revitalization in 1979, wise city planners drew heavily on public opinion through questionnaires, interviews, and live television "design-a-thons."

Orientation

Roanoke's rapid blooming has left it a rather scrambled city. The easiest way to navigate is by landmarks and highway exits. Heading south on I-81 from I-81, exit 4 sits between the Roanoke Civic Center on the east and the tan spire of St. Andrew's Catholic Church, one of the highest points in the city. Next, look for the unmistakable Tudor bulk of the Hotel Roanoke & Conference Center, followed by the spaceship tower of the First Union Bank.

Exit 5, onto Williamson Road, carries you past the H&C coffeepot billboard and the Dr. Pepper bottlecap clock on Salem Ave. Park at one of the lots along Williamson Rd. and head toward

Market Square along Campbell or Salem Ave.

To reach Mill Mountain and the Blue Ridge Parkway, hop on Walnut Ave. from either Jefferson St. south.

SIGHTS

Market Square

Begun in the 1880s with only a handful of vendors, this is one of Virginia's oldest markets. After following the city's boom-and-bust cycles through most of the 20th century, the market became the center of Roanoke's recent downtown renaissance. Today, permanent awnings shade sidewalk stands brimming with country market staples: fresh produce in season, baskets of flowers, eggs, dairy products, and meats. Old Victorian shops, now nouveaux country stores, have shelves that groan under gourmet wines, cheeses, and preserves, while for blocks around restaurants, gift shops, and art galleries take up any extra space.

The historic **City Market Building,** erected in 1922, is home to a neon-lit international food court featuring everything from sushi to Cuban sandwiches. Local legend has it that anyone who drinks form the small **Dog Mouth Fountain,** at Salem and Market St., will someday return to Roanoke.

Center in the Square
This converted warehouse at the southwest corner of Market Square houses five floors of southwest Virginia's finest cultural attractions. The **Art Museum of Western Virginia,** tel. (540) 342-5760, features Appalachian folk art in the midst of permanent and rotating collections of regional and national artists from the 19th and 20th centuries. Open Tues.-Sat. 10 a.m.-5 p.m., Sunday 1-5 p.m.; free. Ten thousand years of local goings-on, from Native Americans to the present day, are covered in the **Roanoke Valley History Museum,** tel. (540) 342-5770. Open Tues.-Fri. 10 a.m.-4 p.m., Saturday 10 a.m.-5

p.m., Sunday 1-5 p.m.; $2 adults, $1 children (free the second Friday of each month 3-4 p.m.).

Hop the elevator to the **Science Museum of Western Virginia,** tel. (540) 342-5710, a place full of noises, voices, and flashing lights that proves that museums can be anything but boring. Hands-on exhibits geared toward kids but fun for anyone include holograms, fiber optics, a giant xylophone, and a "body tech" exhibit for budding anatomists. The Hopkins Planetarium and a tank full of live marine animals from the Chesapeake Bay help the museum maintain its consistent status as one of the best in the region. Open Mon.-Sat. 10 a.m.-5 p.m., Sunday 1-5 p.m. Admission is $5 for adults ($6.30 with a planetarium show) and $3 for children ($4.30 with show), but it's free the second Friday of each month 3:30-7 p.m.

Each museum also has a gift emporium on the first floor—try dragging your child (or parent) away from the **Science Museum Shop,** next to the **History Museum Store** and the **Art Museum Store.**

ROANOKE VALLEY

To Natural Bridge, Lexington

To The Homeplace

To Salem

To Salem

To Lynchburg

To Smith Mountain Lake

To Buck Mountain Grill

© MOON PUBLICATIONS, INC.

0   2.5 mi

0   2.5 km

ROANOKER MOTOR LODGE

LA MAISON DU GOURMET

CROSSROADS MALL

VALLEY VIEW MALL

SUPER 8 MOTEL

HOLIDAY INN-AIRPORT

ROANOKE AIRPORT MARRIOTT

ROANOKE REGIONAL AIRPORT

ROANOKE ANTIQUE MALL

ECONO LODGE

GREYHOUND STATION

WALNUT HILL B&B

MINIATURE GRACELAND

Mill Mountain Star and Zoological Park

The Library Restaurant

STEPHEN'S Restaurant

ROANOKE MTN CAMPGROUND

GRANDIN THEATER

TOWERS MALL

ROANOKER RESTAURANT

THE COFFEE POT

TANGLEWOOD MALL

Virginia's Explore Park

Mill Mountain

Roanoke Mountain

MT. PLEASANT BLVD.

BLUE RIDGE PKWY.

Vinton

WASHINGTON ST.

GUS NICKS BLVD.

DALE AVE.

Roanoke River

13TH ST.

9TH AVE.

HOLLINS RD.

PLANTATION RD.

WILLIAMSON RD.

AIRPORT RD.

PETERS CREEK RD.

GREEN RIDGE RD.

COVE RD.

HERSHBERGER RD.

SALEM TPKE.

MELROSE

ELECTRIC RD.

ROANOKE BLVD.

24TH ST.

SHENANDOAH AVE.

ORANGE AVE.

10TH ST.

JAMISON AVE.

BRANDON AVE.

GRANDIN RD.

COLONIAL AVE.

BRAMBLETON

APPERSON DR.

MAIN ST.

Roanoke River

ELECTRIC RD.

FRANKLIN RD.

ORANGE AVE.

WASHINGTON ST.

ROANOKE AREA CLIMATE

SNOWFALL — MAXIMUM TEMP.
RAINFALL — MINIMUM TEMP.

An outstanding example of the possibilities of regional theater, the **Mill Mountain Theater** shows original works, classics, and children's plays. They also oversee the more experimental **Theater B** at 20 E. Church Ave. Call (800) 317-6455 or (540) 342-5740, for the latest schedule and ticket prices.

For more information on Center in the Square, call (540) 342-5700 Mon.-Sat. 10 a.m.-5 p.m., Sunday 1-5 p.m. p.m. (also e-mail: cits@cits.org, Web site: www.cits.org). In the same building, the **Arts Council of the Blue Ridge,** tel. (540) 342-5790, can supply information on regional events.

Other Museums

The **Virginia Museum of Transportation,** 303 Norfolk Ave. and 3rd St., tel. (540) 342-5670, Web site: www.vmt.org, serves as a monument to the glorious methods of simply getting from one place to another. Inside the restored freight station straddling the train tracks three blocks west of Market Square are an O-scale model railroad, a gift shop, and a gorgeous collection of antique autos, including a 1934 Ford V-8 Model A Sedan and a 1950 Studebaker Landcruiser, more spaceship than car. Dozens of train engines and cars—a few of which are open to visitors—fill the lot out back. Steam engines, diesel locomotives, post office cars and a classic caboose cover virtually the entire history of rail travel. Open Mon.-Sat. 10 a.m.-5 p.m., Sunday noon-5 p.m.; $5 adults, $3 children 3-18.

The Harrison School, opened in 1916 as the city's first public high school for African-American students, has reserved a few downstairs rooms for the **Harrison Museum of African-American Culture,** 523 Harrison Ave. NW, tel. (540) 345-4818, fax 345-4831. Changing exhibits relating to African-American culture focus on the Roanoke area, and African crafts fill the gift shop. Open Tues.-Fri. 10 a.m.-5 p.m., Saturday, Sunday 1-5 p.m.; free.

Roanoke was home to the country's first volunteer emergency rescue squad, organized in 1928 by a railroad worker who as a child had watched helplessly as two men drowned in the Roanoke River before help could arrive. That small group evolved into today's national EMT system, pioneering the use of CPR and modern lifesaving techniques along the way. Over 50 exhibits (many interactive) at the **To The Rescue Museum,** Tanglewood Mall, 4428 Electric Rd., tel. (540) 776-0364, include a memorial to emergency medical technicians killed in the line of duty. Open Mon.-Sat. 10 a.m.-9 p.m., Sunday 1-6 p.m.; $2 adults, $1 children.

The curator of the Met probably wouldn't deem it a museum, but **Miniature Graceland,** 605 Riverland Dr., tel. (540) 427-4254, is certainly a memorial—even a shrine—and the product of hours of loving work. Don and Kim Epperly have filled their modest backyard with doll-sized replicas of major buildings in Elvis' life, topped by Graceland itself, complete with car museum. This pop culture landmark passes through various stages of repair and disrepair. It's also right next to their house, so walk softly and make a donation.

Mill Mountain

Sandwiched between the city and the Blue Ridge Parkway sits this lone peak, disconnected from the rest of the Appalachian chain. A trolley to the summit was built in 1910 but soon abandoned because people preferred to drive up winding Walnut Ave. instead. At the peak stands the **Mill Mountain Star,** Roanoke's most famous landmark. At 100 feet tall, it's the World's Largest Man-Made Illuminated Star, with 2,000 feet of neon tubing visible for 60 miles. Airplane pilots navigate by it occasionally, and even Elvis Presley once snuck up here after a concert to take a closer look. The view of the city and valley from the base of the star, and the picnic area nearby, are excellent on a clear day.

A short walk away, the **Mill Mountain Zoological Park,** tel. (540) 343-3241, is a small but professional zoo with many exotic, endangered species including tree kangaroos from New Guinea, a Nepalese red panda, and Ruby, a huge Siberian tiger with whom the zoo eventually hopes to start a tiger breeding center. Children will love the prairie-dog village, petting zoo, and the miniature Zoo-Choo train that circles the park. Open daily 10 a.m.-5 p.m.; $5 adults, $3 children under 12.

Virginia's Explore Park

An authentic hill settlement from the early 19th century has been opened to the public off the Blue Ridge Parkway at milepost 115. Reenactors portraying Native Americans and frontier families tend the working farm and its crops and animals but are happy to demonstrate colonial skills including loading and firing flintlock muskets, flint-and-steel firemaking, crafts, and cooking. Eight miles of trails loop past the homes and one-room schoolhouse into the surrounding countryside. Special events include a Native American powwow in early May and traditional Blue Ridge music in early Sept. Open May.-Nov. Mon.-Sat. 10 a.m.-6 p.m., Sun noon-6 p.m., (only Fri.-Mon. in April); $6 adults, $4 children 6-18. For more information call (540) 427-1800, fax 427-1880.

ACCOMMODATIONS

Inexpensive

Take I-81 exit two west to reach the **Super 8** motel, 6616 Thirlane Rd. NW, tel. (540) 563-8888 ($44-50), or east along Peter's Creek Rd. for the **Roanoker Motor Lodge,** 7645 Williamson Rd., tel. (540) 362-3344. An **Econo Lodge,** 308 Orange Ave. and Williamson Rd., tel./fax (540) 343-2413, sits off exit four.

Moderate

The **Best Western Inn at Valley View,** tel. (540) 263-2400, fax 263-2400 ext. 499, is in the Valley View Mall at 5050 Valley View Dr. Just south of the airport is the **Holiday Inn-Airport,** 6626 Thirlane Rd. NW, tel. (540) 265-8961, fax 366-1637.

© MOON PUBLICATIONS, INC.

Surprisingly, there's only one B&B in Roanoke proper: the **Walnut Hill B&B,** 436 Walnut Ave. SE, tel. (540) 427-3312, fax 427-0273. The front lawn overflows with flowers, and a veranda runs the length of the front of this elegant house, decorated with photos of the host and his late wife (who helped him open the place) during their travels around the world.

Premium

Two pools, a spa, tennis courts, and a gym fill the Mediterranean-style **Roanoke Airport Marriott,** 2801 Herschberger Rd., NW, tel. (800) 228-9290 or (540) 563-9300. Inside are two eateries: gourmet Remington's and airy Lily's (featuring an excellent Sunday brunch).

Luxury

With a history almost as long as the city itself, the **The Hotel Roanoke & Convention Center,** 110 Shenandoah Ave., tel. (800) 222-TREE (800-222-8733) or (540) 985-5900, fax 853-8264, Web site: www.doubletreehotels.com, has anchored Roanoke's downtown for over a century. It was built in a wheat field in 1882, and, thanks to its popularity with vacationers, it's outlasted the railroads that financed it. In the 1930s, major alterations changed the exterior style from Queen Anne to the current classic Tudor. Anyone who's anyone passing through the area has stayed here, from presidents to celebrities, Amelia Earhart to Elvis. The hotel was donated to Virginia Tech in 1989 and underwent a complete facelift.

Even if you're staying elsewhere, a peek inside the lobby is worth the walk across the glassed-in Market Square Walkway over the train tracks. Florentine marble floors set off vaulted ceilings, while Southern idyll paintings on the walls and ceilings make the Palm Court off the lobby perfect for afternoon tea. Guests enjoy a fitness center, pool, the Regency Room's famous peanut soup, and the hotel's trademark fresh-baked cookies on arrival.

Dating to between the World Wars, the **Radisson Patrick Henry Hotel,** 617 S. Jefferson St., tel. (800) 767-1664 or (540) 345-8811, fax 342-9908, is also listed on the National Register of Historic Places. Renovations in 1991 preserved the wrought iron, brass, wood, and crystal accents in the lobby area. Most of the rooms include kitchenettes, and suites are also available.

Camping

The **Roanoke Mountain Campground,** tel. (540) 982-9242, is off the Mill Mountain Rd. between the Mill Mountain Star and the Blue Ridge Parkway. Tent and trailer campsites ($10) are first-come, first-served. Open May-September.

FOOD

City Center

Blink and you just might miss **Eden's Way,** 104 Church Ave. SE at Williamson, tel. (540) 344-EDEN (540-344-3336), a tiny nook serving vegetarian carry-out with spiritual reverence. Everything here is animal-free and excellent, especially the bread. Open Mon.-Fri. 10 a.m.-4 p.m. On the other hand, you *can't* miss the **Star City Diner,** 108 S. Jefferson St. at Campbell, tel. (540) 343-9301, with its sidewalk sign that orders you to "Get in here and eat." Classic 1950s styling includes neon and pinup art. Burgers and banana splits aren't health food, but they hit the spot.

Other local favorite burger joints are the **Texas Tavern,** 114 Church Ave., tel. (540) 342-4825, a no-frills, post-midnight kind of place with great chili and actual bottled sodas (open 24 hours a day, seven days a week), and the more upscale **Billy's Ritz,** 102 Salem Ave. SE, tel. (540) 342-3927, serving steaks and pastas near the oak bar and in an open courtyard (open daily for dinner).

A virtual United Nations of eateries fills the Market Square food court, packed at lunch with the downtown crowd. Try the **Asian French Cafe,** tel. (540) 345-5593, offering well-prepared Vietnamese dishes in the food court side or in the elegant dining room. **Chico & Billy's Prestigious Pizza and Pasta Palace,** tel. (540) 342-1197, serves gourmet pizza.

Ask around for Roanokers' favorite place for dinner and chances are good that **Carlos Brazilian & International Cuisine,** 312 Market St. at Church, tel. (540) 345-7661, will come up more than once. Casually classy styling, good prices, and outstanding food make this one so popular you'll need reservations on weekends. Try the authentic Brazilian *feijoada*—a full meal that's the national dish—on Saturday. Entrées run $5-7 at lunch and $7-17 for dinner, open Mon.-Sat.

One of the city's best night spots has nothing to do with dancing or alcohol, though intoxicating drinks are still a cornerstone. **Mill Mountain Coffee & Tea,** 112 Campbell Ave. SE, tel. (540) 342-9404, is easily the best coffee shop in town, if not this part of the state. Beans roasted here are served in a good strong brew, alongside dozens of flavors of teas, Italian sodas, and desserts to diet for. Open to midnight (1 a.m. Fri.-Sat.). For a quick bite, try one of Roanoke's best bagels at **Five-Boro Bagels,** 206A Market Square, tel. (540) 342-1494.

Elsewhere in Town

The **New Yorker,** 2802 Williamson Rd., tel. (540) 366-0935, is a true Manhattan-style deli with great submarine sandwiches and cheesecake. Head to the **Hatteras Seafood Company,** in the Valleyview Mall, tel. (540) 362-FISH (540-362-3474), for key lime pie—theirs is voted best in town. A raw bar features catch of the day, and they serve cocktails until 11 p.m. or midnight.

Speaking of seafood and awards, **Stephen's,** 2926 Franklin Rd. SW, tel. (540) 344-7203, serves Roanoke best—and only—authentic Creole cuisine, with fresh seafood flown in for the gumbo and étoufée and softshell crabs and crawfish in season. Dinner (entrées $12-20) is served Mon.-Sat. And the Best Place to Eat With Your Mother, according to a recent poll, is the **Roanoker,** 2522 Colonial Ave. at Wonju, tel. (540) 344-7746, a local favorite since 1941. City residents pack several dining rooms for down-home staples like the biscuits-and-gravy breakfast, homemade breads, and fresh vegetables.

La Maison du Gourmet, 5732 Airport Rd., tel. (540) 366-2444, sits in a converted Georgian mansion (c. 1929) near the airport. Fine French dining features escargot, rack of lamb, special homemade Virginia seafood sausage, and changing daily specials. Dinner entrées are $10-30, and reservations are suggested (casual dress, though). Open Mon.-Sat. for dinner and Sunday brunch.

With an entryway lined with awards, **The Library,** Picadilly Square, 3117 Franklin Rd. SW, tel. (540) 985-0811, is easily one of the state's 10 best restaurants. Top-notch service, an extensive wine list, and the candlelit atmosphere of book-lined walls set off exceptional French cuisine. Dinner (entrées $13-25) is served Tues.-Sat., and reservations are recommended.

Out of Town

Eating at **The Homeplace,** Rt. 311 near Salem, tel. (540) 384-7252, is like nothing more than dinner at grandma's. This old country home features a set menu of classic country items—fried chicken, roast beef, or country ham, mashed potatoes, beans, fresh flaky biscuits, slaw, gravy, and cobbler for dessert—and they'll keep bringing it out until you beg them to stop. Meals are $9-10, served Thurs.-Sat. 4-8 p.m., Sunday 11 a.m.-6 p.m. To get there take I-81 exit 140 or 141 to 311 north, and it's seven miles farther on your left.

Off the Blue Ridge Parkway, the **Buck Mountain Grill,** 5002 Franklin Rd. (US 220), tel. (540) 776-1830, featuring American and Mediterranean cuisine with fresh seafood a specialty. Steak and vegetarian options round out the menu, with main courses for $8-18. Open Tues.-Sun. for lunch and dinner.

SHOPPING

Aside from the farmer's market in Market Square, a wide range of shops provide enough spending opportunities for days. **Gallery 3,** 213 Market

---

SOUTHWESTERN VIRGINIA WINERIES

Château Morrisette
tel. (540) 593-2865

Near Meadows of Dan; at Blue Ridge Parkway milepost 171.5, west on Rt. 726 (Black Ridge Rd.), left onto Rt. 777 (Winery Rd.), 0.25 miles

French country restaurant. Fruity white Our Dog Blue, in blue bottle, is one of state's best sellers.

Dye's Vineyard
tel. (540) 873-4659

Near Honaker; US 19, west on Rt. 80, left onto Rt. 620, 0.5 miles

Villa Appalaccia
tel. (540) 593-3100

Near Floyd; on Blue Ridge Parkway between milepost 170 and 171

St. SE, tel. (540) 343-9698, stocks local art and handicrafts, while 18 artists have studios and shops in the **Studios on the Square Gallery,** 206 Market Square, tel. (540) 345-4076. Gourmet country foods are the specialty of **Sumdat Farm Market,** 209A Market St. SE, tel. (540) 982-2164, and **Wertz's Country Store & Wine Cellar Inc.,** 215 Market St. SE, tel. (800) 767-3110 or (540) 342-5133.

Lee & Edwards Wine Merchants, 309 S Jefferson St., tel. (540) 343-3900, carries the largest collection of local and international wines in this part of the state, along with beer and home-brewing supplies. For books and music, stop by **Books Strings & Things,** 202 Market Square, tel. (540) 342-5511, where people who come for one or the other usually end up leaving with both.

Campbell Ave. is home to no fewer than three quality antique stores: **Russell's Yesteryear,** 109 W. Campbell Ave., tel. (540) 342-1750, **12 E. Campbell Antiques & Collectibles,** 12 E. Campbell Ave., tel. (540) 343-7946, and **Barbara's Antiques,** 125 E. Campbell Ave., tel. (540) 342-6864. For the largest selection, try the **Roanoke Antique Mall,** 2302 Orange Ave. NE (Rt. 460) at Gus Nicks Blvd., tel. (540) 344-0264, with over 100 dealers open daily until 6 p.m. And if *that's* not enough, the **Roanoke Antique and Collectable Expo,** tel. (804) 431-9500, rolls into the Salem Civic Center one weekend a month, bringing close to 1,000 dealers, food, and outlet stores ($2 pp).

ENTERTAINMENT

Three of Roanoke's major cultural institutions have offices in the Jefferson Center at 541 Luck St.: the **Roanoke Symphony Orchestra,** tel. (540) 343-6221 or 343-9127; the **Roanoke Ballet Theater,** tel. (540) 345-6099; and **Opera Roanoke,** tel. (540) 982-2742. Call each for the latest performance listings. On a more visceral level, the **Roanoke Civic Center** hosts rock concerts and home games with the Roanoke Express pro hockey team. Phone (540) 981-1201 for the box office or (540) 989-GOAL (540-989-4625) for hockey tickets.

Four of the city's shopping malls—Valley View, Tanglewood, Towers, and Crossroads—have multiplex theaters inside or nearby. For a more personal experience, though, head out to the **Grandin Movie Theater,** 1310 Grandin Rd., tel. (540) 345-6177. The Grandin is an ornate theater in a style that's all but disappeared (it took a benefit by Bill Murray to keep this one alive). They run current and older films and still occasionally offer $1 ticket specials.

A "Cigar & Billiards" sign outside the **Corned Beef & Co. Bar and Grill,** 107 S. Jefferson St., tel. (540) 342-3354, advertises the restaurant's major draw after hours, when live and DJ music drifts through the haze in the scotch and cigar lounge toward the pool tables. Established in 1936, **The Coffee Pot,** 2902 Brambleton Ave., tel. (540) 774-8256, is a Virginia historic landmark and the oldest club in town, hosting acoustic, R&B, and southern rock on occasion. Look for the big coffee pot on top of the building.

Formerly famous as the Iroquois, **The Ghost of Hollywood,** 324 Salem Ave., tel. (540) 982-8979, draws hard rock, metal, and blues, while **Lowell's,** 2328 Melrose NW, tel. (540) 344-4884, keeps things cooler with R&B and light jazz. **The Park,** 615 Salem Ave. SW, tel. (540) 342-0946, is a gay and straight dance club open until the wee hours of the morning on Saturday and Sunday.

EVENTS

Roanoke isn't called the Festival City of Virginia for nothing. For two weeks beginning Memorial Day, the **Festival in the Park,** tel. (540) 342-2640, ushers in summer with riverboat races, parades, a black-tie gala, and a carnival at the Civic Center. Also in May, the **Virginia State Championship Chili Cook-Off,** tel. (540) 342-2028, has participants begging for water at the farmer's market the first Saturday of the month. This often coincides with Roanoke's **Strawberry Festival,** tel. (540) 563-5036.

Preserves and cobbler are only two of the ways to enjoy the **Virginia Mountain Peach Festival,** tel. (540) 342-2028, held downtown the first weekend in August. The small town of Vinton, just east of Roanoke via US 24 or US 460, is the home of the **Vinton Old-Time Bluegrass Festival and Competition,** tel. (540) 345-8548, held mid-month in the Vinton Farmer's Market and accompanied by crafts and a carnival.

During the last weekend in Sept., Elmwood Park, at the corner of Jefferson St. and Elm Ave., hosts the **Henry Street African-American Heritage Festival**, tel. (540) 345-4818. Southwest Virginia's fabulous fall colors serve as a flaming backdrop to Roanoke's mid-October **Harvest Festival**, tel. (540) 342-2028, with horse-drawn carriage rides, antique cars, and music. It's held downtown at Century Square. The first Saturday of the month, the **Roanoke Symphony Polo Cup**, tel. (540) 387-6359, raises funds for the Roanoke Youth Symphony. The national-level tournament is held in Green Hill Park in West Salem, and costs $10 pp.

TRANSPORTATION

Getting Around
The **Valley Metro** bus network, 1108 Campbell Ave. SE, tel. (540) 982-2222, serves the entire city from its main transfer point at Campbell Court, 17 W. Campbell Ave. Buses run Mon.-Sat. 5:45 a.m.-8:45 p.m., and route maps are available at the visitors center. For cab service, try the **Yellow Cab Co. of Roanoke**, tel. (540) 345-7711, or **Liberty Cab**, tel. (540) 344-1776.

Getting There and Away
The **Roanoke Regional Airport**, 5202 Aviation Dr. NW, tel. (540) 362-1999, is the only large airport in southwest Virginia. It's served by Delta Connection, United Express, USAirways, USAirways Express, and Northwest Airlink. A number of car rental agencies have offices: Avis, tel. (540) 366-2436; Dollar, tel. (540) 563-8055; Hertz, tel. (540) 366-3421; and National, tel. (540) 563-5050. **Roanoke Airport Limo**, tel. (540) 345-7710, charges $12 to take one person downtown (add $2 for each additional person).

There's a **Greyhound** station at 26 W. Salem Ave. SW, tel. (800) 231-2222. **Amtrak's** nearest station is in Clifton Forge, 45 miles northwest. For information on a thruway bus there, call (800) 872-7245.

INFORMATION

The Roanoke Valley **Visitor Information Center,** 114 Market St., tel. (800) 635-5535 or (540) 345-8622, fax 342-7119, Web site: www.visitRoanokeVA.com, is on the east side of Market Square. It's open daily 9 a.m.-5 p.m. and offers walking-tour brochures.

NEAR ROANOKE

Dixie Caverns
This hole in the earth was discovered by a pair of Civil War soldiers whose dog disappeared while chasing an animal across the hillside. They found the hole it had disappeared into (still visible today) and managed, with lanterns and rope, to rescue the canine. The caverns the dog—named Dixie—unwittingly discovered creep upwards into the mountain instead of down, so for most of the tour you're actually *above* the parking lot where you started.

Fifty-minute tours leave whenever a large enough group materializes. Hundreds of couples have been married beneath the 57-ton Wedding Bell formation (a statement on the beauty of the union or the weight of the commitment—you be the judge). Notice where early tours broke off small stalactites for souvenirs—a practice that would get you thrown in jail today.

The caverns are off I-81 exit 132 just west of Salem, tel. (540) 380-2085. Open daily 9:30 a.m.-6 p.m.; $6.50 adults, $3.50 children 5-12. Tent ($5 pp) and RV ($16) campsites are available.

Dragon's Tooth
A jagged prow of rock juts from the peaks of the Jefferson National Forest, offering great views from a moderately strenuous 2.6-mile climb just off the Appalachian Trail. Take Rt. 311 north 8 miles from I-81, exit 141, and look for the parking area on the left just past the Catawba Grocery. For more information on this and other hikes in the area, contact the Blacksburg Ranger District of the National Forest, tel. (540) 552-4641.

Ferrum
This tiny town erupts every fall with the **Blue Ridge Folklife Festival,** the largest showcase of rural tradition in the state. Animals are the stars, from the State Championship Mule Jumping Contest to coon dog competitions and border collie herding demonstrations. Visitors enjoy all the deep-fried, golden-brown, down-home cook-

the beautiful Blue
Ridge Parkway

ing they can fit down—barbecue, apple pie, pork rinds, spare ribs, and fried chitterling sandwiches, for starters—while listening to gospel, country, and blues music. Storytellers and a petting zoo will keep the kids busy as parents peruse the quilts and crafts displays.

The festival is held the fourth Saturday in October 10 a.m.-5 p.m., rain or shine; $6 adults, $4 children. For more information and directions call the Blue Ridge Institute of Ferrum College, at (540) 365-4418 or 365-2865.

Floyd
One of the more interesting counties in the state, Floyd, south of Roanoke, shelters a small pocket of the 1960s—apparent in subtle but distinct signs. Earthships (houses made of recycled materials and earth), gasohol, and tie-dyed T-shirts in crafts stores all reflect a countercultural legacy. There's only one stoplight in the town of Floyd itself, which makes it easy to find **Cockram's General Store,** tel. (540) 745-4563, famous for its weekly Flatfooting Jamboree. Every Friday at 7 p.m., the display cases are pushed aside and the floor given over to country music and shuffling feet. The store is the fourth building on the right to the west of the stoplight, and the show is free.

Across Locust St., **The Harvest Moon, Inc.,** tel. (540) 745-4366, may be the best-smelling store in the state, full of spices, candles, herbs, produce, and greeting cards. Upstairs wait a coffee and wine shop and a quiet sitting room. Al-

most next door is the **New Mountain Mercantile,** tel. (540) 745-4ART (540-745-4278), with local crafts, an art gallery, and new-age body-and-mind products. The **Floyd County Chamber of Commerce,** tel. (540) 745-4407, is happy to supply more information on their area.

Southern Blue Ridge Parkway
At mile 169, the **Rocky Knob Recreation Area** has a Visitor Contact Station, tel. (540) 745-9662, and a campground, tel. (540) 745-9664, with 100 sites for $10 each (open late April through October). Housekeeping cabins with fully furnished kitchens and linens are available for $50. For reservations contact National Park Concessions, Inc., Route 1, Box 5, Meadows of Dan, VA 24120-9603, tel. (540) 593-3503.

A National Recreational Trail winds 11 strenuous miles down into Rock Castle Gorge, 1,500 feet deep and studded with outcroppings of quartz. The Black Ridge Trail offers a more moderate hike of 3.1 miles from the visitors center to Black Ridge and Grassy Knoll. A one-mile loop trail also leaves from the parking lot.

Seven miles farther south is **Mabry Mill,** tel. (540) 952-2947, centered on a gristmill operated commercially from 1910 to 1935. Fresh-ground cornmeal is sold near a restored sawmill and blacksmith shop. There's also a campground, coffee shop, and gift shop (open late April-Oct.)

Cool nights and loamy soil give the **Meadows of Dan** the distinction of raising the sweetest cabbage in the world. The fourth Saturday of every August, more than 3,000 people arrive for the **Cabbage Festival,** at Poor Farmers Farm, tel. (540) 952-2560, with country music, games for the kids, and, of course, plenty of cabbage.

Keep going almost to the North Carolina state line to reach the **Blue Ridge Country Hostel,** mile 214.5, tel. (540) 236-4962. It's a little over one mile north of the intersection with Rt. 89 and has rooms for $13.50 for HI members ($16.50 non-members).

BLACKSBURG AND VICINITY

A quiet town on the surface, Blacksburg harbors the secret heart of one of the fastest-growing, most progressive communities in Virginia. Its scenic setting, on a plateau right at the edge of farm country, seduces all ages—Blacksburg is rated one of the best places in the country to retire, while the 22,000 students of Virginia Tech make up over 60% of the town's population.

It's this influx of brainpower that makes Blacksburg a bit difficult to classify. The town celebrated its bicentennial in 1998—a year after a number of downtown tattoo parlors hosted the two-day Piercefest VIII. The municipal bus system has won national awards, yet the town lends itself so well to strolling. The wings of Virginia Tech, southwest Virginia's major learning center, spread over the community. The town was one of the first to be wired to the Internet, and Hokie basketball and football are NCAA Division 1 mainstays.

HISTORY

This gorgeous slice of Appalachia was originally the farming settlement of Draper's Meadow, a mixed community of European settlers and the first permanent English-speaking colony west of the Alleghenies. Much of the land was granted in 1748 to Colonel James Patton's Woods River Company.

A Shawnee attack in July 1775 left all but four settlers dead, wounded, or captured; Patton himself was shot after cutting down two attackers with his sword. One captive managed to escape and make an incredible trek back to the settlements. Another, Mrs. John Draper, was adopted by the chief's family and remained a prisoner until she was ransomed in 1781.

Colonel William Preston arrived in 1772 and built Smithfield Plantation, which still stands on the edge of the Virginia Tech campus. Blacksburg was founded in 1798 on 38 acres donated by William Black and set up as a 16-block grid bounded by today's Draper Rd., Wharton St., Jackston St., and Clay St.

Dr. Henry Black petitioned the Virginia General Assembly in 1872 to establish a land-grant university in the area. It opened with a single building and 43 students; a century and a quarter later, it thrives as southwest Virginia's largest university and employer.

VIRGINIA TECH

The original Virginia Agriculture and Mechanical College has become Virginia Polytechnic Institute and State University, known as Virginia Tech, or simply "Tech." It's one of the state's powerhouse universities, ranking among the nation's best in research and scholarship. A yearly research budget of $100 million makes it easy to understand why there are more computers on campus than phones. Close to 24,000 undergraduate and graduate students study within eight colleges, including Agriculture, Veterinary Medicine, and Forestry.

Stately limestone neo-Gothic architecture dots the 3,000-acre campus in the heart of Blacksburg. Burruss Hall presides over the huge grassy drill field, and the tree-lined duck pond, west of the central campus, provides a peaceful spot to escape the pressures of academics.

Tech's **Museum of Geological Sciences,** 2062 Derring Hall, contains the largest collection of Virginia minerals in the state, alongside full-scale dinosaurs, gemstones, and other fossils. Open Mon.-Fri. 9 a.m.-4 p.m.; free admission. The university also maintains a **Museum of Natural History** at 428 N. Main St., with a permanent collection of North American mammals and a hands-on Discovery Corner for kids. Open Wed.-Sat. 11 a.m.-5 p.m.; free admission. For information on either museum call (540) 231-3001.

THE ELECTRONIC VILLAGE

One of the most remarkable things about Blacksburg isn't visible to the naked eye. Some might say it doesn't even exist. But plenty of others—including most of the town's residents—point out that the Blacksburg Electronic Village (Web site: www.bev.net), an Internet counterpart to the living, breathing town, is fun and useful, making it one of the most famous and successful small-town networks in the world.

The idea began, of course, at Virginia Tech in 1991. With a stated goal to "foster a virtual community to complement and enhance the physical community," the cooperative venture between the city, the university, and Bell Atlantic got off the ground only a few years later. Everybody in town was given free access to the Internet, electronic mail, and a host of other Web tools to play with. Two-thirds of the town hopped aboard immediately, either through public-access library terminals or private computers in dorms, offices, or homes (special high-speed phone lines were offered by Bell Atlantic as part of the deal).

Soon the snowball began to roll: restaurants put their menus and coupons on-line, bands proffered sound clips, and local galleries uploaded images in their collections. The entire range of daily life began to reflect itself in the ether, from businesses' advertising sales to obituaries and birth announcements. Blacksburg's "town within a town" has attracted worldwide attention as a model of a successful Internet community and has drawn personal visits from government officials coming from as far away as Japan.

Not all the attention has been positive, though. Critics have voiced worries that the town's shadow twin will actually erode person-to-person connections in the real village. They point out that you don't bump into your neighbors shopping for groceries on-line and you can't make eye contact in a virtual chat room. The silicon doppelgänger may end up driving a wedge between residents who have computers and those who don't.

But an overwhelming percentage of users (185 out of 219 in one USA Today poll) say that the network enhances connections that already exist outside the net. Public polling for town projects is now a snap. Especially in education, the benefits are hard to deny: schoolkids can correspond with other students overseas, and parents can keep in touch with teachers and track classroom activities.

The key point seems to be Blacksburg's small size. It was already a tightly knit community, so the electronic village serves to bring it closer. Paul Saffo, director of the Institute for the Future in Menlo Park, CA, said of the community, "They are very lucky nerds to live there."

Smithfield Plantation

Follow signs down Duck Pond Drive to reach this classic plantation home built by Scots-Irish immigrants William and Susanna Smith Preston in 1772. Over the years, two Virginia governors, James Patton Preston (1816-19) and John Bucanan Floyd (1849-52), have been born here. Today, the Tidewater-style mansion is a living museum, with costumed reenactors leading tours of the house and the garden, which is planted with culinary and medicinal herbs.

One-hour tours run April-Dec., Thurs.-Sun. 1-5 p.m.; $4 adults, $1.50 children and students. **Smithfield Plantation Days,** in June, include militia demonstrations, arts and crafts, and children's activities. Over the holidays, candles replace lamps for tours of the home. Call (540) 231-3947 for more information.

ACCOMMODATIONS

Inexpensive

The **Red Carpet Inn,** 1615 S. Main St., tel. (540) 552-4011, is the least expensive in town. For slightly more, the **Best Western Red Lion Inn,** 900 Plantation Rd., tel. (540) 552-7770, fax 552-6346, offers a pool and tennis courts.

Moderate

The **Comfort Inn,** 3705 South Main St., tel. (540) 951-1500, has a pool and exercise room for $66. The **Blacksburg Marriott,** 900 Prices Fork Rd., tel. (540) 552-7001, fax 552-0627, adds tennis courts and another pool for $90.

Blacksburg has surprisingly few guesthouses, considering how many students and parents come and go over the course of the year. A number of buildings make up the **Clay Corner Inn,** 401 Clay St. SW, tel. (540) 953-2604 or 951-0543, e-mail: claycorner@aol.com, from the main home (c. 1929) to the Huckleberry House at 404 Clay St., with a fireplace in every room and an outdoor jacuzzi. Twelve rooms provide enough space for the entire Hokie football team, which has stayed here in the past. There's a heated swimming pool out back and a patio perfect for warm-season breakfasts. Rates include breakfast.

Expensive

Ten minutes outside of town you'll find the popular **Brush Mountain Inn Bed and Breakfast,** 3030 Mt. Tabor Rd., tel. (540) 951-7530, e-mail: brushmtn@vt.edu, Web site: www.bbonline.com/va/brushmtn. When it's too cold to enjoy the 20-acre property, head indoors for a cup of hot chocolate in front of the 20-foot stone fireplace.

FOOD

Coffee Shops and Snacks

Settle into **The Easy Chair Coffee Shop,** 801 University City Blvd., tel. (540) 951-1628, for healthy sandwiches, gourmet java, tea, and desserts daily until midnight. **Mill Mountain Coffee and Tea,** 700 N. Main St., tel. (540) 552-7442, is a sibling to the downtown Roanoke standby. Local landmark status is claimed by **Carol Lee Doughnuts,** 133 College Ave., tel. (540) 552-6706. Founded over 25 years ago, Carol Lee still serves glazed and iced doughnuts for a quarter, along with an economical breakfast. Cakes, pies, and bagels are the manna of **Our Daily Bread,** 1317 S. Main St., tel. (540) 953-2815. They've expanded to offer daily sandwiches and salads, and even full entrées on Thursdays.

Student Favorites

Sidle up to the counter of **Souvlaki,** 201 College Ave., tel. (540) 951-0555, for one of their surprisingly inexpensive foot-and-a-half sandwiches or gyros (don't unwrap until the last bite). And remember, as the sign says, you can't complain about the service: there isn't any. **PK's,** 432 N. Main St., tel. (540) 552-1577, operates on

a pastel-Caribbean Jimmy-Buffett theme. Subs and sandwiches (including, yes, a Paradise cheeseburger platter) run $5, with dinner entrées around $10. It's open daily from 11:30 a.m. or noon to 2 a.m.

Techies say **The Cellar,** 302 North Main St., tel. (540) 552-9545, has one of the best price-to-volume ratios in town, but is quick to add that the food is good as well as plentiful. Italian and Greek entrées are $5-7, with normal and specialty pizzas for $6-13. The Cellar is also one of the most popular night spots in Blacksburg. And speaking of cellars and the goodies therein, the **Vintage Cellar,** 1313 S. Main St., tel. (540) 953-CORK (540-953-2675), stocks over 750 labels of wine and a few hundred kinds of beer, along with specialty foods and homebrewing supplies.

A Little Fancier

Ipanema, 107 Ellett Rd., tel. (540) 951-4501, brings a taste of Brazil to the south end of town. Appetizers such as their trademark *sopa de feijão* (bean soup), cost $3-5. Entrées fall in the $12 range, with a handful of vegetarian options for around $9. Wash it all down with a *capirinha* (lime juice, sugar, and vodka) or a Guaraná soda from the Amazon.

Other mid-priced options include **Zeppoli's Italian Restaurant,** tel. (540) 953-2000, serving excellent fresh pastas in the University Mall, and **Boudreaux's Restaurant,** 205 M. Main St., tel. (540) 961-2330, with Cajun food, lots of seafood, and a Sunday brunch.

ENTERTAINMENT AND RECREATION

Nightlife

For live music, **Top of the Stairs,** 217 W. College St., tel. (540) 953-2837, books mostly alternative bands. **The Cellar Restaurant** offers a little cooler atmosphere, with jazz and a great bar. **Champs Sports Bar,** 111 N. Main St., tel. (540) 951-2222, straddles the line: fans whoop it up in front of the TVs while jazz groups play downstairs. On College Ave. next to Carol Lee Doughnuts, the **Lyric Theater,** tel. (540) 951-0604, is an old-style movie house showing films with a university-town inclination toward the unusual and innovative.

THE GREAT FRONTIER ESCAPE

Mary Draper Ingles, wife of frontiersman William Ingles, was captured in the Shawnee raid of July 1775 and taken to a spot near Big Bone Kick, KY. There, she managed to escape her captors and struck out for home.

Bearing news of a planned second Shawnee attack, this determined woman followed rivers east and managed to cross 850 miles of some of the wildest country east of the Mississippi before showing up in Adam Harman's cornfield in Giles Country, VA, in late November.

Her story was dramatized in a play by Earl Hobson Smith, called the official Historical Outdoor Drama of the Commonwealth (Big Stone Gap already had claim to the Official *State* Outdoor Drama). It's been performed since 1971 at the Ingles Homestead Amphitheater in Radford, off US 11 about 20 miles southwest of Blacksburg, tel. (540) 639-0679, Web site: www.bev.net/community/NRAC/perform/longwayhome/. The play runs from mid-June to the end of August, Thurs.-Sun. at 8:30 p.m. Ticket prices ($10 adult, $5 children 12 and under) include a tour of Mary's cabin and a short walk down a section of the Wilderness Road to Ingles Ferry Landing.

At the College

Virginia Tech **football** is almost a way of life for die-hard fans, who nearly keeled over with joy in 1995 when the hometown Hokies capped their best season ever with a victory over Texas in the Sugar Bowl. Games against the archrival Cavaliers of the University of Virginia fill parking lots at either school with tailgate parties and boisterous alumni. For tickets, call (540) 231-6931

Art happenings on campus range from nationally known musicians and speakers to Virginia Tech's Theater Arts Programs and Audubon Quartet. Call the main campus number, tel. (540) 231-6000, for a current schedule.

Outdoors

Both **Blue Ridge Outdoors,** 211 Draper Rd., tel. (540) 552-9012, and **Back County Ski & Sports,** 3710 South Main St., tel. (540) 552-6400, sell outdoor gear and can provide you with information on outfitters in the area.

MOUNTAIN LAKE AND VICINITY

In the shadow of 4,200-foot Bald Knob, Mountain Lake is Virginia's highest—and one of only two natural lakes in the state (the other lies in the Great Dismal Swamp). No one is quite sure how it formed here, at 4,000 feet, high enough to record the lowest temperatures in the state (it hit -30° F in 1985). One theory holds that a small rockslide blocked a natural outlet sometime during the late 19th century, back when the spot was called Salt Pond by farmers looking for salt for their cattle.

Mountain Lake Resort

It was also around the late 19th century that the first hotel was built on the shore of the chilly lake, providing lodging for people making the east-west trip through the mountains. In the hands of the Porterfield family near the turn of the century, the hotel became known as a luxury stop. Guests were allowed to build their own cottages until the main stone lodge was built in 1936. The movie *Dirty Dancing* was filmed here in 1986, two years after major renovations, and brought the hotel's classic mountain character to the attention of the world.

Guests have no excuse to cry boredom. The daily roster overflows with things to do, starting with hikes on a network of trails of different difficulty levels around the lake and into the surrounding hills. You can wander to the Mountain Lake Biological Station, run by the University of Virginia, or as far as Minnie Ball Hill, named for small-caliber Civil War cannonballs still found here a century and a half after a Union general abandoned his supply wagons because his horses couldn't pull them up the steep grade. Some trails are open to mountain bikes, which are available for rent—as is equipment for volleyball, horseshoes, and croquet.

During warmer months, the small sandy beach is packed with swimmers, while the farther reaches of the lake are open to boats and canoes. Relaxation comes in the form of massages at the health spa, a day camp for the children, or simply enjoying the view from a deck chair while families compete at lawn chess nearby.

While you're browsing the row of shops and galleries, notice Bob Evans' whittled wooden Nobbits ("cousins to Hobbits"). He bases them on the German legend of Wurtzelgrabbers (root diggers), said to run around carving their own likenesses out of roots and leaving them on the doorsteps of friends to bring good luck. At the height of fall comes Oktoberfest, with Teutonic food, beer, and live polka music.

Rates: Rooms start at $115 d, with suites available for $145-235. Cottages come with one bedroom ($95-155), two ($150-285), or three ($200-335). For reservations and information contact, Mountain Lake Hotel, 115 Hotel Circle, Pembroke, VA 24136, tel. (800) 346-3334.

To get here, take US 460 west (actually north) from Blacksburg, turning right onto Rt. 700, a precipitous backroad that winds through seven gorgeous miles of rural Virginia. As you chug uphill, keep in mind that this was included in a recent Tour De Pont bicycle race as a Category One climb—as hard as it gets.

Near Mountain Lake
This corner of the state conceals one of the wilder chunks of the Jefferson National Forest,

marked by high, windswept ridges blanketed with hemlock and spruce. Steep ravines within the 10,000-acre **Mountain Lake Wilderness** conceal stands of centuries-old white oak, with mushrooms, bogs, and berry bushes in more moderate valleys. The **Peters Mountain Wilderness** spreads farther north to intersect with the Appalachian Trail, skirting the West Virginia border near the **White Rocks Recreation Area** off Rt. 613. All three wild areas are open only to primitive camping. For more information, contact the Blacksburg Ranger District of the Jefferson National Forest, 110 Southpark Dr. in Blacksburg, tel. (540) 552-4641.

A few miles west of the Mountain Lake turnoff waits the **Cascades Recreation Area,** known for a four-mile loop trail up Little Stony Creek Gorge. Wooden bridges span the creek as the trail climbs through hemlocks and birch trees to a 60-foot waterfall. Trout fishing is good in the creek. To get here, take a right turn (north) off US 460 onto Rt. 623 in Pembroke, following signs four miles to the Recreation Area.

NEW RIVER VALLEY

WYTHEVILLE

First of all, it's pronounced "WITH-vul," and has been ever since the town was incorporated in 1839 along the Wilderness Road (part of which serves as modern Main Street). During the Civil War, Wytheville saw plenty of action, as troops from both sides passed through on a regular basis. A Union attack in 1863 was beaten back by a local militia, but by the end of the war most of the town lay in ruins.

Sights
Whytheville's two museums sit next to each other near the intersection of Monroe and Tazewell Streets. The **Rock House Museum,** tel. (540) 223-3330, was built of limestone in 1823 and served as a hospital during the Civil War—bloodstains are still visible on the floor of one of the second-story bedrooms, along with a bullet hole in a front parlor window frame. Inside are heirlooms from the Haller-Gibboney family, who owned the house for a century and half. Out back, an herb garden showcases plants used for medicine in

the 1800s. Open Wed.-Fri. 10 a.m.-3 p.m., plus Saturday noon-4 p.m. from July-Aug.; $2 adults, $1 children. Tours are given April-Oct.

The historical collection in the **Thomas J. Boyd Museum,** 295 Tazewell St., includes the towns' first fire truck (1855), Civil War uniforms, and hands-on displays of local history for children. Hours, admission, and telephone number are the same as for the Rock House.

Accommodations
The **Travel Lite Motel,** 655 E. Main St. tel. (540) 228-5574, is the most central and least expensive. Look for the pink doors near 7th St. Budget. The **Boxwood Inn Bed & Breakfast,** 460 E. Main St., tel. (540) 228-8911, falls in the moderate category, along with the **Best Western Wytheville Inn,** 355 Nye Rd., tel. (540) 228-7300, fax 228-4223, and the **Holiday Inn,** 1800 E. Main St., tel. (540) 228-5483, fax 228-5417.

Just east of town is the **Wytheville KOA Kampground,** tel. (540) 228-2601. To get there take exit 77 off I-81/I-77, then head south half a mile on Rt. 758. Year-round sites are $20-24, and Kamping Kabins are $25-35. The U.S. For-

SOUTHWESTERN VIRGINIA AREA CLIMATE

SNOWFALL — MAXIMUM TEMP.
RAINFALL — MINIMUM TEMP.

est Service maintains the **Stony Fork Campground,** tel. (540) 228-5551, eight miles north on US 52 and 0.3 miles east on Rt. 717. Fifty-three sites cost $8 each.

Food
The **1776 Log House Restaurant,** tel. (540) 228-4139, preserves a touch of creaky country charm at 520 E. Main St. After your meal (entrées cost $8-11), wander to the gardens out back, where you'll find crafts shops and Fran's Deli. At exit 73 off I-81 is **Mom's Country Store Restaurant,** tel. (540) 228-4379. Sugar-baked ham, country-fried steak and eggs—you get the picture.

Shopping
Both **Snooper's Antique & Craft Mall,** tel. (540) 637-6441, and the **Old Fort Antique Mall,** tel. (540) 228-GIFT, are located on the service road between exits 77 and 80 off I-81. They're both

open daily year-round, stocking industrial quantities of antiques, collectibles and snacks.

Information
The **Wytheville-Bland Chamber of Commerce,** tel. (540) 223-3360 or 223-3365, fax 223-3315, e-mail: chamber@naxs.com, Web site: www. wytheville.org/chamber, runs an information center in the city municipal offices at 150 E. Monroe St. at 1st, open Mon.-Fri. 8 a.m.-5 p.m. For details on the many hikes in the Jefferson National Forest north of town, stop by the **Wytheville Ranger District** office, 155 Sherwood Forest Rd., tel. (540) 228-5551.

Near Wytheville
North of town the Appalachians crest with surprising speed, forcing I-77 to dive into a tunnel through Big Walker Mountain within a few miles. A small loop beginning at exit 47 has been deemed a Scenic Byway: take Rt. 717 west to the junction with US 52, which you'll climb to the **Big Walker Lookout,** tel. (540) 228-4401, e-mail: scenicbeauty@naxs.som. The 100-foot tower sits at 3,405 feet, commanding an Olympian view of the surrounding hills. Admission tickets ($2.50 adults, $1.50 children) are sold in the combination gift shop and deli at the base. Open April-Memorial Day, Thurs.-Sun. 10 a.m.-5 p.m.; Memorial Day-Labor Day, Tues.-Sun. 10 a.m.-6 p.m., and Tues.-Sun. 10 a.m.-5 p.m. in September and

JULIAN SMITH

Walker Mountain Baptist Church

THE BIRTHPLACE OF MOUNTAIN DEW AND DR. PEPPER

Southwest Virginia claims parenthood of not one, but two famous soft drinks within miles of each other. Mountain Dew was created about midway between Wytheville and Abingdon, in Marion (I-81 exit 45), where its original spokesman was a hillbilly shouting, "Ya-hoo, Mountain Dew!" Every Fourth of July, a Chili Cookoff and Mountain Dew Day celebrates the soda.

Just up the highway, at exit 60, pharmacist Dr. Charles Pepper was experimenting with caramel-flavored soda water in the Rural Retreat Drug Store (now a flower shop), but, as the story goes, his young assistant fled for Texas with the formula after falling in love with one of the pharmacist's daughters. He did, however, eventually name the final product in honor of his former employer.

October. Afterward, dispel your vertigo by following US 52 north and east back to I-77, crossing Walker Creek along the way.

GALAX

Early Scots-Irish settlers would have been proud to know that their fiddles and bagpipes still echo in Galax (GAY-lacks), the current World Capital of Old Time Mountain Music. The quiet village is brought to raucous life during the annual **Old Time Fiddler's Convention and Fiddlefest,** the oldest (inaugurated in 1935) and largest mountain music convention in the country. The clack of clogs and the slap of flatfoot combine with the usual arts, crafts, and food booths the second weekend of August.

For more information, contact the Old Fiddler's Convention, P.O. Box 655, Galax, VA 2433, tel. (540) 236-8541, or the **Galax-Carroll-Grayson Chamber of Commerce,** 405 N. Main St., tel. (540) 236-2184.

Sights
Turn off the US 58/221 strip (a.k.a. E. Stuart Dr.) onto Main Street to the center of town to reach the massive brick **Grayson County Courthouse,**

built near the turn of the century when the town first sprang to life as Bonaparte. From Main Street, head west on Oldtown St., then south on Old Stuart Dr. to reach the **Jeff Matthews Museum,** 606 W. Stuart Dr., tel. (540) 236-7874. Barely across the threshold you're accosted by the biggest stuffed bear you've ever seen, an 8.5-foot Kodiak grizzly from Alaska, presiding over enough animal carcasses to stock a taxidermy shop. Set aside a few hours to browse through everything a turn-of-the-century family (or three) would need to survive, including a fully stocked country store, a 1902 Sears & Roebuck catalog, an 1899 map of Virginia, over 1,000 knives, and an 800-pound whetstone. Don't miss the antique hair curler, straight out of a Frankenstein movie. Two reconstructed cabins out back, furnished with period artifacts, date to the mid-19th century. Open Wednesday, Thursday, Friday 1-5 p.m., Saturday 11 a.m.-4 p.m., Sunday 1-4 p.m.; free, but donations are welcome.

This end of the **New River Trail State Park** can be entered from the intersection of US 58/221 and Thomas George Vaughan Jr. Rd.

Accommodations and Food
Pickings are slim. Both the **Knights Inn,** 312 W. Stuart Dr., tel. (540) 236-5117, fax 236-0652, and the **Super 8,** 303 N. Main St., at Washington, tel. (540) 236-5127, have rooms in the budget range. Cheap camping is possible in the **Crooked Creek Wildlife Management Area,** three miles east of town.

The **Country Line Cafe,** 956 E. Stuart Dr., tel. (540) 236-3201, is also a deli, open daily at 6 a.m. for breakfast. A reasonably authentic Mexican meal runs $6-10 at **Tloquepaque,** 500 E. Stuart Dr. at Caldwell, tel. (540) 236-5060.

NEW RIVER TRAIL STATE PARK

This flagship example of a new kind of park, called a greenway, protects a 40-mile stretch of the misnamed waterway and her banks. For just over 50 miles, from Galax to Pulaski, you'll find people hiking, biking, riding horseback, and skiing down the old railroad bed, with occasional stops to fish or admire the cliffs and forest along the river.

Park headquarters, tel. (540) 699-6778, are in **Shot Tower Historical State Park,** 17 miles south of Wytheville by either I-77 (exit 24) or US

52. Here, a 70-foot tower was used in the 19th century for making lead rifle shot. From the top, molten metal was poured down through the tower and a 75-foot shaft beneath into a kettle of water at the bottom. The perfectly round balls were then recovered through a horizontal tunnel from the river's edge. Parking ($1) and restrooms are available at the base of the tower, and a loop trail gives access to the New River Trail ($2 adults, $1 children). Open daily April-Nov., 8 a.m.-dusk. Tours are given weekends and holidays from Memorial Day-Labor Day.

Seven other access points stretch along the river from Galax (see below) to Draper on I-81 near Pulaski.

Outfitters

In Wytheville, **New River Adventures,** 1007 N. 4th St., tel. (540) 228-8311, has a full-service bike shop and backpacking and fishing equipment for sale. Daily rental of bikes ($15), canoes ($30), kayaks ($30), and inner tubes ($10) should about cover it. For shuttle service, add another $10. Overnight canoe and fishing trips can be arranged. They have an outlet near Shot Tower State Park. **New River Bicycles,** in Draper, tel. (540) 980-1741, rents bikes by the day ($15) and half-day ($10), and also has a shuttle service.

Guided fishing trips for smallmouth bass are $125 pp (two minimum) with **Tangent Outfitters,** 1055 Norwood St., Radford, tel. (540) 674-5202. Canoe rentals range from $30 per day to $110 per week, and they organize combination bike/canoe trips for $55 pp per day. **New River Canoe and Campground, Inc.,** on US 21 4 miles south of Independence, tel. (540) 773-3412, rents canoes ($35 including shuttle service) and offers tent sites ($12) and cabins ($22) along the river. Near the entrance to Shot Tower the **Cherry Creek Cyclery & More,** tel./fax (540) 699-2385, e-mail: shop@cccyclery.com, Web site: www.cccyclery.com, has a bike shop, with snacks and fishing supplies for sale.

MOUNT ROGERS
NATIONAL RECREATION AREA

To some people—especially residents of the western U.S.—the idea of a "wilderness" back east tends to elicit mild scoffs. Places such as the Mount Rogers National Recreation Area, though, prove that there are still spots this side of the Mississippi as wild and gorgeous as any in the country. Throughout the 120,000 acres of the area, massive stone protrusions called balds jut skyward from high, wild alpine meadows ringed by fir and spruce forests.

Within the Recreation Area tower Virginia's two tallest mountains. Mt. Rogers (5,729 feet), near the center of the Lewis Fork Wilderness, is covered with enough trees to block any sweeping vistas from the top. Whitetop Mountain (5,344 feet) is more representative of the gently rounded "southern balds" found in Georgia and North Carolina. Some of the best views in the region come from the top of Wilburn Ridge, a mile from Mt. Rogers. Named for an 18th-centruy hermit and bear hunter, the ridge offers views stretching up to 100 miles.

Hiking

Bring your boots. More than 70 hiking trails creep through the area, offering 400 miles of easy-to-difficult wandering. Most famous of these paths is the **Virginia Creeper National Recreation Trail,** which winds 34 miles along Whitetop Laurel Creek from Abingdon through Damascus to Whitetop Station at the North Carolina line. What began centuries ago as an Indian footpath had been claimed as a railroad bed by the turn of the century. Timber and passengers were ferried from Abingdon to West Jefferson, North Carolina, up grades so steep the engines would slow to a crawl—hence the name.

The last train whistle split the forest silence in 1977, and since then the Virginia Creeper has become a shining example of the nationwide rails-to-trails initiative. It's relatively flat from Abingdon to Damascus—and packed with hikers and horseback riders on weekends. Mountain bikers love to drive to the top of White's Mountain and glide back toward Abingdon. For more information on the trail, contact the Abingdon visitor center or the Virginia Creeper Trail Club, P.O. Box 2382, Abingdon, VA 24210, tel. (540) 783-5196.

Along with the Creeper, the Appalachian Trail snakes through the entire Recreation Area, 64 miles from end to end. The nine-mile Mt. Rogers trail is difficult and doesn't reward you with a view at the end.

Other Recreation and Events

Although some of the best riding around is found in Grayson Highlands State Park (see below), Mt. Rogers offers the **Virginia Highlands Horse Trail,** running the entire length of the Recreation Area. It's maintained by the Virginia Horse Council, P.O. Box 72, Riner, VA 24149, tel. (540) 783-5196. Horses are also permitted on the Virginia Creeper Trail and the Iron Mountain Trail within the boundaries of the Recreation Area (the Virginia Highlands Horse Trail lies just outside). Mountain bikes are welcome on many of the same trails.

Even if you don't get out of your car, you can still enjoy the prettiest drive in this part of the state. The **Mount Rogers Scenic Byway,** consisting of 34 miles of US 58 from Damascus to Volney, earns the title of highest road in Virginia as it climbs the flank of Whitetop. A 23-mile side branch of Rt. 603 to Volney passes closer to Mt Rogers itself. Anglers can find trout in Hale Lake and 14-acre Beartree Lake, which also has a small sandy beach for swimming. Whitetop Laurel Creek is popular with fly-casters.

In late March, the **Whitetop Mountain Maple Festival,** tel. (540) 388-3294, brings two weekends of country music, maple-tapping demonstrations, art and crafts, and food. The **Mount Rogers Ramp Festival,** tel. (540) 388-3257, salutes the ramp, a wild relative of the onion, the third weekend in May. This often coincides with the **Mount Rogers Naturalist Rally,** tel. (540) 783-2125, with speakers and guided hikes.

Outfitters

In Damascus, the **Blue Blaze Bike and Shuttle Service,** tel. (540) 475-5095, e-mail: blueblaze@naxs.com, rents mountain bikes ($15-20 half day, $25-30 full day) and runs a bike shuttle service departing on Saturday and Sunday. Also in Damascus are **Mount Rogers Outfitters,** tel. (800) 337-5416 or (540) 475-5416, offering the same services plus backpacking gear, and **Virginia Creeper Bike Rental,** tel. (540) 475-5416, with canoes, cross-country skis, and fishing and backpacking equipment.

The **Mount Rogers High Country Outdoor Center,** on Rt. 603 near Troutdale, tel. (540) 677-3900, is a family-run business with guided day and overnight trips on foot, horseback, or in covered wagons. **Virginia Creeper Fly Fishing,** on US 58 just south of the intersection of I-81 and US 11, Abingdon, tel. (540) 628-3826, has guides and gear available and runs float trips. If you didn't happen to bring your own horse, consider a trip aboard a South American camelid with **Treasure Mountain Farm Llama Trekking,** 10436 Echo Lane, Glade Spring, VA 24340, tel. (540) 944-4674 or 628-4710, running $60 per day including lunch.

Camping

The Recreation Area has 10 camping areas, eight of which charge a fee. Most have water but only three have showers. Three camps—Fox Creek, Raven Cliff, and Hussy Mountain—are linked by the Virginia Highlands Horse Trail and have equestrian facilities. For reservations at any call (800) 933-7275.

Information

The **W. Pat Jennings Visitor Center,** tel. (800) 628-7202 or (540) 783-5196, sits off Rt. 16 six miles south of Marion (I81 exit 45). It's open 8 a.m.-4:30 p.m., daily in season and Mon.-Fri. year-round. In Damascus there's a small information station called the Caboose.

Grayson Highlands State Park

On the southern side of the Mount Rogers National Recreation Area is this hidden gem, a horse-lover's paradise off US 58 just west of Volney. Virginia's only state park with horse camping facilities has 25 campsites and stalls for over 50 horses. Special orange-blaze equestrian trails climb Haw Orchard Mountain—named for the prickly hawthorne trees found there in abundance—for 360-degree views from Big Pinnacle and Little Pinnacle.

The wingbeats of wild turkeys thunder in the underbrush, while wild ponies—part of a herd of 150 released years ago—may sidle up looking for handouts. The ponies are rounded up twice a year and checked for disease, and some are sold through a public auction during the **Grayson Highlands Fall Harvest Festival** at the end of September, which also includes Appalachian crafts and music

A day-use fee of $1 ($2 on weekends) allows access to Grayson Highlands; campsites cost $11 per night ($15 with hookups). Information is available from park headquarters in Mouth of Wilson, tel. (540) 579-7092, where they can also tell you about rock climbing, rappelling, and backpacking courses offered for $95 per person.

Maps

Two topographical maps cover both areas: the 1:24,000 "Mount Rogers High Country and Wilderness" ($3.25) and the less detailed "Mount Rogers National Recreation Area Sports Map" ($4.25). Both are available through the US Forest Service, tel. (800) 628-7202.

ABINGDON

As the oldest English-speaking settlement west of the Blue Ridge Mountains, Abingdon is the genteel nexus of southwest Virginia, a town very aware and proud of its history. Abingdon centers on the historic streets of Main—split into East and West at Court Street—and Valley, more residential but just as charming. In places it seems as though every building along the rolling brick sidewalks is an antique, either original or restored to its former grandeur through the careful ministrations of its latest owners. Along with two of southwest Virginia's biggest draws—the Barter Theater and the Martha Washington Inn—Abingdon is the nearest town of substance to the Mt. Rogers National Recreation Area, making this quiet burg of about 7,000 one of the area's most popular destinations.

HISTORY

Abingdon's first name, Wolf Hills, came during a visit by Daniel Boone in 1760, when a group of wolves attacked the dogs in his hunting party near where the town is today. The name stuck until 1774, when Joseph Black erected Black's Fort on this site to protect hundreds of local settlers from Cherokee raids. Abingdon proper, named for Martha Washington's home parish, in Oxfordshire, England, was established two years later as the seat of Washington County.

The early 19th century saw Abingdon bloom into a focal point of southwest Virginia, handling most of the mail and traffic to the western frontier along the Wilderness Road. It escaped the damage of the Civil War until December 1864, when 10,000 Federal troops under the command of Gen. George Stoneman burned a number of buildings, including the depot and the town jail, that were being used to store Confederate supplies. Over the years, other fires have claimed other historic structures, but many more still remain standing.

SIGHTS

A good place to start your stroll down Main St. is at **The Arts Depot,** tel. (540) 628-9091, in Depot Square at W. Main St. and Russell Rd. Built in the late 19th century as a loading point for the Virginia & Tennessee Railroad, the old freight station was abandoned for years before being rescued and claimed by Abingdon's visual, performing, and literary artists. You can watch artists at work in their studios, browse the sales galleries, or attend various workshops and lectures held throughout the year. Both the Sow's Ear

the Washington County Courthouse in Abingdon

Press and the Appalachian Center for Poets and Writers operate out of the building, too. Open Thurs.-Sat. 11 a.m.-3 p.m.

More exhibits and classes are held in the **William King Regional Art Center,** 415 Academy Dr., tel. (540) 628-5005. An affiliate of the Virginia Museum of Fine Arts, the center concentrates on the artistic heritage of Appalachia but also hosts the works of national artists along the lines of Ansel Adams, Andrew Wyeth, and Winslow Homer. Open Tuesday, Wednesday, and Friday 10 a.m.-5 p.m., Thursday 10 a.m.-9 p.m., Saturday 10 a.m.-3 p.m., and Sunday 1-5 p.m.; suggested admission $3 pp.

Head east to the **Fields-Penn House,** at 208 W. Main St., tel. (540) 676-0216. James Fields built many of the homes in the area in the mid-19th century, including the Washington County Courthouse farther down Main St. This building dates to 1860 and was home to Fields and his wife, their eight children, and a maiden Aunt Jane. It's now a period museum open April-Dec., Wed.-Sat. 1-4 p.m.

A block away stands **Camberley's Martha Washington Inn,** one of the town's outstanding landmarks (and a functioning inn). Across the street is Abingdon's other landmark, the **Barter Theater.**

East Main Street starts to dip and rise as it reaches the old commercial and administrative center of town. Soon you'll pass the **Washington County Courthouse,** the fifth such building to stand at Main St. and Court St. This one was built in 1869 and boasts a WW I-memorial stained glass window designed by the Tiffany studio. In the "jockey lot" behind the courthouse, horse merchants used to gather on the first Saturday of each month while court was in session for a boisterous day of trading and gambling (women and children were encouraged to keep their distance).

A short walk farther brings you past **The Tavern,** Abingdon's oldest building and finest restaurant. It'll take a bit longer to get to **White's Mill,** 12291 White's Mill Rd., tel. (540) 676-0285. Southwest Virginia's only remaining water-powered grist mill sits a short drive or moderate bicycle ride into the countryside north of town. Built around 1840, it's painfully photogenic and literally redolent of history, with a great musty smell, creaking floorboards, and antique ma-

White's Mill is Virginia's last remaining water-powered grist mill.

chinery filling four floors. It's open more or less regularly (free, though donations are welcome) and still grinds flour and cornmeal offered for sale across the street in White's Mill Mercantile.

ACCOMMODATIONS

Camberley's Martha Washington Inn

Known locally as "the Martha," this gargantuan structure, tel. (540) 628-3161, fax 628-8885, fills an entire block of W. Main St. with true colonial class. It began in 1832 as the home of Gen. Francis Preston, who built the original central brick structure for himself and his family. Preston made his fortune on the nearby salt mines, allowing him to shell out $15,000—a huge sum at the time—for the construction. In 1858, the building became the Martha Washington College, a high-class school for young women.

During the Civil War, students served as nurses for soldiers wounded in skirmishes near Abingdon, and the Martha became a makeshift hospital while the Washington Mounted Rifles trained on the grounds outside. By 1934, the place had become a true hotel, housing actors in town for productions at the Barter Theater and such presidential luminaries as Harry Truman, Eleanor Roosevelt, Lady Bird Johnson, and Jimmy Carter. An $8 million renovation in 1984 transformed the Martha into a fully modern luxury inn while preserving much of the original architecture and antebellum appeal.

The building's changing roles over the years reverberate through the various rooms. The west parlor, formerly the master bedroom, became a study hall for the college. The lobby was the original family dining room before serving as the school library. On Washington's birthday, student belles would descend the central staircase in full colonial costume to dance the Virginia reel in the parlors.

Antique treasures wait around almost every corner Notice the marble fireplaces, crystal chandeliers, and the beautiful paintings in the Grand Ballroom, formerly the school chapel. Other paintings on the walls of the entranceway are copies of ones in the White House, depicting Niagara Falls, Natural Bridge, Boston Harbor, West Point, and New York City as they looked in the 1830s. Oscar Bachtecit, designer of Rockefeller Center in Manhattan, fashioned the 16-foot brass and silver table in the dining room. The oval glass weighs 300 pounds, and the entire table has been appraised at $100,000. For more history—including a few hotel ghost stories—track down Pete Sheffey, a walking encyclopedia of Martha lore who has served as a bellhop for the past three decades.

Fifty-one rooms and 10 suites are filled with rich fabrics and antiques. Luxury rates include daily continental breakfast and afternoon tea on weekends. Some suites have fireplaces and jacuzzis.

Inexpensive

The classic 1960s-era **Alpine Motel**, 822 E. Main St., tel. (540) 628-3178, fax 628-4217, offers well-kept rooms with mountain views and cable TV. For a more generic stay, there are the **Comfort Inn Abingdon**, 170 Jonesboro Rd., tel. (540) 676-2222, fax. 576-2222, and a **Super 8**, 282 Towne Center Dr., tel./fax (540) 676-3329.

Moderate and Up

Joyce Ferratt was born in the same house in which she and her husband, Jack, now operate the **Shepherd's Joy Bed & Breakfast,** 254 White's Mill Rd., tel. (540)-628-3273. The friendly couple runs a small sheep farm out back, complete with well-trained sheep dogs. The house is decorated with family heirlooms and a sheep motif. Just next door, the **White Birches Inn,** 268 White's Mill Rd., tel. (800) BIRCHES (800-247-2437) or (540) 676-2140, fax 676-2146, e-mail: whitebirches@naxs.com, Web site: www.whitebirchesinn.com, features three rooms named after playwrights who traded words for food at the Barter Theater: Tennessee Williams, Thornton Wilder, and Noël Coward. Just off the back porch, a small pond is stocked with koi and goldfish.

The **Victoria and Albert Inn,** 224 Oak Hill St., tel. (540) 676-2797, e-mail: v&ainn@naxs.com, Web site: www.naxs.com/victoria&albertinn, sits across from the town library. It was built in 1892 and features rooms named for the deep colors of their walls: blue, raspberry, gold, and burgundy.

Rates: $75-120. A large front deck graces the **Summerfield Inn B&B,** 101 West Valley St., Abingdon, VA 24201, tel. (540) 28-5905 or (800) 668-5905, e-mail: suminn@naxs.com., Web site: www.naxs.com/abingdon/suminn. The entire house is sunny and spacious, with four large rooms in the main Parsonage and three more-modern ones in the newer Cottage, featuring whirlpools. Rates for some rooms rise to premium.

The original **Crooked Cabin** at 303 E. Main St., tel. (540) 628-9583, was built in 1780, making it one of Abingdon's oldest buildings. Today it's a cozy, self-contained cottage appointed with antiques and quilts, featuring three bedrooms, a dining room, and a patio and garden out back. Prices start at $185 per night for up to six people and include continental breakfast. Other meals can be arranged from the Abingdon General Store next door.

Camping

The **Riverside Campground,** tel. (540) 628-5333, sits seven miles north of town on Rt. 19, then two miles east on Rt. 611. Eighty tent and RV sites ($14-18) are open April-Oct.

THE SALTVILLE MASSACRE

Not as visible as men or munitions but almost as important, salt played a major role in the Civil War. It was used in medicine and gunpowder, and to preserve meat for army rations. Only two spots in the entire South produced significant amounts—one mine near Atlanta and one here, the "Salt Capital of the Confederacy."

Saltville also saw one of the war's worst massacres, on October 3, 1864. The day before, about 3,600 Union troops—including 400 members of the U.S. Colored Cavalry—had been beaten back repeatedly as they tried to take the town from 2,800 ragtag Confederates under Capt. Champ Ferguson and Brig. Gen. Felix Robertson. By nightfall, hundreds of Federal wounded covered the ground after the rest had retreated.

The next morning, Confederate soldiers advanced across the field, shooting black soldiers as they lay helpless. It's uncertain exactly how many were killed this way, but accounts from both sides put the total at well over 100.

Union troops managed to occupy and level much of the town within a few months, but justice took time. Ferguson was eventually captured, tried, and hanged for murder in October 1865. Robertson, amazingly, not only escaped punishment but lived well into the 20th century. He died, the last surviving Confederate general, in 1928.

FOOD

Starters and Light Fare

The **Virginia Creeper Bakery,** 284 W. Main St., tel. (540) 623-BAKE (540-623-2253), offers a wide range of baked goods and coffees. The specialty is breads—the gingerbread with lemon sauce is excellent. A gift shop and gourmet deli fill **The Abingdon General Store and Gallery, Inc.,** 301 E Main St., tel. (540) 628-8382, fax 623-1414. Fresh ingredients fill the sandwiches in the deli, while farther back are two restaurants open in different seasons: the Plum Alley Eatery, downstairs, opens for the summer, and the Dumbwaiter, upstairs, serves during winter. Prices range $4-8.

Vegetarians and carnivores alike say that the **Secret Garden Restaurant,** 130 Pecan St., tel.

(540) 623-1111, is worth discovering (open Tues.-Sat., reservations accepted). It's inside **Max and Kathy's International Gourmet,** the largest gourmet food market in the area with hundreds of kinds of beers and wine. If the walk down Main St. has you overheated and peckish, stop by the **Carriage Creamery** at 153 W. Main St., a brightly colored wagon with a full menu of ice cream confections.

More Substantial

Typical American fare fills the bill at the **Hardware Company Restaurant,** 260 W. Main St., tel. (540) 628-1111. Sandwiches run $4-7, and dinner entrées $7-18. The great old wooden bar, decorated with brass and old signs, is open until midnight for aprés-Barter drinks. The **Hunan Restaurant,** 558 Cummings St., tel. (540) 676-2875, is in a shopping center near I-81 exit 17. Here the service is gracious, the prices reasonable, and the food tasty.

Serious Dining

Abingdon's oldest building (and that's saying something) houses **The Tavern,** serving excellent continental food with a German flair. It was built in 1779 as a tavern and overnight stop for stagecoach traffic on the Wilderness Road. President Andrew Jackson and Louis Phillippe, king of France, were both among the many guests. The first post office west of the Blue Ridge operated out of the east wing, where the mail slot is still visible in the door.

Over the years the building passed through various incarnations as a private residence, general store, bank, barber shop, bakery, and, oh yes, tavern. During the Civil War, wounded soldiers from both armies were tended to on the third floor—the charcoal numbers for each bed are still visible on the plaster walls. In 1984, it was restored using original materials and techniques, including hand-forged hinges, hand-planed lumber, and handmade bricks in the two-foot walls. It was reopened in 1994 by German native Max Harmann with his wife, Kathy, from nearby Damascus. Tilted tables, rustic fixtures, low ceilings, and dark worn wood evoke the informal air of an old tavern, but the food is excellent. German standbys like wiener schnitzel and kasseler rippchen occupy the menu along with salmon, jam-

balaya, and ostrich. Prices range $7.50 for lunch sandwiches to about $15 for dinner entrées.

On one corner of Depot Square, the **Starving Artist Cafe,** 134 Wall St., tel. (540) 628-8445, displays works by local artists as a background to a high-powered menu featuring seafood and some sandwiches. Dinner entrées range $10-23. With the layout of a deli but the feel of a Soho bistro, the cafe belies its name.

ENTERTAINMENT AND RECREATION

Barter Theatre

In 1933, aspiring but frustrated Virginia actor Robert Porterfield opened a theater in this structure, built in 1832 as a church on W. Main St. and College St., with the novel idea of bringing theater to the masses. Not only would hungry, out-of-work actors and playwrights be given a place to perform their works, but theatergoers short of the cash for a ticket could exchange produce for seats. Playwrights would be given a Virginia ham for the use of their works. The barter system caught on, and farmers and townspeople began exchanging "hams for Hamlet" along with, perhaps, cabbages for Coward and spinach for Shaw (who was a vegetarian). The first season's profits amounted to $4.35 in cash, two barrels of jelly, and a collective weight gain among the actors of over 300 pounds.

Declared the State Theater of Virginia, the Barter stage has hosted stars including Ernest Borgnine, Gregory Peck, and Kevin Spacey over the decades, making it the longest-running professional repertory theater in the country. Productions, including many world premieres, range from musicals to farce and Shakespeare. Between productions, storytellers take the stage to entertain children. Visitors hail from around the world; the guests coming the longest distance receive a door prize every evening. Tickets run $16-24 for adults, $2 less for children, and any unsold seats go for $10 to students 15 minutes before the curtain goes up. Major renovations (to the tune of $1.7 million) in the mid-1990s resulted in a vastly improved—yet still intimate—theater. Call the box office at (800) 368-3240 or (540) 628-3991, for information and ticket sales.

Tours

Horse-drawn carriage tours of historic Abingdon cost $5 pp for 25 minutes, leaving Wed.-Sun. Sign up at the Carriage Creamery or phone (540) 669-6522.

Outdoor Recreation

The western end of the **Virginia Creeper Trail** starts off Pecan Alley just across the train tracks, near the huge Norfolk and Virginia locomotive—the last one to run these rails. **Highlands Ski & Outdoor Center,** on E. Main St., tel. (540) 628-1329 or 628-9672, rents full-suspension mountain bikes for $30 per day or $20 per half-day. It also stocks camping, hiking, and climbing gear for anyone eager to tackle Mt. Rogers.

EVENTS

As if it didn't already have enough going for it, Abingdon also hosts one of the top 100 tourist events in North America, known as the **Virginia Highlands Festival.** Officially a showcase for Appalachian musicians, artists, craftspeople, and writers, the festival—held for two weeks near the beginning of August—features one of the largest antique markets in the southeast, wine-tasting, garden workshops, and a hot-air balloon rally. For kids, there's storytelling, writing workshops, puppetry, and interactive theater.

Get down to music from rock to swing, funk to Celtic, in between sampling food from around the world and choosing your favorites from the exhibits of local and national artists. About 200,000 people pack the town during the festival, so make reservations as early as possible.

During the second week in September, the **Washington County Fair and Burley Tobacco Festival** brings country music and the sounds of livestock to the fairground on US 11 west of town. Carnival rides, tractor pulls, and the Miss Washington County pageant round out the fun.

Call the Abingdon Convention and Visitors Bureau for more information on either festival.

SHOPPING

Close to a dozen antique shops line Main St. in the center of town. The largest is probably the **Highlands Antique Mall,** 246 W. Main, tel. (540) 676-4438. Craftaholics shouldn't miss the **Cave House Crafts Shop,** 279 E. Main St., tel. (540) 628-7721, named for the cave beneath the store, from which, according to legend, the wolves that attacked Daniel Boone's dogs emerged. The historic home, built in 1858, was used in the 1950s and 1960s to house Barter Theater actors and is graced with a three-story walnut stair railing and a solid burled walnut mantel. In 1971, the Holston Mountain Arts and Crafts Cooperative moved in and began selling crafts of every description: quilts, musical instruments, clothing, baskets, pottery, and toys, to name a few.

Across from the Martha, **153 West Booksellers & Gallery,** 153 W Main St., tel. (540) 628-1232 (bookstore) and 628-4506 (gallery), exhibits fine handicrafts, especially pottery, alongside a peaceful bookstore. **Dixie Pottery** is a warehouse full of crafts and pottery—enough to justify the slogan, "Shop the World." It's five miles south of the center of Abingdon on US 11, near I-81 exit 13. It's open daily but there's no phone number—just stop on by.

INFORMATION AND TRANSPORTATION

The Abingdon Convention and Visitors Bureau runs a **visitors center** at 335. W. Cummings St., tel. (800) 435-3440 or (540) 676-2282, fax 676-3076, e-mail: acvb@naxs.com, Web site: www.naxs.com/abingdon/tourism.

Greyhound has a station at 465 W. Main St., tel. (540) 628-4409.

FAR SOUTHWEST

TAZEWELL AND VICINITY

From Marion, drive north on Rt. 16—a gorgeous corkscrew of a road—to the hub of Tazewell (TAZ-wul) County, incorporated in 1866 after a fistfight settled a dispute over where to establish the local government seat. Before, between, or after visiting the two sights in the area, stop by the **Piggy Bank Cafe**, tel. (540) 988-2560, on Main St. in the Old Clinch Balley Bank building—which explains the Prime Rate Burger, Default Dog, and BLT (Bank Loan Transaction).

Crab Orchard Museum and Pioneer Park of Southwestern Virginia

Nearly every phase of the state's history finds a voice on this 110-acre archaeological site, three miles west of Tazewell on US 19/460, tel. (540) 988-6755. Mastodon fossils and frontier furniture and weapons fill the central gallery building, while the nearby Pioneer Park consists of log homes dating to the 1800s. Park staff discuss crops typical of the pioneer era and explain the uses of various buildings, including a blacksmith shop, lardhouse, and dairy. Near a recently discovered Cherokee burial ground, descendants of local Cherokee groups have built indigenous houses typical of the 16th century. Farther on, a barn contains horse-drawn farm equipment and antique cars.

In early September, the **Southwest Blue Ridge Highlands Storytelling Festival** packs visitors in for tall tales and country music, and **Pioneer Days,** around July 4, brings more living history demonstrations, music, crafts, and food. Other events toward the end of the year include a Halloween haunted village, a pot-luck Pioneer Thanksgiving, and a Frontier Christmas.

The park is open Mon.-Sat. 9 a.m.-5 p.m.; $6 adults, $2 children 6-11, $3 children 12-17, and $15 for a family.

Pocahontas Exhibition Coal Mine

Some time during the 19th century, a blacksmith discovered a small outcropping of coal poking out of a nearby hillside. Finding himself with more than enough to power his forge, he amiably allowed neighbors to take home wagonloads for their own homes—despite his wife's warning him that there soon wouldn't be enough even for them. In 1882, the Pocahontas Coalfield opened with the arrival of the Norfolk & Western Railroad, giving birth to the town. Over the next 73 years, it would produce more than 44 million tons of "world-famous" Pocahontas Coal, chosen by the U.S. Navy for its ships for its clean burning.

Today, a short section of the mine is open to the public, providing a fascinating glimpse into the industry that underpinned the economy of this section of Appalachia for most of the past century. In the Coal Heritage Museum, tel. (540) 945-2134 or 945-9522, Web site: wwweb.com/www/pocohontas_mine, formerly the power house for the mine, visitors learn just how dangerous the industry was. Peruse accounts of the coal-dust explosion in March 1884 that killed everyone in the mine, filling the cemetery on the other side of town. Look for the mine-accident diagrams in the old shower room.

Tours into the mine begin with a video on modern mining. Then you enter the shaft itself, lined with rusted equipment and the famous 13-foot coal seam. As interesting as the tunnel he leads you through is guide Raymond Comer, who retired in 1994 ("$100 in debt") after three decades in the mines. The shaft remains cool (52° F) year-round, so wear a coat.

To get here, take Rt. 102 nine miles northwest from Bluefield on the West Virginia border. The mine is on the other side of the town of Pocahontas, over the bridge and railroad track. Open April 1-Oct. 31, Mon.-Sat., 10 a.m.-5 p.m., Sunday noon-6 p.m.; $6.50 adults, $3.50 children.

BREAKS INTERSTATE PARK

What could break a mountain? In this case, it took the Russell Fork River and a few hundred eons to carve through Pine Mountain on the border between Virginia and Kentucky. The result is said to be the deepest canyon in the country east of the Mississippi. Numerous overlooks line

KING COAL

The legendary coal deposits of Appalachia began taking shape hundreds of millions of years before Loretta Lynn's daddy ever made a living out of the side of a mountain. Over the centuries, organic matter was compressed, dried, and hardened into the black substance known as bituminous or "soft" coal, the most common type still found in the Norton formation, which underlies Kentucky, West Virginia, Tennessee, and Virginia.

Coal mining took off with the country's economic expansion after the Civil War—especially at the turn of the 20th century, when fresh-cut passages through the hills allowed railroads to transport the fuel to ships and factories for the first time. Demand for coal peaked in the 1920s, both to power vehicles and to make coke, a precursor to the steel used in gleaming new structures that sprouted from the heart of expanding metropolitan cities. The industry declined after WWII as oil and natural gas began to take over the market, but in the 1970s—about the time women began to work in the mines—the worldwide oil crisis drove demand—and coal prices—back up. The most recent trend has been back down, as worldwide competition, the decline of the steel industry, and a decreasing demand for electric power have all cut demand for coal.

The Industry in its Infancy

Conditions during the early heyday of mining in southwest Virginia (roughly 1910-30) were brutal and dangerous—labor was cheap, and mining was often the only work around. Miners had to supply their own tools, which included a soft hat, carbide lamp, and low-vein shovel, so-called because its shallow bend allowed a miner to work under a ceiling only a few feet high. A strong worker could swing a short, double-pointed miner's pick at 40 strokes per minute.

Mines were laid out in grids, with long "main streets," or "headings," crisscrossed by "cross streets," or "rooms," up to 20 feet wide and 60 feet high. The 50-foot square pillars of coal in between were mined (or "robbed") last, to keep the ceiling up as long as possible. In the meantime, hand-cut timbers supported the ceiling, at least most of the time.

To blast out the coal, a miner would drill holes by hand using a six-foot breast auger braced against his sternum. A tamping bar was used to place the explosive charge, filled with the miner's own black powder and ignited with a small firecracker-type charge called a "squid." The final steps were to light the fuse and run for cover.

The resulting broken pieces of coal were then loaded into carts pulled to the surface by ponies or mules, a method that persisted into the 1950s. Miners noted bitterly that the animals seemed more valuable than they did—and beasts of burden were certainly harder to replace. The horses and mules were brought out of the mines on weekends to keep them from going blind in the darkness (though many still did).

Flammable methane, which seeps naturally from exposed coal, was the most immediate danger in the mines. The slightest spark could ignite the invisible gas and set fire to coal dust or the coal itself, causing explosions of awesome power. One blast in the Pocahontas mine in March 1884 killed at least 114 people beneath the surface and hurled coal cars out the mouth of the tunnel with enough force to dash them to pieces against the distant bank of a ravine. Such explosions were frighteningly common, and were economic as well as human disasters, as noted in the official report of the Pocahontas explosion: ". . . it being the wish of those in authority to have the fullest and widest publicity given to the facts of the circumstances attending this sweeping calamity . . . instantly deprived so many human beings of life and blighted . . . the fair prospects of a mining company just as it was entering upon a career of prosperity." It was the unenviable job of the fire boss to track down methane pockets with the help of caged canaries (who succumbed to the odorless fumes more quickly than humans) and ignite them before they became too big.

Other dangers included falling rocks and "widowmakers"—petrified tree stumps that slid from the ceiling with surprising frequency. The most insidious threat by far, though, was black or miner's lung (pneumoconiosis), a chronic pulmonary condition caused by breathing coal dust.

For all this, miners received an average of $2.15 per hour in 1952—which works out to less than $1 for a hand-blasted load of 2.5 tons of coal. Sometimes they were paid in company scrip good only in the overpriced company store, with the excuse that real U.S. currency was hard to come by in such rural areas.

Modern Mining

Plastic hard hats and electric lamps have replaced leather and carbide, and self-rescue kits with 30-minute breathing filters are now carried by every miner. Six-foot roof bolts are epoxied into holes drilled in the ceiling, and blasting has become a less hazardous activity thanks to safety fuses, detonating cords, and electric blasting caps.

The days of digging by hand are also long gone. Massive machines called shearers, armed with twin cutting drums, can gouge out 50 tons of coal—enough to supply the electricity needed by one household for 15 years—each *minute*. Hydraulic roof supports called shields, each of which can support 500 to 1,000 tons, are electronically controlled to follow the shearer and set themselves in place. A typical shearer can work strips up to 1,000 feet wide and two miles long, eating through 30-40 inches at a time over a period of 9-12 months.

Dust controls imposed by the government in 1969 have cut cases of miner's lung dramatically, and digital methane and oxygen monitors make sure the underground environment is safe. Pay has improved significantly as well, but a few things haven't changed: miners still rid themselves of coal dust in the bathhouse with common kitchen detergent, which has always worked better than regular soap.

---

this five-mile gorge along a broad curve in the river, so deep that you can't even hear the class V whitewater 1,600 feet below the famous pyramidal Towers.

The Cherokee once hunted here, though by 1769 (only a few decades after English silversmith John Swift supposedly buried a fortune in silver near the Towers) they had relinquished rights to the area. Daniel Boone passed through twice on a reconnaissance mission through the canyon, carving his name in trees in both 1767 (coming) and 1771 (going). Shawnee raids during the late 18th and early 19th centuries only slowed the inevitable influx of settlers.

Park headquarters, tel. (800) 982-5122 or (540) 865-4413/4, are in the village of Breaks, eight miles north of Haysi on Rt. 80.

Accommodations and Food

Overnight guests can choose from among 140 **campsites** ($7 each, slightly more for hookups) or more permanent accommodations. The **Breaks Motor Lodge** has 34 rooms overlooking the canyon ($65-70). Two-bedroom **cottages** are available for $350 per week and can hold up to four people. The **Rhododendron Restaurant** boasts an impressive view from its deck and serves all meals.

Recreation

It may be hard to spot from the top, but the Russell Fork River rages within the confines of the park. Class III-V+ rapids make the run one of the most challenging on the Eastern Seaboard.

Russell Fork Whitewater Adventures, tel. (540) 530-7243 or 530-7044, and **Wahoo's Adventures,** tel. (800) 444-RAFT (800-444-7238), fax (704) 264-6242, send rafts and kayaks downstream. Water levels depend on releases from the John W. Flanagan Reservoir upstream—call (540) 835-9544 for current schedule.

Twelve miles of short hiking trails lead down to the river or out to overlooks (Clinchfield Overlook has the best view of the gorge here but is outshone by the Towers Overlook). Twelve-acre Laurel Lake is stocked with bluegill and bass, and boats can be rented Memorial Day through Labor Day. Likewise, horse rentals and a pool are limited to the summer season.

Information

A **visitor's center** is open daily year-round, 7 a.m.-10 p.m. (April-Oct.) or 8 a.m.-6 p.m. (Nov.-March). A parking/entrance fee of $1 per car is charged Memorial Day through Labor Day. Inside is a small museum on the history of the area, with a focus on coal mining.

BIG STONE GAP

Southwest Virginia's "other" gap has played second fiddle to Cumberland since the early days of the republic, when passages through the mountains were few and precious. The various names of its central town over the years reflect its strategic location. Initially called Three Forks, for tributaries of the Powell River that meet in or near the town center, the settlement became Mineral City from 1882 to 1888, thanks to major coalfields nearby. By the end of the late 19th century three separate railroads served the gateway settlement, hauling out the black gold and leaving a rather drab mining town behind.

Sights and Entertainment

Big Stone Gap's favorite son, John Fox, Jr., made this corner of Appalachia famous in the 19th century with his short stories and novels, most notably in *The Trail of the Lonesome Pine*. The bare-knuckled romance between the Virginia mountain girl and the Eastern mining engineer has metamorphosed into the Official State Outdoor Drama of Virginia, presented at the **June Tollivar Playhouse**, Clinton Ave. near E. 4th St., tel. (800) 362-0149 or (540) 523-1235, named for its real-life heroine. A rollicking mix of humor and heartbreak, folk music and fantasy, the melodrama unfolds Thursday, Friday, and Saturday evenings at 8 p.m. July-Aug.; $10 adults, $7 children.

The mountain girl is also memorialized at the **June Tollivar House & Craft Shop**, Jerome St. at Clinton St., tel. (540) 523-4707. The historic home is open Tues.-Sat. 10 a.m.-5 p.m., Sunday 2-6 p.m., with free tours throughout the day. Like most other sights in town, the Tollivar house is run by volunteers, so hours may vary.

The author himself is immortalized in the **John Fox, Jr. Museum**, Shawnee Ave. between E. 2nd St. and E. 3rd St., tel. (540) 523-2747 or 523-4707, built in 1888. Ask the employees about Fox's wife, the opera star Fritzi Scheff (a.k.a. Mademoiselle Modiste), who, according to one account, "dazzled the world with jewels, gowns, pompadour, wasp waist, and sprightly charm." She married Fox less than 24 hours after divorcing her previous husband, a baron, but didn't last long in this decidedly un-cosmopolitan neck of the woods. Open Tuesday and Wednesday 2-5 p.m., Thursday and Saturday 2-6 p.m., Sunday 2-5 p.m.; admission $3 adults, $1 children.

One of southwest Virginia's best regional museums is called, fittingly, the **Southwest Virginia Museum**, W. 1st St. and Wood Ave., tel. (540) 523-1322. This former mansion of a state attorney general houses well-presented exhibits tracing the boom-and-bust cycles of the area's coal and iron industries, along with the household utensils, clothes, and furniture of everyday citizens. Open Memorial Day-Labor Day, Mon.-Thurs. 10 a.m.-4 p.m., Friday 9 a.m.-4 p.m., Saturday 10 a.m.-5 p.m., Sunday 1-5 p.m.; admission $3 adults, $1.50 children. Finally, the **Harry W. Meador, Jr. Coal Museum**, Shawnee Ave. and E. 3rd St., tel. (540) 523-4950, concentrates on Big Stone Gap's bituminous legacy. You'll know the place by the hulking mine equipment rusting out front, courtesy of the Westmoreland Coal Co., which also runs the museum. Open Wed.-Sat. 10 a.m.-5 p.m., Sunday 1-5 p.m.; free admission.

Accommodations and Food

Two budget motels sit along US 23 on the way into the center of town: the **Trail Motel**, tel. (540) 523-1171, and the **Country Inn Motel**, tel. (540) 523-0374, which also has camper sites. Fast food has taken over Big Stone Gap, with the usual plastic-roofed representatives scattered about. Across the Powell River from the center of town, **Stringer's Restaurant**, 412 E. 5th St., tel. (540) 523-5388, is family run and moderately priced.

Information

Interstate Private Railroad Car #101 was built in 1870, but today it houses Big Stone Gap's **Regional Tourist and Information Center**, tel. (540) 523-2060, on US 23 next to the Country Inn Motel. The wooden car is open Mon.-Fri. 9 a.m.-5 p.m., offering walking tour maps and assistance galore.

NATURAL TUNNEL STATE PARK

Another monument to geological persistence has been carved by modest little Stock Creek, whose carbonic acid gradually dissolved an 850-foot tunnel through limestone bedrock. The southern entrance opens off the Amphitheater, a semicircular gallery with sheer walls that drop 150 feet to creek level. The gaping hole is large enough for the creek and a pair of train tracks, installed in the 19th century to take advantage of the natural passageway to and from the coalfields.

A number of short trails, open until dusk, lead to the bottom and around the rim. Careful near the edge at Lover's Leap, where an ancient myth holds that an Indian and his love, prohibited from

COUNTRY MUSIC'S LEGENDARY CARTER FAMILY

One of the taproots of American country music reaches all the way back to Maces Spring in southwest Virginia. It's well worth a side trip to visit the music center, especially if you're already in the vicinity of Natural Tunnel State Park.

It all began with carpenter Alvin Pleasant "A.P." Carter, who grew up here and operated a grocery store on Rt. 614. His true passion, though, was collecting and playing the pure, haunting mountain music that recorded the loves, losses, and everyday events of life in Appalachia.

In 1927, Ralph Peer, a talent scout from RCA Victor Records, discovered A.P. playing in a trio with his wife Sara and sister-in-law Maybelle. They soon had a contract to record, turning out the "Bristol Sessions," which are today considered a watershed in commercial country music. Between 1927 and 1942, the Carter Family recorded more than 300 songs, including classics such as "Bury Me Under the Weeping Willow," "I'm Thinking Tonight of Blue Eyes," and "Keep on the Sunny Side," which is inscribed on A.P.'s tombstone in a cemetery just down the road from his store.

In addition to the songs the family wrote, A.P. also collected songs on countless forays into the hills, where he'd obsessively scribble down lyrics and memorize tunes with the help of Sara and their daughter, Jeanette. This priceless form of musical anthropology introduced dozens of timeless tunes—including "Will the Circle Be Unbroken?"—to the country and the world.

The trio's career ended in 1940 with the breakup of A.P. and Sara's marriage, but its effect on country music still echoes. In 1993, their faces appeared on US postal stamps along with Patsy Cline, Hank Williams, and others. That same year, Rounder Records began to re-release the complete Carter Family Victor recordings, a nine-CD set that includes almost 150 songs recorded 1927-34.

A.P.'s grocery store fell into disrepair, serving briefly as a tobacco warehouse, before Jeanette cleaned it up and began to hold regular concerts in an effort to preserve the family legacy. Soon the crowds drawn to the Saturday-night shows were packing the place to the roof. So with the help of friends and relatives (including Johnny Cash, who married Maybelle's daughter, June), the Carter Family Fold was erected in 1976 and has been going strong ever since.

Shows begin every Saturday at 7:30 p.m. ($4 adults, $1 children 6-12), presenting a wide range of traditional acoustic mountain music, including gospel and bluegrass. Jeanette still MCs, introducing local and regional artists and occasionally stepping aside while her brother Joe warms the crowd up with a humorous "coon tale." Up to 900 people can squeeze into the dirt-floored arena, although 200-400 is more typical. On summer evenings, the sides and back are opened to the night air, cooling down the cloggers and buck dancers who gyrate on the small concrete dance floor. A concession stand sells drinks and snacks, but no alcohol—it's strictly prohibited, as are swearing and misbehaving.

A.P.'s old store is now the **Carter Family Museum,** open every Saturday 6 a.m.-7:30 p.m. for 50 cents pp. Alongside A.P.'s work clothes and tools you'll find Jeanette's first autoharp, bought at age 13 with her earnings from performing with the family (25 cents per show); original 78 rpm records; photographs; and show clothes including those worn by Johnny Cash and June when they performed for President Nixon in 1970.

Every August, even more music lovers congregate in Maces Spring for the **Carter Family Memorial Festival,** held to commemorate the family's first recording session. Banjos, fiddles, guitars, and bass fill the Fold all weekend 2-11 p.m., while local artisans set up booths outside. National acts bring slightly higher prices ($10 pp per day).

Call the Center at (540) 386-9480 or 386-6054 for show lineups and other questions. To get to Maces Spring from Clinchport, take US 23/58/421 southeast to Weber City, then US 58/421 east from Weber City to Hiltons (17 miles). From Hiltons, take Rt. 709 north to Rt. 615, also known as the A.P. Carter Highway. Maces Spring is three miles farther, and you can't miss the Fold.

marrying by their warring tribes, leapt to their deaths. A chairlift runs into the gorge 10 a.m.-6 p.m. on Saturday and Sunday ($2 pp). About 10 coal trains a day still chug through the tunnel, so a guided tour is the only way to explore beyond the entrance. Tours leave at 2 p.m. on Saturdays, Sept.-Oct.

At the top, a visitor's center, tel. (540) 940-2674, houses a gift shop and a small museum on the geology and history of the immediate area. It's open 10 a.m.-2 p.m. Mon.-Fri., 10 a.m.-6 p.m. Saturday, Sunday. Campgrounds on the hilltop by the entrance cost $11 for tents and $15 with water and electric hookups, and include use of the pool (both open March-Nov.).

Natural Tunnel State Park is off Rt. 871 off US 23 between Clinchport and Duffield.

CUMBERLAND GAP NATIONAL HISTORICAL PARK

One of frontier America's most famous landmarks is more accurately an absence of land: a break in the long Appalachian chain that allowed migrating deer and buffalo, Native Americans, and pioneers alike to pass through into the Ohio River Basin. It was discovered by European settlers in the mid-18th century to be the easiest way to the Kentucky Territory, easing crowding east of the mountains. Named after the Duke of Cumberland, son of King George II, the pass had already been called the Warrior's Path, for the Cherokee raiding parties that came from as far as North Carolina to attack western tribes.

Daniel Boone made the pass famous, and vice versa. In 1796, the budding frontiersman set his legend on track when he and 30 "axe-men" hacked out the Wilderness Road through the gap. Also known as Boone's Trace, the historic highway was barely a rutted track in spots as it wound from Kingsport, TN, to Boonesborough, KY. Still, hundreds of thousands of settlers made the trek as the new nation spread west.

Today this rugged corner of the Cumberland Mountains is preserved in the nation's second-largest historical park (20,271 acres). It's also one of the least-visited, so any trip to the corner of Kentucky, Tennessee, and Virginia is automatically a step away from crowds as well as into the past.

Visiting the Gap
The visitor center is actually over the border in Middlesboro, Kentucky, tel. (606) 248-2817, Web site: www.nps.gov/cuga. It's open daily 8 a.m.-5 p.m. and contains exhibits and films on the history and geology of the park. Close to 50 miles of trails wind through hemlock, pine, and oak forests (lusher here than farther north, since scouring glaciers didn't make it this far south). Views from the 21-mile Ridge Trail and the Pinnacle Overlook (reached by road) can be spectacular, weather permitting—on a clear day it's possible to see all three states spread out below, and even as far as the Great Smoky Mountains in North Carolina.

Other spots on the itinerary include Hensley Settlement, a self-sufficient homestead dating to the turn of the century and now under restoration by the Park Service. Countless caves creep underground, including Cudjo Caverns, possibly Virginia's largest and containing what may be the world's largest stalagmite (closed for renovations as of 1997). On the Virginia side, 160 campsites with restrooms and hot showers are available for $10 (28 have hookups for $15). Backcountry camping is free but requires a permit from the visitors center.

A $265 million pair of tunnels completed in 1996 rerouted US 25 to the south of the original mountain pass, which is being restored to its unpaved, "Boone-era" condition. Once the roadbed is removed, the trail will be narrowed and replanted with native shrubs and trees, allowing visitors to cross the gap much as their frontier predecessors did. Work is scheduled to be completed around 2010.

THE SHENANDOAH

Virginia naturalist Henry Heatwole described Virginia's rolling, off-center spine as a place full of "small and subtle pleasures," which raises the question—what *is* the Shenandoah, exactly? In name, it's the lazy-winding river—two, actually—that join near Front Royal before flowing north into the Potomac. In legend, it's the wide, fertile valley dividing the Blue Ridge Mountains from the Alleghenies, elevated to near-mythic status by some of the most dramatic fighting of the Civil War. In essence, it's a state of mind, embodied in the odors of rich farmland in morning mist, snow on rugged granite peaks, and the simple pleasures of small-town hospitality evident even in the larger cities.

History
Herds of buffalo once roamed the "Valley of the Daughter of the Stars," as early native inhabitants called it. Scattered villages of Shawnee here were prey to frequent raids by Catawbas from the south and Delawares from the north. Later, first- or second-generation German farmers moved down from Pennsylvania to the promising valley—where, it was said, the summer grass grew high enough to tie across a horse's saddle. During the Civil War, the valley's productivity and strategic importance almost proved its undoing. Over three years, the area endured more

battles than any other region in the country. Traditionally isolated from the political centers of the Piedmont and the coast, the Shenandoah was long considered the domain of backwoods "clay-eaters," causing many an argument over how much trade and money for development should be sent from the east.

Highlights
Aside from its intangible enticements of atmosphere, the Shenandoah is replete with things to do and see. Cultural attractions tend toward the historic, led by places affected or begotten by the Civil War. The apple city of Winchester saw the most action, while Stonewall Jackson lived briefly in the antique college town of Lexington before being buried there. Battlefields like New Market and Cedar Creek keep the valley's past alive in year-round displays and annual reenactments.

Stretch your legs with a hike or ride through the seemingly endless George Washington National Forest, then relax with a soak at The Homestead in Hot Springs, the most venerable and lavish resort hotel in the state. In the winter, skiing at Bryce and Massanutten Resorts is respectable for being this far south, while during the warmer months the region's countless streams and rivers attract anglers in canoes, rafters in

CIVIL WAR IN THE SHENANDOAH

As the Civil War slowly tore through Virginia, the strategic value of the Shenandoah made it crucial to the strategies of both sides. The valley was not only the fertile "breadbasket" of the Confederacy but could also allow troops to march unseen practically to the steps of Washington, D.C.—or, in the other direction, to flank Richmond. Stonewall Jackson declared, "If the valley is lost, Virginia is lost." And Jackson would add his own legend to the two short but bloody years that would transform a pastoral landscape into a smoking wasteland.

Spring 1862:
Jackson's Valley Campaign

Robert E. Lee's orders to Jackson were quite simple: defend the valley, and prevent Federal reinforcements from joining the attack on Richmond. With that in mind, Jackson pitted his 17,000 troops against heavy odds in an incredible display of cunning, endurance, courage, and luck. In seven weeks, Jackson's famous "foot cavalry"—consisting of the 2nd, 4th, 5th, 27th, and 33rd Virginia infantry regiments and the elite Rockbridge Artillery—fought four battles and six skirmishes, marched over 600 miles, and eventually immobilized and inflicted twice its casualties on some 60,000 Federals.

Jackson believed, "There are two things never to be lost sight of by a military commander: always mystify, mislead, and surprise the enemy if possible . . . [and] never fight against heavy odds, if by possible maneuvering you can hurl your own force on only a part, and the weakest part, of your enemy and crush it." Not surprisingly, he employed a strategy of surprise and deception—which suited the uneven terrain perfectly—as he kept his dogged troops showing up when- and wherever they were least expected.

CIVIL WAR IN THE SHENANDOAH

Cool Spring (JULY 1864)

Winchester (MAY 1862, SEPT. 1864)

Kernstown (MARCH 1862, JULY 1864)

Shenandoah River

N. Fork Shenandoah River

Front Royal (MAY 1862)

Strasburg (OCT. 1864)

Fishers Hill (SEPT. 1864)

WEST

Toms Brook (OCT. 1864)

VIRGINIA

Shenandoah Mountain

Valley

Luray

Massanutten Mountains

New Market (MAY 1864)

TOWNS AND CITIES IN BOLD DESIGNATE BATTLE SITES

Harrisonburg

0   10 mi

0   10 km

Port Republic (JUNE 1862)

S. Fork Shenandoah River

Blue Ridge

Waynesboro (MARCH 1865)

Staunton

McDowell (MAY 1862)

To Charlottesville

© MOON PUBLICATIONS, INC.

Jackson had quickly realized that speed was of essence and once led his troops 350 miles in 30 days. And his tactics worked: as of 1864, the Stonewall Brigade had yet to be driven from a field that its valiant men defended.

At the First Battle of Kernstown, on March 23, Jackson attacked a force he thought to be only a few regiments strong but which turned out to be Gen. James Shields' entire division. Both sides raced for the cover of a wall in the middle of an open field. The Confederates won, though they eventually had to retreat in the face of overwhelming numbers. The Rebels did, however, manage to keep Shields from joining McClellan's peninsular campaign.

On May 3, Jackson mystified even his own subordinates when he ordered half his army to march eastward out of the valley. Almost to Charlottesville, the troops suddenly found themselves herded onto railroad cars and shipped back to Staunton. There they disembarked and marched off for a surprise attack at McDowell on May 8, forcing Union troops under Gen. Robert Milroy to flee into West Virginia.

General Philip Sheridan

With help from the spirited spy Belle Boyd, the Confederates captured Front Royal on May 23 after joining with Jubal Early's command in a surprising move and passing through a gap in Massanutten Mountain. During this battle, members of the 1st Maryland Division from each side found themselves facing, greeting, and then fighting their own neighbors and relatives.

The First Battle of Winchester, on May 25, followed a race toward the important supply city lost by Union Maj. Gen. Nathaniel Banks. At sunset, Banks, believing the fighting ended, had gone upstairs to take a bath. Under Jackson, Confederate attacks continued, though, sending the Union troops scurrying in retreat toward Washington, D.C. (When asked by Banks if he loved his country, one retreating soldier replied, "Yes sir, and I'm trying to get back to it as fast as I can.") Pursuit was eventually called off because Jackson's men were too worn out from marching the previous nights.

Two more victories in June near Port Republic secured the Confederate hold on the valley. On June 8, Gen. Richard S. Ewell sent a larger army under Gen. John C. Fremont packing, and the next day Jackson defeated Brig. Gen. Erasmus Tyler.

In a tragic irony, Jackson was killed by his own men following the Rebel triumph at Chancellorsville one year later.

Summer 1864: The Tide Turns

As the war continued to drag on, Lincoln and his Union commanders realized they would have to bring the South to its knees by any means possible to keep the war from dragging on indefinitely. Soon after the Battle of New Market, on May 15, in which 10 VMI cadets were killed, Union Lt. Gen. Ulysses S. Grant began a massive statewide offensive intended to end the war once and for all. Lee sent Lt. Gen. Jubal Early to defend the valley. Early's Maryland Campaign, as it became known, began with successes, at Cool Spring on July 19 and the Second Battle of Kernstown on July 24. By August, Early had his sights set on Washington, D.C., itself.

Embarrassed by the continued defeats and alarmed by the threat to the capital, Grant realized that the Union had to win the valley at all costs. He sent Maj. Gen. Philip Sheridan south with orders to raze the Shenandoah so completely "that a crow flying over it will have to carry his provender with him." Sheridan's Valley Campaign spelled doom for the area as surely as Jackson's had meant its temporary salvation, and Early's 12,000 remaining troops found themselves facing 40,000 Union soldiers who advanced down the valley slaughtering countless livestock, ruining fields, and putting buildings to the torch. Scattered stone foundations still recall the frenzy of destruction remembered for generations simply as "The Burning."

The Battle of Opequon (Third Winchester), on September 19, was the largest in the valley, leaving 5,000 Federals and 3,500 Confederates dead in its wake. Despite the numbers, it was still considered a Union victory. Three more wins—Fishers Hill, on September 22, Toms Brook, on October 9, and Cedar Creek (near Strasburg), on October 18—marked the beginning of the end for the Confederate hold on the valley. At the Battle of Waynesboro, on March 2, 1865, Sheridan crushed Early's remaining forces and condemned the South to defeat.

DOVER PUBLICATIONS, INC.

kayaks, and hungover college students in inner tubes. The Shenandoah is also home to most of the state's commercial caves, led by Luray Caverns, the largest and most spectacular on the East Coast. You could easily take a week driving from Front Royal to the North Carolina border along the crest of the Blue Ridge, following Skyline Drive—the linchpin of Shenandoah National Park—and the Blue Ridge Parkway.

Access

Interstate 81 runs the length of the valley along the well-worn route of the Old Valley Pike, once worn deep into the soil by native tribes, European settlers, and Civil War troops. That older, more scenic route (Old Valley Pike) lives on as US 11, worlds away from the interstate though the two are often within sight and sound of each other. The Blue Ridge is pierced by one interstate (I-66, roughly paralleled by the Amtrak line from Charlottesville to West Virginia via Staunton) and a number of smaller roads (US 211 from Luray, US 33 from Harrisonburg, and US 60 from Lexington). Interstate 66 leads to Winchester and the mountains for the weekend hordes from Washington, D.C.

Resources

The **Shenandoah Valley Travel Association,** PO Box 1040, New Market, VA 22844-1040, tel. (540) 740-3132, fax 740-3100, can provide more information on touring the area. E-mail: svta@shentel.net, Web site: www.svta.org. For detailed listings of local inns and B&Bs, try the **Blue Ridge Bed &**

THE SHENANDOAH

© MOON PUBLICATIONS, INC.

Breakfast Reservation Service, Rocks and Rills Farm, Route 2, Box 3895, Berryville, VA 22611, tel. (800) 296-1246 or (540) 955-1246, fax 955-4240, or **Bed and Breakfasts of the Historic Shenandoah Valley,** 402 N. Main St., Woodstock, VA 22664, tel. (540) 459-4828.

WINCHESTER AND VICINITY

Known for its apple blossoms and Civil War battles, Winchester (pop. 22,000) has alternately enjoyed and endured its position as the gateway to the northern Shenandoah Valley. The largest city in Virginia's apple heartland of Frederick and Clarke Counties, Winchester is surrounded by acres and acres of orchards, filled with delicate buds in the spring and teams of migrant harvest workers in the fall. From padded shoulder buckets to wooden crates in the backs of rumbling trucks, the fruit eventually makes its way to dozens of processing plants near town that infuse the air with the sweet smell of cider,

vinegar, apple butter, and applesauce in the making. Over half of each yearly crop of 200-300 million pounds is sold fresh across the country.

A number of natives of this region have gone on to nationwide fame, including progressive 1920s Governor Harry Byrd and author Willa Cather *(Death Comes for the Archbishop)*. Country singer Patsy Cline was born at 608 S. Kent St. in 1932, worked in Gaunt's Drug Store at the corner of S. Loudoun St. and Valley Ave., and is buried on a boulevard named in her honor east of the interstate.

A quiet pedestrian mall in the center of downtown (Loudoun St. between Piccadilly and Cork) is crowded with restaurants, bookstores, coffeeshops, and gift stores within a few blocks. Sadly, many empty windows and "For Rent" signs attest to competition from malls and gigantic depot-type stores farther out of town.

SHENANDOAH AREA CLIMATE

SNOWFALL
RAINFALL
MAXIMUM TEMP.
MINIMUM TEMP.

History

Virginia's oldest city west of the Blue Ridge, Winchester began as a Shawnee campground, and was settled by Pennsylvania Quakers in 1732. Settlers soon arrived from all over Europe, including Scots-Irish, Welsh, English, and French. Germans left their mark in trim houses set flush against sidewalks and with tidy gardens in back.

In 1748, an eager red-haired 16-year-old arrived to survey thousands of rolling acres belonging to Lord Fairfax. Within a decade, George Washington had set about building Fort Loudoun to protect the frontier town from Indian attacks and French encroachment. Soon he was elected to his first political office, in the House of Burgesses.

During the Civil War, Winchester saw as much action as any city in Virginia. On the cusp of the valley with Maryland, less than 50 miles to the north, Winchester changed hands 72 times during the course of the war—13 times in one day. Some of these capitulations were, of course, questionable—a single soldier left in town after the oppo-

WINCHESTER

DETAIL

COLONIAL ART & CRAFT SHOP
PICCADILLY ST.
AMHERST ST.
TUCANO BRAZILIAN RESTAURANT
KURTZ CULTURAL CENTER
WOLFE ST.
BOSCAWEN ST.
CORK ST.
HANDS ON POTTERY
WASHINGTON'S OFFICE MUSEUM

STONEWALL JACKSON HEADQUARTERS MUSEUM

SEE DETAIL

NATIONAL CEMETERY

STONEWALL CEMETERY

GAUNT'S DRUG STORE

VISITORS CENTER
ABRAM'S DELIGHT

To Berryville

EXIT 315

To Cafe Sofia   To Middletown   To Patsy Cline Gravesite and Memorial   To White Post

© MOON PUBLICATIONS, INC.

0   0.5 mi
0   0.5 km

sition retreated, for instance—but no fewer than five major battles were fought within the city limits. The Third Battle of Winchester (a.k.a. Opequon), on Sept. 19, 1864, was the largest fought in the valley. Confederate forces under Lt. Gen. Jubal Early killed over 5,000 of Sheridan's Federal troops, but the battle was still considered a Union victory. Thousands of wounded were brought here from Gettysburg and Antietam, helping fill close to 8,000 graves in two major cemeteries along Woodstock Lane—Stonewall for the Confederates, National for the Federals.

SIGHTS

Block tickets to Winchester's three main historical sights can be purchased at any of the three ($7.50 adults, $4 children 6-12, $20 family). In-

dividual admission is also available, for $3.75 adults, $1.75 children ($2 adults, $1 children for George Washington's office). Each location is open April-Oct., Mon.-Sat. 10 a.m.-4 p.m., Sunday noon-4 p.m., and informative tours are given about every half-hour.

Abram's Delight, 1340 S. Pleasant Valley Rd., tel. (540) 662-6519, sits across from the visitors center. The oldest home in the city, it began in 1734 as the log house of Quaker settler Abraham Hollingsworth, who called his 582 acres "a delight to behold." It originally stood downtown but was dismantled there, reassembled here, and filled with tools, a loom, and other well-worn artifacts.

The limestone main house next door was built in 1754 by Abraham's son Isaac and served as the city's first Quaker meeting house. Five generations of Hollingsworths used beautiful an-

PATSY CLINE CHRONOLOGY

1932 ......Born Virginia Patterson Hensley in Winchester

1957 ......Breaks into show business by winning Arthur Godfrey talent program performing "Walkin' After Midnight"

1958 ......Joins Grand Ole Opry

1961-62...#1 Female Recording Artist

1962 ......#1 song: "I Fall to Pieces"

1963 ......Dies in plane crash in Tennessee at age 30

1973 ......Inducted into Country Music Hall of Fame

1993 ......Commemorative stamp issued

1994 ......Inducted into Cowgirl Hall of Fame

1995 ......Greatest Hits album sells six million copies

tiques including a melodeon (a small reed organ), a 1790 walnut plantation desk, and a solid cherry butler's desk with mahogany veneer dating to 1800. Rope beds upstairs had to be tightened every night with a special crank (hence the phrase "sleep tight"). Abraham's ghost is said to move things around when nobody's looking.

The 1854 Gothic Revival building that served as **Stonewall Jackson's Headquarters,** 415 N. Braddock St., tel. (540) 667-3242, originally belonged to Lt. Col. Lewis Moore, great-grandfather of Mary Tyler Moore (who donated the reproduction gilt wallpaper). It was taken over by the Confederate general from late 1861 to the start of his Valley Campaign in 1862. Civil War-era furniture and relics include original Confederate flags, uniforms, and Jackson's prayer book and camp table. Heft an 1861 Springfield rifle and try to figure out whether *you* could have handled the percussion caps, minnie ball bullets, and ramrod quickly enough to load and fire it three times in one minute.

Between September 1755 and December 1756, future Founding Father George Washington, still a 23-year-old colonel in the Virginia militia, organized the frontier town's Revolutionary War defenses from a three-room structure preserved today as **George Washington's Office Museum,** 32 W. Cork St., tel. (540) 662-4412. The oldest surviving structure in town, the museum is filled with Revolutionary War and Civil War memorabilia, antique surveying tools, and a model of Fort Loudoun. Bloodstains under one window bear witness to one of the city's many battles.

At the corner of Braddock and Piccadilly in front of Kimberly's Linens and Gifts sits the **World's Largest Apple,** built to top a 5,200-pound monument in rival apple town Cornelia, GA (actually a 1927 gift from Winchester). A few blocks over on the downtown mall, children can try their hand at a mock apple-packing center, one of the many interactive exhibits at the **Shenandoah Valley Discovery Museum,** tel. (540) 722-2020. Open Tues.-Sat. 9 a.m.-5 p.m., Sunday 1-5 p.m.; $3 pp. Browse the museum shop for free.

ACCOMMODATIONS

The most interesting lodgings in the area are outside the city, in Berryville, White Post, and Middletown (see below).

Budget
The **Echo Village Budget Motel,** 3632 Valley Ave., tel. (540) 869-1900, has sat off I-81's exit 310 for half a century. "Special rates for honest

and clean people" are advertised by the **Tourist City Motel,** 214 Millwood Ave., tel. (540) 662-9011 or 662-0607. The **Mohawk Motel,** 2754 Northwestern Pike, tel. (540) 667-1410, sits on US 50 west of downtown.

Inexpensive to Moderate

Exit 313 onto US 50 off I-81 has most of Winchester's mid-level hotels, including the **Hampton Inn,** 1655 Apple Blossom Dr., tel. (540) 667-8011, fax 667-8033, and the **Best Western Lee-Jackson,** 711 Millwood Ave., tel. (540) 662-4154, fax 662-2618. In addition to its rooms, the **Travelodge of Winchester,** 160 Front Royal Rd., tel. (540) 665-0685 has a heated pool and eight efficiencies.

FOOD

Downtown Mall

Starting at the north end, the **Violino Restaurante Italiano,** 181 N. Loudoun St. at Piccadilly, tel. (540) 667-8006, serves creative Italian fare that earned four stars in one local review. Franco and Marcella Stocco from Turin offer classical northern cuisine, graced by excellent sauces, in the $7-10 range, including many vegetarian plates. Lunch and dinner are served daily in the main dining room, decorated with instruments, or on the small patio facing the mall.

Half a block down is the **Snow White Grill,** tel. (540) 662-5955, a diner usually crammed with locals in for ice cream and cheap eats ($2-3). Closed Sunday. The **Old Town Cafe,** at Loudoun and Boscawen, tel. (540) 665-1805, does the diner tradition a bit more justice with generous lunch specials for $4-5 served Tues.-Sun.

At the same intersection two coffee shops coexist peacefully side by side. The **Daily Grind,** tel. (540) 662-2115, offers java, light food, Internet access, and live music on Friday and Saturday nights. Readings, discussions groups, and acoustic jams are more the style at the **Satisfied Mind Coffeehouse and Bookstore,** tel. (540) 665-0855, e-mail: satmind@mnsinc.com. Ginseng and ginkgo elixirs give a pot of tea extra zing.

Open daily at 6:30 a.m., the **Chelsea Bagel Bakery,** 24 S. Loudoun St., tel. (540) 678-4637, churns out fresh bagels, sandwiches, and great homemade soups for under $5. Keep going to the southern end of the mall and take a right to

the **Cork Street Tavern,** 8 W. Cork St., tel. (540) 667-3777. This snug place, housed in a building dating to 1830, serves burgers ($4), award-winning ribs and other entrées ($9-14) in front of a big stone fireplace and bar.

Elsewhere in Town

Just a block off the mall sits the **Tucano Brazilian International Restaurant,** 12 S. Braddock St., tel. (540) 722-4557. Brazilian dishes with a worldly flair, including *aves* (poultry), *paixes* (fish), and *pratos vegetarianos* (vegetarian plates), are $4-6 for lunch, Mon.-Fri., and $9-14 during dinner Mon.-Sat.

One of the few authentic Slavic restaurants in the country, **Cafe Sofia,** 2900 Valley Ave., tel. (540) 667-2950, is warmed by a log fireplace and filled with Eastern European weavings, baskets, dolls, and plates. Entrées such as *pierogi* (a type of savory turnover) and goulash are often served in bread bowls accompanied by Bulgarian wine, and range from $7-10 for lunch (Tues.-Fri.) and $14-30 for dinner (Tues.-Sat.). Don't forget to save room for apple strudel or *palachinka* crepes for dessert.

EVENTS

To usher in spring and its acres of blooming orchards, normally conservative Winchester erupts with pink and green clothing, parades, music, and parties. The first **Apple Blossom Festival** was organized in 1924, and except for a break during WW II it's been going strong ever since. Five days of marching entertainment, food, and fun, including a circus and the coronation of the Apple Blossom Queen, take place every May the weekend before Mother's Day. For more information call (540) 662-3863, or try their Web site: www.apple-blossom.com.

May is also the month of the **Spring Fly-In** at the Winchester Regional Airport, tel. (540) 662-4786, featuring antique, homebuilt, and experimental planes. On the second Saturday in August, the **Great American Duck Race,** tel. (540) 662-4118, waddles into Jim Barnett Park with music, food, and, of course, duck races. The end of the apple season in September is occasion for its own celebration: the **Apple Harvest Arts and Crafts Festival,** tel. (540) 665-8060, with square dancing and every kind of apple food imaginable the third weekend of the month. The **Old Town Farmer's Market** is held at the south end of the mall during growing season (roughly May-Oct.).

SHOPPING

At the north end of the mall, **Handworks,** tel. (800) 277-0184 or (540) 662-3927, sells unusual and beautiful handicrafts from all over the world, including handcrafted wooden boxes from Poland, batik masks from Indonesia, and Peruvian carved gourds. World music and beads galore lead toward the Global Village tearoom in back. Wrought iron decorates the porch of an old mansion at 25 W. Piccadilly St., home to the **Colonial Art & Craft Shop,** tel. (540) 662-6513. This is the kind of place that comes to mind with the phrase "bull in a china shop," stocked from creaking floor to ceiling with porcelain, crystal, and other country gifts. **Hands on Pottery,** 15 E. Boscawen St., tel. (540) 772-2610, contains the studio and gallery of potter Alicia White Daily. Solid, graceful stoneware is for sale along with local drawings and paintings.

INFORMATION

The **Winchester/Frederick County Visitors Center,** 1360 S. Pleasant Valley Rd., Winchester, VA 22601, tel. (800) 662-1360 or (540) 662-4135, fax 722-6365, occupies a former grist mill near a small park and lake. Open daily 9 a.m.-5 p.m., it has videos of the area and of Patsy Cline, a small shrine to the singer, and brochures of walking and driving tours. E-mail: wfcedc@globalcom.net, Web site: www.globalcom.net/wfcedc. Near the downtown mall the **Kurtz Cultural Center,** Cameron and Boscawen, tel. (540) 722-6367, is more of a local museum, with exhibits on the valley's role in the Civil War and a gift shop. Open Mon.-Sat. 10 a.m.-5 p.m., Sunday noon-5 p.m.

NEAR WINCHESTER

Berryville
For a change of pace from the usual hotels, motels, and B&Bs, consider a spiritual stay at the **Holy Cross Abbey,** tel. (540) 955-3124, one of 17 working Trappist monasteries in the country. Twenty-one members of the Cistercian Order of the Strict Observance live a quiet life on 1,200 acres in the rolling Blue Ridge foothills alongside the Shenandoah River. The monastery's main means of support is a bakery, where the monks find time, between their six daily services, to turn out 24,000 famous fruitcakes a year.

An elegant guesthouse a short distance from the monastery holds 15 rooms, rented for retreats Mon.-Fri. ($90-180) or Fri.-Sun. ($60-90). Guests are welcome to join in the services, sung liturgy, and family-style meals. Reservations should be made far in advance. A gift shop sells Cistercian publications and monastery products including Trappist preserves, creamed honey, fudge, and bread.

To get there, follow Rt. 7 east from Berryville, turning left immediately before crossing the Shenandoah River onto Rt. 603, and watch for a sign on the right after one mile.

White Post
Eight miles south of Winchester at the intersection of US 522, US 340 and Rt. 277 looms **Dinosaur Land,** tel. (540) 869-2222, a Jurassic-themed landmark that's been around for decades. Thirty-five dinosaur replicas, including a brontosaurus, stegosaurus, yaleosaurus, and saltoposuchus, stand next to a 60-foot shark, a 70-foot octopus, and a homely cave couple. Open daily 9:30 a.m.-5:30 p.m.; $3 adults, $2.50 children.

In the same town but at the other end of the cultural spectrum is **L'Auberge Provençal,** Route 340, tel. (800) 638-1702 or (540) 837-1375, fax 837-2004. Innkeepers Alain and Celeste Borel have created a small, charming French country inn in the middle of the fields and pastures of the Shenandoah. Three buildings huddle near an expansive flower garden, full of tulips in the spring and sunflowers every fall.

Alain, the French-born chef, draws regular visitors from as far as Washington, D.C., for a taste of his native Avignon in the dining rooms of the 18th-century stone manor house. Fresh fruit and herbs from the gardens add the final touch to five-course gourmet candlelight dinners featuring foie gras, smoked rabbit, and fresh Shenandoah trout—and that's just for appetizers. Breakfast is almost as impressive: scones, salmon, poached eggs, and croissants may all grace your plate.

Provençal fabrics, canopy beds, and fireplaces fill 10 guest rooms, each with private garden view and entrance. Rooms with breakfast are $145-175 per night, with dinner another $58 pp. Afternoon cooking classes ending in dinner are $155.

Middletown

Antique stores and a curious mix of old and new houses line US 11, called Main Street as it passes through the center of Middletown. At number 7783 you'll find the **Wayside Inn,** tel. (540) 869-1797, fax 869-6038, one of the oldest inns in the United States. It received its first guests in 1797, when it was Wilkerson's Tavern, and later served as a stagecoach rest stop and waystation for soldiers from both sides of the Civil War. With the arrival of the automobile, it became America's first motor inn, regaining much of its antique charm during a restoration in the 1960s.

An antique parlor welcomes guests with chiming clocks, and brick and stone fireplaces. Antiques and books are everywhere, including a combination chess and cribbage board. The stately colonial dining room of Larrick's Taverns dates to the 1720s, with lunch entrées for $7-9 and daily specials. Each of the 24 rooms has a distinct personality, and the hotel offers popular romantic escapes for honeymoons and anniversaries that include champagne, breakfast in bed, and a special late checkout. Expensive to premium.

Just south of the inn, the small, intimate **Wayside Theater,** tel. (800) 951-1776 or (540) 869-1776, began as a movie house in the 1940s before being converted with a stage in 1962. It's now under the management of a nonprofit community foundation, which has welcomed actors such as Susan Sarandon, Kathy Bates, and Stacy Keach. Tickets are $15-20 adults, $7.50 children.

Two sisters run **McSylvie's Restaurant and Cafe,** 7843 Main St., tel. (540) 869-1911, a cheerily floral place set in a turn-of-the-century bank building (notice the vault door in back protecting the iced tea and coffee). Lunch sandwiches such as swordfish and crabcakes are tasty for $5-6, with dinner entrées such as quiche and pasta in the $13-16 range.

Cedar Creek Battlefield

In the pre-dawn mist of October 19, 1864, 21,000 Confederates under Lt. Gen. Jubal Early made a surprise attack on 32,000 sleeping Union troops. The Rebels soon had the larger force on the run to the north of Middletown, but Maj. Gen. Philip Sheridan, hearing the roar of cannons, managed to gallop from Winchester in time to rally his forces. The Federals pushed their opponents back to the south and eventually out of the valley altogether, signaling the end of Confederate military power in the Shenandoah. Over three times as many Confederate soldiers were killed or wounded as Union soldiers, whose ranks included Rutherford B. Hayes, William McKinley, and George Armstrong Custer.

Today a **visitors center,** tel. (540) 869-2069, Web site: www.winchesterva.com\cedarcreek, is open April-Oct., Mon.-Sat. 10 a.m.-4 p.m., Sunday 1-4 p.m., one mile south of Middletown. It's run by a nonprofit organization, not the National Park Service, so the $2 suggested donation is appreciated. The fields have changed little in the years since the battle (which is reenacted every year the weekend closest to October 19). Over 2,500 participants take part under the gaze of 15,000 spectators, who are allowed on the actual battlefield (prohibited in National Historical Parks). It costs $8 to watch; call (540) 869-2064 for more information.

Belle Grove Plantation, tel. (540) 869-2028, sits in the middle of the battlefield opposite the visitors center. Once one of the valley's most prestigious homes, it was built in 1794-7 by Major Isaac Hite, Jr., with design help from Thomas Jefferson. Sheridan used the mansion as his headquarters for his devastating march down the valley, and ended up burning many of the farm buildings. James and Dolley Madison later honeymooned here.

Extensive renovations to the main house were underway in 1997, soon after the gardens had been resurrected by the Garden Club of Virginia. A quilt and fabric shop fills the basement, and Colonial craft demonstrations are held in the smokehouse, icehouse, and blacksmith shops. Open March-Oct., Mon.-Sat. 10:15 a.m.-3:15 p.m., Sunday 1:15 a.m.-4:15 p.m.; $5 adults, $2.50 children 12-18.

There's a **campground** 1.4 miles north of I-81 exit 298 on US 11, tel. (540) 869-1888. Sites costs $14-17, and include a pool, playground, recreation room, and laundry.

SOUTH FROM WINCHESTER (THE NORTHERN VALLEY)

FRONT ROYAL

Called Hell Town during its frontier days, this riverside city is thought to have been unintentionally renamed by an exasperated colonial drill sergeant. His repeated orders for his troops to "front the royal oak" in the center of town (oaks were considered the royal tree of England) struck someone's fancy, and the name stuck. In the Civil War, Front Royal was captured in May 1862 by Stonewall Jackson with the help of spy Belle Boyd.

Today, a long bridge over the Shenandoah leads to tree-lined Royal Avenue (US 340). Turn left onto E. Main St. at the Warren County Courthouse to reach the Village commons with its gazebo, big red caboose, and the town visitors center. Front Royal serves as the northern gateway to Shenandoah National Park and the Blue Ridge, which rises to the south of town.

Sights

A local chapter of the United Daughters of the Confederacy owns and operates the **Warren Rifles Confederate Museum,** 95 Chester St., tel. (540) 636-6982, containing a large collection of arms, uniforms, flags, pictures, and personal items that evoke the Civil War exploits of Stonewall Jackson, Mosby's Rangers, J.E.B. Stuart, and Robert E. Lee. Open April 15-Oct., Mon.-Sat. 9 a.m.-4 p.m., Sunday noon-4 p.m.; $2 adults.

Learn more about life during the days of Belle Boyd, along with details about the spy herself, at the **Belle Boyd Cottage,** 101 Chester St., tel. (540) 636-1446. Open May-Oct., Mon.-Fri. 10 a.m.-3:30 p.m.; $2 adults, $1 children. There's an interesting **elephant mural** by nationally known artist Patricia Wondrow entitled *The Not So National Zoo* on the side of a barn at High St. and Jackson St. To see more murals, head down High St. toward Wondrow's **gallery,** at the Main St. intersection. If her wooden likeness is on the sidewalk, she's at work inside.

Accommodations

The **Blue Ridge Motel,** 1370 N. Shenandoah Ave., tel. (540) 636-7200, is the least expensive in town. Budget. A small step up is the **Twin Rivers Motel,** 1801 Shenandoah Ave., tel. (540) 635-4101 or the **Quality Inn Skyline Drive,** 10 Commerce Ave. (US 522), tel. (540) 635-3161, both moderate.

Architecture is one highlight of the **Chester House B&B,** 43 Chester St., tel. (800) 621-0441 or (540) 635-3937, fax 636-8695. The 1905 Georgian-style home sits amid two acres of lily ponds, garden mazes, and imported fountains and statuary. Three sitting rooms inside are warmed by fireplaces with marble mantels. The Carriage House out back has a kitchen, loft bedroom, and wide windows overlooking the gardens. Moderate-premium. E-mail: chesthse@rma.edu, Web site: www.chesterhouse.com.

Innkeepers Susan and John Lang run the Edwardian mansion known as **Killahevlin,** 1401 North Royal Ave., tel. (800) 847-6132 or (540) 636-7335, fax 636-8694, built by a local limestone baron on one of the highest perches in town. A strong Irish influence pervades, from the reproduction wallpaper to the private pub with oak bar and Irish beer on tap. Premium (two three-room suites in the Tower House out back, near the koi pool and gazebos, qualify as luxury). E-mail: kllhvln@shentel.net, Web site: www.vairish.com.

Camping

Campers should head two miles south of town on US 340 to the **Front Royal/Washington D.C. West KOA,** tel. (540) 635-2741, fax 635-4089, reservations tel. (800) KOA-9114, e-mail: FrntRylKOA@aol.com. Campsites are $23 ($29 with full hookups), and Kamping Kabins cost $40-50.

Food

Set in the old Proctor Biggs building next to the town park, **The Feed Mill Bar and Grill,** 500 E. Main St., tel. (540) 636-3123, serves BBQ and

BELLE BOYD: THE CONFEDERACY'S MATA HARI?

Born on May 9, 1843, in Martinsburg, Belle Boyd, the Confederacy's most colorful secret agent, reveled in attention from an early age. With the arrival of the Civil War, the vivacious young woman found her niche, using her feminine charms and quick mind to coax military secrets from Union troops and pass them on to Confederate officers. By age 21, she had achieved a measure of infamy within Union forces: she had been reported 30 times, arrested six or seven, and thrown in jail twice. During one stay in Washington, D.C.'s Old Capital Prison, Boyd put intelligence messages in India rubber balls and threw them to an accomplice waiting outside her window.

Fellow Southern belles were shocked at Boyd's life of risk—Union authorities twice sent her back behind Confederate lines with stern warnings to stay there. She often traveled alone, meeting with officers from both sides in their private tents with little concern for decorum. Refusing to disguise her handwriting or encode her messages, the socialite spy found herself an international celebrity called "La Belle Rebelle" in France and "That Secesh Cleopatra" in New York.

Front Royal served as her main base of operations. When a Federal regiment under Gen. Nathaniel P. Banks occupied the city in May 1862, Boyd invited the officers to a ball and plied them for information. After her guests had fallen asleep, she reportedly rode 30 miles in the dead of night to pass the intelligence to Stonewall Jackson, who attacked the next morning and captured three-quarters of the Union forces.

After the war ended, Boyd tried her hand at acting and gave public lectures on her secretive adventures. In 1865, she published *Belle Boyd in Camp and Prison*, a dramatic tell-all of her life as a female secret agent. She died on June 11, 1900, in Wisconsin.

club sandwiches on homemade bread ($4-6) and, on weekends, hearty Belgian waffle breakfasts in the $3 range. Dine inside by the animal paintings or out on the porch. Open daily for lunch and dinner.

Schnitzel and wurst are the standbys of **Stadt Kaffe,** 300 E. Main St., tel. (540) 635-8300, run by local Teutonic transplant Elke Cafter. Vegetarians can enjoy cheese spaetzle and there's plenty of German beer to go around. Open Thurs.-Tue. for lunch ($3-9) and dinner ($10-15). Next to the Royal Cinema sits the **Cinema Grill,** 127 E. Main St., tel. (540) 635-2562, a diner with daily breakfast and lunch in the $2-4 range. **L Dee's Pancake House,** 522 E. Main St., tel. (540) 635-3791, offers "breakfast all day" starting at $2.

Recreation
A number of local outfitters take advantage of the fact that one of Virginia's favorite rafting rivers flows practically through their backyard. Most operate campsites down the South Fork of the Shenandoah for overnight visitors during the floating season of March-November. Prices should include equipment, brief instruction, maps, and shuttle service.

The **Front Royal Canoe Co.,** tel. (800) 270-8808 or (540) 635-5440, has day trips for $26-42 along with longer excursions. E-mail: frcanoe@rma.edu, Web site: www.frontroyalcanoe.com. In Bentonville, eight miles south on US 340, **River Rental Outfitters,** Rt. 613, tel. (540) 635-5050 or (800) RAPIDS1 (800-727-

4371), rent canoes for $20-42 per day, kayaks for $16-22, and tubes for $10-12. They also have a fishing and camp store. The **Downriver Canoe Company,** 884 Indian Hollow Rd., tel. (800) 338-1963 or (540) 635-5526, fax 622-2656, has overnight trips from $74-100 for two days to $146 for four days. E-mail: somebody@downriver.com, Web site: www.downriver.com.

Events
Front Royal is home to the **Virginia Mushroom and Wine Festival,** held the third Saturday of May. Contact the Chamber of Commerce for more information.

Shopping
On summer weekends and holidays, the **Front Royal Antique and Flea Market,** tel. (540) 635-7336, is *the* place for assorted treasures, junk, and crafts spread among 100 booths. It's on the US 522 bypass between the Quality Inn and Rt. 55. Alternatively, you can browse year-round through **Valley Vintage Antiques,** 217 E. Main St., tel. (540) 635-2402, specializing in furniture, china, and glass.

Information
The **Front Royal/Warren County Visitor Center,** 414 E. Main St., tel. (800) 338-2576 or (540) 635-3185, fax 635-9758, sits in the restored train station in the town park. They have a well-done walking tour brochure and are open daily 9 a.m.-5 p.m. E-mail: coc@frontroyal.com, Web site: www.frontroyal.com.

Adventure Nearby
Opened to the public in 1939, **Skyline Caverns,** tel. (800) 296-4545 or (540) 635-4545, were discovered a few years earlier by means of a giant sinkhole where the parking lot now sits. The highlight of these caves, otherwise overshadowed by their southern neighbors, are glittering calcite formations called anthodites. These delicate spikes are found in only one other cave in the U.S. (and there in much smaller quantities). They grow one inch every 7,000 years, either pure white or stained brown by iron oxide. Skyline Cavern's crop sprouted in a vacuum left by a receding underground pool.

Through the rest of the cave, high, smooth passages evoke slot canyons of the American southwest. Kids love the Skyline Arrow, an outdoor miniature train that crawls near the entrance. Open daily 9 a.m.-4 or 6:30 p.m., depending on season; $10 adults, $5 children 7-13.

STRASBURG

One of the earliest settlements in the valley, Strasburg has been a crafts center since being chartered in 1761. A tradition of earthen and stoneware pottery was once manifest in six shops going at once in a section called Pot Town. Antiques are now the main draw of the self-proclaimed "Antiques Capital of Virginia," with local ceramics running a close second.

Try any of the dozen or so shops in town for furniture, clothing, folk art, and rugs, including **Vilnis and Company Antiques,** 305 N. Massanutten St. (US 11 and US 55), tel. (540) 465-4405, **Heritage Antiques,** 102 Massanutten St., tel. (540) 465-5000, and **Trousseau Treasures,** 136 E. King St., tel. (540) 465-3534. For a more mass-market approach, stop by the **Strasburg Emporium,** 110 N. Massanutten St., tel. (540) 465-3711, one of the largest antiques centers in the state with over 100 dealers sharing an old former silk mill.

WEST OF THE INTERSTATE

Bryce Resort
Only a few miles from the West Virginia border, this small resort features eight ski slopes ranging from beginner to expert. Nearly 9,000 square feet were added to the lodge in 1997, where lift tickets sell for $25-35. The ski instruction program, developed by German National certified instructor Horst Locher, start with children as young as four. Night skiing ($15), ski rentals, and snowboarding are all options. In the summer, an 18-hole, par 71 golf course enjoys mountain views and all the amenities, and guests can also choose from horseback riding, mountain biking, tennis, grass skiing, and boating in a small nearby lake.

To get here, take I-81 exit 273 onto Rt. 263 and head eleven miles to the entrance on the right. For more information on the resort and lodging options contact (800) 821-1444 or (540) 856-

2121, fax 856-8567, e-mail: bryce@bryceresort. com, Web site: www.bryceresort.com.

Orkney Springs

Five weekends between May and the end of August are filled with symphony, big band, jazz, and folk music during the **Shenandoah Valley Music Festival** in this tiny town in the hills. A benefit ball kicks things off, and ice cream socials and special children's concerts are parts of the program. Tickets are $11-16 for individual events for both reserved seating and general admission, available at the gate or from the festival office in Woodstock, 102 N. Main St., tel. (800) 459-3396 or (540) 459-3396, fax 459-3730, e-mail: svmf@shentel.net, gpsolutions.com/shen-valley-music.

The concerts have been held since the early 1960s at the Shrine Mountain Retreat and Conference Center, a venerable mineral springs resort dating to the turn of the century. The town is 15 miles west of I-81 exit 273 via Rt. 263.

NEW MARKET AND VICINITY

Two major Indian pathways gave this spot on the upper North Fork of the Shenandoah its first official name—Cross Roads. The first inhabitants, the Senedo tribe, were wiped out by the Catawbas from the south when their paths crossed around 1700. In 1796, the town of New Market was established, named after the city in England with the famous racetrack (mirrored in one that once stood here to the west of the settlement). A famous Civil War battle nearby left the town with memories of cannons in the rain and a three-inch shell hole in a post at the intersection of Breckinridge Lane and Congress St. (US 11 through town).

Accommodations

The **Blue Ridge Inn,** 2251 Old Valley Pike, tel. (540) 740-4136, has more character than most motels in the inexpensive-to-moderate price range. It's one mile north of I-81 exit 264, along with a **Budget Inn,** 2192 Old Valley Pike, tel. (540) 740-3105 (moderate). At the same exit you'll find a **Quality Inn Shenandoah Valley,** 162 W. Old Cross Rd., tel. (540) 740-3141, fax 740-3250, offering a pool, sauna, and miniature golf (moderate).

A Touch of Country, 0029 Congress St., tel. (540) 740-8030, has rooms inside the main house and in two separate carriage houses (inexpensive to moderate). Dating to the end of the 18th century, the **Red Shutter Farmhouse B&B,** tel. (800) 738-8262 or (540) 740-4281, sits on 20 acres off Rt. 793 near Endless Caverns. Inexpensive to moderate. The **Cross Roads Inn Bed & Breakfast,** 9222 John Sevier Rd., tel. (888) 740-4157 or (540) 740-4157, fax 740-4255, was built in 1925 for Claude Hoover, one of the driving forces behind Shenandoah National Park. The late Victorian home is run by an Austrian couple who serve afternoon tea with authentic homemade apple strudel. Six rooms range from inexpensive to expensive and include use of an outdoor jacuzzi. E-mail: freisitz@shentel.net, Web site: www.shenwebworks.com:8001/crossroads.

Camping

Seven sites at the **Harrisonburg-New Market KOA,** 3.3 miles east on Rt. 608 from I-81 exit 257, tel. (540) 896-8929, are $20-23 each. The **Rancho Campground,** 2.1 miles S on US 11 from I-81 exit 264, tel. (540) 740-8313, has 60 sites for $18 each.

Food

Apple pie á la mode is one standby of the **New Market Cafe,** 9478 Congress St., tel. (540) 743-8433, open Tues.-Sun. with breakfast from 5 a.m. on. Lunch sandwiches are $2-6, with entrées in the $6-12 range. The **Battlefield Family Restaurant,** 9403 Congress St., tel. (540) 740-3664, also serves dependable, inexpensive fare, including sausage and eggs, steaks, and vegetarian platters. With a real 1950s-diner feel, the **Southern Kitchen,** 9579 Congress St., tel. (540) 740-3514, has sandwiches for $3-6 and dinners for $10 (open daily 7 a.m.-9 or 10 p.m.).

Shopping

A handful of antique stores lines Congress St. within a few blocks of the center of town at Old Cross Rd., stocking everything from pottery to Civil War relics. Try **B&B Valley Antiques,** 9294 Congress St., tel. (540)740-8700, **New Market Antiques,** 9298 Congress St., tel. (540) 740-4446, or the **Nickelodeon Antique Mall,** 9466 S. Congress St., tel. (540) 740-3424.

Shenandoah Valley Crafts & Gifts, 9365 Congress St., tel. (540) 740-3899, sells quilts, baskets, and Virginia hams. Farther down the street is **Paper Treasures,** 9595 Congress St., tel. (540) 740-3135, a captivating place to spend hours browsing among thousands of used books, old comics, records, prints, and magazines dating to the 19th century.

New Market Battlefield Historical Park

On May 15, 1864, one of the last Confederate victories in the valley featured a famous charge by 257 VMI cadets against a line of Union artillery under Maj. Gen. Franz Sigel. The well-preserved battlefield is easily understood and absorbing, whether or not you think children in war is something worth celebrating.

Bypass the private museum on your left to reach the Hall of Valor, run by a nonprofit organization under the authority of VMI. Inside is a visitors center, tel. (540) 740-3101, and a museum dedicated to the cadets. Two short films give some background on Stonewall Jackson's Valley Campaign and the cadets themselves.

Pick up a walking-tour brochure and step outside to begin the mile-long loop trail. Imagine yourself as one of the students—as young as 15—your spirits high at being called to defend your home, then drenched by four days' march in the rain. A headlong charge takes you through the buildings of the Bushong farm, where the terrified family hides in the basement, and across the mud-clogged Field of Lost Shoes toward the deafening thunder of the Union guns.

A 200-foot vista over the peaceful Shenandoah River marks where the trail turns back. Ten cadets died in the process of capturing one cannon, an event honored in a formal ceremony every May 15 at VMI. The costumed reenactment of the battle and the cadets' charge is one of the oldest in the country, held around the same date. Open daily 9 a.m.-5 p.m.; $5 adults, $2 children 6-15.

Shenandoah Caverns

North of New Market (I-81 exit 269), these caverns were unearthed in 1884 during the construction of the valley railroad and opened to the public in 1922. They're the only ones in the state with an elevator, and feature tempting flowstone slabs called the Bacon Formations. American Celebrations on Parade, a personal collection of decades' worth of window displays from around the country, can be visited for a separate

VMI Cadets Thomas G. Jefferson and Moses Ezekiel were among those killed at New Market Battlefield.

admission ($6 adults, $3 children) or as part of a discounted package. Open daily 9 a.m.-5 p.m.; $11.50 adults, $5.50 children 5-14, tel. (540) 477-3115.

Endless Caverns

The largest billboard in the eastern United States points off I-81 toward this serpentine network of passages and tunnels discovered in 1879 by two boys hunting a rabbit. Five miles have been mapped so far, with no end in sight, giving Endless Caverns, tel. (540) 896-2283, the most untamed feel of Virginia's caves. Refreshments are available in the 1920s limestone lodge, and 100 campsites cost $15 for a full hookup. Open daily 9 a.m.-4 or 7 p.m., depending on season; $11 adults, $5.50 children 3-12.

LURAY

The seat of Page County is known for what it's near: the central entrance for Shenandoah National Park, and the most impressive caverns in the east. The US 211 Bypass serves as Main Street, divided into east and west at Broad St. (US 340).

Luray Caverns

By far the most impressive of the valley's commercial caves, this U.S. Registered Natural Landmark encloses the most-visited caverns in the East. From the very start, the ceilings bristle, the floors bulge, and the walls flow in a scale that makes you wish the tour lasted longer than an hour. Fifty-foot drapery is pulled so thin some parts are translucent, near pure white calcite columns and a 170-ton fallen stalactite the size of a school bus. Dream Lake, 2,500 feet square, is only 1-6 inches deep.

The most famous feature of Luray Caverns, though, is only half natural: a "stalacpipe organ," which produces tones with electronically controlled rubber mallets striking stalactites to produce sounds oddly like those of a marimba. Covering 312 acres, the organ is listed in the Guinness Book of World Records as the largest natural instrument in the world.

Back out in the fresh air is an Antique Carriage and Car Museum, with 140 models as old as 1625 (included in admission). And no cav-

ern resort complex would be complete without a gas station, airport, restaurant, golf course, and gift shop, selling everything from cheap pottery to handcuffs. Open daily 8:30 a.m.-4 to 7 p.m., depending on season; 13 adults, $5 children 7-13, tel. (540) 743-6551.

Other Diversions and Recreation

The **Luray Reptile Center and Dinosaur Park,** tel. (540) 743-4113, is home to one of Virginia's largest scaly collections, both extinct and living. Cobras, alligators, and 20-foot pythons coexist with tropical birds and a monkey along Rt. 211 half a mile west of town, with a petting zoo for the children and herpetophobes. Open Tues.-Sun. 10 a.m.-5 p.m.; $5 adults, $4 children 3-12. A carillon of 47 bells fills the **Luray Singing Tower** on West Main St. opposite the caverns. Free live

---

SHENANDOAH AREA WINERIES

Deer Meadow Vineyard
tel. (540) 877-1919 or (800) 653-6632
Near Winchester; Rt. 629 off Rt. 608, 6.5 miles south of US 50/US 55 intersection

Guilford Ridge
tel. (540) 778-3853
Near Luray; Rt. 632 off 211 south of town

Landwirt Vineyard
tel. (540) 833-6000
Near Harrisonburg; Rt. 806 3 miles west of US 11

North Mountain Vineyard and Winery
tel. (540) 436-9463
Near Maurertown; Rt. 655 south of Strasburg

Peaks of Otter Winery
tel. (540) 586-3707
Near Bedford; Rt. 680 near Penick's Mill off Rt. 43
Known for fruit wines.

Shenandoah Vineyards
tel. (540) 984-8699
Near Edinburg; Rt. 675 (S. Ox Rd.)

Rockbridge Vineyard
tel. (540) 377-6204
Near Raphine; Rt. 606
Harvest Fest in October

concerts are given in the spring and fall Saturday, Sunday at 2 p.m. and during the summer on Tuesday, Thursday, Saturday, and Sunday at 8 p.m. For a "taste of Nashville" stop by the **Shenandoah Jubilee,** 750 Middleburg Rd., tel. (540) 778-1933. The two-hour country-music and comedy show is performed April-Dec. on Thursday and Sunday; $13 adults, $7 children 6-13.

The South Fork of the Shenandoah from Luray to Front Royal is known for great **bass fishing,** packing the placid waters with canoes, tubes, and private boats on busy weekend afternoons from spring to fall. **Shenandoah River Outfitters, Inc.,** 6502 S. Page Valley Rd. (Rt. 684), tel. (800) 6CANOE2 (800-622-6632) or (540) 743-4159, offers rentals and trips along the river 10 miles northwest of town. Canoes are $46 per day, kayaks $30, and tubes $14, including shuttle service. A special canoe and steak dinner trip (groups only) can be arranged for $42 pp, including lunch. They also operate a number of fully furnished cabins ($100-120) and campgrounds ($5 pp) along the way. E-mail: canoes@shenandoah-river.com, Web site: www.shenadoah-river.com.

Accommodations

The nearly identical **Luray Caverns Motel East,** 831 W. Main St., tel. (540) 743-4531, and **Luray Caverns Motel West,** US 211 W, tel. (540) 743-4536 range from inexpensive to moderate. **The Mimsyln,** 401 W. Main St., tel. (800) 296-5105 or (540) 743-5105, opened in 1931 on top of a commanding hill just outside the center of town. The "Grand Old Inn of Virginia" sits amid 14 acres of lawns and gardens overlooked by a terrace and solarium. Through the front doors a red carpet flows down the central staircase. An antique and art gallery houses works by Virginia artist P. Buckley Moss. Moderate to expensive.

A long driveway leaves the bustle of the US 11/Broad St. intersection, passing horses grazing in fenced pastures, to reach **The Ruffner House B&B,** 440 Ruffner House Rd., tel. (540) 743-7855. Built in 1840 to replace an original 1739 log cabin, the spacious house features high ceilings, wide hallways, and four gigantic guest rooms. Outside are gardens and a pool. Expensive. Rooms in the **Ramada Inn Luray,** US 211E Bypass, tel. (540) 743-4521, fax 743-6863, are decorated with antiques and some feature whirlpools. Expensive.

Head five miles east on the US 211 bypass to reach **The Cabins at Brookside,** 2978 US 211E, tel. (800) 299-2655 or (540) 743-5698, fax 743-1326, in the heart of the rich farmlands of the Shenandoah foothills. Eight rooms fill private log cabins—formerly a 1940s-era filling station—next to a rushing stream, most of which have fireplaces and kitchens but no phones or TVs (honeymoon cabins have hot tubs). The nearby **Brookside Restaurant** will do for guests who don't want to make the trek back into town. Moderate to luxury. Other, more remote cabins are available on a longer (week-to-week) basis. Contact the Page Country Chamber of Commerce for more details.

Camping

Yogi Bear's Jellystone Park, tel. (540) 743-4002, sits off Rt. 211 three miles east of town. Campsites are $22.50 ($28 with full hookups), and cabins range from inexpensive for "barebones" to moderate for "comfort." On hand are a stocked fishing pond, pool, camp store, and laundromat. **The Country Waye RV Resort,** tel. (540) 743-7222, offers furnished cabins for $35-40 and 78 campsites for $18-22. All the amenities are included: pool, hot tub, game room, and laundry. Maintained by the National Forest, **Camp Roosevelt,** tel. (540) 984-4101, has 10 basic sites for $6 each, 8.5 miles northwest of Luray on Rt. 675.

Food

Virginia wines and a view of the Massanutten Mountains are two reasons to stop by the **Parkhurst Restaurant,** tel. (540) 743-6009, on Rt. 211 2.5 miles west of the caverns. The menu covers all the bases—chicken, pasta, fish, and beef—with a cozy colonial flair, making reservations for dinner (entrées $18-27) a good idea. Open Tues.-Sat. The **Sundowner Cafe,** in the Ramada Inn, is also said to be good, with a weekday lunch buffet for $4-7 and dinner entrées in the $7-15 range.

Events

Luray's **Mayfest,** the third Saturday of May, fills the streets with pony and llama rides, antique dealers, and food vendors. A traditional maypole dance and historic home tours are also part of the festivities. Around Columbus Day in October, the **Page County Heritage Festival** has been known for arts and crafts since 1060.

Information

For the most up-to-date information on either festival and any other activities in town, contact the **Page County Chamber of Commerce**, 46 C. Main St., tel. (540) 743-3915, e-mail: page-cofc@shentel.net, Web site: www.pen.k12.va.us/Anthology/Div/Page/pcounty.html. The chamber also operates a visitors center, open daily 9 a.m.-5 p.m.

SHENANDOAH NATIONAL PARK

One of the country's most popular national parks protects close to 300 square miles of the Appalachian Mountains, from some 60 rough-edged peaks to all the stream-filled nooks and wildflower crannies in between. Zipping it all together is the Skyline Drive, stretching for 105 miles along ridgetops from Front Royal to Waynesboro. Probably the most beautiful drive in the eastern U.S., this meandering byway continues as the Blue Ridge Parkway south toward North Carolina and the Smoky Mountains.

Few visitors venture far off the road, either because they're content with the countless overlooks or because they're in a hurry to move on. Those who do leave their cars discover gushing spring waterfalls, quiet oak glades, and mountaintop views that beat anything available from the asphalt. It may take some effort to put the miles between you and the high-season crowds, but you won't be disappointed.

All mileposts are measured from 0 at Front Royal.

HISTORY

The idea of protecting a large swath of Virginia's mountains had been around since the turn of the century, but it took Governor Harry Byrd's creations of a state conservation and development commission in 1926 to get the ball rolling. Without federal money to buy land, the Virginia State legislature passed an act that required landowners to sell their plots within 10 years. The project received the enthusiastic support of President Hoover, who spent every moment he could spare at a fishing camp on the upper Rapidan River within the borders of the proposed park.

Ground was broken for the Skyline Drive in 1931, supposedly after Hoover got the idea during a horseback ride along the crest of the mountains. Local farmers provided the labor in exchange for money from drought-relief funds, while Franklin Delano Roosevelt's Civilian Conservation Corps pitched in with the construction of scenic overlooks, picnic areas, and landscaping. Four thousand mountain residents had found somewhere else to live by the time the park was dedicated in 1936. When the road was finished three years later, the land was slowly allowed to return to its natural state—so much so that in 1976 Congress declared two-fifths of the park wilderness.

HABITATS

Flora

With elevations ranging from 600 feet at the northern entrance to over 4,000 feet on mountain peaks, Shenandoah National Park encloses mostly mature deciduous forest. Close to 100 tree species and 47 species of mosses and ferns blanket the slopes. A chestnut blight near the turn of the century wiped out most of that native species, leaving oak and hickory the most common trees in the park. Pines and scrub oak grow on drier slopes, while ash and basswood line many streams. Rhododendrons and azaleas fill the understory.

At the right time of year, meadows sparkle with wildflowers and berries—especially Big Meadows, which are thought to have been burned clear by Native Americans looking to attract game and create more room for berry bushes. Higher elevations help the spring blossoms of violets, chickweeds, and bloodroots persist after summer heat has claimed the Piedmont. Periwinkles and columbines flower in April, followed by gaudy yellow cowslips in May and black-eyed Susans and Queen Anne's lace in August.

Fauna

Lucky hikers may spot a bobcat or wild turkey among the trees, while unlucky ones may have a too-close encounter with a timber rattler or copperhead. At dawn and dusk, white-tailed deer congregate in open areas, particularly Big Meadows, browsing on tender plants until spooked by a car or breeze.

Shenandoah National Park has one of the highest densities of black bears of any park in the country—about one per square mile. It's rare to see more than paw prints or scat, though, unless you leave your empty tuna cans outside the tent at night. A few colonies of beavers live along the Thornton and Rapidan Rivers.

Two hundred species of birds include permanent residents such as the barred owl and ruffed grouse. Migratory woodcocks arrive in the early spring, while warblers, thrushes, tanagers, and flycatchers move in during the summer. A hawk or six-foot turkey vulture circling the updrafts is a common sight along the Skyline Drive. Virginia's first breeding pair of peregrine falcons in 40 years was found nesting in the park in 1994.

ACCESS

Shenandoah National Park is divided into three sections by roads bisecting the Skyline Drive. The Northern District stretches from Front Royal (milepost 0) to Thornton Gap (milepost 31.5), where US 221 connects Luray to the Piedmont. The Central District continues south to US 33 at Swift Run Gap (milepost 65.7), and Rockfish Gap and I-64 mark the boundary of the Southern District, the park, and the Skyline Drive.

Each road entrance has an information booth where you can pay your admission fee and receive a map of the park and a copy of *Shenandoah Overlook* magazine. Various hiking trails enter the park from the base of the mountains on either side, often continuing as far as the crest and the Skyline Drive.

Fees

Shenandoah National Park's early years—when it cost 25 cents to enter and $1 for an annual pass—are long gone. In the mid 1990s, national park fees were raised throughout the country in an effort to make up for chronic underfund-

ing and to direct more dollars back into the parks themselves. Today, a pass (good for seven consecutive days) costs $10 per car and $5 per pedestrian or bicyclist.

A year-long Shenandoah Passport is now $20, and a Golden Eagle Passport—good at any national park for a year—is $50. US Citizens over 62 can buy a Golden Age Passport ($10) for lifetime access to any national park, and a visitor with a disability can receive a free Golden Access Passport with similar privileges. Fees in all national parks are suspended on August 25 for Founders Day, celebrating the establishment of the National Park Service.

When To Go

Lying only 72 miles from Washington, D.C., can seem a curse on weekends and holidays in the summer and fall, when traffic on the Skyline Drive crawls along at well below the 35-mph speed limit and RVs seem to jam every turnoff. This also happens to be the time when haze from power plants in the Ohio Valley can almost obscure the view. For the height of the fall foliage display it may be necessary to make accommodation reservations as much as a year in advance.

The best time to avoid the two million people who visit per year, then, while still getting the view, vegetation, and wildlife you came for, is in the spring and on weekdays during the summer and fall. In the winter, most facilities shut down, staffing is reduced to a minimum, and parts of the Skyline Drive are often closed due to weather. You'll have most of the park to yourself, then, which can be a magical experience if you're prepared. Bring a full tank of gas, tire chains or snow tires, water, and warm clothing—even for a drive.

HIKING

Close to 500 miles of trails crisscross the Shenandoah, usually uphill or downhill, and occasionally precipitous. Over a dozen waterfalls accessible only on foot are a highlight of any hot ramble. Remnants of early settlements are visible in crumbling walls and chimneys and mossy cemeteries hidden in the underbrush.

Each visitors center has free maps of each of the 112 trails, along with PATC topos and a detailed one-sheet map of the entire park pub-

THE APPALACHIAN TRAIL

North America's most famous footpath winds 2,155 miles from Maine to Georgia, connecting Appalachian ridges and river valleys, pristine wilderness and stoplight suburbia like an enormous green zipper. All but three percent of the greenway is protected by government-owned land or private rights-of-way; the U.S. Forest Service administers 850 miles, and 14 states oversee another 420 miles.

As classic as it is, the AT isn't a historic trail. The "impossible" idea began as a 1921 proposal by Massachusetts regional planner Benton MacKaye, who envisioned it as an escape for residents of the increasingly populated east. (Even today, close to two thirds of the population of the U.S. lives within 500 miles of the trail.) The Appalachian Trail Conference (ATC.), a loose organization of local hiking clubs, was formed in 1925. Thanks to its unpaid efforts, the first continuous trail opened in 1937, but various highways, extreme weather, and the privations of WW II almost buried the project. In the early 1950s, the entire pathway was relocated, cleared, and marked, and in 1968 it was declared the nation's first National Scenic Trail (akin to a linear National Park, but without the funding).

At its northern end, the trail starts at the peak of Maine's Mt. Katahdin (5,267 feet), winding its most isolated miles through the Maine backwoods. From there it passes through the White Mountains of New Hampshire and the Green Mountains of Vermont before clipping off the western ends of Massachusetts and Connecticut. Southern New York state, where the trail crosses the Hudson River, marks the beginning of the trail's least rural section. Northern New Jersey is next, followed by the Cumberland Valley in eastern Pennsylvania. (At the C&O Canal in Maryland, the **Big Blue Trail** heads off in a 144-mile loop to the west, crossing the Potomac and curving south the meet up with the AT again at Matthews Arm, in Shenandoah National Park—contact the Potomac Appalachian Trail Club for more information) Soon A.T.C. headquarters in Harper's Ferry, WV, comes into sight, where through-hikers sign a logbook and have their pictures taken, foot-weary but smiling.

Virginia contains a quarter of the AT and some of its most breath-taking scenery. Winding down around the Skyline Drive through Shenandoah National Park, the trail then steers west to touch the West Virginia line. It crosses the Blue Ridge Parkway only twice on its way through some of the state's best wilderness, including the Mount Rogers National Recreation Area. South of Virginia, the AT follows the state line between Tennessee and North Carolina on its way through the rugged undulations of the Great Smoky Mountains National Park. The finish line (or starting point, if you're heading north) comes at the peak of Springer Mountain (3,782 feet), in Georgia's Chattahoochee National Forest. White painted blazes mark the path the entire way, doubled at turns and junctions.

Through-hiking, as difficult and expensive as it is (4-6 months and thousands of dollars each way), has become a way of life for some people ever since Early Shaffer first hiked the entire length of the trail in 1948. Hikers ranging from a six-year-old to octogenarians have completed the journey, including a blind man led by his seeing-eye dog. Decades of experience in regulating the trail have resulted in a time-proven set of regulations and strong suggestions. No motorized traffic, horses, or pack animals are allowed on the trail, and dogs must be on a leash (they're prohibited in the Smokies, and discouraged in general). Stay on the trail, since much of the surrounding land is private, and leave no trace; camp at established sites and build no campfires. Overnight camping permits are necessary in the two national parks. Try not to hike alone, since solitary travelers have met with harassment and worse.

Information

Two organizations serve as information clearinghouses and administrative centers for the Appalachian Trail. The 5,500-member **Potomac Appalachian Trail Club,** 118 Park St. SE, Vienna, VA 22180-4609, concentrates on the 200 miles of trail from Pennsylvania to Virginia. It maintains 80% of the trails in Shenandoah National Park, along with seven huts and six public cabins along the AT Each primitive cabin holds 8-12 people ($12 weeknights, $15-

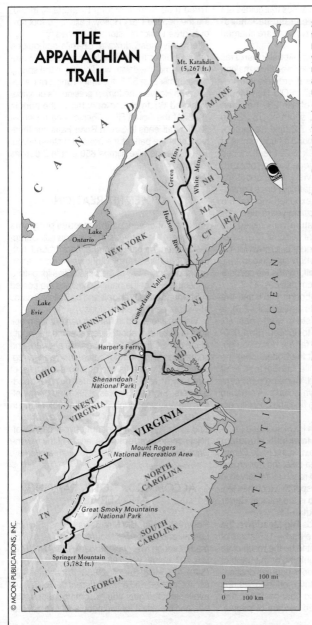

20 weekends and holidays for the first five people). Membership is $25 per year, including access to nine more private cabins and a subscription to the monthly newsletter, the *Potomac Appalachian*. There are dozens of maps and guidebooks available from the headquarters, which you can reach at tel. (703) 242-0693, fax 242-0968, e-mail: wriley1226 @aol.com, patc.simplenet. com.

The **Appalachian Trail Conference,** 799 Washington St., P.O. Box 807, Harpers Ferry, WV 25425, works to maintain the trail and to preserve the natural habitats and inhabitants of the surrounding buffer zone. Membership is $30 pp or $35 per couple per year, and comes with a year's subscription to *Appalachian Trail News* and discounts in their Ultimate Trail Store (e-mail: sales@ atconf.org). Its booklist includes 11 official guidebook/map sets for different sections of the trail, the *AT Thru-hikers' Companion,* and the *AT Data Book,* updated yearly. Other volumes cover natural history, hikers' memoirs, geology, and history of the trail. Contact the ATC at tel. (304) 535-6331, e-mail: info@atconf.org, Web site: www.atconf.org.

lished by Trails Illustrated. Various trail guides are available at the bookstore in the park head-quarters building near Luray. Fees are charged at a few trailheads.

A 101-mile segment of the Appalachian Trail threads its way down the Skyline Drive, making it ideal for short hikes as it crosses and recrosses the road. The trail to Old Rag Mountain leaves a parking lot off Rt. 231 between Sperryville and Madison, south of US 221 to the east of the park. The 7.2-mile (roundtrip) trail winds up, over, and around a huge jumble of granite boulders to the peak (3,291 feet), dotted with water-filled depressions called "buzzard baths." As you enjoy the view, think about the fact that the rock you're standing on is considered some of the oldest exposed rock on the East Coast—around 1.1 billion years old.

An easy self-guided nature walk called the **Traces Nature Trail** starts at milepost 22.2, passing old settlements and mature oak forest for 1.7 miles roundtrip. Another short self-guided trail, the **Stony Man Nature Trail,** climbs the second-highest peak in the park from milepost 41.7.

Just south of Skyland Lodge you'll find the trail to **White Oak Canyon** (milepost 42.6), a spectacular hike down a steep gorge past six waterfalls ranging from 35 to 85 feet. The 1,000-foot climb gets harder the farther down you go, but there are campsites at the bottom near the town of Syria. The 1.2-mile **Limberlost Trail** also leaves from Skyland, heading past centuries-old hemlocks and white oaks. A crushed stone walkway makes it the first and only fully accessible trail in the park.

A steep path leaves from Hawksbill Gap (milepost 45.6) to the top of **Hawksbill Mountain** (4,049 feet), the highest point in the park. Climbing 1,557 feet in less than a mile, the trail crosses a heavily logged area to reach an observation tower at the peak (a great spot to watch hawks). Sharing the same trailhead is the track to **Cedar Run Falls,** 3.5 miles roundtrip.

Near milepost 51 spreads **Big Meadows,** the largest treeless area in the park—150 acres of fields and wetlands thought to be the result of an ancient fire, either from lightning or the hand of man. This is one of the most popular destinations along the Skyline Drive, offering various visitor facilities and a good chance of spotting herds of deer unimpressed by cars or people.

Three trails lead to different waterfalls, including the popular Dark Hollow Falls, a 70-foot flow over green volcanic stone (1.4 miles roundtrip). Alternately, head down a 1.8-mile self-guided nature trail or the half-mile path to Big Meadows Swamp, filled with wildflowers in the spring.

From milepost 52.5, the **Mill Prong Trail** leads to Camp Hoover, the former president's unofficial weekend White House donated to the park in 1933. At the South River Picnic Area (milepost 62.8) a trail leads to **South River Falls,** the third-highest in the park at the head of a steep gorge. The moderate hike climbs 850 feet in 2.6 miles roundtrip.

OTHER RECREATION

Park staff offer various **interpretive programs** throughout the spring, summer, and fall. Campfire talks on the park's cultural background, naturalist-led hikes, and wildflower identification walks are only a few of the possibilities for getting under the skin of the park. Schedules are posted in **Shenandoah Overlook** and on bulletin boards at visitors centers and lodges.

Visitors interested in **fishing** can pursue brook trout in dozens of short, steep streams the length of the park. Only artificial lures are allowed, and some streams are under catch-and-release regulations. Pick up a fishing brochure and a list of streams at any visitors center or park headquarters. Skyland Stables at Skyland Lodge offers the only opportunity for **horseback riding** in the park—down a handful of yellow-blazed trails. And even if you don't get out of your car, 75 official **scenic overlooks** the length of the Skyline Drive are more than enough to fill an entire day.

ACCOMMODATIONS, CAMPING, AND SERVICES

Reservations for Big Meadows Lodge, Skyland Lodge, and the Lewis Mountain Cabins can be made through reservations via **ARAMARK,** P.O. Box 727, Luray, VA 22835, tel. (800) 999-4714 or (540) 743-5108, fax 743-7883. Prices are highest in October, and a few different packages are available. One gets you accommodations, dinner, and breakfast for two people for two days for

$239 (add $15 for tickets to Luray Caverns).

The park's three campgrounds feature tent, trailer, and RV sites (no water or electric hookups) for $12-14. A 14-day limit is in effect June-Oct. The Potomac Appalachian Trail Club maintains huts and cabins along the Appalachian Trail. Backcountry camping is free, but you'll need a permit from one of the visitors centers, entrance stations, or park headquarters (also available by mail). Most facilities are open from March or April to Oct. or Nov., so call ahead if you plan to visit at either end of the season.

Starting from Front Royal, the **Elkwallow Wayside** (milepost 24.1) has a restaurant, tel. (540) 999-2253, snack bar, grocery store, gas station, and gift shop. At **Thornton Gap** (milepost 31.5), the Panorama Restaurant, tel. (540) 999-2265, serves three square meals daily. **Skyland Lodge,** tel. (540) 999-2211, began as Stoneyman Camp in 1894. At 3,680 feet it's the highest point on Skyline Drive (milepost 41.8), which means great views from most of the 117 rooms. "Rustic" cabin rooms are inexpensive to moderate, motel-style rooms in the main lodge range from moderate to expensive, and suites climb into the luxury range. None have phones, but some have TVs. The glass-walled restaurant lets you enjoy steaks, trout, and other honest fare while looking out over the forest, and the Tap Room has live entertainment on summer nights. Guided horseback rides from the stables, tel. (540) 999-2210, run $20 per hour, with ponies available for children over a certain height.

Built in 1939, the **Big Meadows Lodge,** tel. (800) 999-4714 or (540) 999-2221, has a cozier feel, thanks to stone walls paneled with native chestnut wood. The sitting room features a fireplace and outdoor deck with the requisite gorgeous vista; otherwise, the facilities are similar to those at Skyland. Rooms in the main lodge are moderate, as are 11 cabins. Separate apartments and suites are moderate to premium. At the same turnoff (milepost 51.2) is the park's largest and most popular campground with 237 sites. This is the only place you can reserve sites in advance (up to eight weeks ahead) through MISTIX, P.O. Box 85705, San Diego, CA 92138, tel. (800) 365-CAMP

(800-365-2267). Next door are a coffee shop, gas station, camp store, and ranger station.

Lewis Mountain (milepost 57.6) has cabins with one or two rooms, ranging from inexpensive to moderate. All are heated and provide linens, but they don't have phones or TVs. Cooking is done outdoors on a grill. Budget tent cabins are also available. Thirty-one campsites are first-come, first-served, right next to the information center, gift and food shop, showers, and laundry. At **Loft Mountain** (milepost 80), you'll find a Wayside and Campstore, tel. (804) 823-4515, with showers, laundry, and a grill with a limited food selection. Over 200 campsites are first-come, first-served.

INFORMATION

The park has two **visitor centers:** Dickey Ridge (milepost 4.6) and the Harry F. Byrd, Sr. Visitors Center in Big Meadows. Each is open April-Oct. daily 9 a.m.-5 p.m., with reduced hours through the end of November. Both are stocked with information, exhibits, maps, and books. **Park Headquarters,** tel. (540) 999-3500 or (800) 828-1120 (TDD), are four miles east of Luray on US 211, open Mon.-Fri. 9 a.m.-5 p.m. The same building is home to the **bookstore** of the Shenandoah Natural History Association, tel. (540) 999-3582, with a large selection of books on the flora, fauna, trails, and history of the park. The Association also rents Explorer Backpacks for children, complete with field guides, binoculars, magnifying glasses, and notepaper. Shenandoah National Park's **emergency number** is (800) 732-0911, and the **haze hotline,** tel. (540) 999-3500, can give you an up-to-the-minute report on viewing conditions Mon.-Fri. after 2 p.m.

An excellent map of the park is printed by **Trails Illustrated,** P.O. Box 4357, Evergreen, CO 80437, tel. (800) 962-1643, fax 626-8676, e-mail: xyz-topo@aol. com, Web site: www.trailsillustrated.com. The map costs $9. Visit the park on the Internet at www.nps. gov/shen, or at www.American ParkNetwork.com/parkinfo/ sh/index.html.

The Official AT Answer Shirt

1. 15-20 miles a day
2. Yes, I've seen bears
3. Mac & cheese
4. 50 lbs. or so
5. In a tent
6. 4-6 months, over 2,000 miles
7. Yes, I WALKED here

HARRISONBURG AND VICINITY

The urban center of the northern Blue Ridge is home to 34,000 people and some 20 major industries. Surrounding Rockingham County is number-one in the state in production of beef, dairy products, and poultry (only one county in the nation produces more turkeys annually) and leads four other Virginia counties and three in West Virginia who come to Harrisonburg to shop and invest. Thousands of local farmers come together in huge farmers' markets. At these, you might find yourself parked next to a black horse-drawn buddy carrying a family of Old Order Mennonites—about 1,000 live in the area in a severe, simple lifestyle similar to Pennsylvania's Amish, with whom they share a common Anabaptist religious heritage. Three of the Shenandoah's largest schools—James Madison University (JMU), Bridgewater College, and Eastern Mennonite University—have campuses in the city.

HISTORY

Harrisonburg was founded in the 1740s by Thomas Harrison near the intersection of the Spotswood Trail and the main Indian road down the valley. Strict Methodists started the city's first school in 1794, outlawing gaming and "instruments of music" and decreeing that no student be "permitted on any account whatever to wear Ruffles or powder his hair." The Battle of Harrisonburg, on June 6, 1862, saw the death of Gen. Turner Ashby, one of Stonewall Jackson's most trusted and respected officers.

SIGHTS

Court Square
The heart of downtown rings the limestone-faced Rockingham County Courthouse. Dating from the turn of the century, the imposing building is the fifth to sit on the original 1.5-acre plot of land donated by Thomas Harrison in 1779. Look for the copper dome of the **springhouse** at the southwest corner, an exact replica, erected in 1995, of the original watering hole and meeting place.

Virginia Quilt Museum
Both traditional and modern masters of the art of quilting have works on display in the 1855 **Warren-Sipe House,** 301 S. Main St., tel. (540) 434-4762. People began making quilts—blanket covers made out of scraps—out of necessity, since new bedclothes were expensive, but quilting has evolved into its own art form. Three rotating exhibits per year feature some wild, colorful examples edging towards fabric impres-

GHOSTS OF HARRISONBURG

On December 1, 1900, an aunt was checking on a baby in an upstairs bedroom when she bent to blow out an oil lamp. Low on oil, the lamp suddenly exploded, igniting the woman's dress and burning her so badly that she died the next day. Local legend holds that glowing hand prints from the unlucky aunt appear on the wall of the old house, now part of the Willow Hill subdivision. Previous owners have witnessed the door to the master bedroom slamming shut on its own.

Residents of the Funk House on Mason Street—usually college students—tell of blasts of cold air gusting through rooms, and doors closing without visible assistance. One person reported that in the early 1970s she woke up in the middle of the night feeling as if she were suffocating and couldn't get out of bed. As a possible explanation, folklore scholars point out the old English custom of "mattressing," in which poor families piled mattresses on sick or elderly people they couldn't afford to take care of and sat on them until they suffocated.

Harrisonburg's most famous specter is said to be Colonel Warren, of the Warren-Sipe House, killed during the Battle of the Wilderness by a bullet in the head. A number of witnesses have spotted his ghost at the first landing of the stairway, standing in full uniform with its head wrapped in wide bandages.

WASHINGTON D.C. AND VICINITY

MARYLAND

Potomac River

Rock Creek Park

NATIONAL ZOOLOGICAL PARK

WASHINGTON NATIONAL CATHEDRAL

WASHINGTON, D.C.

Anacostia River

National Arboretum

NEW YORK AVE.

RFK STADIUM

CONSTITUTION AVE.

KENILWORTH AQUATIC GARDENS

JACK KENT COOKE STADIUM

ARLINGTON NATIONAL CEMETERY

E. CAPITOL ST.

CONGRESSIONAL CEMETERY

East Potomac Park

NATIONAL AIRPORT

VIRGINIA

GEORGE WASHINGTON MEMORIAL PKWY.

CAPITAL BELTWAY

MARYLAND

CAPITAL BELTWAY

0   2 mi

0   2 km

© MOON PUBLICATIONS, INC.

sionism. Notice the one made from old Bull Durham tobacco pouches. Open Monday, Thur.-Sat. 10 a.m.-4 p.m., Sunday 1-4 p.m.; $4 adults, $2 children 6-12.

James Madison University

Twelve thousand students call this beautiful 472-acre campus home for as many years as it takes to complete a bachelor's or master's degree in the sciences, arts, business, health, or education. The well-rounded public university also supports a number of successful sports teams that make regular appearances in the NCAA playoffs. Information is available in Wilson Hall, tel. (540) 568-6989, Mon.-Fri. 8:30-4:30 p.m.

On campus, the **Life Science Museum,** 17 Grace St., tel. (540) 568-6378, is small but has high quality natural-history displays including

live reptiles and insects that children will love. Open Mon.-Fri. 9 a.m.-3 p.m. JMU also administers the **arboretum** on University Blvd. Thirty-three acres of mature natural forest surround ponds and landscaped plots of shrubs and flowers. Nature trails weave through the leaves and across little Monet-esque bridges over a stream. It's open dawn to dusk for free, with occasional tours, lectures, and workshops. Call (540) 568-6340 for more information.

ACCOMMODATIONS

Inexpensive

Shoney's Inn, 45 Burgess Rd. (I-81 exit 247), tel. (540) 433-6089 or 433-6385, offers a heated indoor pool, sauna, whirlpool, exercise room. The *a Harrisonburg firefighting company in the early 20th century*

Ramada Inn, 1 Pleasant Valley Rd., tel. (540) 434-9981, fax 434-7088, is off I-81 exit 243. Head south past I-81 exit 243 into the countryside to reach the **Rockingham Motel,** 4035 S. Main St. (US 11), tel. (540) 433-2538, fax 433-0832, and the **Village Inn,** tel./fax (540) 434-7355.

Expensive

The Joshua Wilton House, 412 S. Main St., tel. (540) 434-4464, claims the titles of both best hotel and best restaurant in the city. The Victorian mansion was built in 1888 by the owner of a hardware store on Court Square, who went on to start the local electric company. Wilton's residence, naturally, was the first in town with electricity—even before it had plumbing.

Much of the original materials and craftsmanship remain, including the leaded glass in the front door and the parquet floor and banister in the main hall. Five bedrooms feature period antiques, four-poster beds, and faux-marble fireplaces. Enjoy the inn's award-winning cuisine in the two front rooms, where a five-course prix fixe menu is $40 ($55 with wine). More casual fare is served in three back rooms and on an outdoor patio cafe, with smoked salmon and crayfish cakes appetizers ($5-7) and entrées such as Cornish game hen and buckwheat crepes ($10-19). Rates include breakfast. E-mail: jwhouse@rica.net, Web site: www.rica.net/jwhouse/.

FOOD

Coffee and Snacks

A piano, couches, and funky local art on the walls make **The Artful Dodger,** 47 W. Court Square, tel. (540) 432-1179, a classic coffeehouse. It also serves desserts and light food for lunch (Mon.-Fri.) and dinner (Mon.-Sat.), and has live music at night on occasion. Look for the 20-foot ice cream cone in front of **Kline's Dairy Bar,** 58 E. Wolfe St., tel. (540) 434-6980, serving soft-serve ice cream, sundaes, and shakes (in the same building as the Smokin' Pig BBQ).

Inexpensive Fare

Jess' Lunch, 22 S. Main St., tel. (540) 434-8282, is an old city standby with the best hot dogs in town. Low-priced breakfast and lunch are served Mon.-Sat. in diner booths and at the counter. **Nancy's Cafe,** 68 W. Water St., tel. (540) 433-6393, is another plain but pleasant place with sandwiches and breakfast for $2-3 and burgers and entrées for $4-6. They offer three meals from 5:30 a.m. Mon.-Fri., and breakfast and lunch on Saturday. "Home cooking from scratch" is the calling card of the **L&S Diner,** 255 N. Liberty St., tel. (540) 434-5572. The bright-red diner recalls the Happy Days of the 1940s and 1950s, with counter seating only for three meals Mon.-Sat.

Ethnic

Gyros (YEE-rose), souvlaki, and homemade soups and salads keep **Dave's Taverna,** 95 S. Main St., tel. (540) 564-1487, in business. Sandwiches are $4.50, and pizzas run $6.50-11.50. The popular **Indian and American Cafe,** 91 N. Main. St., tel. (540) 433-1177, cooks up spicy curries, *chapatis, somosas,* and chutneys. Dishes cost $5-6 during lunch and $7.50-11 for dinner, and can be prepared with or without meat.

Both restaurants are open for lunch and dinner Mon.-Sat.

Fine Dining
Aside from The Joshua-Wilton House, Harrisonburg's only other establishment of note is the **Olympic Room,** at the Four Points Hotel Harrisonburg, 1400 E. Market St., tel. (540) 433-2521. Continental food is served in an elegantly relaxed setting for three meals daily, including a Sunday brunch. Entrées are $8-11 for lunch and $10-21 for dinner.

ENTERTAINMENT

James Madison University
The university's College of Arts and Letters supports various **music and drama** offerings throughout the year, from the Richmond Ballet and jazz to opera and touring Broadway musicals. There's a box office in Harrison Hall, Room A103, tel. (540) 568-3330, open Mon.-Fri. 1-5 p.m. Tickets to JMU Dukes **football** and **basketball** games can be ordered by calling (540) 568-DUKE (540-568-3853).

SHOPPING

A Touch of the Earth, 163 S. Main St., tel./fax (540) 432-1894, e-mail: desk@rica.net, stocks a little bit of everything from far-off corners of the planet. Afghani carpets, southwestern Indian pottery, Balinese carvings, and a roomful of drums are only the beginning. If you can't find it there, swing by **Gift & Thrift,** 227 N. Main St., tel. (540) 433-8844, covering the rest of the globe with Salvadoran painted boxes, Vietnamese ceramics, and Philippine shell ornaments. Half thrift shop and half international crafts store, this fascinating place is run by the Mennonites as a nonprofit organization.

James McHone Antique Jewelry, 75 S. Court Sq., tel. (540) 433-1833, e-mail: chiago@rica.net, specializes in estate jewelry both new and antique, with a great selection of pearls and Wedgewood cameos. For stained glass and country pieces try **Villager Antiques,** 673 N. Main St., tel. (540) 433-7226. Over 50 dealers fill the **Rolling Hills Antique Mall,** 779 E. Market St., tel.

(540) 433-8988, stuffed to the rafters with everything from kitchen collectibles to "automobilia."

EVENTS

The Rockingham County Fairgrounds keep busy year-round, hosting the **Spring Arts and Crafts Show and Sale** in March, the **Annual Antique Bottle and Collectible Show** in April, and the **Shenandoah Valley Food & Business Fair** and **Annual Memorial Day Horse Fair & Auction** in May. **Summerfest,** tel. (540) 434-1777, rolls into Hillandale Park in June. Biggest of all is the **Rockingham Country Fair,** tel. (540) 434-0005 in August, an agricultural expo rated as one of the top 10 in the country by the *Los Angeles Times.* Competitions in flowers, crops, livestock, and art compete with country music, tractor pulls, and demolition derbies for a week near the middle of the month.

INFORMATION

The **Harrisonburg-Rockingham County Visitors Center,** is at 10 East Gay St., tel. (540) 434-2319, fax 433-2293, e-mail: info@harrisonburgrockingham.com, open Mon.-Fri. 9 a.m.-5 p.m. and weekends May-December. Walking-tour maps are available for people who can't make the **guided tour** of the downtown that leaves from the Municipal building Wednesday at 10 a.m.

NEAR HARRISONBURG

Farmer's Markets
The flowing valley farmland surrounding Harrisonburg sets the stage for two examples of the original rural version of the shopping mall. Follow S. Main St. out of town as it turns into US 11 to reach the **Shenandoah Heritage Farmer's Market** between I-81 exits 240 and 243, where you can browse Civil War memorabilia, antique tractors, model trains, crafts, and furniture as well as produce. It's open year-round weekdays and some weekends—call (540) 433-3929 for current hours. A few miles farther south on Rt. 42 between Bridgewater and Dayton is the **Dayton**

Farmer's Market, tel. (540) 879-2613 or 879-9885. Homemade breads, cheese, and jellies fill about 20 booths next to country hams, jams, and toys. Take a break from shopping with a bite at **Huyard's Country Kitchen.** This one is open year-round Thur. 9 a.m.-6 p.m., Friday 9 a.m.-8 p.m., and Saturday 9 a.m.-5 p.m.

Dayton

The centerpiece of the **Shenandoah Valley Folk Art and Heritage Center,** 382 High St. tel. (540) 879-2681, is a huge electrified map tracing the comings, goings, and clashings of Stonewall Jackson's Shenandoah Valley Campaign. A 20-minute narrated tape explains things in dramatic tones. Regional ceramics, textiles, paintings, and sculptures fill the folk art section, close to a genealogy research library. Open Monday, Wed.-Sat. 10 a.m.-4 p.m., Sunday 1-4 p.m.; $4 adults, $1 children 5-18.

Green Valley Book Fair

Some 25 years ago Kathryn and Leighton Evans got the idea of selling surplus new and used books out of an old family barn. Today the idea has evolved into a huge affair filling three floors with half a million volumes on all subjects. New titles from most major publishers are 60-90% off retail—enough to entice buyers from nearby states. The sale is held six weekends a year in Mt. Crawford off I-81 exit 240. Head east onto Rt. 682 for 1.5 miles, then take a left on Rt. 681 at the Green Valley sign. Contact the organizers at tel. (800) 385-0099 or (540) 434-0309, Web site: www.gvbookfair.com, for specific dates.

Massanutten Resort

Some of the state's best skiing waits east of Harrisonburg in a natural depression behind Massanutten Peak. With the longest vertical drop in Virginia (1,100 feet), Massanutten boasts 14 runs ranging from green to black, and five lifts including one quad. Other attractions include night skiing, a snowboard park, kids programs, and NASTAR races. Lift tickets cost $28-36 adults, $23-30 children, with a day at the state's first and only snow tubing park for $18 ($12 half day). Ticket/rental/instruction packages on ski or snowboard are $45-65.

During the rest of the year Massanutten keeps busy with an 18-hole golf course, pool, tennis, in-line skating rink, and an indoor fitness complex. Ski lifts run to the top during limited hours in the summer ($4 adults, $2 children) for outstanding views from the rough limestone peak. Outside of operating hours it's possible (and well worthwhile) to hike up, and a mountain bike makes the trip back down a blast. As a matter of fact, over the July Fourth weekend the Grundig/UCI Mountain Bike World Cup Downhill—the only downhill World Cup event held in the continental U.S.—takes over the slopes.

The resort is 10 miles from Rt. 33 on Rt. 644. For information on activities and lodging contact the resort at tel. (800) 207-6277 or (540) 289-9441, e-mail: skimass@shentel.net, Web site: www.massresort.com.

Natural Chimneys Regional Park

Seven limestone towers 65-120 feet tall form the nucleus of this small park near Mt. Solon (I-81 exit 240). The columns used to be part of the same block of limestone left from when Virginia was covered by an inland sea, but a layer of harder rock on top protected them from erosion. Natural Chimneys' other claim to fame is the **jousting tournament** held the third Saturdays of June and August since 1821, making it one of the oldest continually held sporting events in the country. No one crashes to the ground in full armor here, though—the tournaments are based on accuracy, with contestants aiming their lances through small rings at full gallop. A **campground** has 132 sites for $15 each, along with a pool, store, hot showers, and playground. The park is open daily 9 a.m.-dusk for $3 pp or $6 per car. For more information call (540) 350-2510.

Grand Caverns Regional Park

Up there with Virginia's best, this network of caves includes huge Cathedral Hall, one of the largest underground rooms in the east, and the 5,000-square-foot Grand Ballroom, where dances were actually held in the early 1800s. This one was discovered in 1804 by a 17-year-old looking for a raccoon trap and was once visited by Thomas Jefferson on horseback from Monticello. Signatures on the walls record the quartering of Stonewall Jackson's troops near here during the Valley Campaign. Over 200 formations called "shields" are a mystery to geologists.

East at I-81 exit 235, the caverns are open April-Oct. daily 9 a.m.-5 p.m., and some weekends in March. Admission is $10 adult, $6 children 3-11, and the park also encloses picnic shelters, hiking and biking trails, a pool, tennis courts, and a miniature golf course.

STAUNTON AND VICINITY

One of the oldest cities in the Shenandoah Valley, Staunton (pop. 24,500) is a pretty, if hilly, town to amble through for an afternoon or two. Since it was spared from Civil War destruction, the city still claims 19th-century architecture to rival that of any city in the state. Faded advertisements for feed, fertilizer, and hardware on brick buildings give the downtown a railroad-era look, while grand private homes fronted by sloping lawns line West Frederick. Intense restoration efforts have resurrected the train station and are now being focused on the warehouses of the adjacent Wharf area.

HISTORY

. . . of patients treated during the last ten years, 23 became deranged because of 'the war'—from disappointed love 7; from intemperance and dissolate habits, 30; from religious excitement, 1; from the use of tobacco, 5; jealousy, 4; idleness, 5.
—1866 newspaper report on Staunton's Western State Hospital

Staunton ("STAN-ton") first served as a waystation at the intersection of the old Valley Pike and the westbound Midland Trail, where travelers could rest themselves and their horses and stock up on supplies. Hundreds of hogs once churned the muddy streets as they were driven to markets east of the Blue Ridge. In 1787 it served briefly and unexpectedly as the capital of Virginia when the General Assembly fled Charlottesville ahead of the British.

A little over half a century after the town was chartered, in 1801, the Central & Ohio Railroad arrived, beginning Staunton's transformation from a rural outpost to a thriving commercial city. Woodrow Wilson was born here to the wife of a local Presbyterian minister in 1856. Staunton served as a supply base during the Civil War.

SIGHTS

A total of five National Historic Districts spread through the city. The cobble-lined **Wharf Area** includes the turn-of-the-century train depot (now an Amtrak station), with old cabooses at the end of a long platform. Many of the nearby warehouses and mill buildings have been turned into galleries and antique shops. Beautiful Victorian buildings from the boom years of 1860-1920 fill the **Beverly** district, along the street of the same name between Lewis St. and Market Street. West of Lewis St. is **Newtown,** the city's oldest residential area, home to prominent citizens and their less wealthy neighbors who labored in local factories.

Woodrow Wilson
Birthplace and Museum
Only a few original presidential birthplaces are still open to the public (that cabin in Kentucky probably isn't the one where Lincoln was born), and this modest city boasts one of them. The original home of the 28th president features pe-

"MAD ANN" BAILEY

Indian attacks took a heavy toll in the early years of Augusta County. When one Richard Trotter fell to flying arrows, his wife went on the warpath herself. Ann, who had arrived in America as an indentured servant, quickly became one of the area's most renowned Indian fighters. Dressed in men's clothes and carrying a rifle, tomahawk, and knife, she did her best to even the score as a messenger, scout, and spy. According to one account she "halways carried a hax and a hauger and could chop as well as hany man" and was said to have "killed more than one person's share of Indians." She lived to be 83 years old.

riod furniture, personal belongings, and Wilson's favorite 1919 Pierce-Arrow limousine. Boxwood gardens outside were restored in 1993 by the Garden Club of Virginia. Guided tours trace his life from here to Princeton and the White House. The museum is on Coalter St., tel. (800) 496-6376 or (540) 885-0897. Open March-Nov. daily 9 a.m.-5 p.m., Dec.-Feb. daily 10 a.m.-4 p.m.; $6 adults, $2 children 6-12.

Statler Brothers Complex

The famous family of country singers has its offices and a miniature museum in the building where they once went to school, at 501 Thornrose Ave. near Norfolk Ave., tel. (540) 885-7927. Gifts sent by fans fill one room, while another has been set up as it looked when the brothers were learning their ABCs. Free tours are given Mon.-Fri. at 2 p.m., and a gift shop is open Mon.-Fri. 10:30 a.m.-3:30 p.m.

Other Landmarks

The cream-brick **Augusta County Courthouse,** on the corner of Johnson St. and Augusta St., is the fifth such structure on this particular site. Its classic design includes large stone columns supporting a dome topped by a weather-greened statue of Justice. Dating to 1855, the Gothic-revival **Old Trinity Church** replaced one that hosted the Virginia General Assembly in 1787. The lime-green **St. Francis of Assisi Catholic Church** sits on the highest hill in town.

Mary Baldwin College was founded by the Rev. Rufous Bailey in 1842 as the Augusta Female Seminary, making it the oldest continually operating women's college in the South. The Greek revival structure sits on Sycamore St. overlooking downtown. Tennis courts, playgrounds, a golf course, and a swimming pool fill **Gypsy Hill Park,** northwest of downtown along Churchville Ave. On Monday nights during

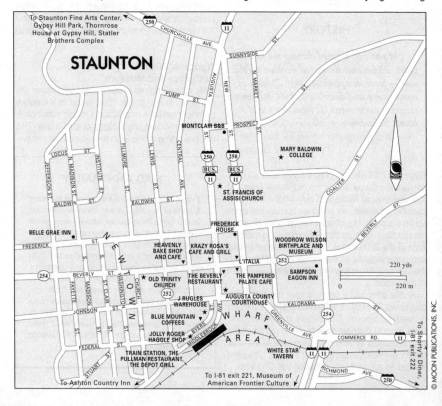

MUSEUM OF AMERICAN FRONTIER CULTURE

In the 1700s, three ethnic groups—English, German, and Scots-Irish—dominated the small-scale farming settlements of the Shenandoah Valley frontier. Over the next two centuries their distinctive traditions would blend into a uniquely American heritage that lives on, alongside its roots, in this fascinating living-history center that focuses on the common man rather than the patrician. Ignore the traffic hum from I-81 and it's easy to be carried back in time by the smells of fresh-cut hay and open-hearth cooking and the sounds of cows lowing, pigs rooting, and the clank of hammer on anvil.

At the **visitors center,** tel. (540) 332-7850, e-mail: mafcinfo@cfw.com, films and a small museum tell you about the colonial cultures you're about to experience. (The **Staunton/Augusta Travel Information Center,** tel. (800) 332-5219 or (540) 332-3972, fax 332-3807, is in the same building.) Step outside to begin a 5/8-mile self guided walking loop through four distinct settlements. All the buildings are original, disassembled where they stood, shipped here, and reassembled on site. Everything was re-created as authentically as possible, down to bringing in thatchers from Ulster to roof the Irish cottage.

Costumed interpreters keep each farm running, from planting and harvesting crops to tending rare, authentic breeds of cattle and making cast-iron implements by hand. They're not re-enactors, but they know all about what life for their antecedents was like and are happy to explain what they're doing. A long list of daily demonstrations varies throughout the year, including fabric weaving, sheep shearing, woodworking, and cooking. Some of the more popular activities require special admission fees and pre-registration.

The 17th-century German farm from the Rhineland-Palatinate region is first. A framework of thick posts and beams is covered with wattle and daub (woven sticks covered with a mixture of soil, water, sand, lime, and manure). This style became common in colonial America, though wooden planks would eventually replace the twigs and fertilizer.

Twin walls of whitewashed stone separated by a layer of rubble make up the early 19th-century Scots-Irish cottage and outbuildings, one of which encloses a working forge. A small field is planted every spring with flax to make linen, a common crop in northern Ireland at the time.

The 17th-century English farmhouse from West Sussex is the most substantial so far, a two-story wooden building with an elaborate brick chimney. Furniture inside is carved from oak and walnut.

Last comes an entry from Botetourt County near Roanoke. The clapboard-covered log house features a full-length back porch and an open hearth that doubled as furnace and kitchen. Among the eight farm buildings you won't find an outhouse—chamber pots were still emptied outdoors in the 19th century.

The museum is on US 250 west of I-81 exit 222 (follow signs). It's open daily March 16-Nov.30, 9 a.m.-5 p.m., and Dec.1.-March 15,10 a.m.-4 p.m.; $8 adults, $4 children 6-12. Most of the grounds and buildings are wheelchair accessible, and electric golf carts and hand-pulled wagons for the kids are available for rent.

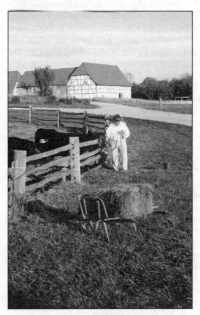

The museum's four distinct settlements contain original buildings.

the summer the local Stonewall Brigade Band gives free jazz concerts at the bandstand

ACCOMMODATIONS

Inexpensive
Both the **Econo Lodge Staunton,** 1031 Richmond Ave., tel. (540) 885-5158, fax 885-5281, and the **Super 8 Motel,** 1015 Richmond Ave., tel. (540) 886-2888, fax 886-7432, are off I-81 exit 222.

Moderate
Foxhunt decor marks the **Montclaire B&B,** 320 N. New St., tel. (540) 885-5761. Sheri and Mark Bang run the Italianate home (c. 1880), which features three guest rooms, a library, and private sitting rooms. Across the street from Gypsy Hill Park sits the stately Georgian **Thornrose House,** 531 Thornrose Ave., tel. (800) 861-4338 or (540) 885-7026, fax 885-6458, Web site: www.bbhsv.org/thornrose. Fireplaces warm the dining room and a guest parlor decorated with family heirlooms and oriental rugs. Relax on a rocking chair on the wraparound veranda or stroll through the grounds and gardens or the park across the street.

    Frederick House, 28 N. New St., tel. (800) 334-5575 or (540) 885-4220, is a small European-style inn with an attached tearoom (enter from the parking lot on New Street). The building, some parts of which date to 1810, features a federal-style curving stairway. Eight rooms and six suites are spread between the main house and nearby cottages and townhouses. Prices range up to premium. Up on the high western end of Frederick St. perches the **Belle Grae Inn,** 515 W. Frederick St., tel. (888) 541-5151 or (540) 886-5151. Originally part of a 200-acre farm on the edge of town, the "Old Inn" was opened to the public in 1983. A front veranda and 12-foot ceilings grace the first of three federal stories, and azaleas bloom in the garden in back. Fifteen rooms and suites are shared between the main building and the adjacent townhouse, both erected in the 1870s. The Belle Grae Inn offers a number of dining choices (see below). Expensive-premium.

Expensive
Frank and Laura Mattingly have garnered repeated awards and recommendations as one of the best inns in the state, if not the country, with **The Sampson Eagon Inn,** 238 E. Beverly St., tel. (800) 597-9722 or (540) 886-8200. A porch swing and period antiques enhance the 1840s inn, known for its gourmet "skip-lunch" breakfasts. Laura's delectable Grand Marnier pancakes and Belgian Kahlua waffles might make you want to skip that jog around town as well—or at least postpone it. Both rooms and two suites have canopied beds, TV/VCRs, and a/c. E-mail: eagoninn@rica.net.

    The **Ashton Country House,** 1205 Middlebrook Ave., tel. (800) 296-7819 or (540) 885-7819, sits one mile southwest of the center of town. Three verandas and a 40-foot central hall are only the beginning. Pine and maple floors, brick interior walls, high ceilings, and 25 bucolic acres complete with farm buildings and animals give a convincing taste of what this Greek revival mansion must have been like in its heyday in the latter 19th century. Of the five bedrooms, four have fireplaces and one is fully accessible to visitors with disabilities. Expensive-premium.

FOOD

Beverly Street
Starting at the east end and working west, **The Pampered Palate Cafe,** 26-28 E. Beverly St., tel. (540) 886-9463, offers quiches, pita sandwiches, and New York-style bagels for $4-6. Many vegetarian and lowfat options are balanced by a gourmet goodie/coffee/wine shop. Open Mon.-Sat. for breakfast and lunch. Regional dishes like Veal Sorrentina and Steak alla Pizziada are a specialty of **L'Italia Restaurant,** 23 E. Beverly St., tel. (540) 885-0102. Casual lunches ($6-10) and dinners ($9-13) served Tues.-Sun. are enlivened by occasional jazz on weekend nights. **The Beverly Restaurant,** 12 E. Beverly St., tel. (540) 886-4317, serves homestyle cooking including chicken and dumplings, ham hocks and cabbage, and chipped-beef gravy breakfasts. Both their chocolate milkshakes and the homemade pecan pies are said to be "the best you'll ever eat" (let me know *your* verdict). Open Mon.-Sat. 6 a.m.-7 p.m.

    Passing Augusta St. your next stop is **Krazy Rosa's Cafe and Grill,** 9 W. Beverly St., tel. (540) 886-0052, an unpretentious Mexican place serving lunch and dinner Mon.-Fri. ($6-10) and dinner on Saturday. The **Heavenly Bake Shop and Cafe,** 101 W. Beverly St., tel. (540) 886-4455, offers sandwiches, salads, pastries, and libations under a cloud-filled sky painted on the ceiling. Open for lunch Tues.-Sat., and dinner on Friday.

Elsewhere Downtown

Today, more people head to the old C&O depot to try one of the two restaurants there than to board a train. The centerpiece of **The Pullman Restaurant,** tel. (540) 885-6612, is an 1880s Victorian soda fountain and ice cream bar. Tiffany lampshades, marble counters, and antiques evoke an old-time railroad atmosphere. Cuisine is Cajun and Creole inspired. Entrées run $5-8 for lunch and $12-19 for dinner, both served daily (Sunday brings a buffet brunch). Farther down the platform, **The Depot Grill,** tel. (540) 885-7332, boasts a marvelous 40-foot bar rescued from a luxury hotel demolished in Albany, NY. Seafood is also a favorite here, starting with shrimp, crab legs, and crawdads at the steamer bar. Sandwiches are $6-10, and entrées $10-17. Open Mon.-Fri. for lunch and dinner

Also in the Wharf district, **Blue Mountain Coffees,** 18A Byers St., tel. (540) 886-4506, serves muffin- and bagel-type fare for breakfast and lunch Mon.-Sat. The **Belle Grae Inn,** 515 W. Frederick St., tel. (888) 541-5151 or (540) 886-5151, offers two dining options. Fine dining in the Old Inn means appetizers such as sweet potato and crawfish bisque ($5-7) and entrées for $17-22. Floor-to-ceiling windows in The Bistro make á la carte dining a sunny affair (entrées for $9-14, sandwiches slightly less). In fine traditional style, tea is served every afternoon at 4 p.m. with cookies and cakes. Non-guests should call ahead.

Beyond Downtown

Mrs. Rowe's Family Restaurant and Bakery, US 250 just east of I-81 exit 222, tel. (540) 886-1833, opened in 1947 and has been serving three hearty meals daily ever since. Bread, biscuits, and pies are all baked fresh from her original recipes. The gleaming metal exterior of **Shorty's Diner,** 1013 Richmond Rd., tel. (540) 885-8861, goes well with the retro-chic red vinyl seats and CD jukebox. An order of Your Mama's Chicken Soup or Three Alarm Chili might

leave room—barely—for blue-plate specials ($6-8) such as meatloaf and country-fried steak. Shakes, malts, and pies are also on the menu, of course. Open daily 6 a.m.-midnight, with breakfast for $2 and up.

ENTERTAINMENT AND TOURS

J Rugles Warehouse, 18 Byers St., tel. (540) 886-4399, is a bar/restaurant with local and regional music tending toward blues and acoustic. The **White Star Tavern,** 123 S. New. St., tel. (540) 885-5887, hosts live jazz and rock. Local artists are thankful for the **Staunton-Augusta Art Center,** tel. (540) 885-2028, at the intersection of Churchill Ave. and Thornrose Ave. near Gypsy Hill Park. Crafts such as paintings, pottery, jewelry and scarves are sold near the holidays. Open Mon.-Fri. 9 a.m.-5 p.m.; free. From late May to late Oct. free guided **walking tours** leave from the Woodrow Wilson Birthplace and Museum every Saturday at 10 a.m. Brochures are also available for self-guided excursions. Contact the Historic Staunton Foundation, tel. (540) 885-7676, or the Staunton/Augusta Travel Information Center.

EVENTS

In mid-May, Gypsy Hill Park blooms with **Art in the Park,** tel. (540) 885-2028, an outdoor show organized by the Art Center with over 100 artists of all ages, children's activities, food, and entertainment. On the second weekend of the same month the **Virginia Mushroom and Wine Festival,** tel. (800) 338-2576 or (540) 635-3185, rolls into town with many of the same activities (but fancier eats).

SHOPPING

Staunton's most interesting spot to browse is unquestionably the **Jolly Roger Haggle Shop,** 27 Middlebrook Ave., tel. (540) 886-9527. Leave an hour or more to do justice to roomfuls of old lunch boxes, turquoise jewelry, antique tools, books, militaria, and coins piled to the ceiling. They advertise "over 1,000,000 items," and it's easy to believe. Other craft/antique stores are clustered near Beverly St. and New St., including the **Naked Creek Pottery Gallery,** 112 S. New St., tel. (540) 885-5721, and the **White Swan Gallery,** 107 E. Beverly St., tel. (540) 886-0522.

INFORMATION
AND TRANSPORTATION

Look for the **Staunton/Augusta Travel Information Center,** tel. (800) 332-5219 or (540) 332-3972, fax 332-3807, in the Museum of Frontier Culture.

Greyhound has an station on 1143 Richmond Rd., tel. (540) 886-2424. Trains leave the **Amtrak** station for Charlottesville and Clifton Forge.

WAYNESBORO

Take exit 94 off I-81 to reach this industrial town just west of a major pass through the Blue Ridge. Accommodations await two blocks off Main St. at the **Belle Hearth B&B,** 320 S. Wayne Ave., tel. (800) 949-6993 or (540) 943-1910, fax 942-2443, e-mail: bellehrth@aol.com, Web site: www.inngetaways.com/va/belle.html. Adorned with a gabled roof and wraparound porch, the turn-of-the-century building is filled with Victorian furnishings and no fewer than seven fireplaces. Three rooms and one suite fall within the moderate category.

The **P. Buckley Moss Museum,** 150 P. Buckley Moss Dr. (US 340), tel. (540) 949-6473, houses dozens of works by the well-known local artist. Her distinctive "Valley Style," inspired by the scenery and people of the Shenandoah, is marked

THE GREAT OIL HOAX OF 1895

In 1895, a sly group of entrepreneurs proclaimed they had found oil near Waynesboro. They sold stock and even made a convincing show of drilling. With every day that passed without producing any black gold, though, the townspeople grumbled more.

Sales of the stock picked up again when several barrels of oil were poured into the ground surreptitiously one night, prompting several investors to retire in anticipation of their newfound wealth. In time, the scam was unearthed, and the only thing that ever came out of the hole that wasn't dumped there was clean drinking water.

by bare, wiry trees, sensuous horses, chunky Canadian geese, and elongated portraits of Amish and Old Order Mennonite farmers. There's a gift shop downstairs, where prices for even small prints start in the hundreds. Open Mon.-Sat. 10 a.m.-6 p.m., Sunday 12:30-5:30 p.m.; free.

The Association of Virginia Artisans runs the **Fine Craft Gallery,** 327 W. Main St., tel. (540) 943-9282, stocked with glassware, weavings, ceramics, and beadwork by regional artists. You can watch brass and iron pieces being sandcast at the factory showroom of **Virginia Metalcrafters,** 1010 E. Main St., tel. (540) 949-9432. The rest of the building is filled with any and all kinds of metal accessories imaginable, from sundials and garden animals to lamps, trivets, and candlesticks. They also have an outlet store in Waynesboro Outlet Village (Building 16B) on Rosser Ave. (Rt. 340), tel. (540) 949-8190.

ALLEGHENY HIGHLANDS

Encompassing Highland, Bath, and parts of Augusta and Alleghany Counties, this wrinkled western spur is surprisingly accessible for such a wild area. Long, narrow peaks of the Allegheny Mountains ripple off into West Virginia, split by river valleys running arrow-straight southwest to northeast. With fewer than 3,000 people spread over 455 square miles, Highland County doesn't lack for open space. Most of it is over 4,000 feet above sea level, giving it the highest average elevation of any county east of the Mississippi. Many residents live off the land as their ancestors did, still referring to locations as "three mountains over."

Bath County, in contrast, is one of the richest in Virginia, thanks to the fully realized resort possibilities of a series of thermal springs to which native tribes once ascribed healing powers. In 1750, a visiting doctor wrote, "The spring is very clear and warmer than new milk . . . The settlers would be better able to support travelers was it not for the great number of Indian warriors that frequently take what they want from them, greatly to their prejudice." Over the next few centuries, the wealthy residents of the Piedmont learned that the mountains and waters were the perfect escape from the unbearable summer mugginess of their own region. Thus began a tradition of lavish seasonal retreats, which is carried on today in The Homestead—possibly the grandest in the state.

Outdoor Recreation

Fishing is one of the top draws in this part of the state, attracting anglers from hundreds of miles away in search of bass (largemouth, smallmouth, and rock), trout, catfish, crappie, and muskies. A number of Virginia's major rivers have their headwaters in these choppy hills. Almost any of the streams and rivers flowing southwest, including the Maury, Bullpasture, and Cowpasture, offer great casting. The Jackson River flows into Lake Moomaw, a 12-mile flood-control reservoir with some of the best fishing in the state (bass in the three-to-four-pound range love the clear waters). The 60-acre Douthat Lake in Douthat State Park offers fee fishing for stocked trout.

Many wildlife management, recreation, and wilderness areas present endless opportunities for **hiking and camping** amid the spruce and northern hardwood forests. Pocahontas County, just over the border in West Virginia, is a top-five national destination for **mountain biking**, and this side of the border is almost identical, though largely unexplored by knobby-tire enthusiasts. Finding your own track should be a cinch.

Access

Possibly the prettiest road to the highlands—or anywhere in the state, for that matter—is Rt. 39 from Lexington to Warm Springs via Goshen Pass. A 150-foot suspension bridge over the Maury River leads into tens of thousands of

ALLEGHENY HIGHLANDS AREA CLIMATE

SNOWFALL
RAINFALL
MAXIMUM TEMP.
MINIMUM TEMP.

HUMPBACK COVERED BRIDGE

The only original covered bridge left in the U.S. spans Dunlap Creek, three miles west of Covington on US 60. Built in 1835, Humpback Covered Bridge was used until 1929. In 1953, it was restored for foot traffic, and the surrounding land was set aside as a park and picnic area.

Ropes dangle underneath for (illicit) swings into the water, and the inside of the bridge is, sadly, defaced by graffiti. Social anthropologists call this "idiot sign," or should; it's left wherever idiots congregate.

acres administered by the state. Frequent pull-offs can easily turn this 42-mile drive into a half-day trip. US 250 from Staunton to Monterey comes in a close second, passing through the quaint burg of Churchville (with its church-lined Main St. and 40-cent soda machines) before becoming a rising corridor through the George Washington National Forest. A great view at the crest welcomes you to Highland County before the road inches its tortured way down the other side of the ridge, only to rise, and fall, again and again. Finally, no-nonsense I-64 heads from Lexington straight into West Virginia.

There's an **Amtrak** station on Ridgeway St. in Clifton Forge, with trains to Staunton and White Sulphur Springs, WV, and through bus service to Roanoke. Call (800) USA-RAIL (800-872-7245) for information.

MONTEREY

Coming over the mountain at just the right time can make the Highland County seat a vision, nestled as it is in a narrow, gently sloping valley. It's a small town, with about 250 people at last count and only one traffic light (a flashing one, at that). US 250 turns into Main Street as it runs through the center of town, lined with dozens of old buildings from the turn of the century or before. The Landmark House, across from the courthouse, was built from logs in 1790 and renovated in 1977.

Accommodations

The pink stone **Montvallee Motel,** tel. (540) 468-2500, offers 1950s-style charm at the intersection of US 250 and US 220. Budget to inexpensive. Farther on into town sits the Victorian **Highland Inn,** tel. (888) 466-4682 or (540) 468-2143, built in 1904 as a vacation getaway. Gingerbread trim decorates the twin front porches where rocking chairs sway in the breeze. Seventeen guest rooms range from inexpensive to moderate, including continental breakfast. A dining room and tavern are inside.

Keep going through town to reach the **Curry-Alexander B&B,** tel. (540) 468-2055, e-mail: curryalx@cfw.com, four blocks past the courthouse on your right. Dark wood paneling, Victorian furnishings, and a claw-foot bathtub in the hall bathroom evoke the turn of the century. The owners serve breakfast on fine china in the dining room and run a special-order bake shop out of the kitchen. Tea and lunch can be arranged for non-guests ahead of time. Moderate to expensive. The **Cherry Hill Bed & Breakfast,** tel. (540) 468-1900, perches on Mill Alley one block off Main St. Bay windows look out over a wraparound porch to a great view of the town and valley, and a hammock sways in the quiet flower garden out back. Moderate to premium.

Food
Look for the fish on the roof of the **Maple Restaurant,** tel. (540) 468-2684, one block off Main St. past the courthouse on the right. Simple dishes including country ham and fried chicken start at $5 for a full dinner plate, with sandwiches as low as $1. They're open the latest in town—until 9 p.m. **High's Restaurant,** tel. (540) 468-2700, across from the Highland Inn, is similar and even cheaper. Try **Royal Pizza & Subs,** tel. (540) 468-3333 for ice cream, sandwiches, and pizza, plus a look at a mural of the valley by local artist Anne Witschey. It's behind the Texaco station.

Recreation
For guiding and instruction in caving, rock climbing, mountain biking, and camping contact **Highland Adventures,** P.O. Box 151, Monterey, VA 24465, tel. (540) 468-2722. The Lions Club **city pool,** on US 250 past the Curry Alexander B&B, is fed by mountain streams. It's open during the summer Mon.-Fri. 1-5 p.m., 6-8 p.m., Saturday, Sunday noon-5 p.m.; free.

Events
Fans of Virginia fairs know Monterey's **Highland Maple Festival** is one of the first major ones of the year. Held the second and third weekends in March, the festival centers on the fact that Highland is the only county in Virginia that produces maple syrup and all its tasty byproducts. Some 50,000 people eager to see the sun after being inside all winter make the trek to enjoy crafts and an all-you-can-eat pancake breakfast—topped with fresh maple syrup, of course.

Shopping
Opposite the courthouse sit the **H&H Cash Store,** tel. (540) 468-2570, an old-fashioned mercantile stocking maple sugar candy, buckwheat flower, tools, and clothing. **The Personal Touch,** tel. (540) 468-2145, carries stained glass, fabric arts, and dolls by local artisans in a historic house on Main St.

Information
The **Highland County Chamber of Commerce,** tel. (540) 468-2550, fax 468-2551, has an office on Main St. You can also contact it at e-mail: highcc@cfw.com.

Near Monterey
The 374-acre **Laurel Fork Preserve,** part of a 10,000-acre special management area, covers the very tip of the point sticking into West Virginia. This pristine area shelters "relic communities" left over from cooler times, including rare species such as the endangered Virginia northern flying squirrels—which soar through the red spruce forests. Almost 30 miles of trails roam through the craggy hills, many following old railroad grades. Popular ones include the Laurel Fork, Buck Run, and Locust Springs Run Trails. A campground has shelter for up to six people. To get there, take Rt. 642 east from Blue Grass. Contact the Warm Springs Ranger District of the George Washington National Forest, tel. (540) 839-2521, for more information.

If even Monterey isn't far enough away for you, consider staying at the **Endless Mountain Retreat Center,** an environmentally focused lodge so far into the hinterlands you could throw a rock and hit West Virginia. The center welcomes everyone from individuals to groups of up to 25, who can stay in simple, snug pine cabins with shared bathhouse or the Post and Beam Lodge, which feels straight out of the Wyoming foothills. The lodge has a large common room with a piano, cooking facilities, and spectacular views from the wide windows and wraparound porch. Seminars on flora, fauna, animal tracking, and edible plants are held year-round, and the owners can also organize expeditions to go fly fishing, horseback riding, mountain biking, or snowshoeing through their hundreds of untouched acres. Relax in the evening in front of the woodburning stove in the main room or in the sand-floored sauna. Moderate rates include breakfast, but additional meals can be prepared with advance notice. For more information and detailed directions contact the lodge at HC-2, Box 141, Hightown, VA 24465, tel. (540) 468-2700, e-mail: endless@cfw.com.

W.S. Heindl is proprietor and guide at the **Rainbow Springs Reteat,** tel. (804) 353-1112, a fly-fishing nirvana four miles north of Monterey on US 220. In the heart of the "trout capital of the Southeast," Rainbow Springs offers brown, wild rainbow, and native brook trout in six stocked ponds and close to a mile of private stream. Catch-and-release is the rule, and a license is required. A 19th-century log lodge sits on 62 acres, complete with washer, dryer, dishwasher, fireplace, porch, and patio with grill. Six beds and two baths can hold up to eight guests, with a weekly price of $750 and Fri.-Sun. packages for $375 (linens and food not included). Guided fishing is $175 per day for one person and $250 per day for two.

RAMSEY'S DRAFT WILDERNESS AREA

Some of the most isolated and craggy territory in the George Washington National Forest fill this preserve, which you enter off US 250 about 21 miles east of Monterey. Thousands of acres of virgin forest—spared the axe thanks to their inaccessibility—include yellow poplar, white oaks, and hemlocks. The seven-mile Ramsey's Draft Trail winds alongside a stream of the same name, and a National Forest campground, tel. (540) 828-2591, sits 9 miles north of US 250 on Rt. 715 (continue one mile northeast on Forest Road 95, then one mile southwest on Forest Road 95b). Sixteen sites are $3 each. Call the Deerfield Ranger district of the U.S. Forest Service in Staunton, tel. (540) 885-8028, for more information.

WARM SPRINGS

The Bath County seat nestles in a valley near a small set of natural thermal springs. Eighteenth-century buildings, many white with green trim, constitute the original town center—known as "Old Germantown"—off Rt. 39 just west of US 220.

Accommodations and Food
The **Warm Springs Inn,** tel. (703) 839-5351, occupies a hillside right at the intersection of US 220 and Rt. 39 across the street from the springs.

The sprawling structure began as a log jail built in 1792 and a stone courthouse (1796), replaced with brick in 1842. It's been augmented over the years with other buildings and architectural styles, resulting in an interesting mix of Victorian inn and funky motel. Huge porcelain vases and other antiques fill the main foyer, which leads to the Courtroom Restaurant (where, pasta, beef, and seafood entrées are $13-17). A sunny glassed-in porch looks out over a swing bench in a tree out front. Inexpensive to moderate. Take Old Germantown Road (Rt. 692) off Rt. 39 toward the center of Warm Springs to reach the **Anderson Cottage Bed & Breakfast,** tel. (540) 829-2975, fax 839-3058, on your left. The two buildings are among Bath County's oldest, having served over the years as a tavern, a girl's school, and a summer inn. They've been in the present owner's family since the 1870s. Rates range from moderate to expensive, including a separate guest cottage, formerly an early 19th-century brick kitchen.

To find **The Inn at Gristmill Square,** tel. (540) 839-2231, fax 839-5770, look for the waterwheel on Old Mill Rd. (Rt. 645) in the heart of Warm Springs. A mill has stood here since 1771, but the present buildings date to the 19th century. Janice and Jack McWilliams, who bought the place in 1981, have added tennis courts, a pool, and a sauna in the process of restoring four buildings for guests: the Blacksmith Shop, containing the offices and two rooms (one of which started as a hayloft); the Miller House (four rooms), the Steel House (four); and the Hardware Store (six rooms and one apartment). All have woodburning fireplaces and are tastefully furnished with antiques and exotic curios. Rates (expensive) include continental breakfast. Apartments are premium to luxury. Fine food is served with a country flair in the adjacent **Waterwheel Restaurant.** Dinner, served daily, features expensive but savory dishes such as roast duck with apricots and veal picatta. Sunday brunch is also available.

Three **campgrounds** can be found west on Rt. 39 into the George Washington National Forest. Hidden Valley (1.5 miles west, one mile north on Rt. 621) and Blowing Springs (nine miles west) are both $4 per night, and the Bolar Mountain Campground ($10-12) is 13 miles west, then seven miles south on Rt. 600.

Recreation

A pair of oddly shaped buildings at the Rt. 39/US 220 intersection house the **Jefferson Pools,** owned by the Homestead (see below). These large stone pools of naturally warm water were built in the late 18th century, when the Virginia elite would make the round of different pools in the area. Thomas Jefferson may have lent his design flair to the structures: the men's pool house has eight sides and the women's has 22. As you relax in the 98° F water, be thankful fashions have changed—according to one account, the stylish bather of the 1830s had to don "a large cotton gown of a cashmere shawl pattern lined with crimson, a fancy Greek cap, Turkish slippers and a pair of loose pantaloons." For a change of pace, try hydrotherapy, where part of the 1,200-gallon-per-minute flow is released on your back as you sit in a special chamber outside and below the pool. The pools are open daily 10 a.m.-6 p.m.; free to guests of the hotel and $12 pp for the public.

At the foot of Courthouse Hill just off US 250 the **Warm Springs Gallery,** tel. (540) 839-2985 or 839-2912, houses both permanent collections (don't miss Tom Ferguson's stoneware pottery) and rotating exhibits by regional artists ranging from paintings to metalwork.

ON THE ROAD TO HOT SPRINGS

Virginia novelist Mary Johnson (To Have and To Hold) built the central part of **Three Hills Inn & Cottages,** tel. (888) 23HILLS (888-234-4557) or (540) 839-5381, fax 839-5199, in 1913. Today the hotel, reached by a winding driveway from US 220, commands an impressive view from 38 acres of hillside just south of the Rt. 39/US 220 intersection. Rooms in the main house are moderate to expensive, and a number of cottages with kitchenettes can hold up to six people for $139-189. Duplex townhouses are being planned. Rates include breakfast (full on weekdays and continental on weekends). The Muse Restaurant in the main house is a bistro-style eatery serving "creative contemporary" cuisine such as portabello sandwiches, lobster pierogi, and the occasional wild-game-and-wine dinner. Entrées are $15-20.

This neck of the woods also happens to be home to one of Virginia's most celebrated musical venues—**Garth Newel Chamber Music Center.** Classical concerts are held on Saturday and Sunday afternoons from July 4 through Labor Day. Call (540) 839-5018 or fax 839-3154 for current schedule and prices.

Three miles north of Hot Springs on Rt. 220, the **Roseloe Motel,** tel. (540) 839-5373, is a friendly place run by Dan and Merrie Jo Perkuchin. It's as nice as motels get. Some rooms have kitchenettes. Moderate.

HOT SPRINGS

The Homestead

Virginia's premiere resort is more like a richly endowed university than a hotel. So big that US 220 curves around it and you need little arrows to navigate the hallways, this world-class resort covers 15,000 acres of Bath County with spotless grounds, stately brick buildings, and one of the finest mountain golf courses in the country.

The first lodge here was built in 1766 by Lt. Thomas Bullitt, a frontier militiaman. The facilities were improved to the status of "modern hotel" in the mid-19th century, just in time to serve as a field hospital during the Civil War. The first spa and golf and tennis courses were opened in 1892, but most of the buildings vanished in a fire in 1901 and were rebuilt.

Inside the main structure, the cavernous Great Hall is lined with fireplaces surrounded by cozy chairs. The opulent President's Lounge has a view of the inner courtyard, and the Jefferson Parlor features wall paintings of Thomas Jefferson and the Homestead itself. For meals, guests can choose between the formal main dining room and the more casual Casino Grill or one of two Cascades Clubs. The Cafe Albert, serving snacks in a deli setting, has an outdoor deck. Cottage Row off the Great Hall contains a small mall's worth of shops selling fine gifts, children's items, and gourmet foods. Golf, ski, and tennis shops elsewhere in the complex rent and sell sporting goods.

The Homestead offers more than enough activities to keep guests busy year-round, both indoors and out. Three golf courses—including the regular top-100 contender Cascades Course—draw the most visitors. One boasts the oldest first tee in the country, in use since 1890. Instruction and full equipment services are available for golfers and patrons of the hotel's nine tennis courts. Canoeing, mountain biking, and 100 miles of hiking trails lure hikers into the hills, and there's a four-mile private trout stream and a shooting club for the sporting types. One of the first European-style spas in the country is an old standby, offering aroma-, hydro-, and massage therapy, facials, and an indoor spring-fed pool opened in 1903. Bowling alleys and a movie theater keep night owls busy, while the Homestead Kid's Club occupies the children. In the winter, a small ski area—the South's first—has nine slopes, a snowboard park, snowmaking equipment, and a full-service ski shop.

DOVER PUBLICATIONS, INC.

Over 500 rooms and suites are all in the luxury price range. Ski passes are $15 ($27 on weekends and holiday) and rentals $9-12. A weekend ski package including rentals, accommodations, two meals, and lessons is $133-173. Contact the hotel at US 220, Hot Springs, VA 24445, tel. (800) 838-1766 or (540) 839-1776, fax 839-7670, Web site: www.thehomestead.com.

DOUTHAT STATE PARK

Virginia's oldest state park has 40 miles of hiking trails winding through 4,493 rugged acres high in the Allegheny Mountains. Blustery ridges and deep forest surround 50-acre Douthat Lake, stocked twice a week with rainbow trout (as is Wilson Creek below the dam). Three miles of the creek have been designated children-only, giving budding anglers easy access and clearings to perfect their casts into well-stocked pools.

Campsites (open March 1-Dec. 1) are $17 each with no hookups. Reservations are essential on busy weekends from Memorial Day to Labor Day. One-room, one-bedroom, and two-bedroom cabins are priced from inexpensive to moderate. Two five-bedroom lodges can be rented by the week or for a minimum of two nights. **Creasey Lodge** is $275.60 per night for the first and second nights ($82.30 each for 3rd-7th) or $670 per week, and the **Main Lodge** is $1,100 per week or $454.50 per night for the first and second night ($130 each for 3rd-7th). Douthat is the only state park split by a road—Rt. 629, which leaves I-64 north from exit 27. For more information and reservations contact the Virginia Division of State Parks, Route 1, Box 212, Millboro, VA 24460, tel. (540) 862-8100.

LEXINGTON

Take a smallish, mannerly town, steep it in Civil War history, overlay with a nationally recognized college or two, and you'll end up with something approaching this quiet community (pop. 7,100), close to both Natural Bridge and the Blue Ridge Parkway. Crew-cut cadets stroll in full gray dress uniform down tree-shaded streets, while other students jog in red-and-yellow school colors past

grand houses with names and stories going back a century or more. Within the town limits lie two of the most honored heroes of the Confederacy: Robert E. Lee and Stonewall Jackson.

Founded in 1777, Lexington was leveled by fire in 1796 and rebuilt with lottery proceeds. Less than 30 years after its founding, the Virginia Military Institute (VMI) was the target of

LEXINGTON

To I-64 Exit 50, Days Inn

To Lime Kiln Theater

NELSON ST.

LIME KILN RD.

MCLAUGHLIN ST.

MYERS AVE.

WHITE AVE.

MCDOWELL ST.

JORDAN ST.

JACKSON ST.

ROSS LN.

To Boxerwood Gardens

LLEWELLYN LODGE

WHITMORE ST.

WALLACE ST.

TAYLOR ST.

HOUSTON ST.

MAIN ST.

JEFFERSON ST.

WASHINGTON ST.

LENFEST CENTER FOR THE PERFORMING ARTS ★

COCOA MILL CHOCOLATE COMPANY ▼

THE PALMS ▼

CITY SUBS AND STEAKS INC. ▼

FOOD EUPHORIUM ▼

STATE THEATER ★

MILITARY MEMORABILIA MUSEUM ★

VISITORS CENTER ★

HENRY ST.

TUCKER ST.

PRESTON ST.

NELSON ST.

MASSIE ST.

RANDOLPH ST.

DIAMOND RD.

LEWIS ST.

MORNINGSIDE DR.

STONEWALL JACKSON CEMETERY ★

SEVEN HILLS INN ★

SPOTSWOOD ST.

HAMPTON INN COL ALTO ★

BYP. 11

To Applewood Inn, Natural Bridge

SCALE NOT AVAILABLE

Maury River

Woods Creek

VIRGINIA

BARRACKS ★

Parade Grounds

GEORGE C. MARSHALL MUSEUM AND LIBRARY ★

MILITARY

LETCHER AVE.

VMI MUSEUM ★

WASHINGTON AND LEE UNIVERSITY

INSTITUTE

MAIN ST.

LEE CHAPEL ★

WASHINGTON ST.

To Virginia Horse Center, Goshen Pass

© MOON PUBLICATIONS, INC.

LEXINGTON COFFEE ROASTING CO. ★

COUNTRY KITCHEN AND BAKERY ★

WILSON-WALKER HOUSE ★

HARBS' BISTRO ▼

IL PALAZZO ●

MCCAMPBELL INN, HISTORIC COUNTRY INNS ●

MAIN ST.

WASHINGTON ST.

ALEXANDER-WITHEROW HOUSE, ARTISTS IN CAHOOTS ★

VIRGINIA BORN AND BRED ★

FRAMEWORKS ★

RANDOLPH ST.

BLUE HERON CAFE ▼

ARTISANS ON WASHINGTON ST. ★

STONEWALL JACKSON HOUSE ★

Union Gen. David Hunter's guns in June 1864. The barracks and much of town was left in ruin.

SIGHTS

Washington & Lee University
Known as "W and L," this small private college enjoys a national reputation: 90% of students come from the top fifths of their high school classes. It was founded in 1749, and saved from bankruptcy in 1796 by a substantial gift from George Washington. Fresh from Appomattox, Robert E. Lee served as its president from 1865 to 1870. The college honored him in 1871 by renaming itself to join Lee's name to Washington's. Today, 2,000 students enjoy a beautiful central campus (declared a National Historic Landmark in 1972) made up of a row of dark red brick buildings fronted by bright white colonnades. The university's main number is (540) 463-8400.

In the center of the campus stands the **Lee Chapel and Museum,** tel. (540) 463-8768, (not to be confused with the Robert E. Lee Episcopal Church, at Washington Ave. and Lee Ave.). The former Confederate commander supervised its construction in 1867-8 and set up his offices in the lower level. The simple, pretty Romanesque chapel was actually never consecrated, serving instead as a hall for meetings and weddings. Inside is Charles Wilson Peale's portrait of George Washington—the first Washington ever sat for—in the incongruous uniform of a British colonel. A famous Edward Valentine statue of Lee in repose is surrounded by Confederate flags. Notice that Lee is represented not as dead, but resting: his feet are crossed and his hand rests on the hilt of his sword. Downstairs are the Lee family crypt and a small museum, which includes Lee's office just as he left it on 28 Sept. 1870. Lee's horse, Traveler, is buried outside. Open Mon.-Sat. 9 a.m.-4 or 5 p.m., Sunday 2-5 p.m.; free.

Virginia Military Institute
The country's first state military college was founded in 1839 on the site of the Lexington Arsenal with a class of 23. Two and a half decades later, 1864 was a big year for VMI: in May, her cadets fought in the Battle of New Market, and in June the barracks were shelled to the ground by Federal forces. In 1983, female cadets were allowed to endure the infamous freshman "rat line"—which claims 25% of each incoming class—for the first time. The "cadettes" lived on the same floors as men under the ruling that any fooling around would result in the dismissal of both parties. New outdoor security lighting, emergency phones, and modified communal bathrooms made the adjustment slightly easier. In 1998, 23 out of 30 made it through the rat line as part of the institute's first co-ed class without any major incidents to mar the transition.

Crenellations top somber gray buildings around the huge central parade ground where cadets practice sports and military drills. At the southwest corner the **George C. Marshall Museum and**

Robert E. Lee once served as president of the historic Washington & Lee University.

STONEWALL JACKSON

Born Thomas Jonathan Jackson on January 21, 1824, in Clarksburg, VA, the Civil War's most famous field commander found himself an orphan by age seven. He grew up in the house of an uncle, before squeaking in to the U.S. Military Academy at West Point. (The first choice from the local congressional district, it seemed, had quit after his first day.) There he survived, in his own words, "by the skin of my teeth," graduating 17th in a class of 59 in 1846.

During the Mexican-American War, Jackson saw action in Cerro Gordo, Veracruz, and Chapultepec, and his outstanding conduct in the artillery earned him early promotions. In 1851, though, he left the rank of major to become a professor of military tactics and physics at the Virginia Military Institute. Students disliked and derided his dull teaching style and classroom quirks, starting with a shrill voice that belied his six-foot, 170-lb frame. Jackson lived in Lexington for the next decade, joining the Presbyterian Church and local Bible society. Two of those years were spent in the house on Washington Street that is now a museum.

Within weeks of the outbreak of the Civil War, Jackson was back in the ranks, assuming a post as infantry colonel on April 21, 1861. Quickly promoted to brigadier general, the former teacher marched a group of VMI cadets to Richmond to help train the budding Confederate Army. His famous nickname came at the First Battle of Bull Run, in July 1861, soon after Confederate forces had begun to flee the fight. Seeing Jackson's troops holding their ground, Brig. Gen. Barnard E. Bee cried, "There stands Jackson like a stone wall! Rally behind the Virginians!" Bee was killed minutes later, but the tide of battle turned, and the name stuck.

Shortly after being promoted to major general, Stonewall cemented his place in history with his famous Valley Campaign in the spring of 1862, often called one of the most brilliant in military history. He continued to shine through the battles of Antietam and Second Bull Run, where his unorthodox tactics and uncanny rapport with General Lee won him fight after fight. Stonewall worked best when he was free to march and attack at will, pushing his men to the limit and always appearing when and where his opponents least expected.

Through it all, "Old Jack" remained a strange bird, obsessed with secrecy and concealing his plans even from direct subordinates. (Maj. Gen. Richard Ewell eventually concluded that his superior was a few pecks short of a bushel.)

At Chancellorsville in early May of 1863, Jackson detached from General Lee's forces to flank the Federal XI Corps under Maj. Gen. Joseph Hooker. The risky but inspired maneuver routed the enemy troops in one of the most dramatic and decisive Confederate victories of the war. But Stonewall's finest hour was too soon followed by his final one: out riding the evening of May 2, he was fired on by mistake by Confederate guards. Two of his aides were killed and Jackson was shot once in the right hand and twice in the left arm. In a nearby home that served as a field hospital doctors decided to amputate the shattered limb. "He has lost his left arm," Lee said as Jackson lay dying, "but I have lost my right."

Jackson gave a good fight, but pneumonia set in and his condition deteriorated. On May 10, his doctors decided that he wouldn't last until sundown. The Confederacy's star commander died that afternoon after a final request: "Let us cross over the river and rest in the shade of the trees." His valiant Stonewall Brigade, hardened by dozens of battles, was never the same after losing its leader, though eight of its men went on to become generals.

Library, tel. (540) 463-7103, commemorates the 1901 graduate who went on to serve as general of the army, the highest military rank possible. While he was secretary of state, his Marshall Peace Plan for the rebuilding of Europe after WW II won him the Nobel Peace Prize. The museum, open daily 9 a.m.-5 p.m. ($3 adults, $1 children) contains army memorabilia, personal papers, and a narrated map of WW II. The **Virginia Military Institute Museum,** tel. (540) 464-7232, occupies the basement of Jackson Memorial Hall at the opposite corner of the parade ground. Stonewall Jackson's field desk and a statue of his favorite horse, Little Sorrel, are both on display along with period clothes, weapons, and historical VMI artifacts. Open daily 9 a.m.-5 p.m.; $3 pp suggested donation.

Stonewall Jackson House

The only home the Confederate commander ever owned stands in the heart of Lexington, at 8 E. Washington St., tel. (540) 463-2552. Jackson occupied the modest brick town house for two years with his second wife, Anna Morrison, before riding off to war in April 1861, never to return. Restored in 1979, the brick building contains many of his possessions and other Civil War-era pieces along with a gift shop. The kitchen garden has been replanted behind the house. Tours are given every half-hour. Open Mon.-Sat. 9 a.m.-5 p.m., Sunday 1-5 p.m.; $5 adults, $2.50 children 6-18.

Stonewall Jackson Cemetery

After being accidentally killed by his own men at Chancellorsville, "Old Jack" was laid to rest in this burial ground at the south end of Main St. An Edward Valentine statue marks his tomb in the center, surrounded by the graves of other Civil War notables and prominent local citizens. Open dawn to dusk.

Boxerwood Gardens

Local doctor Robert Munger began planting rare trees and shrubs around his house at 963 Ross Rd. in 1952. After his death in 1988, his gardener bought the place and opened it to the public in 1997. More an arboretum than a flower garden, Boxerwood encloses rolling acres of exotic species like Japanese maples and dwarf conifers alongside local dogwoods, rhododendrons, and azaleas, all with a panoramic view of the Blue Ridge Mountains. Everything is labeled but left more raggedly natural than neatly pruned. Maps are available for self-guided tours, but half the fun is simply wandering and seeing what you find. In the center of the gardens, the Orchard House is available for rent. Open March-Nov. Thursday, Friday 9 a.m.-4 p.m., Saturday 9 a.m.-1 p.m., and the first Sunday of each month 1-4 p.m., $4 pp suggested donation. It's a good idea to call ahead at (540) 463-1953 or 463-2697, though, as it's still private property.

Military Memorabilia Museum

Uniforms, weapons, flags, and accouterments from France, Great Britain, Germany, and the United States fill a small gallery at 122 1/2 S. Main St., tel. (540) 464-3041. Open May-Oct. Wed.-Sat. 11 a.m.-5 p.m.; $4 adults, with guided tours available by appointment.

Virginia Horse Center

On Rt. 39 just north of I-64 lies one of the most outstanding equine complexes in the country. Shows, clinics, and sales are held year round, including the Virginia Horse Trials, the National Miniature Horse show, and the Southwest Virginia Hunter/Jumper Association. Call (540) 463-2194, fax 464-3507, for current schedules.

ACCOMMODATIONS

In Town

The **McCampbell Inn,** 11 N. Main St., is administered by Historic Country Inns, tel./fax (540) 463-2044 in the same building, constructed in 1809 by John McCampbell and later expanded into the Continental Hotel. Rooms range from expensive to premium. HCI also manages the **Alexander-Witherow House** across the street, a Georgian structure built in 1789. Suites are premium. John Roberts, the owner of **A Bed & Breakfast at Llewellyn Lodge,** 603 Main St., tel. (800) 882-1145 or (540) 463-3235, fax 464-3122, was born in the Stonewall Jackson house and knows Lexington and the area like the back of his hand—especially the outdoors. He's run the B&B with his wife Ellen for 13 years, making it the oldest in town. Six rooms are moderate to expensive, including a celebrated full gourmet breakfast. E-mail: lll@rockbridge.net.

The stately three-story **Seven Hills Inn,** 408 South Main St., Lexington, VA 24450, tel. (888) 845-3801 or (540) 463-4715, fax 463-6526, is set back from Main St. under a grove of tall trees. Seven rooms are decorated with antiques from Europe, the Far East, and the U.S. Moderate to premium, including full breakfast. An 1827 manor home has been converted into the **Hampton Inn Col Alto,** 401 E. Nelson St., tel. (800) HAMPTON (800-426-7866) or (540) 463-2223, fax 463-9707, graced by a palladian porch and many antiques. Moderate and up, including continental breakfast.

Out of Town

There's a **Super 8 Motel,** tel. (540) 463-7858, near the intersection of Rt. 39 and I-64 (exit 55). Inexpensive. On US 60 4.5 miles west of Lexington, is the **Days Inn Keydet General Motel,** tel. (540) 463-2143. Moderate. **Maple Hall,** tel. (540) 463-6693 or 463-4666, is the third property managed by Historic Country Inns. The 1850s plantation house sits out in the rural countryside off US 11 seven miles north of Lexington accompanied by a pool and tennis courts. Rooms and suites are moderate to expensive, while a guesthouse with living room and full kitchen is premium.

The **Applewood Inn,** Buffalo Bend Rd., tel. (800) 463-1902 or (540) 463-1962, is an environmentally friendly B&B offering 36 acres of rustic comfort south of town. A California redwood hot tub sits on an enclosed porch that's part of the house's solar envelope construction, where a layer of heated air surrounding the entire building provides warmth well into the night. Guests are welcome to use the pool and kitchen, and the owners offer two-hour llama treks to a gourmet luncheon in the hills for guests and day visitors. To get there take Rt. 11 for 4.5 miles south of town and make a right onto Buffalo Bend Rd., following signs for the next 2 miles. Expensive-premium. E-mail: applewd@cfw.com, Web site: www.applewoodbb.com.

The **Orchard House,** in the Boxerwood Gardens (see above), tel. (540) 463-1953 or 463-2697, is a fully furnished cottage with a screened porch, fireplace, full kitchen, and a great view of the Blue Ridge. Price depends on season and how many meals are provided, so call ahead for the latest rates.

Camping

Long's Campground, tel. (540) 463-7672, has sites for $10 (full hookup $17) along with a pool, game room, camp store, hot showers, and movie rentals. It's on Rt. 39 three miles west of the intersection of I-64 and US 11.

FOOD

Breakfast

Omelets, French toast, and waffles are all under $3 at **City Subs and Steaks Inc.,** 159 S. Main St., tel. (540) 463-7827. The deli is open Mon.-Sat. 7:30 a.m.-9 p.m. **Harbs' Bistro,** 19 W. Washington St., tel. (540) 464-1900, offers full breakfast and lunch daily in a cheery atmosphere. Dinner—from red beans and rice to fettuccini, including Harbs' "famous clam chowder"—is served on Friday and Saturday

Sweets and Snacks

Although there may still not be any sign for the **Country Kitchen Bakery,** 8 N. Main St., tel. (540) 463-5691, it's still the best old-fashioned bakery in town. Open Tues.-Sun. from 7 a.m. The **Cocoa Mill Chocolate Company,** 121 W. Nelson St., tel. (800) 431-6220, has shelves dripping with handmade fudge, truffles, and pecan, caramel, or chocolate "snappers"—and free samples to start you off. **Lexington Coffee Roasting Co.** 22 W Washington St., tel. (540) 464-6586, serves a hearty cup of joe along with pastries and Italian sodas. Open daily until 4 or 5 p.m. **Washington Street Purveyors,** 9 E Washington St., tel. (540) 464-9463, offers regional and international wines, microbrews, cigars, and gourmet snacks. Wine tastings are held on Friday and Saturday afternoons.

Moderate

Near the top of Lexington's long list of Italian restaurants is **Il Palazzo,** 24 N. Main St., tel. (540) 464-5800. Pastas are $7-9.50 and veal and chicken entrées run $13-14. The place also cooks up pizzas and subs, with lunch specials of any pasta for $5 and any seafood for $6. **Salerno's,** 800 N. Main St., tel. (540) 463-5757, has a $2.50 all-you-can-eat spaghetti special on Monday 5-10 p.m. Open daily for lunch and dinner. Owner/"food goddess" Jaurie Macrae says her **Blue Heron Café,** 4 E. Washington St., tel. (540) 463-2800, is the only completely vegetarian restaurant for miles around. Excellent, healthy plates such as spicy fried noodles topped with nasturtiums are under $5 for lunch served Mon.-Sat. (dinner Friday and Saturday). Meals to go ("like Mother makes") are prepared in the My Kitchen deli in the back of the **Food Euphorium** grocery store, 167 S. Main St., tel. (540) 463-5004.

Fine Dining

Subdued lighting and antique etchings and paintings set the tone in the **Wilson-Walker House Restaurant,** 30 N. Main St., tel. (540) 463-3020, in a beautiful two-story classical revival house (c.1820) with columns and balconies in front. Dinner features standbys including as crab, pasta, and trout along with daily specials and "Creative American" creations such as Tofu Wellington and pecan-crusted pork loin with ginger sauce. An extensive list of Virginia wines ensures that there's always something to pair with your entrée ($14-18). Open Tues.-Sunday.

ENTERTAINMENT AND RECREATION

Theaters

On the outskirts of Lexington, the ruins of a 19th-century kiln have been converted into one of the more unusual and enjoyable places to see a play in the entire mid-Atlantic region. Founded in 1983, the **Lime Kiln Theater,** tel. (540) 463-3074, seems to rise up out of the ground itself amid the vine-covered stones where workers once smelted lime and cut stones. Actors and musicians now perform on summer evenings on one of three stages—two open to the stars and one a tent in case of rain. The theater season runs May.-Sept. with performances Tues.-Sat., while the Coors Summer Concert Series brings folk and rock music from around the country. The theater can be reached from Lime Kiln Rd. off White and McLaughlin from Main St., or via Border Rd. south off US 60 West.

Washington and Lee's **Lenfest Center for the Performing Arts,** US 60 West and Glasgow, tel. (540) 463-8000, also hosts plays and concerts by students and professionals. The **Trubador Theater** [no direct phone] on cam-

pus welcomes indie movies. On Nelson St. just west of Main St. the **State Theater,** tel. (540) 463-3424, is an old-time uniplex, complete with balcony, that screens more mainstream films. Head north on Rt. 39 to reach the classic dinosaur called **Hull's Drive-In Theater,** tel. (540) 463-2621, one of the last left in the state. It's the real thing, sno-cones and all.

Nightlife

Students name **The Palms,** 101 W. Nelson St., tel. (540) 463-7911, as the biggest and most popular bar in town. It's open from lunch (sandwiches and burgers) though dinner (light fare—chicken and pasta) until 1 or 2 a.m. Downstairs at 16 Lee Ave., **The Staircase Bar & Grill,** tel. (540) 464-3157, also draws a crowd.

Tours

From late May to Oct. the **Ghost Tour of Lexington,** tel. (540) 348-1080, guarantees a scare—or at least a shiver—as it takes you on the candlelit rounds of haunted sites around town. The 75-minute tour leaves from the Visitors Center at 8:30 p.m. Tickets are available there or at the Shear Timing Hair Salon on 17 S. Randolph St., Mon.-Fri. 9 a.m.-5 p.m., Saturday 9 a.m.-1 p.m.; $8 adults, $6 children 4-10. A daytime option is a tour of Lexington's major historical sights by horse-drawn carriage with the **Lexington Carriage Company, Inc.,** tel. (540) 463-5647. Its 45-minute tours leave from Washington St. across from the Visitors Center, April-May 10 a.m.-4:30 p.m., June-Aug. 9 a.m.-5 p.m.; $10 adults, $6 children 7-13.

Outdoors

Narrow but pretty **Woods Creek Park** follows the creek of the same name for two miles the length of Lexington. At the northern end where it reaches the Maury River you can pick up the **Chessie Nature Trail,** a seven-mile stretch of the old Chesapeake and Ohio rail line through rural countryside to Buena Vista. Damage from Hurricane Camille in 1969 caused the line to be abandoned, allowing the Nature Conservancy to acquire it in 1978. Along the way you'll pass old canal locks and cross a 235-foot bridge over the South River near its confluence with the Maury River. To reach the starting point, cross US 11 near VMI Island using the foot bridge;

the pedestrian trail begins near the north end of the US 11 bridge.

Rockbridge Outfitters Limited, 112 W. Washington St., tel. (540) 463-1947, rents Specialized and Gary Fisher mountain and road bikes for $4 per hour and $24 per day. It also sells bike, outdoor gear, and USGS topographical maps. **Kellys Corner,** tel. (540) 463-5452, offers hand-tied flies custom-designed for the area, along with fly-fishing equipment, snacks, fishing licenses, and advice. It's on Rt. 60, 2.5 miles west of Lexington. Afternoon canoe and kayak trips on the Maury and James Rivers can be arranged through the **James River Basin Canoe Livery Ltd.,** 1870 E. Midland Trail, tel. (540) 261-7334, for $23-42 pp. Longer trips are also possible. E-mail: information@canoevirginia.com. The **Wilderness Canoe Company,** tel. (800) 4-CANOE-4 (800-422-663) or (540) 291-2295, will send you off down the James River in a canoe ($45 per day) or kayak ($30) including shuttle service, maps, and equipment. Finally, there's a **U.S. Forest Service Information Center** in front of the Stonewall Inn at Natural Bridge.

EVENTS

On the third Monday in January, **Lee-Jackson Day,** commemorates the birthdays of Robert E. Lee (Jan. 19) and Stonewall Jackson (Jan. 21) with celebrations throughout the South, but particularly in Stonewall's hometown. Free tours of Jackson's home and other festivities honor the local hero. In March of election years, Lexington comes alive with Washington & Lee's famous **Mock Convention,** tel. (540) 463-8460, an outrageous parade and party that also happens to be one of the most accurate predictors of presidential politics in the country. Since William Jennings Bryan defeated John A. Johnson in 1908, the counterfeit caucus has correctly predicted presidential nominees 15 out of 20 times. In spite of the festive atmosphere, a year's worth of serious research goes into keeping up such a good track record (last broken in 1972, when Ted Kennedy was chosen for the Democratic nomination over

George McGovern). The convention happens early in the actual races, giving it serious political sway that attracts national interest.

The Virginia Horse Center hosts the **Virginia Horse Festival** the third weekend in April, showcasing dozens of different breeds with demonstrations, seminars, and equestrian merchandise and art for sale.

SHOPPING

Local artists have formed a cooperative gallery in the Alexander Witherow House called **Artists in Cahoots,** tel. (540) 464-1147, showcasing beautiful crafts from photography and stained glass to hand-painted silks and delicate carved birds. Some artists also work here. **Virginia Born and Bred,** 16 W. Washington St., tel. (540) 463-1832, stocks Americana including hand-carved nutcrackers and folk art alongside jellies, hams, and wines. Textiles and ceramics, both Virginian and non-, fill **Artisans on Washington Street,** 22 W. Washington St., tel. (540) 464-3625, while **Frameworks,** 1 N. Main St., tel. (540) 464-6464, is a frame shop with a back room full of Civil War relics, prints, and paintings.

Lexington has too many antique stores to mention—practically one on every block—but for sheer volume you can't beat the **Lexington Antique and Craft Mall,** tel. (540) 463-9511, with 250 dealers spread over 40,000 square feet. It's in the College Square Shopping Center, southwest of the center of town on Rt. 672 (Enfield Rd.).

INFORMATION AND TRANSPORTATION

Lexington's well-organized **Visitors Center,** 106 E. Washington St., tel. (540) 463-3777, features a miniature museum, slide show, and helpful employees. It's open daily Sept.-May. 9 a.m.-5 p.m., June-Aug. 8:30 a.m.-6 p.m.

There is a **Greyhound** bus terminal, tel. (800) 231-2222, on US 11 north of the Maury River bridge.

SOUTH OF LEXINGTON

NATURAL BRIDGE

Rockbridge County derives its name from a 215-foot-tall limestone span—all that remains of a huge cavern carved out over thousands of years by tiny Cedar Creek. Thomas Jefferson, who once owned Natural Bridge, called it "so beautiful in archeology, so elevated, so light, and springing as it were up to Heaven, [that] the rapture of the spectator is really indescribable" (brochure literature names it as one of the dozen or so Seven Wonders of the World). Thousands of tourists make the pilgrimage annually.

Natural Bridge is spectacular, to be sure—one of Virginia's most impressive natural sights—but almost as fascinating is the marketing spectacle that has evolved around it. Interstate billboards are stacked like dominoes for hundreds of miles in every direction, and even ticket sellers can't keep a straight face describing the nightly *Drama of Creation* colored-light show, complete with music and solemn narration intoning the origins of the universe. If you run out of money, there's an ATM; if you find religion, there's a Baptist church. In the end, the whole package—which has little to do with the bridge itself—gives a new shade of meaning to the slogan "The Wonder of It All."

History

According to native legend, the "Bridge of God" materialized to help a band of Monocan Indians in flight from raiding Shawnee and Powhatans. In 1749, British Lord Fairfax hired Col. Peter Jefferson—who, six years earlier, had fathered a son destined to become president—to survey the land around today's Rt. 11. One young assistant carved his initials on the stone wall; the faint "GW" is still visible, making George Washington the only president to have officially defaced a Virginia landmark. In 1773, Thomas Jefferson gained title to the bridge and 157 surrounding acres from King George III for 20 shillings ($2.40 today). Near the base he built a log cabin and installed a "sentiment" book in which prominent visitors could record their im-

pressions. During the Revolutionary War, soldiers made bullets by pouring molten lead from the bridge into the creek below and mined saltpeter from nearby caves for gunpowder.

The Bridge

All visits start at the **main ticket building,** which encloses a gargantuan gift shop, indoor pool, miniature golf course, ATM, and post office. Brochures in French, German, Spanish, Russian, Chinese, and Japanese describe what you're going to see as soon as you've decided which ticket package to buy. Options include the bridge only ($8 adults, $4 children 6-15); the bridge, cave, and wax museum ($15 adults, $7.50 children); any two ($12 and $5.50); or the cave or museum only ($7 and $3.50). A full-season pass is $25 for adults and $12.50 for children. Alternately, you can drive over the bridge for free—Rt. 11 heading east toward the Blue Ridge Parkway crosses right over it—but you can't see anything from above. Open daily 8 a.m.-7 p.m., tel. (800) 533-1410 or (540) 291-2121, e-mail: natbrg@aol.com, Web site: www.naturalbridgeva.com.

Walk downhill or take a shuttle bus to the beginning of the trail, where the **Summer House Cafe** offers light fare in an open patio alongside the creek. Children's voices echo up the deep, wooded gorge where you'll get your first glimpse of the sheer size of the thing. At 215 feet tall, 50-150 feet wide, and 90 feet long, it's massive—but surprisingly graceful for 36,000 tons of stone. The trail continues along the creek, a pleasant walk when it's not too crowded. Past an open space where Easter sunrise services have been held since 1947 are an old saltpeter mine, picnic areas, and the Lace Waterfalls.

Other Sights

George Washington, Daniel Boone, and Robert E. Lee share quarters with some 175 others in the **Natural Bridge Wax Museum & Factory.** Narrated historic scenes include a theatrical presentation of Leonardo da Vinci's *Last Supper.* An explanation of the making of wax figures is part of the tour. It's said that the ghost of a woman haunts the **Natural Bridge Caverns,** tel. (540) 291-2121,

JULIAN SMITH

*the impressive limestone span for which the
town was named*

the deepest cave on the East Coast. Guided tours
to spots including the Wishing Well Room, Colossal Dome Room, and Mirror Lake leave every
half-hour. **Natural Bridge Zoo,** tel. (540) 291-
2420, harbors the usual—giraffes, camels, bears,
and monkeys—along with rare and endangered
species such as a white tiger born in 1997. It also
boasts the largest petting zoo in the state. Don't let
the kids hear about the $2.50 elephants rides on
weekends or you'll have no choice but to stop
by; $6 adults, $4 children 3-12.

Accommodations and Food

Next to the ticket building, the **Natural Bridge
Inn & Conference Center,** tel. (800) 533-1410 or
(540) 291-212, fax 291-1551, has a wide range of
choices. Rooms in the hotel itself range from inexpensive to moderate, with an Olympic-sized
pool and a restaurant offering lots of buffets like
prime rib ($16), seafood ($16), and a Sunday
country feast for $13. Other options under the
same management include the Stonewall Inn

across the road (budget to inexpensive) and nine
cabins behind it (budget to moderate). A two-night package including dinner, breakfast, and
tickets to the bridge, caverns, and wax museum
is $115-152 for two people, and family deals for
two adults and two children is $169-189.

**Camping: The Campground at Natural
Bridge,** tel. (540) 291-2727, e-mail: campnb1@
aol.com, has full-hookup sites for $21 and cabins for $35 per night. They rent boats, canoes,
and tubes to enjoy the nearby James River, and
charge a small fee for fishing in their stocked pond.
To get there take Rt. 130 east from I-81 exit 175 for
4.5 miles, take a right onto Rt. 759, then your first
left onto Rt. 782. Tent sites at the **Natural Bridge
KOA Kampground,** tel. (540) 291-2770, fax 291-
2770, are $19, with RV campsites for $21.50-
23.50 and Kamping Kabins for $34-42. They're
just off I-81 exit 180 on Rt. 11. A short drive up into
the Jefferson National Forest brings you to the
Cave Mountain Lake Recreation Area, tel. (540)
265-5100, where 42 sites near the cold, clear lake
are $8 each. Take Rt. 130 east from I-81 exit 175
or 180 for 3.2 miles, turn south onto Rt. 795 for another 3.2, and turn right onto Rt. 781 for 1.6 miles
to the recreation area's paved entrance road.

BLUE RIDGE PARKWAY

Like a vine connecting two ripe grapes, this
scenic highway unites the Shenandoah and
Great Smoky Mountains National Parks in one
long, lovely stretch of Appalachia. It was begun
during the Great Depression as a federal public-works project and finished within a decade. Designers took liberties with the philosophy of the
shortest distance between two points, choosing
instead to follow the wandering 3,000-foot ridge-line wherever it chose to go. Of the parkway's
469 miles, 217 are in Virginia, and the first 114,
between Waynesboro and Roanoke along the
crest of the Blue Ridge Mountains, are widely
thought to be the most impressive. Miles of tranquil farm scenes are punctuated by crumbling
graveyards and gaps which open to grand
panoramas in either direction.

Access

The parkway is open year-round, though few
facilities outside Peaks of Otter are open be-

yond May-Oct., and parts of the road may be closed due to weather. Entry is free. Between I-64 at Waynesboro and US 460 at Roanoke drivers can reach the road via US 60 near Buena Vista, Rt. 30 and Rt. 501 east of Natural Bridge, and Rt. 43 east of Bucanan.

Flora and Fauna

Vegetation along the parkway is more southern (i.e., drier) than in Shenandoah National Park. Forests of white pine, hemlock, and hawthorn burst into color during an extended fall season, thanks to the wide range of altitudes along the road (649 to 6,047 feet). In the autumn spectrum, reds are probably maples or dogwoods, yellows hickory, and orange sassafras. Spruce, fir, and pine provide a green backdrop. Spectacular flame azalea blooms between Roanoke and the Smokies in May and June, followed by purple Catawba rhododendron near Peaks of Otter. Many of the larger animals come out at dusk and are gone by dawn, leaving daytime to the groundhogs, squirrels, and chipmunks. White-tail deer, bobcats, raccoons, and black bears all make occasional appearances.

Camping

Of the four campgrounds along the Blue Ridge Parkway, two (Otter Creek and Peaks of Otter) are north of Roanoke. All are open roughly May-Oct., but call ahead during other months since they might keep a few sites going year-round. Campsites are first come, first served, $10 per site for two adults, and limited to 14 days' maximum stay between June and Labor Day. Some campsites are accessible to visitors with disabilities. Trailers up to 30 feet are permitted, and there are dumpstations at all campgrounds (but no water or electrical hookups). Pets must be on leashes. Off the parkway, backcountry camping is permitted in the George Washington National Forest.

Rockfish Gap to Roanoke

All locations along the parkway are measured in mileposts (milepost), from 0 at the southern terminus of Shenandoah National Park at Rockfish Gap to 218 at the North Carolina border. The speed limit along the entire parkway is 45 mph, but traffic can crawl during high season. In emergencies, call (800) PARKWATCH (800-727-5928).

At the **Humpback Rocks Visitor Center,** milepost 5.8, tel. (540) 943-4716, a self-guided trail leads through a reconstructed historic farmstead. Across the road, a steep three-quarter-mile trail climbs to the jagged top of Humpback Rocks for a 270-degree view of the Blue Ridge Mountains. Sunrise from the top of Humpback with a box of donuts and a steaming thermos of coffee is one of my personal favorites in the whole state. Past **Devil's Knob** (3,851 feet) is a turnoff to Rt. 664 toward Wintergreen Ski Resort. The **Sherando Lake Recreation Area** is next, centered on a pair of lakes created in the early 1900s by the Civilian Conservation Corps for recreation and flood control. The 25-acre lower lake is open to swimming and boating, while the seven-acre lake above it is known for trout, bass, and bluegill fishing. A total of 63 campsites are open April-Oct. for $15 per day, and hot showers are available in the bathhouse near the 200-yard beach. Almost 20 miles of forest roads and singletrack make up the Sherando Lake Loop, including a 1,000-foot climb from the lake through "Big Levels" to the Bald Mountain Overlook. For more information, contact the George Washington National Forest office in Harrisonburg, tel. (540) 433-2491.

At **Tye River Gap** (2,969 feet), take Rt. 56 east to the head of the **Crabtree Falls Trail,** leading to the highest waterfall east of the Mississippi. Five cascades tumble over 1,200 feet in all. Pass the **Whetstone Ridge Ranger Station** and a basic restaurant near milepost 29 to reach **Yankee Horse** at milepost 34.4, named for an unfortunate Union mount that had to be shot after it fell from exhaustion. Here an overlook trail leads along a remnant of an old logging railway from the 1920s to 30-foot Wigwam Falls in a shady grove. **Otter Creek** (milepost 60.8) rolls down the hillside toward the James River, lined by blooming mountain laurel in May and June. A campground has 67 sites, a coffee shop, and a service station.

There is a visitors center at **James River Overlook,** milepost 63.6, tel. (804) 299-5496, the lowest point on the parkway. A self-guiding trail leads over a footbridge and along the river bluff to restored locks along the Kanawha canal. The **Peaks of Otter Recreation Area,** milepost 86, encloses a visitor center, tel. (540) 586-4357, and the **Peaks of Otter Lodge,** tel.(800) 542-5927 or (540) 586-1081, fax 586-4420, the only place on the parkway guaranteed to be open year-round. Sixty-three rooms overlooking Abbott Lake each have two double beds but no TVs or phones. The view from the dining room is justly famous, and the hotel also has a coffee shop, lounge, and gift shop. Moderate. E-mail: peaksotter@aol.com, Web site: www.imall.com/stores/peaks. Trails near the campground lead to the Old Johnson Farm, Harkening Hill, and Flat Top. Long thought to be the highest point in the state, Sharp Top (3,875 feet) can be reached by foot and sweat via a steep 1.5-mile trail, or on a tour bus from the hotel that drops you off near the peak.

Information
The Blue Ridge Parkway is administered by the National Park Service, U.S. Department of the Interior, 400 BB&T Building, Asheville, NC, 28801, tel. (704) 298-0398, Web site: www.nps.gov/blri. Each visitors center sells a number of excellent books detailing hikes, history, and wildlife along the road.

NORTHERN VIRGINIA

Northern Virginia is a study in contrasts. On one hand you have the paved expanses of Arlington and Fairfax Counties: shopping malls, housing developments, and little else; this area once languished in the shadow of the Capitol. On the other hand are miles of undulating pastures dotted with mansions, and farms housing purebred stallions. In one direction, suburbia; in the other, arcadia; in all, a region that's definitely worth a second glance.

Still, the two halves have more in common than may be evident at first. For one, money. Hunt Country is among the nation's wealthiest regions per capita, and dollars have been pouring into local coffers ever since the federal government built the Pentagon on the eve of WW II. Another is the area's vicinity to Washington, D.C. District residents have always looked to places like Old Town Alexandria, Great Falls, and the parks south along the Potomac as refuges from the downside of urban life. Now they're looking even farther west and finding enchanting B&Bs, gourmet restaurants, and quiet, historic towns. Some like it so much they're buying land and relocating—bringing with them (some would say) a wave of development that inches along the Dulles Greenway one subdivision at a time.

Highlights

History fans will be surprised at the pockets of the past hidden among the high-rises in northern

Virginia. Over 2,000 buildings in Old Town Alexandria are listed in the National Register of Historic Places, while George Washington's home at Mt. Vernon retains most of its Revolutionary allure in spite of tourist crowds. Arlington National Cemetery and the Pentagon lie within sight of the capital skyline, and Robert E. Lee's mansion in Arlington National Cemetery overlooks waves of headstones, which are only a short drive from Manassas, site of two major Civil War battles. Travelers interested in things modern will enjoy Frank Lloyd Wright's Pope-Leighey House at Woodlawn and the cutting-edge Newseum in Arlington.

For outdoor recreation, running from Arlington to Purcellville there's the Washington & Old Dominion Trail, a scenic success of converting a former railroad bed into a multiuse trail. A visit to horse-happy Hunt Country, centered around Leesburg, will show you why the American foxhound is the Virginia state dog, while a sea-kayak paddle around Mason Neck might net you a bald eagle sighting.

Access

Inside the Beltway (the loop of I-495 and I-95 around the nation's capital), the **Metrorail,** tel. (202) 637-7000, Web site: www.wmata.com, provides a clean, quiet, and quick way to get around. Three lines enter northern Virginia from Washington. The orange and blue cross the Potomac together into northern Arlington; from there the orange heads west as far as Vienna, while the blue turns south past Arlington National Cemetery to join with the yellow (spanning the river next to I-395) at the Pentagon. This pair continues south to the King Street Station before splitting for a final stop or two.

Trains run until midnight from 5:30 a.m. on weekdays and 8 a.m. on weekends. Fares depend on distance and whether or not you're traveling during rush hour (weekdays 5:30-9:30 a.m. and 3-8 p.m.). Passengers ages four and up have to buy a magnetic paper fare card with enough computerized value to get where you're going (a minimum of $1.10). **Metrobuses** connect with Metrorail stations for travel to outlying areas. Fares are similar, but transfers are only 25 cents and one-day passes cost $5.

Arlington's **National Airport,** tel. (703) 572-2700, recently had Ronald Reagan's name officially attached to it, but most people ignore the Gipper and still call it by the old name of Washington National Airport. The blue and yellow Metro lines both stop at the airport. **Washington-Dulles International Airport,** tel. (703) 572-2700, is about a half-hour drive (depending on traffic) from Arlington National Cemetery.

Washington Flyer Airport Shuttles, tel. (703) 685-1400 or (888) 927-4359, run taxis and limousines to D.C. and northern Virginia from both airports. Transportation from Dulles to the West Falls Church Metro stop is $8 one-way, and a ride between airports will run you $16 one-way. To get to downtown D.C., call **Super Shuttle,** tel. (800) 258-3826; **Capitol Taxi,** tel. (202) 546-2400; or **Yellow Cab,** tel. (202) 544-1212.

NEAR D.C.:
ARLINGTON COUNTY AND VICINITY

At just under 26 square miles, Arlington County is the third smallest in the U.S. Still, 185,000 residents call it home, mostly in the north and west. Even with four bridges connecting it to the Capital, Arlington has started to grow out of its role as a D.C. appendix, full of "bedroom communities" that lie empty during the day. Computer and communications industries have set up shop in neighborhoods (the county has no incorporated cities) such as Clarendon, Ballston, and Crystal City, sparking the birth of the Internet and sparing local employees the cross-river commute. Federal buildings and monuments still concentrate in the eastern portion, along with high-rise condos and most of the county's 37 hotels.

Together with Fairfax County, Arlington is part of a region many Virginians consider almost another state. Closer in demeanor and skyline to the nation's capital than to most of the rest of Virginia, this part of the Old Dominion is one of the few areas that consistently votes Democratic in presidential elections. It *is* part of Virginia, though, and has more than a few spots that merit a visit.

Without any true urban centers, Arlington County hotels and restaurants are spread throughout the area. To find out what's going on here, as well as in D.C., pick up a copy of the *Washington Post's* "Weekend" section (out on Friday) or the *Washington City Paper,* a free weekly.

History
Originally part of the arbitrary diamond of the District of Columbia, Arlington County was ignominiously trimmed in 1847 when District planners decided no territory was needed across the Potomac. Both the Custis (as in Martha Custis Washington) and Lee (Robert E.) families—which eventually merged—had extensive landholdings here in the 18th and 19th centuries. The Lee family mansion gave the county its name. By the 20th century, war offices and commuter homes for capital workers had started to replace farmlands, setting the stage for high-tech businesses and defense industries.

ARLINGTON NATIONAL CEMETERY

The country's most famous burial grounds embrace 612 acres of hills, grass, and endless, mesmerizing rows of white marble headstones. Almost a quarter of a million American veterans

WEST VIRGINIA

MARYLAND

Lovettsville

Hillsboro
Waterford

Morven
Park

WHITE'S
FERRY

BALL'S BLUFF BATTLEFIELD
AND NATIONAL CEMETERY

Purcellville
Hamilton

Leesburg

CLARKE
Bluemont

Potomac

River

LOUDOUN

DULLES GREENWAY

OATLANDS
ESTATE

Riverbend
Park

Great
Falls

Upperville

Glenwood
Park

Great Falls
Great Falls Park

Herndon

Sky Meadows
State Park

Middleburg

WASHINGTON-DULLES
INTERNATIONAL
AIRPORT

Wolf Trap
Farm Park

Vienna

The
Plains

Fairfax

Manassas National
Battlefield Park

GREAT
MEADOWS

Haymarket

Gainesville

Bull Run
Regional Park

Bull Run
Creek

FAIRFAX

FAUQUIER

Manassas

Occoquan
River

Warrenton

RAPPAHANNOCK

PRINCE WILLIAM

CULPEPER

Occoquan
Reservoir

Prince William
Forest Park

QUANTICO MARINE

CORPS BASE

CAROLINE

0   5 mi

0   5 km

© MOON PUBLICATIONS, INC.

Shenandoah

River

NORTHERN VIRGINIA

from every war are buried here, and the graves are visited by four million mourners and sightseers every year.

Even with the crowds and circling Tourmobiles, Arlington National Cemetery is a somber place. Most visitors heed the numerous signs for quiet and respect, leaving a silence punctuated only by birdcalls, the infrequent crack of a rifle salute, and the plaintive notes of "Taps."

History

The cemetery began as an estate surrounding Arlington House, built from 1802-17 by George Washington Parke Custis, grandson of Martha Washington (née Custis). In 1831, the house and property changed owners when Mary Custis, George's granddaughter, married Robert E. Lee, who had often come to visit from his home in Alexandria. Robert and Mary lived in Arlington House for 30 years until, on April 22, 1861, Lee accepted the command of Virginia's forces in the war against the Union.

In 1864 the 1,100-acre estate was confiscated by the federal government when Martha couldn't appear in person to pay the property taxes. Quartermaster Gen. Montgomery Meigs, a Georgian who had remained loyal to the Union, considered Lee the worst kind of traitor and came up with a scathing revenge: the burial of Union dead, literally, in Lee's backyard. Meigs crossed the

---

D.C.'S MISSING PIECE

The otherwise perfect diamond of the District of Columbia once extended as far south as Alexandria, donated by Virginia along with part of Fairfax County to form the newly organized Capital district in 1789. Residents welcomed the honor at first, but started to grumble when the government prohibited the construction of public buildings south of the Potomac and denied District residents congressional representation and the right to vote for president (the former grievance, amazingly, is still an issue). The threat of a ban on slavery in the District was the final straw. Several petitions later, in 1847, the region was given back to Virginia leaving a ragged bite out of D.C.'s southern border.

SPRAWL

Urban sprawl is a little like pornography—offensive to many, hard to define exactly, but one of those things that you know when you see it. In city-planner jargon, it's large-lot residential subdivisions beyond the edge of service and employment areas. To those who experience it every day, it's a land-devouring invasion of single-use zones that separate homes from businesses, shopping areas, schools, and parks, resulting in cities delineated only by stoplights, endless strip-style commercial developments along indistinguishable highways, and a subtle social malaise that can make conglomerations out of communities—or out of nothing at all. Virginia's worst-hit sprawl areas are inside the Beltway and in the Hampton Roads/Tidewater region. And with populations in both expected to skyrocket over the next few decades, more and more people are starting to look around, and look ahead, and worry.

Sprawl is the direct result of poor planning. Developers, looking to make a quick buck, steamroll their plans through local political systems, which are often willing to share in the profits as they sell community interests down the river. People moving to the suburbs to live in "the country" and to flee the (often-imagined) crime of urban centers

leave inner cities with declining tax bases and crumbling infrastructure. Cities spread outward instead of upward, squelching farmland and empty acres under parking lots, bypasses, and office buildings.

As a result, everyone has to drive everywhere. People who thought they left urban gridlock behind find themselves trapped in their cars for more hours than before. Interstate freeway systems, designed to carry drivers in and out of downtown areas, become useless for suburb-to-suburb commuters (currently estimated at 39 million people, or 44% of all American commuters). Beltways become packed—in 1981 the average speed on I-495 was 47 mph; 10 years later it was 23 mph—and commuters looking for shortcuts through local roads get in more and more accidents. Billions of dollars in fuel and work time go up in a carbon monoxide haze.

The environmental costs are just as high. Sediment from building sites and fertilizers from acres of lawns overload local ecosystems with nutrients, which build up to toxic levels without the filtering and water-holding capacity of the wetlands and forests they replaced. One study in 1995 placed Virginia among the country's top 10 states

---

Potomac to personally oversee the interment of the first Union soldiers in Martha's rose garden. Eventually 16,000 soldiers were buried in the fields around Arlington House, ensuring that Lee would never live there in peace again.

After the war, Lee's grandson, George Washington Custis Lee, sued the U.S. government for possession of the estate and won after taking the case to the Supreme Court. In 1883, he turned around and sold it back to the government for $150,000. Two hundred acres were set aside to start the cemetery.

Sights

At the main entrance gate, the **Women in Military Service for America Memorial** contains an education center and theater dedicated to all women serving in the armed forces in war and peace. A short uphill walk brings you to the eternal flame at the grave of former president **John F. Kennedy.** This is the most visited sight in Ar-

lington. A low marble wall engraved with his "Ask not" speech faces a view of the Potomac and the Capitol. The resting places of **Jaqueline Kennedy Onassis** and her two infant sons lie nearby, as does that of **Robert F. Kennedy,** whose grave, as requested in his will, is marked only by a single white wooden cross and excerpts from two of his speeches on civil rights.

On the hilltop above the Kennedys presides **Arlington House,** Web site: www.nps.gov/arho, the Greek revival mansion that Robert E. Lee described as the spot "where my affection and attachments are more strongly placed than at any other place in the world." In 1933, the house was transferred to the care of the National Park Service and filled almost to its 12-foot ceilings with Lee-era antiques and reproductions. The Marquis de Lafayette called the view of the Potomac and the Capitol "the finest view in the world" in 1824. Today the Memorial Bridge heads straight from Arlington House toward the Lin-in extreme danger of losing its native ecosystems, and named suburban sprawl as one of the major factors. All these people need to drink, so huge reservoirs are created, in the process drowning thousands of more acres.

Sprawl almost always ends up costing more in the long run. Infrastructure must be extended to service outlying areas, so counties and towns have to shell out more and more money for new roads, water and sewage lines, fire and police services, libraries, schools, and parks. Even though people are pouring in, their tax dollars aren't enough to cover the costs, so municipalities have to keep raising taxes or go into debt. It's estimated that some $8.5 billion for roads alone may be required to service new suburbs in Tidewater and northern Virginia by 2020, and guess who's going to be footing *that* bill. Not the developers who got the ball rolling. Thanks to million-dollar incentive packages, they're often only liable for 12-15% of the new infrastructure costs their creations necessitate—often over half the total price of development.

Sprawl's most insidious effect is also its most indirect. By spreading people so thinly over such a faceless space, it threatens the quality of community life. Impersonal corridors of glass and gray replace nature's browns and greens, and residents of impersonal tract houses find they often don't know who lives right next door.

The Alternative

Through the strategy of "smart growth"—basically, planning ahead—local governments can avoid the side effects of sprawl, protect their environment, and save money. If development is kept compact and close to existing social centers, infrastructure costs plummet as fewer sewer mains and electrical wires, and less pavement are needed. Buffer zones can protect sensitive natural areas like shores, streams, and wetlands, both for the enjoyment of citizens and the preservation of the local ecological balance. By building a range of housing types near each other and near schools, offices, and shopping areas, builders can increase the odds of pedestrian neighborhoods where people actually bump into each other on the street.

Planners have their work cut out for them. Almost $50 billion worth of road projects are in the blueprint stages in Virginia in the coming decade, and currently established sprawl has to be addressed. Future transportation and water-supply issues must be solved, and somebody has to figure out, quite simply, where to put all these people. But with foresight and restraint, sprawl is anything but inevitable.

---

coln Memorial in a symbolic link between the two former adversaries (Lee and Lincoln). Pierre Charles L'Enfant, Revolutionary War veteran and designer of the Capitol, was reburied in front in 1909. Behind the house stands one of the last wooded areas left in the cemetery, which puts it at the center of a debate over where to put more bodies as empty space runs out. Open daily April-Sept., 9:30 a.m.-6 p.m., Oct.-March 9:30 a.m.-4:30 p.m.

Look for the white marble **Memorial Amphitheater** and pass behind it to reach the **Tomb of the Unknowns,** where unidentified bodies from WW I, WW II, the Korean War, and the Vietnam War are guarded round the clock by the U.S. Third Infantry in an amazing display of discipline and precision. Each guard paces back and forth in 21 unerring steps, snapping his or her heels at every turn, often under the gaze of hundreds of people. Three people take part in the changing of the guard (every 30 minutes April-Sept., every hour otherwise), in which one gives the orders as two others march in step, inspect weapons, and transfer orders.

Dozens of other memorials are scattered about Arlington, including the **Mast of the Battleship** *Maine,* whose mysterious explosion on February 15, 1898, in Havana Harbor sparked the Spanish-American War; the **Tomb of the Unknown Dead of the Civil War,** guarding 2,111 bodies; and the **Challenger Memorial,** for the crew of the downed space shuttle.

Visiting Arlington National Cemetery

The **visitors center,** tel. (703) 692-0931 is open daily Oct.-March 8 a.m.-5 p.m., April-Sept., 8 a.m.-7 p.m.; free. Narrated **shuttle tours** aboard the Tourmobile start from here and visit the John F. Kennedy gravesite, the Tomb of the Unknowns, and Arlington House for $4.75 for adults, $2.25 for children 3-11. Passengers can buy tickets from the driver and get on or off different buses all day. Call (202) 554-5100 for information on optional extensions to Mt. Vernon ($37 for adults, $18.50 children) and Washington, D.C. ($14 adults, $7 children).

NEAR ARLINGTON NATIONAL CEMETERY

On the cemetery's northern border stands the **Netherlands Carillon,** given in 1960 from the people of Holland in gratitude for American help against the Nazis in WW II. Concerts here, starting Easter Sunday and running through September, feature the ringing of all 50 bells. Call (703) 285-2598 for a schedule. Just to the north the **U.S. Marine Corps War Memorial** depicts Joe Rosenthal's Pulitzer Prize-winning photograph of marines raising the U.S. flag over Iwo Jima during the Battle for the Pacific in 1945. The memorial is the largest cast bronze statue in the world, erected in memory of all marines who have died serving their country since 1775. Open daily, 24 hours; free.

A footbridge connects the Virginia side of the Potomac with **Theodore Roosevelt Island,** tel. (703) 285-2598 or 285-2225, an 88-acre bird sanctuary dedicated to the 26th president. The island, crossed by the Theodore Roosevelt Bridge (I-66), is open daily 8 a.m.-dusk. Farther south along the George Washington Memorial Parkway an abrupt exit (look carefully for the sign) leads to the peaceful, 15-acre **Lyndon B. Johnson Memorial Grove** at the southern end of Lady Bird Johnson Park.

THE PENTAGON

The headquarters of the Department of Defense occupies the largest office building in the world, just to the south of Arlington National Cemetery. Though no longer the hot spot it was during the Cold War—employees once half-jokingly called the center courtyard "ground zero"—the Pentagon is still one of the most impressive structures you'll ever see.

Designed in just one weekend in 1941 by the U.S. Army Corps of Engineers, it was built over a filled-in swamp after only 16 months, and came complete with a host of monolithic statistics. The

ARLINGTON COUNTY AND VICINITY

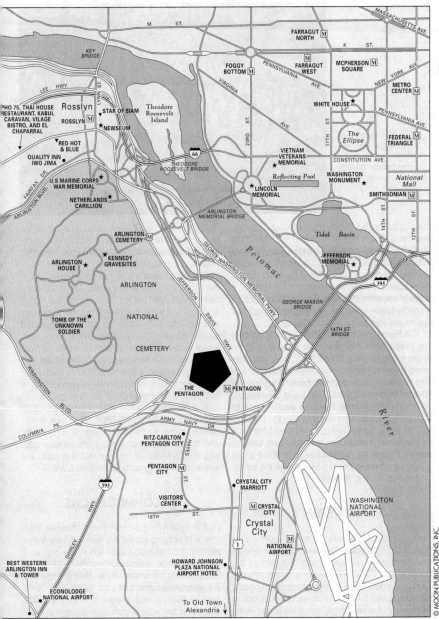

MASSACHUSETTS AVE.

M ST.

FARRAGUT NORTH Ⓜ

KEY BRIDGE

K ST.

FOGGY BOTTOM Ⓜ

PENNSYLVANIA AVE.

FARRAGUT WEST Ⓜ

MCPHERSON SQUARE Ⓜ

NEW YORK AVE.

METRO CENTER Ⓜ

LEE HWY.

VIRGINIA

Rosslyn

PHO 75, THAI HOUSE RESTAURANT, KABUL CARAVAN, VILLAGE BISTRO, AND EL CHAPARRAL

ROSSLYN Ⓜ ★ STAR OF SIAM

NEWSEUM

Theodore Roosevelt Island

WHITE HOUSE ★

PENNSYLVANIA AVE.

RED HOT & BLUE

23RD ST.

AVE.

17TH ST.

The Ellipse

FEDERAL TRIANGLE

QUALITY INN IWO JIMA

VIETNAM VETERANS MEMORIAL

CONSTITUTION AVE.

FAIRFAX DR.

THEODORE ROOSEVELT BRIDGE

Reflecting Pool

WASHINGTON MONUMENT ★

National Mall

SMITHSONIAN Ⓜ

U.S MARINE CORPS WAR MEMORIAL ★

★ LINCOLN MEMORIAL

ARLINGTON BLVD.

NETHERLANDS CARILLION ★

14TH ST.

12TH ST.

ARLINGTON MEMORIAL BRIDGE

Tidal Basin

ARLINGTON CEMETERY Ⓜ

Potomac

JEFFERSON MEMORIAL ★

ARLINGTON HOUSE ★ ★ KENNEDY GRAVESITES

GEORGE WASHINGTON MEMORIAL PKWY.

395

ARLINGTON

JEFFERSON DAVIS HWY.

NATIONAL

GEORGE MASON BRIDGE

TOMB OF THE UNKNOWN SOLDIER ★

14TH ST. BRIDGE

CEMETERY

River

WASHINGTON BLVD.

THE PENTAGON

Ⓜ PENTAGON

COLUMBIA PK.

ARMY NAVY DR.

RITZ-CARLTON PENTAGON CITY

HAYES ST.

PENTAGON CITY Ⓜ

395

CRYSTAL CITY MARRIOTT

WASHINGTON NATIONAL AIRPORT

VISITORS CENTER ★

18TH ST.

Ⓜ CRYSTAL CITY

Crystal City

SHIRLEY HWY.

1

NATIONAL AIRPORT Ⓜ

BEST WESTERN ARLINGTON INN & TOWER

ECONOLODGE NATIONAL AIRPORT

HOWARD JOHNSON PLAZA NATIONAL AIRPORT HOTEL

To Old Town Alexandria ↓

© MOON PUBLICATIONS, INC.

The gravestones of Arlington National Cemetery attest to the magnitude of lives lost in American wars.

building covers 6.5 million square feet spread over five floors. Each of the five sides is longer than the U.S. Capitol, and the whole thing is covered by 7.1 acres of glass. About 23,000 employees (half military and half civilian) tell time by 4,200 clocks, drink from 691 water fountains, and navigate 17.5 miles of corridors that were planned so well it supposedly takes only seven minutes to walk between any two points in the building.

The Pentagon, tel. (703) 695-1776, is open to the public Mon.-Fri. 9:30 a.m.-3:30 p.m. Free tours are given every half hour, and you may need to sign in to reserve a spot a half hour before departure. U.S. citizens should bring a photo ID and foreign visitors must have a passport. Although employees have 16 parking lots to choose from, your best bet is to take the Metro or to park along Army-Navy Dr., reached from Rt. 1 or Hayes St. north from the Arlington visitors center. Park in the commercial lot or at the shopping mall (cheaper), and walk through the tunnel under I-395 to the Pentagon.

NEWSEUM

One of Virginia's newest museums presents a high-tech, interactive look at the media and its profound effect on our society. Funded by the nonpartisan Freedom Forum, an international foundation dedicated to "free press, free speech, and free spirit," the Newseum starts with a look at the history of news from Sophocles to satellites.

Along the way you'll learn about journalistic integrity, consider the effects of reporting accuracy, and behold mesmerizing images from this century's top stories.

Check out what's going on back home, wherever that may be, with the display of 70 daily newspaper front pages from around the world, and find out what the headlines were the day you were born. Peek in the working broadcast studio; it's near the 126-foot video news wall, which faces a display of famous news photos, both beautiful and wrenching. Downstairs you can try your hand at playing anchor in front of the TelePrompTers in the mock newsroom, and even buy a tape of yourself on camera.

The Newseum, 1101 Wilson Blvd., tel. (703) 284-3725 or (888) 639-7386, Web site: www.newseum.org, is open Wed.-Sun., 10 a.m.-5 p.m. and is free. Educational programs include talks with the Journalist of the Day. Refreshments are available in the (groan) News Byte Cafe.

ACCOMMODATIONS

Lodgings in Arlington are often a cheaper alternative to staying across the river, with the Metro providing a quick and easy link to the capital. A central toll-free reservation number, (888) 743-8292, covers the whole county. **Bed & Breakfast Accommodations Ltd.,** tel. (202) 328-3510, fax 332-3885, e-mail: bnbaccom@aol.com, Web site: www.bnbaccom.com, can arrange stays in about 10 private homes, guest houses, inns, and small hotels in northern Virginia (moderate and up). The **Alexandria and Arlington Bed & Breakfast Network,** tel. (703) 549-3415 or (888) 549-3415, e-mail: aabbn@erols.com, also sets up accommodations.

The **Arlington/Washington Travelodge Cherryblossom,** 3030 Columbia Pike, tel. (703) 521-5570, fax 271-0081, and the **Econo Lodge-National Airport,** 2485 S. Glebe Rd., tel. (703) 979-4100, fax 979-6120, both fall in the moderate category. The **Quality Inn Iwo Jima,** 1501 Arlington Blvd., tel. (703) 524-5000, fax 522-5484, is convenient to Arlington National Cemetery, and there's an **Econo Lodge-Metro Arlington,** 6800 Lee Hwy., tel. (703) 538-5300, fax 538-2110, farther west on I-66 near its intersection with Lee Hwy./Rt. 29. Both are expensive.

Higher-end accommodations are concentrated to the south in Crystal City and Pentagon City. All offer complimentary shuttle service to National Airport. The **Howard Johnson Plaza National Airport Hotel,** 2650 Jefferson Davis Hwy., tel. (703) 684-7200, fax. 684-3217, is just across the George Washington Memorial Parkway from the airport. Premium. The **Best Western Arlington Inn & Tower,** 2480 S. Glebe Rd., tel. (703) 979-4400, fax 685-0051, sits a few blocks west. Premium.

At the **Crystal City Marriott,** 1999 Jefferson Davis Hwy., tel. (703) 413-5500, fax 413-0192, guests can choose from three restaurants, including Tuscany's, serving northern Italian fare at the top of a six-story skylit atrium. A short passage connects the hotel with a shopping mall and the Crystal City Metro stop. Luxury. Tops in the area is the **Ritz-Carlton Pentagon City,** in the Fashion Centre complex at 1250 S. Hayes St., tel. (703) 415-5000, fax 415-5061, laden with antiques, paintings, and every amenity you could ask for. The elegant Grill restaurant gets four stars from AAA, and the Pentagon City Metro Station is minutes away. Luxury.

FOOD

Rosslyn is a good place to take advantage of Arlington's increasing ethnic diversity. A little plaza off the 1700 block of Wilson Blvd., Rosslyn has no less than five options—choosing, and parking, are the only problems. All are open daily for lunch and dinner. **Pho 75,** tel. (703) 525-7355, is a popular nook with low-priced, tasty Vietnamese food, and the **Thai House Restaurant,** tel. (703) 527-5772, serves it up good and spicy. Middle Eastern rugs and a huge samovar decorate **Kabul Caravan,** tel. (703) 522-8394, which offers Afghani fare heavy on the rice and lamb. Dinner entrées are in the $15 range, with lunch plates for around $9. Pasta, fish, and meat dishes are served next door at the **Village Bistro,** tel. (703) 522-0284, which has some outside seating. **El Chaparral,** tel. (703) 527-3388, a Latin grocery, rounds things out.

Curries are a specialty of **Star of Siam,** 1735 N. Lynn St., tel. (703) 524-1208, opposite the Rosslyn Metro station. Bona fide Thai is served for lunch Mon.-Fri., dinner daily. For a more "local" meal, try the Memphis pit BBQ at **Red Hot & Blue,** 1600 Wilson Blvd. at N. Pierce St., tel. (703) 276-7427. Opened by the late Lee Atwater, blues guitarist and chairman of the Republican National Committee, this patriotically painted place draws rave reviews and visitors from across the Potomac for their wet and dry ribs, smoked ham and chicken, and homemade sides. Open daily for lunch and dinner.

Down Wilson Blvd. into Clarendon is **Queen Bee,** 3181 Wilson Blvd., tel. (703) 527-3444, another Vietnamese restaurant that's packed as often as Pho 75. They have vegetarian dishes and a mouth-watering *pho* (noodle soup). The **Rio Grande Cafe,** 4301 N. Fairfax Dr., tel. (703) 528-3131 has authentic Mexican food complete with plenty of *cerveza fría* (cold beer) and patio seating.

ENTERTAINMENT AND RECREATION

Nightlife

Steer toward Rosslyn once again for the best bars and clubs. There's a car protruding from the wall of the **Bardo Rodeo Brewpub,** 2000 Wilson Blvd., tel. (703) 527-1852 or 527-9399, a hip, smoky place with live music and a delicious line of homebrewed beers. Try a pint of James Brown Ale, Beat My Wheat, or Tibetan Sasquatch to wash down something off the short but enter-

WASHINGTON &
OLD DOMINION TRAIL

The Washington & Old Dominion Trail (technically the W&OD Railroad Regional Park) links northern Virginia's split personalities in a 45-mile stretch from the suburbs of Arlington County to Loudoun County's rural reaches. A train ran this route 1859-1968, but today all you'll encounter on the way from condos to meadows, or vice versa, are other walkers, bikers, and riders on horseback.

The asphalt path begins at the intersection of Shirlington Rd. and Four Mile Run Dr. in Arlington County, two blocks north of I-395 exit 6. From here it noses west through Falls Church in Fairfax County. A parallel bridle path joins in Vienna, and the double trail continues through Reston, Herndon, and Leesburg before ending at Purcellville west of Leesburg, on 21st St. (Rt. 690) one block off Main St. (Rt. 7).

Camping isn't allowed along the trail, but plenty of hotels and motels on the way make it possible to spend a few days making the whole trip. For more information contact the **Friends of the W&OD Trail** office at 21293 Smiths Switch Rd., Ashburn, VA 22011, tel. (703) 729-0596. The group also sells a 56-page guide and REI map.

---

taining menu. **Galaxy Hut,** 2711 Wilson Blvd., tel. (703) 525-8646, also has a long list of beer on tap and features live local bands. They charge a door admission, as does **Iota,** 2832 Wilson Blvd., tel. (703) 522-8340, which hosts everything from folk to alternative rock. For blues, try **Whitlow's on Wilson,** 2854 Wilson Blvd., tel. (703) 276-9693, or **Red Hot & Blue,** 1600 Wilson Blvd. at N. Pierce St., tel. (703) 276-7427.

Outdoor Activities

Bikers, joggers, strollers, and stroller-pushers flock to the **Mt. Vernon Trail,** which runs for 18 miles along the George Washington Memorial Parkway from Memorial Bridge south to Mt. Vernon, passing the Lyndon B. Johnson Memorial Grove and Old Town Alexandria along the way. You can stop to watch jets taking off from National Airport, boaters sliding their crafts into the river, and capital lights as they start to sparkle in the evening.

To the north, the unpaved **Potomac Heritage Trail** continues along the Virginia side of the river for 10 miles from Theodore Roosevelt Island to the Beltway. This one sees much less traffic, even though it passes through a riverside wilderness, along clifftops, and across countless streams gurgling toward the Potomac. It's blazed in blue, and you can reach it from the parking lot off the George Washington Memorial Parkway near the island. The **Washington & Old Dominion Trail** (see special topic) begins in Shirlington off of I-395.

Call the Arlington County Department of Parks and Recreation, tel. (703) 228-4747, for more details.

EVENTS

Clarendon hosts the **Virginia State Championship Chili Cookoff,** tel. (703) 276-0228 in early June. The winner goes on to the national competition in Texas. Later that same month the D.C. Blues Society co-sponsors the **Columbia Pike Blues Festival,** tel. (703) 892-2776, at the Patrick Henry Elementary School, 701 S. Highland St., north of the intersection of Columbia Pike and Walter Reed St.

August brings 60,000 people or more to enjoy the rides, music, crafts, and international food of the **Arlington County Fair** at the Thomas Jefferson Center, 3501 S. 2nd St., tel. (757) 358-6400. The **Rosslyn Jazz Festival,** tel. (703) 522-6628, swings through Gateway Park in mid-September, followed by the **Marine Corps Marathon,** tel. (800) RUN-USMC (800-786-8762), Web site: www.marinemarathon.com, in late October. Seventeen thousand runners huff through Arlington, Georgetown, and Washington, D.C., in the country's fourth-largest marathon, which begins and ends at the Iwo Jima Memorial.

TRANSPORTATION

Northern Virginia does prove one sprawl theory true: driving can be a nightmare, especially on major highways during the weekday rush hours of 6-9 a.m. and 4:30-7 p.m. A maze of highways and swarms of traffic lights sometimes only seem to slow things down (one gate guard answered my directional question with a laugh: *"Quickest* way? Where are you from?"). Simply turning around can be a chore, and don't get caught driving alone in an HOV (high-occupancy vehicle) lane, marked with white diamonds, or you'll get a hefty fine.

With three lines and eleven stations spread throughout the county, the **Metrorail** is by far the easiest way to get around Arlington. The orange line serves Rosslyn, Clarendon, and Ballston. It crosses the Potomac north of Theodore Roosevelt Island along with the blue line, which brushes against Arlington National Cemetery before joining the yellow line at the Pentagon to head south toward Old Town Alexandria. Trains run until midnight from 5:30 a.m. on weekdays and 8 a.m. on weekends. Fares depend on distance and whether or not you're traveling during rush hour. The minimum fare is $1.10, electronically recorded on a mandatory magnetic paper fare card; be sure to put enough money on the card to get where you're going. **Metrobuses** connect rail stations with locations farther into the 'burbs. These cost only 25 cents for a transfer, $5 for a one-day pass. **Greyhound/Trailways,** tel. (703) 998-6312, has a station at 3860 S. Four Mile Run Dr. near Walter Reed Dr. in South Arlington.

If you choose to fly into the Arlington area, two airports are there to serve you: **National Airport,** tel. (703) 572-2700, where both blue and yellow Metro lines stop, and **Washington-Dulles International Airport,** tel. (703) 572-2700, about a half-hour drive (depending on traffic) from Arlington National Cemetery. **Washington Flyer Airport Shuttles,** tel. (703) 685-1400 or (888) 927-4359, have taxis and limousines that go to D.C. and northern Virginia from both airports.

INFORMATION

The **Arlington County visitors center,** 735 S. 18th St., tel. (800) 677-6267 or (703) 228-5720, e-mail: acvs@us.net, Web site: www.co.arlington.va.us/acvs, is open daily 9 a.m.-5 p.m. To find it, leave the Jefferson Davis Hwy. (US 1) in Crystal City onto 20th St. heading west, take a right on Eads St., a left on 18th St., and it's at the corner of a park where Hayes St. leaves 18th Street.

OLD TOWN ALEXANDRIA

Less than an hour from downtown D.C., one of the country's oldest port cities (pop. 116,000) preserves a core little changed, at least cosmetically, from the days when George Washington and a young Robert E. Lee called it home. Tall, narrow houses in brick or pastel clapboard line cobblestone streets, embellished by ivy escaping over the walls of small front gardens. In all, over 2,000 buildings from the 18th and 19th centuries give Old Town a dignified colonial aura, from the smallest "spite" or "mother-in-law" house to the red brick mansions of Captain's Row along Prince Street.

District residents escape to Old Town for more than a history lesson, though—scores of shops and restaurants keep the sidewalks crowded and the parking spaces filled on most weekend evenings. The restored waterfront area along the Potomac, which once echoed with the hammers of shipbuilders and the cries of tobacco auctioneers, now features the famous Torpedo Factory Arts Center, riverside parks, and the oc-casional America's Cup contender, paddlewheeler, or old-style sailboat.

HISTORY

In 1669, British Gov. Sir William Berkeley granted 6,000 acres along the Potomac to English ship captain Robert Howsing, as a reward for bringing 120 settlers to the area. Less than a month later Howsing sold the land to John Alexander, a Scottish captain, for "six thousand pounds of Tobacco and Cask." In 1748, the town of Alexandria, organized by Scottish merchants William Ramsay and John Carlyle, was named in his honor. A year later, the 60-acre plot was surveyed by John West, Jr., and, according to local tradition, a 17-year-old George Washington. Washington liked the location so much he returned to buy a house and a pew in Christ Church, and later he drilled troops in Market Square and served as worshipful master of the local Masonic Lodge.

OLD TOWN ALEXANDRIA

© MOON PUBLICATIONS, INC.

Plantations flourished into the 18th century, turning Indian trails into "rolling roads" on which horse and ox teams rolled hogsheads of tobacco to public warehouses along the water. As the last good anchorage before the falls upriver, Alexandria grew into an important shipping port complete with taverns, shipyards, and a public ferry. Soon hemp and wheat became as important exports as tobacco, drawing caravans of "flour wagons" from as far as Winchester for shipment to England. A French visitor in 1796 called Alexandria "beyond all comparison the handsomest town in Virginia—indeed . . . among the finest in the United States."

Light Horse Harry Lee, Robert E. Lee's father, brought his family to Alexandria in 1810. By the mid-19th century, so many of Robert E. Lee's relatives lived near the corner of Oronoco and Washington Streets that it became known as "Lee Corners." The future general himself spent the first few decades of his life in his father's house in the heart of town.

Soon after receiving city status in 1852, Alexandria saw much of its oceangoing trade lured away by Baltimore and its clipper ships. The 20th century has seen an influx of out-of-towners (once called the "Foreign Legion") drawn by old houses just dying for renovation.

ORIENTATION

The George Washington Memorial Parkway becomes Washington Street as it passes through downtown, intersecting with the major east-west thoroughfare of King Street. Rt. 1 splits into one-way northbound (Patrick St.) and southbound (Henry St.) stretches a few blocks west. Traffic and parking can be tough, espcially at night, so it's usually best to park your car in a lot or on the street (the visitors center has free passes) and walk. Hard downpours can flood the waterfront area along Union St. to a few feet deep, so consider parking elsewhere if it looks like rain.

SIGHTS

Note: Many of Alexandria's historic sites are closed on Monday.

Old Town

George Washington, Thomas Jefferson, and the Marquis de Lafayette were among the many patrons of **Gadsby's Tavern,** 134 N. Royal St., tel. (703) 838-4242, since it opened at the end of the 18th century. The tavern and the adjacent City Hotel have been restored and converted into a museum on dining, drinking, and dozing in the heart of colonial America. While you're in the mood, stop by the colonial restaurant of the same name next door. A lavish ball and banquet commemorating the first president's birthday has been held in the upstairs ballroom since 1797. Tours are given Tues.-Sat. 11 a.m.-4 p.m., Sunday 1-4 p.m.; $3 adults, $1 children 11-17.

Established in 1792, the **Stabler-Leadbeater Apothecary,** 105-107 S. Fairfax St., tel. (703) 836-3713, operated for almost a century and a half, making it the second-oldest shop of its kind in the country. George and Martha Washington shopped here, as did Robert E. Lee, who bought paint for his house. A five-minute taped tour points out the finest collection of medicinal bottles in America, pill machines, original cash registers, and jars filled with native cures such as dandelion, sassafras, and snakeroot. Colored water fills a pair of two-foot show globes in the windows, which are said to have served as an early version of Open/Closed signs. Red indicated "stay away: plague," blue or green meant "all clear, come on in." Open Mon.-Sat. 10 a.m.-4 p.m.; $2 adults, $1 children 11-17.

Scottish merchant John Carlyle built **Carlyle House,** 1212 N. Fairfax St., tel. (703) 549-2997, for his blushing bride Sara Fairfax in 1753. Two years later, Maj. Gen. Edward Braddock met here with five colonial governors to organize a tax on the colonies to pay for Britain's role in the French and Indian War. Local governments refused to pay, marking one of the first serious rifts between England and America. Today the property remains an outstanding 18th-century manor home, furnished with period furniture and sheltering a small but radiant garden out back. Tours are given every half hour until closing. Open Tues.-Sat. 10 a.m.-4:30 p.m., Sunday noon-4:30 p.m.; $4 adults, $2 children 10-17.

The Northern Virginia Fine Arts Association has found a home in the Greek revival **Athenaeum,** 201 Prince St. at Lee St., tel. (703) 548-0035, built in 1850 as a banking house. National and local art exhibits are open to the public for free Tues.-Sat. 10 a.m.-4 p.m., Sunday 1-4 p.m.

Head toward the croak of gulls perched on riverfront pilings to find the **Torpedo Factory Arts Center,** 105 N. Union St., tel. (703) 838-4565. The name is no hyperbole: shell casings for torpedoes were built here during the first part of the century. The factory was reopened in 1983 as one of Virginia's first and best artistic cooperatives. About 150 painters, potters, sculptors, glassmakers, photographers, and fiber artists turn out artwork both fine and fun. The artists occupy 84 studios and four galleries in exchange for opening their creative process and workspaces to the public. Colorful painted factory pipes add an artsy-industrial touch. Open daily 10 a.m.-5 p.m., free. **Alexandria Archeology,** tel. (703) 838-4399, maintains a museum and research lab on the third flood dedicated to unearthing the town's long history. Open Tues.-Fri. 10 a.m.-3 p.m., Saturday 10 a.m.-5 p.m., Sunday 1-5 p.m.; free.

If you're lucky you'll also find the **Schooner Alexandria,** tel. (703) 549-7078, hove to at the foot of Prince Street. The three-masted Scandinavian ship, built in 1929, measures 125 feet long with over 7,000 square feet of red sails. Originally a Baltic trader, the schooner has been rechristened as a passenger vessel used for sailing education.

The **Old Presbyterian Meeting House,** 321 S. Fairfax St., tel. (703) 5449-6670, has been in use for all but 60 years since it was built in 1774. George Washington attended services here in 1798, a year before ministers preached at his memorial service. Twin balconies bracket the plain, almost severe interior, and many of the stones in the graveyard behind have weathered into near-illegibility. Several of Washington's friends and local luminaries, including William Ramsay and John Carlyle, are buried near the Tomb of the Unknown Soldier of the American Revolution. Open Mon.-Fri. 8:30 a.m.-4:30 p.m.; free.

Built in 1839 in the style of a Doric temple, the pale orange **Lyceum,** 201 S. Washington St., tel. (703) 838-4994, served as a hall for meetings, debates, and lectures on literature, history, and science. Today the imposing, two-story columns flank the entrance of a museum, which covers Alexandria's history from Native Americans to the 20th century. Open Mon.-Sat. 10 a.m.-5 p.m., Sunday 1-5 p.m.; free. A block west, the **Friendship Firehouse,** 107 S. Alfred St., tel. (703) 838-3891 or 838-4994, commemorates the city's first organization to battle blazes, founded in 1774. Washington's involvement is debated by historians, but around here it's taken for granted. Antique firefighting equipment, including an engine, is open to the public Friday and Saturday 10 a.m.-4 p.m., Sunday 1-4 p.m.; free.

Historians do agree that the first president and his wife attended services beneath the distinctive octagonal tower of **Christ Church,** 118 N. Washington St. at Cameron St., tel. (703) 549-1450. Established in 1773, the church served as the setting for Robert E. Lee's confirmation and the church still holds Episcopal services. Both the Washington and Lee family pews remain inside. Grave markers in the surrounding burial ground (the only one in town until 1805) don't necessarily mark actual gravesites; many were moved by Union soldiers during the Civil War to make room for campfires and grazing horses. The restored Old Parish Hall next door contains a gift shop and small historical museum. Open Mon.-Sat. 9 a.m.-4 p.m., Sunday 2-4:30 p.m.; free.

The **Boyhood Home of Robert E. Lee,** 607 Oronoco St., tel. (703) 548-8454, housed the future Confederate hero from age five until he left for West Point in 1867 at age 18. Renovations have left the federal-style mansion without any original furnishings but many echoes of the Lee heritage, starting with a portrait of Robert as a handsome teenager ready to take on officer's school and the world. The museum's collection of 19th-century artifacts includes an intricately carved ivory chess set in the parlor and a custom-made washing stand and commode in the upstairs bedroom, portable enough to be carried along in a coach. Open daily 10 a.m.-4 p.m., Sun 1-4 p.m.; $4 adults, $2 children 10-17, free tours.

Across the street stands the **Lee-Fendall House,** 614 Oronoco St., tel. (703) 543-1789, built in 1785 by a relative of Lighthorse Harry Lee. It was renovated in 1850 in the Greek revival style, and remained in the Lee family until 1903. Free tours are given every hour until 3 p.m. Open Tues.-Sat. 10 a.m.-4 p.m., Sunday noon-4 p.m.; $4 adults, $2 children 10-17.

George Washington Masonic National Memorial

Beyond Old Town

Head west on King past the Metro stop to reach the monumental neoclassic spire of the **George Washington Masonic National Memorial,** 101 Callahan Dr., tel. (703) 683-2007. Towering atop Shuter's Hill—a potential site for the U.S. Capitol when Alexandria was part of the District of Columbia—the memorial encloses a 25-foot bronze statue of the first worshipful master of Alexandria Lodge No. 22 gazing over the city and the Potomac. Three-story marble columns and heroic murals on either side make this a monument on the D.C. scale. A museum on the fourth floor contains Washington memorabilia like the clock stopped by his physician at 10:20 p.m., the moment of his passing, along with the largest oriental carpet in the world. Keep going to the ninth-floor observatory for a spectacular view clear across the river. Guided tours are given about every 45 minutes. Open daily 9 a.m.-5 p.m.; free.

During the Civil War, Washington, D.C., was one of the most heavily defended locations in the nation. Thirty-six guns and 162 earthwork forts and batteries bristled from hillsides around the capital, all awaiting the all-out Confederate assault that never came. Today, part of those fortifications are preserved in the **Fort Ward Museum and Historic Site,** 4301 W. Braddock Rd., tel. (703) 838-4848, a 45-acre park enclosing restored earthwork bastions, six guns, and a Civil War-era museum. To get there take King St. west, then bear left onto West Braddock, and it's on the right near I-395 exit 4. Open Tues.-Sat.

9 a.m.-5 p.m., Sunday noon-5 p.m.; free. (The park and its picnic facilities are open until sunset.)

ACCOMMODATIONS

The **Alexandria and Arlington Bed & Breakfast Network,** tel. (703) 549-3415 or (888) 549-3415, e-mail: aabbn@erols.co, can help with lodgings in Old Town.

Moderate

A **Days Inn Alexandria,** 110 S. Bragg St., tel./fax (703) 354-4950, sits near the intersection of Duke St./Little River Tpk. and I-395 west of Old Town. Head south along Rt. 1 (first called the Jefferson Davis Hwy., then Richmond Hwy.) to find the **Red Roof Inn-Alexandria,** 5975 Richmond Hwy., tel. (703) 960-5200, fax 960-5209. Keep going for the **Best Western-Mount Vernon,** 8751 Richmond Hwy., tel. (703) 360-1300, fax 799-7713, seven miles south, and the **Econo Lodge-Mount Vernon,** 8849 Richmond Hwy., tel. (703) 780-0300 or 780-0842, half a mile farther.

Expensive

There's a **Holiday Inn Hotels & Suites-Historic District Alexandria,** 625 First St., tel. (703) 548-6300, fax 548-8032, off the George Washington Memorial Parkway just east of the intersection of 1st St. and Washington St. The **Howard Johnson Hotel-Alexandria/Olde Towne,** 5821 Richmond Hwy., tel. (703) 329-1400 or 329-1424, sits on the border of Alexandria proper just south of the I-95/I-495 intersection.

Alternatively, **Princely Bed & Breakfast Reservation Service,** tel. (800) 470-5588 or (540) 343-0100, fax 343-6450, can arrange stays in 31 private historic residences in Old Town for expensive to premium rates including continental breakfast.

Luxury
The small but luxurious **Morrison House,** 116 S. Alfred St., tel. (703) 838-800 or (800) 367-0800, fax (703) 684-6283, evokes a Colonial manor house—from the butler at the top of the curving entrance staircase to the federal period reproductions in its 45 rooms and suites. English tea is served every afternoon near the first-floor library and parlor, occasionally graced by a pianist in the lounge. The Elysium Restaurant serves a sophisticated Mediterranean menu, while the Grill Bar offers more casual fare.

The refined historic feel of the **Holiday Inn Select Old Town,** 480 King St., tel. (703) 549-6080, fax 684-6508, may be a surprise to guests expecting another off-the-rack hotel. Six floors of rooms smack in the middle of Old Town top a heated indoor pool, sauna, exercise room, restaurant, and cocktail lounge.

FOOD

Standards
The former chef of the Watergate Hotel moved here to open the unpretentious **Lite "N" Fair,** 1018 King St., tel. (703) 549-3717. It may not be much to look at, but the menu's mix of French, Italian, Asian, and German draw raves for quality and value. Open for lunch Mon.-Sat., dinner Tues.-Saturday. Stained glass and a gigantic James Dean poster decorate the playful **Ecco Cafe,** set in an 18th-century tobacco warehouse on 220 N. Lee St., tel. (703) 684-0321. Pick a wine from the daily board to go with your homemade pasta, gourmet pizzas, and fresh grilled seafood, all served in generous portions for moderate prices. Open daily for lunch and dinner, with a jazz brunch on Sunday.

Catie Archuleta added German and French accents to an Italian bistro to come up with

Cate's Bistro, 715 King St., tel. (703) 549-0533, perfect for a romantic date or a family dinner. Everything from the bread and pasta to soup and desserts is homemade, with dinner entrées in the $13-18 range. Steaks and seafood are staples of **The Chart House,** 1 Cameron St. on the waterfront, tel. (703) 683-5080. Diners can stay inside under the cavernous ceiling or opt for outside in nicer weather overlooking the Potomac. Dinner entrées run $17 and up. Open for dinner daily, plus Sunday brunch.

Head west a few blocks to reach the **Fish Market,** 105 King St., tel. (703) 836-5676, where big pots of chowder on the bar, checkered tablecloths, and an open, clattering kitchen are all clues to some of the best seafood in town. Prices range from $5 sandwiches to $14 platters. Open daily for lunch and dinner. A block west is **Two-Nineteen,** 219 King St., tel. (703) 549-1141, offering fine dining, Cajun-style. Catfish, Cajun fried oysters, jambalaya and seafood gumbo are all served with Southern flair, ranging from $10 for lunch to $15-25 for dinner. The Bayou Room downstairs serves less expensive meals, and the Basin St. Lounge whoops it up on weekends.

A Bit Unusual
Cross a roadhouse with a funhouse, add neon, and you'll end up with something like **King Street Blues,** 112 N. St. Asaph St., tel. (703) 836-8800. Voted the best BBQ, burger, and "cheap eats" in town, this art-bar serves up sammies, po' boys, and blue-plate specials amid riotous paintings and sculptures. Open daily for lunch and dinner. **Gadsby's Tavern,** 138 N. Royal St. at Cameron St., tel. (703) 548-1288, re-creates the 18th century in its pewter plates, creaking wood floor, and costumed waiters. The food is just as authentic, with strolling minstrels providing entertainment during dinner. Open daily for lunch and dinner.

Snacks
One of seven in the D.C. area, **Bread and Chocolate,** 611 King St. between Washington and St. Asaph Sts., tel. (703) 548-0992, is a European-style bakery/cafe selling espresso drinks and delicacies like bread pudding, macaroons, and linzer torte. Enjoy homemade ice cream and frozen yogurt beneath stained glass lampshades at **The Scoop Grill,** 110 King St., tel.

(703) 549-4527, which also offers breakfast specials. A handful of inexpensive lunch options fill the glass-walled **Torpedo Factory Food Pavilion** by the river.

International

Le Refuge, 127 N. Washington St., tel. (703) 548-4661, serves authentic French fare with street signs and cheese boxes on the walls adding atmosphere. A three-course meal deal ($11 lunch, $17 dinner) includes soup or salad, entrée, and dessert. Look for the wooden Gallic heads outside **Le Gaulois,** 1106 King St., tel. (703) 739-9494, a southern French-style bistro with quiches, casseroles, and a Pot Au Feu special. Both are open daily for lunch and dinner.

Simple, effective southwestern decor sets the stage for the chile rellenos and chipotle chicken **Santa Fe East,** 110 Pitt St. S, tel. (703) 548-6900, while **East Wind,** 809 King St., tel. (703) 839-1515, offers that incomparable blend of Chinese, French and Japanese influences known as Vietnamese cooking. For fine Italian try **Landini Brothers,** 115 King St. between Lee and Union Sts., tel. (703) 836-8404, a dark, quiet, cozy place with entrées in the $12 range and antipasti for $5-7.50. A menu full of Ks marks the **Taverna Cretekou,** 818 King St., tel. (703) 548-8688, as the real thing. Greek specialties like mousakka, spanakopita, and baklava are $6 for lunch, $11-19 for dinner, both served Tues.-Sun.

It's in a shopping strip a little ways out of town, but the **Bombay Curry Company,** 3110 Mount Vernon Ave., tel. (703) 836-6363, rewards those who venture this far with unusually tasty tandooris and curries for rock-bottom prices. Sunday afternoon buffets include a little of everything for $7. Open daily for lunch and dinner.

ENTERTAINMENT AND RECREATION

Nightlife

Two-Nineteen's **Basin Street Lounge,** 219 King St., tel. (703) 549-1141, hops with swing and big-band jazz on weekends, and **King St. Blues** hosts live music in its first-floor bar on Thursday evenings. **The Birchmere,** 3701 Mt. Vernon Ave., tel. (703) 549-7500, features nationally known bluegrass, folk, and country acts. To get

there head west on Pendleton to West St., turn right, then quickly left onto Braddock, and finally right onto Mt. Vernon. It's just south of Glebe Rd. Tickets are available at the door or through Ticketmaster, tel. (202) 432-7328.

The **Virginia Beverage Company,** 605-607 King St., tel. (703) 684-5397, offers home-brewed beer and the largest collection of single-malt scotches and bourbons in northern Virginia, along with pasta, steaks, and burgers. Look for the copper brew machinery in the front windows. For a pint of Old-Country stout try **Ireland's Own,** 132 N. Royal St., tel. (703) 549-4535, and **Murphy's Irish Pub,** 713 King St., tel. (703) 548-1717. The latter was voted one of 50 best bars in the D.C. area, thanks to its roaring fireplace, generous pub fare, and nightly Irish and Welsh sing-alongs. This is what's known as a "happy bar" in technical parlance, meaning they've been known to go through 10 kegs of Guinness on a Saturday night.

Both the **Laughing Lizard Lounge Comedy Club,** 1322 King St., tel. (703) 548-2582, and the **Fun Factory,** 3112 Mt. Vernon Ave., tel. (703) 684-5212, are good for a laugh.

Tours

The Old Town Experience, tel. (703) 836-0694, offers daily guided walking tours of major sites in Old Town with tidbits of legends and folklore along the way. The tour leaves from Ramsay House from late March-Nov. for $4 pp. With a spectral slant is **Doorways to Old Virginia,** tel. (703) 548-0100, which leads a lantern-lit Ghost & Graveyard Tours with guides in period costume. The one-hour walks leave from the visitors center on Fri.-Sun. nights, March-Nov., and end up in a graveyard ($5 adults, $3 children 7-17). Experience Old Town in true colonial style in a carriage with **Old Towne Horse and Carriage, Inc.,** tel. (703) 765-8976, leaving from King and Lee Sts. on Tues.-Sun. evenings May-Aug.

The **Potomac Riverboat Co.,** tel. (703) 548-9000, offers a variety of floating tours from the city marina near the Torpedo Factory; these run April-Oct. A 40-minute narrated tour of Alexandria from the water aboard the **Admiral Tilp** is $7 adults, $4 children. They also send boats to the Washington, D.C., monuments, ($14 adults, $6 children) and Mt. Vernon ($22 adults, $10 children). The *Dandy,* tel. (757) 683-6090, Web site:

www.dandydinnerboat.com, is a 100-ton restaurant cruise ship that leaves from Waterfront Park at the end of Prince St. Three-course lunches ($26-32) and five-course dinners ($52-63) compete with the D.C. monuments for your attention on three-hour cruises up to the capital.

Outdoors

With the **Mt. Vernon Trail** ending just to the north, Alexandria sees plenty of foot and bike traffic in the sunny months. **Big Wheel Bikes,** 2 Prince St., tel. (703) 739-2300, rents hybrid bicycles for $25 per day, and you can contact the **Alexandria Park Planning Office,** tel. (703) 838-5040, for a free map of bike routes around town.

Judy Lathrop's **Atlantic Canoe & Kayak Company,** 1201 North Royal St., Alexandria, tel. (800) 297-0066 or (703) 838-9072, e-mail: ackcinc@atlantickayak.com, Web site: www.atlantickayak.com, leads well-praised sea kayak classes and tours ranging from day trips up both sides of the Potomac to overnights on the Eastern Shore. Their tours, including sunset and full-moon excursions, start at $50 per day and are open to paddlers of all experience levels.

EVENTS

For details on any of the following events, contact the Alexandria Convention and Visitors Association's **Special Events Hotline** at (703) 838-4200, ext. 4. Most charge a small admission fee.

Both Light Horse Harry and his son are honored during the **Lee Birthday Celebrations** the third Sunday in January with special tours, refreshments, and period music at the Lee-Fendall House and The Boyhood Home of Robert E. Lee. The third weekend in February brings another party, this time for **George Washington's Birthday.** On Saturday, a black-tie/colonial-costume **Birthnight Ball** at Gadsby's Tavern commemorates George and Martha's attendance there in 1798 and 1799. A Revolutionary War encampment at Fort Ward follows on Sunday, including a mock skirmish between British and Revolutionary troops. On Monday, the nation's largest parade snakes through here and Arlington, honoring Alexandria's prodigal son with colonial drums and bugle musters.

At the end of May, the **Memorial Day Jazz Festival** fills Jones Point Park southeast of Old Town. The fourth weekend of July brings the **Virginia Scottish Games,** one of the premiere Celtic events in the U.S. Two days of fiddling, bagpiping, Scottish food, and a national-level heptathalon all happen at the Episcopal High School. The theme continues with the **Scottish Christmas Walk** the first Saturday in December, with a parade through Old Town and traditional Highland dancers. Then the holiday spirit rolls right into the **Old Town Christmas Candlelight Tour** the next weekend, passing through three museums and Gadsby's Tavern.

SHOPPING

Alexandria abounds with places to shop, so serious browsers will simply want to start at the **Torpedo Factory** and work their way west. **The Virginia Company,** 104 S. Union St., tel. (703) 836-3160, stocks Virginia crafts, food, and wines. Inside the Carriage House, 215 S. Union St. between Prince and Duke Sts., you'll find **Rocky Road to Kansas,** tel. (703) 683-0116, a quilt shop with antiques, rugs, and bags, and the aromatic **Olde Town Coffee, Tea & Spice,** tel. (703) 683-0856.

Colonial-style folk art fills **The Blue Cottage,** 217 Cameron St. at Fairfax, tel. (703) 683-0028, while **Bird in the Cage Antiques,** above the Scoop Grill at 110 King St., tel. (703) 549-5114, offers jewelry, furniture, and vintage clothing. **The Silver Parrot Ltd.,** 113 King St., tel. (703) 549-8530, stocks silver and jewelry from around the world. You'll find everything from handcarved decoys to historic reproduction brass, linens, and porcelain at **The Pineapple, Inc.,** 132 King St. at S. Lee St., tel. (703) 836-3639, and **The Winterthur Museum Store,** 207 King St., tel. (703) 684-6092, has more historical reproductions along with garden goods and jewelry.

The southern section of Market Square is home to the Alexandria Saturday-morning **farmer's market,** tel. (703) 838-4770. It's been going since 1753, making it one of the oldest continuously operating markets in the country. Early morning is best time to go, and on cold days it's moved inside the lobby of city hall. Keep

*a street in
historic Old Town*

going to **Boxwood Antiques & Fine Art,** 303 Cameron St., tel. (703) 518-4444, for colonial and federal items from the 19th and 20th centuries, along with porcelain and sterling. **Elder Crafters of Alexandria, Inc.,** 405 Cameron St., tel. (703) 683-4338, is a nonprofit store that sells hand-crafted quilts, clothes, toys, jewelry, and pottery all made by the elderly. Offerings at **Funk & Junk,** 106 1/2 N. Columbus St., tel. (703) 836-0749, on the other hand, span the hip scale from the '50s to generation X (which seem to be converging lately according to the whims of fashion). They bill "Cool stuff for cool people at cool prices"; this includes vintage clothes, TV and cartoon items, and art deco knickknacks. Crafts from the developing world are the specialty of **Ten Thousand Villages,** 824 King St., tel. (703) 684-1435, which also has a gourmet coffee shop.

TRANSPORTATION

The yellow and blue Metro lines converge at the **King Street station,** west on King St. just before the George Washington Masonic Memorial. From here you can hop a Metrorail Appalachian Trail-2 or Appalachian Trail-5 DASH bus to the visitors center. This also doubles as the Alexandria **Amtrak** station, tel. (703) 836-4339. There's another yellow/blue Metro stop at **Braddock Rd.;** to reach it head west on Wythe St., jig right on West St.

and then left on Braddock Road. For tips on navigating Old Town, see **Orientation,** above.

INFORMATION

Alexandria's Convention and Visitors Association runs a **visitors center** in the Ramsay House, 221 King St. at Fairfax St., tel. (703) 838-4200 or 838-5005, e-mail: acva@erols.com. The building itself, the oldest in town, was built in 1749 by Scottish merchant William Ramsay, a friend of George Washington and one of the founders of Alexandria. Over the years it served as a tavern, grocery store, cigar factory, and rooming house, and is thought to have been brought here on a barge from its original location some 30 miles downriver.

Along with brochures, walking tour maps, and lists of hotels, restaurants, and shops, the visitors center hands out free 24-hour parking permits for two-hour metered street zones, which can be renewed each day. They also sell discounted block tickets to area sights: the Old Town Tour ($12 adults, $5 children 11-17) covers Gadsby's, Carlyle House, Stabler-Leadbeater Apothecary, the Boyhood Home of Robert E. Lee, and the Lee-Fendall House; the Lee Corner Tour ($6 adults, $2 children) includes the last two; and the Market Square Tour ($7 adults, $3 children) includes the first three.

NEAR THE BELTWAY

McLEAN

Claude Moore Colonial Farm
The homestead of a family of poor tenant farmers circa 1771 is brought to life inside the Beltway at this small but respectable living-history enclave. A one-room log farmhouse anchors the 100-acre site, surrounded by a barn and fields of tobacco, wheat, flax, corn, and rye. Split-rail "worm fencing" keeps the turkeys, hogs, and chickens out of the kitchen gardens and the quarter horse out of the orchard. Costumed historical interpreters are on hand to explain the care and feeding of the Devon cattle and the use of 18th-century tools and clothing.

The best times to stop by are during **market fairs** in May, July, and October, when visitors can buy homegrown produce, bob for apples, try period food, and take the kids to a puppet show. Other special events include the **wheat harvest** in June, the **tobacco harvest** in August, **threshing day** in November, and **wassail** near the winter solstice in late December. Eighteenth-century skills are taught in workshops throughout the year.

To get there take Rt. 738 off Old Dominion Dr. (Rt. 309) into McLean, turn north onto Chain Bridge Rd. for half a mile, then east on Dolley Madison Blvd. (Rt. 123). After two miles turn north on Georgetown Pike (Rt. 193), and make an immediate right on Colonial Farm Rd. It's on the left. The farm is open April-Dec. Wed.-Sun. 10 a.m.-4:30 p.m.; $2 adults, $1 children 5-12.

Evans Farm Inn
Another working farm in the area serves up its produce in a setting that's amazingly rural for being so close to the capital. Flagstone floors, waiters in costume, and antique furniture and utensils give the main dining room a colonial atmosphere. Water from the spring and flowers, herbs and vegetables from 40 cultivated acres go into dishes like plantation chicken, Smithfield ham, and leg of lamb. Lunch entrées are $9-15, including a $12 buffet, and dinner runs $15-25. Downstairs the **Sitting Duck Pub** re-creates a dark, cozy English tavern complete with a fireplace and coats of arms on the wall. Sandwiches, steaks, and seafood are served à la carte for lunch Mon.-Fri. and dinner Mon.-Sat. Piano and guitar music accompany Friday and Saturday dinners and Sunday brunch.

The inn, tel. (703) 356-8000, is at 1696 Chain Bridge Rd., south of the main intersection in McLean.

GREAT FALLS PARK

The Potomac would have been the perfect transport route for goods between the ocean and the heart of the colonies, except for one small detail: a 77-foot drop over a quarter mile as the river seethes over the unyielding shelf of the fall line. Now this source of historical headaches is one of the most natural places within an hour of the capital (traffic permitting), combining trails, historic ruins, rugged rocks, and whitewater.

History
Great Falls stood as a barrier between the open water and important Maryland ports until 1802, when a firm founded by George Washington (is there anything he *didn't* do?) opened the Patowmack Canal parallel to the river on the Virginia side. Elevator locks were hewn from solid rock, and a small settlement sprang up around the steady trade. In 1828, the Chesapeake & Ohio (C&O) Canal took over on the opposite bank from downtown D.C. to Cumberland, MD. By the mid-19th century, a million tons of goods a year flowed through the C&O's 75 locks, but the opening of the Baltimore & Ohio Railroad in 1924 spelled the end of water transport on both sides.

Visiting Great Falls
Start at the **visitor center,** tel. (703) 285-2966, which has exhibits on the geology and human and natural history of the area. There's a snack bar downstairs and picnic table nearby. Many **trails** wind along the edge of the steep cliffs above the river. Be careful on the slippery rocks near the edge, as fatal falls happen every year.

Notice the posts indicating high-water marks of floods which have covered the falls completely about once a decade, occasionally reaching as high as the visitors center. It's possible to hike a 5.1-mile loop, passing the ruins of the canal locks and the original trade village of Matildaville. Along the way you'll pass skunk cabbage and jewelweed in the swampy former riverbed, and upstream you might spot a red-shouldered hawk, osprey, or great blue heron.

Fishing and **cross-country skiing** are other seasonal possibilities. Great Falls is the most popular spot in the state for **rock climbing,** with over 100 climbs up to 5.12 in difficulty. Needless to say, swimming and boating are prohibited over the falls, though of course a few suicidal thrill-seekers have snuck in and done it. On the Maryland bank, the **C&O Canal National Historical Park** contains the historic Great Falls Tavern and a footbridge to an island in the middle of the torrent. Mule-drawn barge trips run April-Oct. Call (301) 722-8226 for more information.

The park is open daily dawn to dusk, with visitor facilities open 10 a.m.-5 p.m. Admission is $4 per car, $2 per pedestrian or cyclist May-Oct. To get there take I-495 exit 13 to Georgetown Pike (Rt. 193). Follow this four miles west to Rt. 738, and take a right into the park.

RIVERBEND PARK

Adjoining Great Falls to the north, this small reserve encloses a calmer section of river inhabited by animals rare for the area, such as foxes, minks, river otters, and the infrequent bald eagle. Ten miles of hiking, biking, and equestrian trails explore the park's 400 acres of meadows and forest, including two miles along the river and a short paved trail for disabled visitors. Huge beech, elm, birch, and poplars grow along the 1.7-mile Potomac Heritage Trail (which shares its name with one farther south).

To reach the park, keep going west past the Great Falls entrance to Riverbend Rd., take a right, and another right on Jeffrey Rd. Another right after two miles brings you to the riverbank and the **visitor center,** tel. (703) 759-9018, with small museum displays, trail maps, and brochures (open Wed.-Mon. 9 a.m.-5 p.m.). Outside are picnic areas, fishing spots, and a boat

ramp, and a **Nature Center,** tel. (703) 759-3211 is just down Jeffrey Rd. An entrance fee of $4 per car is charged on summer weekends and holidays; otherwise entrance is free.

GREAT FALLS TOWN

Two special eateries make this otherwise unassuming town, centered at the intersection of Georgetown Pike (Rt. 193) and Walker Rd. (Rt. 681), an appetizing place to stop before or after visiting the falls. The **Serbian Crown Restaurant,** 1141 Walker Rd., tel. (703) 759-4150, serves authentic Serbian and Russian fare along with a wide selection of iced vodka (a.k.a. Siberian gasoline) to top things off. They're open daily for dinner and for lunch on Thursday and Friday, and reservations are recommended on weekends. Take Walker Rd. south from Georgetown Pike for two miles to find it.

François Haeringer's **L'Auberge Chez François,** 332 Springvale Rd., tel. (703) 759-3800, holds a special place in the heart of Washingtonians, who vie for reservations weeks ahead of time. An *auberge* is a small local restaurant traditionally run by a chef/owner and his family, and this Alsace-meets-Virginia version measures up well. Copious four-course dinners in the $40 range include entrées like salmon in pastry crust with crab and lobster, real Dover sole with wild mushrooms, pheasant, and Alsatian specialties like *matelote* and **choucroute.** Outdoor tables under the trees are first-come first-served, and the wine list draws, naturally, from France and Virginia. Open for dinner Tues.-Sat., and Sunday 1:30-8 p.m. To get there head west of the main intersection about a mile to Springvale Rd., turn right, and it will be on the left after 2.5 miles.

WOLF TRAP FARM PARK

The country's only national park dedicated to the performing arts offers a wide array of performances throughout the year, both indoors and under the stars. Jazz, opera, folk, country, and popular music concerts are held in the **Filene Center,** tel. (703) 255-1860, a partial outdoor amphitheater, during the summer, and inside at **The Barns at Wolf Trap,** tel. (703) 938-2404, Oct.-May. The 18th-century barns, relocated from upstate New York, are half a mile down Trap Rd. from Filene Center. Children's programs, from mime to storytelling, happen in the **Theater-in-the-Woods,** tel. (703) 255-1827, in July and August, and an International Children's Festival spans three days over Labor Day weekend.

Dining options include **Ovations Restaurant,** tel. (703) 255-4017, serving à la carte or buffet meals nightly two hours before evening performances, or The Barns' drink and snack bar. You're welcome to bring your own picnic to the Filene Center, or you can order one ahead of time from **Fresh Fields** in Vienna, tel. (703) 281-6616, and have it waiting at Wolf Trap.

Tickets are available through the park's Web site (see below) or from ProTix, tel. (800) 955-5566 or (703) 218-6500. Prices range from $7 for lawn space to $70 for up-front orchestra seats. Children's shows are free but reservations help. The park is on Trap Rd. off Rt. 7 north of Vienna. For Filene Center performances a **shuttle bus,** tel. (202) 637-7000, runs to and from the West Falls Church Metro station (on the orange line) for $3.50 pp roundtrip. For more information contact the **Wolf Trap Foundation,** tel. (703) 255-1900, e-mail: wolftrap@wolf-trap.org, Web site: www.wolf-trap.org.

HUNT COUNTRY

Some of Virginia's choicest acres pick up where the Beltway sprawl ends, stretching all the way to the Shenandoah. From the banks of the upper Potomac—one of the wildest urban rivers in the East—to the foothills of the Blue Ridge, Hunt Country is a mix of tiny villages and huge estates, with a few modest farms still holding on in between. Old stone walls crawling with honeysuckle curve into neat lines of black and white fences along dirt lanes sunken with centuries of use. Cows and horses speckle emerald fields among silver silos, red barns, and white farmhouses.

Ever since Lord Fairfax first rode off behind a braying pack of hounds, both Loudoun (LOUD-un) and Faquier (fah-KEER) Counties have been known as Virginia's Hunt Country. Presidents from Washington to Kennedy have fled the bustle of the capital to chase foxes through the early-morning tranquillity of the countryside. Some of the richest people in the world breed, show, train, and race thoroughbreds on multimillion-dollar estates, popping into towns like Middleburg and Upperville to repair a harness or pick up a quart of oil for the Mercedes.

Fox hunts remain popular in northern Virginia

VIRGINIA TOURISM CORPORATION

The development juggernaut, though, rolls slowly nearer. High-tech industries moving west from Arlington and Fairfax have made Loudoun one of the fastest-developing counties in the country. Huge tracts of land not yet swallowed up by office parks and housing developments stand on the brink, not yet urbanized but no longer rural. Hunt Country holds its future in its hands, and if its performance with Disney is any indication, it will be a while before these farmlands are paved. The Mouse (the Walt Disney Co.) wanted to build a $650 million-dollar history theme park on 3,000 acres of Fairfax and Loudoun Counties. Concerns surfaced over visitor impact (it would have been only four miles from the Manassas Civil War battlefields) and good taste (how would Disney portray slavery?). Despite Governor George Allen's support, the plan fell to an organized opposition led by an unlikely coalition of Ralph Nader and Old Money.

MANASSAS NATIONAL BATTLEFIELD PARK

The gently rippled hills north of Manassas, still almost as rural as they were a century and a half ago, saw two major Civil War battles. The first opened the war with a horrific bang, and the second set the stage for Lee's invasion of the North three years later.

First Battle of Bull Run (First Manassas)

In 1861, Manassas was a vital railroad junction only 30 miles from Washington, D.C. Union Gen. Irvin McDowell found himself under pressure from a populace flush with patriotism and the romance of a clean, quick war to send his inexperienced troops against the equally untried Confederate army. On July 18, McDowell led 35,000 Federals against 22,000 Confederates under Brig. Gen. P.G.T. Beauregard, his West Point classmate. Ten thousand more Rebels fresh from the Shenandoah Valley under Gen. Joseph E. Johnston joined the fray, which climaxed on Henry House Hill, where 85-year-old Judith Henry refused to leave her home despite Confederate sharpshooters firing from her windows.

Union gunfire killed Ms. Henry and began to crumble the Rebel lines when Gen. Thomas Jackson incited his men to hold the hill, earning him the nickname "Stonewall" and turning the tide of battle. Reinforcements arrived, and the Confederate army was able to send the Federals into retreat even though they were too exhausted to pursue. Three-fifths of the 4,900 casualties were members of the Union Army, which by July 22 was back in Washington, D.C. George McClellan soon replaced McDowell as general, and the war had begun in earnest.

Second Battle of Bull Run (Second Manassas)

A little over a year later Robert E. Lee, having pushed McClellan back from the gates of Richmond, attacked 62,000 Union soldiers under Gen. John Pope in hopes of crushing the Federals before McClellan could arrive with reinforcements. Together with Stonewall Jackson and Gen. James

---

HUNT COUNTRY RECREATION

Perhaps the best way to get a sense of the pastoral sweep of the land here is from above, with only the occasional roar of the gas burner to keep you moving with the wind. **United Balloon Ventures,** tel. (540) 439-8621, sends hot-air balloons aloft at sunrise and sunset from their farm between Warrenton and Bealeton in Faquier County. One-hour flights are $350 for two people. **Balloons Unlimited,** tel. (540) 281-2300, Web site: www.balloon-sunlimited.com, is based in the Hunter Mill Shopping Center in Oakton. It operates in the Middleburg area as well as the Shenandoah Valley. Sunrise and sunset flights are $150 pp.

Get a taste of the equine world during the **Hunt Country Stable Tour** on Memorial Day weekend. During the self-driven auto tour you can visit barns, stables, and training facilities on exquisite country estates where thoroughbreds are raised and ridden. Chat with a re-enactor along the way and introduce the kids to various breeds of horses, foxhounds, and livestock in hands-on demonstrations at the historic estate of the late Mr. Jack Kent Cooke. Tickets are $15 pp, and all proceeds go to charity. Order them ahead of time from the Trinity Episcopal Church in Upperville, tel. (540) 592-3711, fax 592-3408, Web site: www.middleburgonline.com/stabletour.

JULIAN SMITH

A statue in the park commemorates Jackson's stand.

Longstreet, Lee had 55,000 men, plus the advantage of Pope's poor judgment. On August 30, the Union general ordered a pursuit when the Rebels weren't retreating and watched his line crumble under Longstreet's counterattack. During hand-to-hand fighting in an unfinished railroad bed, Confederate soldiers threw rocks when they ran out of ammunition. A nighttime retreat avoided a complete Union rout, but the army still again lost half as many as the Confederates. Pope, blaming his officers for conspiring against him, was relieved of command, and Lee rode the momentum of victory as far north as Antietam, MD.

Visiting the Park
The **Henry Hill Visitors Center,** 6511 Sudley Rd., tel. (703) 361-1339, is on Rt. 234 south of its intersection with Rt. 29. It's open daily 8:30 a.m.-

5 p.m. ($2 pp), with slide programs every half hour and tour maps of the battlefields. You can walk the loop trail of First Manassas in about 45 minutes, passing reconstructed houses and a muscular statue of Jackson commemorating his bold stand. Nine sites of Second Manassas are linked by a driving tour. Visit the park on the Internet at www.nps.gov/mana.

BULL RUN REGIONAL PARK

A thousand wooded acres along Bull Run Creek include the northern end of the **Bull Run-Occo-quan Trail,** which traverses four regional parks in 17.5 rural miles along the river and Occoquan Reservoir. Wood thrushes, scarlet tanagers, hooded warblers, and red-eyed vireos all appear along the blue-blazed trail. It's moderately strenuous and open to hikers and horses. Inside the park, the 1.5-mile **Bluebell Nature Loop** erupts with countless Virginia bluebells in mid-April.

The park, tel. (703) 631-0550, has a camp store, pool, miniature-golf course, playground, and 11 picnic areas open March-Dec. Entrance is $4 per vehicle. There are also 150 campsites for $12-14. If these are full try the **Haymarket Farm Family Campground,** 14004 Shelter Ln. in Haymarket, tel. (703) 754-7944, for $18-24, or the **Hillwood Camping Park,** 14222 Lee Hwy. in Gainesville, tel. (703) 754-4202, for $20.

LEESBURG

Poised between the weight of the past and modern development pushing from the east, the largest city in Hunt Country noses up against the Potomac at the far horizon of D.C.'s suburban spread. One of northern Virginia's oldest cities, it began as little more than a cluster of log houses at the intersection of two settler's roads. It served as an outfitting post during the French and Indian War, and was eventually named for Robert E. Lee's ancestors. During the War of 1812, 22 wagonloads of government documents, including the Declaration of Independence and the Constitution, were brought here for safekeeping as the British put D.C. to the torch.

Leesburg's Historic District, enclosed by the original 1878 boundaries, is chock full of antique stores and rows of narrow 18th- and 19th-century buildings, usually with one or two residential levels over a ground-floor shop or apartment. Freestanding houses with picket fences, small lawns, and Victorian-style architecture line quiet streets.

Sights

The **Market Station** complex, at Loudoun and Harrison Sts. on the site of Leesburg's former "waterless wharf," consists of nine historic buildings including a freight depot, an 18th-century mill, and a log cabin dating to the mid-19th century. Among

and inside these are various shops, offices, the visitors center, and one of the town's most popular restaurants. Parking at the garage at Market and Wirt Sts. is free for the first three hours.

Stop by the **Loudoun Museum,** 16 W. Loudoun St., tel. (703) 777-7427, for a walking tour brochure. While you're there, look over the collection of artifacts spanning Leesburg's three centuries of history; $1 adults, 50 cents children 5-18. A restored 1767 log cabin across the street houses a gift shop. Both are open Mon.-Sat. 10 a.m.-5 p.m., Sunday 1-5 p.m.

Other notable buildings include the Classical revival **Thomas Balch Library,** 208 Market St., tel. (703) 779-1328, built in 1922, and the **Loudoun County Courthouse** at the corner of Market and King Sts, dating to 1894. The courthouse, topped by an octagonal tower, was the third built on this site. General George C. Marshall's late 19th-century federal-style **Dodona Manor,** 217 Edward's Ferry Rd., tel. (703) 777-1880, was undergoing restoration in 1998.

Accommodations

The **Best Western Leesburg-Dulles,** 726 E. Market St., tel. (703) 777-9400, fax 777-5537, is a short way east of the town center on Rt. 7. Keep going to reach the **Holiday Inn** at 1500 E. Market St., tel. (703) 771-9200, fax 771-1575, with 126 rooms and four suites in historic Carradoc Hall that range into the expensive and premium categories.

Once described as the finest tavern in town, the **Laurel Brigade Inn,** 20 W. Market St., tel. (703) 777-1010, was built in stone in the early 1800s to replace an older version dating to 1759. Period antiques and French marble mantelpieces decorate the modest house, which has six guest rooms. The Laurel Brigade Restaurant, open for lunch and dinner Tues.-Sun., overlooks a graceful garden and gazebo in back. Sandwiches are $6-7 and entrées like lamb stew and crab cakes anywhere from $15 to $25, depending on whether you order à la carte or from the full-meal menu. Moderate.

Part of the **Leesburg Colonial Inn,** 19 S. King St., tel. (800) 392-1332, (703) 478-8503 or (703) 777-5000, date to the late 1700s, but its 10 guest rooms were all refitted in 1998 with canopied beds and Persian carpets. Some have whirlpool baths and fireplaces. Downstairs are the Colonial Inn Restaurant and the less formal Georgetown Cafe and Bakery, a fitting place for afternoon English tea. Expensive.

Persian cats claim the sunny upstairs sitting room of **The Norris House Inn,** 108 Loudoun St. SW, tel. (800) 644-1806 or (703) 777-1806, fax 771-8051. Rooms in the 1760 federal home have brass and feather beds and the odd fireplace (premium with full breakfast), and the Stone House Tea Room across the garden serves afternoon tea Mon.-Fri. Pam and Don McMurray also run the Tri-State Bike Trail Group, and offer a guide to

B&Bs and bike trails in Virginia, West Virginia, and Maryland. E-mail: inn@norrishouse.com, Web site: www.norrishouse.com.

Four miles east of Leesburg on Rt. 7, the **Landsdowne Resort,** 44050 Woodridge Pkwy., tel. (800) 541-4801 or (703) 729-8400, fax 729-4096, has 305 deluxe guest rooms and 14 suites overlooking the Potomac River valley, along with a Robert Trent Jones, Jr., championship golf course, a full-service spa and salon, health club, tennis courts, and indoor and outdoor pools. Dining options include the Potomac Riverside Hearth, serving all meals with a view of Sugarloaf Mountain, the Potomac Grill and Fairways on the golf course, and Stonewalls Tavern off the lobby. Luxury.

Food

For colonial food aficionados it doesn't get much more authentic than **The Green Tree,** 15 S. King St., tel. (703) 777-7246. Four months' research in the Library of Congress unearthed a menu's worth of 18th-century recipes which are prepared to the letter for lunch and dinner daily. Choose from salmagundi salad once served at Monticello, Welsh rarebit, calf's liver, and green herb soup with 21 herbs and spices. Finish things off with a real hot buttered rum in the cherry-wood-paneled pub, a bread pudding, or brandied peaches over ice cream. Solid oak tables and pewter candlesticks seem like they came with the 200-year old building.

Another popular option is the **Tuscarora Mill Restaurant,** tel. (703) 771-9300, housed in an 1899 mill building in Market Station. Moved here and restored in 1985, the structure still feels like an antique with its bare wood beams adorned with plants and quilts. Delicious, varied entrées like smoked chicken or lobster and sea scallop pasta are $7-14 for lunch and $15-20 for dinner. Open daily.

The **King's Court Tavern,** 2D Loudoun St., tel. (703) 777-7747, continues the colonial tradition with a short menu of entrées for $16-19. Head downstairs and forward a century or so to the **Ball's Bluff Tavern** with its Civil War recipes and relics. Both are open daily for lunch and dinner. The **Lightfoot Cafe,** 2 W. Market St., tel. (703) 771-2233, serves a light, healthy menu with plenty of salads in a spare, elegant setting. Lunch and dinner are offered Tues.-

Sunday. They have a meal/movie deal with the Tally Ho Theater across the street, with dinner and a movie ticket for $20 pp on Tues.-Thurs. and Sunday.

No-nonsense breakfasts ($5), sandwiches ($4-5) and dinner plates ($8-11) can be found at the **Leesburg Restaurant,** 9 S. King St., tel. (703) 777-3292. The **Leesburg Vintner,** King St. and Loudoun St., tel. (703) 777-3322, combines a wineshop with a gourmet deli serving sandwiches and bagels. **For Goodness' Sake,** Market Station lower level, tel. (703) 771-7146, is a natural food store with sandwiches, books, and gifts.

Entertainment and Recreation

Both **King's Court Tavern** and **Ball's Bluff Tavern** host live music nightly (Ball's Bluff has been voted best live entertainment in the county), and the **Americana Stage** at the Leesburg Restaurant presents original acoustic music. Having survived a fire in 1998, **Payne's Biker Cafe** is as real a biker bar as you're likely to find in Loudoun County. It faces the courthouse (a neon sign reads, Better off here than across the street), and has pool tables, a jukebox, and a bar menu—look for it on the wall next to the beer posters.

Budding zoologists, along with anyone interested in the natural world, should stop by the **Smithsonian Naturalist Center,** in the Leesburg Airpark Business Center at 741 Miller Dr. SE, Suite G-2, tel. (800) 729-7725 or (703) 779-9712, fax 779-9715, e-mail: natcenter@aol.com. It's a small branch of the National Museum of Natural History, and houses a great study collection of 30,000 items from mounted bugs to a horse skeleton and a full-sized stuffed polar bear. Lab equipment and a reference library are also available. Open Tues.-Sat. 10:30 a.m.-4 p.m.; free.

Leesburg Ghost Tours, tel. (703) 913-2060, offers a 1.5-hour walk around Leesburg's historic area, leaving from in front of the Georgetown Cafe and Bakery Saturday evenings at 7 and 9 p.m., April-Oct.; $6 adults, $4 children under 12. The tours go rain or shine, since bad weather does make for a good ghost story. The **Washington & Old Dominion Trail** passes through town south of the historic district, crossing King St. about three blocks south of Loudoun St. You can rent bikes at **Bicycle Outfitters,** 19

Catocpin Circle NE, tel. (703) 777-2148, for $5 per hour and $20 per day.

Maintree Farm, 40252 Thomas Mill Rd., tel. (703) 777-3279, offers group riding lessons and trail rides for $15 per hour. During foxhunting season you might be able to follow along on a mock hunt on Sunday morning—call ahead for details and a schedule.

Events

The **Leesburg Flower and Garden Show,** tel. (703) 777-1262, blooms in late April, and June-Aug. the **Bluemont Concert Series,** tel. (703) 777-6306, brings everything from big bands to folk music to the courthouse lawn. Concerts are held Sundays at 7 p.m., so bring a blanket or chair and a picnic. Ask at the Loudoun Museum for details on the **Cornwall Garden Tour** in June. A costumed street fair, Revolutionary War encampment, and 18th-century crafts and music are all part of **Court Days,** held the third weekend in August.

See **Vicinity of Leesburg,** below, for more annual happenings in the area.

Shopping

With over 100 shops in town—and most of these sell antiques—Leesburg has plenty of options for browsing and buying. **Global Gifts and Crafts,** 10 S. King St., tel. (703) 777-3555, sells candles, clothing, blown glass, pottery, and jewelry made by local, national, and international artisans. At **Golden Bee Collectibles,** 14 S. King St., tel. (703) 443-1061, you can peruse Celtic jewelry, sterling silver, porcelain, crystal, and china.

Antique stores have taken over Leesburg's historic center like an occupying army. Start at the **Leesburg Antique Gallery of Shoppes,** 7 Wirt St. SW, tel. (703) 777-2366, with over 50 dealers operating out of an 1884 church. The **Leesburg Downtown Antique Center,** 27 S. King St., tel. (703) 779-8130, also has a large selection. After that, if you still have time and energy, you might try **Vinegar Hill Antiques,** 106 Harrison St. SE, tel. (703) 777-3502, or **Uncle Sam's Attic,** 2B Loudoun St. SW, tel. (703) 777-5588.

Information

The **Loudoun Tourism Council** has a visitors center in the lower level of Market Station, tel.

(800) 752-6118 or (703) 771-2170. It's open daily 9 a.m.-5 p.m.

VICINITY OF LEESBURG

Ball's Bluff Battlefield and National Cemetery

On the evening of Oct. 20, 1861, a Union reconnaissance force of 1,000 mistook a row a haystacks for Confederate tents, exposing themselves to an actual enemy force in their confusion. The next day, the Federals crossed the Potomac into disaster, finding themselves trapped between the water and a row of high bluffs as Confederate rifle fire mowed them down from above. Nine hundred Union troops died in the skirmish, including their commander, Gen. Edward Baker, a U.S. senator and friend of Lincoln. Bodies floating downriver to Washington galvanized the U.S. government into organizing its forces in earnest.

A three-quarter-mile self-guided interpretive trail loops to the top of the bluff and back, passing a tiny cemetery ringed by Virginia bluebells and white trout lilies in the spring. Open daily dawn-dusk. The adjacent **Ball's Bluff Regional Park** claims a mile-long stretch of riverbank; for

NORTHERN VIRGINIA WINERIES

Farfelu Vineyard
tel. (703) 364-2930
Near Flint Hill; Rt. 6 exit 27, 12.5 miles west on Rt. 647 (13058 Crest Hill Rd.)

Grey Ghost Vineyards
tel. (540) 937-4869
Near Amissville; 11 miles west of Warrenton on Rt. 211 (14706 Lee Hwy.)

Hartwood Winery
tel. (703) 752-4893
Near Fredericksburg; 345 Hartwood Rd.

Linden Vineyards
tel. (540) 364-1997
Near Linden; I-66 exit 13 at Linden, one mile east on Rt. 55, right onto Rt. 638 for two miles (3708 Harrels Corner Rd.)

Loudoun Valley Vineyard
tel. (540) 882-3375
Near Waterford; from Leesburg Rt. 7 west two miles to Rt. 9 west, five miles

Meredyth Vineyards
tel. (540) 687-6277
Near Middleburg; 2.5 miles south to Rt. 628, right, 2.5 miles

Naked Mountain Vineyard
tel. (540) 364-1609
Near Markham; I-66 exit 18N, 1.5 miles on Rt. 688

The Oasis Winery
tel. (540) 635-7627; e-mail:oasiswine@aol.com
Near Hume; I-66 exit 27 at Marshall, four miles on Rt. 647, right onto Rt. 635 for 10 miles
Cafe. "Polo, Wine & Twilight Dine" on Friday, June-September.

Piedmont Vineyards
tel. (540) 687-5528
Near Middleburg; three miles south on Rt. 626

Shaddwell-Windham Winery
tel. (540) 668-6464
Near Hillsboro; 14727 Mountain Rd. (Rt. 690)

Spotted Tavern Winery and Dodd's Cider Mill
tel. (540) 752-4453
Near Hartwood; from Rt. 17/I-95 intersection, five miles north on Rt. 17, right onto Rt. 612 for four miles
Antique cider press.

Swedenburg Estate Vineyard
tel. (540) 687-5219
Near Middleburg; one mile east on US 50 south

Tarara Vineyard & Winery
tel. (703) 771-7100
Near Leesburg; Rt. 15 north eight miles to Lucketts, right on Rt. 662, three miles
Hosts Wines and Cheeses of the World Festival in May.

Willowcroft Farm Vineyards
tel. (703) 777-8161
Near Leesburg; south on Rt. 15, right onto Rt. 704, left onto Rt. 797, three miles

information on activities such as fishing, mountain biking, and ranger-led walks contact the Northern Virginia Regional Park Authority, 5400 Ox Rd., Fairfax Station, VA 22039, tel. (703) 729-0596.

White's Ferry

The only cable-guided ferry on the East Coast has been hauling people and cargo across the Potomac since the 1820s. Today the *General Jubal Early* carries cars and bicycles across the quarter-mile stretch from Rt. 655 to Maryland. On the opposite bank the C&O Towpath runs downriver toward the capital, and a snack bar/souvenir store has fishing supplies and boats for rent. The ferry runs daily 5 a.m.-11 p.m., weather permitting, and is occasionally closed due to flooding. Call (301) 349-5200 for information.

Morven Park

The 1,200-acre estate of Governor Westmoreland Davis, who was elected in 1918, centers on a Greek revival mansion where lavish parties once filled the Renaissance Great Hall with laughter, music, and candlelight. Paintings, tapestries, and sculptures acquired by Mrs. Davis in her travels through Asia and Europe adorn the Jacobean dining room and French drawing room.

In the north wing, a **Museum of Hounds and Hunting** displays art, photos, clothes, and artifacts from centuries of fox chasing, including a 1731 hunting horn carried by a colonial governor. The estate's **Winmill Carriage Collection** contains over 100 antique coaches, one of the largest personal collections in the world. Wrought-iron gates and a reflecting pool set off the impressive boxwood gardens surrounded by the original brick walls.

Events: Morven's **International Equestrian Center** has a full calendar of shows, competitions, schools, and steeplechase races throughout the year, including spring and fall horse trials. The third weekend in June the **Potomac Celtic Festival,** one of the country's best, brings Highland games, music, artisans, and a historical reenactment of life in 200 B.C. Kids activities include storytelling and games, and for the adults there's single-malt whiskey tastings and the caber toss. Call the Loudoun Tourism Council for more information. Morven's **Christmas Open House** lights the mansion with roaring fireplaces

and a 12-foot tree in the great hall the entire month of December.

Visiting the Park: Morven Park, tel. (703) 777-2414, fax 771-9211, e-mail: office@morvenpark.com, Web site: www.morvenpark.com, is northwest of Leesburg. Take Rt. 7 west one mile from the town center, make a right onto Morven Park Rd., then a left onto Old Waterford Rd. Open April-Oct. Tues.-Fri. noon-5 p.m., Saturday 10 a.m.-5 p.m., Sunday 1-5 p.m. The grounds are free, and mansion tours are $6 adults, $3 children 6-12.

Waterford

A gorgeous drive along Rt. 662 deposits you in this village on the bank of Catoctin Creek. Most of the town has been declared a National Historic Landmark. Almost painfully pretty, Waterford is a diametric opposite to the soulless suburbs near the capital. Mossy stone walls, gravel lanes, big trees, and sloping lawns set off dozens of 18th- and 19th-century homes in a smorgasbord of architectural styles. Granted, there aren't any video stores or McDonald's—but that's the point.

Some 40,000 visitors descend for the **Waterford Homes Tour and Crafts Exhibit,** tel. (703) 882-3085, the first weekend in October to enjoy house tours, street performers, and over 100 juried craftspeople exhibiting their wares.

Bluemont

Previously (and unenviably) known as Pumpkintown and Snickersville, Bluemont is home to the **Bear's Den Hostel,** tel. (540) 554-8708, half a mile south of Rt. 7 on Rt. 601. The snug stone building, only minutes from the Appalachian Trail, has dorm rooms ($12 pp for Hostelling International members, $15 otherwise), a full kitchen, dining room, laundry facilities, and camp store. Camping spots are $3-6.

Oatlands Estate

George Carter, the great-grandson of planter baron Robert "King" Carter, built a boxy Greek revival mansion here in 1803. Refugees, both black and white, sought shelter on the 3,000-acre plantation during the Civil War, which was later operated as a guest retreat until mounting debt forced its sale in 1897. William Corcoran and Edith Morton, a pair of affluent Washingtonians, bought the place and restored it as an English country

THE GRAY GHOST OF LOUDOUN COUNTY

Born on December 6, 1833, in Edgemont, VA, John Singleton Mosby was raised near Charlottesville and entered the University of Virginia in 1849. During his stay he shot and wounded a few other students, for which he had to serve a short jail term before graduating in 1852. His imprisonment sparked an interest in the law; three years later he was admitted to the bar and practiced law in Bristol until the start of the Civil War.

Mosby saw action as a scout with J.E.B. Stuart's Confederate cavalry in First Bull Run and the Seven Days Campaign, where it was his idea to ride completely around McClellan's Union Army. In January 1863, with nine men, he began the guerrilla attacks that would make him famous. Under the Partisan Ranger Law, Mosby's Rangers began to attack isolated Union posts in Maryland and northern Virginia. Dressed in his trademark ostrich-plumed hat and red-lined cape, the dashing horseman led lightning-quick cavalry strikes to disrupt communication and supply lines. Anywhere from 20 to 80 volunteers, convalescents, and civilians made up the Rangers, whose officers were chosen by merit and dismissed when ineffective. Men furnished their own uniforms, weapons, food, and horses and divided captured goods evenly among themselves. When danger threatened they melted into the night, sheltered in the homes of private families or living in the hills near Middleburg. At any given moment, bragged Mosby, he could gather his band at a predetermined time and place "like Children of the Mist," ready for their next raid.

As a result, Mosby estimated that he kept at least 30,000 Union soldiers on his tail instead of at the front. Loudoun County became known as Mosby's Confederacy, and Union generals were livid at the guerrillas' audacious exploits and rising fame.

DOVER PUBLICATIONS, INC.

house to entertain weekend guests from the capital. The formal gardens, designed by Carter, are so lavish that Morton was said to have bought the place after one look without even seeing the house. Don't miss the 1920s tea house, reflecting pool, and boxwood bowling allée.

Oatlands, tel. (703) 777-3174, fax 777-4427, is six miles south of Leesburg on Rt. 15, open March-Dec., Mon.-Sat. 10 a.m.-4:30 p.m., Sunday 1-4:30 p.m. Tours of the house and garden are $6 adults, $5 children 12-18, and admission to the gardens only is $3. Oatlands hosts antique fairs in January, April, and September, and in May the **Sheepdog Trials/Farm Days & Crafts Fair** includes border collie demonstrations.

MIDDLEBURG AND VICINITY

Leesburg may be the commercial center of Hunt Country, but Middleburg captures its essence.

Established in 1787, it began as a local commercial center halfway along the stagecoach route from Alexandria to Winchester (hence the name). Today Middleburg is still a one-stoplight place with fewer than 1,000 residents, but it's sure worth more than the original $2.50 an acre. This is barn jacket and Range Rover territory, surrounded by huge estates whose owners pay well to live in one of northern Virginia's most beautiful small towns—and international equestrian center, no less. Upscale shops sell fine cigars, antique jewelry, and everything horse-related right next to the big incongruous Safeway stuck in the center of town.

Accommodations
The **Red Fox Inn,** 2 E. Washington St. at Madison St., tel. (800) 223-1728 or (540) 687-6301, fax 687-6053, began as Mr. Chinn's Ordinary in 1728 (making it the second-oldest tavern in the country). A young George Washington stopped

Ulysses S. Grant ordered all supplies and forage in Loudoun County destroyed and all men under the age of 50 arrested to prevent them from joining the Rangers. Federal officials regarded the cavaliers as criminals rather than soldiers—for their habit of keeping captured spoils—and put a price on their heads. (When the Rangers also started hanging prisoners without trial, though, the order was rescinded.) Grant even considered taking the families of known Rangers hostage.

On March 9, 1863, Mosby led 29 men through the Federal lines at Fairfax Court House, where corpulent Union Brig. Gen. Edwin Stoughton sat surrounded by mountains of food and wine. The Confederates captured Stoughton, 33 men, and 58 horses (to which Lincoln said, "For that I am sorry, for I can make brigadier generals, but I can't make horses."). They also made off with a canvas sack holding $350,000 worth of gold and silver coins and jewelry, which Mosby and a companion were forced to bury during hot pursuit by Union troops. Mosby was never able to return for loot, which by his recall was stashed somewhere between Haymarket and New Baltimore in a shallow hole between two tall pine trees. His partner was eventually captured and hung, and the treasure has never been found.

The "leather-bed soldiers" were mustered into the regular army on June 10, 1863, where the "Gray Ghost" continued to attract followers and earn praise from Stuart and Robert E. Lee. In late 1864, Maj. Gen. Philip Sheridan sent Capt. Richard Blazer and 100 men armed with Spencer repeating rifles to hunt down the marauding band at all costs. The Rangers suffered 18 casualties before killing or wounding all but two of Blazer's party and capturing their rifles. By April 1865, Mosby had been promoted to colonel, wounded seven times, and sat in command of eight well-trained companies. His last raid came on April 10, the day after Robert E. Lee surrendered at Appomattox. He disbanded his men soon after, urging them to turn themselves in and seek individual pardons as he did himself two months later.

After the war, Mosby returned to practicing private law in Warrenton. His legendary status followed, dimmed only slightly by his support of Republican candidate Ulysses S. Grant, who had become an admirer himself, for president. Mosby wrote two books during terms as U.S. Consul to Hong Kong and assistant attorney in the Justice Department: *Mosby's War Reminiscences and Stuart's Cavalry Campaigns* (1887), and *Stuart's Cavalry in the Gettysburg Campaign* (1908). He died in Washington, D.C. on May 30, 1916.

by on a surveying trip, and on June 17, 1863, John Mosby met here with J.E.B. Stuart to discuss the upcoming Gettysburg campaign. The latter left his name on a room where JFK occasionally held press conferences. It's been known as the Red Fox since 1937, and houses 20 rooms in four buildings. A restaurant on the first floor, open daily, offers a short but high-powered menu in a fox-hunt ambiance. Premium to luxury, with various romantic getaway packages. E-mail: innkeeper@redfox.com, Web site: www.fedfox.com.

An old carriage stands in front of the **Middleburg Country Inn,** 209 E. Washington St., tel. (800) 262-6082 or (540) 687-6082, fax 687-5603, where a night in one of eight period rooms comes with the outdoor hot tub in back, full country breakfasts and five-course gourmet dinners on weekends. Fireplaces and four-poster beds are included, too. Expensive to premium. E-mail: midcountryinn@middleburgonline.com, Web site: www.midcountryinn.com.

Food

Tutti Perricone's **Back Street Cafe,** 4 E. Federal St., tel. (540) 687-3122, is a local favorite for its zesty cooking and live jazz on weekend evenings. Pizzas, salads, sandwiches, and pasta are served inside and on the outdoor deck. Open for lunch and dinner Mon.-Saturday. A block away the **Hidden Horse Tavern,** 7 W. Washington St., tel. (540) 687-3828, occupies a 200-year-old building. Seafood and other Hunt-Country standbys are offered daily for lunch and dinner. For breakfast or a midday snack try **Huckleberry's,** 3 W. Washington St., tel. (540) 687-6142, with a full range of sandwiches, gourmet ice cream, coffee, tea, and Jelly Bellys.

Events

The **Middleburg Hunt Point-to-Point Race** gallops through in April, followed by **A Taste of Middleburg,** with wine tastings, food, and crafts on the second weekend in May. The **Middleburg Garden Tour** happens in June.

Shopping

Middleburg has to have one of the highest antique store-to-resident ratios in the state. **The Shaggy Ram,** 3 E. Washington St., tel. (540) 687-3546, sells English and French antiques; **Estates & Estates Garden,** 105 B West Washington St., tel. (540) 687-8027, offers furniture, paintings, and oriental rugs; and **Douglas C. Whitesell Antiques,** 13 S. Madison St., tel. (540) 687-5550, specializes in antique clocks. For gifts and general goods visit **The Fun Shop,** a two-story department store on 117 W. Washington St., tel. (540) 687-6590. Outfit your filly at **The Tack Box,** 7 W. Federal St., tel. (540) 687-3231, with riding equipment, clothing, and gifts.

Information

For details on events and anything else about the area, pop in the **Pink Box Visitors Information Center,** 12 Madison St., tel. (540) 687-8888, Web site: www.middleburgonline.com. It really is a pink-hued stone building, surrounded by a white picket fence and open Mon.-Fri. 11 a.m.-3 p.m., Saturday and Sunday 11 a.m.-4 p.m.

Glenwood Park

A long list of annual equestrian events at this track is capped by the Middleburg Spring Races, tel. (540) 687-6545, the state's oldest steeplechase event. On the third Saturday in April, thousands of race fans watch riders compete for a purse totaling $140,000. It's a few miles north of Middleburg off Foxcroft Rd. (Rt. 626).

Great Meadows

Hunt Country's premiere horse-racing venue, tel. (540) 253-5001, lies in the opposite direction near a village called The Plains. Everyone puts on their best and packs the tailgate with gourmet munchies for the **Virginia Gold Cup Races,** tel. (800) 697-2237, held the first Saturday in May. Seven races, held since 1925, draw upwards of 40,000 spectators, including most of Capitol Hill. Order your ticket well ahead of time and arrive early.

The **Virginia Wine Festival,** tel. (800) 277-2675, brings dozens of wineries and hundreds of vendors for the state's oldest celebration of the vintner's art. Food, rides, and music of all kinds round out the fun, held in mid June. The **Middleburg Classic Horse Show** arrives in mid-September, followed by the **International Gold Cup,** another steeplechase, near the end of October.

SKY MEADOWS STATE PARK

Close to 2,000 acres of clover-dotted fields and wildflower pastures were once part of a 7,883-acre tract purchased from Lord Fairfax in 1713. A bridle trail and five foot paths, including 3.6 miles of the Appalachian Trail, head across open meadows ringing with bird calls and into the forested hills beyond. Take the Gap Run Trail to a primitive campground with 12 sites ($8 per night). The **Mount Bleak visitors center,** tel. (703) 592-3556, occupies an early 19th-century farmhouse on a hilltop near a picnic area and fishing pond.

To get there take US 17 south from US 50 for 1.2 miles to the park entrance on Rt. 710. You can also reach US 17 from I-66 exit 18. Open daily 8 a.m.-dusk, $1 per car.

DOWN THE POTOMAC

HUNTLEY MEADOWS PARK

Fairfax County's Hyble Valley hides 1,260 acres of wetlands, meadows, and forests. The Potomac flowed here long ago, leaving behind freshwater marshes dotted by beaver ponds and teeming with birdlife. Local birdwatchers know the wildlife viewing tower is one of the best places in the Washington area to spot yellow-crowned night herons, woodpeckers, and any one of 200 other resident species.

In the spring, park naturalists lead an evening hike along a half-mile interpretive boardwalk trail to the sounds of a frog chorus. Bicycles are allowed on another two-mile trail. The park entrance and visitors center, tel. (703) 768-2525, is at 3701 Lockheed Blvd., reached from US 1. Open dawn-dusk; free.

MOUNT VERNON

Close to a million people visit the home of America's first president every year, making it second only in popularity to the current president's house. If you can avoid or ignore the crowds, though, it's still possible to glimpse those things that made Mount Vernon so dear to George Washington's heart—the view of the Potomac on a misty morning, the wind through the fig trees in the evening, and all the smells and sounds of a practical, prosperous farm estate far from the public eye.

History

In 1726, George's father Augustine Washington obtained half of a 5,000-acre property called Hunting Creek. Nine years later he moved his family, including a three-year-old George, into a cottage he had built on a bluff overlooking the Potomac, but the Washingtons soon moved away again. George returned at age 16 when his half-brother Lawrence inherited the property in 1743. Washington assumed ownership in 1761 after the death of Lawrence's daughter Sarah, the original inheritor.

The current mansion was begun two years later. Washington continually added to the house and property until he owned 8,000 acres surrounding one of Virginia's finest plantations. George's vision of a quiet farming life had to wait through a few interruptions—the Revolutionary War, the Philadelphia Constitutional Convention, becoming the first president of the United States—but by 1797 he was finally able to retire to Mount Vernon for two quiet years, which he spent with his wife Martha until his death from a throat infection on December 14, 1799, at age 67. By the

the home of America's first president

dictates of his will, he was buried in a mausoleum on his beloved estate, and was joined there by his wife in 1802. In 1858, the newly formed Mount Vernon Ladies' Association of the Union raised enough money to purchase the crumbling building and begin to restore it to its former glory.

Visiting Mount Vernon

A wide bowling green leads to the main house, which is flanked by two curved colonnades of outbuildings. The 19-room mansion mixes the original Georgian style with the feel of an English Palladian villa, thanks to its owner's later remodelings. As they were in Washington's time, the outer pine boards have been painted and beveled to resemble masonry, with sand mixed in the paint to simulate stone. The view from the columned riverfront facade, 126 feet over the Potomac, rivals even hilltop Monticello's view.

Many original pieces have been tracked down and returned to rooms painted their original eye-catching shades of Prussian blue and bright green. Lafayette sent Washington the key to the Bastille displayed in the main reception room, and the English harpsichord once played by Martha's granddaughter Nelly Custis sits silent in the "little parlor." Notice the agricultural motifs—wheat, shovel, and scythe—carved into the ceiling plaster in the two-story dining room, and the globe in the study that's missing the yet-un-known continent of Antarctica. Upstairs are the bedroom where French diplomat Lafayette slept on three visits and Washington's bedroom, containing the bed in which he died (possibly because of over-bleeding by his doctors).

The half-moon of outbuildings includes a kitchen, smokehouse, slaves' quarters, stable, and archaeological museum. Don't miss the re-cycling outhouses (known in George's day as "necessaries") and the rebuilt eight-sided barn. Mount Vernon is still a working farm as it was when Washington kept detailed records of his experiments with crop rotation and different strains of plants. A squad of hardworking employees tends flourishing herb and vegetable gardens and a barnyard of horses, sheep, and chickens. Imported English deer mingle with native species in a cleared space by the river. George and Martha's tombs are found south of the vineyard, marked with simple inscriptions: "Washington," and "Martha, consort of Washington."

Mount Vernon, tel. (703) 780-2000, Web site: www.mountvernon.org, is eight miles south of Old Town Alexandria via US 1 or the George Washington Memorial Parkway (Rt. 235). It's open daily 8 a.m.-5 p.m. (April-Aug.), 9 a.m.-5 p.m. (March, September, and October), and 9 a.m.-4 p.m. (Nov.-Feb.). Admission is $8 adults and $4 children 6-11, but on Washington's Birthday (also a national holiday) visits are free and a wreath-laying ceremony takes place at his tomb. Tours are self-guided, but interpreters are ready to explain details of the house and grounds. For more information you can rent a 40-minute audio tour for $2 or buy a 132-page guidebook for $3.50 at the gift shop, in front of the gate near the snack bar, post office, and ATM. Costumed waiters serve colonial food and Virginia wine by the glass at the elegant **Mount Vernon Inn,** tel. (703) 780-0011, open daily for lunch and dinner. Special annual events include garden tours, craft demonstrations, and children's activities (call for a schedule).

Transportation, Tours, and Trails

If you can't drive to Mount Vernon, don't worry—there are plenty of other ways to get there. One option is to take the **Metro** blue or yellow lines to Huntington and catch the 11P bus to the estate. The **Grey Line,** tour company, tel. (703) 780-2000, sends daily buses from the Lyceum in Alexandria ($18 adults, $9 children including admission), and the *Spirit of Washington,* tel. (202) 554-8000, motors out of Pier 4 at 6th St. and Water St. SW in Washington, D.C. The boat leaves at 9 a.m. Tues.-Sun., arrives at Mount Vernon at 10:30, and heads back two hours later. The cost is $25.50 adults, $7 children 6-12 including admission. The **Mount Vernon Trail** parallels the George Washington Memorial Parkway from here to north of Alexandria. See **Near D.C.: Arlington County and Vicinity** above, for more on the trail.

WOODLAWN PLANTATION

A pair of homes reflecting very different eras share a part of the original Mount Vernon estate grounds to the west. **Woodlawn Mansion** was presented to Washington's nephew Lawrence Lewis on his marriage to Eleanor

Parke Custis, Martha's granddaughter by her first marriage. Built 1800-05, the brick building was designed in part by William Thornton, one of the architects of the U.S. Capitol. Period antiques set off carved marble mantels and the walnut rail lining the winding central staircase. The gardens include an exceptional collection of 19th-century roses.

Frank Lloyd Wright designed the low, angular **Pope-Lighey House,** in 1914 as an example of his Usonian style, meant to be an affordable, tasteful home for middle-income families. Originally near Falls Church, the L-shaped building was rescued from destruction in 1964, dismantled, and rebuilt here. Inside it's snug but comfortable thanks to high ceilings, warm cypress walls, and strategic windows.

Both buildings, at the intersection of the Mount Vernon Memorial Parkway (Rt. 235) and US 1, are open daily 9:30 a.m.-4 p.m. March-Dec., weekends January and February. Separate admission is $6 adults, $4 for children under 12, or a combination ticket is $10 adults, $7 children. Tours of both are included. The mansion hosts the country's oldest **Needlework Show** in March, along with a **Quilt Exhibition** in the fall. Call (703) 780-4000 for details.

MASON NECK

Pohick Bay Regional Park
The first stop on this stubby peninsula offers a huge pool, a campground with hookups ($12-14), camp store, boat access, a golf course, picnic areas, and nature trails. The park, tel. (703) 339-6104, is open year-round daily 8 a.m.-sunset for $4 per car. The pool is open Memorial Day-Labor Day for separate admission. Take Rt. 242 from US 1, and the entrance is on the left.

Gunston Hall Plantation
A short distance farther sits an 18th-century plantation built for George Mason, one of the nation's undersung founding fathers. Mason was a friend of George Washington and the author of the Virginia Declaration of Rights, whose words Thomas Jefferson borrowed for the Declaration of Independence. Even though he helped write the U.S. Constitution, Mason refused to sign the

document because it didn't abolish slavery or include a bill of rights.

A certain serenity pervades the Georgian mansion and 550 acres of grounds, all that's left of the original 5,500-acre tobacco and wheat plantation. Stop by the **visitors center** to see a short film on Mason before taking a tour of the house, built 1755-60. Many of the furnishings are original, as are the remarkable decorative woodcarvings done by a young British indentured servant named William Buckland. Mason himself designed the formal boxwood gardens. Visitors can follow the nature trail through the wooded deer park to the Potomac, and visit the grave of Mason and his wife Ann.

Gunston Hall, tel. (703) 550-9220 or (800) 811-6966, fax (703) 550-9480, e-mail: Historic@GunstonHall.org, Web site: www.GunstonHall.org, is open daily 9:30 a.m.-5: p.m.; $5 adults, $1.50 children under 17. A museum holds a gift shop and a cafeteria serving an inexpensive lunch. Call ahead for information on interpretive activities such as cooking and harvest demonstrations, and the Kite Festival in March.

Mason Neck National Wildlife Refuge
Six miles of shoreline, 2,000 acres of hardwood forest, and northern Virginia's largest marsh fall within the first national wildlife refuge created specifically to protect the habitat of bald eagles. The majestic raptors feed in the 245-acre Great Marsh alongside a 1,000-pair colony of great blue herons, ducks, and 200 varieties of songbirds. Trails lead through fern-filled glades and over streams to the marsh edge. Open year-round, dawn to dusk, free. Call (703) 690-1297 for more information.

Mason Neck State Park
In 1969, the state of Virginia purchased 1,800 acres from The Nature Conservancy, leaving the national wildlife refuge split into two sections on either side of Belmont Bay. The Dogue Indian tribe once hunted and fished here among the oak, ash, and maples. Today you can view ospreys, great blue herons, and a quarter of the Chesapeake Bay's 250 nesting pairs of bald eagles from a number of short trails and walkways over marshy areas. A **visitors center,** tel. (703) 550-0362, operates a museum and can provide information on guided canoe trips in the day-

light and moonlight ($6-10 pp). Guided eagle-spotting walks leave on Saturday at 4 p.m. Open year-round, dawn to dusk, with an entrance fee of $1 per car ($2 on weekends and holidays).

PRINCE WILLIAM FOREST PARK

Inhabited as early as 4,500 B.C., the watershed of Quantico Creek was home to Potomac Indian villages from A.D. 700 until the arrival of English colonists. After centuries of severe erosion from over-farming, it was turned over to the National Park Service in 1948 to become a wooded oasis between the Quantico Marine Base and metropolitan northern Virginia.

Hardwoods and pines dominate 18,500 acres straddling a transition between cooler northern and warmer southern climates. A wide variety of plants (95 species) and birds (152 species) include great horned owls and the rare whorled pogonia orchid.

Start at the **Pine Grove visitors center,** tel. (703) 221-7183, Web site: www.nps.gov/prwi, on Rt. 619 from I-95 exit 150. Ask here for directions to the fishing ponds and picnic areas and for information on interpretive programs and the 35 miles of trails. Open year-round, daily 8:30 a.m.-5 p.m.; $4 per car.

Campers have a number of choices. The Turkey Run Ridge and Oak Ridge tent campgrounds charge $7 for up to six people. The Chopawamsic Backcountry Camp, three miles west of the town of Triangle on Rt. 619, is even more basic. For hookups, steer toward the **Prince William Travel Trailer Village,** tel. (703) 221-2474, off Rt. 234 a few miles west of I-95 exit 152, where sites run $17-20 with electricity and water.

SIDETRIP TO D.C.

HISTORY

On June 20, 1783, hordes of unpaid soldiers descended on Philadelphia demanding back pay from the War of Independence. A nervous Congress was quickly convinced that the fledgling United States needed a federal city where its lawmakers could govern in relative peace. Creating one though, would be no easy task: the 13 colonies were united in freedom but divergent in interests; there was no president yet; and the war had left the national coffers nearly empty.

Nonetheless, the location for the country's new capital was decided by a combination of political compromise and pragmatism. Southern states, who helped bail out their northern brethren after the war, insisted in return that the city be located to the south. Newly elected president George Washington decided on a spot near where the Anacostia River meets the Potomac, for its economic potential near the tobacco market of Georgetown and a planned canal across the Cumberland Gap to the western frontier.

French engineer and Revolutionary volunteer Pierre L'Enfant was given the task of designing the nation's capital, which he planned on a grand scale in the spirit of his beloved Paris. A bold grid pattern, anchored by great parks and monumental squares, was overlaid with diagonal avenues named for the states and radiating outward from the White House and the Capitol building, both of which were begun in 1793. In October 1800, the governmental archives and general offices were shifted to Washington from Philadelphia, president John Adams moved into the White House, and Congress met for the first time in the Capitol.

Critics soon began to attack D.C.'s seemingly arbitrary location. What was conceived as a "city of magnificent distances" was derided as the "Capitol of Miserable Huts," and members of both Congress and the national press tried to have the capital moved to a more accessible location. National outrage over the British invasion in 1814, however, firmly seated Washington,

WASHINGTON D.C. AND VICINITY

MARYLAND

Potomac River

Rock Creek Park

Anacostia River

NATIONAL ZOOLOGICAL PARK

WASHINGTON NATIONAL CATHEDRAL

WASHINGTON D.C.

National Arboretum

NEW YORK AVE

RFK STADIUM

KENILWORTH AQUATIC GARDENS

JACK KENT COOKE STADIUM

CONSTITUTION AVE.

ARLINGTON NATIONAL CEMETERY

E. CAPITOL ST.

CONGRESSIONAL CEMETERY

East Potomac Park

WASHINGTON NATIONAL AIRPORT

VIRGINIA

MARYLAND

GEORGE WASHINGTON MEMORIAL PKWY.

CAPITAL BELTWAY

CAPITAL BELTWAY

0   2 mi

0   2 km

© MOON PUBLICATIONS, INC.

D.C., as America's capital in the minds of her citizens. The city's key role in the Civil War, as the heart and brain of the victorious Union, further solidified its symbolic image.

A sudden influx of 40,000 freed slaves more than doubled D.C.'s population and set it on a course of racial diversity that eventually would embrace immigrants from every country in the world. Into the 20th century, the capital's identity continues to evolve and mutate, as wealthy neighborhoods stand next to slums, and homeless people sleep in the shadows of the country's greatest monuments. Our most monumental, symbolic, and international city serves as a reminder of all that is desirable—and much that is not—in the country it embodies.

THE MALL SIGHTS

The area between Constitution Avenue NW and Independence Avenue SW is truly America's backyard. The grassy expanse, wide as a football field, stretches for 2.5 miles, from the Capitol at the east end to the Lincoln Memorial at the west. Along both sides stand many of the Smithsonian museums, and just to the north is the White House. The Mall itself encompasses the Washington Monument, the Vietnam veterans war memorial, outstanding national gardens, the Reflecting Pool, and even a charming merry-go-round.

For information on any of the free attractions on the Mall, call or write: Superintendent, National Capital Parks Central, 900 Ohio Dr. SW, Washington, DC 20242; tel. (202) 485-9880.

USING THE METRO IN D.C.

LOCATION	METRO STATION/LINE
Adams-Morgan	Dupont Circle/Red
Botanical Gardens	Federal Center SW/Blue or Orange
FBI Building	Archives-Navy Memorial/Yellow or Green
Federal Triangle	Federal Triangle/Blue or Green
Folger Shakespeare Library	Eastern Market/Blue or Green
Ford's Theater	Metro Center/Blue, Orange, or Red
Georgetown	Foggy Bottom/Blue or Orange (walk west along Pennsylvania Ave.)
Rosslyn	Foggy Bottom/Blue or Orange (walk north across Francis Scott Key Bridge)
Kennedy Center/Watergate	Foggy Bottom/Blue or Orange (walk south along New Hampshire Ave.)
Library of Congress	Capitol South/Blue or Green
MCI Center Gallery Place	Gallery Place/Green, Red, or Yellow
National Aquarium	Federal Triangle/Blue or Green
National Archives	Archives-Navy Memorial/Yellow or Green
National Building Museum	Judiciary Square/Red
National Mall	Smithsonian/Orange or Blue
National Museum of American Art	Gallery Place/Green, Red, or Yellow
National Portrait Gallery	Gallery Place/Green, Red, or Yellow
Shakespeare Theatre	Gallery Place/Green, Red, or Yellow
Union Station	Union Station/Red
Washington National Cathedral	Woodley Park-Zoo/Red (walk west along Woodley Rd.)
White House	Metro Center/Blue, Orange, or Red
Zoological Park	Woodley Park-Zoo/Red

Metro Transfer Stations include Federal Center SW, Gallery Place, King Street, Metro Center, Pentagon, Rosslyn, Stadium-Armory

Constitution Gardens

The last of the unsightly "temporary" buildings marring the Mall was finally removed in the mid-1970s and replaced by this tranquil oasis of landscaped gardens, meandering footpaths, and a duck pond. A willow-shrouded island at the center of the pond contains a roster of the signers of the Declaration of Independence, inscribed on a granite-and-gold plate.

Lincoln Memorial

While more than a century elapsed before the Washington Monument moved from contemplation to completion, the Lincoln Memorial was built in 60 years. Henry Bacon's white marble temple is another D.C. testimonial to the Greeks, while the 19-foot statue of Lincoln by Daniel French that sits inside bears signs of Roman influence, especially in the chair arms bearing *fasces,* symbols of Roman imperial power. Although the 1922 unveiling ceremonies were segregated, the site began a long association with the civil rights movement 17 years later when African-American Marian Anderson sang from the steps after she was barred from performing at nearby Constitution Hall. Ms. Anderson ascended the steps again in 1963, preceding the Rev. Martin Luther King, Jr.'s, momentous "I Have a Dream" speech.

During WW II, the Lincoln Memorial was the only edifice in D.C. to come under friendly fire: a nervous trooper manning the big guns atop the Department of the Interior building managed to blow off bits of the marble rooftop. Located at the west end of the Mall, the memorial is best visited at night, when the spirit of the place is most alive. Like other Mall attractions, the Lincoln Memorial is open all day every day. Rangers are on duty 8 a.m. to midnight daily except Christmas Day.

Korean Veteran's Memorial

Washington's newest memorial, dedicated in 1995, honors veterans of the Korean War. The centerpiece is the triangular "field of service," depicting a wedge of soldiers slogging through the countryside. This symbolic patrol of 19 stainless-steel figures is made up of members from each of the four main branches of the armed services. The memorial is most haunting when the seven-foot-tall soldiers are softly illuminated at night. Staffed by park rangers 8 a.m.-midnight every day except Christmas, the memorial is located just south of the Reflecting Pool near FDR Memorial Park.

Vietnam Veterans Memorial

The revolutionary work that designer Maya Lin described simply as "a rift in the earth" doesn't trumpet the glory of struggle or the legacy of some lauded general. Instead it lists, in neat, simple, endless columns, the name of every person killed in America's longest war. More than 58,000 names are carved into the 492-foot wall of black granite, the polished surface of which reflects the faces of those who visit to pay homage. The names are listed chronologically in the order of death, and at each end of the memorial are paperback registers listing the names alphabetically with a key to their location on the wall.

Vietnam veteran Jan Scruggs raised the funds to construct the memorial through a nonprofit organization, and today it is America's most potent shrine, a place of grief and cleansing where every year tens of thousands of people bring offerings of poems and rings, harmonicas and sardines for lost friends, lost sons, or for the parent they never knew. Some leave only their thoughts for future generations, such as, "Understand that if the time comes when you must kill it will destroy you for all of this life."

Vietnam Women's Memorial

This bronze sculpture portraying three women and an injured soldier was dedicated on November 11, 1993. Artist Glenna Goodacre honors the women who served in Vietnam with a solid, uncomplicated piece that communicates the emotional bond that formed between the male soldiers and women who served primarily as nurses and support staff.

Washington Monument

According to federal law, no structure in the capital can be built higher than the 555-foot tapered shaft of the Washington Monument. In 1783, the Continental Congress first suggested a monument honoring the nation's first president, but more than a century passed before the idea be-

came reality; from cornerstone to completion took 40 years. During one embarassing interlude from 1854 to 1876, the obelisk languished as an unsightly stump of 150 feet, described by Mark Twain as "a factory chimney with the top broken off."

When work began again, the marble originally drawn from a Maryland quarry had been exhausted; thus the noticeable change in shade of the remaining 400 feet. The monument finally opened in 1888 with women and children dutifully trudging up the 898 steps (the elevator designed by Mr. Elisha G. Otis was considered patently dangerous, braved only by men). Today everyone rides the elevator, ascending to 360-degree views of the capital's historic heart through narrow windows.

The monument is open daily 9 a.m.-5 p.m., every day except Christmas, with extended summer hours for nighttime viewing. Depending on the availability of staff, summer weekend walking tours down the steps are also offered. For more information call (202) 426-6839 or 485 9880, or write: Superintendent, The Washington Monu-

© MOON PUBLICATIONS, INC.

ment, 1100 Ohio Dr. SW, Washington, DC 20242.

National Gallery of Art

In the 1930s, this museum's west wing sprang full-grown from the wallet of rapacious banker Andrew Mellon, who wisely declined to append his name to the edifice. I.M. Pei designed the angular east wing, which was built in 1978. Both wings are constructed of pink Tennessee marble, but there the similarity ends: the east displays 20th-century works by the likes of Miro, Magritte, and Matisse, while the homier, more crowded west wing is the domain of classic art by the likes of Raphael, Rembrandt, and Renoir. Historians of the presidency are invariably drawn to the West Wing, which sits over the bones of the old B&P Railroad Station where, in 1881, President James A. Garfield was shot twice in the back by Charles Guiteau. The gallery, at 600 Constitution Ave. NW, Washington, DC 20565, tel. (202) 737-4215, is open Mon.-Sat.10 a.m.-5 p.m., Sunday 11 a.m.-6 p.m. Closed New Year's Day and Christmas Day; free admission.

Mall Merry-Go-Round

On the grounds of the south side of the Mall, a small carousel offers a pleasant respite from the solemnity of its monumental surroundings. A circular journey or two aboard gaily painted horses, serenaded by cheery carnival tunes, can serve as a bracing antidote to historic dates and endless museum rounds. The carousel spins just east of the Smithsonian Castle and is open daily 9 a.m.-5 p.m., depending on the weather, closed major holidays. General admission is $1.00.

SMITHSONIAN INSTITUTION

Smithsonian Castle

In 1829, eccentric English chemist James Smithson passed on, leaving to the United States—a country he had never seen—105 bags of gold sovereigns "to found an establishment for the increase and diffusion of knowledge." After no small amount of puzzlement and a fair amount of wrangling, Congress decided in 1846 to spend Smithson's largess on an institute of scientific research. In 1855, James Renwick completed the fairytale red sandstone structure popularly known as the Castle.

The institution quickly outgrew these grand confines, and today the building serves simply as an information center guiding visitors to the Smithsonian's scattered holdings. Smithson's dusty remains rest in a crypt beneath the castle, his corpse having gained these shores at last in 1904. The majority of the Smithsonian attractions are on the Mall. The National Museum of American Art, the National Portrait Gallery, the Anacostia Museum, and the National Zoological Park are elsewhere in the city. The Castle sits at 1000 Jefferson Dr. SW, Washington, DC 20560, tel. (202) 357-1300, and is open daily 10 a.m.-5:30 p.m. Closed Christmas Day.

National Air and Space Museum

Year after year, this is the most visited attraction in the city. People just can't get enough of the model of Sputnik, the 1903 Wright Brothers *Flyer*, Lindy's *Spirit of St. Louis*, a knockoff of the Hubble space telescope, and a walk through a full-scale reproduction of the Skylab space station. Perhaps the most popular item on display is the four-billion-year-old shard of lunar rock brought back by the astronauts of Apollo 17; hardly anyone can resist running fingers over this chunk of another world. The museum is open daily 10 a.m.-5:30 p.m. with extended summer hours determined annually; closed Christmas Day. Admission is free, though a fee of $2-7 is charged to view IMAX films in the museum's Albert Einstein Planetarium and Samuel P. Langley Theater. Visit the Castle or call (202) 357-1300 for more information.

Arthur M. Sackler Gallery

This three-tiered subterranean museum at 1050 Independence Ave. SW, tel. (202) 357-4880, houses 5,000 years of Asian art. Highlights of the Sackler's permanent collection include Chinese bronze, jade, and lacquerware; delicate Persian paintings; Near Eastern works in silver, gold, bronze, and clay; and a pantheon of Buddhist and Hindu deities executed in stone and bronze. Open daily 10 a.m.-5:30 p.m., closed Christmas Day. Admission is free. Write Office of Public Affairs, Arthur M. Sackler Gallery, MRC 707, Smithsonian Institution, Washington, DC 20560, for information.

Arts and Industries Building

At the conclusion of the 1876 U.S. International Exposition in Philadelphia, most exhibiting nations and many U.S. states craftily donated their exhibits to the U.S. government, thus saving the costs of shipping them home. It took 60 trains to transport all these objects to the Smithsonian, increasing its holdings fourfold, and requiring the construction of this Victorian edifice to house it all. Today, the Arts and Industries Building features a reproduction of that 1876 Exposition, with an appealing hodgepodge of artifacts ranging from Kansas wheat to California wines, and some terrifying 19th-century medical and dental tools. The Smithsonian can never bear to throw anything away, hence nothing is too big—witness the full-size elevators, steam engines, and locomotives—or too numerous, as evidenced by the 100 nosegay posy holders. Located at 900 Jefferson Dr. SW, the museum is open daily 10 a.m.-5:30 p.m., and closed Christmas Day. Admission is free. For more information visit the Castle or call (202) 357-1300, fax 357-2700.

Freer Gallery of Art

Charles Lang Freer raked in millions designing railroad cars, then began to spend his accumulated wealth on fine art. Freer first became enamored of the prints, pastels, oils, and watercolors of James Whistler, then, at the artist's urging, began accumulating Asian art. When Freer died in 1919, his entire collection went to the Smithsonian; this gallery opened four years later. Today the Freer houses over 26,000 objects, including more than 1,200 works by Whistler, the largest collection of the artist's work found anywhere. On Jefferson Dr. SW, tel. (202) 357-4880, the gallery is open daily 10 a.m.-5:30 p.m., closed Christmas Day. Admission is free. Visit the Smithsonian Castle for more information or write Office of Public Affairs, Freer Gallery—MRC 707, Washington, DC 20560.

Hirshhorn Museum and Sculpture Garden

Created to quiet critics who complained the Smithsonian cared only for classic art, the Hirshhorn is built around the extensive 11,000-piece modern art collection of uranium tycoon Joseph Hirshhorn. The museum's revolving exhibitions are dedicated to promulgating appreciation for "the art of our time." The museum, located on Independence Ave. SW, is open daily 10 a.m.-5:30 p.m. (the garden is open 7:30 a.m.- dusk) and closed Christmas Day. Admission is free. Call or visit the Castle for more information.

National Museum of African Art

Founded as a private institution in 1964 and absorbed by the Smithsonian in 1979, this underground museum focuses primarily on the traditional arts of sub-Saharan Africa. Permanent exhibits include pieces from the royal court of the kingdom of Benin as it was before British colonial rule; traditional and modern ceramic

the Castle, c. 1862

works from varying regions of the continent; a display of utilitarian objects, each an example of the aesthetics found in daily African life; and a small collection of objects from the ancient city of Kerma, the oldest known African city south of Egypt, on loan from Boston's Museum of Fine Arts. Located on Independence Ave. SW, the museum is open daily 10 a.m.- 5:30 p.m., and closed Christmas Day. Admission is free. For more information call or visit the Castle, or go to Web site: www.si.edu/nmafa.

National Museum of American History

Living up to the nickname "America's attic," this museum is as big, rich, and sprawling as the country it collects. The sheer quantity of material is staggering; it would require several hours to appreciate the intricate, painstaking, exhaustively informative lightbulb display alone. Nothing is too big for the museum's curatorial staff, who have hauled in a fullsize gunboat and an entire post office, among other things. See Foucault's pendulum, proof the earth still turns; and the tattered fabric Francis Scott Key immortalized as *The Star-Spangled Banner,* proof the flag *is* still there. Discover the charge in a kiss in the Hall of Electricity, and on the third floor review the heartbreaking collection of effects left at the Vietnam Memorial. It's located at 14th St. and Constitution Ave. NW, and is open daily 10 a.m.-5:30 p.m. with extended summer hours determined annually. Closed Christmas Day. For more information call or visit the Castle, or go to www.si.edu/nmah on the Internet.

National Museum of Natural History

Here you'll find an endless amalgamation of artifacts—animal, vegetable, and mineral, from the jaws of a prehistoric shark large enough to swallow entire automobiles to the Hope diamond. A 13-foot stuffed African elephant and a great stone head from Easter Island round out the collection. An extensive exhibit on Native Americans inspired Rudyard Kipling to ponder "the wonder of a people who, having extirpated the aboriginals of their continent more completely than any other modern race had ever done, honestly believed that they were a Godly little New England community, setting examples to brutal mankind." Hands-on displays in the Discovery Room (open afternoons by ticket only) are geared toward children. The museum, located on Constitution Ave. NW, is open daily 10 a.m.-5:30 p.m., and closed Christmas Day. For more information go to Web site: www.mnh.si.edu, or write National Museum of Natural History, Smithsonian Institution—MRC 106, Washington, DC 20560, or call or visit the Castle.

MORE CAPITAL SIGHTS

TIDAL BASIN
AND THE WATERFRONT

Seperating West Potomac Park from East Potomac Park, the Tidal Basin was originally dredged as a reservoir but soon proved popular as a recreational area. From 1917 to 1925, white Washingtonians flocked to a segregated beach located where the Jefferson Memorial now stands. Today the basin is famous worldwide for the 1,300 cherry trees along its banks. The first batch, a peace offering from the warlords of Japan, arrived in 1909, but the trees were contaminated with insects and were immediately destroyed. In 1912, a second shipment fared better and thrived through WW II, notwithstanding occasional efforts by enraged citizens to fell them with chainsaws. These days it is possible to cruise the basin on rented paddleboats, available 10 a.m.-7 p.m.; for information call (202) 479-2426. Being a public area, there is no admission to the Tidal Basin area, which is officially open 8 a.m.-midnight daily, but again, being an outdoor public area, it never really closes. For more information write: Information—Superintendent, National Capital Parks Central, 900 Ohio Dr. SW, Washington, DC 20242, or call (202) 485-9880.

FDR Memorial

Composed of four outdoor rooms, one for each of Franklin Delano Roosevelt's terms in office, this granite structure spreads along the banks of the Tidal Basin in West Potomac Park. Visitors to the memorial enter past an inscribed FDR quote—"This generation of Americans has a rendezvous with destiny"—and a bronze bas-relief of the presidential seal as it appeared at FDR's first inauguration in 1933. The interiors of each room include waterfalls, plants, shrubs, and trees, as well as sculpture and inscriptions highlighting FDR's accomplishments as president, from bringing the nation out of the Great Depression to leading the United States during WW II. The fourth room includes FDR's "four freedoms:"

Freedom of Speech, Freedom of Worship, Freedom from Want, Freedom from Fear—symbolizing what the U.S. was fighting for during the war. It also presents the contributions of First Lady Eleanor Roosevelt as U.N. ambassador after her husband's death.

There was some controversy over the memorial at its unveiling. Initially the memorial completely neglected the fact that Roosevelt used a wheelchair for most of his life due the polio he contracted as a child. After protests by historians and the disabled community, the memorial's designers agreed to include images of FDR in his wheelchair. Park staff are on duty 8 a.m.-midnight every day but Christmas. Admission is free. Information—Superintendent, National Capital Parks Central, 900 Ohio Dr. SW, Washington, DC 20242, or call (202) 485-9880.

Jefferson Memorial

Though the Jefferson Memorial has stood only since 1942, it is today under almost constant repair, its columns cracked by the effects of auto exhaust and acid rain. Nevertheless, the 19-foot hollow bronze of Thomas Jefferson in furs is undeniably impressive, centered in an open-air rotunda surrounded by massive ionic columns, an architectural copy of Jefferson's own rejected plans for the White House. The interior walls are crammed with quotes from Jefferson's voluminous writings, although not all are accurate: there are more than a dozen errors in the excerpt from the Declaration of Independence alone. Located on the south shore of the Tidal Basin, the memorial is open all day, every day. Park staff are on duty 8 a.m.-midnight every day but Christmas. Admission is free. For more information write: Information—Superintendent, National Capital Parks Central, 900 Ohio Dr.SW, Washington, DC 20242, or call (202) 485-9880.

"The Awakening"

Brave the gauntlet of joggers and golfers in East Potomac Park to arrive at J. Seward Johnson's bold, boisterous sculpture of a great bearded giant angrily erupting from the chains of the earth. Only the head and portions of each naked limb have broken through the grass at the tip of Hains Point, but the wild look in his eyes promises a great awakening indeed. Children can't resist reaching inside the great shouting mouth. Located at Hains Point in East Potomac Park at the southernmost point of Ohio Dr. SW, "The Awakening" is viewable all day, every day. For more information write: Superintendent, East Potomac Park, Ohio Dr. SW, Washington, DC 20024, or call (202) 485-9880.

Theodore Roosevelt Island

Those proposing a memorial for the nation's 26th president decided nothing less than an en-

tire island would do, choosing 88 wilderness acres in the middle of the Potomac. Three miles of flat, easy trails wander through the swampy, wooded expanse of willow and ash, mud and muskrat. Rocky beaches with D.C. city views compete for visitors' attention with Paul Manship's 17-foot bronze statue of the conservation-minded Roosevelt. There is but one way to get to the island: drive from D.C. into Virginia across the Theodore Roosevelt Bridge, veer right onto the northbound lanes of George Washington Parkway, pull into the poorly signed Roosevelt Island lot, and walk across the pedestrian footbridge that provides the only access to the island. The island memorial to the Bull Moose

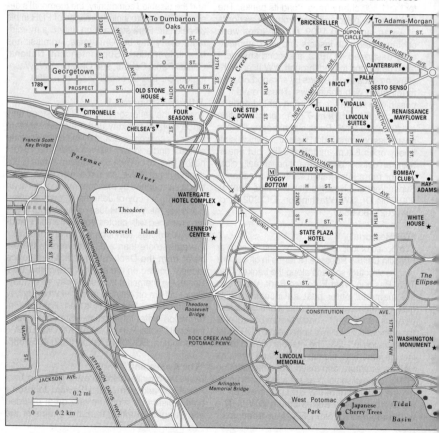

candidate is open 8 a.m.-dusk daily, and closed New Year's Day and Christmas Day. Admission is free. For nature/historical tours call (703) 285-2600 at least seven days in advance, no winter tours are offered. For more information write: Information—District Ranger, Theodore Roosevelt Island, George Washington Memorial Pkwy. c/o Turkey Run Park, McLean, VA 22101, or call (703) 285-2598.

Bureau of Engraving and Printing

Here some 2,300 people labor around the clock to produce more than $100 billion in paper currency each year. Through plates of thick glass visitors can watch workers inking, stacking, cut-

ting, and examining millions of dollars a day. There's also an interesting exhibit on the curious history of money, and yes, bags of shredded bills are for sale in the gift shop (*everyone* considers trying to glue them back together, but it's futile). The Bureau, located at 14th and C Sts. SW, is open Mon.-Fri. 9 a.m.-2 p.m., and closed federal holidays. Admission is always free, though tickets, available inside the building, are required from Easter to Labor Day.

United States Holocaust Memorial Museum

A truly wrenching experience, the Holocaust Museum is one of the most moving exhibits in this or any other city. From the outside the building intentionally resembles the high brick ovens used to dispose of the bodies of millions of European Jews; inside, exhibits methodically trace the rise of Nazi Germany and its systematic implementation of its policy of genocide. The displays make very clear that government officials in the U.S. and elsewhere were well aware of Hitler's implementation of the final solution, but chose to do nothing. Visitors will witness many depictions of horrific atrocities, certainly, but perhaps the most affecting items are the heaps of personal effects collected by the Nazis from those they murdered: mute piles of shoes, brushes, hair.

It's located at 100 Raoul Wallenberg Pl. SW (formerly 15th St.) at Independence Ave. right off the Mall, tel. (202) 488-0400, Web site: visit www.ushmm.org. The museum is open daily 10 a.m.-5:30 p.m. Admission is free, though you must have tickets to enter. There are two ways to get tickets: reserve tickets in advance from Ticketmaster, which charges a service charge: from D.C. call (202) 432-7328, from Baltimore call (410) 481-7328, outside of D.C. (800) 551-7328, or get same-day tickets at the museum box office. Allow yourself at least four or five hours to visit this museum.

CAPITOL HILL

Library of Congress

In 1800, the nation's legislators allocated a modest $5,000 "for the purchase of such books as may be necessary for the use of Congress." The collection was contained in a single room, and was consulted as much to settle bets as to divine fine points of law. In 1814 the British put the entire nascent library to the torch. Fortunately for the nation, Thomas Jefferson was suffering through one of his periodic spasms of acute financial distress around the same time, and so sold to Congress his entire personal library of 6,500 volumes.

Today "Mr. Jefferson's Library" consists of more than 28 million books, with an additional 80 million holdings of film, photographic, music, and other media. The library complex consists of three structures; start at the stunning Jefferson Building, completed in 1897 and offering a feast of mosaics and murals, sculptures and bas reliefs. The Main Reading Room, with 236 desks arranged in an elegant circular pattern beneath a 160-foot dome, is one of the most beautiful sights in the city. The Library of Congress is not a lending library—materials must be perused on-site. Located on 1st St. SE between Independence Ave. and East Capitol St., the library is open Mon.-Fri. 8:30 a.m.-9:30 p.m., Saturday 8:30 a.m.-6 p.m., and closed New Year's Day and Christmas Day.

Union Station

When it was completed in 1907, Union Station, modeled after the Baths of Caracalla in Rome, was the largest train station in the world. For the next 50 years most visitors to the city first set foot in D.C. upon the station's elegant marble floors. By the 1970s, however, the place had become a national embarrassment: the floors buckled, torrential rains caved in portions of the roof, and a runaway train had slammed into the station, scattering spiraling shards of cars.

In 1981, Union Station was shut and sealed, until a business/government consortium invested $160 million to restore it to its former grandeur. Today visitors revel in acres of white marble floorings, bronze grills, coffered ceilings, gold leaf, Honduran mahogany, and a plethora of stone carvings and statues. Being a working train station, Union Station is open all day, every day, and there is no admission. Visit Union Station at 40 Massachusetts Ave. NE, tel. (202) 371-9441.

U.S. Capitol

Any first-time visitor to D.C. should take advantage of the opportunity to peek at our elected congressional officials at work. The small but well-appointed Senate chamber offers each senator a private desk separate from the rest; whereas House representatives are jammed together in long curved pews. The rest of the building presents its own peculiar charms: halls and rotundas stuffed with statues, and the frenzied frescoes of Constantino Brumidi, whose work was incisively described by Mark Twain as "the delirium tremens of art." A word of warning: much of the Capitol is off limits to non-officeholders, and visitors must heed the guidance of Capitol police.

To observe the House and Senate in session, U.S. citizens must obtain passes from the office of their senator or representative. International tickets are available in the Capitol for visitors from foreign countries (picture identification is required for visits to the House gallery). Another option is simply to cruise through the congressional office buildings across from the Capitol, where you're often more likely to experience the hustle and bustle of the political scene. The Senate buildings are to the north, on Constitution Ave., and the House buildings are south of the Capitol on Independence Ave. The Capitol is open to visitors daily 9 a.m.-4:30 p.m., and closed New Years Day, Thanksgiving Day, and Christmas Day. Free guided tours depart every 10-20 minutes from the information desk beneath the rotunda. Reservations are recommended. For more information write Information—United States Senate/House of Representatives, U.S. Capitol Building, Washington, DC 20510 (20515 for the House), or call (202) 224-3121.

Capital Children's Museum
The guiding principle of this elaborate, realistic educational experience is encapsulated in the Chinese proverb, "What I hear, I forget; what I see, I remember; what I do, I understand." From learning how to make animated cartoons to sliding down a fire pole, children learn how the world works by taking the controls. Luckily, there's enough here to keep most grown-ups interested, too. Climb inside a soap bubble (adults welcome), visit Mexico, and tour the ice age in a collection of exhibits that change almost daily. The museum is open 10 a.m.-6 p.m. seven days a week. Admission is $6, $5 for AAA members, and $4 for seniors. Kids under two are admitted free. Located at 800 Third St. NW, right at the Union Station Metro stop on the red line, the Capital Children's Museum fits easily into a tour of the Capitol Hill area. Tel. (202) 675-4120, Web site: www.ccm.org on the Internet.

Folger Shakespeare Library
The bard lives at this research library/museum/theatre, brimming with art, music, and literature. Inside is an eerie and delightful working reconstruction of an Elizabethan theatre, where family events are held and the Shenandoah Shakespeare Express performs Shakespeare's finest. Poetry readings attract the likes of Robert Haas, Czeslaw Milosz, Octavio Paz, and John Updike. The Folger Consort, a chamber music ensemble, performs works from the 12th through the 18th century. The marmoreal facade of this great museum fits neatly between the imposing Library of Congress and the august Supreme Court building. The Folger is open Mon.-Sat. 10 a.m.-4 p.m. at 201 E. Capitol St. SE. Admission is free. Call (202) 544-4600 for more information, or visit www.folger.edu on the Internet.

United States Supreme Court
Completed in 1935, this structure is incongruously opulent, with lush curtains, grandiose statues, and portentous inscriptions at every turn. The main chamber is particularly impressive, with the seats of the nine justices placed high above the rest of the court.

From October through April, the Court hears oral arguments twice a month on Monday, Tuesday, and Wednesday 10 a.m.-3 p.m., and in May and June the justices read opinions from the bench each Monday at 10 a.m. The public is welcome to attend, but there is limited seating, allocated on a first-come, first-served basis to those willing to line up outside the building. When the Court is not in session visitors can attend courtroom lectures on the half-hour 9:30 a.m.-3:30 p.m. The Supreme Court Building, at 1 First St. NE, 20543, tel. (202) 479-3030, is open Monday through Friday 9 a.m.-4:30 p.m., and closed on federal holidays. Admission is free.

Congressional Cemetery
In the early 19th century, D.C. was a remote, pestilential city, which sometimes proved fatal to those sent to govern from it. Congressional corpses faced weeks of daunting travel on slow roads and primitive waterways to reach hometown interment, so it was much easier to bury them in the city itself. In 1812, Congress purchased 100 plots in a five-year-old cemetery, which eventually held 14 senators and 60 representatives.

A peaceful, rarely visited, and ultimately desolate place, the cemetery is mostly full of children, due to the high infant mortality rate in 19th-century. Others among the 60,000 souls laid here to rest include FBI director J. Edgar Hoover and his longtime companion Clyde Tolson; Taza and Push-ma-ta-ha, two native chiefs felled by disease while visiting D.C.; and David Herold, hung for his role in the assassination of Lincoln and quietly buried in a grave unmarked to this day. Dozens of cenotaphs honor congress-members actually buried elsewhere. In this working cemetery, someone can usually be found around the small gatehouse just inside the E St. entrance; ask for the walking tour brochure. The cemetery is open daily 6:45 a.m.-dusk. For more information write: Information—Association for the Preservation of Historic Congressional Cemetery, 1801 E St. SE, Washington, DC 20003, or call (202) 543-0539.

United States Botanic Garden

Another lovely idea of Thomas Jefferson's, this humid haven has enchanted visitors since 1820. Wander amidst a wealth of tropical, subtropical, and desert plants; guide dinosaur-entranced young ones to the garden of the Jurassic; or picnic on a flowery terrace overlooking the Capitol reflecting pool. Located at 100 Maryland Ave. SW, tel. (202) 225-8333, near the east end of the Mall, the gardens are open daily 9 a.m.-5 p.m., and closed Christmas Day. For more information write: Information—United States Botanic Garden, 100 Maryland Ave. SW, Washington, DC 20024.

THE WHITE HOUSE

First occupied by John Adams, the mansion at 1600 Pennsylvania Ave. NW was known as the President's House until it was whitewashed to cover smoke damage from the 1814 British burning of the city. It's not nearly as accessible today as it was during Jefferson's time, when enthusi-

astic dairymen would bustle in to deposit huge cheeses in the East Room. Nevertheless, it's the only chief executive's abode in the world that opens itself to tourists five days a week. When visiting the White House, don't step across the boundary ropes or make other foolish moves—those friendly men patrolling the halls suddenly can turn very serious.

Tours of the White House are free, though tickets are required in spring and summer. Tickets are available at the White House visitor's center at the corner of 15th and E Sts., tel. (202) 456-7041, open 7:30 a.m.-4 p.m. Arrive early if you plan on touring the mansion the same day; there are usually no more tickets available after 8:30 a.m. The White House itself is open Tues.-Sat.10 a.m.-12 noon, and closed major holidays and for official functions. For more information write: Information—White House Historical Association, 740 Jackson Pl. NW, Washington, DC 20560; or call (202) 737-8292.

OLD DOWNTOWN
AND THE FEDERAL TRIANGLE

The area enclosed by Pennsylvania Ave., Constitution Ave., and 15th St. is home to such stern, solemn edifices as the IRS and Justice Department buildings. For many years the area was the most notorious neighborhood in D.C., popularly known as "Murder Bay." During the Civil War, the region was redubbed "Hooker's Division" in honor of the prostitutes encamped there. The place didn't get straight until the U.S. government bought up the land in the 1930s, razing the shacks and replacing them with grim granite.

The area north of Federal Triangle, between the White House and the Capitol Building, and bordered to the north by New York and Massachusetts Avenues, was the city's original downtown area. Popular restaurants and theaters, fashionable tailors' shops, and other, more practical business kept those in office from having to stray too far from their seats of power for dining, entertainment, and life's necessities. Between the time that the buildings of the Federal Triangle were built and the late '60s, the area became quite rundown, gaining the name "Old Downtown" to separate it from "New Downtown"—the area north of the White House, where new businesses opened shop next door to vendors fleeing run-down Old Downtown. The entire Old Downtown area, especially Pennsylvania Ave., gained a major facelift in the '80s. Today, the area again boasts popular restaurants and galleries, as well as landscaped plazas and memorials.

National Building Museum

In 1885, the general-cum-architect Montgomery Meigs erected the Pension Building. Damned at its dedication as an "unsightly monstrosity," the structure is recognized today as a masterpiece. Built of more than 15 million bricks, it features a 1,200-foot-long terra cotta frieze of Union soldiers forever filing for pensions. Eight central Corinthian columns, the largest in the world, dominate a great hall big enough to contain a 15-story building.

Today the eccentric old edifice is home to the National Building Museum, the only institution in the U.S. dedicated to architectural achievements. On permanent display are exhibits dedicated to D.C. and the Pension Building itself. Recent temporary shows covered the humble, classic American barn and the aftermath of the April 1995 bombing of the federal building in Oklahoma City. Located at 401 F St. NW, the museum is open Mon.-Sat.10 a.m.-4 p.m., Sunday noon-4 p.m., and closed New Year's Day, Thanksgiving Day, and Christmas Day. Tel. (202) 272-2448 or fax 272-2564, or go to www.nbm.org on the Internet.

National Museum of American Art

Housed in an imposing edifice Philip Johnson once adjudged "the greatest building in the world," this eclectic collection of two centuries of American art includes truly marvelous works in the folk and ethnic traditions. See especially D.C. janitor James Hampton's *The Throne of the Third Heaven of the Nations' Millennium General,* the fruit of some 15 years of cementing together found objects such as light bulbs, electrical cables, and aluminum foil; and the spirit-rich *Man on Fire* by Luis Jiminez, sprung from a legend of an unlucky Aztec man put to the torch by 16th-century conquistadores. Additional offerings include giraffes constructed solely of bottlecaps and the psychedelic stain paintings of Morris Louis.

At 8th and G Sts. NW, the museum is open daily 10 a.m.-5:30 p.m., and closed Christmas Day. Admission is free. For more information write: Information—Smithsonian Information Center, 1000 Jefferson Dr. SW, Washington, DC 20560, call (202) 357-2700, or visit Web site: www.nmaa.si.edu.

National Portrait Gallery

Upon the site where D.C. designer Pierre L'Enfant once wished to build a national cathedral stands this fascinating gallery of America's heroes and villains portrayed in sculptures, paintings, and photographs. See especially the self-portraits serious and sardonic, the dizzying diversity of the Gallery of Notable Americans, and the treasury of 19th century black-and-white photography. At 8th and F Sts. NW, the gallery is open daily 10 a.m.-5:30 p.m., and closed Christmas Day. For information write: Information—Smithsonian Information Center, 1000 Jefferson Dr. SW, Washington, DC 20560, call (202) 357-2700, or visit www.npg.si.edu on the Internet.

The National Aquarium

Besides the usual collection of fish tank fare, the nation's oldest public aquarium offers belligerent fiddler crabs banging on the glass, sleepy sloe-eyed alligators, gape-mouthed eels exuding yellow slime, and pale moist axolotl salamanders. A touch pool allows young ones to gently maul the likes of horseshoe crabs, while a small sign puts the whole shark business in perspective: people kill and consume 4.5 million sharks each year, while sharks eat only a few dozen of us annually. The aquarium holds shark feedings Monday, Wednesday, and Saturday at 2 p.m., and piranha feedings Tuesday, Thursday, and Sunday. Regular hours are 9 a,m.-5 p.m. daily. Admission is $2 adults and 75 cents for children (ages 2-10) and seniors. The entrance to the aquarium, which is located in the basement of the Commerce Building, is on 14th Street. There is no street address, but you can write to: U.S. Department of Commerce Building, Room B-037, Washington, DC 20230, or call (202) 482-2825 for more information.

J. Edgar Hoover FBI Building

The free one-hour tour of FBI headquarters offers an extremely selective history of the bureau, including Dillinger, drugs, and a firearms demonstration by an FBI sharpshooter. Guided tours (mandatory) depart eight times a day Mon.-Fri. 8:45 a.m.-4:25 p.m. The tour entrance is on E St. NW, and reservations are recommended during peak seasons. Arrange your visit by phoning the bureau or through your congressional representative. For more information call (202) 324-3447. Closed federal holidays.

District of Columbia Courthouse

This Greek Revival edifice originally served as Washington's first city hall; it also saw duty as a hospital, patent office, and slave market. For well over a hundred years it's been the D.C. courthouse, the place where accused local lawbreakers are processed through the criminal justice system. In 1881, the lunatic assassin of President James Garfield, Charles Guiteau, babbled and bellowed through his trial in these rooms, then ascended the gallows reciting poetry until he was stopped by the rope. There are information pamphlets at the Public Information Desk to the left of the entrance. Stop here, after passing through the metal detector, for the lowdown on the juicy trials of the day. The courthouse is open Mon.-Fri.8:30 a.m.-5 p.m., and closed all federal holidays. Admssion is free. Located at 500 Indiana Ave. NW, Washington, DC 20001, tel. (202) 879-1010.

Old Post Office

When it was completed in 1899, this former home of the U.S. Postal Service was denounced as a monstrosity, "a cross between a cathedral and a cotton mill." These days, surrounded by the abominations of modern architecture, the old joint looks pretty good, housing federal workers for such agencies as the NEA and NEH. Take the glass elevator to the clock tower; at 315 vertical feet, it offers the finest aerial view in the city. It's located at 1100 Pennsylvania Ave.NW, tel.(202) 289-4224; admission to the building is free. The tower is open daily April-Oct. 8 a.m.-11 p.m., Nov.-March 9 a.m.-5 p.m.; the shops are open Mon.-Sat.10 a.m.-8 p.m., Sunday noon-6 p.m., closed Christmas Day.

National Archives

Preservationists of "the nation's memory," archivists here determine the worth of billions of documents generated annually by the world's busiest government. Pride of place goes to the Declaration of Independence, the Constitution, and the Bill of Rights, which are displayed daily, then mechanically lowered into a 50-ton vault to shield them from the dangers of vandals and nuclear attack. Famous primarily as a center of genealogical research, the Archives have in recent years become a pilgrimage site for those wishing to listen to Nixon's Watergate tapes. At 8th St.and Constitution Ave. NW, the Archives are open daily 10 a.m.- 5:30 p.m., sometimes extended during summer, and closed Christmas Day. Reservations are required, and are available by appointment only. Call (202) 501-5205 for details. For more general information write to the archives (zip code 20408), or call (202) 501-5400.

Ford's Theatre National Historic Site

In one of history's tragic ironies, President Abraham Lincoln was shot in a box in Ford's Theatre just five days after Confederate Gen. Robert E. Lee surrendered at Appomattox. Today the basement of the theater is a shrine to the martyred president, while upstairs the show goes on. See the bronze of a slumping, exhausted Lincoln; the simple contents of his pockets at the time of his death, from an Irish linen handkerchief to Confederate money; and the .44 single-shot derringer used by assassin John Wilkes Booth. Located at 511 10th St. NW, the theater is closed to visitors during rehearsals and matinees (usually Thursdays and weekends), but the museum is always open. Admission to the museum is free. For theater box office information call (202) 347-4833. The box office is open daily 9 a.m.-5 p.m., and closed Christmas Day. For more information write: Information—Superintendent, National Capital Parks Central, Washington, DC 20242, tel. (202) 485-9880, or visit www.nps.gov/foth on the Internet.

Petersen House

After his shooting by John Wilkes Booth, Abraham Lincoln was carried from his box in Ford's Theatre across 10th St. to the boardinghouse of William Petersen, a German-born tailor. Today, three rooms of the Petersen domicile are preserved as they were that night in April 1865; the front bedroom that Secretary of War

*Ford's Theatre,
c. 1865*

Edwin Stanton turned into a temporary White House; the parlor where Mary Lincoln waited and prayed; and the room where Lincoln died, which had been commandeered from William T. Carl, a young man out on the town that night celebrating the end of the war. The house is open daily 9 a.m.- 5 p.m., and closed Christmas Day. Admission is free. For more information write: Information—Superintendent, National Capital Parks Central, 900 Ohio Dr. SW, Washington, DC 20242, or call (202) 485-9880.

ADAMS-MORGAN

Adams-Morgan is D.C.'s version of New York City's East Village, only smaller. Most of this teeming quarter's nightlife takes place along two main drags: Columbia Rd. and 18th St., joined together in a V at their northern apex. A little bit tony, a little bit tawdry, Adams-Morgan a place where Washingtonians feel free to step outside the bars of their pin-striped suits.

Where yankee-doodle Washington is built on a monumental scale, Adams-Morgan is a concrete redoubt, an urban refuge. The streets actually become more crowded after 6 p.m., while the rest of D.C. rolls up its sidewalks. Here it's safe to be neurotic, to be gay, to be straight, to stay up late, to drink too much, to pretend.

Once a row of tired Ethiopian restaurants scrunched cheek-by-jowl into red brick townhouses, Adams-Morgan has hip-hopped into its own over the last decade, as Washington discovered that there was life after legislation. This is an immigrant neighborhood, a largely Hispanic enclave that is also home to wealthy Anglos and a veritable United Nations of other ethnicities.

When the world starts getting you down, there's room enough for two (and plenty more) on Adams-Morgan's roofs, rooftop partying is de rigueur. There's Perry's, for instance, a restaurant at 1811 Columbia Rd., tel. (202) 234-6218, that offers sashimi by starlight. There's also Roxanne's at 2319 18th St., where you can enjoy an eclectic Cajun cuisine under the stars.

One way to get your bearings in Adams-Morgan is by zigging and zagging. Best to zig down to 18th St. and to zag up to Columbia Rd. Such an erratic route will take you up and down (mostly up, for Adams-Morgan is hilly) delightfully leafy lanes lined with elegant townhouses, many of which come with huge picture windows.

A big problem is that there are no convenient Metro stops. It's a long walk from the nearest station, DuPont Circle, to the heart of the quarter. It's best to pay for taxis or, better yet, let a friend drive: finding a parking spot in Adams-Morgan has been known to reduce would-be visitors to tears. There is one convenient 200-space parking lot at 2419 18th St., tel. (202) 452-9600. But beware—while it's easy to get into the lot before 8 p.m., it's also easy to get parked in after 10 p.m.

Club Heaven, 2327 18th St. NW, tel. (202) 667-4355, provides an antidote for the fiendish parking. Appropriately, Club Heaven shares its townhouse venue with—you guessed it—Club Hell, downstairs. (And just in case you're wondering about the afterlife, Club Hell has the trendier crowd—and a larger dance floor.)

In addition, Adams-Morgan offers a wide variety of good restaurants and entertainment. This is the only area of town apart from Georgetown where it's possible to shop, relax over drinks, then walk down the street to find dinner. Afterwards, you can stroll up the block to a club to close the night, unwind with some dancing or just relax and listen to good music.

UPPER NORTHWEST

A series of residential neighborhoods, arranged in a succession of rings, gives the Upper Northwest its own distinct character and allure. Arguably, **DuPont Circle** marks the center of the area that fills the district's borders between Adams-Morgan and the Maryland state line. On one side of the circle sits some of the city's great think tanks, such as the Brookings Institution, 1775 Massachusetts Ave., established in 1927. Near the circle along Connecticut Ave., you'll find good restaurants in a variety of price ranges. To the north, **Kramerbooks & Afterwords,** 1517 Connecticut Ave., NW, tel. (202) 387-1462, is a D.C. institution. The bookstore offers a cafe in back, where, after browsing the aisles you can hear live music Wed.-Saturday. On Friday and Saturday, Kramerbooks stays open 24 hours for late-night literary binges.

One ripple out from DuPont Circle is **Woodley Park,** known principally for the National Zoo (see below). The area also claims to be home to more international restaurants than anywhere in D.C., which in this international metropolis is saying a lot.

Beyond Woodley Park is exclusive **Cleveland Park,** where former President Grover Cleveland built his "summer White House," and consequently lent his name to the neighborhood.

Today, the area is home to former Sen. Bill Bradley, Jim Lehrer of the News Hour, and satirist Mark Russell. If you're here at lunchtime, try the local Irish pub **Ireland's Four Provinces,** 3412 Connecticut Ave. NW, tel. (202) 244-0860, serving shepherd's pie and Irish brew.

Heading farther north, the campus of **American University,** alma mater of Willard Scott and novelist Anne Beattie, covers 84 acres in the area known as Tenleytown. The final reaches of the Upper Northwest extend out to Friendship Heights and Chevy Chase at the border of Maryland. **Friendship Heights** is a busy entertainment/shopping district offering the tony urban mall known as Mazza Gallery, and **Chevy Chase** is an exclusive address where you'll find one of the best movie palaces in Washington: the **Cineplex Odeone Avalon 2,** built in 1925, with 679 seats in the main theatre.

Washington National Cathedral

Medieval cathedrals frequently required centuries to complete, so perhaps it's not so embarassing that 199 years passed before this one was considered finished. In 1791, D.C. designer Pierre L'Enfant envisioned a "church intended for national purposes, and assigned to the special use of no particular Sect or denomination, but equally open to all." In 1893 Congress finally allocated funds for the edifice, and in 1990 the last stone was placed atop a west front pinnacle.

The cathedral is a truly magnificent structure, and its stone and wood carvings, stained glass, and metalwork are unsurpassed on these shores. The Gothic wonderment is constructed of Indiana limestone, with all details carved from the walls by hand. High above dwell angels, gargoyles, and grotesques; outside, visitors to the 57-acre grounds can stroll a medieval walled garden of roses and herbs. The cathedral is located at Massachusetts and Wisconsin Sts. NW, tel. (202) 537-6207. There is no admission fee to the cathedral, which is open Mon.-Sat.10 a.m.-4:30 p.m., Sunday 7:30 a.m.-4:30 p.m. Services are held at 7:30 a.m. every day, and the Chapel of the Good Shepherd is always open.

National Zoological Park

Under the auspices of the Smithsonian Institution, the National Zoo is one of the nation's more humane animal parks. Over three miles of trails wander past 5,000 animals caged on 163 hilly acres at the edge of Rock Creek. Visitors will find no class hierarchy here: paramecia and leafcutter ants are displayed as proudly as lions, tigers, and bears. An enclave of naked mole rats even get exposure via the Internet with the zoo's live naked mole rat Web-cam (www.si.edu/organiza/museums/zoo/hilights/webcams/molerat1/nmcam.htm).

Visitors can "ooh" and "aah" over such rarities as giant pandas and Komodo dragons, watch the cuttlefish transform from a mass of transparent jelly into a voracious predator, or ponder the ways animals use their brains described in the Think Tank exhibit. The rainforest environment of the Amazonia exhibit approaches D.C.'s own August heat and humidity. Admission to the zoo, at 3001 Conncecticut Ave. NW, is free, though there is a somewhat steep charge for onsite parking (maximum $10.50); tel. (202) 673-4800, Web site: www.si.edu/natzoo. The zoo grounds are open daily April 15-Oct.15, 8 a.m.-8 p.m., Oct. 16-April 14, 8 a.m.-6 p.m. (closed Christmas Day). Zoo buildings are open 9 a.m.-4:30 p.m. year-round.

Rock Creek Park

These 1,750 acres were purchased in 1890 by Congress for the "pleasant valleys and ravines, primeval forests and open fields, its running waters, its rocks clothed with rich ferns and mosses, its repose and tranquility, its light and shade, its ever-varying shrubbery, its beautiful and extensive views." Rock Creek Park still offers all that, as well as over one million wildflowers.

Bordering the Upper Northwest to the east, the city's largest park comprises a magical ribbon of green. Here hikers, horse-back riders, and joggers have the right of way, and on Sunday, with long sections of the park's roads closed to cars, they take control. Rock Creek Park offers some 15 miles of hiking trails, from toddler-friendly to quite rugged. Trail maps are available at both the park headquarters and at the nature center. An 11-mile bike path, from the Lincoln Memorial to the Maryland border, runs the full length of the park; it's paved the entire distance, and closed to vehicular traffic on weekends and holidays. Numerous access points make visiting the park on bike or on foot an easy day's outing. Horse rentals ($21) are available at the **Rock Creek Park Horse Center,** 5100 Glover Rd. NW, tel. (202) 362-0118.

The cemetery in Rock Creek Park is the oldest in the city and home to one of the most arresting statues in D.C. In 1883, Marian Adams, wife of historian Henry Adams, downed enough photographic chemicals to end her own life. Her husband interred her in Rock Creek Cemetery, then commissioned sculptor Augustus Saint-Gaudens to create a monument in bronze, instructing that "no attempt is to be made to make it intelligible to the average mind." When the work was ready the gravekeepers were horrified, saying they wanted no part of it. But Adams persisted, and the cloaked, hooded lady was set among holly and ivy in section E. Adams called it *The Peace of God,* the sculptor *The Mystery of the Hereafter,* but most visitors agree with Mark Twain that the most appropriate designation is simply *Grief.*

The cemetery is located on Rock Creek Church Rd. NW and open daily 7:30 a.m.-dusk. Admission is free. The nature center is open Tues.-Sunday 9 a.m.-5 p.m. Pierce Mill, a working cornmeal and wheatflour gristmill, is open Wed.-Sun. 9 a.m.-5 p.m. Here visitors can purchase the mill's products, make the flour and meal themselves in small hand-held grinders, or just come in and watch. Both the nature center and mill are closed on major holidays. For more information write: Rock Creek Park Superintendent, 5000 Glover Rd. NW, Washington, DC 20015, call (202) 426-6832, or visit Web site: www.nps.gov/rocr.

Society of the Cincinnati

Established in 1783 by George Washington and the officers in his Continental Army, the Society still limits membership to only one direct descendant per original officer. For 15 hours each week (Tues.-Sat. 1-4 p.m.; closed federal holidays), the society's beautiful beaux arts mansion is thrown open to the public, and visitors may walk among elegant furnishings and priceless artwork, or peruse the excellent Revolutionary-era reference library. Admission to Anderson House, 2118 Massachusetts Ave. NW, tel. (202) 785-2040, is free.

GEORGETOWN

President Kennedy lived in Georgetown 1957-61 during his pre-presidential term as a U.S. senator and before becoming president. Syndicated columnist George Will keeps his office here. The latter was a New Deal Democrat, then later a staunch Republican. Still, they hailed from the same place, a neighborhood sandwiched between Rock Creek and the Potomac River known as Georgetown. No one is certain who named the quarter: some it was named after one of the King Georges, or one or another of the area's founders. Georgetown didn't become part of the District of Columbia until after the Civil War.

Since then, it has had ups and downs, good times and bad, but the present moment is decidedly up. Between the peaceful towpaths of the old C&O Canal to the south and what has come to be known as "the most civilized square mile in America" to the north abides some of the most expensive real estate on earth. An average-sized, even smallish house in Georgetown runs into the millions of dollars. Like Beverly Hills in Los Angeles, the homes in Georgetown are pedigreed, known by their former famous owners, like the house at 3017 N St. where Jacqueline Kennedy lived for a time.

History and personality blend in Georgetown's streets. Many great authors, such as Katherine Anne Porter and Sinclaire Lewis, have called the neighborhood home. Herman Wouk still lives here, as does celebrity biographer Kitty Kelly. Historical figures such as Alexander Graham Bell called Georgetown home, as did Dr. Walter Reed, the American Army surgeon who proved yellow fever was carried by mosquitoes.

Georgetown's main crossroads are M St. and Wisconsin Ave., a bustling area of boutiques, jazz clubs, and good restaurants. Just south of Wisconsin on M St., **Canal Square**, built in 1842, was first used as a grain warehouse, then as a cooperage, and finally as home to a census bureau contractor known as the Tabulating Machine Company. Though its heaquarters are currently in Armonk, NY, you'll recognize the company's more recent acronym: IBM.

From Canal Square, a block south of M St. toward the Potomac you'll find lock number 4 of the **Chesapeake & Ohio Canal.** Operated by National Park Service rangers dressed in 19th century costumes, a barge takes visitors under the bridge and through the locks on a half-mile mule-towed journey through the past. A bit farther south is **Washington Harbor,** known by some as "Baghdad on the Potomac." This terraced extravaganza is a riverfront development of condominiums, shops, and restaurants. Once something of a joke, the Harbor has grown into a delightful and popular setting of nightspots. With lots of fun restaurants, gushing fountains, bright lights, fluttering flags, fabulous river views, and a romantic promenade, the harbor makes for great people-watching.

Despite being 20 minutes by foot from the nearest Metro station, Georgetown definitely deserves, and can easily consume, a day or more of touring. Walk the historic homes, idle at Dumbarton Oaks, and dine in town.

Dumbarton Oaks

The crown jewel of Georgetown is Dumbarton Oaks, 1703 32nd St. NW, tel. (202) 342-3200, a former estate that is now a museum and 43-acre garden spot. In 1944, as WW II moved into its final climactic phase, the leaders of the U.S., Britain, China, and the Soviet Union met here to lay the groundwork for what was to become the United Nations.

For visitors to Dumbarton Oaks, it's easiest to think of the estate in three parts. The first is the 16-acre compound owned by Harvard University and known as the Dumbarton Oaks Research Library and Collection. Here you'll find the estate's renowned collection of some 1,500 eastern Mediterranean artifacts dating from 330 to1453 A.D. The library holds more than 12,000 Byzantine coins, one of the most complete collections in the world. Next comes the 27-acre Dumbarton Oaks Park, tel. (202) 338-8278 (open daily until dusk). Ten acres of the park are given over to one of the finest examples of European-styled formal gardens in America, with nearly 1,000 rose bushes, 10 pools and nine fountains. The entrance is on R street, and it's open April-Oct.; $2 admission, $1 seniors and children. The remaining 17 acres of the Dumbarton Oaks estate are covered by well-groomed parkland.

Georgetown University

Another cornerstone of the community is the 104-acre main campus of Georgetown Univer-

the Old Stone House, c. 1896

sity, one of the nation's premier schools for law and international affairs, and the oldest Catholic university in the nation. Free maps and brochures on the campus and environs are available at the main gate, 37th and O Sts. NW. Be sure to visit the Gaston Hall collections of Victorian dolls and Indian artifacts. For more information on the university, check out www.georgetown.edu or call (202) 687-5084.

Old Stone House

The oldest standing structure in the city, the house was built in 1765 by a cabinetmaker named Christopher Layman in what was then the Town of George. Over the years the dwelling also served as boardinghouse, tavern, bordello, and artists' studio. Today its low doorways and lumpy beds are preserved as a relic of working-class life in pre-Revolutionary times. Rumor that Pierre L'Enfant worked here while designing D.C. helped secure congressional protection for the structure in the 1950s. It is said that children are those most likely to encounter the many ghosts inhabiting the structure. The house at 3051 M St. NW, tel. 202-426-6851, is open daily 9:30 a.m.-5 p.m., and closed Christmas and New Year's Day. Admission is free.

EAST OF THE CAPITOL

Kenilworth Aquatic Gardens

This 12-acre haven along the Anacostia River is the only U.S. national park devoted exclusively to water plants. Beginning in 1880, one-armed Civil War veteran Walter Shaw and his industrious daughter methodically dredged a series of ponds here, growing lilies and lotuses that they marketed to plant-happy Washingtonians. The government acquired the property in 1938, and today a network of trails crisscrosses levees separating dozens of bright marshy ponds.

Don't miss the lotus, once thought to be extinct, which was grown from 900-year-old seeds unearthed in a dry Tibetan riverbed; be on the lookout too for frogs, salamanders, snakes, mallards, and turtles. Admission to the gardens, located at 900 Anacostia Ave. NE, tel. (202) 426-6907, is free. The entrance is just off Anacostia Ave. near Quarles and Douglas Streets. Kenilworth Aquatic Gardens is open daily 7 a.m.-4:15 p.m., and closed Christmas and New Year's Day. Tours are offered on summer weekends and holidays at 9 a.m., 11 a.m., and 1 p.m., and evening walks can be made by arrangement.

United States National Arboretum

Along the Anacostia River lies this 444-acre natural jewel, featuring stunning collections of bonsai, dwarf conifer, dogwood, and azalea. There are nine miles of paved roads, but it's more enjoyable to park somewhere and get out and walk. At the center of the arboretum are 22 ghostly Corinthian columns rising from a grassy knoll; for 125 years they supported the east portico of the Capitol. Other highlights of the arboretum include the National Herb Garden, containing over 800 useful herbs from around the world, and the National Grove of State Trees, a perfect place for picnicking. The arboretum staff is currently attempting to reintroduce bald eagles to the nation's capital. Admission to the arboretum is free, 3501 New York Ave. NE, tel. (202) 245-2726, fax 245-4575, Web site: www.ars-grin.gov/ars/Beltsville/na/. Hours are Mon.-Fri. 8 a.m.-5 p.m., Sat.-Sun. and holidays 10 a.m.-5 p.m., closed Christmas Day.

ACCOMMODATIONS

For the most part, accommodations in the District are pricey. There are exceptions to that rule, though, and your options increase dramatically if you consider staying outside of D.C. in Maryland or Virginia. Some D.C. hotels offer discounts when you make reservations through Capitol Reservations, Web site: www.capitol-reservations.com.

en central staircase groans loudly at the lightest tread. Nevertheless, the willfully eccentric proprietors of the four-story ex-senator's home at **2005 Columbia,** tel. (202) 265-4006, offer what may be the best rates in the city. A favorite of students, conferees, and Bohemians from overseas, 2005 Columbia has 11 air-conditioned rooms (nonsmoking available) for $30 s, $40 d.

BUDGET: UNDER $35

The **Washington, DC Hostel** is centrally located downtown at 11th and K Sts. NW, near the Smithsonian Museums, the White House, and other attractions. Only a three-block walk from Metro Center station, the renovated eight-story hotel offers 250 beds, a kitchen and laundry facilities, lockers/baggage storage area, and wheelchair accessibility. For night owls, the hostel offers 24-hour access; there are also tours, movies, and other special programs. Rates run $18-21. The D.C. Hostel is open year-round and private rooms are available on a limited basis. Groups are also welcome but reservations are required, tel. (202) 737-2333, fax 737-1508, or e-mail DChostel@erols.com. Reservations are accepted by phone or fax with 24-hour advance notice and credit card confirmation, and can also be made using the Hosteling International toll-free number (within the US only); have your credit card ready and dial (800) 909-4776, then enter the D.C. Hostel 2-digit access code—04—to be connected.

In another low-coster, the rooms are spartan, the beds sometimes lumpy, the plumbing occasionally scaldingly unpredictable, and the wood-

MODERATE: $60-85

Located close to DuPont Circle, the cozy **Tabard Inn,** 1739 N St. NW, tel. (202) 331-8528, fax 785-6173, is an unspoiled mark of good taste. This country inn in the heart of Washington offers rooms with shared baths priced as low as $65. Comparable doubles run about $90, but don't be fooled by the bargain. The Tabard's indoor-outdoor restaurant is without peer in this price range.

The **Adams Inn,** 1744 Lanier Place NW, tel. (202) 745-3600, fax 332-5867, consists of three brick townhouses and a carriage house hidden away on a leafy residential street two blocks from the heart of the Adams-Morgan district. Built around 1913, the inn has a definite Victorian feel, from the furnishings to the parlors to the rules: no phones, no TVs, and no smoking. Guests will find plenty of books and games, though, and the lavish continental breakfast included in the price of your stay features truly heaping portions. Rooms ($55 s, $75 d) are available with private or shared baths (the latter on average about $10 less per person). As elsewhere in Adams-Morgan, parking is limited.

The charming, inexpensive **Kalorama Guest House,** 1854 Mintwood Place NW, tel. (202) 745-

3600 or (800) 578-6807, fax (202) 332-5867, is comprised of six Victorian townhouses filled with creative antique furnishings, like brass beds and Oriental rugs, set off by fresh flowers. Enjoy a sherry in front of the fire or lemonade on the patio, then take the short walk to many of the finest restaurants in the city. Really two venues, one at this location in Adams-Morgan and another in Washington's pleasant Woodley Park neighborhood, the guest house offers 31 air-conditioned rooms ($65 s, $75 d), all nonsmoking. Reservations with full payment are required.

Located a few blocks from the White House, the **Center City Hotel,** 1201 13th St. NW, tel. (202) 682-5300 or (800) 458-2817, fax (202) 371-9624, offers 100 traditional-style guest rooms at decent rates ($69 s $79 d). There are free movies in all the rooms, refrigerators in some, and a restaurant on the premises. Non-smoking rooms are available. In regard to pets, the front desk says, "We take small animals, but no snakes!"

The venerable, friendly **Harrington Hotel,** tel. (202) 628-8140 or (800) 424-8532, fax (202) 347-3924, is located downtown at 436 11th St. NW, only two blocks from the Smithsonian. The excellent location makes the Harrington a particular favorite of international travelers. The Harrington also offers a restaurant and pool, and is wheelchair accessible. The 265 rooms and 25 suites must be booked in advance. Parking is available at a lot next door.The large rooms ($70 d/s) are clean and comfortable.

The **Carlyle Suites,** 1731 New Hampshire Ave. NW, tel. (202) 234-3200 or (800) 964-5377, fax (202) 387-0085, is a wonder. The bold exterior and accompanying interior frills are pure art deco, a motif abandoned only in the suites, which are washed in pastels splashed with charcoal and gray. The on-site Neon Cafe is stuck firmly in the 1940s: here you can dig into a large steak while swinging to the sounds of live weekend jazz. Located on a pleasant residential street near DuPont Circle, the eight-story Carlyle features170 guest suites ($70 s/d) with sitting areas, kitchenettes and limited complimentary parking.

EXPENSIVE: $85-100

The Savoy Suites Georgetown, 2505 Wisconsin Ave. NW, tel. (202) 337-9700 or (800) 944-5377, fax (202) 337-3644, features fine, large rooms. The 150 suites, some with excellent views of the D.C. skyline, run $79 s, $89 d. The hotel restaurant, a favorite of the locals, offers outdoor dining in season and also serves as gallery space for area artists. Area transportation services are available at the Savoy, including a D.C. Metro shuttle.

Located hard by the Lincoln Memorial, the Mall, and George Washington University, the **State Plaza Hotel,** 2117 E St. NW, tel. (202) 861-8200 or (800) 424-2859, fax (202) 659-8601, is a favorite among those Kennedy Center performers who aren't staying at the posh and expensive Watergate. The 218 suites ($90 s/d) are pleasant and spacious, with full kitchens. The State Plaza also offers a restaurant on premises, a fitness center, and coin-operated washing machines for those taking a longer stay. Children under 18 stay without charge. For those needing to get out of the city or wishing to visit Arlington Cemetery, the State Plaza is conveniently located just blocks from Memorial Bridge.

The **Washington Courtyard,** 900 Connecticut Ave. NW, tel. (202) 332-9300 or (800) 842-4211, fax (202) 328-7039, is surprisingly affordable for all that it offers: chandeliers in the lobby, mahogany armoires, and phones with modems, for starters. The hotel is also host to the pricey **Claret's** for eats and the club-like **Bailey's** for drinks. Children under 18 sleep with their parents for free. Prices at this 147-room hotel range from $89 s to $160 d depending on the season and availability. Located in Kalorama, an upscale residential neighborhood near embassy row, the hotel hosts many foreign diplomats, who undoubtedly enjoy the marble baths and fax machines of the executive rooms. All guests can enjoy the outdoor pool and the fitness room.

PREMIUM: $100-150

International visitors feel welcome at the **Swiss Inn,** 1204 Massachusetts Av. NW, tel. (202) 371-1816 or (800) 955-7947, by managers who speak a plethora of European languages. The inn's seven air-conditioned apartments ($98 s, $108 d) feature a fridge, bath, and kitchenettes; weekly rates can dip under $75. If you need a ride from the airport or bus stop just give the place a call, and a staff member will come pick you up.

The friendly, 10-story **Hampshire Hotel,** 1310 New Hampshire Ave. NW, tel. (202) 296-7600, fax (202) 293-2476, has 82 spacious rooms, most with two double beds ($99 s, $109 d). This DuPont Circle hotel also features a health club, free in-room movies, and "smart phones" offering access to a bewildering variety of services. All of the rooms allow you to eat in privacy in the kitchen units, which include coffee makers, refrigerators, and microwaves.

D.C.'s only waterfront hotel, the **Channel Inn,** 650 Water St. SW, tel. (202) 554-2400 or (800) 368-5668, fax (202) 863-1164, peers out over Washington Channel towards the island of East Potomac Park. Each of the 98 rooms ($110 s, $120 d) offers a balcony, and some provide fine views of the boats in the harbor. Try the raw bar at the hotel restaurant, the Engine Room.

Situated only five blocks west of the White House, the **Hotel Lombardy,** 2019 I St. NW, tel. (202) 828-2600 or (800) 424-5486, fax (202) 872-0503, provides sumptuous accommodations including cherrywood furnishings, dustrose carpeting, and fine art on the walls. Most of the 85 rooms ($115 s, $130 d) offer fully equipped kitchens, but the Lombardy features a fine restaurant as well. Rates are reduced sharply in the off-season.

Located just two blocks from DuPont Circle, the **Canterbury Hotel,** 733 N St. NW, tel. (202) 393-3000 or (800) 424-2950, fax (202) 785-9581, occupies a site where Theodore Roosevelt once lived with his large family. The lobby is lined with hunting prints, and you can heave darts in the homey English pub, which serves appropriate dinners of fish and chips and finger sandwiches. The 10-story edifice features 99 suites ($125 s, $135 d), breakfast included. Junior suites with kitchenettes are also available; children aged 12 and under stay free. In a town where parking is at a premium, this snug hotel has its own lot.

The **Barcelo Washington Hotel,** 2121 P St. NW, tel. (202) 293-3100 or (800) 333-3333, fax (202) 331-9719, is the first D.C. venture of the Mallorca-based Barcelo chain, offering European service at decent American prices. The 275 marble and mahogany decorated rooms run $135 s, $155 d. The hotel restaurant, Gabriel,

is excellent, and the hotel bar is popular with locals. Enjoy swimming in the roof-top pool while watching the stars.

The 150-year-old **Willard Intercontinental Hotel,** 1401 Pennsylvania Ave. NW, tel. (202) 628-9100, fax 637-7326, is the grand dame of Pennsylvania Avenue, located just around the corner from the White House. Its architect, H.J. Hardenberg, designed New York's prestigious Plaza, but did his best work in Washington. The hotel also features the locally popular Occidental Grill (see below).

LUXURY: $150 AND UP

The 10-story **Doubletree Guest Suites,** 2500 Pennsylvania Ave. NW, tel. (202) 333-8060 or (800) 222-8733, fax (202) 338-3818, offers 123 spacious one- and two-bedroom suites, $149 s, $164 d, with kitchens. If you're absolutely determined not to get away from it all, this is the place: some rooms offer two telephones and two TVs.

The Gaelic place in DC—the **Phoenix Park Hotel,** 520 N. Capitol St. NW, tel. (202) 638-6900 or (800) 824-5419, fax (202) 393-3236—is nine stories of Irish linen, hospitality, finery, and food. The Phoenix Park features 84 rooms ($150 s/d) and regular live entertainment, both scheduled and unscheduled. AAA members can secure drastic rate reductions.

Built by D.C. hotel magnate Harry Wardman, **The Jefferson,** 1200 16th St. NW, tel. (202) 347-2200 or (800) 368-5966, fax (202) 223-9039, offers 68 air-conditioned rooms ($160 s, $175 d). Hailed by some as one of the top 10 hotels in the world, it's the sort of place where, even after a single visit, the staff will recall every detail of your preferences and peculiarities. A favorite since 1923 of arty types such as Vivien Leigh, Van Cliburn, and Leonard Bernstein, the hotel's legendary discretion also made it a favorite of reporters such as Edward R. Murrow and H. L. Mencken.

The **Henley Park Hotel,** 26 Massachusetts Ave. NW, tel. (202) 638-5200 or (800) 222-8474 , fax (202) 638-6740, is a converted 1918 seven-story Tudor structure featuring faux 18th-century furnishings, a facade bristling with 119 gargoyles, and a telephone in every bathroom. The 90 air-conditioned rooms at the Henley Park run

$165 s, $185 d. Ask if there's a four-poster bed available, and be sure to take afternoon tea in the Wilkes Room.

The aristocratic edifice of the **Hay-Adams,** 1 Lafayette Square NW, tel. (202) 638-6600 or (800) 424-5054, fax (202) 638-3803, was erected in 1927, the work of tireless D.C. hotel builder Harry Wardman, who intended it "to provide for the socially elite as well as men who loom large in the country's life." It was named for the structures it replaced, the homes of McKinley cabinetmember John Hay and historian Henry Adams. Years before, Confederate arch-spy Rose Greenhow plied her duplicitous trade on this site. Each of the 117 rooms ($210 s/d) offers luxurious antiques, ornaments, and amenities.

The venerable **Stouffer Rennaissance Mayflower Hotel,** 1127 Connecticut Ave. NW, tel. (202) 347-3000 or (800) 468-3571, fax (202) 466-9082, was snapped up by the Stouffer chain in 1991 for a cool $100 million. Formerly the haunt of political stalwarts such as Huey P. Long and J. Edgar Hoover, the stately Mayflower is Washington's answer to New York City's Waldorf-Astoria. Lines of black limos parked around the hotel signal that government dignitaries have dropped by for a meal or are staying for the night in one of 581 air-conditioned rooms ($230 s/d). Hoover arrived at the Mayflower Grille Room every day of the last 20 years of his life for his regular meal of chicken soup, grapefruit, and cottage cheese. Franklin Delano Roosevelt wrote "the only thing we have to fear is fear itself" in suite 776.

For a price, you can stay in the ritzy hotel wing of the complex that brought down a president. On June 17, 1972, Watergate security guard Frank Wills surprised five men burgling the offices of the Democratic National Committee; a little over two years later the burglars' employer, Richard Nixon, was a disgraced ex-president on his way home to San Clemente. The **Watergate Hotel,** 2650 Virginia Ave. NW, tel. (202) 965-2300 or (800) 424-2736, fax (202) 337-7915, has long been a favorite of the high and mighty—Attorney General John Mitchell, who authorized the Watergate break-in, maintained an apartment here, as did would-be chief executive Robert Dole. Many of the actors, dancers, and musicians who appear at the Kennedy Center across the street enjoy shorter stays in one of the hotel's 148 rooms (270 s, $295 d). On the weekend, singles and doubles start at $155.

FOOD

POLITICALLY CORRECT

Washington's answer to New York's Sardi's, **Palm,** 1225 19th St. NW, tel. (202) 293-9091, features an earnest menu that only occasionally misses the mark. Steaks are another matter—get one. Enjoy the brilliant waiters and see what it feels like to be treated as a powerbroker. Reservations are recommended and make sure you ask for the main dining room.

In French, **La Colline,** 400 N. Capitol St. NW, tel. (202) 737-0400, means "The Hill," as in Capitol Hill. The food is good, the service is solid, but the restaurant itself sometimes suffers from a slight case of the conventional. There always seems to be enough room, so reservations are not usually necessary.

Relaxed but stately, the **Old Ebbitt Grill,** 675 15th St. NW, tel. (202) 347-4801, offers wonderful service and very good food. The bar is long on character and the Kumamoto oysters are magnificent. Call for reservations and ask for the main room to catch the power-lunch scene. Try breakfast; it's a pleasant surprise.

When White House staff members take a break to celebrate a victory, the courtly **Occidental Grill,** 4th & Pennsylvania (part of the Willard Hotel complex, see above), tel. (202) 783-1475, known locally as the "Oxie," is their destination. Straighten your tie, make your reservations and admire the century-old trophy wall of 1,800 photographs portraying Washington's famous faces. Don't miss out on the martini with quail eggs.

Bullfeathers, 410 First St. SW, tel. (202) 543-5005, is beery, a bit overpriced (but still cheap by D.C. standards) and loud, so have a drink at the bar if there's room. It's hamburgers for lunch, and happy hour for those in the nearby House office buildings who need to change their mood.

COLUMBIA HISTORICAL SOCIETY

L.T. Bridwell's Saloon and Oyster Bar, c. 1890

Georgia Brown's, 950 15th St. NW, tel. (202) 393-4499, is unique in Washington for its soul-food version of haute cuisine—collard greens and black-eyed peas never looked this fancy. Enjoy the handsome crowds, smashing ambience, and tantalizing menu descriptions.

EXPENSIVE

Roberto Donna is one of D.C.'s culinary kings. Elegantly Italian with an outdoor terrace to enjoy summer, Donna's flagship restaurant, **Galileo,** 1110 21st St. NW, tel. (202) 293-7191, is a showcase of Piedmontian cuisine. Make reservations for the chef's table and watch a great kitchen at work. **Kinkaid's,** 2000 Pennsylvania Ave. NW, tel. (202) 296-7700, is a gleaming red-white-and-blue answer to a French bistro. Seafood is Chef Bob Kinkaid's specialty—try the tapas or the Carolina shrimp with corn pudding and Virginia ham. **Makoto,** 4822 MacArthur Blvd., tel. (202) 298-6866, could well be among the top five Japanese restaurants in the United States. There are only four tables, with just 10 seats at the sushi bar. Try the "kaiseki" fixed-price (i.e., very expensive) dinner.

The setting at **I Ricchi,** 1220 19th St. NW, tel. (202) 835-0459, is romantic, the service is personable and relaxed (and very professional), and the food would make a Florentine jealous. This is hands down one of the finest and most consistent restaurants in the city.

Vidalia, 1990 M St. NW, tel. (202) 659-1990, is a southern belle of a restaurant known for its roasted Vidalia onion appetizer and manicured southern cooking. But don't be misled: the food here is elegant, imaginative and the menu is a palette for the palate. All this and valet parking, too.

With a glass enclosed wine "cellar" surrounding the newly renovated dining room, **Citronelle,** 3000 M St. NW, in the Latham Hotel, tel. (202) 625-2150, is one of Washington's finest restaurants. If you consider how French wines were reborn in the Napa Valley, then you might imagine how French cuisine would fare when transplanted and ripened to perfection here in Washington.

The setting for **1789,** 1226 36th St. NW, tel. (202) 965-1789, is a Federal-styled townhouse overlooking Georgetown. The oak-walled bar serves perfect silver bullets, while Chef Ris Lacoste conspires to fuse East and West with soys, peanut flavors, and lime marinades.

The **Bombay Club Restaurant,** 815 Connecticut Ave. NW, tel. (202) 659-3727, prepares the best Indian food in Washington, served in a setting as elegant as the best of India's famed Hill Stations. The service is magnificent and courtly, a relief from the earnest and overly eager professionalism in most city restaurants.

FUN

Ah, beer! Miles of beer. The **Brickskeller,** 1523 22nd St. NW, tel. (202) 293-1885, is Washington's monument to the mighty brew, packing over 800 varieties from 50 countries, including 400 from the U.S. alone. The owners claim to have served 5,000 different styles of suds since opening in 1957. Enjoy the upstairs game room and buckets of mussels at good prices.

The cuisine at **Jaleo,** 480 7th St. NW, tel. (202) 628-7949, is Spanish and the tapas are terrific. Heft a jug of sangria and settle in at this exuberant restaurant set in the renewed area near downtown known as Penn Quarter.

If a restaurant can be sexy and reasonably priced, **Sesto Senso,** 1214 18th St. NW, tel. (202) 785-9525, certainly qualifies. The people-watching is excellent, even at lunch: Mick Jagger eats here when in town. Chef Francesco Marra's menu ranges from fair to fine, so take care when ordering.

Kids love **Tony Cheng's Seafood Restaurant,** 619 H St. NW, tel. (202) 371-8669, is the home of kung fu cooking. Patrons circle the huge round griddle that dominates the restaurant, selecting foods from surrounding trays. Chefs then fry up the selections and swipe the finished dinners onto small round plates without dropping so much as a soybean.

Washington has good Ethiopian restaurants and **Red Sea,** 2463 18th St. NW, tel. (202) 483-5000, is one of the city's classics—outdoor dining in summer and great prices all year round. But remember, in Ethiopia, there's nothing between you and dinner, not even utensils. Every dish is finger-food, sopped up with yeasty *injera* bread.

If your imagination runs to the great backroom dives of Tijuana, **Cactus Cantina,** 3300 Wisconsin Ave. NW, tel. (202) 686-7222, manages the atmosphere without any of the grit. A fun place for Sunday brunch or a relaxed dinner.

Chef and owner Elizabeth Bright has managed to create a "real" restaurant in a neighborhood setting. **Coppi's Vigorelli,** 3421 Connecticut Ave. NW, tel. (202) 244-6437, is a local eatery that just happens to serve exquisite food—baby artichokes and sheep's milk cheese. This is serious dining, but casual too.

ENTERTAINMENT AND NIGHTLIFE

CLUBS

The classy **Habana Village**, 1834 Columbia Rd. NW, tel. (202) 462-6310, seemingly offers one activity for each of the its four rooms: food, entertainment, dance and a singles scene. The restaurant ambience is wicker and white wine. Cigars are allowed. Upstairs it's dance and the single-set, and above that two heavenly lounges (with Latin music, of course).

The eclectic heart of the late-night **Ritz Nightclub**, 919 E St. NW, tel. (202) 638-2582, beats to the sound of R&B. Five separate dance floors rock to reggae, go-go, hip-hop, R&B, salsa, soul, funk, and world music. Upstairs is a good lounge for singles, though the bar menu is pedestrian. Covers range up to $10, but big-time acts can raise the range—call ahead.

The timeless **One Step Down Jazz Club**, 2517 Pennsylvania Ave. NW, tel. (202) 955-7141, features live music six nights a week. The club, known locally as "The Step," holds the honor of being America's second oldest surviving jazz club, and seating is limited to 75. The club hosts big-name performers on the weekends and first-rate local talent during the week.

JAZZ/ROCK

A Georgetown landmark (assuming you can find it), **Blues Alley**, 1703 Wisconsin Ave. NW, tel. (202) 337-4141, is a side-street success. The 130-seat club attracts top acts to the town that gave birth to Duke Ellington. Covers are high, from $13 to over $40. Usually you get what you pay for. The **9:30 Club**, 815 V St. NW, concert line tel. (202) 393-0930, hosts the likes of Sean Lennon and Ziggy Marley. This pantheon of punk can hold up to 1,000 dancing, drinking guests within its walls. Parking is secure. Check out the downstairs bar to escape the crush. Visit the club's Web site: www.930.com for concert info and to view the beer list and bar menu.

Looking like nothing so much as a below-ground Paris jazz cave, tiny **U-topia**, 1418 U St. NW, tel. (202) 483-7669, has become a part of the city's U-street scene. U-topia offers a bit of everything, from take-out food to jazz and blues. Decorated with Kremlin leftovers, **State of the Union**, 1357 U St. NW, tel. (202) 588-8810, caters primarily to a younger crowd. The music is loud and there's lots of it. Jazz on Monday, reggae on Wednesday, and no two days are the same, so call ahead.

THEATER/CONCERTS

John F. Kennedy Center for the Performing Arts

This D.C. landmark, New Hampshire Ave. and Rock Creek Pkwy. NW, tel. (202) 467-4600, Web site: www.kennedy-center.org, is home to the **National Symphony Orchestra** as well as the **Washington Opera**. Founded in 1931, the National Symphony Orchestra has enjoyed a succession of brilliant musical directors—Antal Dorati, Mstislav Rostropvoich and, today, Leonard Slatkin. The NSO has promised to visit all 50 states, but don't miss them while in Washington.

Artistic Director Placido Domingo gives the 42-year-old Washington Opera Company the sex appeal and gravitas it so much deserves, making D.C. one of the nation's centers for song. The Kennedy Center Opera House and the center's Eisenhower Theatre, offers a prolific 74 performances of about eight operas annually.

The Kennedy Center also presents Broadway shows, repertory theatre, jazz, Shakespeare, and more. Free performances are held every day at 6 p.m. on the Millenium Stage featuring performers from the local area and around the world. Tours of the center's main theaters and selected art holdings are offered 10 a.m.-5 p.m. during the week, and 10 a.m.-1 p.m. on the weekends.

Other Venues

The **National Theatre**, 1321 Pennsylvania Ave. NW, tel. (202) 628-6161, is Washington's only Broadway-styled theatre, and the city's oldest cultural institution. "West Side Story" had its world premier here, as did "Hello Dolly." The

National Theatre,
c. 1890

theater's accoustics are excellent, but watch out for the distant seats in balcony Two. The Helen Hayes Gallery (a workshop-sized auditorium) hosts free events weekly.

The classical and Shakespearean adaptations for which the **Shakespeare Theatre,** 450 7th St. NW, tel. (202) 393-2700, is known are vivid and non-traditional productions, attracting such big-name actors and actresses as Harry Hamlin and Pat Carrol. The company regularly returns to more traditional presentations, such as Tennessee Williams's "Sweet Bird of Youth."

The **Folger Elizabethan Theatre,** 201 East Capitol St., SE, tel. (202) 544-7077, inside the Folger Library, is a full-scale recreation of a 250-seat Elizabethan theater. Here one can experience life as a "groundling," as well as allowing the children to discover something of the life of Elizabethans—including William Shakespeare.

From repertory classics to musicals, the three stages at the **Arena Stage Theatre,** 1101 6th St. NW, tel. (202) 488-3300, have pulled down 54 prestigious Helen Hayes theatre awards. The Arena was the first theater outside New York to capture a coveted Tony Award. James Earl Jones, Dianne Wiest, Kevin Kline, James Woods, and many others have graced its stages.

The **Woolly Mammoth Theatre,** 1401 Church St. NW, tel. (202) 234-6130, is Washington's off-Broadway-style venue for experimental cutting-edge works. Productions are first-rate and free parking is just across the street. Be careful when buying seats, as the quality of the views range widely.

The **Studio Theatre,** 14 & P Sts. NW, tel. (202) 232-7267, has grown more ambitious each year, and recently renovated its two theaters, the Mead and the Milton, to allow longer show runs. The productions are contemporary and first quality.

COMEDY

Best known as the home to the Capitol Steps, one of the nation's leading singing and performing satirical companies, **Chelsea's,** 1055 Thomas Jefferson St. NW, tel. (202) 298-8222, is a large dinner theater. The Steps are the main attraction, performing Friday and Saturday nights, and reservations are highly recommended. Call ahead for schedules and information on other performances.

Free jazz, blues (Friday and Saturday nights), and beer, **Mr. Henry's,** 1836 Columbia Rd. NW, tel. (202) 945-0744, has only one drawback: it closes at midnight. The burgers are good, and Mr. Henry's patio is a perfect place for a bite.

MORE EVENTS AND ENTERTAINMENT

Located in the heart of Chinatown, the **MCI Center,** 601 F St. NW, tel. (202) 628-3200, is not your typical sports venue. Home to the NHL's Washington Capitals, NBA's Wizards, and WNBA's Mystics, the center features a video center showcasing historic moments in athletics, a sportscasters hall of fame, a sporting goods store, and the Discovery Channel's three-story, 25,000-square-foot, interactive store.

Robert F. Kennedy Memorial Stadium, 2400 East Capitol St. SE, tel. (202) 547-9077, was once home to the Washington Redskins, but now hosts the city's pro soccer team, D.C. United, as well as rock concerts and the occasional outdoor convention. (The Redskins moved out of the city in 1996 and now play at **Jack Kent Cooke Stadium** in Landover, MD.) There are numerous ticket outlets in the D.C. area—check the local yellow pages or call the Redskins ticket office, 1050 Connecticut Ave. NW #1230, at (202) 546-2222. Parking at the stadium costs $12, but extra Metro buses and trains make the

journey to Maryland much more convenient. Call WMATA headquarters, tel. (202) 637-7000, TDD 638-3780, Web site: www.wmata.com, for information.

The 4,200-seat **Carter Barron Ampitheatre,** 4850 Colorado Ave. NW, tel. (202) 426-6837, could host a major tennis tournament but more often offers free concerts during summer. Located along the 16th Street corridor, it is also easily accessible. **Ford's Theatre,** 511 10th St. NW, tel. (202) 347-4833, the site of President Lincoln's last act and still a working theater, produces plays and musicals aimed at portraying the eclectic character of American life.

Washington is a monumental city, a city of lights. A fine way to capture the capital's dramatic sights is by cruising its feisty boundary, the Potomac River. **Odyssey Cruises,** 600 Water St. SW, tel. (202) 488-6000, offers river tours, serving lunch, brunch, or dinner on board. **The Wharf,** at 900 Water St. SW, offers another way to look at the Potomac, through its floating seafood stalls, shelling out everything from octopus to Carolina crabs. The river complex offers historic sites, quality restaurants, and fresh seafood.

TRANSPORTATION

GETTING THERE

By Air
The Washington area is served by three major airports: Dulles International Airport receives both international and domestic arrivals, National Airport primarily takes domestic arrivals, and Baltimore-Washington International Airport (BWI) also receives international and domestic flights. Expect between 20 and 45 minutes driving yourself or in a taxi to reach downtown from any of the airports, longer at rush-hour. Taxis downtown from Dulles (26 miles west in Virginia) and BWI (25 miles northeast in Maryland) will run $40-50, from National (four miles south of downtown) about $15.

Shuttle service is also available from all three airports. The Washington Flyer Express bus runs every 30-60 minutes from National (daily 6 a.m.-9 p.m.; $8 one-way, $14 roundtrip) and from Dulles (daily 5 a.m.-10 p.m.; $16 one-way,

$26 roundtrip) to its city terminal at 1517 K St. NW. There is another Washington Flyer Express bus from Dulles to the West Falls Church Metro Station every 20-30 minutes (Mon.-Fri. 6:30 a.m.-10:30 p.m., Sat.-Sun. 7:30 a.m.-10:30 p.m.; $8 one-way, $14 roundtrip). Trains run from this station to Metro Center station and on to downtown. Courtesy shuttles are available at the Washington Flyer terminal at Dulles to various downtown hotels. The BWI Super Shuttle offers hourly departures (daily 6 a.m.-1 p.m.; $19 one-way, $29 roundtrip) to the 1517 K St. NW terminal.

National is the only airport with direct Metrorail service. The station is across from North Concourse and links directly with Metro Center and other stops along the Yellow Line. From BWI, the MARC commuter line (Maryland Rail Commuter Service) offers peak-hour service (Mon.-Fri. only, 5:30 a.m.-8 a.m. and 3:45 p.m.-6:45 p.m.; $5 one-way, $8.75 roundtrip) to Union Station. Amtrak offers daily service ($12 one-way,

$24 roundtrip) from BWI to Union Station. Both MARC and Amtrak take about 45 minutes to reach the city. For more information on BWI, Dulles, and National Airports, see the Northern Virginia chapter.

GETTING AROUND

Most of the major sightseeing highlights in central Washington—the Mall, the White House, the Tidal Basin area—are within walking distance of each other, so using public transportation is only an option. If you want to see anything away from these areas or need to travel to any of the outlying neighborhoods, Washington has one of the best subway systems of any major city in the world. The related bus service is quite reliable, and there are always plenty of taxis and rental car options. Driving around downtown should always be your last choice: besides the confusing layout of the streets and the accompanying confusion of trying to read a map, parking fees are astronomical.

By Subway
The Washington Metropolitan Area Transit Autority (WMATA) operates the Metrorail, D.C. subway system that's known by residents simply as "the Metro." It covers the downtown area and the suburbs (excepting Georgetown), but expansion is almost constant and new stations are due to open in the next decade. Metro stations are identified by a large letter "M" atop a brown pylon.

You can purchase magnetic **fare cards** from vending machines at your departure station. Simply insert the card into the turnstile and when you get where you're going use the card to exit. The turnstile will magnetically record the remaining value on your fare card. Cards can be purchased for the base fare of $1.10, or for as much as $45. Fare cards purchased for $20 or more receive a 10% value bonus, so a $20-card would actually be worth $22. Should your card not have enough credit for you to exit the station, use one of the special exit-fare machines and try the turnstile again. **Children** under the age of four ride free when accompanied by a paying adult, up to a limit of two children.

On average, expect to pay between $1.10 and $3.25 during peak times (5:30-9:30 a.m. and 3-8 p.m.) and between $1.10 and $2.10 at other times. Metro trains run Mon.-Fri. 5:30 a.m. to midnight, and Saturday and Sunday 8:30 a.m. to midnight, and most public holidays. The trains arrive/depart every 5-6 minutes during peak times and every 10-15 minutes at other times.

The Metro also offers a variety of useful **train passes.** For $5 you can purchase a one-day pass valid from the time of purchase until closing (but not before 9:30 a.m. on weekdays). If you plan on being in the capital for an extended stay, you might consider purchasing the $50 Fast Pass, good for 14 consecutive days of unlimited rail travel. For even longer stays, WMATA offers the $100 28-Day Pass, good for unlimited rail travel for almost a month. Another good option, especially if you plan on riding the Metro buses in addition to the trains, is the $65 Bus/Rail SUPER Pass, good for 14 consecutive days of unlimited bus and rail travel. If you don't want to spend the money or don't plan on staying for two weeks, daily rail-to-bus transfers are available on the train platform for only 25 cents.

Passes are available at the WMATA headquarters, 600 Fifth St. N.W., Washington D.C. 20001, tel. (202) 637-7000, TDD (202) 638-3780, Web site: www.wmata.com; and at the Metro Center station sales office at 12th and F Sts. NW. Some banks, liquor stores, and some Safeway and Giant grocery stores also sell rail and bus passes. Metro **route maps** are available for $2 from the marketing office at WMATA headquarters.

By Bus

Like the subway, the **Metrobus** base fare is $1.10, and buses run at the same times as the trains, although some operate until 2 a.m. Rail-to-bus transfers are available (see above) and so are bus-to-bus transfers (only 10 cents)—simply hand your bus-transfer pass, which you must purchase for each transfer, to the driver of the second bus. Bus fare is acceptable either as cash or in the form of tokens worth $1.10 and available in rolls of 10 or 20. You can also purchase a $25 Flash Pass, good for 14 consecutive days of unlimited bus travel.

By Taxi

Since not every D.C. neighborhood is served by the Metro (most notably Georgtown and Adams-Morgan), the capital's taxi cabs are a nice complement to the subway and bus systems. A few reliable taxi companies include **Super Shuttle,** tel. (800) 258-3826, **Capitol Taxi,** tel. (202) 546-2400, and **Yellow Cab,** tel. (202) 544-1212. For information on cabs and fares in Washington call the Taxicab Commission at (202) 767-8319.

Rental Car

Most rental car agencies have offices at Dulles International Airport, National Airport, and Union Station, although you probably won't need a car if you're planning on staying within the city limits.

BOOKLIST

BACKGROUND

General History

Dabney, Virginius. *Virginia: The New Dominion.* Charlottesville, VA: University of Virginia Press, 1983. The consummate state history.

Jefferson, Thomas. *Notes on the State of Virginia.* University of North Carolina Press, 1982. Jefferson's only full-length book, called "an American classic," opens a vivid window into the author's personality and life in the 18th century.

McGraw, Mary Tyler. *At the Falls: Richmond, Virginia, and Its People.* Chapel Hill: University of North Carolina Press, 1994. Beautiful photos, prints, and engravings enhance this comprehensive history of the state capital.

Smith, John. *The Complete Works of Captain John Smith.* Chapel Hill: University of North Carolina Press, 1986. Includes *A True Relation of Such Occurrences and Accidents of Note as Hath Happened in Virginia* (1608), and *A Generall Historie of Virginia* (1624).

Civil War History

Catton, Bruce. *America Goes to War: The Civil War and Its Meaning in American Culture.* Wesleyan University Press, 1992. Catton also wrote a compelling three-volume account of the war, consisting of *The Coming Fury, Terrible Swift Sword,* and *Never Call Retreat.*

McPherson, James. *Battle Cry of Freedom.* New York: Oxford University Press, 1988. Dense (900 pages), but probably the best single-volume history of the war.

Ward, Geoffrey C., Ric Burns, and Ken Burns. *The Civil War: An Illustrated History.* New York: Alfred A. Knopf, 1990. The lavishly illustrated companion volume to Ken Burns' award-winning PBS series.

RECREATION

Civil War Touring

Braselton, Susan, ed. *Official Guide to the Civil War Discovery Trail.* Arlington, VA: The Civil War Trust, 1996. A handy guide that covers the entire theater. Published by Macmillan Travel (Simon and Schuster).

Lawliss, Chuck. *The Civil War Sourcebook: A Traveler's Guide.* New York: Harmony Books, 1991. Excellent background and touring information.

Hiking

Adkins, Leonard. *50 Hikes in Northern Virginia.* Woodstock, VT: The Countryman Press (Backcountry Publications), 1997. For rambles near D.C., from the mountains to the bay.

Adkins, Leonard. *Walking the Blue Ridge.* Chapel Hill, NC: University of North Carolina Press, 1996. Details every trail that touches the Blue Ridge Parkway, 122 in all. Plus descriptions of flora, fauna, history, and geology, and a roadside bloom calendar.

de Hart, Allen. *The Trails of Virginia: Hiking the Old Dominion.* Chapel Hill, NC: University of North Carolina Press, 1995. The authoritative work, covering every trail in the state from Civil War battlefields to backcountry.

Johnson, Randy. *Hiking Virginia.* Helena, MT: Falcon Press, 1992. Formerly *The Hiker's Guide to Virginia,* this guide includes a 50-hike sampler of the state's best walks, from the cities to the wilderness, along with maps and photos.

Gildart, Robert. *Hiking Shenandoah National Park.* Helena, MT: Falcon Press Publishing Company, Inc., 1998. Gildart is also the author of *Best Easy Day Hikes Shenandoah.*

Bicycling

Adams, Scott. *Mountain Bike Virginia.* Springfield, VA: Beachway Press, 1995. Comprehensive, including 120 maps for 40 rides from the seashore to the mountains.

Parham, Jim. *Off the Beaten Track Vol. V: A Guide to Mountain Biking in Northern Virginia.* Almond, NC: Milestone Press, Inc., 1995. Actually covers the northern part of the Shenandoah Valley. Slim enough to take along.

Porter, Randy. *A Cyclist's Guide to the Shenandoah Valley.* Birmingham, AL: Menasha Ridge Press, Inc., 1993. Focuses on scenic rural routes, with many interesting sidebars.

Porter, Randy. *Mountain Bike! Virginia: A Guide to the Classic Trails.* Birmingham, AL: Menasha Ridge Press, Inc., 1998. Exhaustive, with maps and a good range of rides from beginner to single-track.

Skinner, Elizabeth and Charlie. *Bicycling the Blue Ridge.* Birmingham, AL: Menasha Ridge Press, Inc., 1990. Covers both Skyline Drive and the Blue Ridge Parkway.

Rafting

Corbett, Roger. *Virginia's Whitewater.* Out of print but recommended.

Grove, Ed. *Appalachian Whitewater Vol. 2: The Central Mountains.* Birmingham, AL: Menasha Ridge Press, Inc., 1987. Grove is also the author of *Classic Virginia Rivers: A Paddler's Guide to Premier Whitewater and Scenic Floats Trips in the Old Dominion,* another excellent but out-of-print source. Amazon (www.amazon.com) might be able to locate a used copy of this latter one.

Fishing

Camuto, Christopher. *A Fly Fisherman's Blue Ridge.* New York: Holt & Co., 1992. The author, an angler and naturalist, traces one year of fly fishing in the Blue Ridge. A good read for anyone interested in fishing or the natural history of streams.

Gooch, Bob. *Virginia Fishing Guide.* Charlottesville: University Press of Virginia, 1992. Revised edition.

Miller, Skip. *Tidewater Fishing; The Complete Guide to Eastern Virginia Waters.* Soho Press, 1996. Focuses on the shore and the Chesapeake Bay.

Slone, Harry. *Virginia Trout Streams: A Guide to Fishing the Blue Ridge Watershed.* Woodstock, VT: The Countryman Press, Inc., 1994. Second edition, revised and expanded.

Climbing

Watson, Jeff. *Virginia Climber's Guide.* Mechanicsburg, PA: Stackpole Books, 1998. Covers the entire state in detail.

Natural History

Badger, Curtis. *A Naturalist's Guide to the Virginia Coast.* Mechanicsburg, PA: Stackpole Books, 1996. Great beach reading, split between background and visiting information. Heavy on birding.

Duda, Mark. *Virginia Wildlife Viewing Guide.* Helena, MT: Falcon Press Publishing Company, Inc., 1994. Details 80 outstanding areas to view Virginia's plants and animals, from whales along the coast to warblers in the mountains.

Frye, Keith. *Roadside Geology of Virginia.* Missoula, MT: Mountain Press, 1986. Includes general information on the state's geologic history, plus guides to those parts visible along major highways throughout the sate.

Gupton, Oscar. *Wildflowers of the Shenandoah Valley and Blue Ridge Mountains.* Charlottesville: University Press of Virginia, 1979. Gupton also wrote *Trees and Shrubs of Virginia* (UPV, 1989), *Wildflowers of Tidewater Virginia* (UPV, 1989), and *Wild Orchids of the Middle Atlantic States* (University of Tennessee Press, 1987).

Experienced naturalists know it's hard to beat the illustrated **Peterson Field Guides** series, published by Houghton Mifflin (Boston), the straightforward standard for amateur and professional alike. Covering the mid-Atlantic are *A Field Guide to the Mammals* (William H. Burt, 1998), *A Field Guide to Animal Tracks* (J. Murie, 1998), *A Field Guide to the Birds* (Roger Tory Peterson, 1998), and *A Field Guide to Reptiles & Amphibians: Eastern & Central North America* (Roger Conant and Joseph Collins, 1998).

FICTION

Crane, Stephen. *Red Badge of Courage.* New York: HarperCollins, 1996. The battle of Chancellorsville as seen by an idealistic, frightened young Union recruit. A classroom classic for a reason.

Styron, William. *The Confessions of Nat Turner.* New York: Random House, 1993. Pulitzer-prizewinning account of the abortive 1831 slave uprising in Southampton County.

NONFICTION

Barden, Thomas, ed. *Virginia Folk Legends.* Charlottesville: University of Virginia Press, 1991.

Blake, Allison. *The Chesapeake Bay Book.* Lee, MA: Berkshire House Publishers, 1997. A great book for those interested in exploring the bay up into Maryland.

Dillard, Annie. *Pilgrim at Tinker Creek.* New York: HarperCollins, 1988. Metaphysical, beautifully written observations on life and the universe set in the Roanoke valley.

Garrison, Webb. *A Treasury of Virginia Tales.* Nashville, TN: Rutledge Hill Press, 1996. Subtitled "Unusual, Interesting, and Little-Known Stories of Virginia."

Jameson, W.C. *Buried Treasures of the Appalachians.* Little Rock, AR: August House, 1991. Forty tales of lost wealth, gathered from interviews with those who have searched for it. Even includes maps!

Lautman, Robert. *Thomas Jefferson at Monticello: A Photographic Portrait.* New York: The Monacelli Press, 1997. Gorgeous, atmospheric black-and-white photos.

Mariner, Kirk. *Off 13: The Eastern Shore of Virginia Guidebook.* New Church, VA: Miona Publications, 1994. Available locally and full of native nuggets.

Nock, Anne. *Child of the Bay.* Charlottesville: Hampton Roads Publishing Co., 1992. The past and present on the eastern shore, available at bookstores in Virginia, Maryland, Delaware, Pennsylvania, and D.C.

Warner, William. *Beautiful Swimmers: Watermen, Crabs and the Chesapeake Bay.* New York, NY: Viking Penguin, 1977. Pulitzer-prizewinning account of life on the bay.

Washington, Booker T. *Up From Slavery.* New York: Viking Penguin, 1986. A vivid account of the struggle faced by African-Americans at the turn of the century.

Whitehead, John Hurt, III. *The Watermen of the Chesapeake Bay.* Centerville, MD: Tidewater Publishing, 1979. Photographic account of watermen in the 1980s, interspersed with colorful quotations.

Whitman, William. *The Wines of Virginia: A Complete Guide.* Warrenton, VA: Virginia Heritage Publishers. Best ordered directly from the publisher, tel. (540) 341-1951.

INDEX

ARTS/CRAFTS

BATTLES/BATTLEFIELDS/MONUMENTS

COLLEGES/UNIVERSITIES

HIKING

HISTORIC HOMES/BUILDINGS

PARKS/RECREATION AREAS

RAFTING/ KAYAKING/CANOEING

TRAILS

ABOUT THE AUTHOR

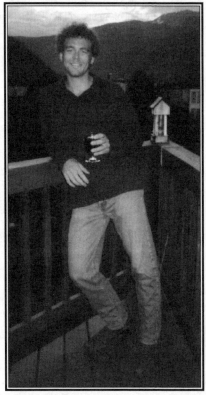

MARNIE BOREN

Born and raised in downstate New York, Julian Smith has been writing since he could read and traveling since the first family summer in Cape Cod as a child. A serious affection for the Old Dominion sprouted during four years at the University of Virginia, during which he wrote for local publications, played in a few bands, explored the Blue Ridge, and managed to wrangle a B.A. from the biology department. Another year in idyllic Charlottesville left him the proud parent, along with two partners, of *On Your Own in El Salvador,* the first travel guide to the country. Moon's *Ecuador Handbook* came two years later.

Along the way he's found himself freezing atop Kilimanjaro, meditating in a Japanese zen temple, and exploring the misty heights of Machu Picchu and the depths of southern Utah's canyonlands. An affinity for risky, expensive sports like snowboarding, mountain biking, and rock climbing keeps things interesting in the incomparable desert southwest, where he lived while writing the *Virginia Handbook.* Who knows where he'll be by the time you read this, but wherever it is, you can bet the days are just packed with good books, travel plans, funky music, and lots—we're talking months on end—of sunshine.

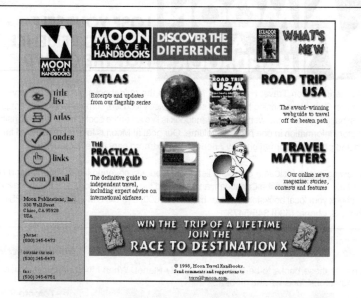

www.moon.com

Enjoy our travel information center on the World Wide Web (WWW), loaded with interactive exhibits designed especially for the Internet.

ATTRACTIONS ON MOON'S WEB SITE INCLUDE:

ATLAS
Our award-winning, comprehensive travel guides cover destinations throughout North America and Hawaii, Latin America and the Caribbean, and Asia and the Pacific.

PRACTICAL NOMAD
Extensive excerpts, a unique set of travel links coordinated with the book, and a regular Q & A column by author and Internet travel consultant Edward Hasbrouck.

TRAVEL MATTERS
Our on-line travel zine, featuring articles; author correspondence; a travel library including health information, reading lists, and cultural cues; and our new contest, **Destination X,** offering a chance to win a trip to the mystery destination of your choice.

ROAD TRIP USA
Our best-selling book, ever; don't miss this award-winning Webguide to off-the-interstate itineraries.

Come visit us at: **www.moon.com**

MOON TRAVEL HANDBOOKS

LOSE YOURSELF IN THE EXPERIENCE, NOT THE CROWD

For 25 years, Moon Travel Handbooks have been the guidebooks of choice for adventurous travelers. Our award-winning Handbook series provides focused, comprehensive coverage of distinct destinations all over the world. Each Handbook is like an entire bookcase of cultural insight and introductory information in one portable volume. Our goal at Moon is to give travelers all the background and practical information they'll need for an extraordinary travel experience.

The following pages include a complete list of Handbooks, covering North America and Hawaii, Mexico, Latin America and the Caribbean, and Asia and the Pacific. To purchase Moon Travel Handbooks, check your local bookstore or order by phone: (800) 345-5473 M-F 8 am.-5 p.m. PST or outside the U.S. phone: (530) 345-5473.

"An in-depth dunk into the land, the people and their history, arts, and politics."
—*Student Travels*

"I consider these books to be superior to Lonely Planet. When Moon produces a book it is more humorous, incisive, and off-beat."
—*Toronto Sun*

"Outdoor enthusiasts gravitate to the well-written Moon Travel Handbooks. In addition to politically correct historic and cultural features, the series focuses on flora, fauna and outdoor recreation. Maps and meticulous directions also are a trademark of Moon guides."
—*Houston Chronicle*

"Moon [Travel Handbooks] . . . bring a healthy respect to the places they investigate. Best of all, they provide a host of odd nuggets that give a place texture and prod the wary traveler from the beaten path. The finest are written with such care and insight they deserve listing as literature."
—*American Geographical Society*

"Moon Travel Handbooks offer in-depth historical essays and useful maps, enhanced by a sense of humor and a neat, compact format."
—*Swing*

"Perfect for the more adventurous, these are long on history, sightseeing and nitty-gritty information and very price-specific."
—*Columbus Dispatch*

"Moon guides manage to be comprehensive and countercultural at the same time . . . Handbooks are packed with maps, photographs, drawings, and sidebars that constitute a college-level introduction to each country's history, culture, people, and crafts."
—*National Geographic Traveler*

"Few travel guides do a better job helping travelers create their own itineraries than the Moon Travel Handbook series. The authors have a knack for homing in on the essentials."
—*Colorado Springs Gazette Telegraph*

MEXICO

"These books will delight the armchair traveler, aid the undecided person in selecting a destination, and guide the seasoned road warrior looking for lesser-known hideaways."

—*Mexican Meanderings* Newsletter

"From tourist traps to off-the-beaten track hideaways, these guides offer consistent, accurate details without pretension."

—*Foreign Service Journal*

Archaeological Mexico	**$19.95**
Andrew Coe	420 pages, 27 maps
Baja Handbook	**$16.95**
Joe Cummings	540 pages, 46 maps
Cabo Handbook	**$14.95**
Joe Cummings	270 pages, 17 maps
Cancún Handbook	**$14.95**
Chicki Mallan	240 pages, 25 maps
Colonial Mexico	**$18.95**
Chicki Mallan	400 pages, 38 maps
Mexico Handbook	**$21.95**
Joe Cummings and Chicki Mallan	1,200 pages, 201 maps
Northern Mexico Handbook	**$17.95**
Joe Cummings	610 pages, 69 maps
Pacific Mexico Handbook	**$17.95**
Bruce Whipperman	580 pages, 68 maps
Puerto Vallarta Handbook	**$14.95**
Bruce Whipperman	330 pages, 36 maps
Yucatán Handbook	**$16.95**
Chicki Mallan	400 pages, 52 maps

LATIN AMERICA AND THE CARIBBEAN

"Solidly packed with practical information and full of significant cultural asides that will enlighten you on the whys and wherefores of things you might easily see but not easily grasp."

—*Boston Globe*

Belize Handbook	**$15.95**
Chicki Mallan and Patti Lange	390 pages, 45 maps
Caribbean Vacations	**$18.95**
Karl Luntta	910 pages, 64 maps
Costa Rica Handbook	**$19.95**
Christopher P. Baker	780 pages, 73 maps
Cuba Handbook	**$19.95**
Christopher P. Baker	740 pages, 70 maps
Dominican Republic Handbook	**$15.95**
Gaylord Dold	420 pages, 24 maps
Ecuador Handbook	**$16.95**
Julian Smith	450 pages, 43 maps
Honduras Handbook	**$15.95**
Chris Humphrey	330 pages, 40 maps
Jamaica Handbook	**$15.95**
Karl Luntta	330 pages, 17 maps
Virgin Islands Handbook	**$13.95**
Karl Luntta	220 pages, 19 maps

NORTH AMERICA AND HAWAII

"These domestic guides convey the same sense of exoticism that their foreign counterparts do, making home-country travel seem like far-flung adventure."

—*Sierra Magazine*

Alaska-Yukon Handbook	**$17.95**
Deke Castleman and Don Pitcher	530 pages, 92 maps
Alberta and the Northwest Territories Handbook	**$17.95**
Andrew Hempstead and Nadina Purdon	530 pages, 72 maps,
Arizona Traveler's Handbook	**$17.95**
Bill Weir and Robert Blake	512 pages, 54 maps
Atlantic Canada Handbook	**$17.95**
Nan Drosdick and Mark Morris	460 pages, 61 maps
Big Island of Hawaii Handbook	**$15.95**
J.D. Bisignani	390 pages, 23 maps

Boston Handbook	**$13.95**
Jeff Perk	200 pages, 20 maps
British Columbia Handbook	**$16.95**
Jane King and Andrew Hempstead	430 pages, 69 maps
Colorado Handbook	**$18.95**
Stephen Metzger	480 pages, 59 maps
Georgia Handbook	**$17.95**
Kap Stann	370 pages, 50 maps
Hawaii Handbook	**$19.95**
J.D. Bisignani	1,030 pages, 90 maps
Honolulu-Waikiki Handbook	**$14.95**
J.D. Bisignani	400 pages, 20 maps
Idaho Handbook	**$18.95**
Don Root	610 pages, 42 maps
Kauai Handbook	**$15.95**
J.D. Bisignani	320 pages, 23 maps
Maine Handbook	**$18.95**
Kathleen M. Brandes	660 pages, 27 maps
Massachusetts Handbook	**$18.95**
Jeff Perk	600 pages, 23 maps
Maui Handbook	**$15.95**
J.D. Bisignani	420 pages, 35 maps
Michigan Handbook	**$15.95**
Tina Lassen	300 pages, 30 maps
Montana Handbook	**$17.95**
Judy Jewell and W.C. McRae	480 pages, 52 maps
Nevada Handbook	**$18.95**
Deke Castleman	530 pages, 40 maps
New Hampshire Handbook	**$18.95**
Steve Lantos	500 pages, 18 maps
New Mexico Handbook	**$15.95**
Stephen Metzger	360 pages, 47 maps
New York Handbook	**$19.95**
Christiane Bird	780 pages, 95 maps
New York City Handbook	**$13.95**
Christiane Bird	300 pages, 20 maps
North Carolina Handbook	**$14.95**
Rob Hirtz and Jenny Daughtry Hirtz	275 pages, 25 maps
Northern California Handbook	**$19.95**
Kim Weir	800 pages, 50 maps
Oregon Handbook	**$17.95**
Stuart Warren and Ted Long Ishikawa	588 pages, 34 maps
Pennsylvania Handbook	**$18.95**
Joanne Miller	448 pages, 40 maps

Road Trip USA	**$22.50**
Jamie Jensen	800 pages, 165 maps
Santa Fe-Taos Handbook	**$13.95**
Stephen Metzger	160 pages, 13 maps
Southern California Handbook	**$19.95**
Kim Weir	720 pages, 26 maps
Tennessee Handbook	**$17.95**
Jeff Bradley	530 pages, 44 maps
Texas Handbook	**$18.95**
Joe Cummings	690 pages, 70 maps
Utah Handbook	**$17.95**
Bill Weir and W.C. McRae	490 pages, 40 maps
Virginia Handbook	**$15.95**
Julian Smith	340 pages, 30 maps
Washington Handbook	**$19.95**
Don Pitcher	870 pages, 113 maps
Wisconsin Handbook	**$18.95**
Thomas Huhti	590 pages, 69 maps
Wyoming Handbook	**$17.95**
Don Pitcher	610 pages, 80 maps

ASIA AND THE PACIFIC

"Scores of maps, detailed practical info down to business hours of small-town libraries. You can't beat the Asian titles for sheer heft. (The) series is sort of an American Lonely Planet, with better writing but fewer titles. (The) individual voice of researchers comes through."

—Travel & Leisure

Australia Handbook	**$21.95**
Marael Johnson, Andrew Hempstead, and Nadina Purdon	940 pages, 141 maps
Bali Handbook	**$19.95**
Bill Dalton	750 pages, 54 maps
Bangkok Handbook	**$13.95**
Michael Buckley	244 pages, 30 maps
Fiji Islands Handbook	**$14.95**
David Stanley	300 pages, 38 maps
Hong Kong Handbook	**$16.95**
Kerry Moran	378 pages, 49 maps
Indonesia Handbook	**$25.00**
Bill Dalton	1,380 pages, 249 maps

Micronesia Handbook	$14.95
Neil M. Levy	340 pages, 70 maps
Nepal Handbook	**$18.95**
Kerry Moran	490 pages, 51 maps
New Zealand Handbook	**$19.95**
Jane King	620 pages, 81 maps
Outback Australia Handbook	**$18.95**
Marael Johnson	450 pages, 57 maps
Philippines Handbook	**$17.95**
Peter Harper and Laurie Fullerton	670 pages, 116 maps
Singapore Handbook	**$15.95**
Carl Parkes	350 pages, 29 maps
South Korea Handbook	**$19.95**
Robert Nilsen	820 pages, 141 maps
South Pacific Handbook	**$22.95**
David Stanley	920 pages, 147 maps
Southeast Asia Handbook	**$21.95**
Carl Parkes	1,080 pages, 204 maps
Tahiti-Polynesia Handbook	**$15.95**
David Stanley	380 pages, 35 maps
Thailand Handbook	**$19.95**
Carl Parkes	860 pages, 142 maps
Vietnam, Cambodia & Laos Handbook	**$18.95**
Michael Buckley	760 pages, 116 maps

OTHER GREAT TITLES FROM MOON

"For hardy wanderers, few guides come more highly
recommended than the Handbooks. They include
good maps, steer clear of fluff and flackery, and offer
plenty of money-saving tips. They also give you the
kind of information that visitors to strange lands—on
any budget—need to survive."

—*US News & World Report*

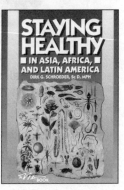

Moon Handbook	$10.00
Carl Koppeschaar	141 pages, 8 maps
The Practical Nomad: How to Travel Around the World	**$17.95**
Edward Hasbrouck	575 pages
Staying Healthy in Asia, Africa, and Latin America	**$11.95**
Dirk Schroeder	230 pages, 4 maps

THE PRACTICAL NOMAD

✈ TAKE THE PLUNGE

"The greatest barriers to long-term travel by
Americans are the disempowered feelings
that leave them afraid to ask for the time off.
Just do it."

✈ TAKE NOTHING FOR GRANTED

"Even 'What time is it?' is a highly politicized
question in some areas, and the answer may
depend on your informant's ethnicity and
political allegiance as well as the proximity of
the secret police."

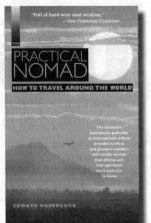

"Full of hard-won road wisdom."
—*San Francisco Examiner*

$17.95   576 pages

✈ TAKE THIS BOOK

With experience helping thousands of his globetrotting clients plan their trips
around the world, travel industry insider Edward Hasbrouck provides the
secrets that can save readers money and valuable travel time.
An indispensable complement to destination-specific travel guides,
The Practical Nomad includes:

airfare strategies

ticket discounts

long-term travel considerations

travel documents

border crossings

entry requirements

government offices

travel publications

Internet information resources

WHERE TO BUY MOON TRAVEL HANDBOOKS

BOOKSTORES AND LIBRARIES: Moon Travel Handbooks are distributed worldwide. Please contact our sales manager for a list of wholesalers and distributors in your area.

TRAVELERS: We would like to have Moon Travel Handbooks available throughout the world. Please ask your bookstore to write or call us for ordering information. If your bookstore will not order our guides for you, please contact us for a free catalog.

> **Moon Travel Handbooks**
> **P.O. Box 3040**
> **Chico, CA 95927-3040 U.S.A.**
> **tel.: (800) 345-5473, outside the U.S. (530) 345-5473**
> **fax: (530) 345-6751**
> **e-mail: travel@moon.com**

IMPORTANT ORDERING INFORMATION

PRICES: All prices are subject to change. We always ship the most current edition. We will let you know if there is a price increase on the book you order.

SHIPPING AND HANDLING OPTIONS: Domestic UPS or USPS first class (allow 10 working days for delivery): $4.50 for the first item, $1.00 for each additional item.

Moonbelt shipping is $1.50 for one, 50 cents for each additional belt.

UPS 2nd Day Air or Printed Airmail requires a special quote.

International Surface Bookrate 8-12 weeks delivery: $4.00 for the first item, $1.00 for each additional item. Note: We cannot guarantee international surface bookrate shipping. We recommend sending international orders via air mail, which requires a special quote.

FOREIGN ORDERS: Orders that originate outside the U.S.A. must be paid for with an international money order, a check in U.S. currency drawn on a major U.S. bank based in the U.S.A., or Visa, MasterCard, or Discover.

TELEPHONE ORDERS: We accept Visa, MasterCard, or Discover payments. Call in your order: (800) 345-5473, 8 a.m.-5 p.m. Pacific standard time. Outside the U.S. the number is (530) 345-5473.

INTERNET ORDERS: Visit our site at: www.moon.com

ORDER FORM

Prices are subject to change without notice. Be sure to call (800) 345-5473,
or (530) 345-5473 from outside the U.S. 8 a.m.–5 p.m. PST for current prices and editions.
(See important ordering information on preceding page.)

Name: _____ Date: _____

Street: _____

City: _____ Daytime Phone: _____

State or Country: _____ Zip Code: _____

QUANTITY	TITLE	PRICE

Taxable Total_____

Sales Tax (7.25%) for California Residents_____

Shipping & Handling_____

TOTAL_____

Ship: ☐ UPS (no P.O. Boxes) ☐ 1st class ☐ International surface mail

Ship to: ☐ address above ☐ other _____

_____

Make checks payable to: **MOON TRAVEL HANDBOOKS**, P.O. Box 3040, Chico, CA 95927-3040
U.S.A. We accept Visa, MasterCard, or Discover. **To Order**: Call in your Visa, MasterCard, or Discover number,
or send a written order with your Visa, MasterCard, or Discover number and expiration date clearly written.

Card Number: ☐ **Visa** ☐ **MasterCard** ☐ **Discover**

☐ ☐ ☐ ☐ ☐ ☐ ☐ ☐ ☐ ☐ ☐ ☐ ☐ ☐ ☐ ☐

Exact Name on Card: _____

Expiration date:_____

Signature: _____

U.S.~METRIC CONVERSION

1 inch = 2.54 centimeters (cm)
1 foot = .304 meters (m)
1 yard = 0.914 meters
1 mile = 1.6093 kilometers (km)
1 km = .6214 miles
1 fathom = 1.8288 m
1 chain = 20.1168 m
1 furlong = 201.168 m
1 acre = .4047 hectares
1 sq km = 100 hectares
1 sq mile = 2.59 square km
1 ounce = 28.35 grams
1 pound = .4536 kilograms
1 short ton = .90718 metric ton
1 short ton = 2000 pounds
1 long ton = 1.016 metric tons
1 long ton = 2240 pounds
1 metric ton = 1000 kilograms
1 quart = .94635 liters
1 US gallon = 3.7854 liters
1 Imperial gallon = 4.5459 liters
1 nautical mile = 1.852 km

To compute celsius temperatures, subtract 32 from Fahrenheit and divide by 1.8. To go the other way, multiply celsius by 1.8 and add 32.